1948 - 58
Series I

WORKSHOP
MANUAL

FOR PETROL

AND DIESEL

MODELS

By Appointment to
Her Majesty
Queen Elizabeth II

Manufacturers
of Motor Cars and
Land-Rovers

By Appointment to
Her Majesty
Queen Elizabeth
the Queen Mother

Suppliers
of
Motor Cars and
Land-Rovers

THE ROVER CO. LTD . SOLIHULL . WARWICKSHIRE . ENGLAND

PART No. 4291

"THE LAND-ROVER 86 and 88"

"THE LAND-ROVER 107 and 109"

Please note that all prices and specifications are subject to alteration without notice.

THE ROVER COMPANY LTD.
SOLIHULL, WARWICKSHIRE, ENGLAND

SERVICE AND SPARES DEPT.:
SOLIHULL, WARWICKSHIRE
ENGLAND

Telephone: *Telegrams:*
021-743 4242   Rovrepair, Solihull, England
Telex: 33-156

2nd Edition

Part No. 4291

March **1960**
Reprinted October 1963
Reprinted March 1966
Reprinted November 1969
Reprinted October 1971

Year and Model		Car and Chassis Commencing Numbers	Engine Commencing Number	Gearbox Commencing Number	Front axle Commencing Number	Rear axle Commencing Number
1948-49						
L-R Basic Home R.H.D.		R860001 to 863000 and R8660001				
L-R Basic Export L.H.D.	Series I '80'	L860001 to 863000 and L8660001	860001	860001 R.H.D. L860001 L.H.D.	860001 R.H.D. L860001 L.H.D.	860001
L-R S.W. Home R.H.D.		R8670001				
L-R S.W. Export L.H.D.		L8670001				
L-R S.W. Export R.H.D.		R8670001				
L-R Welder Home R.H.D.		R8680001				
L-R Welder Export L.H.D.		L8680001				
L-R Welder Export R.H.D.		R8680001				
1950						
L-R Basic Home R.H.D.		R06100001				
L-R Basic Export L.H.D.		L06100001				
L-R Basic Export R.H.D.		R06100001				
L-R S.W. Home R.H.D.		R06200001				
L-R S.W. Export L.H.D.		L06200001	06100001 R.H.D.	06100001 R.H.D.	06100001 R.H.D.	
L-R S.W. Export R.H.D.	Series I '80'	R06200001	L06100001 L.H.D.	L06100001 L.H.D.	L06100001 L.H.D.	06100001
L-R Welder Home R.H.D.		R06300001				
L-R Welder Export L.H.D.		L06300001				
L-R Welder Export R.H.D.		R06300001				
L-R C.K.D. L.H.D.		L06100001				
L-R C.K.D. R.H.D.		R06100001				
L-R 50 Prototype 2 litre		07100001	07100001	06100001	06100001	06100001
1951						
L-R Basic Home R.H.D.		16100001				
L-R Basic Export L.H.D.		16130001				
L-R Basic Export R.H.D.		16160001				
L-R S.W. Home R.H.D.		16200001				
L-R S.W. Export L.H.D.	Series I '80'	16230001	16100001 R.H.D.	16100001 R.H.D.	16100001 R.H.D.	
L-R S.W. Export R.H.D.		16260001	16130001 L.H.D.	16130001 L.H.D.	16130001 L.H.D.	16100001
L-R Welder Home R.H.D.		16300001				
L-R Welder Export L.H.D.		16330001				
L-R Welder Export R.H.D.		16360001				
L-R C.K.D. L.H.D.		16630001				
L-R C.K.D. R.H.D.		16660001				
1952						
L-R Basic Home R.H.D.		26100001				
L-R Basic Export L.H.D.		26130001				
L-R Basic Export R.H.D.		26160001	26100001 R.H.D.	26100001 R.H.D.	26100001 R.H.D.	
L-R Welder Home R.H.D.	Series I '80'	26300001				26100001
L-R Welder Export L.H.D.		26330001	26130001 L.H.D.	26130001 L.H.D.	26130001 L.H.D.	
L-R Welder Export R.H.D.		26360001				
L-R C.K.D. L.H.D.		26630001				
L-R C.K.D. R.H.D.		26660001				
1953						
L-R Basic Home R.H.D.		36100001				
L-R Basic Export L.H.D.		36130001				
L-R Basic Export R.H.D.		36160001	36100001 R.H.D.	36100001 R.H.D.	36100001 R.H.D.	
L-R Welder Home R.H.D.	Series I '80'	36300001				36100001
L-R Welder Export L.H.D.		36330001	36130001 L.H.D.	36130001 L.H.D.	36130001 L.H.D.	
L-R Welder Export R.H.D.		36360001				
L-R C.K.D. L.H.D.		36630001				
L-R C.K.D. R.H.D.		36660001				
1954						
L-R Home R.H.D.		47100001				
L-R Export L.H.D.		47130001	47100001 R.H.D.	47100001 R.H.D.	47100001 R.H.D.	
L-R Export R.H.D.	Series I '86'	47160001				47100001
L-R C.K.D. L.H.D.		47130001	47130001 L.H.D.	47130001 L.H.D.	47130001 L.H.D.	
L-R C.K.D. R.H.D.		47660001				
1954						
L-R Home R.H.D.		47200001			47100001 R.H.D.	
L-R Export L.H.D.		47230001	47100001 R.H.D.	47100001 R.H.D.	47130001 L.H.D. 10" brakes	47100001 10" brakes
L-R Export R.H.D.	Series I '107'	47260001			47200001 R.H.D.	47200001 11" brakes
L-R C.K.D. R.H.D.		47760001	47130001 L.H.D.	47130001 L.H.D.	47230001 L.H.D.	
L-R C.K.D. L.H.D.		47730001			11" brakes	

Year and Model		Car and Chassis Commencing Numbers	Engine Commencing Number	Gearbox Commencing Number	Front axle Commencing Number	Rear axle Commencing Number
1955						
L-R Home R.H.D.		57100001, 57110001 and 170600001	57100001, 57110001 and 170600001 R.H.D.	57100001, 57110001 and 170600001 R.H.D.	57100001, 57110001 and 170600001 R.H.D.	57100001, 57110001 and 170600001
L-R Export L.H.D.	Series I '86'	57130001, 57140001 and 173600001	57130001, 57140001 and 173600001 L.H.D.	57130001, 57140001 and 173600001 L.H.D.	57130001, 57140001 and 173600001 L.H.D.	
L-R Export R.H.D.		57160001, 57170001 and 176600001				
L-R C.K.D. L.H.D.		57630001, 174600001				
L-R C.K.D. R.H.D.		57660001, 177600001				
1955						
L-R Home R.H.D.		57200001, 57210001 and 270600001	57100001, 57110001 and 170600001 R.H.D.	57100001, 57110001 and 170600001 R.H.D.	57200001, 57210001 and 270600001 R.H.D.	57200001, 57210001 and 270600001
L-R Export L.H.D.	Series I '107'	57230001, 57240001 and 273600001	57130001, 57140001 and 173600001 L.H.D.	57130001, 57140001 and 173600001 L.H.D.	57230001, 57240001 and 273600001 L.H.D.	
L-R Export R.H.D.		57260001, 57270001 and 276600001				
L-R C.K.D. L.H.D.		57730001, 274600001				
L-R C.K.D. R.H.D.		57760001, 277600001				
1956						
L-R Home R.H.D.		111600001	170600001 R.H.D.	170600001 R.H.D.	170600001 R.H.D.	170600001
L-R Export R.H.D.		112600001				
L-R C.K.D. R.H.D.	Series I '88'	113600001				
L-R Export L.H.D.		114600001	173600001 L.H.D.	173600001 L.H.D.	173600001 L.H.D.	
L-R C.K.D. L.H.D.		115600001				
1956						
L-R Home R.H.D.		121600001	170600001 R.H.D.	170600001 R.H.D.	270600001 R.H.D.	270600001
L-R Export R.H.D.		122600001				
L-R C.K.D. R.H.D.	Series I '109'	123600001				
L-R Export L.H.D.		124600001	173600001 L.H.D.	173600001 L.H.D.	273600001 L.H.D.	
L-R C.K.D. R.H.D.		125600001				
1956						
L-R S.W. Home R.H.D.		870600001	170600001 R.H.D.	170600001 R.H.D.	270600001 R.H.D.	87060001
L-R S.W. Export L.H.D.		873600001				
L-R S.W. Export R.H.D.	Series I '107' S.W.	876600001				
L-R S.W. C.K.D. L.H.D.		874600001	173600001 L.H.D.	173600001 L.H.D.	273600001 L.H.D.	
L-R S.W. C.K.D. R.H.D.		877600001				
1957						
L-R Home R.H.D.		111700001	111700001 R.H.D.	111700001 R.H.D.	111700001 R.H.D.	111700001 Semi-floating
L-R Export R.H.D.	Series I '88' Petrol	112700001				
L-R C.K.D. R.H.D.		113700001				
L-R Export L.H.D.		114700001	114700001 L.H.D.	114700001 L.H.D.	114700001 L.H.D.	111780001 Fully-floating
L-R C.K.D. L.H.D.		115700001				
1957						
L-R Home R.H.D.		116700001	116700001 R.H.D.	116700001 R.H.D.	111700001 R.H.D.	111700001 Semi-floating
L-R Export R.H.D.	Series I '88' Diesel	117700001				
L-R C.K.D. R.H.D.		118700001				
L-R Export L.H.D.		119700001	119700001 L.H.D.	119700001 L.H.D.	114700001 L.H.D.	111780001 Fully-floating
L-R C.K.D. L.H.D.		120700001				
1957						
L-R Home R.H.D.		121700001	111700001 R.H.D.	111700001 R.H.D.	121700001 R.H.D.	121700001
L-R Export R.H.D.	Series I '109' Petrol	122700001				
L-R C.K.D. R.H.D.		123700001				
L-R Export L.H.D.		124700001	114700001 L.H.D.	114700001 L.H.D.	124700001 L.H.D.	
L-R C.K.D. L.H.D.		125700001				
1957						
L-R Home R.H.D.		126700001	126700001 R.H.D.	126700001 R.H.D.	121700001 R.H.D.	121700001
L-R Export R.H.D.	Series I '109' Diesel	127700001				
L-R C.K.D. R.H.D.		128700001				
L-R Export L.H.D.		129700001	129700001 L.H.D.	129700001 L.H.D.	124700001 L.H.D.	
L-R C.K.D. L.H.D.		130700001				

NOTE: The fifth digit of 1957 Land-Rover '88' rear axle number indicates a fully-floating axle.

Year and Model		Car and Chassis Commencing Numbers	Engine Commencing Number	Gearbox Commencing Number	Front axle Commencing Number	Rear axle Commencing Number
1957						
L-R S.W. Home R.H.D.	Series I '107' S.W.	131700001	111700001 R.H.D.	111700001 R.H.D.	121700001 R.H.D.	131700001
L-R S.W. Export R.H.D....		132700001				
L-R S.W. C.K.D. R.H.D.....		133700001				
L-R S.W. Export L.H.D.....		134700001	114700001 L.H.D.	114700001 L.H.D.	124700001 L.H.D.	
L-R S.W. C.K.D. L.H.D.....		135700001				
1958						
L-R Home R.H.D.	Series I '88' Petrol	111800001	111800001 R.H.D.	111800001 R.H.D.	111800001 R.H.D.	111800001 Semi-floating
L-R Export R.H.D.		112800001				
L-R C.K.D. R.H.D.		113800001				
L-R Export L.H.D.		114800001	114800001 L.H.D.	114800001 L.H.D.	114800001 L.H.D.	111880001 Fully-floating
L-R C.K.D. L.H.D.		115800001				
1958						
L-R Home R.H.D.	Series I '88' Diesel	116800001	116800001 R.H.D.	116800001 R.H.D.	111800001 R.H.D.	111800001 Semi-floating
L-R Export R.H.D.		117800001				
L-R C.K.D. R.H.D.		118800001				
L-R Export L.H.D.		119800001	119800001 L.H.D.	119800001 L.H.D.	114800001 L.H.D.	111880001 Fully-floating
L-R C.K.D. L.H.D.		120800001				
1958						
L-R Home R.H.D.	Series I '109' Petrol	121800001	111800001 R.H.D.	111800001 R.H.D.	121800001 R.H.D.	121800001
L-R Export R.H.D.		122800001				
L-R C.K.D. R.H.D.		123800001				
L-R Export L.H.D.		124800001	114800001 L.H.D.	114800001 L.H.D.	124800001 L.H.D.	
L-R C.K.D. L.H.D.		125800001				
1958						
L-R Home R.H.D.	Series I '109' Diesel	126800001	126800001 R.H.D.	126800001 R.H.D.	121800001 R.H.D.	121800001
L-R Export R.H.D.		127800001				
L-R C.K.D. R.H.D.		128800001				
L-R Export L.H.D.		129800001	129800001 L.H.D.	129800001 L.H.D.	124800001 L.H.D.	
L-R C.K.D. L.H.D.		130800001				
1958						
L-R S.W. Home R.H.D.	Series I '107' S.W.	131800001	111800001 R.H.D.	111800001 R.H.D.	121800001 R.H.D.	131800001
L-R S.W. Export R.H.D....		132800001				
L-R S.W. C.K.D. R.H.D....		133800001				
L-R S.W. Export L.H.D....		134800001	114800001 L.H.D.	114800001 L.H.D.	124800001 L.H.D.	
L-R S.W. C.K.D. L.H.D....		135800001				

NOTE: The fifth digit of the 1958 Land-Rover '88' rear axle number indicates fully-floating axle.

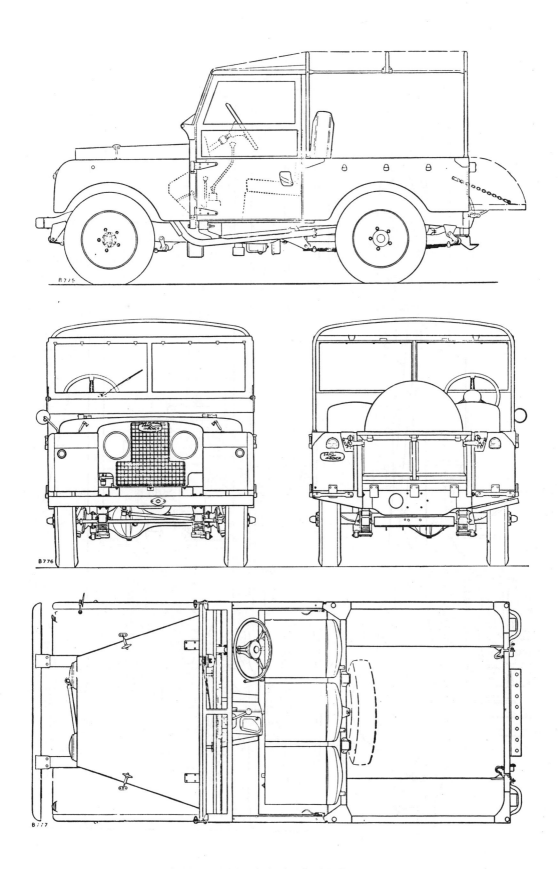

GENERAL ARRANGEMENT — LAND-ROVER 88

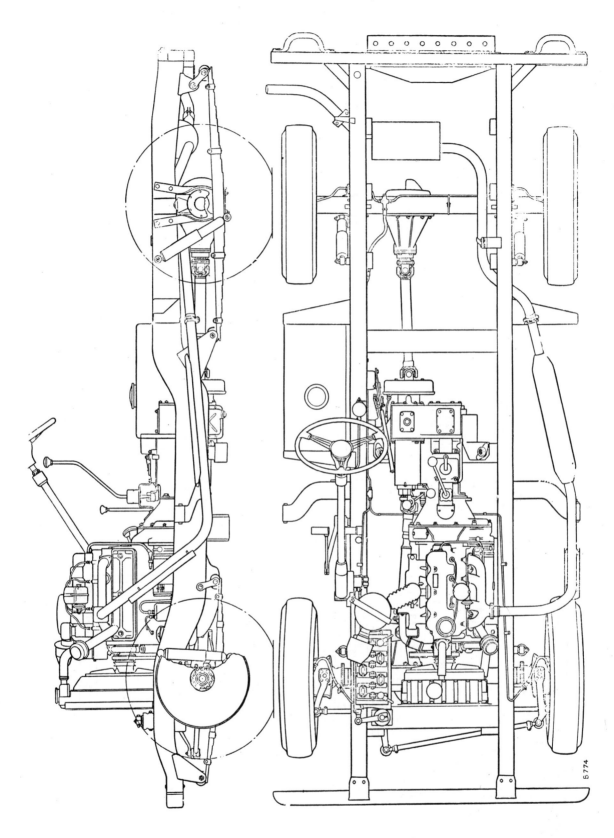

GENERAL ARRANGEMENT — LAND-ROVER 86 AND 88

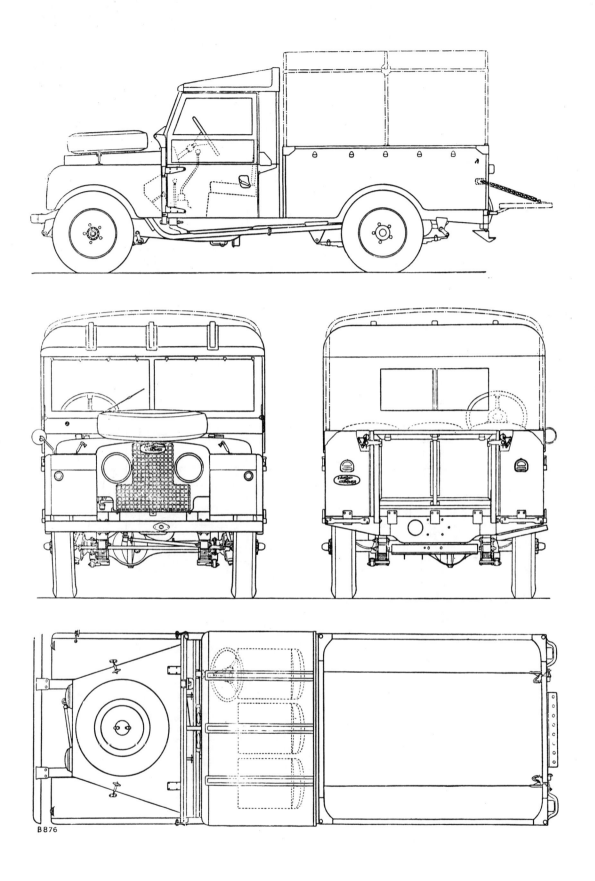

GENERAL ARRANGEMENT — LAND-ROVER 107 AND 109

B 876

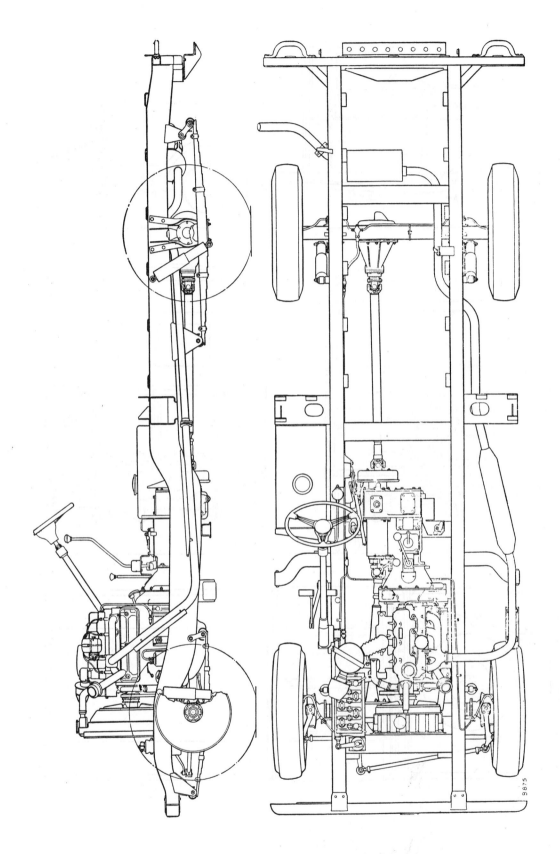

GENERAL ARRANGEMENT — LAND-ROVER 107 AND 109

12

Introduction

This Workshop Manual is designed to assist those responsible for the maintenance and overhaul of the Land-Rover.

The subject matter is sectionised as detailed in the index on the next page, and the pages are numbered within those sections. At the beginning of each section will be found a sub-index for that section.

NOMENCLATURE

As this manual covers both right- and left-hand drive models, reference is made throughout the text to the "left-hand" and "right-hand" sides of the vehicle, rather than to the "near-side" and "off-side". The "left-hand" side is that to the left hand when the vehicle is viewed from the rear; similarly, "left-hand drive" models are those having the driving controls on the left-hand side, again when the vehicle is viewed from the rear.

CAPACITIES

All capacities are quoted in Imperial and Metric measure; to ascertain the U.S. equivalent, multiply the Imperial figure by 1.2.

MEASUREMENTS

All measurements are given in Imperial measure; the Metric equivalent is added where possible, but in certain cases, such as cylinder rebore sizes, this is of course not practicable, and the Imperial figure must be used.

VEHICLE SERIAL NUMBERS

The vehicle serial number will be found on the transfer box instruction plate on the dash panel over the gearbox cover. It is the same as the chassis number, which is stamped on the right-hand front spring shackle bracket.

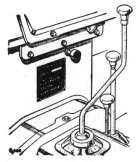
Fig. 1.
Vehicle serial number.

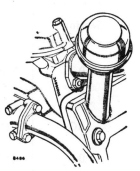
Fig. 2.
Engine serial number petrol models.

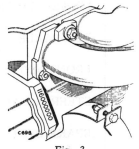
Fig. 3.
Engine serial number Diesel models.

The full vehicle serial number must be quoted in all correspondence; the registration number of the vehicle is of no use whatever to us.

The engine serial number, **which need not be quoted in correspondence** unless specifically asked for, is stamped on the left-hand side of the cylinder block at the front.

Other units bear serial numbers as detailed below, but they should not be quoted unless specifically requested:—

Gearbox number: Right-hand side of gearbox casing.

Rear axle: On top of axle casing on left-hand side.

Front axle: On top of axle casing on left-hand side.

Note that this book incorporates all Workshop Manual information appertaining to Land-Rovers circulated by means of combined Rover Service News Letters numbered up to 117 and Land-Rover Service News Letters numbered up to 22.

Index to Sections

See section title pages for detailed operation indexes

Section	Title	Pages
A	ENGINE 2 litre petrol 2 litre Diesel	A-1 to A-18 A-37 to A-57
AO	LUBRICATION SYSTEM	AO-1 to AO-7
B	CLUTCH	B-1 to B-11
C	GEARBOX	C-1 to C-27
D	PROPELLER SHAFTS	D-1 to D-3
E	REAR AXLE	E 1 to E-7
F	FRONT AXLE	F-1 to F-17
G	STEERING AND LINKAGE	G-1 to G-11
H	BRAKE SYSTEM	H-1 to H-17
J	SUSPENSION	J-1 to J-5
K	CHASSIS	K-1 to K-4
L	COOLING SYSTEM	L-1 to L-9
M	FUEL SYSTEM	M-1 to M-28
N	EXHAUST SYSTEM	N-1 to N-4
P	ELECTRICAL SYSTEM	P-1 to P-22
Q	INSTRUMENTS AND CONTROLS	Q-1 to Q-9
R	BODY	R-1 to R-19
S	WHEELS AND TYRES	S-1 to S-3
T	EXTRA EQUIPMENT	T-1 to T-56
V	RECLAMATION SCHEMES	V-1

Detailed Index

Component	Section	Component	Section
Air cleaner	M	Brakes, foot	H
Air cleaner support	K	Brake, transmission	H
Accelerator pedal and linkage	Q	Brush gear dynamo	P
Accelerator pedal housing	Q	Brush gear starter motor	P
Accelerator pump carburetter	M	Bump rubber, road spring	J
Accelerator shaft	Q	Bumper, front	K
Adaptor, external oil filter	A		
Adaptor, power-take-off	T		
Adjuster, timing chain	A	Cab	R
Ammeter	Q	Cable clips	P
Anchor plate, brake, foot	H	Cable harness, dash	P
Anchor plate, brake, hand	H	Cable harness, frame	P
Approved lubricants	AO	Cable harness, headlamp	P
Apron, front	R	Cable harness, main	P
Arm, drop	G	Cable, fuel tank	P
Arms, steering	F	Cable, speedometer	Q
Attachments, towing	T	Cables, high tension	P
Axle casing oil seal	F	Camshaft	A
Axle, front	F	Camshaft bearing	A
Axle, rear	E	Camshaft chain	A
Axle shaft, rear	E	Camshaft chain adjuster	A
Axles, stub	F	Capacity, cooling system	L
		Capacity, lubrication system	AO
		Capstan winch, front	T
Back leakage, fuel	M	Carburetter	M
Back light, cab	R	Carrier, battery	K
Back rest, rear seat	T	Carrier, spare wheel (on bonnet)	T
Back rest, seat	R	Casing, gearbox	C
Balance weight, road wheel	S	Catch, bonnet	R
Batteries	P	Centre cover panel	R
Battery and air cleaner support	K	Centre power take-off	T
Bearings, camshaft	A	Chaff guard	L
Bearings, centre propeller shaft, 107 and 109	D	Chain, tailboard	R
Bearings, connecting rod	A	Chain, timing	A
Bearings, gearbox	C	Change speed lever, main	C
Bearings, main	A	Change speed lever, transfer	C
Bearings, transfer box	C	Chassis frame	K
Bearings, steering column thrust	G	Check strap, rear spring	J
Bearings, swivel pin	F	Cleaner, air	M
Bearings, valve rockers	A	Clutch unit	B
Belt, fan	A	Clutch linkage	B
Bell housing	C	Clutch pedal unit	B
Board, tail	R	Clutch operating levers	B
Body, rear	R	Clutch plate	B
Body mounting	R	Clutch withdrawal mechanism	B
Body repairs	R	Coil, ignition	P
Body sides	R	Connecting rods	A
Bonnet	R	Control box, voltage	P
Bonnet carrier for spare wheel	T	Control, mixture	Q
Bonnet catch	R	Control tube, steering	G
Brake cylinder, master	H	Control quadrant, engine governor	T
Brake cylinder, wheel	H	Control quadrant, engine speed, Diesel	Q
Brake drum, foot	H	Cooler, oil	T
Brake drum, hand	H	Cooling system	L
Brake, hand	H	Cover, gearbox	R
Brake lever, hand	H	Cover plate, universal joint	T
Brake pedal	H	Cover plate, wing valance	R
Brake pipes	H	Crankcase sump	A
Brake shoe, foot	H	Crankshaft	A
Brake shoe, hand	H	Cushion, seat	R
Brake supply tank	H	Cushion, seat, rear	T

Component	Section
Cut-off control	Q
Cylinder block	A
Cylinder, brake, master	H
Cylinder, brake, wheel	H
Cylinder head	A
Cylinder liners	A
Dampers, hydraulic	J
Damper, vibration	A
Dash panel	R
Data, axles	E & F
Data, brakes	H
Data, clutch	B
Data, coolant system	L
Data, electrical	P
Data, engine	A
Data, extras	T
Data, fuel	M
Data, gearbox	C
Data, lubrication	AO
Data, steering	G
Data, suspension	J
Decarbonising	A
Differential, front	F
Differential pinion oil seal	F
Differential, rear	E
Dip switch	P
Distributor	P
Distributor housing	A
Door	R
Door hinges	R
Door locks	R
Doors and fittings	R
Drag link	G
Drawbar, rear	K
Driven plate, clutch	B
Driving shaft, front axle	F
Drop arm	G
Drum, foot brake	H
Drum, hand brake	H
Dynamo	P
Engine	A
Engine governor	T
Engine support, front	A
Engine support, rear	C
Exhaust manifold	A
Exhaust pipe, front	N
Exhaust rocker shaft	A
Exhaust silencer	N
Exhaust valves	A
Extra equipment	T
Fan	L
Fan belt	A
Fan driving pulley	A
Fastener, windscreen	R
Filler cap, petrol	M
Filter, injection pump	M
Filter, fuel pump	M
Filter, oil external	A
Filter, oil internal	A
Filters, fuel oil	M
Fire fighting equipment	T
Flashing indicators	T

Component	Section
Floor, front	R
Flywheel	A
Flywheel reclamation	V
Foot pedal	H
Frame alignment	K
Frame harness	P
Front axle	F
Front axle half shaft	F
Front bumper	K
Front capstan winch	T
Front exhaust pipe	N
Front hub	F
Front output shaft	C
Front shock absorber	J
Front wing	R
Fuel, gauge, instrument panel	Q
Fuel level unit	P
Fuel pump, 2 litre petrol	M
Fuel pump, Diesel	M
Fuel tank	M
Fuse box	P
Gauge unit, fuel tank	P
Gearbox	C
Gearbox bearings	C
Gearbox cover	R
Gearbox units, power take-off	T
Gear change levers	C
Gears, main gearbox	C
Gears, rear power take-off	T
Gears, transfer box	C
Glass, hard top, cab	R
Glass, windscreen	R
Governor, engine	T
Grille, radiator	R
Grommet, bell housing	C
Gudgeon pins	A
Half shaft	F
Hand brake	H
Hand throttle	T
Hard top	R
Harness, dash	P
Harness, frame	P
Harness, main	P
Headlamps	P
Heater plugs	P
Heater unit	T
Hinge, bonnet	R
Hinge, door	R
Hinge, locker lids	R
Hinge, ventilator	R
Hood, full length	T
Hood socket	T
Hood stick	T
Hood, three-quarter length	T
Horn	P
Horn button	P
Housing, accelerator pedal	Q
Housing, clutch withdrawal	B
Housing, distributor	A
Housing, front output	C
Housing, rear mainshaft bearing	C
Housings, swivel pin	F
Housing, universal joint	F

(iv)

Component	Section
Hub, front	F
Hydraulic dampers	J
Ignition switch	Q
Ignition timing	A
Indicators, flashing	T
Inlet manifold	A
Inlet rocker shaft	A
Inlet valves	A
Injection nozzle	M
Injection pump	M
Inner tubes	S
Instruments	Q
Lamp, head	P
Lamp, number plate	P
Lamp, rear	P
Lamp, side	P
Lamp, stop	P
Lamp switch	Q
Layshaft	C
Level gauge, fuel	Q
Level unit, fuel tank	M
Lever, change speed, main	C
Lever, change speed, transfer	C
Lever, hand brake	H
Levers, steering	F
Lever, steering relay	G
Light, warning, instrument panel	Q
Liners, cylinder	A
Link, drag	G
Linkage, accelerator	Q
Linkage, clutch	B
Linkage, hand brake	H
Linkage, steering	G
Lock, door	R
Lock stop, steering	F
Longitudinal tube, steering	G
Lubricants, recommended	AO
Lubricating system	AO
Main bearings	A
Main gear change lever	C
Mainshaft bearing housing, rear	C
Mainshaft, gearbox	C
Manifold, exhaust	A
Manifold, inlet	A
Master cylinder, brake	H
Mixture control	Q
Mixture control thermostat switch	P
Mounting, body	R
Mountings, engine	A & C
Nozzle, cleaning	M
Nozzle, flushing	M
Nozzle, injection	M
Nozzle, testing	M
Number plate lamp	P
Oil cooler	T
Oil filter, external	A
Oil filter, internal	A
Oil pressure gauge	T
Oil pressure release valve	A
Oil pump	A & AO
Oil seal, axle casing	F
Oil seal, pinion housing	F
Oil seal, swivel pin housing	F
Operating levers, clutch	B
Output shaft, front	C
Paint, touch-up process	R
Panel light switch	Q
Panel lights	Q
Pedal, accelerator	Q
Pedal, brake	H
Pedal, clutch	B
Petrol pipes	M
Petrol pump	M
Petrol sediment bowl	M
Petrol tank	M
Petrol level gauge	Q
Petrol tank level unit	P
Pins, gudgeon	A
Pins, shackle	J
Pins, swivel	F
Pipes, brake	H
Pistons	A
Plate clutch drive, starter	P
Plate, toe	R
Plate, tow	T
Plug, hot, Diesel	A
Plug, heater, Diesel	M
Plugs, sparking	A
Power take-off, centre	T
Power take-off, gearbox units	T
Power take-off, rear	T
Power take-off, rear pulley	T
Priming fuel system	M
Propeller shaft joint cover plates	T
Propeller, shaft, front	D
Propeller shaft, power take-off	D & T
Propeller shaft, rear	D
Pulley, power take-off	T
Pump, accelerator	M
Pump, oil	A
Pump, fuel	M
Pump, water	L
Radiator	L
Radiator grille panel	R
Rear axle	E
Rear axle shaft	E
Rear body	R
Rear capstan winch	T
Rear drawbar	K
Rear drive pulley	T
Rear lid, hard top	R
Rear number plate lamp	P
Rear power take-off	T
Rear seats	T
Reboring, petrol models	A
Recommended lubricants	AO
Relay unit, steering	G
Relief valve, oil	A
Resistance, heater plugs	P
Reverse stop, gearbox	C
Rings, piston	A
Riveting body panels	R
Road spring, front	J
Road spring, rear	J
Road wheels	S
Rocker shafts	A
Rod, connecting	A

(v)

Component	Section	Component	Section
Rod, hand brake	H	Switch, starter	P
Rod, track	G	Switch, stop lamp	P
Roof, hard top	R	Switch, direction indicator	T
Roof, tropical	R	Swivel pins	F
Rubber grommet, electrical	P	Swivel pin housings	F
		Synchronising clutch	C
Seat base	R	Tailboard	R
Seat cushions	R	Tailboard chain	R
Seats, rear	T	Tail lamps	P
Seats, standard vehicle	R	Tank, brake supply	B & H
Sediment bowl, fuel	M	Tank, fuel	M
Selector, four-wheel drive	C	Tappet adjustment	A
Selector, power take-off	T	Thermostat	L
Selector shaft, gear	C	Throttle control, hand	T
Shackle pins	J	Thrust bearings, crankshaft	A
Shaft, brake lever	H	Timing	A
Shaft, front axle	F	Timing chain tensioner	A
Shaft, gearbox selector	C	Toe plates	R
Shaft, output, front	C	Towing jaws	T
Shaft, propeller, front	D	Tow plates	T
Shaft, propeller, power take-off	D	Track rod	G
Shaft, propeller, rear	D	Transfer box	C
Shaft, front axle	F	Transfer shaft housing	C
Shaft, rear axle	E	Transmission brake	H
Shafts, rocker	A	Tropical roof panel, hard top and cab	R
Shock absorber, front	J	Tyre pressures	S
Shock absorber, rear	J	Tyres	S
Shoe, foot brake	H		
Shoe, hand brake	H	Units, power take-off	T
Side lamps	P	Universal joint cover plates	T
Side screen	R	Universal joint, front half shaft	F
Silencer, exhaust	N	Universal joint housing	F
Sleeve, clutch withdrawal	B		
Solenoid, starter motor	P	Valves	A
Spare wheel carrier (on bonnet)	T	Valves, fuel pump, petrol models	M
Sparking plugs	A	Valves, fuel pump, Diesel models	M
Speedometer	Q	Valve guides	A
Speedometer cable	Q	Valve rocker shafts	A
Spray form, Diesel nozzle	M	Valve seats, exhaust	A
Spring, road, front	J	Valve timing	A
Spring, road, rear	J	Vehicle heater	T
Starter drive	P	Ventilator, windscreen	R
Starter motor	P	Vertical drive shaft gear	A
Starter switch	P	Vibration damper	A
Steering column thrust bearing	G	Voltage regulator	P
Steering drag link	G		
Steering longitudinal tube	G	Warning lights, instrument panel	Q
Steering relay unit	G	Water pump	L
Steering track rod	G	Water temperature gauge	T
Steering unit	G	Wheel alignment	G
Steering wheel	G	Wheel brakes	H
Stop lamps	P	Wheel cylinder, brake	H
Stop lamp switch	P	Wheels, road	S
Stub axles	F	Wheel, steering	G
Stub shaft	F	Wheel support, spare (on bonnet)	T
Sump, crankcase	A	Winch, capstan, front	T
Sump filter	A	Window glass, hard top	R
Supply tank, brake and clutch	B & H	Windscreen	R
Support, air cleaner	K	Windscreen fastener	R
Support, engine front	A	Windscreen ventilator	R
Support, engine rear	C	Windscreen wiper	P
Support, spare wheel	T	Windtone horn	P
Switch, dip	P	Wing, front	R
Switch, ignition	Q	Wing valance cover plate	R
Switch, lamps	Q	Wiring diagram, flashers and trailers	T
Switch, panel lights	Q	Wiring diagram, general	P
		Withdrawal mechanism, clutch	B

(vi)

Section A — ENGINE — PETROL MODELS

INDEX

	Page
Camshaft	
Removal	A-4
Fitment	A-5
Camshaft bearings	
Removal	A-4
Fitment	A-5
Camshaft chain wheel	
Removal	A-3
Fitment	A-10
Connecting rod	
Removal	A-4
Fitment	A-6
Connecting rod bearings	
Removal	A-4
Fitment	A-6
Crankshaft	
Removal	A-4
Fitment	A-5
Crankshaft bearings	
Removal	A-4
Fitment	A-5
Crankshaft chain wheel	
Removal	A-3
Fitment	A-10
Cylinder head	
Removal	A-3
Fitment	A-9
Data	A-16
Decarbonising	A-13
Defect location	A-15
Engine removal from chassis	A-2
Engine dismantling procedure	A-2
Engine assembly procedure	A-5
Fan belt adjustment	A-12
Flywheel	A-4 and 8
Gudgeon pins	
Removal	A-4
Fitment	A-7
Ignition timing	A-12
Liner fitment	A-7
Oil filter—external	
Removal	A-14
Fitment	A-14
Pistons and piston rings	
Removal	A-4
Fitment	A-6
Push-rod	
Removal	A-3
Fitment	A-9
Reboring	A-7
Rocker gear, exhaust	
Removal	A-4
Fitment	A-9
Rocker gear, inlet	
Removal	A-3
Fitment	A-9
Tappet adjustment	A-10
Timing chain	
Removal—engine removed	A-3
Fitment—engine removed	A-10
Renewal—engine installed	A-14
Timing chain tensioner	
Removal	A-3
Fitment	A-10
Valves	
Removal	A-4
Fitment	A-9
Valve guides	
Removal	A-8 and 9
Fitment	A-8 and 9
Valve timing	A-10
Vibration damper	A-11

LIST OF ILLUSTRATIONS

Fig.		Page
A-1	Oil pressure relief valve	A-2
A-2	Timing chain and tensioner	A-3
A-3	Clip for timing chain tensioner	A-3
A-4	Removing camshaft chainwheel	A-3
A-5	Exhaust rocker shafts and distributor housing location bolts	A-4
A-6	Camshaft bearing location bolts	A-4
A-7	Removing gudgeon pin	A-4
A-8	Checking main bearing nip	A-5
A-9	Checking crankshaft end-float	A-5
A-10	Guide in position on cylinder block (oil seals)	A-5
A-11	Checking big-end bearing nip	A-6
A-12	Checking piston clearance	A-6
A-13	Checking piston ring gap	A-7
A-14	Fitting gudgeon pin	A-7
A-15	Reboring, jig block	A-7
A-16	Fitting cylinder liner	A-7
A-17	Checking flywheel run-out	A-8
A-18	Fitting exhaust valve guide	A-8
A-19	Removing exhaust valve seat	A-8
A-20	Fitting exhaust valve seat	A-8
A-21	Early and late type valve seals	A-9
A-22	Drilling oil feed holes, inlet rockers	A-9
A-23	Tightening cylinder head bolts	A-9
A-24	Tappet adjustment	A-10
A-25	Exhaust valve fully open position	A-10
A-26	Timing chain and tensioner	A-10
A-27	Checking vibration damper run-out	A-11
A-28	Balancing vibration damper	A-11
A-29	Oil pressure relief valve	A-11
A-30	Order of tightening cylinder head bolts	A-13

ENGINE REMOVAL AND DISMANTLING PROCEDURE

Removing engine   **Operation A/2**

1. If fitted, remove the spare wheel from bonnet panel.

2. Remove the bonnet panel.

3. Disconnect the battery leads.

4. Disconnect the air intake pipe from the carburetter and remove air cleaner.

5. Drain the coolant from system (one tap at bottom L.H. side of radiator and one tap at L.H. side of cylinder block).

6. Disconnect the side lamp leads at snap connectors at each side of the grille panel assembly and the front lamp harness from the junction box at R.H. side of scuttle, then pull the wiring clear to front of engine.

7. Detach the top hose at radiator header tank and the bottom hose from water pump inlet.

8. Remove the fan blades.

9. Remove the bolts securing the grille panel to the front cross member and front wings.

10. Lift the radiator, grille panel and headlamps assembly upward, then forward to clear the vehicle.

11. Disconnect the exhaust pipe from exhaust manifold.

12. Disconnect the heater pipes (if fitted) at the engine side of scuttle.

13. Disconnect the petrol pipe at carburetter.

14. Disconnect the throttle return spring, throttle linkage (at a ball joint) and the cold start control cable at carburetter and clamp. If fitted, disconnect the engine governor operating rod. Section T.

15. Disconnect:
Dynamo wiring; ignition coil leads; starter lead from switch; oil pressure switch wire; mixture control switch wire (at rear of cylinder head).

16. Secure a sling to the engine and with suitable lifting tackle just take the strain.

17. Remove the front floor and gearbox cover.

18. Support the gearbox assembly with a jack or packing blocks.

19. Remove the remaining nuts and washers securing the gearbox to the flywheel housing.

20. Remove the bolts from engine front support brackets and allow the engine to move forward and thus clear the gearbox input shaft. Ensure that the speedometer cable and all wires, etc., are clear, then hoist the engine gently from the vehicle.

21. Drain the oil from sump.

22. Bolt the engine to a suitable stand.

DISMANTLING ENGINE

Externals   **Operation A/4**

1. Disconnect the accelerator linkage (at a ball joint), distributor vacuum pipe and remove carburetter. Detach sparking plug covers and leads, remove locating screw and withdraw the distributor. Remove sparking plugs.

2. If fitted, disconnect the heater pipe and flow control tap from cylinder head.

3. Remove the exhaust rocker cover.

4. Remove the dynamo and starter motor.

5. Remove the exhaust and inlet manifolds.

6. Remove the external full flow oil filter complete.

7. Disconnect the oil feed pipe—gallery to cylinder head.

8. Remove the dipstick and tube, then drain and remove sump.

Oil pump   **Operation A/6**

1. Slacken the locknut securing oil pressure adjusting screw, then remove screw, washer, spring, plunger and ball (which may remain in the pump and can be removed when the pump complete is withdrawn).

2. Remove the pump locating screw.

3. Withdraw the pump, leaving the drive shaft in position.

4. If necessary, withdraw the oil pump drive shaft. Operation A/18.

Note: See Section AO for details of oil pump strip and assembly.

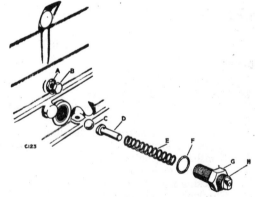

Fig. A-1—Oil pressure relief valve

A—Locknut   E—Spring
B—Locating screw—oil pump   F—Washer
C—Ball   G—Locknut
D—Plunger   H—Adjusting screw—oil
                                        pressure

Vibration damper Operation A/8

1. Remove the starter dog, using spanner Part No. 263055 or 530102.
2. Withdraw the vibration damper complete.
3. Remove the plate, shims (if fitted), rubber disc, driving flange and second disc from the damper flywheel. Six set screws.
4. If necessary, remove the flywheel bush.

Water pump and front cover Operation A/10

1. Remove the thermostat housing from the cylinder head complete with thermostat, outlet pipe, inlet elbow and joint washer.
2. Remove the copper tube and rubber joint ring from either the bottom face of the thermostat housing or the top face of the water pump casing.
3. Remove the water pump complete with joint washer and inlet pipe; as the pump casing is spigoted in the block, it will be necessary to oscillate it slightly as it is removed.

   To strip water pump completely for overhauling purposes, refer to Section L.
4. Remove the securing bolts and remove the front cover.

Timing chain tensioner and chain wheels Operation A/12

1. Remove the crankshaft oil thrower.
2. Release the pawl from the ratchet, compress the tensioner spring by lifting the jockey pulley arm as far as possible, and fit clip, Part No. 262748, over the tensioner.

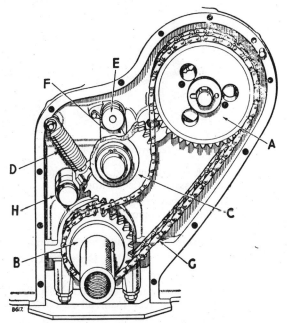

Fig. A-2—Timing chain and tensioner

A—Camshaft chainwheel E—Pawl
B—Crankshaft chainwheel F—Ratchet
C—Jockey pulley G—Timing chain (driving side)
D—Hydraulic tensioner H—Jockey pulley arm

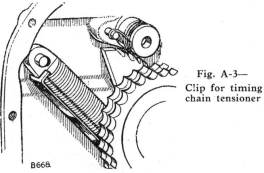

Fig. A-3—
Clip for timing
chain tensioner

3. Remove the jockey pulley; remove the driving chain.
4. Withdraw the jockey pulley arm and tensioner.
5. Carefully remove the special clip and part the tensioner spring, piston, cylinder and, if necessary, extract the ball and the two retaining springs from the cylinder.
6. If necessary, extract the pawl pivot pin (5/16 in. B.S.F. tapped hole); remove the pawl and pawl spring.
7. Remove the camshaft chainwheel, using extractor, Part No. 262750, or Part No. 507231.

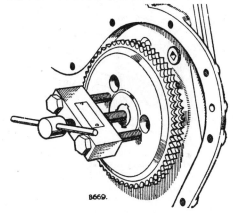

Fig. A-4—Removing camshaft chainwheel

8. If necessary, remove the crankshaft chainwheel, using a claw extractor.
9. Wash and dry all tensioner components and renew any worn part.

Cylinder head and inlet rocker gear Operation A/14

1. Remove the inlet rocker cover.
2. Remove the rocker shaft complete with all components.
   Note: The 3/8 in. (spanner size) nuts have 7/16 in. threads.
3. Remove the components and lay out in the following order: Rear bracket (located by set screws); spring; R.H. rocker; bracket; L.H. rocker; two brackets; spring; R.H. rocker; bracket; L.H. rocker; spring; front bracket.
4. Withdraw the push rods and insert them in a piece of cardboard pre-pierced and marked.
5. Loosen the securing bolts evenly and lift the cylinder head clear.

6. Using a valve spring compressing tool, Part No. 276102, remove the valve assemblies. The valves should be inserted in a piece of cardboard pre-pierced and marked. Retain the springs in pairs; they are selected to ensure an interference fit.

Exhaust valves   Operation A/16

1. Slacken the tappet adjusting screws right back.

2. Set each rocker on the back of its cam, and using a valve spring compressing tool, Part No. 276102, remove the valve assemblies. The valves should be inserted in a piece of cardboard pre-pierced and marked. Retain the springs in pairs; they are selected to ensure an interference fit.

Exhaust rocker shafts and distributor housing
Operation A/18

1. Remove the plug and fibre washer from the flywheel end of the cylinder block.

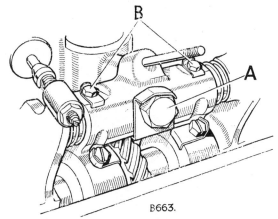

B663.

Fig. A-5—Exhaust rocker shaft and distributor housing location bolts

A—Distributor housing location bolt.
B—Exhaust rocker shaft location bolts.

2. Remove the location bolts; two for the rocker shafts and a hollow bolt for the distributor housing. Withdraw the distributor housing, and remove oil pump drive shaft.

3. Withdraw the rear shaft using extractor, Part No. 262749.
Lay out the components in order:—
Spring; R.H. rocker; washer; R.H. cam follower; washer; L.H. rocker; spring. Same order applies to both rocker shafts.

4. Repeat for the front shaft.

Camshaft and camshaft bearing removal
Operation A/20

1. Remove the camshaft thrust plate.

2. Remove the bolt and lock washers locating each of the three front bearings.

3. Withdraw the camshaft until the third bearing is clear of No. 2 bearing housing; split the bearings and lay aside. Remove the camshaft and front bearing.
Split the front bearing and remove.

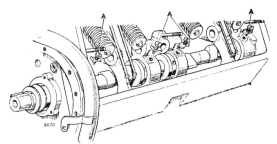

B670

Fig. A-6—Camshaft bearing location bolts
A—Location bolts

4. If necessary, remove the bolt and lock washer from the rear bearing. Remove the rear camshaft cover.

5. Remove the rear bearing; preserve all bearings in their respective pairs.

Flywheel   Operation A/22

1. Remove the clutch assembly, then the flywheel securing bolts and withdraw the flywheel. The primary pinion bush may be extracted if necessary.

Pistons and connecting rods   Operation A/24

1. Remove the connecting rod caps, bearings and bolts.

2. Push each connecting rod up and turn, in order to engage the slots at the bottom of the cylinder bore. Remove the circlips; withdraw the gudgeon pin, using extractor, Part No. 278668; remove the piston.

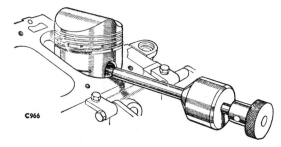

C966

Fig. A-7—Removing gudgeon pin

3. Lower each connecting rod, turning the crankshaft as necessary to effect withdrawal.

4. Remove the piston rings.
Note: Mark all components in sets.

Crankshaft, main bearing and rear bearing
oil seal   Operation A/26

1. Remove the flywheel housing.

2. Remove the main bearing caps and shells. The lower half of the rear main oil seal may be removed complete with rear main bearing cap.

3. Lift out the crankshaft and remaining bearing halves. The bearing halves must be preserved in pairs. Ensure that the thrust washers are retained in original housings if used again.

ENGINE ASSEMBLY

Camshaft   Operation A/28

Note: The bearings must be fitted dry and must be a hand push fit in the cylinder blocks; they must always be renewed in paired halves and the numbers stamped on one of the end faces of each of the bearing halves must be adjacent.

The rear bearing is provided with four lateral holes.

1. Checking bearing clearance on camshaft, if new bearings are fitted, make sure that they can be dismantled and assembled without difficulty.

2. Insert the camshaft partly into the cylinder block, assemble the bearings on to the shaft with the locating holes in line with the holes in the housing, and push the shaft into position.

3. Line up the locating holes in the bearings and housings, and before replacing the set bolts, squirt oil down the holes to lubricate the bearings until oil pressure is built up. Replace set bolts. See Fig. A 6.

4. Fit the camshaft thrust plate and chain wheel. The camshaft should have .003 in. (0,07 mm) to .005 in. (0,12 mm) end-float, measured between the chain wheel and the thrust plate.

Crankshaft, main bearing and seals
                              Operation A/30

1. To check that the bearing caps have not been filed, first assemble the caps without bearing shells to the crankcase, ensuring that they are correctly located by means of the dowels. Tighten both securing bolts for each cap, then slacken one bolt of each pair right off. There should be no clearance at the joint face.

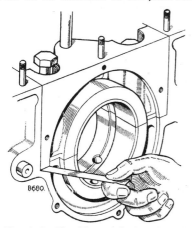

Fig. A-8—Checking main bearing nip

2. Remove the bearing caps and fit the bearing shells, locating by means of the tags. Tighten the caps down and slacken off one bolt of each pair. Check the bearing nip, as illustrated in Fig. A-8, ensuring that the clearance does not exceed .004 to .006 in. (0,10 to 0,15 mm). The nip can be corrected by selective assembly of bearing shells; these are available in slightly varying thicknesses.

3. When the bearing nip has been checked, remove the caps and bearing shell bottom halves. Position a standard-size thrust bearing at each side of centre bearing shell—top half, and fit the crankshaft.

4. Refit the bearing shell bottom halves and bearing caps. Tighten the securing bolts evenly and check each bearing in turn for correct clearance. The crankshaft should resist rotation when a feeler paper, .0025 in. (0,06 mm) thick, is placed between any one bearing shell and crankshaft journal, and turn freely by hand when the feeler paper is removed. Adjust by selective assembly of bearing shells.

5. Check the crankshaft end-float with a feeler gauge (Fig. A-9); adjust at centre bearing by selective assembly of thrust washers to give .002 to .006 in. (0,05 to 0,15 mm) end-float.

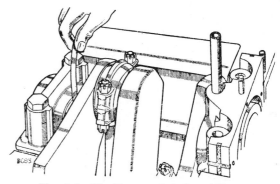

Fig. A-9—Checking crankshaft end-float

6. Remove the bearing caps, bottom half shells and crankshaft.

7. To the rear main bearing cap fit neoprene seals in recess at each side, and on the rear face fit the lower half of crankshaft rear bearing seal.

8. Fit the top half of crankshaft rear bearing oil seal to the crankcase. Lubricate bearing face with Silicone MS4 Compound.

9. If the crankshaft end-float reading, obtained in Item 5, was not within the limits, fit suitable oversize thrust bearings. The variation of thrust bearing thickness at each side must not exceed .003 in. (0,07 mm) to ensure that the crankshaft remains centralised.

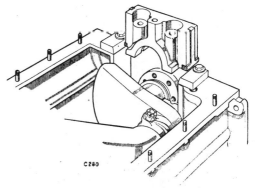

Fig. A-10—Guide in position on cylinder block

Lubricate the crankshaft journals, main bearing shells and thrust bearings, then refit crankshaft.

Smear bearing face of crankshaft rear bearing oil seal with Silicone MS4 compound.

Fitment of the rear main bearing cap with side seals in position, will be facilitated by using a lead tool (Part No. 270304) fitted to the sump studs adjacent to rear bearing cap aperture.

It will be found advantageous to cut a slight lead on to the bottom edges of the side seals, as this will prevent them from folding under the cap during fitment, thus causing an oil leak due to the cap not seating properly. Smear seals with Silicone MS4 Compound when fitting.

Connecting rods   Operation A/32

1. The oil hole in gudgeon pin bush is pre-drilled and care must be taken to ensure that the oil holes of bush and connecting rod will align when the bush is pressed into position. The gudgeon pin bushes should be a .001 to .002 in. (0,02 to 0,05 mm) interference fit in connecting rods. Ream the bush when fitted to connecting rod to allow a .0003 to .0005 in. (0,007 to 0,012 mm) gudgeon pin clearance. Ensure that correct alignment is maintained while reamering.

   This fit is selected to give the smallest possible clearance consistent with a smooth revolving action.

2. Fit each connecting rod to a suitable test rig and check for twist and mal-alignment.

3. To check that the connecting rod has not been filed:—

   Select the correct cap for each connecting rod, as denoted by the number stamped near the joint faces. This number also indicates the crankpin to which it must be fitted.

   Assemble the connecting rods, less shell bearings, with corresponding numbers together. Tighten the securing nuts, then slacken one of them right off and check that there is no clearance at the joint face.

4. Check the bearing nip as follows:—

   Fit the bearing shells and tighten both securing nuts—slacken one nut as before and check the nip with a feeler gauge; this should be .002 to .004 in. (0,05 to 0,10 mm).

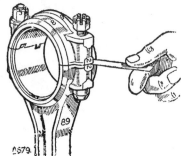

Fig. A-11—Checking big-end bearing nip

5. If the bearing nip is too great, decrease by rubbing down the joint faces of the bearings on fine emery cloth; if the bearing nip is too small, select another pair of bearings, and re-check the bearing nip.

   If the bearing nip is still small, re-check that the connecting rod has NOT been filed (see Item 3).

6. Assemble the big-end of each connecting rod to its respective crankpin, then check for correct end-float, by inserting a feeler gauge between the end face of the rod and the crankpin shoulder. End-float should be .009 to .013 in. (0,23 to 0,33 mm).

7. Remove the connecting rods from the crankshaft, ensuring that the bearing shells are kept with the rods to which they were fitted.

Pistons   Operation A/34

1. When fitting pistons, standard or oversize, the cylinder bore clearance should be in accordance with the dimensions laid down in the data section. When reboring, the block must be honed to suit the selected pistons. In the absence of suitably accurate measuring instruments, a long feeler .0025 in. (0,06 mm) thick may be inserted against the thrust side of the bore as illustrated in Fig. A-12 and the piston located crown downward. The piston should become a tight fit when the top of the skirt (immediately below the bottom scraper ring) enters the bore.

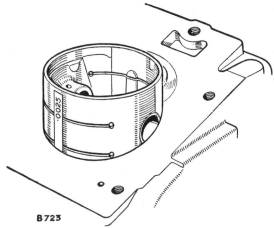

B723

Fig. A-12—Checking piston clearance

Piston ring fitting

Check gap and side clearance. To check gap, support the ring in the cylinder bore with an old piston.

Stepped scraper rings, where used, must be fitted with the larger diameter at the top.

Compression rings are marked "T" or "Top" on one face.

3. The gudgeon pin, when cold and dry, should be an easy sliding fit in the connecting rod and should have a slight interference fit in both piston bores, i.e. so that it can be pressed in by hand, but will not fall out under its own weight.

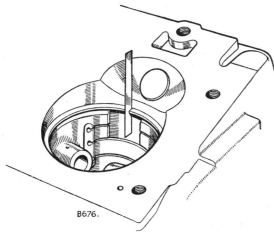

Fig. A-13—Checking piston ring gap

Pistons to connecting rods   Operation A/36

1. Enter the connecting rod, without bolts, up into the cylinder bore and engage in the cylinder block slots.

2. Enter the skirt of the piston into the top of the bore, with the flat top of the piston in line with the oil hole in the connecting rod.

3. Fit the gudgeon pin, using thimble Part No. 272103, to align piston and connecting rod. Lock the pin in position with circlips.

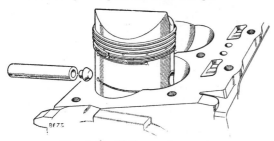

Fig. A-14—Fitting gudgeon pin

Piston and connecting rod to cylinder block and crankshaft   Operation A/38

1. The connecting rod bolts are a tight fit in the rod and must be tapped into place with a 'Z' shaped bar.

2. Turn the crankshaft until the crank journals relative to numbers 1 and 4 cylinders are at B.D.C. Squirt oil on to the journal, refit appropriate bearings to cap and connecting rod, pull the rod down to the journal and fit cap, ensuring that the oil hole in the connecting rod is on the opposite side to the camshaft. Tighten the nuts to 30 lb/ft. (4 mKg) on 1948-53 models and to 40 lb/ft. (5,5 mKg) on 1954-58 models and then turn on to the next split pin hole. Fit split pin.

Re-boring   Operation A/40

1. Re-boring conforms to normal practice. It is necessary to employ a jig block, Part No. 261287, to enable standard equipment to be used.

It should also be noted that on early engines the upper portion of the bores is chromium plated; the chromium is too hard for standard cutters,

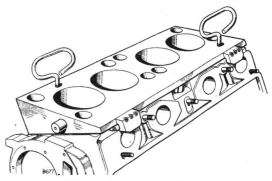

Fig. A-15—Re-boring jig block

so that the first cut, starting from the top of the bore, must be sufficiently deep to cut behind the plating.

2. If the cylinder block has already been bored out to maximum size, cylinder liners may be fitted.

Cylinder liners   Operation A/42

1. Fitting conforms to standard practice; note the following points:—

2. Machine the cylinder block bores as follows:
1948-51 1.6 litre .... 2.937 in. + .001 (74,60 mm + 0,025)
1952-54 2.0 litre .... 3.188 in. + .001 (80,97 mm + 0,025)
1955-58 2.0 litre .... 3.245 in. + .001 (82,42 mm + 0,025)
This gives an interference fit of .003 to .004 in. (0,075 to 0,10 mm).

3. Prior to pressing in the liner, allowance must be made for twist up to 3/16 in. (5 mm) clockwise. To facilitate re-alignment should the liner not be positioned correctly at the first attempt, scribe lines down the sides of the liner from the two peaks and make corresponding marks on the cylinder block.

4. Press in the liner, using press block Part No. 262864, until the top edge is level with the bottom of the exhaust valve pocket. Blend to the shape of the cylinder block.

5. Bore to suit the selected pistons. Operations A/40 and A/34.

Liners for the 1.6 litre engine can be bored out to a maximum of .040 in. (1,00 mm).

Liners for the 2.0 litre engine can only be bored out to suit standard or .010 in. (0,25 mm) oversize pistons.

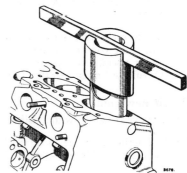

Fig. A-16—Fitting cylinder liner

Flywheel housing and flywheel
Operation A/44

1. Ensure that the rear main bearing oil seal is in good condition, then secure the flywheel housing to cylinder block.

2. Fit the flywheel and tighten the securing bolts to 70 lb/ft (9,8 mKg).

3. Check the run-out on the flywheel face as illustrated by Fig. A-17. The run-out must not exceed .005 in. (0,12 mm) at outer edge of face.

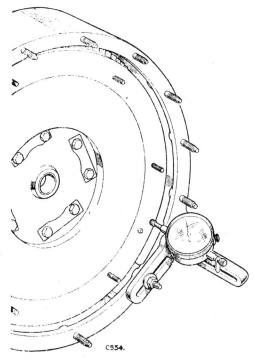

Fig. A-17—Checking run-out on flywheel face

Exhaust valves　　　　　　Operation A/46

1. Grind the seats to $45° + \frac{1}{4}$, using 'Vibro-centric' equipment.

2. Face the valves to $45° - \frac{1}{4}$ and lap into their respective seats.

3. Wash each valve, seat, port and guide in paraffin.

4. Locate each valve into their respective guides and, using compressor Part No. 276102, fit the spring assemblies, caps and split cones. A new 'O' ring seal must be fitted to each guide.

To fit new guides

5. Remove the guide with a drift, Part No. 263051.

6. Pull in the new guide, using tool Part No. 262753, and ream to .3448 in.—.0005 (8,757 mm—0,012)

7. Repeat items 1 to 4 inclusive.

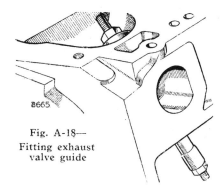

Fig. A-18—
Fitting exhaust
valve guide

To fit new seats

Note.—Special attention is needed to prevent possible injury from flying fragments when the insert is broken.

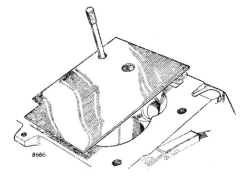

Fig. A-19—Removing exhaust valve seat

8. Secure protection plate, Part No. 263050, over the appropriate cylinder bore, and cover the opening below the insert with a heavy pad of rag.

9. Break the insert by means of a chisel applied through the hole in the plate.

10. Remove the valve guide by means of a piloted drift, Part No. 263051.

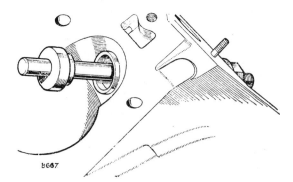

Fig. A-20—Fitting exhaust valve seat

11. Clean the seat recess and pull the new insert into position, using tool Part No. 262752. It is not necessary to heat the block or freeze the insert, but light taps on the tool may be required to ensure that the insert enters smoothly.

12. Continue precautions against fragmentation for a few minutes, as the insert may shatter a short time after fitting.

13. Pull in the new valve guide, using tool Part No. 262753.

14. Repeat items 1 to 4 inclusive.

Exhaust rocker shafts assembly
Operation A/48

Note.—When fitting a replacement rocker or cam-follower, it is essential that the component be fitted with the special protective coating of grease still adhering.

1. Fit new bushes in the rockers and followers as necessary and drill through the 1/16 in. (1,58 mm) oil feed hole. The bush must be a *light drive fit* in the rocker or follower and a *sliding fit* on the shaft. Ream in position to .593 in.+.001 (15,081 mm+0,025).

2. Replace shafts by inserting front shaft through the locating hole and assembling component parts in the following order: spring; R.H. rocker, washer; R.H. cam-follower; L.H. cam-follower; washer; L.H. rocker; spring.

3. Repeat for rear shaft, ensuring that, with both shafts in position, the oil feed holes in the rocker shafts are facing towards the cylinder block. The front of each shaft is marked 'F'.

4. Fit the plugs and fibre washer; for tappet adjustment see Operation A/54.

Inlet valves   Operation A/50

1. Cut the valve seats (in cylinder head) to $30° + \frac{1}{4}$ only when necessary; normally they require cutting only at every second or third decarbonising operation.

2. Face the valves to $30° - \frac{1}{4}$ and lap into their respective seats.

3. Wash each valve, seat, port and guide in paraffin.

4. Locate each valve into their respective guides and, using compressor Part No. 276102, fit the spring assemblies, caps and split cones. A new 'O' ring seal must be fitted to each guide.

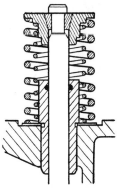 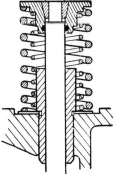

Later seal   Fig. A-21   Early seal

To fit new guides

5. Remove the guide with a drift, Part No. 263051.

6. Press in the new guide, and ream to .3448 in.—.0005 (8,757 mm—0,012).

7. Repeat items 1-4, noting that the seat must be ground in the event of a new guide being fitted.

Cylinder head and rocker gear
Operation A/52

1. Smear the joint face of cylinder block and cylinder head gasket with engine oil, then fit the gasket and cylinder head to cylinder block.

2. Locate head and gasket with the securing bolts, fitting all bolts except those which also secure the rocker shaft pedestals, but do not tighten at this stage.

3. Insert the push-rods into their original position, through cylinder head and locate in the cam-followers.

4. Fit new bushes in the rockers as necessary. The bush must be a *light drive fit* in the rocker and a *sliding fit* on the shaft. Press a new bush in with its shoulder on the same side as the rocker pad; drill through the oil feed holes—7/64 in. (2,77 mm) to the push-rod and 1/16 in. (1,58 mm) in the top of the rocker. Ream in position to .005 in+.001 (12,7 mm+ 0,025).

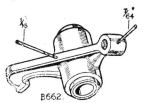

Fig. A-22—
Drilling oil feed holes

5. Fit the component parts to the rocker shafts in the following order:

Rear bracket (located by set screw); spring; R.H. rocker; bracket; L.H. rocker; two brackets; spring; R.H. rocker; bracket; L.H. rocker; spring; front bracket.

6. Fit the rocker shaft to the cylinder head. When in position, the oil feed holes in the rocker shaft must face the push-rods. Tighten all the bolts down in the manner illustrated by Fig. A-23: $\frac{7}{16}$ in. bolts to 50 lb/ft. (7 mKg) ; $\frac{3}{8}$ in. bolts to 30 lb/ft. (4 mKg).

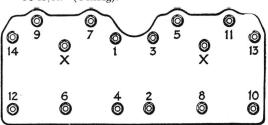

Fig. A-23—
Order of tightening cylinder head bolts. Those marked X also secure the rocker shaft.

Tappet adjustment   **Operation A/54**

The exhaust tappets may be set with the engine hot or cold.

The inlet tappets should be set with the engine at running temperature.

1. Set the valve receiving attention fully open by engaging the starting handle and turning the engine, then rotate the engine one complete revolution, to bring the tappet on the back of the cam.

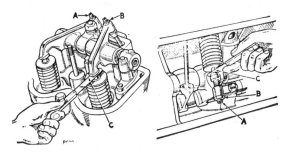

Fig. A-24—Tappet adjustment

A—Tappet adjusting screw   B—Locknut
C—Feeler gauge

2. Slacken the tappet locknut and using a feeler gauge, rotate the adjusting screw to give the correct clearance .010 in. (0,25 mm) inlet and .012 in. (0,30 mm) exhaust, bearing down on the screw to take up all the clearance at the push-rod ends.

Tighten the locknut.

3. Repeat for the remaining tappets.

Chain wheels, timing chain, adjuster and valve timing   **Operation A/56**

1. Fit the crankshaft chain wheel on to shaft and key.

2. Turn the crankshaft in direction of rotation until the E.P. mark on the flywheel is in line with the timing pointer.

3. Replace the camshaft chainwheel and key (do not secure at this stage), rotate the camshaft and set No. 1 exhaust tappet at .010 in. (0,254 mm).

4. If removed, refit the pawl pivot pin, pawl and spring.

5. Fit dial test indicator and bracket, Part No. 262751, so that the "fully open" position of No. 1 exhaust valve can be ascertained in the following manner:—

   (a) Turn the camshaft **in** direction of rotation until the lobe of cam has nearly opened the valve fully, then stop rotation and mark the chain wheel and timing case to record the position.

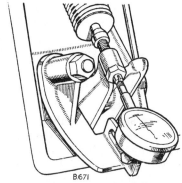

Fig. A-25—Checking exhaust valve fully open position

   (b) Note the reading on dial test indicator, then continue to turn the chain wheel slowly **in** direction of rotation until the needle has again reached the same position.

   (c) Mark the chain wheel at a point opposite to the mark on timing case and make a third mark on the chain wheel, exactly midway between those made previously.

   (d) Turn the camshaft **against** direction of rotation until the third mark is in line with that on timing casing, whereon the valve should be fully open.

Fit the timing chain with "**no slack**" on the driving side. It may be necessary to remove and re-position the camshaft chain wheel to obtain this "no slack" condition on the driving side when the flywheel and camshaft are correctly positioned. The camshaft chain wheel is provided with three irregularly spaced keyways to facilitate accurate timing.

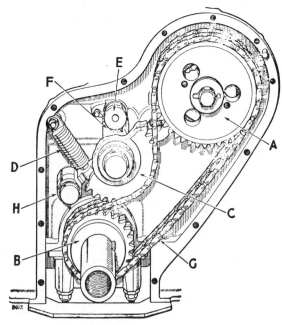

Fig. A-26—Timing chain and tensioner

A—Camshaft chain wheel   E—Pawl
B—Crankshaft chain wheel   F—Ratchet
C—Jockey pulley   G—Timing chain (driving side)
D—Hydraulic tensioner   H—Jockey pulley arm

6. Fit the jockey pulley arm to its locating spindle.

7. Assemble the hydraulic tensioner, compress and retain the spring with clip, Part No. 262748, and fit complete assembly to its locating spindle. Position the ball-end in its seat on the pulley arm, holding the ratchet pawl clear, and push arm upwards to the extent of its travel. Remove the special clip and fit jockey wheel.

8. Release the pulley arm and allow jockey wheel to take up slack in the timing chain.

9. Check the timing by rotating the engine and correct if necessary, by moving the camshaft chain wheel to one of the other key-ways.

10. Finally, secure the tensioner with a split pin and plain washer, secure the jockey wheel with a circlip and secure the camshaft chainwheel by locating the lockwasher in one of the vacant key-ways and bending over the tag. Fit the oil thrower to the crankshaft noting that, correctly located, it curves away from the chain.

Water pump and front cover Operation A/58

1. Renew the joint washer and smear with a light grease.

2. Fit front cover to block (two locating dowels) and secure with bolts.

3. For details of assembly procedure for water pump, refer to Section L.

4. Fit new joint washer, smear with light grease and offer assembly to cylinder block, complete with copper tube and rubber joint ring in recess on top of water pump.

5. Locate securing bolts and tighten.

6. Fit thermostat housing complete with thermostat, outlet pipe, inlet elbow and joint washer, to cylinder head, taking care not to dislodge the copper and rubber washer.

Vibration damper Operation A/60

1. If stripped, examine the flywheel bush. Renew if necessary, noting that it should be a press fit in the flywheel and an easy fit on the driving flange.

2. When reassembling the damper, discard any shims which may have been previously fitted. These have been found to be unnecessary. Tighten the screws fully.

3. Mount the unit on a suitable mandrel, using a slave location key and rotate on centres. Adjust the run-out on the front face by tightening the screws at the point where a dial test indicator gives a minus reading. Secure the screws by staking.

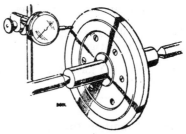

Fig. A-27—Checking vibration damper run-out

4. Balance statically, using putty or similar material. Weigh the putty and drill balancing holes in the flywheel. *Note:* A hole $\frac{3}{8}$ in. (9,52 mm) dia. x $\frac{1}{4}$ in. (6,35 mm) deep represents $1\frac{1}{2}$ grams.

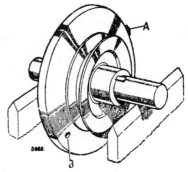

Fig. A-28—Balancing vibration damper
A—Putty   B—Balancing hole

5. Refit damper on crankshaft, securing with a lock washer and starting dog. Tighten the starting dog, using spanner Part No. 263055.

Oil pump Operation A/62

1. For details of assembly procedure for oil pump, refer to Section AO.

2. With the gauze oil strainer secured in position, offer the pump up to the engine.

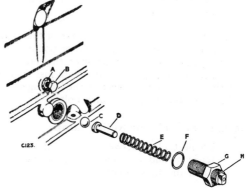

Fig. A-29—Oil pressure relief valve

A—Locknut
B—Locating screw—oil pump
C—Ball
D—Plunger
E—Spring
F—Washer
G—Locknut
H—Adjusting screw—oil pressure

3. Fit the pump locating screw and locknut.

4. Fit the relief valve assembly. Do not tighten the locknut at this stage.

5. Refer to Section AO for details of oil pressure adjustment.

Distributor and ignition timing
Operation A/64

1. Rotate the engine in running direction until the F.A. 15° mark (1948-53 models) or the F.A. 10° mark (1954-58 models) on the flywheel is in line with the pointer, with both valves on No. 1 cylinder closed.

2. Fit the oil pump drive shaft so that when fully engaged in oil pump, the broad segment of driving spigot will be nearest to No. 3 exhaust port. The crankshaft may have to be rotated slightly to allow engagement of driving shaft in oil pump, and when this is necessary, item 1 must be repeated.

3. Secure the distributor housing in position with the hollow oil feed bolt, then fit distributor drive shaft.

4. Locate a cork washer in recess in top of distributor housing.

5. Check the distributor contact breaker clearance and adjust if necessary, .014 to .016 in. (0,35 to 0,40 mm). Set the octane selector so that the fourth line from the L.H. side of the calibrated slide is against the face of distributor body casting.

6. Rotate the distributor spindle until the rotor is at the firing point for No. 1 cylinder. The broad side of the driving spigot should be towards No. 3 exhaust port and vacuum unit facing forward when the distributor is located.

7. Mount distributor and secure to distributor housing.

8. Slacken the pinch bolt at the base of the distributor body; rotate the distributor bodily in the opposite direction to the arrow on the rotor arm, until the contact breaker points are just opening with the fibre cam follower on the leading side of the cam; retighten the pinch bolt.

Checking with 12 volt timing lamp

(a) Connect a lead between the distributor L.T. terminal and the centre pole of the bulb; earth the bulb body.

(b) Rotate the distributor; the bulb will glow exactly when the points begin to open.

9. Adjust as required by slackening the pinch bolt and turning the distributor bodily, or for fine adjustments, by means of the vernier screw.

Externals

1. Fit the oil filter complete and joint washer.

2. Fit the exhaust rocker cover and joint washer.

3. Fit the oil feed pipe, gallery to cylinder head.

4. Fit the exhaust and inlet manifolds, and joint washers.

5. Fit the dynamo and starter motor; adjust the dynamo belt tension to allow the belt to move ½ to ¾ in. (12 to 19 mm) when pressed by thumb between the crankshaft and water pump pulleys.

6. If removed, refit heater pipes, etc., to cylinder head.

7. Fit the inlet rocker cover and joint washer.

8. Fit the sparking plugs, covers and rubber sealing rings, and connect plug leads to distributor.

9. Fit the carburetter, and connect vacuum pipe between carburetter and distributor, connect fuel feed pipe from pump. Connect the accelerator linkage to the carburetter.

10. Fit the oil sump, noting rubber seal, packing strip and three distance pieces at rear.

11. Fit the dipstick and tube.

Engine, to refit Operation A/66

1. Reverse removal procedure—fit new mounting rubbers if necessary. Refill with lubricating oil, 10 imperial pints (5,5 litres), and coolant, 17 imperial pints (9,75 litres).

2. See Section M for details of carburetter adjustments.

3. See Section AO for details of oil pressure adjustment.

4. Check for oil and coolant leaks—rectify as necessary.

MAINTENANCE PROCEDURE

Removing cylinder head   Operation A/68

1. If necessary, remove the spare wheel from the bonnet panel.

2. Remove the bonnet panel.

3. Remove the radiator cap; drain off coolant.

4. Disconnect the battery leads.

5. Remove the air cleaner.   Section M.

6. Disconnect the throttle return spring, throttle linkage (at a ball joint), the mixture control (at the carburetter and clamp) and hand throttle control (if fitted) at the lever and clamp. If fitted, remove the engine governor.   Section T.

7. Disconnect: Oil feed pipe from the cylinder head; petrol pipe at the carburetter; mixture control switch wire (at rear of cylinder head); H.T. wire from the coil; L.T. wire from the distributor.

8. Remove the distributor vacuum pipe.

9. Pull off the plug covers and detach the distributor cap.   Remove the sparking plugs.

10. Disconnect the top water hose at the radiator.

11. Release the dipstick tube bracket.

12. Remove the inlet rocker cover.

13. Remove the inlet rocker shaft complete. *Note:* The ⅜ in. nuts (spanner size) have 7/16 in. threads.   Lift out the push rods.

14. Remove the distributor complete with clamp.

15. Remove the cylinder head complete, together with the rubber seal between the water pump and thermostat housing, which should be preserved.

Fitting cylinder head   Operation A/70

1. Reverse the removal procedure.

2. Renew all joint washers.

3. Pull down the cylinder head bolts evenly to the correct tension in the order shown in Fig. A-29.

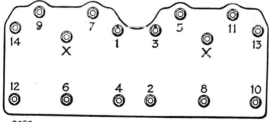

B652

Fig. A-30—Order of tightening cylinder head bolts
Those marked X also secure the rocker shaft.

4. Carry out ignition timing.   Operation A/64.

5. Adjust the tappet clearances.   Exhaust .012 in. (0,30 mm) and inlet .010 in. (0,25 mm).   Operation A/54.

6. Run the engine for a few minutes and check for leaks.

Decarbonising, valve grinding and
lapping   Operation A/72

1. Remove the cylinder head and inlet rocker shaft. Operation A/68.

2. Remove the valves.   Operations A/14 (inlet), A/16 (exhaust).

3. Remove the carbon from the cylinder head face and ports, using a blunt scraper.   Do not use a wire brush or sharp tools.   On no account must the cylinder head be sandblasted.

4. Remove the carbon from the cylinder block combustion chambers, exhaust ports and piston tops, using a blunt scraper.

5. Clean out the small water holes on the right-hand side of the cylinder block and head faces.

6. Renew valve guides or seats as necessary. Operations A/46 and A/50.   Grind in the valves.

7. Check and clean the sparking plugs.

8. Refit the cylinder head.   Operation A/70.

9. Carry out ignition timing.   Operation A/64.

10. Adjust the tappet clearances—exhaust .012 in. (0,30 mm) and inlet .010 in. (0,25 mm).   Operation A/54.

11. Run the engine for a few minutes and check for leaks.

Tappet adjustment   Operation A/74

1. Remove the rocker covers.   The exhaust tappets may be set either hot or cold.   The inlet valves should be set with the engine at running temperature.

2. Engage the starting handle and set the tappet clearance by the method described in Operation A/54.   Exhaust .012 in. (0,30 mm) and inlet .010 in. (0,25 mm).

Rocker gear removal   Operation A/76

1. Remove the rocker covers.

2. To remove the inlet rocker gear, see Operation A/68, items 1, 2, 12 and 13.

3. To remove the exhaust rocker gear, see Operation A/18. *Note:* It is not necessary to remove the oil pump drive shaft.

Rocker gear fitment   Operation A/78

1. Reverse removal procedure and set tappet clearance as directed in Operation A/54. Exhaust .012 in. (0,30 mm) and inlet .010 in. (0,25 mm).

Timing chain renewal   Operation A/80

1. Remove bonnet top.

2. Remove the radiator. Section L.

3. Pivot the dynamo inwards and remove the fan belt.

4. Unscrew the starting dog and remove the damper.

5. Remove the front cover and mark the camshaft and crankshaft chain wheels, then mark the casing opposite these marks.

6. Release the pawl from the ratchet, compress the tensioner spring by lifting the jockey pulley arm as far as possible, then fit clip, Part No. 262748, over the tensioner.

7. Remove the jockey pulley; remove the driving chain and discard.

8. With the marks on chain wheels and casing aligned, fit the new chain with "no slack" on the driving side.

9. Fit the pulley arm and jockey wheel and check that the exhaust valve of No. 1 cylinder is fully open when the timing pointer is in line with the E.P. mark on the flywheel. See Operation A/56.

10. Complete the assembly by reversing the removal procedure.

Piston and connecting rod removal.
                                  Operation A/82

1. Remove cylinder head. Operation A/68.

2. Drain the oil from the sump. Jack the front end of vehicle up, and position suitable stands beneath the chassis side members.

3. Remove sump carefully to avoid damage to the joint washer. Remove the connecting rod caps, bearings and bolts.

4. Push each connecting rod up and turn to engage the slots at the bottom of the cylinder bore. Remove the circlips; withdraw the gudgeon pin, using extractor Part No. 263052; remove the piston.

5. Lower each connecting rod, turning the crankshaft as necessary to effect withdrawal.

Piston and connecting rod—fitment
                                  Operation A/84

1. Reverse the removal procedure, using tool Part No. 263053 to refit the gudgeon pins, noting that when cold and dry, the gudgeon pin should be an *easy sliding* fit in the connecting rod and should have a *slight interference* fit in both piston bores, i.e. so that it can be pressed in by hand but will not fall out under its own weight.

2. Fit the connecting rods with the oil spray hole on the opposite side to the camshaft. Tighten the nuts to 30 lb/ft. (4 mKg) on 1948-53 models and to 40 lb/ft. (5,5 mKg) on 1954-58 models.

3. Refit sump and joint washer. Refit the cylinder head, Operation A/70.

4. Refill with oil.

External oil filter, 1955-58 models—removal
                                  Operation A/86

1. Jack the front end of vehicle up and position suitable stands beneath the side members. Place a drip tray under the filter.

2. Remove the securing bolts and withdraw the filter complete.

External oil filter, 1955-58 models—fitment
                                  Operation A/88

1. Fit a new gasket between the filter head and cylinder block, then reverse removal procedure.

External oil filter element, 1955-58 models—renewal   Operation A/90

1. See item 1 of Operation A/86.

2. Unscrew the bolt at base of container, then remove the element and container complete.

3. Discard the old element and the large rubber sealing ring from filter head.

4. Wash the container thoroughly in paraffin or petrol, fit the new element and rubber sealing ring, ensure that all the sealing washers are in position, and that the container is correctly located in the top cover. Tighten securing bolts in base of container.

External oil filter, to renew, 1948-54 models

1. Disconnect the inlet and outlet pipes from the filter.

2. Slacken the four set bolts securing the filter mounting bracket and clip to the cylinder block; withdraw and discard the filter.

3. Fit the new filter by reversing this procedure, and refill the engine with one of the recommended lubricants.

4. Run the engine for five minutes and inspect and rectify any oil leaks.

5. Check the engine oil level and top up as necessary.

DEFECT LOCATION
(Symptom, Cause and Remedy)

A—ENGINE FAILS TO START

1. Incorrect starting procedure—*See Instruction Manual.*
2. Starter motor speed too low—*Check battery and connections.*
3. Faulty ignition system—*Section P.*
4. Water or dirt in fuel system—*Section M.*
5. Carburetter flooding—*Section M.*
6. Defective fuel pump—*Section M.*
7. Defective starter motor—*Section P.*
8. Starter pinion jammed in flywheel—*Rotate starter shaft with spanner to free pinion.*
9. Starter pinion not engaging—*Clean drive sleeve and pinion with paraffin.*

B—ENGINE STALLS.

1. Low idling speed—*Section M.*
2. Faulty sparking plugs—*Rectify.*
3. Faulty coil or condenser—*Renew.*
4. Faulty distributor points—*Rectify or renew. Section P.*
5. Incorrect tappet clearance—*Adjust.*
6. Incorrect mixture—*Adjust carburetter. Section M.*
7. Foreign matter in fuel system—*Section M.*

C—LACK OF POWER

1. Poor compression—*If the compression is appreciably less than the correct figure, (Page A-16) the piston rings or valves are faulty. Low pressure in adjoining cylinders indicates a faulty cylinder head gasket.*
2. Badly seating valves—*Rectify or renew.*
3. Faulty exhaust silencer—*Renew.*
4. Incorrect ignition timing—*Rectify.*
5. Leaks or restrictions in fuel system—*Section M.*
6. Faulty sparking plugs—*Rectify.*
7. Clutch slip—*Section B.*
8. Excessive carbon deposit—*Decarbonise.*
9. Brakes binding—*Section H.*
10. Faulty coil, condenser or battery—*Section P.*

D—ENGINE RUNS ERRATICALLY

1. Faulty electrical connections—*Rectify.*
2. Defective sparking plugs—*Rectify.*
3. Low battery charge—*Recharge battery. Section P.*
4. Defective distributor—*Rectify.*
5. Foreign matter in fuel system—*Section M.*
6. Faulty fuel pump—*Section M.*
7. Sticking valves—*Rectify or renew.*
8. Incorrect tappet clearance—*Adjust.*
9. Defective valve springs—*Renew.*
10. Incorrect ignition timing—*Rectify.*
11. Worn valve guides or valves—*Renew.*
12. Faulty cylinder head gasket—*Renew.*
13. Damaged exhaust system—*Rectify or renew.*

E—ENGINE STARTS, BUT STOPS IMMEDIATELY.

1. Faulty electrical connections—*Rectify low tension circuit.*
2. Foreign matter in fuel system—*Section M.*
3. Faulty fuel pump—*Section M.*
4. Low fuel level in tank—*Replenish.*

F—ENGINE FAILS TO IDLE

1. Incorrect carburetter setting—*Section M.*
2. Faulty fuel pump—*Section M.*
3. See defect D, 7-12.
4. See defect D, 1-4.

G—ENGINE MISFIRES ON ACCELERATION

1. Distributor points incorrectly set.—*Rectify. Section P.*
2. Faulty coil or condenser—*Renew.*
3. Faulty sparking plug—*Rectify.*
4. Faulty carburetter—*Section M.*

H—ENGINE KNOCKS

1. Ignition timing advanced—*Adjust.*
2. Excessive carbon deposit—*Decarbonise.*
3. Incorrect carburetter setting—*Section M.*
4. Unsuitable fuel—*Adjust octane selector.*
5. Worn pistons or bearings—*Renew.*
6. Distributor advance mechanism faulty—*Rectify. Section P.*
7. Defective sparking plugs—*Rectify or renew.*
8. Incorrect tappet clearance—*Adjust.*
9. Incorrect valve timing—*Adjust.*

J—ENGINE BACKFIRES

1. Ignition defect—*Section P.*
2. Carburetter defect—*Section M.*
3. Incorrect valve timing—*Adjust.*
4. Incorrect tappet clearance—*Adjust.*
5. Sticking valve—*Rectify.*
6. Weak valve springs—*Renew.*
7. Badly seating valves—*Rectify or renew.*
8. Excessively worn valve stems and guides—*Renew.*
9. Loose timing chain—*Rectify tensioner.*
10. Excessive carbon deposit—*Decarbonise.*

K—BURNED VALVES

1. Insufficient tappet clearance—*Adjust.*
2. Sticking valves—*Rectify.*
3. Weak valve springs—*Renew.*
4. Excessive deposit on valve seats—*Re-cut.*
5. Distorted valves—*Renew.*

L—NOISY VALVE MECHANISM

1. Excessive tappet clearance—*Adjust.*
2. Sticking valves—*Rectify.*
3. Weak valve springs—*Renew.*
4. Faulty valve mechanism—*Renew worn parts.*

M—MAIN BEARING RATTLE

1. Low oil pressure—*See N.*
2. Excessive bearing clearance—*Renew bearings; grind crankshaft.*
3. Burnt-out bearings—*Renew.*
4. Loose bearing caps—*Tighten.*

N—LOW OIL PRESSURE

1. Thin or diluted oil—*Refill with correct oil.*
2. Low oil level—*Replenish.*
3. Choked pump intake filter—*Clean.*
4. Faulty release valve—*Rectify.*
5. Excessive bearing clearance—*Rectify.*
6. Excessive camshaft bearing clearance—*Rectify.*
7. Loose or restricted oil line—*Rectify.*

GENERAL DATA

Capacity (piston displacement)
1948-51 models .... 1,595 cc
(97.34 cu.in.)

Capacity (piston displacement)
1952-58 models .... 1,997 cc
(121.9 cu.in.)

Number of cylinders 4
Bore, 1948-51 models .... 69,5 mm (2.736 in.)
Bore, 1952-58 models .... 77,8 mm (3.063 in.)
Stroke .... 105 mm (4.134 in.)
Compression ratio 6.9-1
B.H.P. .... 52 at 4,000 r.p.m.

Maximum torque, 1948-51
models .... 80 lb/ft. (11 mKg)
at 2,000 r.p.m.

Maximum torque, 1952-58
models .... 101 lb/ft. (14 mKg)
1,500 r.p.m.

Firing order .... 1—3—4—2

Compression pressure (at starter motor cranking speed, i.e., 300 r.p.m. with engine hot and carburetter butterfly fully open) .... 125 lb/sq.in.
8,8 kg/cm^2

DETAIL DATA

Camshaft
Journal diameter .... .874 in.—.0005
Clearance in bearing.... .001 to .002 in. (0,025 to 0,050 mm)
End-float .... .003 to .005 in. (0,075 to 0,12 mm)

Camshaft bearings
Type .... Split Mazak die casting
Internal diameter .... .876 in.—.001

Connecting rods
Bearing fit on crankpin .001 to .0025 in. (.025 to 0,063 mm)
Bearing nip .... .002 to .004 in. (0,05 to 0,10 mm)
End-float at big-end .... .009 to .013 in. (0,23 to 0,33 mm)
Gudgeon pin bush fit in small end .... .001 to .002 in. (0,025 to 0,050 mm) interference
Gudgeon pin bush—internal diameter—reamed in position .8755 in.—.0005 (22,187 mm—0,0127)
Fit of gudgeon pin in bush .... .0003 to .0005 in. (0,0075 to 0,0127 mm) clearance

Crankshaft
Journal diameter .... 2.005 in. (50,80 mm)
Crankpin diameter .... 1.875 in. (47,52 mm)
End-float .... .002 to .006 (0,05 to 0,15 mm)

Regrind sizes:

Undersize	Journal dia.	Crankpin dia.
.010 in.	1.990 in.	1.865 in.
.020 in.	1.980 in.	1.855 in.
.030 in.	1.970 in.	1.845 in.
.040 in.	1.960 in.	1.835 in.

Flywheel
Number of teeth 97
Thickness at pressure
face .... 1.094 in.—.010

Maximum permissible run-out on flywheel face .... .005 in. (0,12 mm)
Maximum refacing depth .... .030 in. (0,75 mm)
Minimum thickness after grinding:
88 models, 1956-58.... 1.204 in. (30,5 mm)
Other models, 1948-56 1.047 in. (26,5 mm)
Markings:
T.D.C. .... When opposite pointer, No. 1 piston is at top dead centre

E.P. .... When opposite pointer, No. 1 exhaust valve should be fully open. 114° before T.D.C.

F.A. 15°, 1948-53 models .... When opposite pointer, indicates firing point of No. 1 cylinder

F.A. 10°, 1954-58 models .... When opposite pointer, indicates firing point of No. 1 cylinder.

Primary pinion bush
Fit in flywheel .... .001 to .003 in. (0,025 to 0,075 mm) interference
Internal diameter—reamed in position .878 in. (22,3 mm)
Fit of shaft in bush .003 to .004 in. (0,075 to 0,10 mm) clearance

Gudgeon pin
Fit in piston (selective assembly) .... Zero to .0003 in. (zero to 0,0075 mm) interference
Fit in connecting rod bush (selective assembly) .... .0003 to .0005 in. (0,0075 to 0,0127 mm) clearance

Main bearings
Clearance on crankshaft journal .... .001 to .002 in. (0,025 to 0,05 mm)
Bearing nip .... .004 to .006 in. (0,10 to 0,15 mm)

Pistons

Type .... Light alloy, tin plated

Clearance in bore, measured at bottom of skirt at right angles to gudgeon pin .... .0012 to .0017 in. (0,030 to 0,043 mm)

Clearance in bore, measured at top of skirt at right angles to gudgeon pin .... .0022 to .0027 in. (0,055 to 0,068 mm)

Gudgeon pin bore, early models .... .6872 in. +.0002 in. (17,45 mm+0,005)

Gudgeon pin bore, late models .... .8747 in. +.0002 (22,21 mm+0,005)

Piston rings

Compression (2)

Type .... Taper periphery

Gap in bore .... .015 to .020 in. (0,38 to 0,50 mm)

Clearance in groove .0005 to .002 in. (0,012 to 0,05 mm)

Scraper ring (upper) Early models only

Type .... Stepped

Gap in bore .... .012 to .017 in. (0,3 to 0,4 mm)

Clearance in groove .0005 to .002 in. (0,012 to 0,05 mm)

Scraper ring (lower)

Type .... Slotted, H section

Gap in bore .... .012 to .017 in. (0,3 to 0,4 mm)

Clearance in groove .0005 to .002 in. (0,012 to 0,05 mm)

Rocker gear

Rockers and cam followers:	Inlet	Exhaust
Reamed bore	.500 in.+ .001 (12,7 mm +0,025)	.593 in.+ .001 (15,081 mm +0,025)
Clearance on shaft....	.001 to .002 in. (0,025 to 0,050 mm)	.001 to .003 in. (0,025 to 0,075 mm)

Tappet clearance

Exhaust, engine hot or cold .... .012 in. (0,30 mm)

Inlet, engine at running temperature .... .010 in. (0,25 mm)

Timing chain tensioner

Driving chain

Type .... Endless roller, pre-stretched

Diameter of rollers $\frac{1}{4}$ in. (6,35 mm)

Chain tensioner spring

Free length .... 4.200 in.

Length in position 1.937 in.

Load in position .... $15\frac{1}{2}$ lb$\pm\frac{1}{2}$ (7 Kg$\pm\frac{1}{4}$)

Hydraulic chain tensioner

Inlet valve lifts at .... 4 to 12 lb/sq.in. (0,30 to 0,80 Kg/cm²)

Thrust bearings, crankshaft

Type .... Semi-circular, steel backed, tin plated

Thickness .... .093 in.—.002 (2,36 mm —0,05)

Oversizes .... .0025 in., .005 in., .0075 in. and .010 in.

Torque loadings

Connecting rod bolts 40 lb/ft. (5,5 mKg)

Cylinder head bolts:

7/16 in. B.S.F. .... 50 lb/ft. (7 mKg)

3/8 in. B.S.F. .... 30 lb/ft. (4 mKg)

Main bearing bolts 80 lb/ft. (11 mKg)

Flywheel securing bolts .... 70 lb/ft. (9,7 mKg)

Valves

Inlet valve

Diameter (stem) .... .343 in.—.001

Face angle .... 30°—$\frac{1}{4}$

Exhaust valve

Diameter .... .343 in.—.001

Face angle .... 45°—$\frac{1}{4}$

Valve seat—inlet

Type .... Integral

Angle .... 30°+$\frac{1}{4}$

Valve seat—exhaust

Type .... Removable insert

Angle .... 45°+$\frac{1}{4}$

Fit in cylinder block .005 in. to .007 in. (0,12 to 0,17 mm) interference

Fit of inlet and exhaust valves in guides .... .002 to .003 in. (0,05 to 0,08 mm) clearance

Valve guides

Length—inlet .... 1.968 in.—.016

Length—exhaust .... 2.250 in.—.016

Reamed bore .... .3448 in.+.0005 (8,757 mm+0,012)

35

Valve springs

Free length, inner .... 1.817 in. (46,0 mm)

Free length, outer .... 1.845 in. (46,8 mm)

Compressed length. inner .... 1.469 in. (36,3 mm)

Compressed length, outer .... 1.625 in. (41,2 mm)

Pressure, valve closed, inner .... 10 lb. $\pm\frac{1}{2}$ (4,5 kg $\pm\frac{1}{4}$)

Pressure, valve closed, outer .... 32.8 lb. ±1 (14,8 kg $\pm\frac{1}{2}$)

Pressure, valve open, inner .... 17.9 lb. ±1 (8,1 kg $\pm\frac{1}{2}$)

Pressure, valve open, outer .... 74.0 lbs. $+1$ (33,5 kg $+\frac{1}{2}$)

Valve timing

Inlet opens .... 9° B.T.D.C.
    closes .... 45° A.B.D.C.
    peak .... 83° B.B.D.C.

Exhaust opens .... 42° B.B.D.C.
    closes .... 16° A.T.D.C.
    peak .... 66° A.B.D.C.

Vibration damper

Fit of bush in flywheel .002 to .004 in. (0,05 to 0,10 mm) interference

Clearance of bush or driving flange .... .005 to .007 in. (0,12 to 0,17 mm)

Run-out on front face .005 in. (0,12 mm) maximum

Permissible out-of-balance .... 3 grams

Section A – ENGINE – DIESEL MODELS

INDEX

	Page
Camshaft	
Removal	A-40
Fitment	A-45
Camshaft bearings	
Removal	A-40
Fitment and reamering	A-40
Camshaft chain wheel	
Removal	A-39
Fitment	A-45
Connecting rod	
Removal	A-39
Fitment	A-43
Connecting rod bearings	
Removal	A-39
Fitment	A-43
Crankshaft	
Removal	A-40
Fitment	A-42
Crankshaft bearings	
Removal	A-40
Fitment	A-42
Crankshaft chain wheel	
Removal	A-39
Fitment	A-47
Cylinder head	
Removal	A-39
Fitment	A-46
Data	A-55
Decarbonising	A-52
Defect location	A-54
Engine removal from chassis	A-38
Engine dismantling procedure	A-38
Engine assembly procedure	A-40
Fan belt adjustment	A-51
Flywheel	A-45
Fuel lift pump	
Removal	A-38
Fitment	A-51
Fuel injection pump	
Removal	A-38
Fitment	A-50

	Page
Fuel injection nozzles	
Removal	A-38
Fitment	A-51
Gudgeon pins	
Removal	A-39
Fitment	A-44
Liner, cylinder	
Removal	A-39
Fitment	A-43
Lubricating oil filter—external	A-53
Lubricating oil pump and filter	
Removal	A-38
Fitment	A-50
Pistons and piston rings	
Removal	A-39
Fitment	A-44
Push-rod	
Removal	A-39
Fitment	A-46
Push-rod tubes	
Removal	A-39
Fitment	A-46
Rocker gear	
Removal	A-39
Fitment	A-46
Tappet adjustment	A-48
Tappets, guides and rollers	
Removal	A-39
Fitment	A-45
Timing chain	
Removal—engine removed	A-39
Fitment—engine removed	A-47
Renewal—engine installed	A-52
Timing chain tensioner	
Removal	A-39
Fitment	A-47
Valves	
Removal	A-39
Fitment	A-46
Valve guides	
Removal	A-39
Fitment	A-45
Valve timing	A-47

LIST OF ILLUSTRATIONS

Fig.		Page
A-401	Removing vertical drive shaft gear	A-39
A-402	Outer camshaft bearing removal	A-40
A-403	Inner camshaft bearing removal	A-40
A-404	Fitting camshaft bearings	A-41
A-405	Reamering camshaft bearings	A-41
A-406	Checking main bearing nip	A-42
A-407	Checking crankshaft end-float	A-42
A-408	Fitting rear bearing cap and seal assembly	A-43
A-409	Checking cylinder liner extension	A-43
A-410	Checking big-end bearing nip	A-43
A-411	Checking piston clearance	A-44
A-412	Checking piston ring gap	A-44
A-413	Checking ring clearance in groove	A-44
A-414	Checking run-out on flywheel face	A-45
A-415	Checking camshaft end-float	A-45
A-416	Tappet guide and roller	A-45
A-417	Fitting valve guides	A-46

Fig.		Page
A-418	Correct position of push-rod tubes in relation to hot plugs	A-46
A-419	Compressing valve springs	A-46
A-420	Order of tightening cylinder head bolts	A-47
A-421	Timing pointer	A-47
A-422	Checking exhaust valve "fully-open" position	A-47
A-423	Timing diagram	A-48
A-424	Timing gear arrangement	A-48
A-425	Adjusting tappets	A-48
A-426	Checking vibration damper run-out	A-49
A-427	Sectioned view of vibration damper	A-49
A-428	Driving gear in correct timing position	A-50
A-439	Distributor pump timing marks correctly aligned	A-50
A-430	Position of injection nozzle washers	A-51
A-431	Order of tightening cylinder head bolts	A-52

ENGINE REMOVAL AND DISMANTLING PROCEDURE

Removing engine   Operation A/402

1. If fitted remove the spare wheel from bonnet.

2. Disconnect the bonnet support stay and remove the bonnet.

3. Disconnect the hose from inlet manifold, unscrew the securing wing nut and lift the air cleaner and hose clear.

4. Disconnect the battery leads and remove the L.H. battery.

5. Drain the coolant from system (one tap at bottom L.H. side of radiator and one tap at L.H. side of cylinder block).

6. Disconnect the side lamp leads at each side of the grille panel assembly and the front lamp harness from the junction box at R.H. side of scuttle, then pull the wiring clear to front of engine.

7. Detach the top hose at radiator header tank and the bottom hose from water pump inlet.

8. Remove the fan blades.

9. Remove the bolts securing the grille panel to front cross member and front wings.

10. Lift the radiator, grille panel and headlamps assembly upward, then forward to clear the vehicle. Remove the L.H. battery support.

11. Loosen the bolts securing the intermediate to front exhaust pipe and disconnect the exhaust pipe from exhaust manifold.

12. Disconnect the heater pipes (if fitted) at the engine side of bulkhead.

13. Disconnect the wiring from starter motor, dynamo, oil pressure warning switch and glow-plug lead at resistance on **bulkhead.**

14. Disconnect the fuel inlet and outlet pipes from fuel lift pump and injection pump, then disconnect the three pipes joined at scuttle, lower R.H. side.

15. Remove the accelerator control rod, then the cut-off control cable from the steady bracket on engine and from the lever on injection pump.

16. Fit the engine sling to the support brackets at front and rear of cylinder head and with suitable lifting tackle just take the strain.

17. Remove the front floor and gearbox cover.

18. Support the gearbox assembly with a jack or packing blocks.

19. Remove the clutch slave cylinder bracket from the flywheel housing and pull back the complete assembly as far as possible.

20. Remove the remaining nuts and washers securing the gearbox to the flywheel housing.

21. Remove the bolts from engine front support brackets, allow the engine to move forward and thus clear the gearbox input shaft. Ensure that

the speedometer cable, etc., and all wires are clear, then hoist the engine gently from the vehicle.

22. Drain oil from sump.

23. Bolt the engine to a suitable stand.

DISMANTLING ENGINE

Externals   Operation A/404

1. Disconnect the fuel spill gallery pipe from injectors and remove the fuel feed pipes—injection pump to injectors.

2. Remove the securing straps, then withdraw the injectors and seating washers. Make sure the small steel washer is also removed from out of the orifice in the cylinder head.

3. Release the accelerator pull-off spring and remove the injection pump; disconnect the wiring, then remove heater plugs carefully to avoid damage to element.

4. Remove the inlet and exhaust manifolds, then the starter, fan belt and dynamo.

5. Disconnect the heater pipes and water tap from cylinder head if fitted. Remove the fuel filter from mounting bracket at R.H. front of engine.

6. The rearmost tappet chamber cover and fuel lift pump may be removed as one unit; the foremost tappet chamber cover and oil filler pipe may also be removed together.

7. Remove the external full-flow oil filter complete with oil pressure warning switch.

8. Disconnect the oil feed pipe—gallery to cylinder head and the hose, thermostat to water pump casing.

9. Drain the oil and remove the sump.

Oil pump   Operation A/406

1. Remove the securing bolts and withdraw the pump assembly.

2. Withdraw the driving shaft from the pump upper casing.

3. Unscrew the securing nut and remove the filter gauze assembly.

   Note.—See Section AO for oil pump strip and assembly.

Vertical drive shaft gear   Operation A/408

1. Lift the drive shaft gear and external bush assembly clear, with a pair of snipe-nosed pliers, after removing the locating screw from the external filter adaptor joint face. The split bush may be removed by tapping to release the dowels. Do not remove the aluminium plug in the gear unless absolutely necessary. A new plug must be fitted if the old one has been removed.

Vibration damper   Operation A/410

1. Remove the starting nut and tab washer, then withdraw the vibration damper assembly from crankshaft.

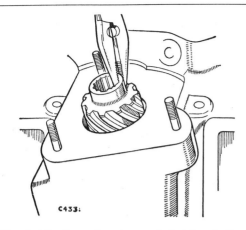

Fig. A-401—Removing the vertical drive shaft gears

2. Unscrew the set bolts securing the back plate to flywheel, withdraw the back plate, rubber discs and shims. Extract the bushes from flywheel and back plate if necessary.

Water pump and front cover
Operation A/412

1. Remove the front cover and water pump assembly. For overhaul of water pump, see Section L.

Timing chain tensioner and chain wheels
Operation A/414

1. Remove the ratchet securing bolt and withdraw the ratchet and spring. Compress the chain tensioner spring and unscrew the lower fixing bolts and remove the chain tensioner assembly. Lift off the timing chain and remove the chain wheels.

2. The screwed plug and ball may be removed from the piston if necessary and the piston pressed from its housing if unduly worn.

3. The tensioner cylinder and bush must be renewed complete if the bush is unduly worn.

4. The bushes in idler wheel and ratchet arm should also be removed if worn beyond reasonable limits.

Rocker gear and cylinder head
Operation A/416

1. Remove the rocker gear cover, unscrew the bolts securing the rocker shaft support brackets, and lift the rocker gear assembly complete from the cylinder head.

2. Unscrew the rocker cover securing studs from the centre and end support brackets and the locating set bolts from the intermediate support brackets. Remove the component parts from the rocker shafts but retain the items in their correct relative positions.

3. Withdraw the push rods and insert them in a piece of cardboard pre-pierced and marked.

4. Remove the cover and joint washer, then lift out the thermostat.

5. Loosen the securing bolts evenly and lift the cylinder head clear.

6. Using a valve spring compressing tool, Part No. 276102, remove the valve assemblies.

7. If necessary remove the hot plugs by inserting a copper drift through the injector aperture, then tap evenly and gently around the inside of hot plug. Avoid using a hammer if possible and thus minimise the possibility of damage. The push rod tubes may also be removed if necessary by drifting them out, using tool Part No. 274399.

8. Drift the valve guides from the cylinder head using tool, Part No. 274401 (exhaust) and 274400 (inlet). Remove and scrap the seals.

Tappet guide, roller and tappet
Operation A/418

1. Remove the locating bolts from R.H. side of cylinder block and lift out the brass tappets.

   With a piece of bent wire remove the rollers; then remove the tappet guide.

   The guide, roller and tappet are marked to ensure correct refitment. The rollers have a chamfer on their front face inside diameter.

Camshaft removal
Operation A/420

1. Remove the camshaft front thrust plate, then withdraw the camshaft.

Flywheel
Operation A/422

1. Remove the clutch assembly, then the flywheel securing bolts and withdraw the flywheel. The primary pinion bush may be extracted if necessary.

Pistons, connecting rods and liners
Operation A/424

1. Turn the crankshaft until the pistons of numbers 1 and 4 cylinders are at B.D.C. Remove the big end bolt securing nuts of numbers 1 and 4 connecting rods, then withdraw the piston and connecting rod assemblies from the top of cylinder block.

   Retain the bearing shells in pairs, preferably taped together on the crankpins from which they were removed, until ready for inspection.

   Repeat for numbers 2 and 3 assemblies.

   Remove the piston rings, gudgeon pin retaining circlips and press out the gudgeon pins; if necessary remove the small end bushes from connecting rods.

2. After marking the top with a scriber to ensure correct refitment, the liners may be withdrawn by hand and the sealing rings removed from the crankcase end of cylinder block bores.

   Note: Ensure that the component parts are retained in their correct relative positions.

Crankshaft, main bearings and rear bearing seal   Operation A/426

1. Remove the main bearing caps, lift the crankshaft clear and place in a suitable stand.

   Retain the shell bearings in pairs adjacent to the journal from which they were removed.

2. The rear bearing seal halves may be removed from the cylinder block and bearing cap.

Camshaft bearing removal   Operation A/427

   Note: When new camshaft bearings are to be fitted, the front and front intermediate bearings must be removed and new ones fitted **before** removing the rear bearings. See Items 1 to 5 of Operation A/428 for bearing fitment.

2. Unscrew the 3½ in. (88,9 mm.) long stud from the joint face at front of cylinder block.

3. Drift the front camshaft bearing in to the foremost tappet chamber using tool, Part No. 274388, then withdraw the bearing from the chamber aperture.

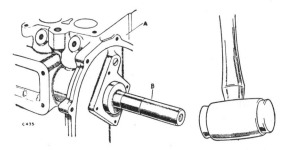

Fig. A-402—Outer camshaft bearing removal
A—Cylinder block.   B—Drift.

The front intermediate bearing is removed by drifting it into the fuel injection pump drive chamber, using the same tool, but it must be collapsed before withdrawing from the drive aperture as illustrated by Fig. A-403.

   Note: The inner bearing should be positioned at the innermost lower side of the chamber, before inserting a suitable bar which should then be tapped lightly against the bearing. Care must be taken to avoid damage to the machined faces in the chamber.

4. Fit new front and front intermediate bearings, Items 1 to 5 Operation A/428, **before** removing the rear bearings by drifting them, using the same tools and method employed when removing the foremost bearings.

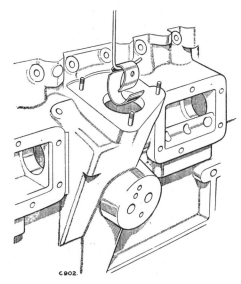

Fig. A-403—Inner camshaft bearing removal

ENGINE ASSEMBLY

Camshaft bearings   Operation A/428

When replacing camshafts it should be noted that 2¼ litre petrol engine camshafts are marked "Petrol" between No. 1 and No. 2 cam lobes. This is to differentiate between Diesel camshafts which are similar in all respects other than the positioning of the cam lobes.

   Note: When new camshaft bearings are to be fitted, the front and front intermediate bearings must be removed and new ones fitted **before** removing the two rearmost bearings. See Items 2 to 4 inclusive of Operation A/420 for bearing removal procedure.

1. Fit a guide tool, Part No. 274385, into the two **old** rearmost bearings with the part of flange marked "TOP" uppermost, then insert three end cover set bolts loosely for location purposes. Position a new bearing on to the handle end of bearing fitting bar, Part No. 274382, and locate by means of the peg and semi-circular cut-out, then slide a spacer, Part No. 274383, on to the fitting bar and engage the locating shoulder

2. Place a new bearing on spigot, Part No. 274384, and position it inside the foremost tappet chamber with the bearing nearest the front intermediate housing.

   Insert the bearing fitting bar into the front bearing housing and feed the spigot on to the bar; withdraw the spigot handle. Turn the

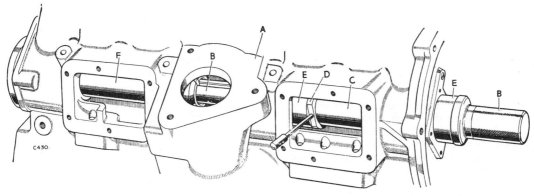

Fig. A-404—Fitting camshaft front bearings

A—Cylinder block.   C—Spacer.   E—New bearings.
B—Bearing fitting bar.   D—Spigot.   F—Guide tube.

spigot to engage the locating shoulder in the spacer, then press the fitting bar inward, turning as necessary to engage the bar slot with the peg in guide tube.

3. When the fitting bar has been pressed in as far as possible by hand, ensure that all locating points are properly engaged, then drive the bearings into position with a hide-faced hammer. Remove the bearing fitting tools and check the oil holes for alignment. Remove the two rearmost bearings—Item 4, Operation A/420.

4. Fit new camshaft **rear** bearings in the same manner as for front bearing fitment, but remove the spacer from fitting bar and use guide tool, Part No. 274386, instead of the guide tube used when fitting front bearings.

5. Locate a guide plug, Part No. 274394, in the front new camshaft bearing and locate, using the end-plate screws. Do not tighten these screws until the reamer, Part No. 274389, is put into position and the guide collar immediately in front of the cutter is entered into the rearmost bearing, which is first to be cut. This precaution is to ensure correct alignment of the reamer.

Before commencing the reamering operation it is necessary to turn the engine block to a vertical position, i.e. front end facing downwards, in order that the weight of the reamer will assist in the cutting operation. As each bearing is cut the reamer should be held steady by the operator whilst an assistant, using a high pressure air line, blows away the white metal cuttings, before allowing the reamer to enter the next bearing.

After the rearmost and the two intermediate bearings have been cut, remove the guide plug Part No. 274394, before cutting the foremost bearing. Remove the reamer handle and carefully remove the reamer, turning it in the same direction as for cutting. Care must be taken to prevent the reamer damaging the foremost bearing as the reamer is removed.

Note: No lubricant is necessary for the reamering operation, best results are obtained when the bearings are cut dry.

Remove the plugs from the ends of oil gallery passage and clean the gallery and oil feed passages to camshaft and crankshaft bearings, using compressed air. Refit the plugs flush with the face of the cylinder block and lock in position.

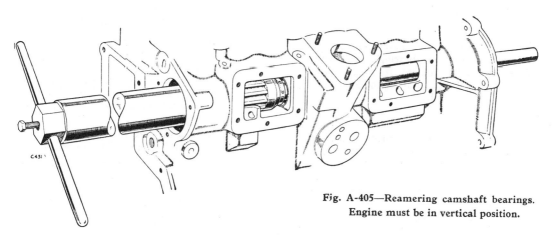

Fig. A-405—Reamering camshaft bearings.
Engine must be in vertical position.

Crankshaft, main bearings and seal
Operation A/430

Note: Crankshafts considered unserviceable because of wear on the journals must not under any circumstances be reconditioned, and no undersize main bearings are supplied.

It is most important, therefore, that when a Diesel crankshaft becomes unserviceable it should be scrapped out, and damaged to ensure that it cannot be subsequently reconditioned. A new crankshaft of the latest type must be fitted.

1. To check that the bearing caps have not been filed, first assemble the caps without bearing shells to the crankcase, ensuring that they are correctly located by means of the dowels. Tighten both securing bolts for each cap, then slacken one bolt of each pair right off. There should be no clearance at the joint face.

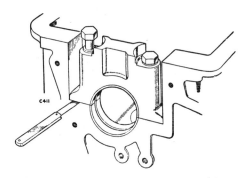

Fig. A-406—Checking main bearing nip

Check the main bearing nip as follows —
Remove the bearing caps and fit the bearing shells, locating by means of the tags. Tighten the caps down and slacken off one bolt of each pair. Check the bearing nip, as illustrated in Fig. A-406, ensuring that the clearance does not exceed .004 to .006 in. (0,10 to 0,15 mm). The nip can be corrected by selective assembly of bearing shells; these are available in slightly varying thicknesses.

2. When the bearing nip has been checked, remove the caps and bearing shell bottom halves. Position a standard size thrust bearing at each side of centre bearing shell—top half, and fit the crankshaft.

3. Refit the bearing shell bottom halves and bearing caps. Tighten the securing bolts evenly and check each bearing in turn for correct clearance. The crankshaft should resist rotation when a feeler paper, .0025 in. (0,06 mm) thick, is placed between any one bearing shell and crankshaft journal, and turn freely by hand when the feeler paper is removed. Adjust by selective assembly of bearing shells.

4. Mount a dial test indicator, then check and note the crankshaft end-float reading which should be .002 to .006 in. (0,050 to 0,15 mm).

5. Remove the bearing caps, bottom half shells and crankshaft.

6. To the rear main bearing cap fit neoprene seals in recess at each side, and on the rear face fit the lower half of crankshaft rear bearing seal.

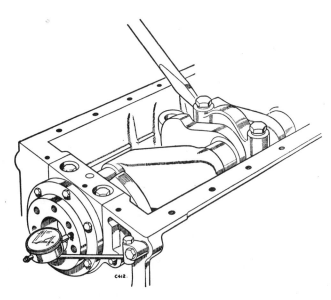

Fig. A-407—Checking crankshaft end-float

7. Fit the top half of crankshaft rear bearing oil seal to the crankcase. Lubricate bearing face with Silicone MS4 Compound.

8. If the crankshaft end-float reading, obtained in Item 4, was not within the limits, fit suitable oversize thrust bearings. The variation of thrust bearing thickness at each side must not exceed .003 in. (0,07 mm) to ensure that the crankshaft remains centralised.

   Note: It will be found advantageous to carry out Items 5, 6 and 7 of Operation A/434 relating to connecting rods at this stage.

9. Lubricate the crankshaft journals, main bearing shells and thrust bearings, then refit crankshaft. Fitment of the rear main bearing cap, with side seals in position, will be facilitated by using a lead tool (Part No. 270304) fitted to the sump studs adjacent to rear bearing cap aperture. See Fig. A-408.

   Smear bearing face of crankshaft rear bearing oil seal with Silicone MS4 Compound.

   It will be found advantageous to cut a slight lead on to the bottom edges of side seals as this will prevent them from folding under the cap during fitment, thus causing an oil leak due to the cap not seating properly. Lubricate seals with Silicone MS4 Compound.

Cylinder liners and seals Operation A/432

1. Smear the sealing ring grooves at the crankcase end of cylinder block bores, and the liner sealing rings, with Silicone MS4 Compound, then fit a ring to the upper and lower grooves of each bore.

   Lightly coat the underside of the liner flange and the mating recess in the cylinder block with Hylomar SQ 32 M sealing compound, using a fairly stiff brush for application.

   The coated joint faces may be allowed to dry thoroughly before assembly if desired, but a minimum drying time of ten minutes must be allowed.

   A small hole is drilled through the cylinder block into the middle groove to provide evidence of coolant leakage past the top sealing ring.

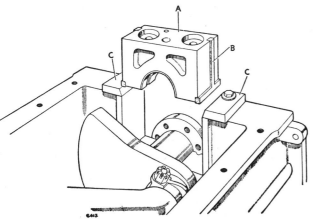

Fig. A-408—Fitting rear bearing cap and seal assembly
A—Bearing cap. B—Seal. C—Lead tool.

2. Press the liners into their respective bores by hand and align the marks made whilst dismantling.

Fig. A-409—Checking cylinder liner extension

3. Clamp each liner in turn in the manner illustrated and tighten the securing bolts to 65 lb/ft. (8,9 Kg/m) torque. Mount a dial test indicator and check that the outer edge of the cylinder liner is from .002 to .004 in. (0,050 to 0,10 mm) above the cylinder head joint face. See Fig. A-410. Adjust if necessary by removing liner and adding a suitable shim washer under the flange. Clamp and re-check liner as described above. Shim washers are available .002 in. (0,50 mm) and .004 in. (0,10 mm) thick.

Connecting rods Operation A/434

1. The oil hole in gudgeon pin bush is pre-drilled and care must be taken to ensure that the oil holes of bush and connecting rod will align when the bush is pressed into position. The gudgeon pin bushes should be a .001 to .002 in. (0,025 to 0,050 mm) interference fit in connecting rods. Ream the bush when fitted to connecting rod to allow a .0003 to .0005 in. (0,0076 to 0,0127 mm) gudgeon pin clearance. Ensure that correct alignment is maintained while reamering.

   This fit is selected to give the smallest possible clearance consistent with a smooth revolving action.

2. Fit each connecting rod to a suitable test rig and check for twist and mal-alignment.

3. To check that the connecting rod and cap have not been filed:—

   (a) Select the correct cap for each connecting rod, as denoted by the number stamped near the joint faces. This number also indicates the crankpin to which it must be fitted.
   Assemble the connecting rods, less shell bearings, with corresponding numbers together.

   (b) Tighten the securing bolts, then slacken one of them right off and check that there is no clearance at the joint face.

   Check bearing nip as follows:—

   (c) Fit the bearing shells and tighten both securing bolts—slacken one bolt as before and check the nip with a feeler gauge; this should be .002 to .004 in. (0,050 to 0,10 mm).

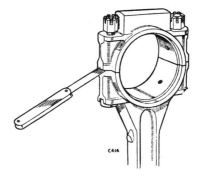

Fig. A-410—
Checking the
big-end bearing
nip

   (d) The nip can be corrected by selective assembly of the bearing shells; these are available in slightly varying thickness. **Do not file the rod or cap.**

4. Fit liner retainers (Part No. 274411) to joint face of cylinder block, then rotate assembly in the stand to bring crankshaft uppermost.

5. Assemble the big-end of each connecting rod to its' respective crankpin, then check for correct clearance.

The connecting rod should resist rotation when a .0025 in. (0,0635 mm) shim paper is fitted between the crankpin and one-half of big-end bearing shell, then move freely by hand when the shim paper is removed. Adjust by selective assembly of bearing shells.

Bearing clearance should be .001 to .0025 in. 0,025 to 0,063 mm).

6. Check the connecting rod end-float on crankpin by inserting a feeler gauge between the end face of rod and the crankpin shoulder. End-float should be .007 to .011 in. (0,177 to 0,279 mm).

7. Remove the connecting rods from crankshaft, ensuring that the bearing shells are kept with the rods to which they were fitted.

Pistons   Operation A/436

1. When fitting pistons, the clearance in liner bore should be in accordance with the dimensions laid down in the Data Section. In the absence of suitably accurate measuring instruments, a long feeler, .004 in. (0,10 mm) thick, may be inserted in the thrust side of the liner bore, as illustrated in Fig. A-411, and the piston located crown downward. The piston should become a tight fit when the bottom of skirt enters the bore.

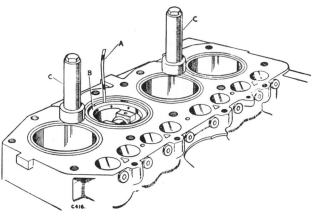

Fig. A-411—Checking piston clearance
A—Feeler gauge.   B—Piston.   C—Liner retainer.

2. The gudgeon pin, when cold and dry, should be a slight **interference** fit in both bores of the piston—see Data. It must be fitted by hand pressure but must **not** be able to fall out of either bore under its own weight.

Lubricate the gudgeon pin when the correct size has been selected for a particular piston, but do not fit and remove the pin from piston unnecessarily thereafter, or the slight interference fit may be lost.

3. Check the piston ring gaps in the liner bores, using an old piston as illustrated in Fig. A-412, to keep the rings square in the bore.

The second and third compression rings are bevel edged and **must** be fitted with the side marked "T" **uppermost**; the top chromium plated compression and the oil scraper ring has a square friction edge and may be fitted either way. Fit the piston rings and check the clearance in ring groove. See Data Section.

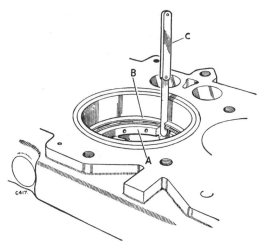

Fig. A-412—Checking a piston ring gap
A—Scrap piston.   B—Piston ring.   C—Feeler gauge.

Note: It will be seen that provision is made for the fitment of two oil scraper rings. The second groove is for service purposes only.

Fig. A-413—Checking ring clearance in groove

Pistons to connecting rods

4. Fit the connecting rod to the piston with the oil spray hole of rod on the same side as the swirl-inducing recess in piston crown. Lock the gudgeon pin in position with circlips.

Piston and connecting rod to cylinder block and crankshaft   Operation A/438

Note: See Items 1 to 6 of Operation A/434 inclusive for gudgeon pin bearing fitment and big-end shell bearing selection.

1. Turn the crankshaft until the crankpins relative to numbers 1 and 4 cylinders are at B.D.C. Insert the connecting rods and pistons for these cylinders from the top of cylinder block, with the oil spray hole in connecting rod and turbulence recess in piston towards the R.H. side of engine—toward the camshaft. Secure the big ends to crankpins, using new nuts and tightening to 35 lb/ft. (4,3 Kgs/m).

2. Repeat Item 1 for numbers 2 and 3 cylinders.

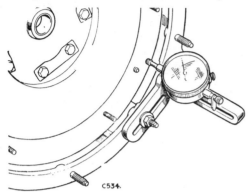

Fig. A-414—Checking run-out on flywheel face

Flywheel housing and flywheel

Operation A/440

1. Ensure that the oil seal is in good condition, then secure the flywheel housing to cylinder block.

2. Fit the flywheel and tighten the securing bolts to 50 lbs/ft. (6,9 Kgs/m) torque.

3. Check the run-out on flywheel face as illustrated by Fig. A-414. The run-out on flywheel face must not exceed .002 in. (0,050 mm).

Camshaft fitment   Operation A/442

Note: For replacement and line boring of camshaft bearing, see Items 1 to 5 of Operation A/428 inclusive.

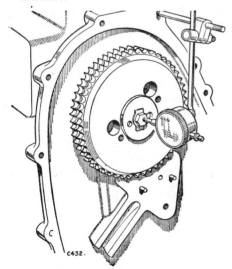

Fig. A-415—Checking camshaft end-float

1. Insert the camshaft—keyed end to extend at front of engine.

2. Fit the front thrust plate and secure the camshaft chain wheel but do not bend up the locking tab for securing bolt at this stage. Check the camshaft end-float with a dial test indicator as illustrated by Fig. A-415 and ensure that the reading is within .0025 to .0055 in. (0,063 to 0,139 mm).

   Adjust by selective assembly of the front thrust plate.

Tappet assembly and fitment

Operation A/444

1. Before fitting the tappet assembly into the block, thoroughly clean all parts and check that the tappet will move freely in the tappet guide when held in the hand and shaken up and down.

2. Fit tappet guides into the cylinder block, ensuring that the locating hole lines up with the hole in the cylinder block.

   The tappet guides must not be too tight in the block or they may be damaged by insertion of the locating screw in cases when they are not properly aligned.

3. Gently insert the roller into the guide, with the chamfer to the front. Do not drop the roller, as it is easily damaged.

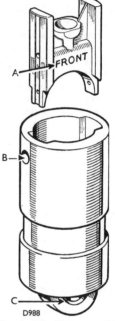

Fig. A-416—Tappet guide and roller

A—Brass tappet slide marked "front".
B—Tappet guide bolt location hole.
C—Roller with chamfer to front.

4. Fit tappet into the guide and locate on to the roller. The tappet is marked " Front " and must be facing the front of the guide.

5. Fit the tappet locating screws and washers; the locating screws must be screwed up with the fingers and then tightened; if they are not free, remove and investigate reason.

6. Lock the locating screws in pairs, using 20 s.w.g. iron wire.

Valve gear, hot plugs and thermostat to cylinder head   Operation A/446

1. Pull the inlet and exhaust valve guides into position, using tool Part No. 274406. Locate an "O" ring seal in each inlet and exhaust valve guide after the valves have been ground and lapped in.

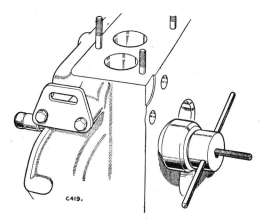

Fig. A-417—Fitting valve guides

2. If the push rod tubes were removed, new tubes complete with new sealing rings, smeared with Silicone M.S.4 Compound, should be pulled into position, using tool Part No. 274402. Ensure that the chamfers on tube and in cylinder head are in full contact and that the "flat" of tube is at right angles to a line drawn between the centre of push rod tube and centre of hot plug, as illustrated by Fig. A-418.

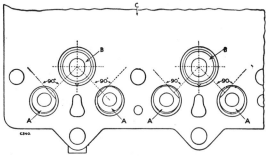

Fig. A-418—Correct position of push-rod tubes in relation to hot plugs
A—Push rod tubes.   B—Hot plug.
C—Cylinder head inverted.

3. Fit the valves, springs, cups and split cotters, ensuring that the components are retained in their original sets and positions.

4. Test the thermostat before fitment to cylinder head, by immersing in hot water. Expansion should commence between 164°F and 173°F and be complete at 193°F.

Insert the thermostat in the housing in cylinder head with rubber 'O' ring and fit the joint washer and cover.

5. If the hot plug and peg assemblies have been removed, these must now be replaced by tapping gently into position with a hide-faced hammer. When fitted they must be checked with a clock gauge to ensure that they do not protrude above the level of the cylinder head face more than .002 in. (0,050 mm) and are not recessed below the level of the cylinder head face more than .001 in. (0,025 mm).

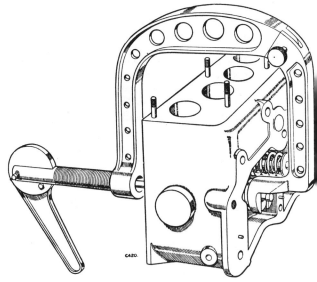

Fig. A-419—Compressing valve springs.

6. The fitment of wooden plugs in the injector nozzle apertures will be found advantageous at this stage.

Cylinder head and valves assembly to cylinder block   Operation A/448

When fitting the cylinder head, dummy studs ($\frac{1}{2}$ in. U.N.F. x 5 in. long) must be used to locate the gasket.

1. Smear the joint face of cylinder block and cylinder head gasket with engine oil, then fit the gasket and cylinder head assembly to cylinder block, using the two studs to facilitate alignment.

   It is strongly recommended that the head should be fitted before fitment of the rocker shaft assembly, otherwise damage to the push rod seats may occur.

2. Locate head and gasket with the securing bolts, fitting all bolts **except** those which also secure the rocker shaft pedestals, but do not tighten at this stage.

Push rods

3. Insert the push rods into their original positions, through cylinder head and locate in the tappets.

Rocker shaft assembly   Operation A/450

1. If necessary, press new bushes into the rockers. The oil holes in the rocker bushes are pre-drilled and care must be taken to ensure that the oil holes of bush and rocker will align when pressed into position.

2. Reamer the bush to .530 in. +.001 (13,4 +0,02 mm) to obtain the correct clearance. The reamer and rocker assembly must be held in such a manner as to ensure the correct alignment of the reamed hole.

3. Align the lubricated rocker shafts, with the bored ends together, and slide a support bracket on to each shaft. The locating hole in each bracket must be positioned immediately above the chamfered hole in shaft, 4.75 in. (120,65 mm) from the plugged end, and then secured with a locating screw and spring washer.

4. Assemble the remaining components with the plugged end of the shafts in the end brackets and the bored end of both shafts located in the centre bracket.

5. Fit the rocker cover securing studs to the rocker brackets.

6. Slacken off all tappet adjusting screws and offer the rocker assembly to cylinder head. Fit the bracket securing bolts, but do not tighten.

7. Tighten down the cylinder head bolts in the order indicated by Fig. A-420. The ½ in. U.N.F. bolts, including those that also secure the rocker brackets must be pulled down to 75 lb/ft. (10,3 Kg/m) whilst the 5/16 in. U.N.F. bolts securing the rocker brackets only are pulled down to 12-13 lb/ft. (1,6-1,7 Kg/m).

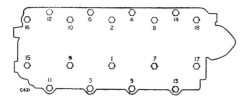

Fig. A-420—Order of tightening cylinder head bolts

8. It is important before rotating the camshaft to adjust all the tappets which are slack. Rotate the camshaft a quarter revolution at a time and after each movement adjust any tappets which are slack. When all excessive clearance has been eliminated adjust the tappets to the correct clearance.

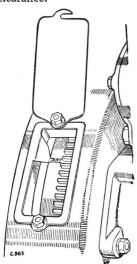

Fig. A-421— Timing pointer

Chain wheels, timing chain, adjuster and valve timing Operation A/452

1. Fit the crankshaft chain wheel on to shaft and key.

2. Turn the crankshaft in direction of rotation until the E.P. mark on flywheel is in line with the timing pointer.

3. Fit a dial test indicator so that the "fully open" position of the valve can be ascertained in the following manner :—

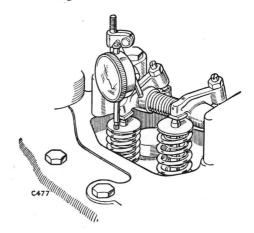

Fig. A-422—Checking exhaust valve "fully open" position

(a) Turn the camshaft in direction of rotation until the lobe of cam has nearly opened the valve fully, then stop rotation and mark the chain wheel and timing casing to record the position.

(b) Note the reading on dial test indicator, then continue to turn the chain wheel slowly in direction of rotation until the needle has again reached the same position.

(c) Mark the chain wheel at a point opposite to the mark on timing casing and make a third mark on the chain wheel, exactly between those made previously.

(d) Turn the camshaft against direction of rotation until the third mark is in line with that on timing casing, whereon the valve should be fully open.

4. Fit the timing chain with "no slack" on the driving side. It may be necessary to remove and re-position the camshaft chain wheel to obtain this "no slack" condition on the driving side when the flywheel and camshaft are correctly positioned.

5. Fit new bushes to the chain tensioner components as necessary; ensure that the fits and clearances are in accordance with those laid down in the Data Section. Position the ball in chain tensioner piston and secure with the retaining clip. Fit the compression spring over piston, locate the cylinder assembly and compress the spring. Place the idler wheel on

bearing arm and offer the assembly to the cylinder block, locating by means of the dowels. Screw the stepped bolt with ratchet and spring in position into cylinder block, then finally secure with two set bolts.

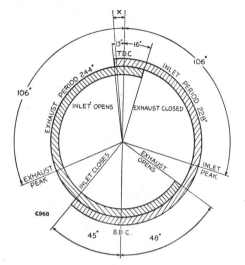

Fig. A-423—Timing diagram

X—Injection point is 17°

6. Turn the flywheel **against** direction of rotation approx. 90° then slowly **in** direction of rotation, checking that the exhaust valve reaches the "fully open" position, as indicated by the dial test indicator, exactly when the "E.P." mark on flywheel is in line with the pointer on flywheel housing.

Adjust if necessary by means of the six irregularly spaced keyways in the timing chain wheel. This arrangement allows a variation of 2° between each position.

Lock the set bolt securing camshaft chain wheel when timing has been set satisfactorily.

7. Secure the timing chain vibration damper to the front of cylinder block.

Tappet adjustment   Operation A/454

Two methods of setting the tappet clearance may be used, the first necessitates revolving the crankshaft 16 times approximately, and the second, two revolutions only.

1. **Method 1**

Turn the crankshaft in direction of rotation until the selected valve is fully open and then continue for a further revolution whereon the tappet concerned will be resting on the cam dwell. Adjust the tappet clearance to .010 in. (0,25 mm) with a feeler inserted between the rocker and valve stem.

Re-check clearance after tightening locknut. Repeat for each valve in turn.

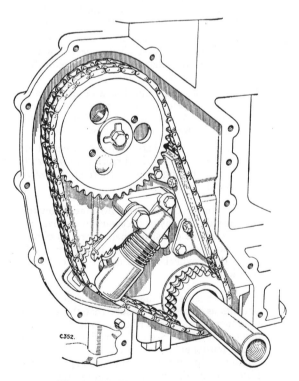

Fig. A-424—Timing gear arrangement.

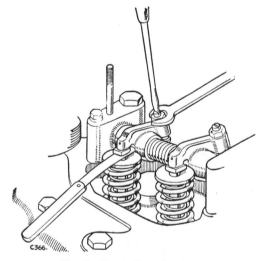

Fig. A-425—Adjusting tappets

2. **Method 2**

Turn the crankshaft in direction of rotation until number 8 valve (counting from front end of engine) is fully open. In this position the tappet for number 1 valve is on the dwell of its cam and the tappet clearance may be set with a .010 in. (0,25 mm) feeler inserted between the rocker and valve stem. Recheck the clearance after tightening the locknut.

The tappets should be set in the following order:

Set No. 1 tappet with No. 8 valve fully open.
Set No. 3 tappet with No. 6 valve fully open.
Set No. 5 tappet with No. 4 valve fully open.
Set No. 2 tappet with No. 7 valve fully open.
Set No. 8 tappet with No. 1 valve fully open.
Set No. 6 tappet with No. 3 valve fully open.
Set No. 4 tappet with No. 5 valve fully open.
Set No. 7 tappet with No. 2 valve fully open.

Water pump assembly and fitment to front cover
Operation A/456

1. See "Coolant System" for water pump assembly.

2. Renew the joint washer, then locate and secure the pump to front cover.

Front cover to cylinder block
Operation A/458

1. Examine the crankshaft oil seal and replace if necessary.

2. Position new joint washers and fit the front cover and water pump assembly to cylinder block.

3. Fit the water pump pulley to hub.

Vibration damper assembly and fitment
Operation A/460

1. If necessary renew the bushes in flywheel and backplate with an interference fit of .002 in. (0,05 mm) to .004 in. (0,10 mm).

2. Bolt the flywheel and backplate together, and reamer the bushes (ensuring that the bore is axially concentric) to allow a clearance fit on driving flange of .001 to .003 in. (0,025 to 0,076 mm).

3. Remove the securing bolts and withdraw the backplate from flywheel.

4. Fit a rubber disc to each side of the driving flange, mount the flywheel and backplate, with the **arrows** on backplate and flange aligned, then fit the set bolts and locking tabs. Discard any shims which may have been previously fitted, as these have been found to be unnecessary. Fit the securing bolts and tighten fully.

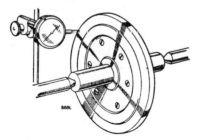

Fig. A-426—Checking vibration damper run-out

5. Mount the unit on a suitable mandrel and rotate between centres. Check the run-out with a dial test indicator and adjust to within .005 in. (0,127 mm) by means of the securing bolts.

Finally bend up the locking tabs to secure the set bolts.

6. Locate the vibration damper on crankshaft and key, then secure with the starting dog and tab washer.

Vertical drive shaft gear assembly
Operation A/462

1. Fit the circlip to groove dividing the upper and lower internal splining and enter the tapered splined plug in the end furthest from gear teeth, small end first.

2. Drift the plug into the gear until it abuts on the circlip.

3. Lubricate the split bush and fit it to the gear with the reduced diameter nearest the teeth.

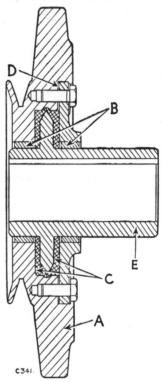

Fig. A-427—Sectioned view of vibration damper
A—Flywheel and pulley.   D—Shims.
B—Bushes.   E—Driving flange
C—Rubber discs.

Injection pump timing
Operation A/464

1. A—Early engines.

   On early engines the flywheel is marked SI.

   (i) Early, unmodified engines.

   In order to time these engines correctly, turn the crankshaft in the direction of rotation, until the timing pointer is exactly in line with the SI mark, with both valves on No. 1 cylinder closed.

(ii) Early engines with latest type pistons and early type hot plugs.

The injection pump timing for these engines must be altered to 17° B.T.D.C. Turn the crankshaft in the direction of rotation, until the timing pointer is .1 in. (2,5 mm) past the SI mark on the flywheel, with both valves on No. 1 cylinder closed.

(iii) Early engines with latest type pistons and hot plugs.

The correct timing for these engines is 16° B.T.D.C.

Turn the crankshaft in the direction of rotation, until the timing pointer is .2 in. (5 mm) past the SI mark on the flywheel, with both valves on No. 1 cylinder closed.

B. Late engines.

On late engines the flywheel is marked 16° and 18°.

(i) Late engines with latest type pistons and early type hot plugs.

The correct timing for these engines is 17° B.T.D.C.

Turn the crankshaft in the direction of rotation, until the timing pointer is exactly between the 16° and 18° mark on the flywheel, with both valves on No. 1 cylinder closed.

(ii) Late engines with latest type pistons and hot plugs.

This type of engine must be timed at 16° B.T.D.C.

Turn the crankshaft until the timing pointer is exactly in line with the 16° mark on the flywheel, with both valves on No. 1 cylinder closed.

Note: Engines fitted with late type hot plugs are identified by a splash of red paint on the cylinder head.

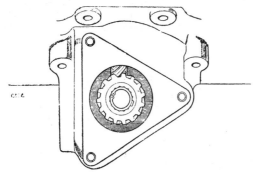

Fig. A-428—Driving gear in correct timing position

2. Insert the driving gear assembly for injection and oil pumps complete with split bushes, then mesh with camshaft gear so that when fully engaged, the master spline is approx. 20° from the centre line of engine (measured from front end) and the locating holes are correctly aligned. Lock the driving gear assembly in position with a grub screw.

It is very important that the backlash in the vertical drive shaft is taken into account when timing the injection.

3. Remove the inspection cover from injection pump and rotate the spindle in direction of rotation until the line marked "A" on driving plate aligns with mark on timing ring.

4. Offer the pump to engine with the fuel inlet connection forward and engage in the splined drive.

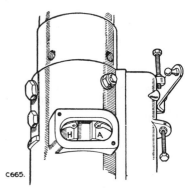

Fig. A-429—Distributor timing marks correctly aligned

Observe the markings through inspection aperture in injection pump side and make any final necessary adjustment by turning the pump body to align the timing marks.

Note 1:
It will be found advisable to use a mirror when checking markings.

Note 2:
It is very important that the injection pump is timed as accurately as possible. Two or three degrees retardation can cause excessive white smoke when starting from cold and running at light load. Two or three degrees advance can cause excessive black smoke at low speed, full load.

The timing must be checked by turning the engine until the timing marks on the pump are dead in line and then checking the timing marks on the flywheel. In this way any slight error is magnified by the 2 : 1 ratio of camshaft to crankshaft and the large diameter of the flywheel. An error of a given width on the pump markings will be 12 times that width if transferred to the flywheel.

5. Tighten pump down and re-check setting. Replace inspection cover on pump and flywheel housing.

Oil pump   Operation A/466

1. Insert the longer splined end of driving shaft into the pump and locate in the driving gear.

2. With the inlet port rearward, and the splined upper end of driving shaft aligned to the vertical drive gear, offer the pump to engine and secure in position.

3. Fit a tab locking washer and seal to the filter gauze and nut assembly. Screw the unit into the pump inlet port and position the filter square with sump bottom; lock in position.

Note: No provision is made for oil pressure adjustment.

Externals

1. Fit the lubricating oil filter assembly and joint washer.

2. Secure the breather pipe and oil filler assembly over the forward tappet chamber aperture, and steady bracket to top of cylinder block.

3. Mount and secure the fuel lift pump and cover plate assembly over the rear tappet chamber aperture.

4. Mount and secure the fuel oil filter assembly.

5. Fit the starter motor.

6. Fit the dynamo driving belt and adjust the tension to allow the belt to move $\frac{5}{16}$ to $\frac{7}{16}$ in. (8 to 11 mm) when pressed by thumb between the camshaft and water pump pulleys.

7. Connect the oil feed pipe and pressure gauge assembly between cylinder head and cylinder block rear end.

8. Secure the coolant pipe to thermostat and water pump casings.

9. Position the joint washer and fit the rocker and valve gear cover.

10. Fit the oil sump.

11. Smear new injector copper joint washers with grease and fit one to each injector. Insert a new corrugated sealing washer into each injector nozzle recess in cylinder head, with the raised portion upward, then locate the injector nozzles; do **not** tighten the clamping straps fully at this stage.

Note: Ensure that the bottom steel washer (corrugated) is replaced correctly, when refitting injectors. See Fig. A-430.

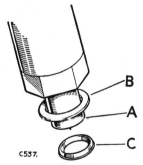

Fig. A-430—Position of injection nozzle washers
A—Nozzle   B—Copper washer   C—Steel washer

Note: For injector assembly and check, see Section M.

12. Connect the injector pipes to the injector pump. Turn the injectors to align with the pipes and connect.

Do not overtighten the clamping strap.

13. Fit the heater plugs to cylinder head and tighten.

Engine, to refit   Operation A/468

1. Reverse removal procedure—fit new mounting rubbers if necessary. Refill with lubricating oil, 11 pints (6 litres) and coolant, 17 pints (9,75 litres).

2. See Section M, Fuel Section, for method of priming injection pump, then Section Q for resetting controls and slow-running adjustment procedure.

3. Check for oil and water leaks—rectify as necessary.

Note:

At all times when the diesel engine is running, it is necessary to ensure that the oil bath air cleaner is fastened securely in the vertical position.

If adjustments are made with the engine running and the oil bath cleaner balanced on top of the engine, it is possible, should the cleaner tip to one side, for oil to be drawn into the intake manifold and hence into the engine, where it will act as a fuel and cause the engine to overspeed out of control and serious damage may result.

Should it be necessary to run the engine with the air cleaner out of the normal position, the rubber hose should be disconnected from the inlet manifold and the whole oil bath removed from the vehicle.

MAINTENANCE PROCEDURE

Removing cylinder head   Operation A/470

1. Open the tap at base of radiator and drain the coolant from this point only.

2. Disconnect the horn leads at the snap connectors adjacent to horn; ensure that the rubber insulators are left fitted to the main harness and thus avoid the danger of "shorting".

3. Remove the pin securing stay to bonnet and lift the bonnet clear of vehicle.

4. Remove the air cleaner and flexible air intake pipe complete.

5. Unscrew the dome nuts securing rocker cover and lift the cover clear.

6. Remove the rocker pedestal securing bolts, then pressing the extreme end pedestals towards the centre of rocker shaft, lift the complete rocker assembly clear.

7. Withdraw the push rods but ensure that they are retained in correct order for refitment.

8. Disconnect the pipes from main fuel filter; the pipe—"filter to injection pump"—must be removed completely to prevent distortion.

9. Remove the bolts securing filter to support bracket at engine, detach the heater plug earth lead and withdraw the filter.

10. Disconnect the fuel "bleed back" pipe from injection nozzle and from union nut on main fuel return pipe.

11. Remove the fuel pipes—injection pump to injection nozzle.

12. Fit aluminium caps to the injection pump outlet unions, to the fuel lift pump outlet, to fuel return pipe union and to the injection nozzle inlet and outlet unions.

13. Remove the injection nozzle securing straps and withdraw the nozzle assemblies.

14. Disconnect the leads and remove the heater plugs.

15. Remove the top coolant hose and the thermostat by-pass hose.

16. Disconnect the oil-feed pipe from rear of cylinder head—R.H. side—and the front exhaust pipe from exhaust manifold.

17. Loosen the cylinder head bolts evenly, then remove them completely and lift the head clear.

18. Remove the inlet and exhaust manifolds if necessary.

Fitting cylinder head   Operation A/472

1. Reverse the removal procedure.

   When fitting the cylinder head, dummy studs ($\frac{1}{2}$ in. U.N.F. x 5 in. long) must be used to locate the gasket. If this procedure is not adopted there is danger of the gasket being nipped on the liner spigot.

   Make sure the injector washers are fitted correctly. See Fig. A-430.

2. Renew all joint washers.

3. Pull down the cylinder head bolts evenly to the correct tension in the order shown in Fig. A-431.

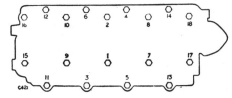

Fig. A-431—Order of tightening cylinder head bolts.

$\frac{1}{2}$ in. bolts to 75 lb/ft. (10,3 Kg/m).
$\frac{5}{16}$ in. bolts to 12 to 13 lb/ft. (1,6 to 1,7 Kg/m).

4. Adjust tappet clearances to .010 in. (0,25 mm)—Operation A-454.

5. Refill radiator.

6. Prime the fuel system. See Section M.

7. Run the engine and check for leaks.

8. It is important that the cylinder head bolts are retightened to the torque figures above after 30 minutes' running.

Decarbonising, valve grinding and lapping   Operation A/474

1. Remove the cylinder head—Operation A/470.

2. Using valve spring compressing tool, part number 276102, remove the valves, valve springs and retaining collets.

Position each valve with its springs and collets together and chalk mark the bench to ensure refitment to the guide from which they were removed.

Inner and outer valve springs are a selected interference fit and must not be interchanged.

3. Remove the carbon from the cylinder head, face, and ports, then from the piston crown and swirl-controlling recess, using a blunt scraper.

4. Examine the valves and valve guides for wear and renew as necessary. The guides may be drifted out using tools, part number 274400 inlet and 274401 exhaust, and new ones fitted with tool, part number 274406. See Fig. A-417—Page A-46.

5. Reface the valves to 45°—$\frac{1}{4}$° and lap them into their seats.

   Use the valve seat re-cutting tools (part number 274413 inlet and 274414 exhaust) only when necessary and then remove the minimum amount of metal.

6. Wash the valves, seats and ports thoroughly with paraffin and wipe dry with a non-furry rag. Fit a new rubber seal to each guide.

7. Refit the valves, springs and collets, then pour paraffin into each port and check the valve seats for tightness.

Tappet adjustment   Operation A/476

1. Disconnect the rubber air intake hose from the induction manifold and from air cleaner.

2. Remove the rocker gear cover.

3. Engage the starting handle and set the tappet clearance to .010 in. (0,25 mm) by either of the methods described under "Tappet adjustment" on Page A-48.

4. Replace the cover and rubber hose.

Rocker gear removal   Operation A/478

1. See Items 2 to 6 of Operation A/470.

Rocker gear fitment   Operation A/480

1. Reverse removal procedure and set tappet clearance to .010 in. (0,25 mm) as directed under "Tappet adjustment", Page A-48.

Timing chain renewal   Operation A/482

1. Lift off bonnet top—Items 2 and 3 of Operation A/470.

2. Remove the radiator—Section L.

3. Pivot the dynamo inwards and remove the fan belt.

4. Unscrew the starting nut and withdraw the vibration damper.

5. Remove the front cover and water pump assembly.

6. Mark the camshaft and crankshaft chainwheels and mark the casing opposite these marks, then remove the timing chain tensioner and timing chain. Discard the old chain.

7. With the marks on chain wheels and casing aligned, fit the new chain with no "slack" on the driving side.

8. Refit the chain tensioner.

9. The timing should be checked to ensure that the exhaust valve of No. 1 cylinder is fully open when the timing pointer is in line with the E.P. mark on the flywheel.

10. Refit the front cover, vibration damper, fan belt, radiator and bonnet top by reversing removal procedure.

11. Refill radiator—17 pints (10,0 litres).

Piston and connecting rod—removal
Operation A/488

1. Drain the oil from sump.

2. Remove the cylinder head—Operation A/470, and fit liner retainers, Part No. 274411.

3. Jack the front end of vehicle up and position suitable stands beneath the chassis side-members.

4. Remove the sump carefully to avoid damage to the joint washer.

5. Turn the crankshaft to bring the connecting rod concerned to B.D.C., then remove the connecting rod cap and push the rod and piston upward to remove.

Piston and connecting rod fitment
Operation A/490

1. With the crankpin at B.D.C., insert the connecting rod and piston assembly from the top of cylinder block with the oil spray hole in connecting rod and turbulence recess in piston towards the R.H. side of engine (nearest the camshaft).

2. Fit new connecting rod cap nuts and tighten to 35 lb./ft. (4,8 Kgs/m) torque.

3. Refit the sump and joint washer.

4. Replace the cylinder head—Operation A/472.

5. Refill with oil—11 pints (6 litres).

Cylinder liner replacement Operation A/492

1. Remove the cylinder head—Operation A/470.

2. Remove piston and connecting rod—Operation A/488.

3. Cover the oil hole in crankpin with masking tape or some similar material to prevent the entry of foreign matter to the crankshaft oilways.

4. Press the liner upward and then withdraw it from the top of cylinder bore.

5. Clean the liner bore spigot at top of cylinder block and the area inside the block immediately surrounding the lower liner bore. Remove and discard the two sealing rings from the grooves at lower bore, wipe the grooves clean and ensure that the small hole drilled through the L.H. side of cylinder block into the middle groove, is clear.

6. Smear the top and bottom grooves and two new sealing rings with Silicone Compound M.S.4, then fit the rings to the top and bottom grooves.

7. Apply a small amount of Silicone Compound M.S.4 to the outer walls of liner and refit to cylinder block.

8. Check the liner extension above cylinder block joint face in the manner instructed by Items 2 and 3 of Operation A/432.

9. Refit the piston and connecting rod—Operation A/490.

External oil filter—removal Operation A/494

1. Jack the front end of vehicle up and position suitable stands beneath the side members. Place a drip tray under the filter.

2. Disconnect the lead at oil pressure switch on filter head.

3. Remove the securing bolts and withdraw the filter complete.

External oil filter—fitment Operation A/496

1. Fit a new gasket between the filter head and cylinder block then reverse removal procedure.

External oil filter element—renewal
Operation A/498

1. See Item 1 of Operation A/494.

2. Unscrew the bolt at base of container, then remove the element and container complete.

3. Discard the old element and the large rubber sealing ring from filter head.

4. Wash the container thoroughly in paraffin, fit the new element and rubber sealing ring, then replace the container.

DEFECT LOCATION

(Symptom, Cause and Remedy)

A—ENGINE FAILS TO START.

1. Incorrect starting procedure—*See Instruction Manual.*
2. Starter motor unserviceable—*Section P.*
3. Batteries in low state of charge—*Remove and charge.*
4. Heater plug circuit broken—*Section P.*
5. Foreign matter in fuel system—*Section M.*
6. Supply of fuel to injection nozzles restricted—*Section M.*
7. Insufficient compression—*Check tappet clearance, cylinder head for tightness, cylinder head gasket, valve seats, valve springs, pistons, piston rings and liners for wear.*
8. Injection nozzles setting incorrect—*Reset—Section M.*
9. Injection nozzle auxiliary spray hole blocked—*Clean—Section M.*

B—ENGINE STALLS.

1. Slow-running incorrectly adjusted.—*See Section Q.*
2. Incorrect tappet clearance—*Adjust.*
3. Injection nozzle setting incorrect—*Reset—Section M.*
4. Injection nozzle auxiliary spray hole blocked—*Clean—Section M.*
5. Insufficient compression—*See item 7 of "A" above.*

C—REDUCED POWER AND ROUGH RUNNING.

1. Broken valve spring—*Renew.*
2. Incorrect tappet clearance—*Reset.*
3. Burnt valve—*Renew, reset tappet clearance and tighten injection nozzles.*
4. Broken piston rings—*Renew damaged parts as necessary.*
5. Compression uneven—*See Item 7 of "A" above.*
6. Injection nozzles burnt—*nozzle valve seating badly—Service—Section M.*
7. Incorrectly timed injection pump—*Check and adjust.*
8. Fuel supply restricted—*Clean filters—Section M.*
9. Injection nozzles improperly tightened—*Check sealing washer and re-tighten.*
10. Fuel pumps not delivering properly—*Section M*

D—ENGINE OVERHEATING.

1. Defective coolant system—*See "Defect Location"—Section L.*
2. Defective lubrication system—*See "Defect Location"—Section AO.*
3. Defective injection nozzles—*See "Defect Location"—Section M.*
4. Incorrect injection pump timing—*Check and adjust.*
5. Restricted fuel supply—*Section M.*

E—LOW OIL PRESSURE.

1. Defective lubrication system—*See "Defect Location"—Section AO.*

F—BLACK SMOKE ISSUES FROM EXHAUST

1. Defective fuel injection nozzle—*Section M.*
2. Injection pump incorrectly timed—*Check and adjust.*

G—WHITE VAPOUR ISSUES FROM EXHAUST.

1. Coolant leaking into combustion chamber—*Ascertain cause.*

   Note:—Do not confuse with the issue of vapour immediately after starting and caused by condensation in the exhaust pipe.

GENERAL DATA

Capacity (piston displacement)	....	.... 2,052 cc.	B.M.E.P.	.... 105 lbs/sq.in. (7,382 Kg/cm²) at 2,000 R.P.M.
Number of cylinders	 4		Maximum torque	.... 87 lbs/ft. (12,00 Kg/m) at 2,000 R.P.M.
Bore	....	.... 3.375 in. (85,725 mm)	Firing order	.... 1 - 3 - 4 - 2
Stroke	....	.... 3.5 in. (88,9 mm)	Piston speed at 3,500 R.P.M.	.... 2,040 ft./min.
Compression ratio	.... 22.5 to 1			
B.H.P.	....	.... 52 at 3,500 R.P.M.		

DETAIL DATA

Camshaft

Journal diameter .... 1.842 in.—.001 (26,70 mm—0,02)

Clearance in bearing.... .001 to .002 in. (0,02 to 0,05 mm)

End-float .... .0025 to .0055 in. (0,06 to 0,14 mm)

Cam lift—inlet .... .262 in. (6,65 mm)

Cam lift—exhaust .... .279 in. (7,10 mm)

Camshaft bearings

Type .... Split—steel backed, white metal lined

Internal diameter (line reamed in position) 1.843 in.+.0005 (46,812 mm+0,012)

Connecting rods

Bearing fit on crankpin .001 to .0025 in. (0,02 to 0,06 mm) clearance

Bearing nip .... .002 to .004 in. (0,05 to 0,10 mm)

End-float at big end .... .007 to .011 in. (0,177 to 0,280 mm)

Gudgeon pin bush fit in small end .... .001 to .002 in. (0,02 to 0,05 mm) interference

Gudgeon pin bush internal diameter— reamed in position 1.1875 in.+.0005 (31,87 mm+0,012)

Fit of gudgeon pin in bush .... .0003 to .0005 in. (0,007 mm to 0,012) clearance

Crankshaft

Journal diameter .... 2.5 in.—.001 (63,5 mm—0,021)

Crankpin diameter .... 2.126 in.—.001 (54 mm—0,02)

End-float (controlled by thrust washers at centre bearing) .... .002 to .006 in. (0,05 to 0,15 mm)

Flywheel

Number of teeth 100

Thickness at pressure face .... 1.375 in.—.015 (85,725 mm—0,39)

Maximum permissible run-out on flywheel face .... .002 in. (0,05 mm)

Maximum refacing depth .... .030 in. (0,76 mm)

Minimum thickness after grinding .... 1.330 in. (33,5 mm)

Markings

T.D.C. .... When opposite pointer, No. 1 piston is at top dead centre

E.P. .... When opposite pointer, No. 1 exhaust valve should be fully open

SI, 17° or 16°. See Pages A-49 and 50 for details .... When opposite pointer, start of injection is indicated.

Primary pinion bush
Fit in flywheel .... .001 to .003 in. (0,02 to 0,083 mm) interference

Internal diameter— reamed in position .875 in.+.002 (22,237 mm+0,0510)

Fit of shaft in bush .001 to .0035 in. (0,02 to 0,08 mm) clearance

Gudgeon pin

Fit in piston .... Zero to .0002 in. (0,005 mm) interference

Fit in connecting rod bush .... .0003 to .0005 in. (0,076 to 0,127 mm) clearance

Injection pump

Type .... Distributor, self-governing

Injection takes place.... SI, 17° or 16°. See pages A-49 and 50 for details

Injector

Type .... C.A.V. Pintaux

Size BDNO/SP6209

Liners

Internal diameter .... 3.375 in. +.001 (85.725 mm +0,02)

Fit in cylinder block

Top—upper .... .005 to .015 in. (0,13 to 0,38 mm) clearance

Top—lower .... .001 to .003 in. (0,02 to 0,08 mm) clearance

Bottom .... .001 to .003 in. (0,02 to 0,08 mm) clearance

Main bearings

Clearance on crankshaft journal .... .001 to .0025 in. (0,02 to 0,06 mm)

Bearing nip .... .004 to .006 in. (0,10 to 0,15 mm)

Push rod tubes

Fit in cylinder head .... .0005 to .002 in. (0,01 to 0,051 mm) interference on large diameter.

Full contact fit at chamfered edges of tube and cylinder head.

Oil pump assembly

Type .... Spur gear

Drive .... By splined shaft from camshaft gear

End-float of gears .... .002 to .005 in. (0,02 to 0,12 mm)

Radial clearance of gears .... .0005 to .002 in. (0,012 to 0,05 mm)

Backlash of gears .... .004 to .008 in. (0,10 to 0,20 mm)

Oil pressure, engine warm at 2,000 R.P.M .... 50 to 60 lbs/sq.in. (3,515 to 4,220 Kgs/cm²)

Relief valve spring

Free length .... 2.840 in. (52,93 mm)

Length in position under a load of 10 lbs. (4,53 Kg) 2.45 in. (61,23 mm)

Pistons

Type .... Light alloy, with recess in crown

Clearance in liner bore, measured at bottom of skirt at right angles to gudgeon pin .... .004 to .005 in. (0,10 to 0,12 mm)

Fit of gudgeon pin in piston .... Zero to .0002 in. (0,005 mm) interference

Gudgeon pin bore .... 1.187 in. +.002 (47,57 mm +0,05)

Piston rings

Compression No. 1

Type .... Square friction edge—chromium plated

Gap in liner bore .... .010 to .015 in. (0,25 to 0,38 mm)

Clearance in groove .0025 to .0035 in. (0,063 to 0,089 mm)

Compression—Nos. 2 and 3

Type .... Bevelled friction edge. Marked 'T' on upper side.

Gap in liner bore .... .010 to .015 in. (0,25 to 0,38 mm)

Clearance in groove .0025 to .0035 in. (0,063 to 0,089 mm)

Scraper No. 4

Type .... Slotted, square friction edge, double landed

Gap in liner bore .... .010 to .015 in. (0,25 to 0,38 mm)

Clearance in groove .0025 to .0035 in. (0,063 to 0,089 mm)

Rocker gear

Bush internal diameter (reamed in position) .... .530 + .001 in. (13,4 + 0,02 mm)

Shaft clearance in rocker bush .... .001 to .002 in. (0,02 to 0,04 mm)

Tappet clearance .... .010 in. (0,25 mm) hot or cold

Timing chain tensioner

Fit of bush in cylinder .003 to .005 in. (0,07 to 0,12 mm) interference

Fit of bush in idler wheel .... .001 to .003 in. (0,02 to 0,07 mm) interference

Fit of idler wheel on stub shaft .... .001 to .003 in. (0,02 to 0,07 mm) clearance

Fit of piston in cylinder bush .... .0005 to .001 in. (0,01 to 0,02 mm) clearance

Thrust bearings, crankshaft

Type .... Semi-circular, steel back, tin plated on friction surface

Standard size, total thickness.... .... .093 in.—.002 (2,362 mm—0,05)

Oversizes .... .0025 in. (0,06 mm) .005 in. (0,12 mm) .0075 in. (0,18 mm) .010 in. (0,25 mm)

Torque loadings

Connecting rod bolts 35 lb/ft. (4,84 Kg/m)

Cylinder head ($\frac{1}{2}$ in. U.N.F.) .... 75 lb/ft. (10,3 Kg/m)

Main bearing bolts (9/16 in. U.N.F.) .... 85 lb/ft. (11,75 Kg/m)

Rocker shaft support bracket bolts (5/16 in. U.N.F.) .... 12 to 13 lb/ft. (1,6 to 1,7 Kg/m)

Flywheel securing bolts 50 lb/ft. (6,91 Kg/m)

Valves

Inlet valve
Diameter (stem) .... .311 in.—.001 (7,92 mm—0,02)
Face angle .... 45°—$\frac{1}{4}$

Exhaust valve
Diameter (stem) .... .343 in.—.001 (8,71 mm—0,02)
Face angle .... 45°—$\frac{1}{4}$

Fit of inlet and exhaust valves in guides .... .0005 to .003 in. (0,01 to 0,07 mm) clearance

Valve seat
Seat angle (inlet and exhaust) .... 45° + $\frac{1}{4}$

Valve springs—inlet

Inner
Length—free .... 1.61 in. (40,89 mm)
Length under 17.5 lbs. (7,9 Kgs) load 1.383 in. (35,12 mm)

Outer
Length—free .... 1.768 in. (44,90 mm)
Length under 46 lbs. (21 Kgs) load .... 1.508 in. (38,30 mm)

Valve springs—exhaust

Inner
Length—free .... 1.61 in. (40,9 mm)
Length under 18.5 lbs. (8,37 Kgs) load 1.372 in. (34,8 mm)

Outer
Length—free .... 1.768 in. (44,9 mm)

Length under 48 lbs. (21,76 Kgs) load 1.497 in. (38,0 mm)

Valve timing

Inlet opens .... 13° B.T.D.C.

Inlet closes .... 45° A.B.D.C.

Inlet peak .... 106° A.T.D.C.

Exhaust opens . .... 48° B.B.D.C.

Exhaust closes .... 16° A.T.D.C.

Exhaust peak .... 106° B.T.D.C.

Vertical drive shaft gear

Backlash .... .006 to .010 in. (0,1524 to 0,254 mm)

Internal diameter of bush .... 1.00 in.+.001 (25,4 mm+0.02)

Fit of gear in bush .....001 to .003 in. (0,02 to 0,07 mm) clearance

Vibration damper

Fit of bushes in flywheel and back plate .002 to .004 in. (0,05 to 0,10 mm)

Internal diameter of bushes (reamed in position) .... 1.917 in. + .001 (47,70 mm + 0,02)

Fit of bushes on driving flange .... .001 to .003 in. (0,02 to 0,07 mm) clearance

Maximum permissible run-out of flywheel .002 in. (0,05 mm)

Section AO — ENGINE LUBRICATION

INDEX

	Page
Approved lubricants:	
Petrol models	AO-3
Diesel models	AO-3
Data, all models	AO-7
Defect location, all models	AO-7

	Page
Filter—external, Petrol models	AO-4
Filter—external, Diesel models	AO-6
Oil pump, Petrol models	AO-1
Oil pump, Diesel models	AO-4
Relief valve adjustment, Petrol models	AO-4

LIST OF ILLUSTRATIONS

Fig.		Page
AO-1	Oil pressure relief valve, Petrol models	AO-1
AO-2	Checking clearance of oil pump gears, Petrol models	AO-1
AO-3	Exploded view of oil pump and driving gear, Petrol models	AO-2
AO-4	Oil pressure adjustment, 1948-54 models	AO-4
AO-5	Engine oil filters, late Petrol models	AO-4

Fig.		Page
AO-6	Exploded view of oil pump and driving gear, Diesel models	AO-5
AO-7	Checking for radial clearance, Diesel models	AO-6
AO-8	Checking end-float of the gears, Diesel models	AO-6
AO-9	Engine oil filters, Diesel models	AO-6

Oil pump, Petrol models

To remove   Operation AO/2

1. Drain the oil and remove sump.
2. Slacken the locknut securing oil pressure adjusting screw, then remove screw, washer, spring, plunger and ball (which may remain in the pump and can be removed when the pump complete is withdrawn).
3. Remove the pump locating screw.
4. Withdraw the pump, leaving the drive shaft in position.
5. If necessary, withdraw the oil pump drive shaft.

   Note: On engines numbered 860001 to 16102271 and 16131648 a cylindrical oil pump filter was fitted into the side of the sump.

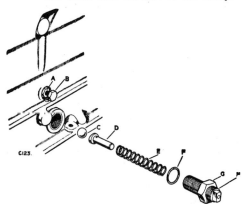

Fig. AO-1—Oil pressure relief valve.

A—Locknut
B—Locating screw—oil pump
C—Ball
D—Plunger
E—Spring
F—washer
G—Locknut
H—Adjusting screw—oil pressure

To overhaul and refit   Operation AO/4

1. Remove the oil strainer from the pump.
2. Remove the oil pump cover and lift out the gears.
3. Remove the idler gear spindle. If necessary, press out the idler gear bush and drive out the bush in the pump body.
4. Clean parts, examine for wear and renew as necessary.
5. If removed, press a new bush into the body and ream in position to .5625 in. +.001 (14,28 mm + 0,025), ensuring correct alignment with the bore at the bottom end of the pump body. The bush should be a *light drive fit* in the pump body.

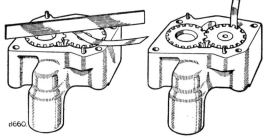

Fig. AO-2—Checking clearance of oil pump gears, Petrol models.

6. Check the radial clearance (.001 to .004 in., 0,02 to 0,10 mm), backlash (.008 to .012 in., 0,20 to 0,30 mm) and end-float (.003 to .005 in., 0,075 to 0,13 mm steel gear, and .004 to .006 in., 0,10 to 0,15 mm aluminium gear) of the gears; renew parts as necessary. If incorrect, oil flow would be insufficient.
7. Complete the assembly.
8. Refit by reversing removal procedure.
9. Adjust the oil pressure. Operation AO/6.

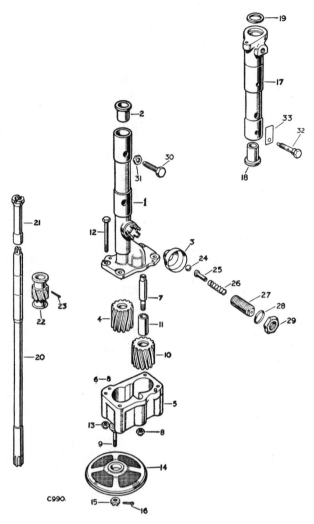

Fig. AO-3—Exploded view of oil pump and driving gear, Petrol models.

1	Oil pump body assembly	
2	Bush for drive shaft	
3	Oil pump shield	
4	Oil pump gear, driver	
5	Oil pump cover assembly	
6	Dowel locating body	
7	Spindle for idler wheel	
8	Self-locking nut ($\frac{3}{8}$") fixing spindle	
9	Stud for oil strainer	
10	Oil pump gear idler assembly	
11	Bush for idler gear	
12–13	Fixings—cover to body	
14	Oil strainer for pump	
15–16	Fixings—oil strainer to pump	
17	Distributor housing assembly	
18	Bush for drive shaft	
19	Cork washer for housing	
20	Oil pump drive shaft	
21	Drive shaft for distributor	
22	Oil pump driving gear	
23	Taper pin, fixing gear to shaft	
24	Steel ball	⎫
25	Plunger	⎪
26	Spring	⎬ For oil pressure
27	Adjusting screw	⎪ release valve
28	Washer	⎪
29	Locknut	⎭
30–31	Fixings—oil pump to cylinder block	
32	Oil feed bolt, locating distributor housing	
33	Locker for bolt	

The chart below covers all currently recommended lubricants for use in engines and all other units.

These recommendations apply to temperate climates, where operational conditions vary between approximately 10°F and 90°F.

PETROL ENGINE								
COMPONENTS	S.A.E.	B.P.	DUCKHAM'S	ESSO	MOBIL	SHELL	WAKEFIELD	REGENT
ENGINE, AIR CLEANER AND GOVERNOR	20W	Energol SAE 20W	Duckham's NOL Twenty	Esso Estra 20W/30	Mobiloil Arctic	Shell X100 SAE 20/20W	Castrolite	Havoline 20/20W

DIESEL ENGINE								
ENGINE AND AIR CLEANER	20W	Energol Diesel D20W	NOL Diesel Engine Oil 20	Essolube HD20	Mobiloil Arctic	Rotella 20/20W	Castrol CR20	RPM Delco Special 20

ALL MODELS								
GEARBOX AND TRANSFER BOX DIFFERENTIALS AND SWIVEL PIN HOUSINGS STEERING BOX AND STEERING RELAY UNIT (SEALED) REAR POWER TAKE-OFF, PULLEY UNIT AND CAPSTAN WINCH	90EP	Energol EP SAE 90	Duckham's NOL EP 90	Esso Expee Compound 90	Mobilube GX 90	Spirax 90EP	Castrol Hypoy	Universal Thuban 90
LUBRICATION NIPPLES	—	Energrease L-2	Duckham's LB 10 Grease	Esso Multi-purpose Grease H	Mobilgrease MP	Retinax A	Castrolease LM	Marfak Multi-Purpose 2

NOTE 1: −20°F = −28°C; 0°F = −17°C; 10°F = −12°C; 32°F = 0°C; 90°F = 32°C.

NOTE 2: The multi-grade oils listed above are recommended for use under the S.A.E. number as shown in the chart; they are also approved for use under the higher range of S.A.E. grades that they cover.

NOTE 3: Information on oil recommendations for use under extreme winter or tropical conditions can be obtained from The Rover Co. Ltd., Technical Service Department.

Oil pressure relief valve, Petrol models

To adjust   **Operation AO/6**

1. Fit a slave oil pressure gauge in place of the warning light switch, run the engine and ensure that there is at least 20 lb./sq.in. (1,4 kg/cm²) oil pressure.

2. Warm the engine to running temperature and adjust the pressure by means of the valve to 55-65 lb./sq.in. (3,8-4,5 Kg/cm²) at 30 m.p.h. (50 k.p.h.) in top gear. Tighten the screw to increase pressure and vice versa. If necessary, renew the release valve spring.

3. Refit the warning light switch and lead.

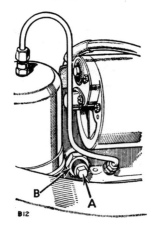

Fig. AO-4—Oil pressure adjustment
1948-54 models

A—Adjusting screw.   B—Locknut.

External oil filter, 1948-54 models, to renew

1. Disconnect the inlet and outlet pipes from the filter.

2. Slacken the four set bolts securing the filter mounting bracket and clip to the cylinder block; withdraw and discard the filter.

3. Fit the new filter by reversing this procedure, and refill the engine with one of the recommended lubricants.

4. Run the engine for five minutes and inspect and rectify any oil leaks.

5. Check the engine oil level and top up as necessary.

External oil filter, 1955-58 Petrol models

Element to renew   **Operation AO/8**

1. Position a suitable drip-tray beneath the filter, then unscrew the bolt at the base of the filter container. Withdraw the container complete with element and large rubber sealing washer. Discard the element and wash the container thoroughly in petrol.

2. Place a new filter element in the container and reassemble the unit, using the new large rubber sealing washer supplied with element. Ensure that the sealing washers are in position and intact and that the container is correctly located.

3. Fill crankcase sump with clean oil—11 pints (6 litres)—to the "high" mark on dipstick, run the engine and check for oil leaks at the filter and then add more oil as necessary. Figure for capacity includes 1 pint (0,5 litre) for filter.

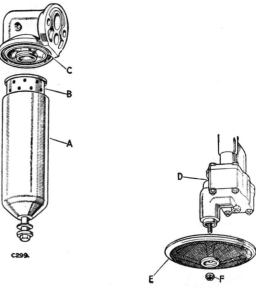

Fig. AO-5—Engine oil filters, late Petrol models

A—Container	D—Oil pump
B—Element	E—Filter gauze
C—Gasket	F—Castellated nut

Filter—to remove and clean   Operation AO/10

1. Remove the bolts securing the filter head to the adaptor, then withdraw complete unit.

2. Unscrew the container bolt and renew element. Operation AO/8.

3. Remove the relief valve, spring and ball from the filter head, then wash these parts thoroughly in petrol.

4. Reverse dismantling procedure and refit the assembly to the cylinder block with a new joint washer interposed.

Oil pump, Diesel models

To remove   **Operation AO/12**

1. Drain the oil and remove sump.

2. Remove the securing bolts and withdraw pump assembly.

3. Withdraw the driving shaft from pump upper casing.

4. Unscrew the securing nut and remove filter gauze assembly.

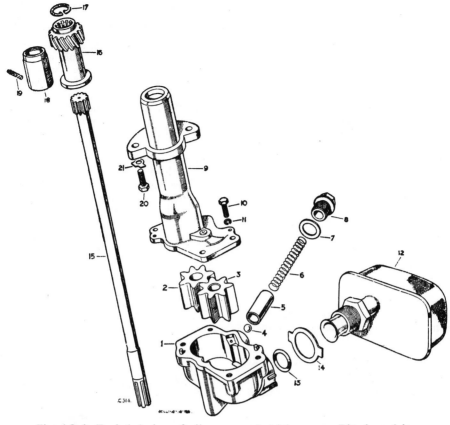

Fig. AO-6—Exploded view of oil pump and driving gear, Diesel models.

1	Lower casing	11	Spring washer for bolt
2	Driving gear	12	Filter gauze assembly
3	Driven gear	13	Oil seal
4	Relief valve ball	14	Tab washer
5	Relief valve plunger	15	Driving shaft
6	Relief valve spring	16	Driving shaft gear
7	Washer	17	Circlip
8	Plug	18	Bush—drive shaft gear
9	Upper casing	19	Locating screw
10	Set bolt for casings	20	Securing bolt

5. Remove the bolts securing the upper casing to lower body, tap them gently apart and withdraw the gears. The idler gear spindle may be removed if necessary.

6. Unscrew the relief valve plug and remove the spring, plunger and ball.

To overhaul and refit   Operation AO/14

1. Check the external diameter of the gears and the internal diameter of the gear housings, using a ring gauge and plug gauge, Part Nos. 276095 and 276094 respectively. With the gauges an exact fit in the bore of the housing, and on the outer diameter of the gears, a radial clearance of .0005 in. (0,01 mm) will exist between the gears and housing.

It should not be possible to interpose a feeler strip of more than .002 in. (0,05 mm) thickness between the gear perimeter and ring gauge, or a feeler strip of more than .003 in. (0,08 mm) thickness between the gear perimeter and gear housing, thus allowing a maximum radial clearance of .003 in. (0,08 mm) between the gear and housing.

2. Press the short, stepped end of idler spindle into the pump body and fit the cast iron idler wheel.

   Mesh the steel gear with the idler gear, inserting the splined end first.

3. Lay a straight edge across the joint face of pump body and check the end-float with a feeler gauge. This should be between .002 and .005 in. (0,0508 to 0,127 mm).

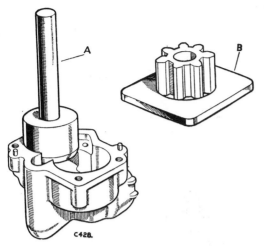

Fig. AO-7—Checking for radial clearance,
Diesel models
A—Plug gauge   B—Ring gauge

4. Smear the joint faces of pump body and cover lightly with suitable jointing compound, then bolt together.

5. Insert the relief valve ball, plunger and spring. Secure with plug and washer.

 Note: No provision is made for oil pressure adjustment.

6. Insert the longer splined end of driving shaft into the pump and locate in the driving gear.

7. With the inlet port rearward, and the splined upper end of driving shaft aligned to the drive gear, offer the pump to engine and secure in position.

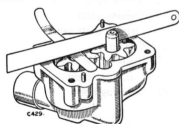

Fig. AO-8—Checking end-float of the gears,
Diesel models

8. Fit a tab locking washer and seal to the filter gauze and nut assembly. Screw the unit into the pump inlet ports and position the filter square with sump bottom; lock in position.

9. Refit the crankcase sump and refill with oil— 13 pints (7 litres)—to the "high" mark on dipstick, run the engine and check for oil leaks at the sump joint face, then add more oil as necessary. Figure for capacity includes 2 pints (1 litre) for filter.

External oil filter, Diesel models
Element—to renew   Operation AO/16

1. Position a suitable drip-tray beneath the filter, then unscrew the bolt at base of the filter container. Withdraw the container complete with the element, which must be discarded.

2. Wash the container thoroughly in petrol, fit a new element, new inner and outer top sealing rings, then replace the container.

3. Fill crankcase sump with clean oil (13 pints (7 litres)) to the "high" mark on dipstick, run the engine and check for oil leaks and then add more oil as necessary. Figures for capacity includes 2 pints (1 litre) for filter.

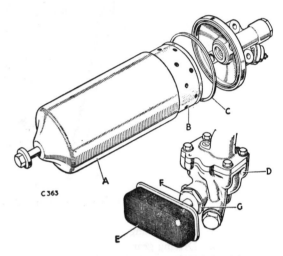

Fig. AO-9—Engine oil filters, Diesel models.

A—Container	D—Oil pump	F—Nut for filter gauze
B—Element	E—Filter gauze	G—Locker for nut
C—Gasket		

Filter—to remove and clean
Operation AO/18

1. Disconnect the leads from the oil pressure switch.

2. Remove the bolts securing the filter head to cylinder block, then withdraw the complete filter assembly.

3. Unscrew the container bolt and renew element. Operation AO/16.

4. Remove the pressure switch, also the relief valve spring and ball from the filter head, then wash these parts thoroughly in petrol.

5. Reverse dismantling procedure and refit the assembly to the cylinder block with a new joint washer interposed.

DEFECT LOCATION

Symptom, Cause and Remedy

A—WARNING LIGHT REMAINS "ON"—ENGINE RUNNING

1. Low oil pressure—*See item* **B.**
2. Oil pressure switch unserviceable—*Renew.*
3. Electrical fault—*Check circuit.*

B—LOW OIL PRESSURE

Ascertained by gauge fitted in place of switch and with sump oil level correct.

1. Dirty gauze filter on pump—*Remove sump, remove filter gauze and clean in petrol with a stiff brush. Refill with clean oil.*
2. Pump body joints loose—*Tighten.*
3. Foreign matter on pump ball valve seat—*Remove and clean.*

4. Relief valve plunger sticking—*Remove and ascertain cause.*
5. Weak relief valve spring—*Renew.*
6. Incorrectly adjusted relief valve (2 litre Petrol only)—*Adjust to 55 to 65 lb/sq. in. (3,8 to 4,5 Kg/cm²)*
7. Gears excessively worn—*See Operations AO/4 and AO/14*
8. Excessively worn bearings—main, connecting rod big-end, camshaft, etc.—*Ascertain which bearings and rectify.*

C—WARNING LIGHT FAILS TO GLOW —

When engine is stopped and ignition (petrol engines) or auxiliary services (Diesel) switch is "on".

1. Bulb filament broken—*Renew bulb. Section Q.*
2. Oil pressure switch unserviceable—*Renew.*
3. Electrical fault—*Check circuit.*

DATA

Oil pump—Petrol models

Type	.... Gear
Drive	.... Skew gear from camshaft

End-float of gears:

Steel gear	.... .003 to .005 in. (0,075 to 0,13 mm)
Aluminium gear	.... .004 to .006 in. (0,10 to 0,15 mm)
Radial clearance of gears	.... .001 to .004 in. (0,02 to 0,10 mm)
Backlash of gears	.... .008 to .012 in. (0,20 to 0,30 mm)

Oil pressure, engine warm

At 2,000 R.P.M. .... 55 to 65 lb./sq.in. (3,8 to 4,5 Kg/cm²)

Oil pressure relief valve

Type	.... Adjustable

Relief valve spring:

Free length	.... 3.050 in. (77,47 mm)
Compressed length at 13 lb. (5,89 Kg) load	.... 1.990 in. (50,54 mm)

Oil pump—Diesel models

Type	.... Spur gear
Drive	.... Splined shaft from camshaft
End-float of gears	.... .002 to .005 in. (0,025 to 0,12 mm)
Radial clearance of gears	.... .0005 to .002 in. (0,012 to 0,050 mm)
Backlash of gears	.... 0.004 to .008 in. (0,10 to 0,20 mm)

Oil pressure, engine warm

At 2,000 R.P.M. .... 50 to 60 lb./sq.in. (3,515 to 4,220 Kg/cm²)

Oil pressure relief valve

Type	.... Non-adjustable

Relief valve spring:

Free length	.... 2.840 in. (52,93 mm)
Compressed length at 10 lb. load (4,53 Kg.)	.... 2.45 in. (61,23 mm)

Section B – CLUTCH UNIT – ALL MODELS

INDEX

	Page		Page
Clutch linkage	B-16	Data	B-21
Clutch operating levers	B-4 and 8	Defect location	B-20
Clutch pedal unit	B-12	Driven plate	B-5 and 10
Clutch unit	B-2 and 6	Withdrawal mechanism	B-11

LIST OF ILLUSTRATIONS

Fig.		Page	Fig.		Page
B-1	Layout of clutch unit, Rover	B-2	B-8	Driven plate, Borg and Beck type	B-10
B-2	Setting operating levers, Stage 2	Rover type B-4	B-9	Setting withdrawal shaft, Borg and Beck type	B-12
B-3	Setting operating levers, Stage 3	B-5	B-10	Cross-section of withdrawal mechanism	B-13
B-4	Driven plate, Rover type	B-6	B-11	Layout of clutch pedal and linkage, 1948-53	B-14
B-5	Layout of clutch unit, Borg and Beck type	B-7	B-12	Clutch adjustment, 1954-58 models....	B-16
B-6	Cross-section of clutch unit	B-9	B-13	Layout of clutch pedal and linkage, 1954-58	B-18
B-7	Setting the operating levers, Borg and Beck type	B-10			

ROVER PATTERN CLUTCH
Clutch unit

To remove   **Operation B/2**

1. Remove the complete gearbox unit as detailed at Section C. If not already done, mark the cover plate and flywheel, so that on re-assembly the plate may be fitted in the same relative position, to preserve the original balance of the unit.

2. Release in rotation the eight self-locking nuts securing the clutch unit to the flywheel until the spring pressure is relieved; remove the nuts and remove the clutch unit (located by two dowels) and driven plate.

To strip   **Operation B/4**

1. Suitably mark the cover plate, pressure plate and operating levers, so that they may be assembled in the same relative positions in order to preserve the original balance.

2. Remove the three operating lever springs.

3. Remove the operating levers and fulcrum pins.

4. Prise up the locking tabs and remove the six bolts securing the oil excluder plate; remove the oil excluder.

5. Remove the three split pins and curved washers from the driving bolts.

6. Using four nuts, pull down the clutch unit and driven plate evenly on to a flywheel or other suitable plate.

7. Withdraw the driving bolts and remove the operating links.

8. Remove the cover and driven plate from the flywheel

9. Remove the cups and springs from the cover.

10. Remove the pressure plate.

11. Remove the fibre inserts from the pressure plate.

To assemble   **Operation B/6**

1. Clean all the components and lay them out for inspection.

2. Renew all parts which show damage or appreciable wear.

3. Examine the pressure plate for signs of scoring or burning and re-grind the pressure face as necessary. The limit for skimming the pressure plate is to .020 in. (0,5 mm) below the nominal thickness (i.e. .730 in. (18,6 mm) minimum overall thickness); if the plate still shows wear when ground to this dimension, it must be discarded and a new part used on assembly. As the leverage of the operating levers is 5 : 1, this 0.20 in. (0,5 mm) skim will reduce the travel of the withdrawal sleeve by $\frac{1}{10}$ in. (2,5 mm), which is the maximum figure allowable without causing serious shortening of the effective life of the clutch unit.

4. Examine the engine flywheel for signs of scoring or burning; if necessary, remove it from the vehicle as detailed in Section A, and re-grind the pressure face.

   The clutch securing bolts and dowels must be removed from the flywheel before skimming, so enabling the entire face to be ground. The policy of grinding only within the bolts, so leaving a pronounced step in the face, is not

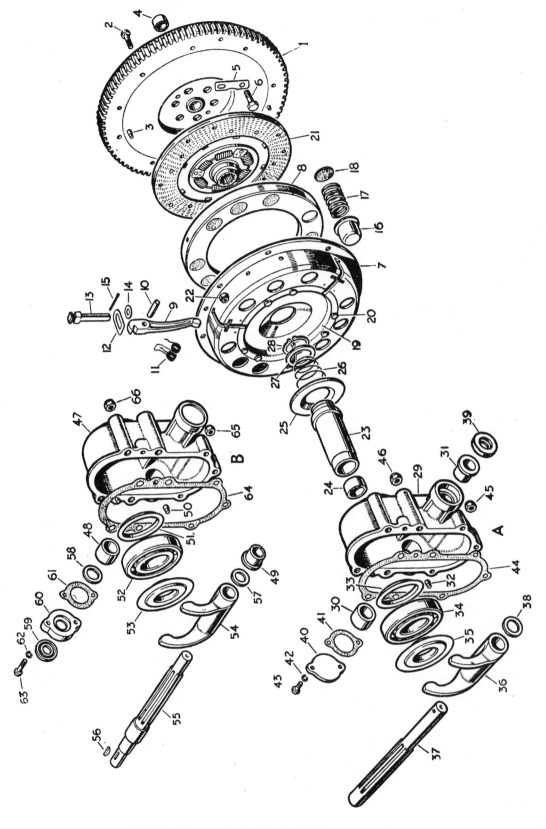

Fig. B-1—Layout of the clutch unit (Rover pattern)

Key to Fig. B-1

1 Flywheel
2 Fitting bolt fixing clutch to flywheel
3 Dowel locating clutch unit
4 Bush for primary pinion
5 Locker ⎫ Fixing flywheel
6 Special bolt ⎬ to crankshaft
7 Clutch cover plate
8 Pressure plate
9 Operating lever
10 Fulcrum pin for lever
11 Return spring for lever
12 Operating link for lever
13 Driving bolt ⎫ Connecting links
14 Curved washer ⎬ to pressure plate
15 Split pin
16 Retaining cup for clutch spring
17 Clutch thrust spring
18 Insert for clutch spring
19 Oil excluder
20 Set bolt fixing oil excluder
21 Clutch driven plate
22 Nut fixing clutch unit to flywheel
23 Withdrawal sleeve

24 Bush for sleeve
25 Outer cup
26 Spring for cup ⎫ For clutch withdrawal sleeve
27 Retaining washer ⎫ For spring
28 Circlip ⎬
29 Withdrawal race housing
30 Bush, large ⎫ For cross-shaft
31 Bush, small ⎬
32 Dowel locating housing
33 Oil drain ring
34 Withdrawal thrust bearing
35 Thrust ring for bearing
36 Operating fork for clutch
37 Cross-shaft for fork
38 Thrust washer for cross-shaft
39 Oil seal for cross-shaft
40 Cover plate for cross-shaft
41 Joint washer for cover plate
42–43 Fixings for cover plate
44 Joint washer for withdrawal housing
45–46 Fixings for housing

} R.H.D. models

47 Withdrawal race housing
48 Bush, large ⎫ For cross-shaft
49 Bush, small ⎬
50 Dowel locating housing
51 Oil drain ring
52 Withdrawal thrust bearing
53 Thrust ring for bearing
54 Operating fork for clutch
55 Cross-shaft for fork
56 Woodruff key for cross-shaft
57 Thrust washer, inner ⎫ For cross-shaft
58 Thrust washer, outer ⎬
59 Oil seal for cross-shaft
60 Housing for oil seal
61 Joint washer for housing
62–63 Fixings for housing
64 Joint washer for withdrawal housing
65–66 Fixings for housing

} L.H.D. models

acceptable, as it results in the driven plate moving forward relative to the clutch cover, so reducing clutch life, and introducing the possibility of "clutch slip" at an early date. The limit for skimming over the whole face is to .030 in. (0,75 mm) below the nominal thickness (*i.e.* 1.063 in. (27 mm) minimum overall thickness); if the flywheel still shows wear when ground to this dimension, it must be discarded and a new part used on assembly.

5. Examine the primary pinion spigot bush in the centre of the flywheel for excessive wear or damage, and renew it as necessary. The new bush must be a *press fit* in the flywheel; its bore should be .878 in.+.0005 and the diameter of the primary pinion .8745 in.—.0005, thus making the pinion an *easy fit* in the bush.

6. Replace the flywheel as detailed in Section A.

7. Check the clutch springs in accordance with the following specification, and renew them as necessary:—

　　Number of coils: 5½
　　Free length: 1.554 in. (39,5 mm)
　　Solid height: 1.040 in. (26,4 mm)
　　Identification: Orange paint
　　Load: 130 lb. ±4 (63 kg. ±1,8)
　at　Working length: 1.164 in. (29,6 mm)

8. Place the driven and pressure plates in position on a spare flywheel or other suitable plate.

9. Replace the fibre spring inserts and clutch springs in the recesses in the pressure plate; place the retaining cups over the springs.

10. Position the cover over the cups and pull it down evenly to the flywheel face by means of four nuts.

11. Insert the driving bolts and operating links.

12. Remove the unit from the flywheel and fit the curved washers and split pins on the driving bolts.

Note: Each split pin should be entered from the recess cut in the clutch cover, and then bent over from the pressure plate side.

13. Replace the oil excluder; secure it by means of six set bolts and turn up the locking tabs.

14. Replace the operating levers, fulcrum pins and return springs.

The clutch unit is now ready for alignment of the operating levers.

Clutch operating levers
To set　　　　　　　　　　　**Operation B/8**

To ensure satisfactory operation of the clutch withdrawal mechanism, it is essential that the thrust faces of the operating levers be set equidistant from the flywheel face.

When assembled in the vehicle, the lever faces must be 1.900 in.+.031 (48,3 mm+0,8) from the flywheel face, but when setting the levers in the way described below, *i.e.* using ⅜ in. (9,5 mm) distance pieces in place of the driven plate, the levers must be set to a dimension of 1.729 in.$^{+.010}_{-.000}$ (43,9 mm $^{+0,25}_{-0,00}$) from the flywheel face.

Owing to the number of accumulated tolerances affecting this dimension, it is unlikely that the setting will be correct on initial assembly, and the following method should be employed to check and rectify any innacuracy present.

1. The equipment required comprises:—
　(a) Clutch unit to be checked.
　(b) A flywheel or other suitable plate.
　(c) Surface plate.
　(d) Scribing block.
　(e) Setting gauge with steps at 1.729 in. (43,90 mm) and 1.739 in. (44,15 mm).

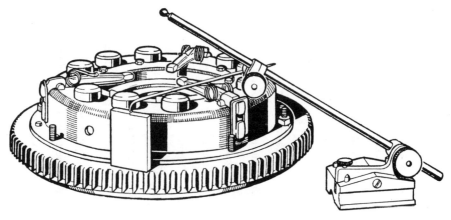

Fig. B-2—Setting the operating levers—Stage 2

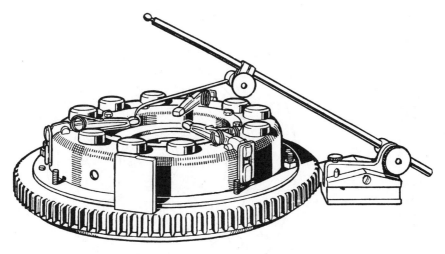

Fig. B-3—Setting the operating levers—Stage 3

This can be made from a piece of flat ¼ in. (6 mm) steel plate.

(f) Three ⅜ in. (9,5 mm) distance pieces; ⅜ in. (9,5 mm) rollers would be suitable.

2. Bolt the clutch unit down to the flywheel with *eight* nuts, with the three distance pieces in place of the driven plate. The driven plate must not be used when setting the levers, as it has an allowable "run-out" of 0.10 in. (0,25 mm).

3. Place the flywheel and clutch assembly on the surface plate and set the scribe to 1.729 in. (43,90 mm) from the flywheel face by using the gauge as in Fig. B-2.

4. Check the heights of the three operating levers (Fig. B-3); those that do not lie between 1.729 in. (43,90 mm) and 1.739 in. (44,15 mm) must be brought into line as described below. The lever return spring must be in position each time a check is made; care should also be taken to **ensure that the lever fulcrum pins are well seated in the cover plate.**

(a) If the lever is too high:

  (i) By selective assembly of levers, or

  (ii) By filing a very small amount from the flat end of the slot in the operating link. As the ratio of the distances of the two ends of a lever from the fulcrum pin is roughly 5 to 1, it will be seen that the removal of .002 in. (0,05 mm) from the link will lower the operating face of the lever by approximately .010 in. (0,25 mm).

(b) If the lever is too low:—

This means that wear is present in the operating lever and/or link and the worn parts must be renewed.

5. When the setting of all three levers is correct, remove the clutch unit from the flywheel after releasing the eight securing nuts in rotation until the spring pressure is relieved.

Driven plate

To reline   Operation B/10

1. Drill out the retaining rivets and remove the old linings; the rivets must not be punched out, as serious deformation of the plate would thereby result.

2. Rivet one new lining in position, using a blunt-ended centre punch to roll the rivet shanks securely against the plate.

3. Rivet the second lining on to the opposite side of the plate with the clearance holes over the rivet heads already formed in fitting the first facing.

4. Mount the plate on a suitable mandrel between centres and check for run-out as near the edge as possible; if the error is more than .010 in. (0,25 mm), press over the high spots until the plate is true within this figure.

Clutch unit

To replace   Operation B/12

1. Place the driven plate in position on the flywheel with the longer end of the central boss away from the engine.

2. Centralise the plate by means of a slave primary pinion or suitable dummy shaft which fits the splined bore of the plate hub and the spigot bearing in the flywheel.

3. Fit the clutch unit with the identification marking adjacent to that on the flywheel; secure it by means of the eight self-locking nuts; the nuts must be pulled down in rotation to prevent distortion of the unit.

4. Remove the centralising shaft.

5. Replace the gearbox assembly as detailed in Section C.

6. Check and adjust the clutch pedal free movement.

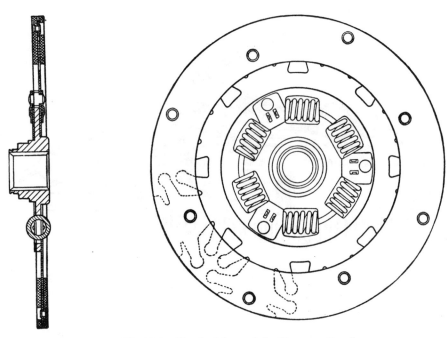

Fig. B-4—Clutch driven plate (Rover pattern)

BORG AND BECK PATTERN CLUTCH
Clutch unit

To remove   **Operation B/14**

1. Remove the complete gearbox unit. Section C. If not already done, mark the cover plate and flywheel, so that on reassembly the plate may be fitted in the same relative position, to retain the original balance of the unit.

2. Release in rotation the self-locking nuts securing the clutch unit to the flywheel, until the spring pressure is relieved; remove the clutch unit and drive plate.

   Note: The release lever adjustment nuts are correctly set and locked when the clutch is assembled, and should not be altered unless the clutch has been dismantled and new parts fitted. Interference with this adjustment would throw the pressure plate out of position and result in clutch judder.

To refit   **Operation B/16**

1. Place the driven plate in position on the flywheel with the longer end of the central boss away from the engine.

2. Centralise the plate by means of a slave primary pinion.

3. Fit the clutch unit with the identification marking adjacent to that on the flywheel; pull down the securing nuts a turn at a time by diagonal selection to prevent distortion of the unit.

4. Remove the centralising shaft.

5. Replace the gearbox assembly. Section C.

6. Adjust clutch pedal free movement. Operation B/44.

To strip   **Operation B/18**

1. Suitably mark the cover plate, pressure plate lugs and release levers, so that they may be assembled in the same relative position, in order to retain the original balance.

2. Place the cover assembly under a press with the pressure plate resting on wooden blocks, so arranged that the cover can move downwards when pressure is applied. Place a block of wood across the top of the cover, resting on the spring bosses.

3. Press the cover downwards and remove the release lever adjusting nuts; slowly release the pressure to prevent the clutch springs from flying out.

4. Lift off the cover.

5. Remove each release lever by holding the lever and eyebolt between fingers and thumb, so that the inner end of the lever and the threaded end of the eyebolt are as near together as possible, keeping the release lever pin in position in the lever. Lift the strut over the ridge on the lever and remove the eyebolt from the pressure plate.

To assemble   **Operation B/20**

1. Clean all the components and lay them out for inspection.

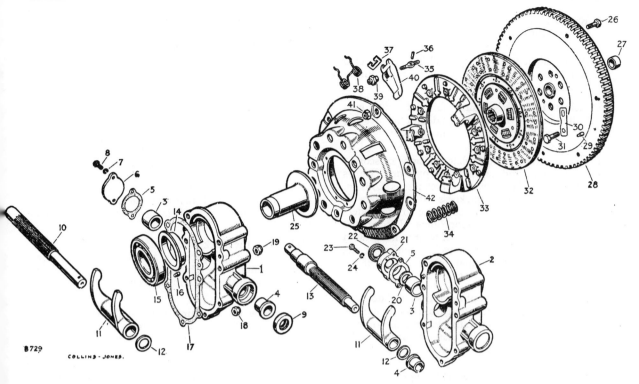

Fig. B-5—Layout of the clutch unit (Borg & Beck type)

1	Withdrawal housing, R.H.D.	22	Oil seal, L.H.D.
2	Withdrawal housing, L.H.D.	23–24	Fixings for oil seal housing, L.H.D.
3	Bush, large } For	25	Withdrawal sleeve
4	Bush, small } cross-shaft	26	Fitting bolt, fixing clutch
5	Joint washer	27	Bush for primary pinion
6	Cover plate	28	Flywheel
7–8	Fixings for cover plate	29	Dowel locating clutch unit
9	Oil seal, R.H.D.	30	Locker } Fixing flywheel
10	Cross-shaft for fork, R.H.D.	31	Special bolt } to crankshaft
11	Operating fork for clutch	32	Clutch driven plate
12	Thrust washer for cross-shaft	33	Clutch pressure plate
13	Cross-shaft for fork, L.H.D.	34	Clutch thrust spring
14	Bush for sleeve	35	Eyebolt
15	Thrust bearing	36	Fulcrum pin for lever
16	Dowel	37	Strut
17	Joint washer for housing	38	Anti-rattle spring
18–19	Fixings for withdrawal race housing	39	Adjustment nut
20	Thrust washer, L.H.D.	40	Release lever
21	Housing for oil seal	41	Nut fixing clutch unit to flywheel

2. Renew all parts which show damage or appreciable wear.

3. A very slight smear of high melting-point grease should be applied to the following parts during assembly :—

Release lever pins, contact faces of struts, eyebolt seats in cover, drive lug sides on the pressure plate and the plain end of the eyebolts.

4. Examine the pressure plate for signs of scoring or burning, and regrind the pressure face as necessary. The minimum thickness is 1.531 in. (38,90 mm). The thickness of the plate is measured from the pressure face to the underside of one of the operating lugs. Discard the plate if it still shows signs of wear when ground to this dimension. Serious shortening of the effective life of the clutch unit will result if the limit for regrinding is exceeded.

Note: The thickness of the pressure plate must always be measured from the underside of the same operating lug and the amount skimmed off the plate stamped on the side of the lug in question.

5. Examine the engine flywheel for signs of scoring or burning; if necessary remove it from the vehicle (Section A) and regrind the face, removing a maximum of .030 in. (0,76 mm).

The clutch securing bolts and dowels must be removed from the flywheel before skimming, so enabling the entire face to be ground. The policy of grinding only within the bolts, so leaving a pronounced step in the face, is not acceptable, as it results in the driven plate moving forward relative to the clutch cover so reducing clutch life and introducing a possibility of clutch slip at an early date. If the flywheel still shows signs of wear when ground it must be discarded and a new part used on assembly.

6. Examine the primary pinion spigot bush in the centre of the flywheel for excessive wear or damage and renew as necessary. The new bush must be a press fit in the flywheel: the bore should be .878 in. + .0005, and the diameter of the primary pinion .8745 in. — .0005, thus making the pinion an easy fit in the bush.

7. Refit the flywheel and tighten the bolts to 50 lb/ft (6,9 mkg).

8. Check the clutch springs in accordance with the data given and renew as necessary.

9. Assemble the release lever eyebolt and lever pin; holding the threaded end of the eyebolt and the inner end of the lever as close together as possible. With the other hand, insert the strut in the slots in the pressure plate lug and insert the plain end of the eyebolt in the hole in the pressure plate. Move the strut upwards into the slots in the pressure plate lug and over the ridge on the short end of the lever, and drop it into the groove formed in the latter. Fit the other two release levers in a similar manner.

10. Place the pressure plate on the wooden blocks under the press and arrange the thrust springs in a vertical position on the plate, seating them on the bosses provided. Lay the cover over the assembled parts, ensuring that the anti-rattle springs are in position and that the tops of the thrust springs are directly under the seats in the cover. Also ensure that the machined portions of the pressure plate lugs are under the slots in the cover and that the parts marked before dismantling are in their correct relative positions.

11. Place the block of wood across the cover, resting it on the spring bosses, and compress the cover, guiding the eyebolts and pressure plate lugs through the holes in the cover.

12. Screw the adjusting nuts on the eyebolts and operate the clutch a few times by means of the press, to ensure that the working parts have settled into their correct positions.

13. Adjust the operating levers as detailed below.

Clutch operating levers

To adjust   **Operation B/22**

Note: This adjustment must be carried out before the clutch is refitted to the engine, and will always be necessary after complete stripping of the unit, or if any new part has been fitted.

1. The setting of the clutch release levers is checked, using ⅜ in. (9,5 mm) distance pieces in place of the driven plate. The levers must be adjusted to a dimension of 1.655 in. (42 mm) from the flywheel face, with a maximum of .010 in. (0,25 mm) difference in height between the three levers. (Fig. B-7.)

2. Place the three distance pieces on the flywheel in place of the driven plate.

3. Fit the cover assembly to the flywheel by tightening all six securing nuts a turn at a time by diagonal selection, until the unit is fully secured.

4. Place the flywheel and clutch assembly on a surface plate and set the scribe to 1.655 in. (42 mm) from the flywheel face using gauge Part No. 262754. Check the height of each operating lever and adjust as necessary, by turning the adjustment nut until the top of the lever is exactly level with the scribe. Adjust the two other levers in a similar manner.

5. Secure the adjusting nuts by staking.

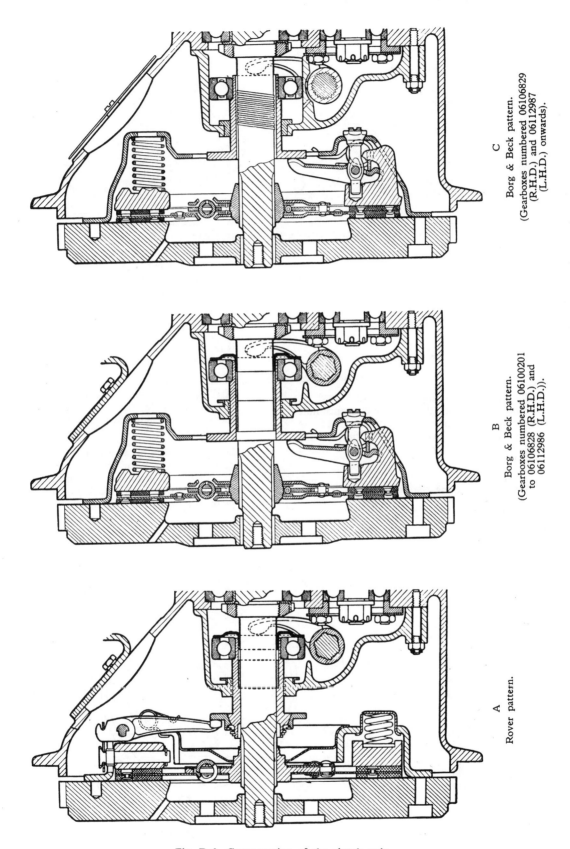

Fig. B-6—Cross-section of the clutch unit

C
Borg & Beck pattern.
(Gearboxes numbered 06106829
(R.H.D.) and 06112987
(L.H.D.) onwards).

B
Borg & Beck pattern.
(Gearboxes numbered 06100201
to 06106828 (R.H.D.) and
06112986 (L.H.D.)).

A
Rover pattern.

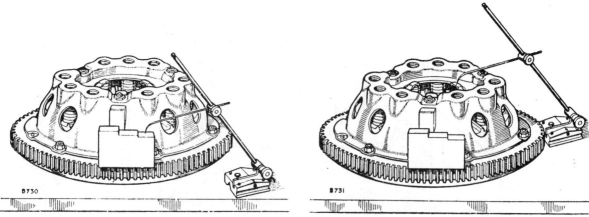

Fig. B-7—Setting the operating levers.

6. Slacken the securing nuts a turn at a time by diagonal selection, and remove the clutch unit from the flywheel.

7. Remove the distance pieces.

Driven plate

To reline   **Operation B/24**

1. Drill out the retaining rivets, using a $\frac{5}{32}$ in. (4 mm) drill inserted through the clearance hole in the opposite lining; each rivet attaches one facing only. The rivets must not be punched out, as serious deformation of the plate would thereby result.

2. Thoroughly examine the segments for cracks; renew as necessary.

3. Place one facing in position with the countersunk holes coinciding with the ones located on the crown or longer side of each segment.

4. Insert the rivets with their heads in the countersunk holes of the facing and roll the shanks over securely against the segments. If a rolling tool is not available, a blunt-ended centre punch will prove satisfactory.

5. Secure the second facing on the opposite side of the plate in a similar manner, matching the countersunk holes with the remaining holes in the segments. The rivet heads should always face outwards.

6. Mount the plate on a suitable mandrel between centres and check for run-out as near the edge as possible; if the error is more than .010 in. (0,25 mm), press over the high spots until the plate is true within this figure.

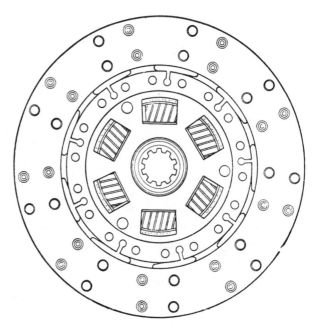

Fig. B-8—Driven plate. Borg and Beck type.

Withdrawal mechanism

Three types of clutch withdrawal mechanism have been used on Land-Rover; they are illustrated at Fig. B-10.

Throughout the overhaul instructions which follow, reference is made to the different types as follows:—

Type A. Fitted to all vehicles equipped with Rover pattern clutch, *i.e.*, gearboxes numbered 860001 to 06100200.

Type B. Fitted to vehicles with Borg & Beck clutch having gearboxes numbered 06100201 to 06106828 (R.H.D.) and 06112986 (L.H.D.).

Type C. Fitted to vehicles with Borg & Beck clutch having gearboxes numbered 06106829 (R.H.D.) and 06112987 (L.H.D.) onwards.

In addition, dust-proofing grommets are fitted to each end of the clutch withdrawal shaft on all gearboxes numbered 06101573 (R.H.D.) and 06104469 (L.H.D.) onwards; these components will also be found on a number of earlier vehicles which have been modified subsequently.

To remove   Operation B/26

1. Remove the gearbox assembly. Section C.

2. **L.H.D. models only.** Remove the clutch operating lever from the withdrawal cross-shaft by removing the retaining set bolt, spring washer and plain washer. Remove the woodruff key from the cross-shaft.

3. Where applicable, remove the blanking grommets from the bell housing.

4. Where applicable, remove the bolt, nut, plain washer, split pin and spring ring retaining the grommet on the other side of the bell housing; remove the grommet from the bell housing.

5. Remove the clutch withdrawal unit from the bell housing.

To strip (R.H.D. models)   Operation B/28

1. Remove the cross-shaft cover plate.

2. Drive out the cross-shaft from right to left, thus releasing the withdrawal fork and a thrust washer.

   Note: Late 1955 models onward have a thrust spring fitted in the bore of the operating fork.

   This spring is removed with the operating fork and does not affect stripping procedure.

3. If necessary, remove the oil seal from the withdrawal housing.

4. If necessary, press off the grommet centre from the housing.

5. Remove the bearing from the withdrawal sleeve and remove the sleeve from the front of the housing.

6. **Rover pattern clutch only.** Remove the circlip from the front of the sleeve, thus releasing the retaining washer, spiral spring and outer cup.

To strip (L.H.D. models)   Operation B/30

1. Remove the oil seal housing grommet centre and joint washer from the withdrawal housing.

2. If necessary, remove the oil seal from its housing.

3. Remove the outer thrust washer from the cross-shaft and withdraw the shaft, thus releasing the withdrawal fork and inner thrust washer.

   Note: Late 1955 models onward have a thrust spring fitted in the bore of the operating fork.

   This spring is removed with the operating fork and does not affect stripping procedure.

4. Remove the bearing from the withdrawal sleeve and remove the sleeve from the front of the housing.

5. **Rover pattern clutch only.** Remove the circlip from the front of the sleeve, thus releasing the retaining washer, spiral spring and outer cup.

To overhaul   Operation B/32

1. If necessary, renew the two small flanged oilite bushes in the right-hand cross-shaft bore of the housing. The bushes must be a *light drive fit* in the housing bore. Renew the cross-shaft if badly worn.

   Note: On L.H.D. models only, it is necessary to drive out the cross-shaft cap before the outer bush can be extracted. The cap should be a *light drive fit* in the withdrawal housing.

2. If necessary, renew the large oilite bush in the left-hand cross-shaft bore of the housing. The bush must be a *drive fit* in the housing bore; press the bush in flush with the outer face of the housing.

3. **Rover pattern clutch and early Borg & Beck type clutch only.** If it is loose or damaged, renew the oil drain ring in the withdrawal housing and secure the new part by "centre-popping". At the same time it is well to ensure that the oil scroll machined in the housing is not damaged; a faulty scroll may result in oil reaching the driven plate and so give rise to clutch slip.

4. **Late type Borg & Beck clutch only.** If necessary, renew the oilite withdrawal sleeve bush in the housing. The bush must be a *drive fit* in the housing. The bush should be a *sliding*

fit on the sleeve. Renew the sleeve if a greater clearance than this is obtained in a new bush.

Ensure that the oil scroll machined on the primary pinion is not damaged; a faulty scroll may result in oil reaching the driven plate and so give rise to clutch slip.

5. **Rover pattern clutch and early Borg & Beck type clutch only.** If necessary, renew the oilite bush(es) in the withdrawal sleeve. The bush(es) must be a *press fit* in the sleeve and a clearance of .0015 in. to .0017 in. must be observed on the primary pinion.

   Note: Two bushes are fitted in gearboxes numbered 860001 to 860913 and in all gearboxes fitted to early Borg & Beck type clutches.

6. **Rover pattern clutch only.** Check that the outer cup slides freely on the sleeve; correct as necessary.

7. Renew the thrust bearing if badly worn or damaged. The bearing must be a *light drive fit* on the sleeve; renew the parts as necessary.

To assemble (R.H.D. models) Operation B/34

1. **Rover pattern clutch only.** Fit the outer cup, spiral spring and retaining washer to the front of the withdrawal sleeve and secure them with a circlip.

2. Replace the withdrawal sleeve in the housing; fit the thrust bearing.

3. Fit the oil seal in the cross-shaft bore, with its knife edge inwards.

4. Fit the grommmet centre over the housing.

5. Place the withdrawal fork and thrust washer in position in the housing and slide in the cross-shaft from left to right. The hole in the outer end of the shaft should be horizontal when the fork is in contact with the bearing.

6. Refit the cover plate and joint washer.

To assemble (L.H.D. models) Operation B/36

1. Replace the withdrawal sleeve in the housing; fit the thrust bearing.

2. Place the withdrawal fork and inner thrust washer in position in the housing and slide in the cross-shaft from the left.

   Late type Borg & Beck clutches. When the rear face of the thrust bearing is set to $\frac{15}{16}$ in.— $\frac{1}{16}$ in. from the joint face of the housing and the fork is resting against the bearing, the hole in the shaft should be horizontal (Fig. B-9).

   Rover pattern clutches and early Borg & Beck type clutches only. The key slot in the shaft should be uppermost when the fork is in contact with the bearing.

3. Replace the outer thrust washer on the shaft.

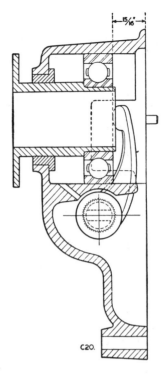

Fig. B-9—
Setting withdrawal shaft.
Late type Borg and Beck clutch

4. Fit the oil seal in its housing, with the knife edge inwards.

5. Replace the oil seal housing, joint washer and grommet centre.

To refit   Operation B/38

1. Refit the withdrawal unit (together with a joint washer).

2. Replace the open grommet over the operating end of the cross-shaft and stick it to the centre and bell housing with a suitable adhesive.

3. Replace the blanking grommet in the other side of the bell housing and stick it with a suitable adhesive.

   L.H.D. models with Rover pattern or early Borg & Beck type clutch. Fit the Woodruff key in the cross-shaft and replace the clutch operating lever; secure it by means of a set bolt, plain and spring washers.

4. Replace the gearbox assembly. Section C.

5. Adjust the clutch pedal free movement. Operation B/44.

Clutch Pedal Unit

To remove   Operation B/40
1948-53 models

1. Remove the pad and rod from the pedal lever by withdrawing the pinch bolt; this action will also release the pedal stop. Lift off the rubber grommet and the felt pad.

2. Remove the cotter securing the pedal lever to the spindle and withdraw the lever.

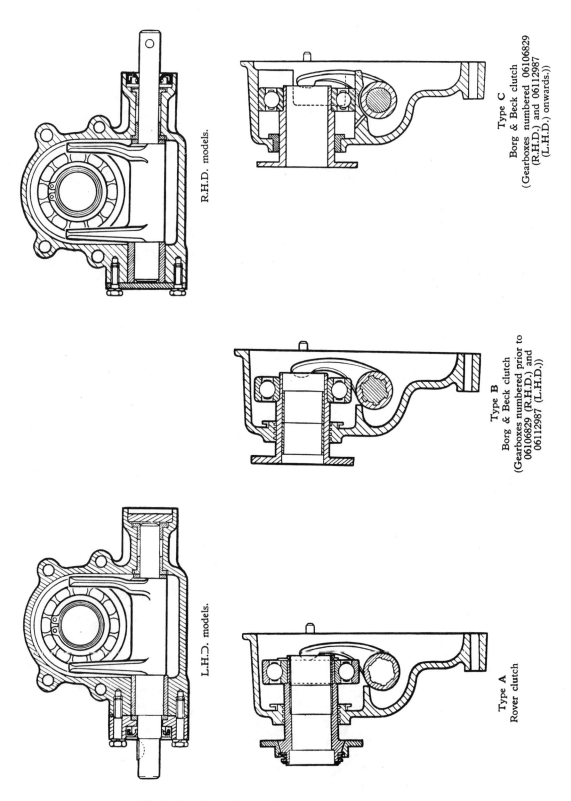

R.H.D. models.

L.H.D. models.

Type C
Borg & Beck clutch
(Gearboxes numbered 06106829
(R.H.D.) and 0611298T
(L.H.D.) onwards.))

Type B
Borg & Beck clutch
(Gearboxes numbered prior to
06106829 (R.H.D.) and
06112987 (L.H.D.))

Type A
Rover clutch

Fig. B-10—Cross-section of the withdrawal mechanism

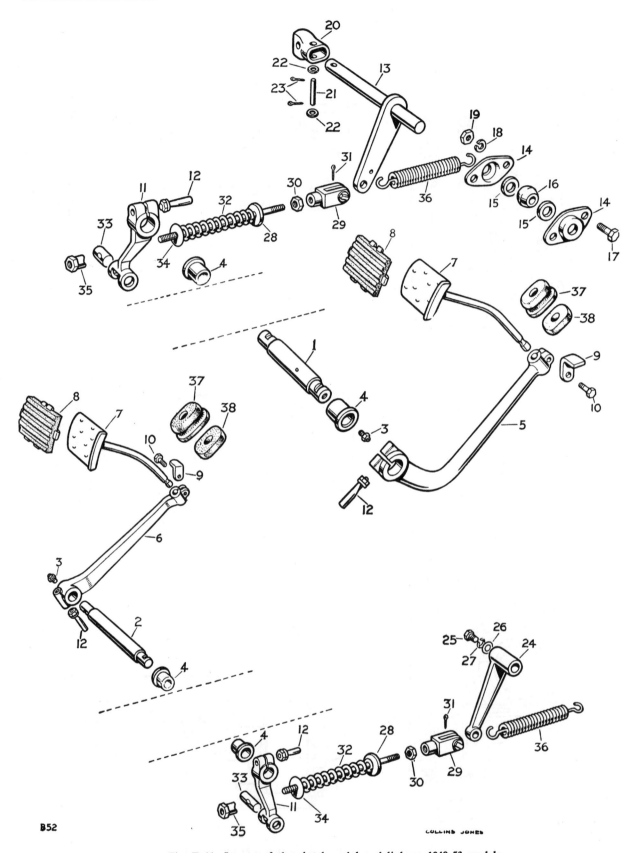

Fig. B-11—Layout of the clutch pedal and linkage, 1948-53 models

Key to Fig. B-11

1	Clutch pedal shaft, R.H.D. models	20	Connecting tube for cross-shaft	
2	Clutch pedal shaft, L.H.D. models	21	Pin	
3	Grease nipple for shaft	22	Plain washers — Fixing connecting tube to shafts	R.H.D. models
4	Bushes for pedal shaft	23	Split pins	
5	Pedal lever, R.H.D. models	24	Operating lever for withdrawal shaft	L.H.D. models
6	Pedal lever, L.H.D. models	25–27	Fixings for operating lever	
7	Clutch pedal rod and pad	28	Operating rod	
8	Rubber pad for pedal (extra equipment)	29	Clevis	
9	Clutch pedal stop	30	Locknut — Fixing rod to withdrawal or cross-shaft lever	
10	Bolt fixing rod and stop to lever	31	Split pin	
11	Operating lever	32	Spring for operating rod	
12	Cotters fixing lever	33	Trunnion	
13	Cross-shaft and lever	34	Plain washer — Fixing rod to operating lever	
14	Housing for cross-shaft bearing	35	Adjusting nut	
15	Felt ring for bearing housing — R.H.D. models	36	Return spring for clutch	
16	Spherical bearing for cross-shaft	37	Rubber grommet — For clutch pedal rod	
17–19	Fixings for bearing housing	38	Felt washer	

3. Remove the adjusting nut from the operating rod, pull the operating lever clear of the rod and withdraw the trunnion from the lever fork.

4. Remove the cotter securing the operating lever to the pedal spindle and withdraw the lever.

5. Remove the oil nipple from the spindle.

6. Tap out the spindle from the chassis frame.

1954-58 models

1. Remove the pad and rod from the clutch and brake pedal levers. Lift off the rubber grommets and felt pads.

2. Disconnect the clutch and brake pedal return springs and the stop light operating spring.

3. Remove the operating rod from the lever on the cross-shaft.

4. Remove the brake pedal from the operating rod.

5. Remove the grease nipple.

6. Remove the circlip securing the brake and clutch pedal levers to the spindle and remove both bronze thrust washers and pedal levers.

7. Remove the top locknut and adjusting nut from the clutch operating rod, pull the pedal lever clear of the rod and withdraw the trunnion from the clutch pedal lever fork.

8. If necessary, remove the bush from the clutch pedal lever.

9. Withdraw the pedal spindle from the chassis side member.

To refit   Operation B/42
1948-53 models

1. The diameter of the pedal spindle should be .935 in.—.001 and the internal diameter of the two flanged oilite bushes in the chassis frame .938 in.—.0005, thus giving a clearance of .0025 in. to .004 If the spindle has excessive play in the bushes, they should be renewed as necessary and reamed in position.

1954-58 models

2. The pedal lever bush is a *press fit* in the lever and a *sliding fit* on the pedal spindle.

 If the spindle has excessive play in the bush, they should be renewed as necessary, reaming the bush in position to the dimension given in the data.

All models

3. Reverse the removal procedure.

 Note: Fit grease nipple to spindle first, then position the spindle so that the nipple points downwards.

4. Adjust pedal free movement. Operation B/44.

5. Lubricate with appropriate oil at grease nipple.

To adjust   Operation B/44

1. Slacken the locknut and screw out the stop bolt (A) until the free movement is correct.

2. Secure with the locknut.
 This action will alter the position of the pedal pad, which can be reset by means of the adjustment provided on the clutch linkage.

3. Slacken the outer locknuts (B) and rotate the inner adjusting nuts (C), both in the same direction, until the pedal is set in a convenient position.

4. Tighten the adjusting nuts and distance pieces against the joint pin and secure with the locknuts.

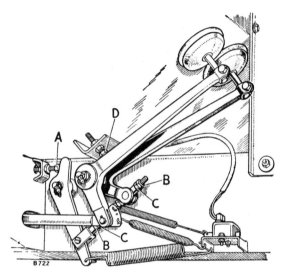

Fig. B-12—Clutch adjustment, 1954-58 models
A—Clutch pedal stop bolt.   B—Locknuts.
C—Adjusting nuts.   D—Brake pedal stop bolt.

Clutch linkage
To remove   Operation B/46
1948-53 L.H.D. models

1. Remove the adjusting nut from the operating rod, pull the operating lever clear of the rod, and withdraw the trunnion from the lever fork.

2. Remove the spring from the operating rod.

3. Remove the return spring, from the chassis cross-member first.

4. Withdraw the split pin and remove the joint pin securing the operating rod to the lever on the cross-shaft.

5. Remove the set bolt, plain and spring washers securing the cross-shaft lever, and withdraw the key-located lever.

1954-58 L.H.D. models

1. If necessary, remove the floor board. Section R.

2. Disconnect the clutch return spring.

3. Remove the operating rod from the relay lever.

4. Remove the top locknut and adjusting nut from the clutch operating rod, pull the rod clear of the pedal lever and remove the trunnion from the clutch pedal lever fork.

5. Remove the connecting tube from the end of the relay inner rod.

6. Remove the circlip and steel thrust washer from inner end of relay shaft and withdraw the complete relay shaft assembly from the chassis side member.

7. Remove distance piece from the relay shaft and tap out pin securing lever to relay shaft.

8. Withdraw inner rod from relay shaft.

9. If necessary, remove bush from relay shaft.

10. If necessary, remove bushes from chassis side member.

11. Remove the grease nipple from the relay lever.

To remove Operation B/48
1948-53 R.H.D. models

1. Remove the adjusting nut from the operating rod, pull the operating lever clear of the rod and withdraw the trunnion from the lever fork.

2. Remove the spring from the operating rod.

3. Remove the return spring, from the chassis cross-member first.

4. Withdraw the split pin and remove the joint pin securing the operating rod to the lever on the cross-shaft.

5. Remove a split pin, plain washer and connecting pin securing the connecting tube to the end of the cross-shaft protruding from the bell housing.

6. Withdraw the split housing from the right-hand chassis side member by removing the two retaining bolts, spring washers and nuts.

7. Remove the cross-shaft and lever complete with two felt seals and the self-lubricating spherical bush.

1954-58 R.H.D. models

1. If necessary, remove the floor board. Section R.

2. Remove brake pedal return spring, stop light operating spring and clutch pedal return spring.

3. Remove the brake pedal lever from the operating rod.

4. Slacken locknut and remove brake operating rod.

5. Remove the clutch operating rod from the relay lever.

6. Remove top locknut and adjusting nut from the operating rod, pull the rod clear of the pedal lever and remove the trunnion from the clutch pedal fork.

7. Push clutch relay shaft dust excluder along the cross-shaft towards bell housing.

8. Remove the connecting tube from the cross-shaft.

9. Remove the universal joint sleeve from the relay shaft and lever.

10. Remove relay lever and shaft from right-hand side of chassis side member and universal joint sleeve steel thrust washer and cross-shaft from the left-hand side.

11. If necessary, remove bushes from chassis side member.

12. Remove the grease nipple from the relay lever and shaft.

To refit Operation B/50
1948-53 models

1. Check the clutch return spring in accordance with the following specification and renew it as necessary:—Load 50 lb. (23 kg) at 2.5 in. (38 mm) extension.

2. Check the operating rod spring in accordance with the following specification, and renew it as necessary:—Load required to compress spring 1 in. (25 mm): 33 lb. (15 kg).

3. **R.H.D. models only.** Renew the felt seals as necessary; grease the spherical bush.

4. Replace the linkage by reversing the sequence of removal operations.

5. Adjust the pedal free movement.

1954-58 models

1. Check clutch return spring and renew as necessary. Load 15 lb. (6,75 kg) at .84 in. (21,3 mm) extension.

2. The relay shaft should be a *sliding fit* in its bushes; they should be renewed as necessary, and reamed in position to the dimension given in the data.

3. L.H.D. models only. The relay inner rod should be a *sliding fit* in the bush in the relay shaft. They should be renewed as necessary, and the bush reamed in position to the dimension given in the data.

4. Replace the linkage by reversing the removal procedure.

   On R.H.D. models the joint pin in the universal joint sleeve should be vertical when the relay lever is against its stop, and on L.H.D. models the hole in the relay inner rod should be horizontal when the lever is against its stop.

5. Adjust pedal free movement. Operation B/44.

6. Adjust brake pedal operating rod. Section H.

7. Lubricate at grease nipple with appropriate oil.

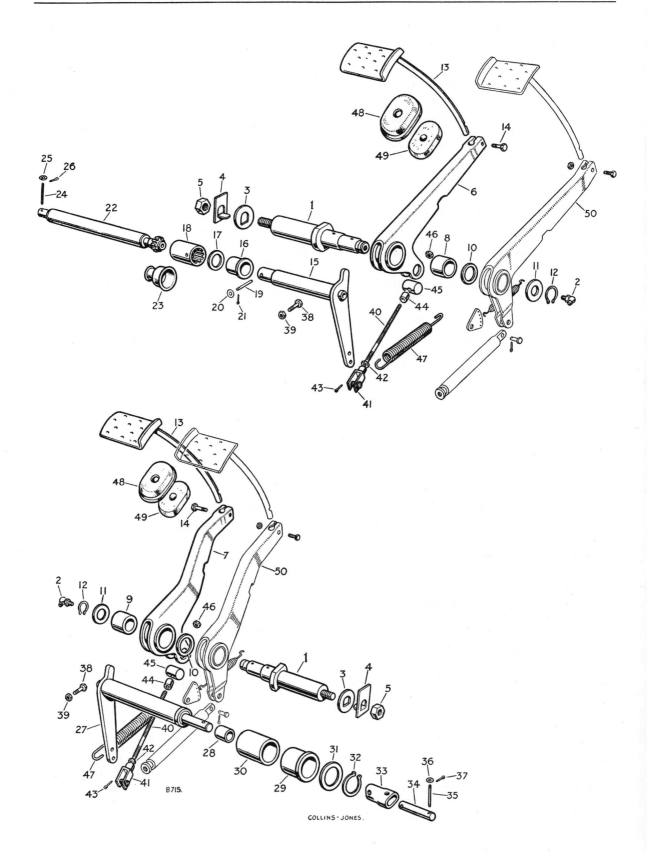

Fig. B-13—Layout of the clutch pedal and linkage, 1954-58 models

Key to Fig. B-13

1	Shaft for clutch and brake pedal
2	Grease nipple for shaft and pedal
3–5	Fixings for pedal shaft
6	Pedal lever for clutch—R.H.D.
7	Pedal lever for clutch—L.H.D.
8	Bush for clutch pedal lever—R.H.D.
9	Bush for clutch pedal lever—L.H.D.
10	Thrust washer for pedal
11–12	Fixings for pedal lever
13	Clutch pedal rod and pad
14	Set bolt fixing rod to lever—R.H.D.
15	Clutch relay shaft
16	Bush for relay shaft
17	Thrust washer for universal joint sleeve
18	Univeral joint sleeve
19–21	Fixings for sleeve
22	Cross-shaft for clutch
23	Dust cover for cross-shaft
24–26	Fixings for cross-shaft to clutch fork

15–26 }R.H.D.

27	Clutch relay shaft
28	Bush for relay shaft, small
29	Bush for relay shaft, large
30	Distance tube for relay shaft
31	Thrust washer for cross-shaft
32	Circlip fixing cross-shaft
33	Connecting tube for clutch
34	Cross-shaft rod for clutch, centre
35–37	Fixings for centre rod
38	Stop bolt for clutch relay
39	Locknut for bolt
40	Operating rod for clutch
41–43	Fixings for rod
44–46	Fixings for rod
47	Return spring for clutch
48	Rubber grommet
49	Felt washer
50	Brake pedal assembly

27–32 }L.H.D.

48–49 }For clutch pedal rod

DEFECT LOCATION
Symptom, Cause and Remedy

A—GRABBING CLUTCH

1. Incorrect release lever adjustment—*Adjust.*

2. Oil on the clutch lining—*Renew.*

3. Worn clutch plates or flywheel—*Renew.*

4. Clutch plate hub sticking on the pinion shaft—*Free off the clutch plate and check for wear and distortion. Check the pinion shaft for wear.*

5. Worn or binding operating levers—*Wear on levers usually indicates a binding withdrawal race thrust bearing. Free off bearing and renew levers.*

6. Worn or glazed linings—*Renew.*

7. Broken or weak pressure springs—*Renew.*

8. Sticking clutch pedal—*Free off the pedal and check for damaged or bent parts. Check the return spring.*

9. Damaged or deteriorated engine mountings, or engine loose in chassis frame—*Re-tighten or renew.*

B—SLIPPING CLUTCH

1. Weak or broken pressure springs—*Renew.*

2. Worn clutch linings—*Renew and check plates for scoring.*

3. Incorrect clutch adjustment—*Adjust.*

4. Oil on the linings—*Renew. Remove drain plug from flywheel housing at regular intervals. Rectify the oil leak.*

5. Warped clutch plate—*Renew.*

6. Scored or damaged pressure plate—*Skim or renew.*

7. Binding withdrawal lever—*Free off the lever and check for wear. Examine the clutch linings, plates and springs for wear or damage and the flywheel for scoring. Renew as found necessary.*

8. Binding clutch pedal mechanism—*Rectify or renew.*

9. Insufficient free movement on the clutch pedal—*Adjust.*

10. Riding clutch—*In the hands of the operator.*

11. Fractured clutch plate—*See Item C (5).*

C—DRAGGING OR SPINNING CLUTCH

1. Oil on the clutch linings—*Remove flywheel housing drain plug at regular intervals. Renew; if necessary rectify oil leak.*

2. Incorrect lever adjustment—*Examine and adjust.*

3. Incorrect pedal adjustment—*Adjust.*

4. Dust or other foreign matter in the clutch—*Clean and renew.*

5. Bent clutch plate—*Ascertain reason for damage, check the remainder of the clutch and renew the plate. A plate may be distorted due to the weight of the gearbox being allowed to hang on the clutch plate during erection. When fitting a new plate, take the weight of the gearbox with a jack or by other suitable means.*

6. Clutch plate hub binding on the pinion shaft—*Rectify or renew.*

7. Primary pinion bush binding—*Rectify.*

8. Clutch withdrawal sleeve sticking—*Rectify and examine all mating surfaces for scoring and wear.*

9. Warped clutch pressure plate and clutch cover—*Renew.*

10. Clutch facings too thick—*Renew.*

11. Broken clutch linings—*Renew. Examine the pressure plate, clutch cover, etc., for distortion and damage.*

D—RATTLING CLUTCH

1. Weak or broken operating lever return spring—*Renew.*

2. Damaged pressure plate—*Ascertain the reason for the damage and rectify. Recondition or renew.*

3. Broken pedal return spring—*Renew.*

4. Pinion shaft or clutch plate splines worn—*Renew.*

5. Worn primary pinion bush—*Renew.*

6. Unequal contact of operating levers—*Adjust.*

7. Incorrect free play in pedal lever—*Adjust.*

8. Damaged clutch plate, loose or broken springs; warped clutch plate—*Renew.*

9. Worn parts in the withdrawal mechanism—*Renew.*

10. Excessive backlash in the transmission—*Rectify.*

11. Normal wear in clutch—*Renew.*

E—SQUEAKING CLUTCH

1. Primary pinion bush binding—*Rectify and renew.*

2. Primary pinion bush turning in the flywheel—*Renew.*

F—VIBRATING CLUTCH OR CLUTCH JUDDER

1. Incorrect clutch balance—*Renew.*

2. Clutch pressure plate incorrectly fitted—*Refit.*

3. Loose engine mountings—*Tighten.*

4. Worn propeller shaft universal joints—*Rectify.*

5. Loose flywheel—*Tighten. Check run-out on flywheel.*

6. Oil or other foreign matter on the clutch lining—*Remove flywheel housing drain plug at regular intervals. Renew.*

7. Contact area of friction faces not evenly distributed—*Rectify or renew.*

8. Bent splined shaft or buckled driven plate—*Renew and check for damage.*

9. Pressure plate out of parallel with flywheel face—*Rectify.*

G—STIFF CLUTCH OPERATION

1. Dry or damaged linkage parts—*Lubricate and renew, if necessary.*

2. Clutch pedal spindle dry—*Lubricate.*

3. Pedal fouling on the floor board—*Rectify.*

H—CLUTCH TICKS OR KNOCKS

1. Clutch plate hub splines worn—*Rectify and renew*

2. Worn primary pinion bush—*Renew.*

J—FRACTURED CLUTCH PLATE

1. See item C (5)—*Rectify and renew.*

K—EXCESSIVE LINING WEAR

Produced by overloading or by slipping clutch—*In the hands of the operator.*

DATA: Rover pattern clutch

Clutch unit:

Type	Single dry plate: spring drive, self-centralising
Diameter	9 in. (230 mm)
Total area of lining	64.8 sq. in. (418 cm²)
Thickness of plate (new)	.330 in. (8,4 mm) ⎤
Thickness of plate fully worn)	.210 in. (5,3 mm) ⎦ Under load

Thrust race	Ball bearing
Number of thrust springs	.... 9 (colour: orange)
Spring poundage	130 lb ± 4 (63 kg ± 1,8) each

Clutch pedal:

Free movement	¾ in. (19 mm)

DATA: Borg & Beck type clutch

Clutch:

Type	.... Single dry plate, spring drive, self-centralising

Thrust race:

Type	.... Ball bearing

Thrust springs:

Number off	9
Free length (Petrol models)	2.680 in. (68 mm)
Free length (Diesel models)	2.688 in. (68,2 mm)
Working length	1.688 in. (43 mm)
Load at working length (Petrol models)	120-130 lb. (54,5-59 kg)
Load at working length (Diesel models)	135-145 lb. (61,3-65,8 kg)
Identification (Petrol models)	Cream paint
Identification (Diesel models)	Yellow paint

Pressure plate:

Re-grinding limit	.010 in. (0,25 mm) under-size
Minimum thickness	1.531 in. (38,90 mm)

Operating levers:

Height from flywheel face using ⅜ in. (9,5 mm) distance piece in place of the driven plate	.... 1.655 in. (42 mm)

Driven plate:

Diameter	.... 9 in. (230 mm)
Thickness of plate, new	.330 in. (8,4 mm)
Maximum permissible wear	.... .120 in. (3,1 mm)
Identification (Petrol models)	.... Red and violet springs
Identification (Diesel models), springs	3 off—Buff and light green
	3 off—Light grey and violet

Withdrawal mechanism:

Clearance of bush on cross-shaft	.002 to .004 in. (0,05 to 0,10 mm)
Fit of oilite withdrawal sleeve bush in housing	Zero to .002 in. (zero to 0,05 mm) interference
Clearance of bush on sleeve	.003 to .007 in. (0,08 to 0,18 mm)
Fit of thrust bearing on sleeve	Zero to .0005 in. (zero to 0,013 mm) interference

Clutch pedal unit:

Pedal free movement....	¾ in. (20 mm) measured at pedal pad
Clearance of bush on pedal spindle	.001 to .002 in. (0,01 to 0,06 mm)
Bush: reamed bore	L.H.D.: ⅞ in. (22 mm)
Bush: reamed bore	R.H.D.: 1 in. (25 mm)

Clutch linkage

L.H.D. models:

Fit of relay shaft bushes in chassis	.001 to .003 in. (0,02 to 0,09 mm) interference
Clearance of bushes on relay shaft	.003 to .004 in. (0,09 to 0,10 mm)
Fit of bush in relay shaft	.001 to .002 in. (0,02 to 0,06 mm) interference
Clearance of bush on inner rod	.002 to .003 in. (0,05 to 0,09 mm)

R.H.D. models:

Fit of relay shaft bushes in chassis	.001 to .002 in. (0,03 to 0,07 mm) interference
Clearance of bushes on relay shaft	.002 to .004 in. (0,05 to 0,10 mm)
Clutch return spring	Load 15 lb. (6,75 kg) at .84 in. (21,3 mm) extension

Section C
GEARBOX UNIT — ALL MODELS

INDEX

	Page			Page
Data	C-35	Main gear change lever		C-15 & 33
Defect location	C-34	Fourwheel drive		C-13 & 30
Gearbox and transfer assembly	C-17 & 22	Freewheel		C-13
		Front output shaft housing		C-30
Gearbox unit mounting rubbers	C-22	Reverse stop		C-16 & 33
Main gearbox	C-23	Transfer box		C-26

LIST OF ILLUSTRATIONS

Fig.		Page	Fig.		Page
C-1	Layout of the gearbox unit: casings	C-2	C-14	Tightening transfer drive gear securing nut	C-25
C-2	Layout of the gearbox unit: shafts and gears	C-4	C-15	Adjusting 2nd speed gear stop bolt	C-26
C-3	Layout of the gearbox unit: front output shaft housing and controls	C-6	C-16	Removing intermediate gear shaft	C-27
			C-17	Fitting transfer box output shaft protection cap	C-27
C-4	Layout of the gearbox unit: main gear change lever and selectors	C-8	C-18	Removing transfer box output shaft front bearing outer race	C-28
C-5	Cross-section of gearbox unit: elevation	C-10	C-19	Removing transfer box output shaft front bearing inner race	C-28
C-6	Cross-section of gearbox unit: plan	C-11	C-20	Adjusting transfer box output shaft end-float	C-29
C-7	Cross-section of gearbox unit: controls	C-12	C-21	Adjusting reverse gear stop bolt	C-30
C-8	Gearbox unit mounting rubbers	C-22	C-22	Setting the link pin	C-31
C-9	Removing the transfer drive gear securing nut	C-23	C-23	Setting transfer and dog clutch selector shaft	C-32
C-10	Removing layshaft rear bearing outer race	C 24	C-24	Cross-section of reverse stop	C-32
C-11	Measuring mainshaft gear end-float	C-24	C-25	Adjusting reverse stop	C-33
C-12	Measuring mainshaft bush end-float	C-25			
C-13	Fitting synchronising clutch assembly	C-25			

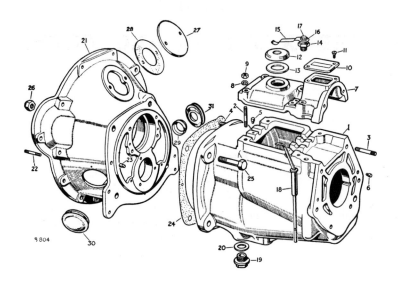

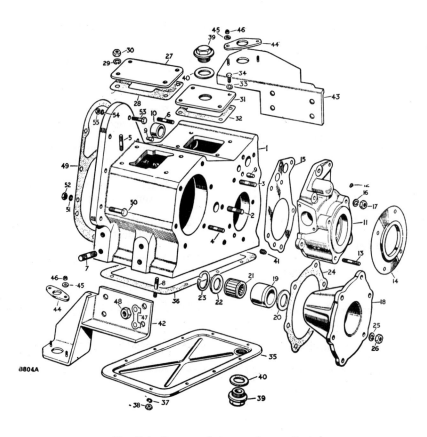

Fig. C-1—Layout of the gearbox unit casings

Key to Fig C-1

1	Gearbox casing assembly	16–17	Fixings for spring
2	Stud for top cover and gear change plate	18	Oil level dipstick
3	Stud, short, for transfer casing	19	Drain plug for gearbox
4	Stud for bell housing	20	Washer for plug
5	Dowel locating top cover	21	Bell housing assembly
6	Dowel locating transfer casing	22	Stud for withdrawal race housing
7	Top cover for gearbox	23	Dowel locating gearbox
8–9	Fixings for top cover	24	Joint washer bell housing to gearbox,
10	Inspection cover plate for selectors	25–26	Fixings for gearbox casing
11	Set screw fixing cover plate	27	Top cover for bell housing
12	Oil filler cap	28	Rubber seal for top cover
13	Joint washer for cap	29	Centre for dust cover
14	Plug for retaining spring	30	Grommet for bell housing hole
15	Retaining spring for cap	31	Grommet for bell housing shaft

1	Transfer box casing assembly	25–26	Fixings for housing
2	Stud for intermediate shaft	27	Cover plate for P.T.O. selector
3	Stud for speedometer housing, short	28	Joint washer for cover plate
4	Stud for mainshaft housing	29–30	Fixings for cover plate
5	Stud for top cover plate	31	Cover plate for transfer gear change
6	Stud, short, for transfer shaft housing	32	Joint washer for cover plate
7	Stud for engine mounting	33–34	Fixings for plate
8	Stud for bottom cover	35	Cover plate, bottom, for transfer box
9	Dowel locating speedometer housing	36	Joint washer for bottom cover
10	Bush for shaft guide	37–38	Fixings for cover
11	Housing assembly for speedometer pinion	39	Plug, top and bottom
12	Insert for pinion	40	Joint washer for plug
13	Stud for transmission brake	41	Oil level plug
14	Mudshield for housing	42	Rear mounting foot L.H.
15	Shim for speedometer pinion housing	43	Rear mounting foot R.H.
16–17	Fixings for housing	44	Adjuster for mounting foot
18	Housing assembly, rear mainshaft bearing	45	Plain washer ⎫ For
19	Bush for housing	46	Self-locking nut ⎭ adjuster
20	Retaining plate, inner	47–48	Fixings for feet
21	Bearing for mainshaft	49	Joint washer, transfer box to gearbox
22	Retaining plate, outer	50–52	Fixings for transfer box
23	Circlip fixing bearing	53–55	Fixings for transfer box
24	Joint washer for bearing housing		

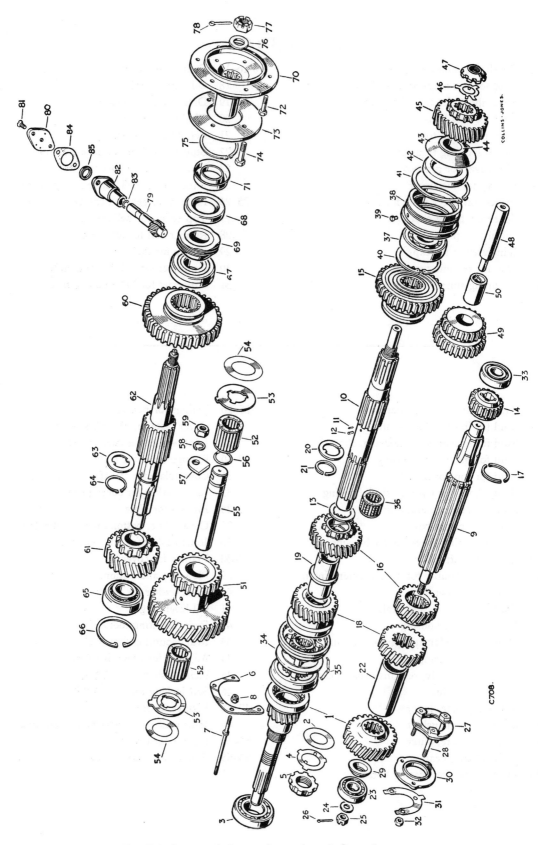

Fig. C-2—Layout of the gearbox units: shafts and gears.

Key to Fig. C-2

1   Primary pinion and constant gear
2   Shield for primary pinion
3   Ball bearing for primary pinion
4–5   Fixings for bearing
6–8   Fixings for bearing
9   Layshaft
10   Mainshaft
11   Peg for 2nd gear thrust washer
12   Peg for mainshaft distance sleeve
13   Thrust washer for 2nd speed gear
14   1st speed layshaft gear
15   1st speed mainshaft gear
16   2nd speed layshaft and mainshaft gear
17   Split ring for 2nd speed layshaft gear
18   3rd speed layshaft and mainshaft gear
19   Distance sleeve for mainshaft
20   Thrust washer for 3rd speed mainshaft gear
21   Spring ring fixing 2nd and 3rd mainshaft gears
22   Sleeve for layshaft
23   Bearing for layshaft, front
24–26   Fixings for bearing to layshaft
27   Bearing plate assembly for layshaft
28   Stud for bearing cap
29   Distance piece for layshaft
30   Retaining plate for layshaft front bearing
31–32   Fixings for cap and bearing
33   Bearing for layshaft, rear
34   Synchronising clutch
35   Detent spring for clutch
36   Roller bearing for mainshaft
37   Ball bearing for mainshaft
38   Housing for mainshaft bearing, rear
39   Peg, housing to casing
40   Circlip, bearing to housing
41   Circlip, housing to casing
42   Oil seal for rear of mainshaft
43   Oil thrower for mainshaft

44   Distance piece, rear of mainshaft
45   Mainshaft gear for transfer box
46–47   Fixings for gear
48   Shaft for reverse gear
49   Reverse wheel assembly
50   Bush for reverse wheel
51   Gear, intermediate
52   Roller bearing for intermediate gear
53   Thrust washer for intermediate gear
54   Shim for intermediate gear
55   Shaft for intermediate gear
56   Sealing ring for intermediate gear
57   Retaining plate for shaft
58–59   Fixings for plate
60   Low gear wheel
61   High gear wheel
62   Output shaft, rear drive
63   Thrust washer for high gear wheel
64   Circlip fixing washer to shaft
65   Bearing for output shaft, front
66   Circlip fixing bearing to case
67   Bearing for output shaft, rear
68   Oil seal for output shaft
69   Speedometer worm complete
70   Flange for output shaft, rear drive
71   Mudshield for flange
72   Fitting bolt for brake drum
73   Retaining flange for brake drum bolts
74   Fitting bolt for propeller shaft
75   Circlip retaining bolts and flange
76–78   Fixings for flange
79   Speedometer pinion
80   Retaining plate for pinion
81   Screw fixing plate to housing
82   Sleeve for pinion
83   Sealing ring for sleeve
84   Joint washer for sleeve
85   Oil seal for pinion

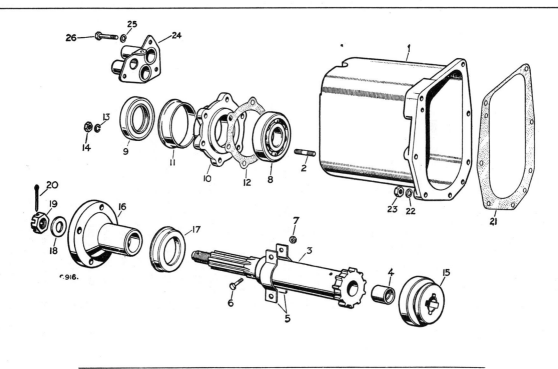

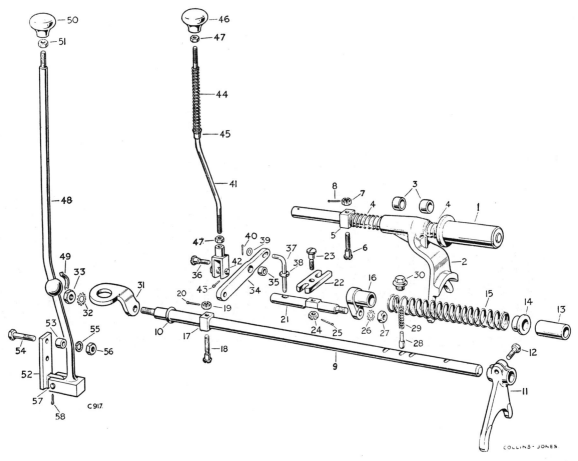

Fig. C-3—Layout of the gearbox unit: front wheel drive, transfer gear controls and front output shaft and housing

Key to Fig. C-3

1	Output shaft housing assembly		12	Joint washer for retainer
2	Stud for oil seal retainer		13–14	Fixings for retainer
3	Front output shaft assembly		15	Locking dog, four wheel drive
4	Bush for shaft		16	Flange for transfer shaft
5	Oil thrower for output shaft		17	Mudshield for flange
6–7	Fixings for oil thrower		18–20	Fixings for flange
8	Bearing for front output shaft		21	Joint washer for transfer housing
9	Oil seal for shaft		22–23	Fixings for housing
10	Retainer for oil seal		24	Dust cover plate for selector shafts
11	Mudshield for retainer		25–26	Fixings for dust cover

1	Selector shaft, four wheel drive		31	Link for selector shaft
2	Selector fork complete, four wheel drive		32–33	Fixings for link
3	Bush for selector fork		34	Lever assembly, four wheel drive
4	Spring for selector fork		35	Bush for lever
5	Block for selector shaft		36	Special bolt, lever to housing
6–8	Fixings for block		37	Locking pin, four wheel drive lever
9	Selector shaft, transfer gear change		38	Sealing ring, four wheel drive locking pin
10	Sealing ring for transfer gear change shaft		39–40	Fixings for locking pin
11	Selector fork, transfer gear change		41	Selector rod, four wheel drive
12	Set bolt fixing fork		42	Clevis complete for rod
13	Distance tube for transfer selector shaft		43	Split pin for clevis
14	Locating bush for selector shaft spring		44	Spring for selector rod
15	Spring for gear change selector shaft		45	Special bush for spring
16	Connector, gear change to pivot shaft		46	Control knob for rod
17	Block for selector shaft		47	Locknut for knob and clevis
18–20	Fixings for block		48	Transfer gear change lever complete
21	Pivot shaft for selector shafts		49	Spring for transfer gear change lever
22	Coupling, selector shafts to pivot		50	Knob for gear change lever
23–25	Fixings for coupling		51	Locknut for knob
26–27	Fixings for pivot shaft		52	Bracket for gear change lever
28	Plunger for transfer selector shaft		53	Distance piece for bracket
29	Spring for plunger		54–56	Fixings for bracket
30	Plug		57–58	Fixings for gear lever

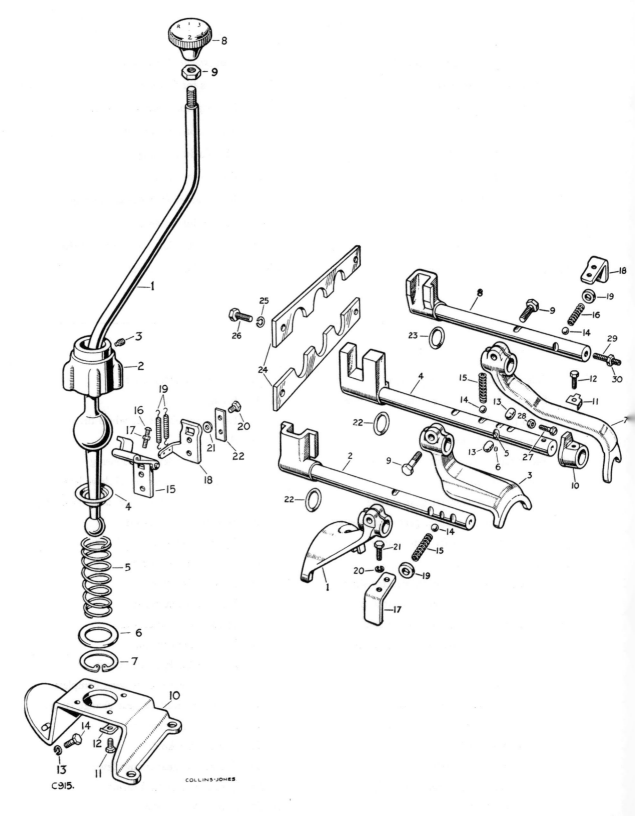

Fig. C-4—Layout of the gearbox unit: main gear change lever and selectors

Key to Fig. C-4

1 Gear change lever
2 Housing for lever
3 Locating pin for lever ball
4 Spherical seat for gear lever
5 Retaining spring for lever
6 Retaining plate for spring
7 Circlip fixing retaining plate
8 Knob for lever
9 Locknut for knob
10 Mounting plate for gear change
11–12 Fixings for housing
13–14 Fixings for mounting plate
15 Reverse stop hinge complete
16 Adjusting screw ⎱ For hinge
17 Locknut ⎰
18 Bracket for reverse stop spring
19 Spring for reverse stop
20–22 Fixings for hinge and bracket

1 Selector fork, 3rd and 4th speed
2 Shaft for fork, 3rd and 4th speed
3 Selector fork, 1st and 2nd speed
4 Shaft assembly for fork, 1st and 2nd speed
5 Interlocking pin
6 Peg fixing interlocking pin
7 Selector fork, reverse
8 Shaft for fork, reverse
9 Set bolt fixing forks to shafts
10 Stop for 2nd speed
11–12 Fixings for stop
13 Interlocking plunger
14 Steel ball for selectors
15 Selector spring, forward
16 Selector spring, reverse
17 Retaining plate L.H. ⎱
18 Retaining plate R.H. ⎬ For selector springs, side
19 Rubber grommet ⎰
20–21 Fixings for retaining plates
22 Seal for selector shafts
23 Cork seal for reverse shaft
24 Retaining plate for sealing ring
25–26 Fixings for retaining plate
27 Set bolt ⎱ In cover for
28 Locknut ⎰ 2nd gear stop
29 Adjustable stop for reverse selector shaft
30 Locknut for stop

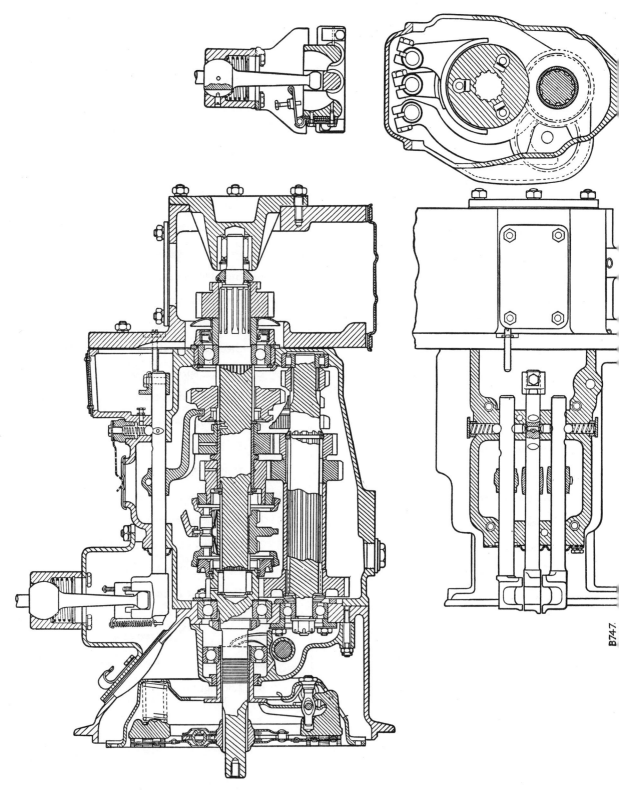

Fig. C-5—Cross-section of gearbox unit: elevation

B747

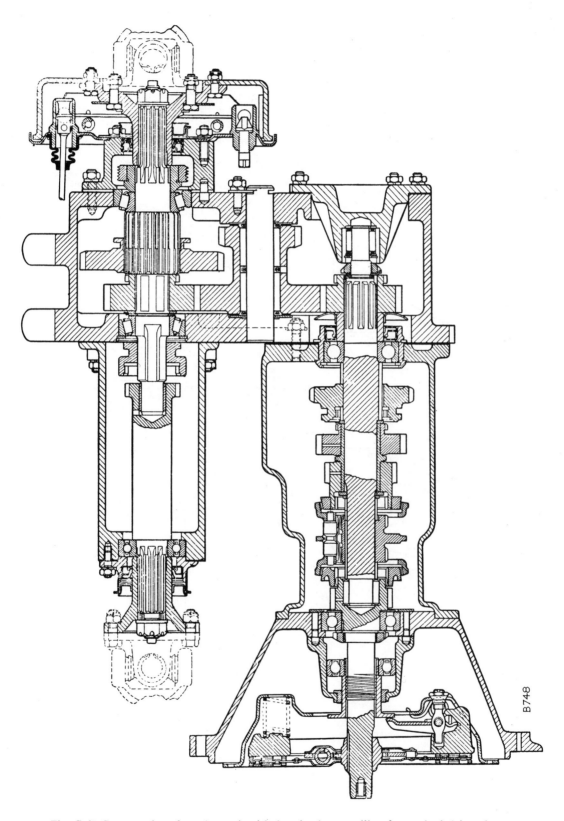

Fig. C-6—Cross-section of gearbox unit with dog clutch controlling front-wheel drive plan.

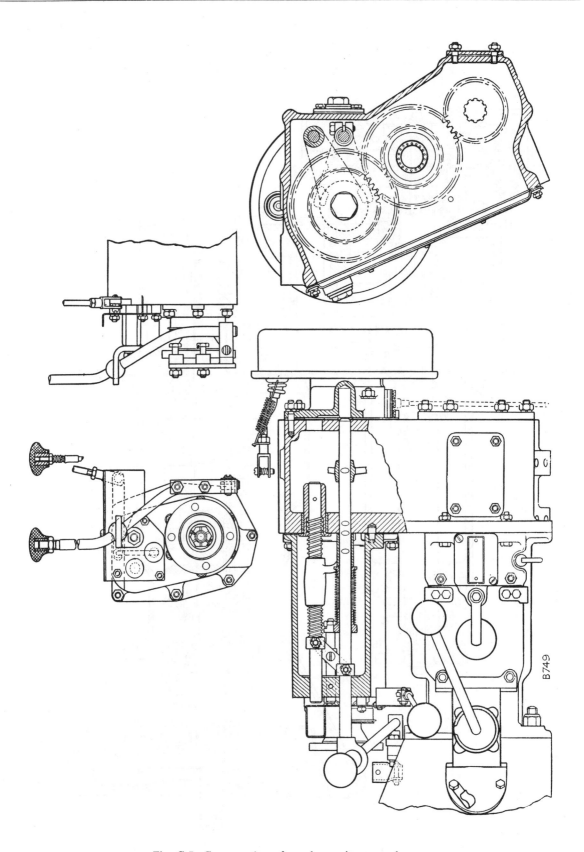

Fig. C-7—Cross-section of gearbox unit: controls.

1948-53 models

Freewheel components (gearbox in position)
To renew Operation C/2
(Gearboxes numbered prior to 16102314 and 16131688)

1. Position the vehicle over a pit or raise it as high as possible with a high-lift jack.

2. Remove the transfer box drain plug and drain off the oil into a suitable receptacle.

3. Place the transfer gear change lever in the low position, *i.e.*, to the rear.

4. Remove the front propeller shaft (see Section D).

5. **R.H.D. models only.** Remove the clutch return spring, from the front end first. Withdraw the split pin and remove the clevis pin connecting the operating rod to the lever on the clutch cross-shaft. Withdraw the split pin and remove the joint pin and two washers securing the cross-shaft to the connecting tube on the clutch shaft. Slide the cross-shaft through the bushes as far as possible towards the chassis side member.

6. Slacken the locknut and remove the freewheel control pivot and eyebolt complete from the output shaft housing.

7. Draw out the freewheel operating rod.

8. Remove the special nut and shakeproof washer securing the transfer control link to the selector shaft and slide the link up the transfer gear change lever.

9. Withdraw the split pin and remove the castle nut and plain washer securing the front axle driving flange; carefully remove the flange, avoiding damage to the oil seal.

10. Remove the plug and joint washer from the left-hand side of the output shaft housing and withdraw the transfer selector spring and ball.

11. Remove the seven nuts and spring washers securing the output shaft housing and carefully remove the housing, complete with joint washer, forward and down below the chassis.

    Note: On gearboxes numbered 860001 to 861988, it is essential that the locking dog remains in the output shaft housing, otherwise it will prevent the unit clearing on removal.

12. Remove the seven nuts and spring washers securing the freewheel housing to the transfer casing; the two upper nuts can be conveniently reached through the seat box centre panel aperture.

13. Slacken the rear engine and gearbox unit mounting bolts.

14. Lever the gearbox unit slightly upwards to allow the bottom freewheel housing boss to clear the chassis and remove the housing, complete with joint washer, in a similar manner to the output shaft housing.

15. Remove the freewheel components as required and rebuild the unit.

16. Re-assemble by reversing the sequence of operations detailed for removal, paying attention to the following points:—

17. Prior to fitting the freewheel housing, ensure that the freewheel operating shaft, guide and spring work freely in the transfer casing.

18. Prior to replacing the output shaft housing, place a suitable guide thimble over the end of the transfer selector shaft, to prevent damage to the oil seal.

19. Check the operation of the transfer and freewheel controls.

20. Refill the transfer box with oil of the correct grade.

1948-53 models

Four-wheel drive mechanism (gearbox in position)
To remove Operation C/4
(Gearboxes numbered 16102314 and 16131688 onwards)

1. Position the vehicle over a pit or raise it as high as possible with a high-lift jack.

2. Remove the transfer box drain plug and drain off the oil into a suitable receptacle.

3. Remove the front propeller shaft (see Section D).

4. **R.H.D. models only.** Remove the clutch return spring, from the front end first. Withdraw the split pin and remove the clevis pin connecting the operating rod to the lever on the clutch cross-shaft. Withdraw the split pin and remove the joint pin and two washers securing the cross-shaft to the connecting tube on the clutch shaft. Slide the cross-shaft through the bushes as far as possible towards the chassis side member.

5. Remove the yellow knob, locknut, spring and bush from the front-wheel drive control rod.

6. Remove the red knob and locknut from the transfer lever.

7. Remove the R.H. floorboard.

8. Withdraw the split pin and remove the castle nut and plain washer securing the front axle driving flange; carefully remove the flange complete with dust seal, avoiding damage to the oil seal.

9. Remove the special nut and shakeproof washer securing the transfer control link to the selector shaft; remove the split pin and spring-loaded clevis pin and remove the transfer lever.

10. Remove the dust cover from the front of the output housing by removing the three nuts, spring washers and distance pieces.

11. Remove the front-wheel drive control lever assembly by withdrawing the special pivot screw.

12. Remove the seven nuts and spring washers securing the output housing to the transfer box (this action also releases an earth lead). Slacken the gearbox mountings and lift under the left-hand support. Withdraw the output housing complete with output shaft, front-wheel drive dog clutch, the dog clutch selector shaft and fork and a joint washer, clear of the chasis cross-member. Withdraw the dog clutch selector shaft and dog clutch from the rear of the housing. Remove the top cover plate from the transfer box, hold in low transfer and remove the output housing upwards through the floorboard aperture. Leave the transfer selector shaft and link in position protruding from the transfer box.

13. Remove the split pin, castle nut and special screw from the transfer selector shaft and remove the block.

14. Slide the following parts from the transfer selector shaft:—

    (a) Link, link pin and connector assembly.

    (b) Spring.

    (c) Spring locating bush.

    (d) Distance tube.

15. Detach the link from the link pin by removing the special screw, castle nut and split pin.

    Note: The connector should not be removed from the link pin unless absolutely necessary, as difficulty will be experienced in effecting correct alignment on re-assembly.

16. Remove the output shaft from the output housing.

17. Remove the split pin, castle nut and special screw from the dog clutch selector shaft and remove the block.

18. Slide the two springs and selector fork from the dog clutch selector shaft.

19. If necessary, remove the two bushes from the selector fork boss.

20. If necessary, remove the spigot bush from the rear end of the output shaft.

21. Remove the six nuts and spring washers securing the oil seal retainer to the front face of the output housing and remove the retainer complete with oil seal and joint washer.

22. If necessary, remove the oil seal from the retainer.

23. If necessary, withdraw the output shaft front bearing from the output housing.

1948-53 models

Four-wheel drive mechanism (gearbox in position)

To replace   **Operation C/6**

(Gearboxes numbered 16102314 and 16131688 onwards)

1. If necessary, replace the output shaft front bearing in the output housing. The bearing must be a **push fit** on the shaft and a **light drive fit** in the housing.

   Renew the shaft, bearing and housing as necessary.

2. If removed, fit a new oil seal in the retainer with its knife edge inwards.

3. If removed, replace the spigot bush in the rear end of the output shaft, pressing it in flush with the face of the shaft. The bush must be reamed in position to .875 in. (22,22 mm) giving .001 in. to .002 (0,02 mm to 0,05) clearance on the transfer box output shaft.

4. If removed, renew the two oilite bushes in the dog clutch selector fork boss; the bushes must be pressed in flush with the end faces of the boss and must have .001 in. to .002 clearance on the selector shaft.

5. Check the two dog clutch selector springs in accordance with the following data and renew as necessary:—

   Free length: 2.750 in. (69,5 mm)
   Solid length: .640 in. (16 mm)
   Maximum load: 13 lb. (5,8 kg)
   Rate: 6⅛ lb./in. (2,7 kg)

6. Check the transfer selector shaft spring in accordance with the following data and renew as necessary:—

   Free length: 7.156 in. (182,7 mm)
   Length in position: 3.875 in. (98,4 mm)
   Load in position: 24 lb. (10,8 kg)
   Rate: 7.31 lb./in. (3,2 kg).

7. Replace the oil seal retainer on the output housing and secure with six nuts and spring washers.

8. Fit the two springs and selector fork (crank to the rear) over the dog clutch selector shaft.

9. Replace the block on the selector shaft and secure by means of the special screw, castle nut and split pin.

10. If the connector has been detached from the link pin, replace it with the hole for the locking peg vertical and the cutaway on the link pin underneath; ensure that the connector is square with the pin and secure lightly with the nut and shake-proof washer.

11. Secure the link to the link pin by means of the special screw, castle nut and split pin. The threaded end of the screw must be downwards and the shorter end of the link towards the transfer selector, with the longer arm of the jaw at the opposite end to the rear.

12. Slide the following parts on the transfer selector shaft:—

    (a) Distance tube.

    (b) Spring locating bush with its smaller diameter to the front.

    (c) Spring.

    (d) Compress the spring and fit the link and connector assembly until the block is over the hole in the shaft. Fit the special screw from the bottom, through the coupling jaw, block and selector shaft and secure with the castle nut and split pin.

13. Fit the dog clutch over the splines on the transfer box output shaft.

14. Fit the dog clutch selector shaft assembly into the bush in the transfer box, ensuring that the link engages the screw correctly.

15. Fit the output housing joint washer. If necessary, tighten the connector on the link pin.

16. Place the housing over the selector shafts (from the top). Before pushing the housing home, select two-wheel drive in high transfer gear (through the transfer box) and fit the output shaft over the transfer box shaft and through the housing. Secure with the seven nuts and spring washers, picking up the earth lead under one of the nuts.

17. Complete the assembly by reversing the sequence of removal operations.

18. Adjust the front-wheel drive rod to ensure efficient extraction and replacement of the locking peg; it is important to avoid the spring becoming coilbound as under such conditions the operation appears correct, but the peg is not extracted sufficiently to engage four-wheel drive.

19. Check the whole assembly for correct operation.

1948-53 models

Main gear change lever

To overhaul   **Operation C/8**

On vehicles numbered 860001 to 861500, the main gear change lever is bolted to the gearbox cover panel, while on later vehicles it is secured directly to the gearbox unit. The overhaul operations differ extensively between the two patterns.

Vehicles numbered 860001 to 861500

1. Remove the gearbox cover panel, complete with the gear change lever and reverse stop, from the vehicle.

2. Remove the five bolts, spring washers and nuts securing the gear change lever to the cover and lift off the lever, complete with shim plates, which should be preserved.

3. Remove the knob and locknut from the lever.

4. Remove the five bolts, anti-rattle springs and nuts securing the ball retainers to the lever and remove the upper (small) and lower (large) ball retainers.

5. Remove the two bolts, spring washers and nuts securing the reverse stop housing to the gearbox cover and remove the housing, spring retainer plate and shim plates, which should be preserved.

6. Remove the detent ball spring, detent ball, plunger and spring from the housing.

7. Renew any worn components.

8. Fit the plunger and spring, detent ball and spring in the reverse stop housing and hold them in position with the retainer plate. Secure the housing and retainer to the cover plate, complete with the shim plates, by means of the two bolts, spring washers and nuts. It may be necessary, at a later stage, to adjust the thickness of shim plates to allow ease of operation of the reverse stop unit; the plates are available .128 in. and .036 in. thick.

9. Fit the upper and lower ball retainers to the gear change lever and secure them with the five bolts, anti-rattle springs and nuts.

10. Replace the locknut and knob on the lever.

11. Fit the complete gear change lever to the gearbox cover panel, together with the shim plates, and secure it by means of the five bolts, spring washers and nuts. After fitting the unit in the vehicle, it may be necessary to adjust the thickness of shim plates, to ensure that the lever selector makes good contact, but does not "bottom" in the gearbox selectors; the plates are available .128 in. and .036 in. thick.

12. Replace the complete gearbox cover panel in the vehicle and check the operation of the gear change lever and reverse stop; adjust the shims as necessary.

Vehicles numbered 861501 onwards

1. Remove the freewheel control ring or front-wheel drive control knob, locknut and spring; remove the knobs and locknuts from the main and transfer gear change levers.

2. Remove the brake pedal rod and pad (see Section H).

3. Remove the clutch pedal and pad (see Section B).

4. Remove the left-hand and right-hand toe plates (see Section R).

5. Remove the gearbox cover.

6. Detach the two springs from the reverse stop hinge. Prise up the locking tabs and remove the two set bolts, lockplate and two plain washers securing the reverse stop to the reverse selector; remove the reverse stop hinge (complete with adjusting screw and locknut) and the spring bracket.

7. Remove the two set bolts, spring washers and distance pieces securing the gear change lever mounting plate to the bell housing and the two nuts and spring washers securing the plate to the gearbox top cover; remove the mounting plate and gear change lever complete.

8. Prise up the locking tabs and remove the four set bolts and lockers securing the gear change lever housing to the mounting plate; remove the plate.

9. Remove the circlip from the lever housing and draw out the spring retaining washer, spring and spherical seat; withdraw the gear lever from the housing. If necessary, remove the lever ball locating pin from the housing.

10. Renew any worn components.

11. Replace the lever ball locating pin in the housing (if removed on stripping) and secure it by "staking".

12. Fit the gear change lever in the housing; replace the spherical seat, spring and retaining washer and secure the whole with a circlip.

13. Fit the housing to the mounting plate and secure it by means of four lockers and set bolts.

14. Fit the mounting plate to the gearbox unit; secure it by means of two spring washers and nuts at the gearbox top cover and two set bolts and spring washers at the bell housing aperture.

15. Fit the reverse stop hinge and spring bracket to the reverse selector and secure them by means of two plain washers, one lockplate and two set bolts (the plain washers should be fitted under the lockplate). Replace the two reverse stop springs.

16. Adjust the reverse stop as described below.

17. Replace the gearbox cover.

18. Replace the left-hand and right-hand toe plates (see Section R).

19. Replace the clutch pedal rod and pad (see Section B).

20. Replace the brake pedal rod and pad (see Section H).

21. Replace the freewheel control ring or front wheel drive control knob, locknut and spring; replace the locknuts and knobs on the main and transfer gear change levers.

1948-53 models
Reverse stop
To adjust   Operation C/10

1. The screw and locknut on the reverse stop hinge should be adjusted so that:
   (a) the hinge rides easily up the gear lever when reverse gear is selected, and
   (b) appreciable resistance is felt on moving the gear lever to the reverse gear position.

2. This adjustment should be carried out on any gearbox removed for attention, before the gearbox cover is fitted.

3. It can also be carried out at any time after:
   (a) detaching the access panel from the right-hand side of the gearbox cover on vehicles fitted with a freewheel control ring, or
   (b) selecting reverse gear and sliding the access panel up the front wheel drive control rod.

1948-53 models
Gearbox dipstick (lower oil level)
To modify   Operation C/12

All main gearboxes numbered prior to 16102100 and 16131500 have an oil capacity of 4 pints (2,5 litres); the oil capacity is reduced to $2\frac{1}{2}$ pints (1,5 litres) on later gearboxes to counteract the possibility of oil passing along the primary pinion and giving rise to clutch slip.

Early gearboxes should be so modified at overhaul as follows:—

1. Make a new "H" mark on the dipstick $\frac{1}{2}$ in, (12,7 mm) below the existing mark, i.e., $5\frac{27}{32}$ in. (148,5 mm) below the handle flange; obliterate the original mark.

2. Alternatively, discard the original dipstick and rebuild the gearbox with a new dipstick, Part No. 235242.

1948-53 models
Transfer box (lower oil level)
To modify   Operation C/14

All 1948 to mid-1950 transfer boxes have an oil capacity of 6 pints (3,5 litres); the oil capacity is reduced on later gearboxes to $4\frac{1}{2}$ pints (2,5 litres) to counteract the tendency for oil to pass from the transfer box to the main gearbox. Early transfer boxes should be modified at overhaul as follows:—

1. The oil level should be lowered by $\frac{7}{8}$ in. (22 mm). Mark off the new position for the level plug on the rear face of the transfer box by scribing a line vertically downwards from the centre of the lower right-hand stud securing the centre power take-off cover plate. Mark off a point $2\frac{1}{4}$ in. (57 mm) below the centre of the stud.

2. Drill a $\frac{3}{16}$ in. (5 mm) hole at this point and tap $\frac{1}{4}$ in. Whit.

3. Fit a suitable $\frac{1}{4}$ in. Whit. set bolt ($\frac{1}{2}$ in. (13 mm) long) and fibre washer to act as a plug.

4. Clean out all swarf from the transfer box.

5. Ensure that an oil flinger is fitted in front of the transfer drive gear on the rear of the gearbox mainshaft (see Fig. C-2).

1948-53 models

Gearbox only

To remove   Operation C/16

1. Disconnect the battery.

2. Remove the hood or hard top, for convenience in working.

3. Remove the centre inspection panel from the seat box.

4. Remove the hand brake lever and linkage (see Section H).

5. Remove the freewheel control ring or the front wheel drive control knob, locknut and spring; remove the knobs and locknuts from the main and transfer gear change levers. (Transfer lever knob only on vehicles numbered 860001 to 861500.)

6. Remove the brake pedal rod and pad (see Section H).

7. Remove the clutch pedal rod and pad (see Section B).

8. Remove the left-hand and right-hand toe plates (see Section R).

9. Remove the gearbox cover. On vehicles numbered 860001 to 861500, the main gear change lever assembly will be removed with the cover.

10. Remove the petrol tank and tool locker lids, by detaching the eight bolts, spring washers and nuts securing the hinges to the back rest panel.

11. Remove the five bolts, spring washers and nuts securing the top fixing angle on the seat box to the back rest panel.

12. Remove the six set bolts, spring and plain washers securing the side fixing angles to the seat box.

13. Remove the two bolts, spring washers and nuts securing the floor sills to the dash.

14. Remove the seat box complete.

15. Remove the rear axle propeller shaft (see Section D).

16. Disconnect the front axle propeller shaft and rear power take-off propeller shaft (if fitted), at the gearbox end in both cases.

17. **R.H.D. models only.** Remove the clutch return spring, from the front end first. Withdraw the split pin and remove the clevis pin securing the clutch operating rod to the cross-shaft lever. Withdraw a split pin and washer and tap out the joint pin connecting the cross-shaft to the connecting tube. Slide the cross-shaft clear of the bell housing, towards the chassis side member.

18. **L.H.D. models only.** Remove the clutch return spring, from the front end first. Withdraw the split pin and remove the clevis pin securing the clutch operating rod to the clutch shaft lever.

19. Disconnect the speedometer cable at the gearbox end either by removing the bolt, spring washer and nut securing the cable to the pinion bush on the drive housing or by detaching the retaining plate and three set bolts and spring washers securing the cable to the drive housing; withdraw the cable clear of the gearbox.

20. Remove the self-locking nuts from the two rear engine and gearbox unit bearer bolts and withdraw the bolts; the bearer rubbers, washers and shims may normally be left in position in the vehicle.

   Note: It may be necessary to remove the right-hand bearer from the transfer casing, as in some cases it will not clear the hand brake bell crank lever.

21. Remove the thirteen nuts and plain washers securing the bell housing to the engine flywheel housing.

22. Place a jack under the rear end of the engine and raise it approximately $\frac{1}{2}$ in. (12 mm) above its normal position; this will enable the bell housing flange to clear the chassis cross-member and also prevent any strain being taken on the primary pinion shaft.

23. Place a suitable sling round the gearbox unit, raise it upwards and to the rear and remove the unit from the vehicle.

1948-53 models

Gearbox only

To replace   Operation C/18

1. Replacement of the gearbox unit is effected by reversing the sequence of operations detailed for removal.

2. Should the engine and gearbox unit mounting rubbers, etc., have been disturbed, they should be fitted as shown at Fig. C-8. The nip on the pads is adjusted by the addition or removal of shims on the top of the central distance tube; it should be checked on replacement and adjusted as necessary. The correct setting is with the top shim approximately $\frac{1}{16}$ in. (1,5 mm) below the top face of the upper rubber pad.

   On early 1952 models onwards, the rear mounting brackets are adjustable laterally, to facilitate alignment with the mounting rubbers.

3. Refill the main gearbox and transfer box with oil of the correct grade.

4. Adjust the transmission brake as described in Section H.

1948-53 models

Gearbox unit

To strip　　　　　　　　**Operation C/20**

Operation C/20 details the differences which will be found on 1948-53 gearboxes. See following pages for main gearbox and transfer box strip and reassembly.

Gearboxes numbered prior to 16102314 and 16131688

1. Mount the gearbox unit on a suitable stand.

2. Remove the drain plugs (and joint washers) from the bottom of the main gearbox casing and transfer casing and drain off the oil into a suitable receptacle.

Remove the controls as follows:

3. **Gearboxes numbered 861501 onwards.** Remove two spring washers and nuts at the main gearbox top cover and two set bolts, spring washers, cover plate and rubber seal at the bell housing and lift off the main gear change lever assembly. Strip the assembly.

   Remove the reverse stop hinge unit.

4. **Gearboxes numbered 860001 to 861500.** Remove the two nuts, spring washers and distance pieces (or cover plate and rubber seal) securing the bell housing inspection cover and remove the cover.

5. Remove the transfer gear change cover plate and joint washer from the transfer casing; this is secured either by four set screws or four set bolts and spring washers.

6. Remove the special screw, spring washer and nut securing the freewheel control pivot to the eyebolt in the front of the output shaft housing; remove the pivot and eyebolt (complete with locknut).

7. Remove the special nut and shakeproof washer securing the transfer selector link to the front of the selector shaft.

8. Remove the split pin and clevis pin securing the transfer gear change lever to the bracket on the bell housing; remove the lever complete with link.

9. Remove the two bolts, spring washers, distance pieces and nuts securing the transfer lever bracket to the bell housing and remove the bracket.

10. Remove the return spring for the freewheel lever; remove the spring anchor from the output shaft housing by withdrawing the set bolt, spring washer and distance piece. Remove the freewheel lever guide by removing the two set bolts and spring washers securing it to the output shaft housing. Remove the special screw and distance piece securing the freewheel lever to the output shaft housing and remove the lever complete with the operating wire or rod.

11. Remove the plug and joint washer from the left-hand side of the output shaft housing and withdraw the transfer shaft selector spring and ball.

12. Remove the front axle drive flange and dust shield from the output shaft, by removing the split pin, castle nut and plain washer.

13. Withdraw the freewheel operating rod from the output shaft housing.

14. Remove the seven nuts and spring washers securing the output shaft housing to the freewheel housing and withdraw the housing complete with joint washer. If necessary, remove the output shaft and selector shaft oil seals from the housing.

15. **Gearboxes numbered 861989 onwards.** The output shaft front bearing will remain on the output shaft protruding from the freewheel housing. Withdraw the bearing from the shaft.

16. **Gearboxes numbered 860001 to 861988.** The front portion of the output shaft ("transfer shaft") will be retained in the output shaft housing. Remove the circlip retaining the front bearing in the housing and drive out the transfer shaft and bearing from the housing; withdraw the bearing from the shaft. Remove the distance washer, locking dog and distance piece from the output shaft in the freewheel housing.

Remove the freewheel unit as follows:

17. Remove the seven nuts and spring washers securing the freewheel housing to the transfer casing and withdraw the housing complete with joint washer. Withdraw the spring guide and freewheel operating spring from the transfer casing.

18. Remove the pinch bolt securing the freewheel operating fork to the operating shaft and remove the fork and shaft.

19. Remove the freewheel locking dog.

20. Remove the circlip retaining the output shaft rear bearing in the freewheel housing; drive out the output shaft and freewheel assembly from the housing.

21. Remove the circlip securing the rear bearing to the output shaft and withdraw the bearing.

22. **Gearboxes numbered 860001 to 861988.** If necessary, remove the bush from the front bore of the output shaft.

23. Remove the spring ring and retaining plate securing the inner member to the outer member. Remove the inner member complete with the fixed cam roller shoes (which can be removed if necessary by removing the securing set screws), nine graded rollers, three free cam roller shoes and three shoe springs. Remove the pilot bearing from the outer member.

24. Prise up the tab washers and remove the six set bolts and two locking plates securing the freewheel outer member to the output shaft.

25. If necessary, remove the operating shaft bush from the freewheel housing.

Gearboxes numbered 16102314 and 16131688 onwards

26. Mount the gearbox unit on a suitable stand.

27. Remove the drain plugs (and joint washers) from the bottom of the main gearbox casing and transfer casing and drain off the oil into a suitable receptacle.

Remove the controls as follows:

28. Remove two spring washers and nuts at the main gearbox top cover and two set bolts, spring washers, cover plate and rubber seal at the bell housing and lift off the main gear change lever assembly. Strip the assembly.

Remove the reverse stop hinge unit.

29. Remove the transfer gear change cover plate and joint washer from the transfer casing (four set bolts and spring washers).

30. Remove the plug and joint washer from the top of the transfer casing and withdraw the transfer shaft selector spring and plunger.

31. Withdraw the split pin and remove the castle nut and plain washer securing the front axle driving flange; carefully remove the flange complete with dust seal, avoiding damage to the oil seal.

32. Remove the special nut and shakeproof washer securing the transfer control link to the selector shaft; remove the split pin and spring-loaded clevis pin and remove the transfer lever.

33. Remove the dust cover from the front of the output housing, by removing the three nuts, spring washers and distance pieces.

34. Remove the front wheel drive control lever assembly by withdrawing the special pivot screw. Remove the split pin and plain washer securing the locking peg to the lever. Disconnect the operating rod from the lever (spring-loaded clevis). If necessary, press out the bush from the lever.

35. Remove the seven nuts and spring washers securing the output housing to the transfer box (this action also releases an earth lead). Withdraw the output housing complete with output shaft, front wheel drive dog clutch, the dog clutch selector shaft and fork and a joint washer. Leave the transfer selector shaft and link in position protruding from the transfer box.

36. Remove the split pin, castle nut and special screw from the transfer selector shaft and remove the block.

37. Slide the following parts from the transfer selector shaft:—

(a) Link, link pin and connector assembly.
(b) Spring.
(c) Spring locating bush.
(d) Distance tube.

38. Detach the link from the link pin by removing the special screw, castle nut and split pin.

Note: The connector should not be removed from the link pin unless absolutely necessary, as difficulty will be experienced in effecting correct alignment on re-assembly.

39. Remove the output shaft, dog clutch selector shaft and dog clutch from the output housing.

40. Remove the split pin, castle nut and special screw from the dog clutch selector shaft and remove the block.

41. Slide the two springs and selector fork from the dog clutch selector shaft.

42. If necessary, remove the two bushes from the selector fork boss.

43. If necessary, remove the spigot bush from the rear end of the output shaft.

44. Remove the six nuts and spring washers securing the oil seal retainer to the front face of the output housing and remove the retainer complete with oil seal and joint washer.

45. If necessary, remove the oil seal from the retainer.

46. If necessary, withdraw the output shaft front bearing from the output housing.

Gearboxes numbered prior to 16102314 and 16131688
Assemble the freewheel unit as follows:

1. Fit the freewheel outer member to the front output shaft and secure it with two lockplates and six set bolts.

2. Place the inner member pilot bearing in the outer member.

3. Fit the inner member, complete with three fixed cam roller shoes, in the bearing; place the nine graded rollers in position and fit the free cam roller shoes and springs.

4. Fit the toothed retaining plate in the outer member and secure it with a circlip.

5. If necessary, press a new operating shaft bush into the freewheel housing and ream it to .625 in.

6. Fit the output shaft rear bearing into the freewheel housing and secure it with a circlip. The bearing must be a **push** fit in the housing.

7. Fit the freewheel assembly into the freewheel housing and press the output shaft through the bearing. The shaft must be a **light press** fit in the bearing. Secure the shaft with a circlip.

8. **Gearboxes numbered 860001 to 861988.** If necessary, renew the oilite bush in the front bore of the output shaft. The bush is a **drive** fit in the shaft; the front (transfer) shaft should be an **easy** fit in the bush bore.

9. Push the freewheel operating shaft through the bush in the freewheel housing, with the spring to the front. Fit the freewheel selector fork on the shaft and secure it with the pinch bolt.

10. Place the locking dog in mesh with the fork and slide the shaft along, so that the freewheel is in the "fixed" position. Ensure that the splines on the inner member and locking dog are in alignment.

11. Slide the freewheel operating spring over the operating shaft guide and fit the guide into the bushes in the transfer casing. Compress the spring and secure it by means of a small peg pushed through the hole in the guide.

12. Fit the complete freewheel, together with a joint washer, to the transfer casing, locating it on two dowels; secure with seven nuts and spring washers.

13. Release the operating spring by removing the peg from the guide and check the freewheel unit for ease of operation.

14. **Gearboxes numbered 861989 onwards.** Drive the output shaft front bearing on to the output shaft until it abuts the shoulder. The bearing must be a **drive** fit on the shaft.

15. **Gearboxes numbered 860001 to 861988.** Fit the transfer shaft bearing in the output shaft housing and secure it with a circlip. The bearing must be a **drive fit** in the housing. Drive the transfer shaft through the bearing until it abuts the shoulder. The shaft must be a **drive** fit in the bearing.

    Replace the distance piece, locking dog and distance washer on the output shaft protruding from the freewheel housing.

16. If necessary, renew the output shaft and selector shaft oil seals in the output shaft housing.

17. Fit a suitable protection thimble over the end of the transfer operating shaft.

18. Fit the complete output shaft housing, together with a joint washer, to the freewheel housing; locate the dowel and secure with seven nuts and spring washers. Remove the thimble.

19. Insert the freewheel operating rod through the seal in the housing and enter it into the operating shaft.

20. Examine the outer diameter of the front axle drive flange for damage which may have caused failure of the original oil seal and rectify or renew the flange as necessary. Fit the flange and dust shield to the output shaft and secure it with a plain washer, castle nut and split pin.

21. Replace the transfer change selector ball and spring in the boss on the left-hand side of the output shaft housing and secure them with a plug and joint washer.

Assemble the controls as follows:

22. If necessary, renew the bush and operating wire in the freewheel operating lever and fit the complete lever to the output shaft housing by means of the special screw; the distance piece should be placed between the lever and the housing.

23. Replace the lever guide and secure it to the top of the housing with two set bolts and spring washers.

24. Secure the lever return spring anchor to the housing by means of a set bolt and spring washer, with the distance piece between the anchor and the housing.

25. Replace the lever return spring.

26. Fit the transfer lever bracket to the bell housing, securing it by means of two bolts, spring washers and nuts, with the distance pieces between the bracket and bell housing.

27. Replace the transfer selector link on the transfer gear change lever.

28. Fit the link over the end of the selector shaft and secure the lever to the bracket by means of a clevis pin and split pin. Secure the link to the selector shaft with a special nut and shakeproof washer.

29. Screw the pivot eyebolt, complete with locknut, into the tapping in the front face of the output shaft housing. Fit the pivot to the eyebolt by means of a special screw, spring washer and nut.

30. Check the operation of the transfer gear change and freewheel controls, adjusting the eyebolt and pivot as necessary, so that:

    (a) With the transfer change lever right forward, high transfer gear is engaged and the freewheel operating rod is pushed to the rear, i.e., the freewheel is "free". In this position the freewheel lever should engage the slot in the operating rod.

    (b) With the transfer change lever pulled halfway back, the transfer box should be in neutral. The freewheel operating rod should be retained in the free position by means of the lever.

    (c) With the transfer change lever right back, low transfer gear is engaged; the freewheel should remain free. When the control wire is pulled or the knob is depressed, so disengaging the lever from the operating rod, the rod should move forward to set the freewheel in the fixed position.

    (d) On returning to high transfer gear, the freewheel rod should be forced to the free position as at paragraph (a).

31. When the controls have been adjusted correctly, complete the assembly as follows:

32. Replace the transfer gear change cover plate and secure it by means of either four set screws or four set bolts and spring washers.

33. **Gearboxes numbered 861501 onwards.** Assemble the main gear change lever. Fit the lever assembly, cover plate and rubber seal to the gearbox unit, securing them by means of two set bolts and spring washers at the bell housing and two nuts and spring washers at the gearbox top cover.

    Fit and adjust the reverse stop hinge.

34. **Gearboxes numbered 860001 to 861500.** Fit the bell housing inspection cover and secure it and the cover plate and rubber seal with two spring washers and nuts.

35. Fill the main gearbox and transfer casing with oil of a suitable grade.

The gearbox unit is now ready for installation in the vehicle.

Gearboxes numbered 16102314 and 16131688 onwards

Assemble the controls as follows:

36. If necessary, replace the output shaft front bearing in the output housing. The bearing must be a **push fit** on the shaft, and a **light drive fit** in the housing. Renew the shaft, bearing and housing as necessary.

37. If removed, fit a new oil seal in the retainer with its knife edge inwards.

38. If removed, replace the spigot bush in the rear end of the output shaft, pressing it in flush with the face of the shaft.

The bush must be reamed in position to .875 in.

39. If removed, renew the two oilite bushes in the dog clutch selector fork boss; the bushes must be pressed in flush with the end faces of the boss and must have .001 to .002 in. clearance on the selector shaft.

40. Check the two dog clutch **selector springs** in accordance with the following data and renew as necessary:—

    Free length: 2.750 in.
    Solid length: .640 in.
    Maximum load: 13 lb.
    Rate: $6\frac{1}{8}$ lb./in.

41. Check the transfer selector shaft spring in accordance with the following data and renew as necessary:—

    Free length: 7.156 in.
    Length in position: 3.875 in.
    Load in position: 24 lb.
    Rate: 7.31 lb/in.

42. Replace the oil seal retainer on the output housing and secure with six nuts and spring washers.

43. Fit the two springs and selector fork (crank to the rear) over the dog clutch selector shaft.

44. Replace the block on the selector shaft and secure by means of the special screw, castle nut and split pin.

45. If the connector has been detached from the link pin, replace it with the hole for the locking peg vertical and the cutaway on the link pin underneath; ensure that the connector is square with the pin and secure lightly with the nut and shakeproof washer.

46. Secure the link pin by means of the special screw, castle nut and split pin. The threaded end of the screw must be downwards and the shorter end of the link towards the transfer selector, with the longer arm of the jaw at the opposite end to the rear.

47. Replace the transfer shaft selector spring and plunger and secure with the plug and joint washer.

48. Slide the following parts on to the transfer selector shaft:—

    (a) Distance tube.

    (b) Spring locating bush with its smaller diameter to the front.

    (c) Spring.

    (d) Compress the spring and fit the link and connector assembly until the block is over the hole in the shaft. Fit the special screw from the bottom, through the coupling jaw, block and selector shaft and secure with castle nut and split pin.

49. Fit the dog clutch over the splines on the transfer box output shaft.

50. Fit the dog clutch selector shaft assembly into the bush on the transfer box, ensuring that the link engages the screw correctly.

51. If they have been separated, the position of the connector and link should now be adjusted as follows:—

52. (a) The most efficient method of carrying out this operation is to use a dummy output housing with a large aperture in the side through which the connector securing nut can be tightened. Place the dummy housing over the selector shafts and locate the link pin by means of a suitable peg. Tighten the connector securing nut and remove the housing.

    (b) If a dummy housing is not available, the actual output housing can be used to align the selectors by sliding it over the shafts back to front. (*Note:* The transfer casing must be detached from the main gearbox, to enable the output housing to clear the bell housing.) Tighten the connector nut with the link in alignment with the two selector shafts. By this method, the locking peg hole in the link pin is not necessarily vertical, a fact which will only appear when the assembly is complete; for this reason the use of a dummy housing is to be preferred.

53. Fit the output housing joint washer.

54. Fit the output shaft in its housing and slide the housing over the selector shafts. Select two-wheel drive in high transfer gear (through the aperture in the transfer casing) and push the housing home; secure with the seven nuts and spring washers.

55. If necessary, renew the bush in the front wheel drive control. Connect the operating rod to the lever and secure the locking peg by means of the plain washer and split pin.

56. Replace the control lever assembly and secure with the pivot screw.

57. Replace the dust cover and secure by means of three nuts, spring washers and distance pieces.

58. Replace the transfer lever and secure with the spring-loaded clevis pin and split pin. Secure the lever to the selector shaft by means of the control link, special nut and shakeproof washer.

59. Examine the outer diameter of the front axle drive flange for damage which may have caused failure of the original oil seal and rectify or renew the flange as necessary. Fit the flange and dust shield to the output shaft and secure it with a plain washer, castle nut and split pin.

60. Check the transfer gear change and dog clutch controls for correct operation and adjust as necessary.

    Adjust the front wheel drive control rod to ensure efficient extraction and replacement of the locking peg; when the gearbox is installed in the vehicle, it is important to avoid the spring becoming coilbound, as under such conditions the operation appears correct, but the peg is not extracted sufficiently to engage four-wheel drive.

61. Replace the transfer gear change cover plate and secure it by means of four set bolts and spring washers.

62. Assemble the main gear change lever.

    Fit the lever assembly, cover plate and rubber seal to the gearbox unit, securing them by means of two set bolts and spring washers at the bell housing and two nuts and spring washers at the gearbox top cover.

    Fit and adjust the reverse stop hinge.

63. Fill the main gearbox and transfer casing with oil of a suitable grade.

    The gearbox unit is now ready for installation in the vehicle.

1954-58 models
Gearbox and transfer box assembly

To remove   **Operation C/22**

1. Remove the hood, hard top or cab, for convenience in working.

2. Remove the front wheel drive control knob, locknut and spring; remove the knob and locknut from the transfer gear change lever.

3. Remove the floor board assembly and gearbox cover. Section R.

4. Remove the seat box complete. Section R.

5. **L.H.D. models only.** Remove the hand brake lever and linkage. Section H.

6. **R.H.D. models only.** Remove the hand brake rod and the expander rod from the relay lever.

7. Disconnect the front axle propeller shaft, rear axle propeller shaft and rear power take-off propeller shaft (if fitted), at the gearbox end.

8. **L.H.D. models only.** Remove the clutch cross-shaft rod from the connecting tubes.

9. **R.H.D. models only.** Disconnect the universal joint sleeve from the clutch relay shaft and the cross-shaft from the connecting tube. Slide the universal joint sleeve together with the rubber dust cover along the cross-shaft and remove the cross-shaft complete with universal joint sleeve and rubber dust cover.

10. Disconnect the speedometer cable at the gearbox and withdraw the cable clear of the gearbox. Disconnect the earth lead at the transfer box.

11. Remove the gearbox unit bearer bolts, top bearer rubbers, washers, shims and distance tubes.

12. Place a suitable sling around the gearbox unit, raise it approximately 1 inch (25 mm).

13. Place a jack under the rear end of the engine; this prevents any strain being taken on the primary pinion shaft.

14. Withdraw the gearbox unit and remove it from the vehicle.

To refit   **Operation C/24**

1. Reverse the removal procedure.

2. The nip on the gearbox unit mounting rubber pads is adjusted by the addition or removal of shims on the top of the central distance tube.

    The correct setting is with the top shim approximately 1/16 in. (1,5 mm) below the top face of the upper rubber pad.

    Note: The rear mounting brackets are adjustable laterally, to facilitate alignment with the mounting rubbers.

3. If necessary, refill the main gearbox, 2½ pints (1,5 litres) and transfer box, 4½ pints (2,5 litres) with oil.

4. Adjust the transmission brake. Section H.

5. Adjust the four-wheel drive control rod. Operation C/48.

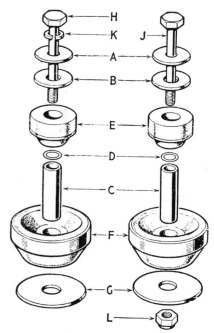

Fig. C-8—Gearbox unit mounting bolts and pads.

A—Plain washer (upper)	G—Plain washer (lower)
B—Rubber washer	H—Front bolt
C—Distance tube	J—Rear bolt
D—Shim	K—Spring washer
E—Top rubber	L—Self-locking nut
F—Bottom rubber	

All models

Main gearbox

To remove   **Operation C/26**

1. For removal procedure, see Operations C/16 and C/22.

To strip   **Operation C/28**

1. Mount the gearbox on a suitable stand.

2. Drain off the gearbox and transfer box oil.

3. Remove the main gear change lever assembly, then the reverse stop hinge. Operation C/50.

4. Remove the transfer box and front output shaft housing complete. Operation C/34.

Dismantle the main gearbox as follows:

5. Disconnect the connecting tube from the clutch cross-shaft.

6. Remove the dust-proofing grommets from the bell housing apertures.

7. Remove and strip the clutch withdrawal unit from the bell housing, Section B.

8. Remove the oil filler cap and joint washer from the gearbox top cover.

9. Remove the filler cap retaining clip.

10. Remove the plug retaining the 1st/2nd speed selector spring in the top cover and withdraw spring.

    Note: To prevent the selector ball falling into the gearbox, with the top cover removed, pack the hole with grease.

11. Remove the retaining plates for the side selector springs, the rubber grommets and the 3rd/4th and reverse selector springs.

12. Remove the selector cover plate from the gearbox top cover.

13. Remove the selector shaft end cover securing set bolts.

14. Remove the gearbox top cover, together with the upper selector end cover. Remove the two selector balls and locking plunger from the gearbox and the 1st/2nd speed selector ball from the top cover. Remove the 2nd gear stop from the top cover.

15. Select 1st gear (centre selector to rear); remove the reverse gear selector by lifting and turning the selector shaft one quarter of a turn to the left. Move the 1st/2nd speed selector to the neutral position and remove it; remove the 3rd/4th selector. Remove the lower selector end cover.

16. Withdraw the reverse selector fork and the sealing ring from the shaft.

17. Remove the 2nd speed stop from the end of the 1st/2nd selector shaft. Withdraw the selector fork and the sealing ring from the shaft.

18. Withdraw the 3rd/4th selector fork and the rubber sealing ring from the shaft.

19. Remove the castle nut from the front of the layshaft. (To lock the shaft for nut removal, select top and 2nd speeds simultaneously.)

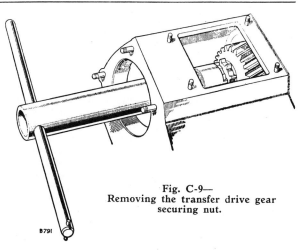

Fig. C-9—
Removing the transfer drive gear securing nut.

20. Remove the nut at the rear of the mainshaft retaining the transfer drive gear. Withdraw the gear and distance piece and oil flinger from the mainshaft.

21. Remove the bell housing complete with joint washer, tapping the layshaft out of the front bearing, so that it remains in the gearbox. Remove the needle roller bearing from the front end of the mainshaft. Remove the constant gear and conical distance piece from the bell housing.

22. Remove the layshaft front bearing retaining plate.

23. Remove the layshaft bearing plate; press out the layshaft front bearing, remove the pinion bearing retaining plate. Press out the primary pinion and bearing from the bell housing. Remove the nut securing the primary pinion bearing; press the bearing and shield off the pinion shaft. (The nut has a left-hand thread.)

24. Remove the synchronising clutch unit from the mainshaft and then withdraw the layshaft complete from the gearbox and strip it as follows:

25. Remove the distance sleeve. Remove the 3rd and 2nd speed gears. Remove the split ring retaining the 2nd speed gear. Press off the rear bearing and 1st speed gear.

26. Drive out the mainshaft complete from the rear and strip it as follows:

27. Remove the 1st speed gear. Prise out the spring ring inside the 3rd speed gear cone and discard it; remove the 3rd speed gear thrust washer and gear. Remove the distance sleeve and 2nd speed gear. Remove the peg locating the distance sleeve and withdraw the located 2nd speed gear thrust washer.

28. Remove the circlip retaining the mainshaft rear bearing housing to the rear face of the gearbox casing. Tap out the peg-located bearing housing complete from the rear. Remove the oil seal from the housing. Remove the circlip retaining the bearing in the housing and press out the bearing.

29. Drive out the reverse gear shaft from inside the gearbox; the gearbox casing must be warmed to facilitate this operation. Remove the reverse

gear and, if necessary, press out the bush from the gear.

30. To remove the outer race of the layshaft rear bearing from the gearbox casing, proceed as follows:

Make a plunger (preferably from hardwood) about 12 in. (300 mm) long and approximately 1 11/16 in. (43,50 mm) in diameter, i.e. to just fit into the outer race. Stand the gearbox casing on end and fill the race housing with thick oil, insert the plunger and tap it down sharply. In most cases the oil will force the outer ring upwards out of the casing; if necessary, the gearbox casing may be warmed to facilitate removal of the race.

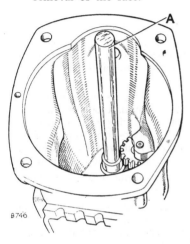

Fig. C-10—
Removing lay-shaft rear bearing outer race.
A—Plunger.

To assemble   Operation C/30

1. Wash all the component parts thoroughly and lay them out for inspection. Renew all lock-washers, split pins, spring rings and joint washers.

2. Check all the bearings for wear and damage, and renew them as necessary.

3. Check all the gears for damage marks and rectify or renew them as necessary. The constant, 2nd and 3rd speed gears are only supplied in mated pairs; all other gears may be replaced singly.

4. Examine the casing for signs of damage or cracks and renew it as necessary. A casing may also be scrap as a result of excessive wear in a bearing bore; such wear will be obvious during the course of assembly.

5. Press the layshaft rear bearing outer race into the gearbox casing with the lipped edge to the rear. It must be a *drive fit*. It may be necessary to warm the casing to assist in this operation.

1948-53 models

Press the layshaft rear bearing outer race into the gearbox casing with the lipped edge to the rear. It must be a *drive fit*. It may be necessary to warm the casing to assist in this operation.

6. If necessary, renew the reverse gear bush, bell out its extremities and ream it in position to .812 in. (20 mm). The bush should be a *press fit* in the gear. Place the reverse gear (with the smaller wheel to the rear) in position in the gearbox and drive the shaft through the gearbox casing and the gear. It will be necessary to warm the casing to assist in this operation. The shaft must be a *drive fit* in the casing.

1948-53 models

If necessary, renew the reverse gear bush and ream it in position to .812 in. (20,63 mm). Place the reverse gear (with the smaller wheel to the rear) on its shaft and drive the shaft into the gearbox casing. It may be necessary to warm the casing to assist in this operation. The shaft must be a *drive fit* in the casing.

7. Press the mainshaft rear bearing into the bearing housing until it abuts the flange in the housing bore; the bearing must be a *press fit* in the housing. Secure the bearing with a circlip.

8. Smear the outer diameter of the oil seal with jointing compound and press it into the other end of the housing, with the knife edge inwards.

9. Fit the location peg in the bearing housing and push the complete housing into the gearbox casing from the inside, until the housing flange abuts the casing. The housing must be a *push fit* in the casing; secure the housing with a circlip.

1948-53 models

Fit the location peg in the bearing housing and push the complete housing into the gearbox casing from the inside, until the housing flange abuts the casing. The housing must be a *push fit* in the casing. Secure the housing with a circlip at the rear face of the casing.

Mainshaft

10. If removed, replace the rear thrust washer. Do not fit the large bush locating peg at this stage.

11. Slide on the mainshaft bush with the large locating slot to the rear, together with the second speed gear, synchromesh cone to the rear.

12. Place the third speed gear on the bush with the gear wheel against the shoulder, and secure with the second thrust washer and the old spring ring.

13. While pressing the third speed gear hard against the bush shoulder, the end-float of the second speed gear, measured between the gear and the bush shoulder, should be .004 to .007 in. (0,10-0,17 mm).

The third speed gear end-float should be the same, measured with the second speed gear pressed hard against the bush shoulder.

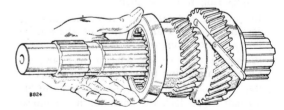

Fig. C-11—Measuring mainshaft gear end-float.

14. If the end-float of either gear is insufficient, a new mainshaft bush must be fitted; if excessive, it may be reduced by rubbing down the end face of the bush.

    Ensure that the correct end face of the bush is rubbed down.

15. Remove the spring ring, take off the thrust washer, bush and gears, and replace the bush and washer, securing with the old spring ring.

16. An end-float of .001 to .008 in. (0,02-0,02 mm) for the mainshaft bush is allowed, but this should be kept as low as possible by the use of the thrust washers, which are supplied in four thicknesses: .125 in., .128 in., .130 in. and .135 in.

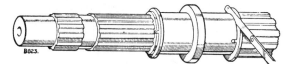

Fig. C-12—Measuring mainshaft bush end-float

17. When the end-floats are correct, fit the rear thrust washer and the bush locating peg. Assemble the bush and gears and slide on the front thrust washer with its groove in line with the small slot in the bush.

18. Secure the assembly with a *new* spring ring.

19. Slide the first speed gear and synchronising clutch on to the rear of the shaft, and drive the mainshaft into the rear bearing, securing with the circlip.

Layshaft

20. Slide the first speed layshaft gear over the splines on the rear of the layshaft with the chamfered end of the teeth to the front and fit the rear bearing inner race on to the shaft. The bearing must be a *tap fit* on the shaft.

    Fit the split ring retaining the 2nd speed gear and slide the gear on to the shaft, with its flange to the front, over the split ring; ensure that the ring beds well into its groove and does not foul or tilt the gear. Slide the 3rd speed gear on to the shaft with its flange to the front, followed by the distance tube, constant gear and conical distance piece. Press the layshaft front bearing on to the end of the layshaft and lock up the whole assembly tightly by means of the plain washer and castle nut. Ensure that the layshaft assembly is locked up tightly and that the gears are not tilted by excessive run-out, either on their faces or those of the distance sleeve.

21. Should the gears have any end-float, this condition must be rectified by fitting a conical distance piece of suitable thickness, chosen from the range available, i.e. .312 in. (7,90 mm), .332 in. (8,40 mm) and .352 in. (8,91 mm) overall thickness.

22. Remove the castle nut, plain washer, bearing, conical distance piece and constant gear from the end of the shaft and fit the rest of the assembly in the gearbox casing, engaging the constant mesh gears.

23. Assemble the primary shaft as follows:
    Press the primary pinion bearing on to the pinion shaft until it abuts the shoulder. The bearing must be a *light press fit* on the shaft. Secure the bearing by means of the lockwasher and locknut.

Assemble the bell housing as follows:

24. Press the primary shaft and bearing into the bell housing. The bearing must be a *press fit* in the housing. It may be necessary to warm the bell housing to assist in this operation.

25. Fit the pinion bearing retaining plate.

26. Press the layshaft front bearing into the bell housing until it is flush with the rear face of the housing. The bearing must be a *press fit* in the housing; it may be necessary to warm the bell housing to assist in this operation. Fit the layshaft bearing plate.

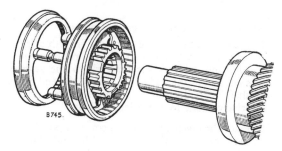

Fig. C-13—Fitting synchronising clutch assembly.

27. Check and renew the synchronising clutch unit detent spring, if necessary. Fit the synchronising clutch assembly over the mainshaft splines, with the recessed portion towards the 3rd speed gear (Fig. C-13).

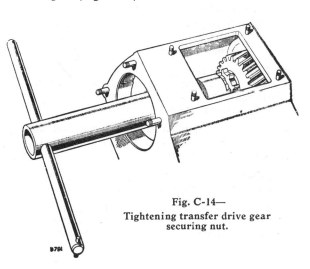

Fig. C-14—
Tightening transfer drive gear securing nut.

28. Place the needle roller bearing over the front of the mainshaft and place the conical distance piece and constant gear in position in mesh with the primary pinion on the rear face of the bell housing. Offer the bell housing and joint washer to the gearbox casing, locating the dowel and entering the housing lip into the casing; the front end of the layshaft is a *sliding fit* in the bearing inner member. Secure the housing to the gearbox casing.

Special fitting bolts are used for securing and locating the gearbox to bell housing.

These bolts are accurately machined and **must not** be replaced by standard bolts.

29. Lock the layshaft by selecting top and 2nd speeds simultaneously and secure it tightly. Fit the retaining plate over the layshaft front bearing.

30. Examine the distance piece for the rear end of the mainshaft, this acts also as a track for the oil seal and must be rectified or renewed if damaged in any way on its outer diameter. Place the distance piece and oil flinger over the shaft and fit the transfer drive gear with its splined flange to the rear; secure the gear with the tab washer, shim and nut using special spanner Part No. 263056 (Fig. C-14).

Assemble the main selectors as follows:

31. Fit the rubber sealing ring and 3rd/4th selector fork to the selector shaft; fit the rubber sealing ring and 1st/2nd selector fork to the selector shaft and fit the 2nd speed stop to the end of the shaft. Fit the rubber sealing ring and reverse selector fork to the selector shaft.

32. Place the lower selector end cover in position on the gearbox. Fit the 3rd/4th and 1st/2nd selectors; move the 1st/2nd selector to the 1st speed position (to the rear) and fit the reverse gear selector; move the 1st/2nd speed selector to the neutral position.

33. Fit the locking plungers between the selector shafts.

34. Fit the gearbox top cover. Fit the upper selector end cover and secure both halves.

    Note: The gearbox casing and top cover are machined together and must not be renewed separately.

35. Replace the reverse and 3rd/4th speed selector balls and springs (the reverse spring is the stronger of the two); fit the rubber grommets and retaining plates.

36. Replace the 1st/2nd speed selector ball and spring in the top cover and fit the filler cap spring plug and spring.

37. Ensure that the operation of the selector mechanism is correct.

38. Fit the set bolt and locknut (acting as a 2nd speed stop) in the top cover. Select 2nd gear and adjust the stop bolt so that there is .002 in. (0,05 mm) clearance between the bolt head and the stop on the selector shaft; tighten the locknut (Fig. C-15). The reverse stop bolt cannot be adjusted until the transfer box has been fitted. Operation C/40.

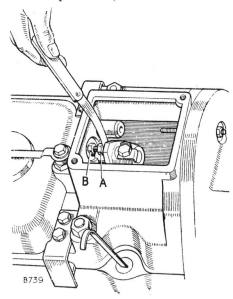

Fig. C-15—Adjusting 2nd speed gear bolt.
A—Stop bolt.   B—Locknut.

39. Assemble the clutch withdrawal unit. Section B.

40. Fit the clutch withdrawal unit to the bell housing.

41. Fit the dust-proofing grommets.

42. Fit the connecting tube to the clutch cross-shaft.

43. Refit the transfer box and front output shaft housing complete. Operation C/40.

44. Refit main gear change lever. Operation C/50.

45. Fit and adjust **reverse stop hinge**. Operation C/52.

To refit   **Operation C/32**

1. Replace the complete gearbox and transfer box assembly in the vehicle. Operation C/24.

Transfer box
To remove   **Operation C/34**

1. Drain off the transfer box oil.

2. Remove the floor board assembly and gearbox cover. Section R.

3. Remove seat box. Section R.

4. Disconnect the front propeller shaft at the output shaft housing end.

5. Disconnect the rear propeller shaft and rear power take-off propeller shaft (if fitted) at the gearbox end.

6. **R.H.D. models.** Disconnect the hand brake expander rod from the relay lever.

7. **L.H.D. models.** Disconnect the hand brake rods from the relay lever. Remove the hand brake cross-shaft. Section H.

8. **R.H.D. models.** Disconnect the universal joint sleeve from the clutch relay shaft and slide the rubber dust cover and universal joint sleeve along the cross-shaft.

9. **L.H.D. models.** Disconnect the outer connecting tube from the clutch cross-shaft rod and relay shaft and slide the connecting tube towards the bell housing.

10. Disconnect the speedometer cable.

11. Remove the transfer box output shaft driving flange complete with brake drum.

12. Remove the brake back plate and shield from the speedometer drive housing.

13. Remove the transfer box bottom cover and joint washer.

14. Remove the nut and spring washer securing the intermediate gear shaft retaining plate; extract the retaining plate stud and remove the plate.

15. Remove the mainshaft rear bearing housing—or, if fitted, the power take-off drive unit assembly (Section T) and joint washer, and extract the intermediate gear shaft, complete with rubber seal, using special extractor Part No. 262772.

16. Remove the intermediate gear cluster through the base of the casing, complete with a needle roller bearing at each end of its bore. Remove the bearings from the gear. Remove also the thrust washer and if fitted, a shim.

17. Disconnect the earth lead at the transfer box.

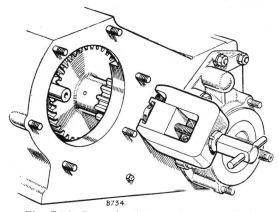

Fig. C-16—Removing intermediate gear shaft.

18. Disconnect the two gearbox unit bearer bolts, the top plain washers, rubber washers, shims, if fitted, top rubbers and distance tubes.

19. Remove the transfer lever from the bracket fixed to the bell housing.

20. Position a jack under the gearbox and raise it sufficiently to enable withdrawal of transfer box and front output shaft housing unit.

21. Detach the transfer casing from the main gearbox, noting *that the three self-locking securing nuts are located inside the transfer casing.* Remove the transfer casing and front output shaft housing unit complete from the vehicle.

To strip Operation C/36

1. Remove the speedometer drive pinion unit. Withdraw the pinion from the sleeve. If necessary, remove the oil seal from the pinion sleeve. Remove rubber 'O' ring if fitted.

2. Remove the speedometer drive housing complete with shims, which should be preserved. If necessary, remove the front output shaft oil seal from the housing.

3. Withdraw the speedometer drive worm from the transfer box output shaft; this is a *sliding fit* on the shaft.

4. Remove the front output shaft housing complete with output shaft, front wheel drive dog clutch, dog clutch selector shaft and fork and the joint washer.

5. Remove the top cover plate from the transfer box.

6. Remove the transfer gear selector fork and shaft.

7. Remove the circlip retaining the front bearing outer race in the transfer casing.

8. Drive out the transfer box output shaft rear bearing outer race from the transfer casing.

   Note: Protect the transfer casing output shaft bearing bores with pads of rag to prevent damage during the following operations.

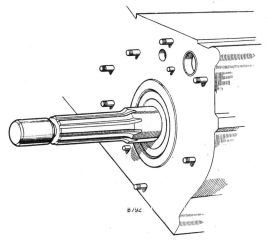

Fig. C-17—Fitting transfer box output shaft protection cap.

9. Fit the protection cap (Part No. 243241) over the threaded portion of the transfer box output shaft and tap the shaft forward as far as possible to drive the front bearing outer race from the casing. Slide the shaft to the rear and insert an appropriate packing piece (Fig. C-18), between the front bearing rollers and the outer race; this packing piece may be fashioned from

a scrap bearing outer race, the outer diameter of which should be ground to give free movement in the transfer box, and a portion cut away so that it may be fitted over the shaft. Tap the shaft forward again, when the bearing outer race should be driven clear of the casing.

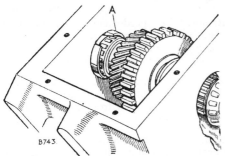

Fig. C-18—Removing transfer box output shaft front bearing outer race.
A—Packing piece.

10. Part the front bearing inner race from the circlip retaining the high speed gear thrust washer by means of a mild steel chisel (Fig. C-19), then drive the front bearing inner race from the output shaft by means of brass drift.

11. Remove the circlip and thrust washer from the output shaft in front of the high speed gear, and push the output shaft through the gears clear of the casing; the high and low speed gears can then be withdrawn through the bottom of the casing.

12. If required, remove the rear bearing inner race from the output shaft by means of a suitable extractor.

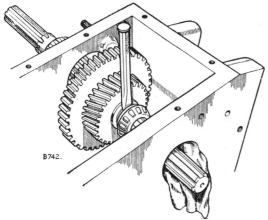

Fig. C-19—Removing transfer box output shaft front bearing inner race.

13. Remove the top cover plate or the power take-off selector assembly (Section T) and joint washer from the transfer casing.

14. Remove the mainshaft rear bearing assembly or the power take-off drive unit assembly and dog clutch (Section T) and joint washer from the rear of the transfer casing.

15. Remove the circlip securing the bearing in the mainshaft housing and withdraw the retaining plate and needle roller bearing. If necessary, remove the hardened steel bush from the housing, when the second plate can be withdrawn.

16. If necessary, remove the engine support brackets from the transfer casing.

17. If necessary, remove the dog clutch selector shaft bush from the transfer casing. If necessary, remove the reverse gear stop bolt and locknut from the transfer casing.

18. If necessary, remove the driving flange complete from the brake drum.

19. If necessary, remove the dust shield, circlip, bolts and retaining plate from the flange.

To assemble   **Operation C/38**

1. If necessary, renew the oilite bush in the transfer casing which carries the dog clutch selector shaft. The bush is made to an *interference* fit in the casing, and must be reamed to 1.148 in. (29,17 mm) after fitting.

2. Fit the two output shaft gears on the shaft and check that they mesh easily at every point of a complete revolution.

3. Remove the two gears from the shaft and place them in position in the transfer casing; the smaller (high-speed gear) should be fitted at the front with its engaging teeth to the rear and the large (low-speed gear) at the rear with its selector flange to the rear.

4. Insert the output shaft through the casing and gears from the rear, engaging the splines in the low-speed gear.

5. Fit the located thrust washer in front of the high-speed gear and secure it with a circlip.

6. Fit the inner members of the two output shaft bearings to the shaft (smaller bearing at the front). The bearings must be a *light press* fit on the shaft.

7. Fit the front bearing outer race and secure it with a circlip. The bearing must be a *drive fit* in the transfer casing.

8. Fit the rear bearing outer race to the transfer casing. The bearing must be a *drive fit* in the casing.

9. Place the protection cap (Part No. 243241) on the threaded portion of transfer box output shaft (Fig. C-17) and drive the shaft until the front bearing is hard against the circlip. Lightly tap the rear bearing outer race until all the end-float of the output shaft has been taken up.

10. Ensure that the high speed gear has .004 to .008 in. (0,10 to 0,20 mm) end-float on the shaft, by checking with feeler gauges between the two gears. The end-float can be increased if necessary, by grinding the located thrust washer.

11. The end-float of the transfer box output shaft must be adjusted to zero by means of shims between the transfer casing and speedometer drive housing. (Fitted at a later stage.)

12. Engage the transfer gear selector fork with the groove in the low speed gear, with the threaded end of the pinch bolt hole to the left-hand side.

13. Slide the selector shaft through the transfer casing and fork and secure the fork.

14. If necessary, renew the transfer box output shaft oil seal in the speedometer drive housing, with the knife edge inwards. The outer diameter of the seal should be smeared with jointing compound and the housing warmed before assembly.

15. If necessary, renew the oil seal in the speedometer drive pinion sleeve; the seal should be fitted with the knife edge inwards. Fit the pinion in the sleeve and fit the assembly to the drive housing, with the "flat" on the sleeve to the bottom. The pinion should be a *sliding fit* in the sleeve. Check that the drive functions correctly. Replace rubber 'O' ring.

16. Slide the speedometer drive worm over the transfer box output shaft with its conical end inwards and fit the dowel-located speedometer drive housing to the transfer casing, complete with suitable shims for adjustment of the transfer box output shaft bearing end-float. The shims, which are available .003 in. (0,08 mm), .005 in. (0,13 mm), .010 in. (0,25 mm) and .015 in. (0,38 mm) thick, should be selected so that the face of the rear bearing lies .002 in. (0,05 mm) below the face of the outer shim, Fig. C-20. Secure the drive housing to the transfer casing. Drive the output shaft towards the rear and ensure that it turns quite freely, but that no end-float is present; check also that the high speed gear end-float is retained.

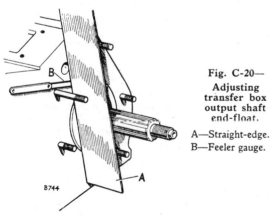

Fig. C-20—
Adjusting
transfer box
output shaft
end-float.

A—Straight-edge.
B—Feeler gauge.

17. Place the two intermediate shaft thrust washers in the transfer casing and retain them with a film of grease; the washers should be fitted with their bronze faces inwards and located in the casing by means of the tabs.

18. Fit the two needle roller bearings in the intermediate cluster gear and offer the gear into position, meshing it with the mainshaft and output shaft gears, i.e., with the larger wheel to the front.

19. Fit the intermediate shaft, from the rear through the casing, thrust washers and gear, tapping it lightly home when the register engages. The shaft must be a *light tap fit* in the casing.

20. Ensure that the gear has .005 in. to .010 in. (0,12 to 0,25 mm) end-float in the casing; if incorrect, the float can be adjusted by grinding the thrust washers or fitting a shim (.010 in. thick) behind one washer. When the end-float is correct, withdraw the shaft and remove the gear cluster from the casing complete with needle rollers and thrust washers.

21. Examine the outer diameter of the rear axle drive flange for damage which may have caused failure of the transfer box output shaft oil seal and rectify or renew the flange as necessary.

22. If removed, insert the six fitting brake drum securing bolts in the outer flange holes and fit the retaining plate over the flange. Fit the four propeller shaft securing bolts in the inner holes and secure them with a circlip.

23. Fit the dust excluder over the outer diameter of the rear axle drive flange, with the open end towards the flange.

24. Replace the front output shaft housing assembly. Operation C/44.

25. Fit the retaining plate and hardened steel bush in the mainshaft bearing housing; fit the needle roller bearing and second retaining plate and secure with a circlip.

26. Fit the complete bearing housing (or power take-off drive unit—see Section T) to the transfer casing, together with a joint washer.

27. Fit the top cover plate (or power take-off selector assembly—See Section T) to the transfer casing, together with a joint washer.

28. Fit the gearbox unit support brackets to the transfer casing.

To refit   **Operation C/40**

1. Fit the complete transfer casing and joint washer to the main gearbox, locating it with two dowels. NOTE—*Three self-locking nuts inside the transfer casing.*

2. Replace the intermediate shaft retaining plate stud in the transfer casing.

3. Fit the intermediate shaft and cluster gear. Operation C/38—(17) and (18).

4. Fit the intermediate shaft together with the retaining plate in its deepest slot through the casing, thrust washers and gear, tapping it lightly home when the register engages.

A rubber seal is fitted to the intermediate gear shaft. This seal must be examined for wear and signs of deterioration. Renew if necessary, before refitment.

5. Fit the transfer casing bottom cover, together with a joint washer and drain plug.

6. Fit the complete transmission brake (Section H) and shield, to the speedometer drive housing, with the expander rod on the right-hand side.

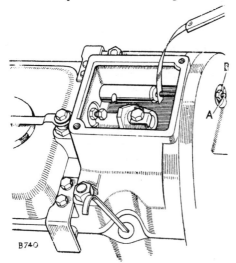

Fig. C-21—Adjusting reverse gear stop bolt.
A—Stop bolt.   B—Locknut.

7. Slide the complete drive flange over the front output shaft and secure.

8. Ensure that the drive flange abuts the speedometer drive worm and gives a positive drive to the pinion.

9. Fit the transmission brake drum. Adjust the brake—Section H.

10. Select reverse gear in the main gearbox, and adjust the stop bolt in the transfer casing so that there is .002 in. (0,05 mm) clearance between the selector shaft and bolt.

11. Replace the oil level dipstick and refill with oil. Fit the main gearbox selector cover plate.

12. Complete the assembly by reversing the removal procedure.

13. Adjust the gearbox unit mounting rubbers. Operation C/24.

14. Adjust the front wheel drive rod. Operation C/44.

1954-58 models

Front output shaft housing assembly

To remove   **Operation C/42**

1. Drain off the transfer box oil.

2. Remove floor board assembly and gearbox cover. Section R.

3. Remove seat box central panel.

4. Remove front propeller shaft. Section D.

5. Remove the hand-brake expander rod from the relay lever.

6. **R.H.D. models only.** Disconnect the universal joint sleeve from the clutch relay shaft and the cross-shaft from the connecting tube. Slide the universal joint sleeve together with the rubber dust cover along the cross-shaft and remove the cross-shaft complete with universal joint sleeve and rubber dust cover.

7. **L.H.D. models only.** Remove the clutch cross-shaft rod from the connecting tubes.

8. Remove the gearbox mounting securing nuts, plain washers, rubber washers, shims (if fitted) and top rubbers.

9. Remove the transfer control link from the selector shaft; remove the transfer lever.

10. Remove the dust cover from the front of the output shaft housing.

11. Remove the front wheel drive control lever assembly. Remove the locking peg from the lever. Disconnect the operating rod from the lever (spring-loaded clevis). If necessary, press out the bush from the lever.

12. Place a jack under the gearbox and raise it as much as possible and remove the front output shaft housing complete with output shaft, front wheel drive dog clutch, the dog clutch selector shaft and fork and a joint washer. Withdraw the dog clutch selector shaft and dog clutch from the rear of the housing. Remove the top cover plate from the transfer box, hold in low transfer and slide the output shaft housing downwards and to the rear, and remove from under the vehicle. Leave the transfer selector shaft and link in position protruding from the transfer box.

To strip   **Operation C/44**

1. Remove the block from the transfer selector shaft.

2. Slide the following parts from the transfer selector shaft:—
Link, link pin and connector assembly, spring, spring locating bush, and distance tube.

3. Detach the link from the link pin.
   Note: The connector should not be removed from the link pin unless absolutely necessary, as difficulty will be experienced in effecting correct alignment on reassembly.

4. Carefully remove the front axle drive flange complete with mudshield, avoiding damage to the oil seal.

5. Remove the output shaft from the output shaft housing.

6. Remove the block from the dog clutch selector shaft.

7. Slide the two springs and selector fork from the dog clutch selector shaft.

8. If necessary, remove the two bushes from the selector fork boss.

9. If necessary, remove the spigot bush from the rear end of the front output shaft.

10. Remove the oil seal retainer complete with oil seal, joint washer and mudshield.

11. If necessary, remove the oil seal from the retainer.

12. If necessary, remove the mudshield from the oil seal retainer.

13. If necessary, withdraw the output shaft front bearing from the front output shaft housing.

14. Remove the rubber seals in front output shaft housing for transfer gear change shaft and four-wheel drive locking pin.

To assemble   **Operation C/46**

1. If necessary, replace the front output shaft front bearing in the front output shaft housing. The bearing must be a *push fit* on the shaft and a *light drive fit* in the housing. Renew the shaft, bearing and housing as necessary.

   Examine the rubber seals for transfer gear change shaft and four-wheel drive locking pin, for signs of wear or deterioration. Renew seals if necessary and replace in respective bores.

2. If removed, fit a new oil seal in the retainer with its knife edge inwards. The external diameter of the oil seal must be smeared with jointing compound and the retainer warmed before assembly.

3. If removed, replace the mudshield on the oil seal retainer.

4. If removed, replace the spigot bush in the rear end of the front output shaft, pressing it in flush with the face of the shaft.

   The bush must be reamed in position to .875 in. (22,2 mm), and should be a *sliding fit* on the transfer box output shaft.

5. If removed, renew the two oilite bushes in the dog clutch selector fork boss, pressing them flush with the end faces of the boss. They must be reamed in position to .625 in. (15,8 mm) and should be a *sliding fit* on the selector shaft.

6. Check the two dog clutch selector springs and renew as necessary. Free length should be 2.75 in. (69,8 mm).

7. Check the transfer selector shaft spring and renew as necessary. Free length should be 7.156 in. (181,76 mm).

8. Replace the oil seal retainer on the front output shaft housing.

9. Fit the two springs and selector fork (crank to the rear) over the dog clutch selector shaft.

10. Replace the block on the selector shaft.

11. If the connector has been detached from the link pin, replace it with the hole for the locking peg vertical and the cutaway on the link pin underneath; ensure that the connector is square with the pin and secure *lightly* with the nut and shakeproof washer.

12. Secure the link to the link pin by means of the special screw, castle nut and split pin. The threaded end of the screw must be downwards and the shorter end of the link towards the transfer selector, with the longer arm of the jaw at the opposite end to the rear.

13. Replace the transfer shaft selector spring and plunger and secure with the plug and joint washer.

14. Slide the following parts on to the transfer selector shaft:—

    Distance tube, spring locating bush with its smaller diameter to the front, and spring. Compress the spring and fit the link and connector assembly until the block is over the hole in the shaft. Fit the special screw from the bottom, through the coupling jaw, block and selector shaft and secure with the castle nut and split pin.

15. If they have been separated, the position of the connector and link pin should now be adjusted as follows:—

16. (a) The most efficient method of carrying out this operation is to use a dummy front output shaft housing with a large aperture in the side through which the connector securing nut can be tightened. Place the dummy housing over the selector shafts and locate the link pin by means of the locking peg. Tighten the connector securing nut, withdraw the peg, and remove the housing.

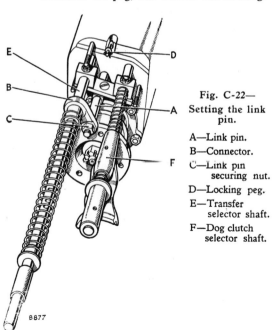

Fig. C-22—
Setting the link pin.

A—Link pin.
B—Connector.
C—Link pin securing nut.
D—Locking peg.
E—Transfer selector shaft.
F—Dog clutch selector shaft.

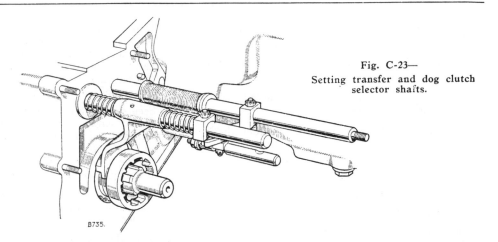

Fig. C-23—
Setting transfer and dog clutch selector shafts.

B735.

(b) If a dummy housing is not available, the actual output shaft housing can be used to align the selectors by sliding it over the shafts back to front. Proceed as follows:— Remove the pinch bolt securing the selector fork to the transfer selector shaft and withdraw the shaft. Engage the transfer selector shaft, link pin and dog clutch selector shaft into the front face of the front output shaft housing ensuring that the link engages the pivot screws of the transfer and dog clutch selector shafts. Locate the link pin in the housing by means of locking peg and tighten the connector nut.

Remove the locking peg and withdraw the shafts and link pin from the housing. Slide the transfer selector shaft through the transfer casing and fork, and secure the fork.

17. Fit the output shaft in its housing. Examine the outer diameter of the front axle drive flange for damage which may have caused failure of the original oil seal; rectify or renew as neces-sary. Fit the flange and dust shield to the front output shaft.

To refit   **Operation C/48**

1. Fit the front output shaft housing joint washer.

2. Engage the dog clutch selector fork with the groove in the locking dog.

3. Engage the selector shaft into the bush in the transfer box, and at the same time slide the dog clutch over the splines on the transfer box output shaft, ensuring that the link engages the screw correctly.

4. Select low transfer (through the aperture in the transfer box). Place the housing over the selector shafts (from under) and secure to the transfer casing, picking up the earth lead under one of the nuts.

5. If necessary, renew the bush in the front wheel drive control. Connect the operating rod and locking peg to the lever.

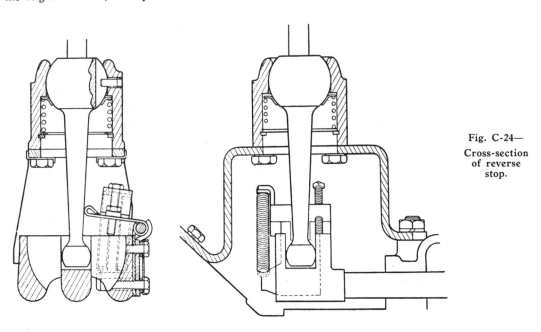

Fig. C-24—
Cross-section of reverse stop.

6. Replace the control lever assembly.

7.*The joint faces of dust cover shield and front output shaft housing should be smeared with Bostik sealing before refitment. Secure cover using three set bolts.

8. Replace the transfer lever. Secure the lever to the selector shaft by means of the control link.

9. Reconnect hand brake expander rod to the relay lever.

10. Replace the transfer gear change cover plate.

11. Refill the transfer box with oil of the correct grade.

12. Complete the assembly by reversing the sequence of removal operations.

13. Adjust the gearbox unit mounting rubbers. Operation C/24.

14. Adjust the front wheel drive rod to ensure sufficient extraction and replacement of the locking peg; proceed as follows:—

(a) Depress the four-wheel drive control rod.

(b) Screw down the knob locknut until the compressed spring length is $2\frac{5}{16}$ in.—$\frac{1}{16}$ (58,73 mm—1,58).

(c) Fit knob and tighten locknut.

1954-58 models

Main gear change lever

To overhaul   **Operation C/50**

1. Remove front wheel drive control knob, locknut and spring; remove the knob and locknut from the transfer gear change lever.

2. Remove the floor board assembly and gearbox cover—Section R.

3. Remove the gear change mounting plate and gear change lever complete.

4. Remove the gear change lever housing from the mounting plate.

5. Remove the circlip from the lever housing and draw out the spring retaining washer, spring and spherical seat; withdraw the gear lever from the housing. If necessary, remove the lever ball locating pin from the housing.

6. Detach the two springs from the reverse stop hinge. Remove the reverse stop hinge (complete with adjusting screw and locknut) and the spring bracket from the reverse selector.

7. Renew the worn components.

8. Replace the lever ball locating pin in the housing (if removed on stripping) and secure it by staking.

9. Fit the gear change lever in the housing; replace the spherical seat, spring and retaining washer and secure the whole with a circlip.

10. Fit the housing to the mounting plate with the locating pin on the right-hand side.

11. Fit the reverse stop hinge and spring bracket to the reverse selector and secure them by means of two plain washers, one lockplate and two set bolts (the plain washers should be fitted under the lockplate). Replace the two reverse stop springs.

12. Fit the mounting plate to the gearbox unit.

13. Adjust the reverse stop. Operation C/52.

14. Replace the floor board assembly and gearbox cover—Section R.

15. Replace the front wheel drive control knob, locknut and spring; replace the locknut and knob on the transfer gear change lever.

1954-58 models

Reverse stop

To adjust   **Operation C/52**

1. The screw and locknut on the reverse stop hinge should be adjusted so that:—

(a) The hinge rides easily up the gear lever when reverse gear is selected, and

(b) Appreciable resistance is felt on moving the gear lever to the reverse position.

2. This adjustment should be carried out on any gearbox removed for attention, before the gearbox cover is fitted.

3. It can be carried out at any time after:
selecting reverse gear and sliding the access panel up the front wheel drive control rod.

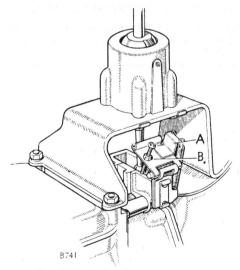

B741

Fig. C-25—Adjusting reverse stop.
A—Adjusting screw.   B—Locknut.

* On 1954-55 models locate three distance pieces to securing studs and refit dust cover.

DEFECT LOCATION
Symptom, Cause and Remedy

A—GEARBOX NOISY IN NEUTRAL

1. Primary pinion bearing worn—*Renew*.
2. Constant mesh gears incorrectly matched or badly worn—*Renew*.
3. Layshaft bearing worn—*Renew*.
4. Insufficient oil in gearbox or incorrect grade of oil—*Replenish*.

B—GEARBOX NOISY IN GEAR.

1. Worn speedometer gears—*Renew*.
2. If the gearbox is noisy in all gears except top, the constant mesh gears may be worn or incorrectly paired or the layshaft bearings may be worn—*Renew the constant mesh gears or the layshaft bearings*.
3. Noise in either the 1st, 2nd or 3rd speed gear only, due to wear—*Renew the gear or pair of gears*.
4. Noise in all gears in all probability denotes worn primary or mainshaft bearings—*Renew bearings and check gear teeth for wear*.

C—OIL LEAKS FROM THE GEARBOX

1. Lubricant level too high—*Correct level*.
2. Damaged, incorrectly fitted or missing joint washers—*Renew*.
3. Damaged or incorrectly fitted oil seals—*Renew*.
4. Drain or level plugs loose or threads damaged—*Rectify*.
5. Cracked or broken gearbox housing—*Renew*.

D—DIFFICULTY IN ENGAGING GEARS

1. Incorrect adjustment of the gear change mechanism—*Adjust*.
2. Failure to release the clutch completely—*In the hands of the operator*.
3. Clutch spinning or sticking on the pinion shaft—*Section B*.

E—DIFFICULTY IN DISENGAGING GEARS

1. Incorrect adjustment of the gear change mechanism—*Adjust*.
2. Failure to release the clutch completely—*In the hands of the operator*.
3. Distorted or damaged mainshaft splines—*Renew*.

F—DIFFICULTY IN ENGAGING REVERSE

1. Bush loose in gear—*Replace*.
2. Faulty stop setting on selector forks—*Adjust*.

G—GEAR LEVER GOING INTO REVERSE TOO EASILY AND NOT INTO FIRST

1. Stop requires setting on selector shafts—*Adjust*.

H—TRANSFER OF OIL FROM TRANSFER BOX TO GEARBOX, TO CLUTCH

1. Faulty oil seal, gearbox to transfer box—*Fit new seal and sleeve*.

J—JUMPING OUT OF HIGH TRANSFER

1. Selector spring too weak—*Renew*.

K—JUMPING OUT OF LOW TRANSFER

1. Transfer selector fork assembled wrongly on shaft—*Assemble fork with set towards rear of vehicle*.
2. Too much end-float on intermediate gear—*Adjust*.
3. Selector spring too weak—*Renew*.

L—NOISY TRANSFER BOX

1. Too much end-float on intermediate gear—*Adjust*.
2. End-float on output shaft—*Adjust*.
3. Worn bearings—*Renew*.

M—CANNOT ENGAGE FOUR-WHEEL DRIVE

1. Maladjustment of return spring for yellow knob—*Adjust*.
2. Shafts sticking in bores of casing—*Rectify*.

GENERAL DATA

Main gearbox:

Type .... Four speed and reverse
Oil capacity .... $2\frac{1}{2}$ pints (1,5 litres)
Dipstick position .... L.H. rear of casing

Gear ratios:

Top .... 1 to 1
Third .... 1.377 to 1
Second .... 2.043 to 1
First .... 2.996 to 1
Reverse .... 2.547 to 1

Transfer gearbox:

Type .... Two-speed gear in main gearbox output, in unit with main gearbox

Oil capacity .... $4\frac{1}{2}$ pints (2,5 litres)

Gear ratios:

High .... 1.148 to 1
Low .... 2.888 to 1

Overall gear ratios:

MAIN GEARBOX	TRANSFER BOX			
	High ratio		Low ratio	
	Axles numbered up to 861319	Axles numbered from 861320 onwards	Axles numbered up to 861319	Axles numbered from 861320 onwards
Top gear	5.612	5.396	14.122	13,578
Third gear, gearboxes numbered up to 06106000	8.362	8.039	21.042	20.229
Third gear, gearboxes numbered from 06106001	—	7.435	—	18.707
Second gear	11.466	11.026	28.852	27.742
First gear	16.814	16.171	42.310	40.688
Reverse gear	14.295	13.745	35.970	34.585

Front axle drive:

Type .... Dog clutch in transfer box
To engage .... Depress yellow knob on gearbox cover
To disengage .... Automatic by selecting low transfer, then reverting to high transfer. Automatically engaged on selection of low transfer

Speedometer drive:

Ratio .... 5 to 11
Position .... At rear of transfer box

Transmission brake:

Type .... Mechanical. (See Section H.) On transfer box output shaft.

DETAIL DATA

Main gearbox:

Reverse gear bush—

    Reamed bore   .... .812 in. + .001 (20 mm + 0,025 mm)

Mainshaft bush—

    Fit in gears   .... .0015 to .002 in. (0,037 to 0,051 mm) clearance

    Fit on shaft   .... .005 to .002 in. (0,0125 to 0,051 mm) clearance

    End-float   .... .001 to .008 in. (0,025 to 0,20 mm)

2nd and 3rd speed gears—

    End-float on distance sleeve   .... .004 to .007 in. (0,10 to 0,177 mm)

Synchronising clutch-load   .... 15-20 lb. (6,5-9 kg)

2nd gear stop—

    Adjustment   .... .002 in. (0,05 mm) clearance

Reverse gear stop—

    Adjustment   .... .002 in. (0,05 mm) clearance

Transfer gearbox:

Dog clutch selector shaft bush—

Reamed bore:

Large bush   .... 1.148 in. — .001 (29,17 mm — 0,025)

Small bush (with freewheel only) .... .625 in. — .0005 (15,8 mm — 0,012)

Output shaft front and rear bearings—

    End-float   .... Zero

High-speed gear—

    End-float   .... .004 to .008 in. (0,10 to 0,20 mm) (after adjusting output shaft end-float)

Intermediate gear—

    End-float   .... .005 to .010 in. (0,12 to 0,25 mm)

Front output shaft housing assembly:

Transfer selector shaft, spring—

    Free length   .... 7.156 in. (181,76 mm)

    Length in position   3.875 in. (98,43 mm)

    Load in position   .... 24 lb. (10,89 kg)

Dog clutch selector springs—

    Free length   .... 2.75 in. (69,8 mm)

    Solid length   .... .64 in. (16,2 mm)

    Maximum load   .... 13 lb. (5,9 kg)

Section D – PROPELLER SHAFTS – ALL MODELS

INDEX

				Page
Data, general	....	....	....	D-3
Defect location	....	....	....	D-3
Propeller shafts	....	....	....	D-1

LIST OF ILLUSTRATIONS

Fig.		Page	Fig.		Page
D-1	Construction of propeller shaft	D-1	D-4	Removing the splined sleeve or shaft	D-2
D-2	Removing a yoke bearing, Stage 1	D-2	D-5	Removing the flange yoke	D-2
D-3	Removing a yoke bearing, Stage 2	D-2			

Propeller shaft (front and rear axle drives)

Wear on the thrust faces of the bearings can be located by testing the lift in the joint, either by hand or with the aid of a length of wood suitably pivoted.

Any circumferential movement of the shaft relative to the flange yokes indicates wear in the roller bearings or the splined joint.

Lubricant may seep from the bearings after a lengthy period of service, owing to failure of the bearing seals.

If an oil leak is severe, or is neglected, failure of the needle roller bearings may result.

If any of these defects are apparent, the complete shaft should be removed from the vehicle and rectified as described.

To remove   Operation D/2

1. Disconnect the propeller shaft from the differential input flange.

2. Disconnect the propeller shaft from the transfer box output flange.

3. Withdraw the propeller shaft complete.

Propeller shaft (rear power take-off drive)

To remove   Operation D/4

See Section T.

To strip   Operation D/6

1. Unscrew the dust cap and withdraw the sliding joint from the splined shaft.

   Dismantle each universal joint as follows:

2. Clean the enamel and dirt from the four circlips and the tops of the bearing races.

3. Remove the circlips.

4. Hold the joint in the left hand with one of the splined sleeve (or shaft) yoke lugs uppermost and tap the radius of the yoke lightly with a soft-nosed hammer.

   The top bearing should then begin to emerge from the yoke. (Fig. D-2.)

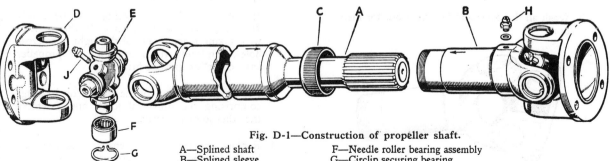

Fig. D-1—Construction of propeller shaft.

A—Splined shaft
B—Splined sleeve
C—Dust cap
D—Flange yoke
E—Journal spider
F—Needle roller bearing assembly
G—Circlip securing bearing
H—Lubrication nipple for splined joint
J—Oil nipple for universal joint

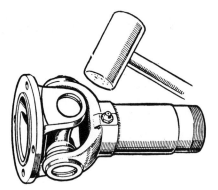

Fig. D-2—Removing a yoke bearing. Stage 1.

5. Turn the joint over and withdraw the bearing. (Fig. D-3.)

   Always remove a bearing downwards, to avoid dropping the needle rollers. It may be necessary to tap the bearing race from the inside with a small drift; in such cases, care should be taken to prevent damage to the bearing race.

6. Repeat these operations for the opposite bearing.

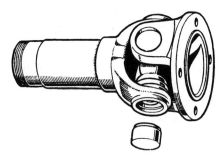

Fig. D-3—Removing a yoke bearing. Stage 2.

7. The splined sleeve (or shaft) yoke can now be removed (Fig. D-4).

8. Rest the flange yoke on a short piece of tubing of suitable diameter (slightly larger than the bearing race) and drive out the two remaining bearings, using a brass drift Fig. D-5).

9. Wash all the parts and lay them out for inspection.

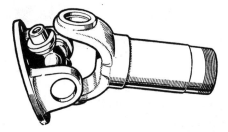

Fig. D-4—Removing the splined sleeve or shaft.

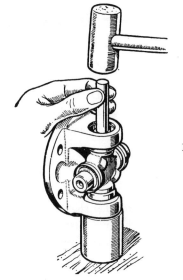

Fig. D-5—
Removing the flange yoke.

To assemble   Operation D/8

The parts most likely to show signs of wear after long usage are the bearing races and the spider journals. Should looseness in the fit of these parts, load markings or distortion be observed, they must be renewed complete, as oversize journals or bearing races are not supplied. Replacement journal assemblies comprise a spider complete with cork oil seals and four bearings.

The other parts likely to show signs of wear are the splined sleeve yoke and splined shaft. A total of .004 in. (0,1 mm.) circumferential movement, measured on the outside diameter of the splines, should not be exceeded. If wear beyond this limit has taken place, a new propeller shaft complete must be fitted.

1. Assemble the needle rollers in the bearing races, if necessary using a smear of vaseline to retain them in place. About half fill the races with oil (S.A.E. 140).

2. Insert the journal in the flange yoke holes and, using a brass drift slightly smaller in diameter than the hole in the yoke, lightly tap the first bearing into position.

   It is essential that the bearing races be a *light drive fit* in the yoke trunnions. In the event of wear taking place in any of the eight yoke cross holes, rendering them oval, a new propeller shaft complete must be fitted.

3. Repeat the operation for the other three bearings comprising the universal joint, and assemble the other joint similarly.

4. Replace the circlips and ensure that they are firmly located in their grooves. If the joint appears to bind, tap the ears slightly with a soft-nosed hammer.

5. Liberally smear the splines of the sliding joint and splined shaft with oil and replace the joint on the shaft, making sure that the arrows marked on the splined sleeve yoke and shaft are in line (Fig. D-1).

6. Screw up the dust cap as far as possible by hand.

Centre bearing assembly (rear power take-off drive—109 only)

To strip   **Operation D/10**

1. Remove the rear driving flange from the front shaft.

2. Drift off the flange from the splined shaft.

3. Hold the centre bearing housing firmly in a vice and drift the shaft, complete with the bearing and dust plate, from the housing. Remove the two Woodruff keys from the shaft.

4. Press the centre ball bearing and dust plate off the shaft.

5. Wash all the parts and lay them out for inspection.

To assemble   **Operation D/12**

1. Reverse the stripping procedure.

2. Insert the bolts securing the front and rear propeller shafts together, in the rear flange, before fitting the flange on the splined shaft.

3. The centre ball bearing must be a *light drive fit* on the shaft; if a new bearing is loose on the shaft, the complete shaft must be renewed.

4. The centre ball bearing must be a *press fit* in the housing; if a new bearing is loose in the housing, the complete housing must be renewed.

Propeller shaft (front and rear axle drives)

To refit   **Operation D/14**

1. Wipe the faces of the transfer box and differential flanges clean.

2. Replace the propeller shaft and ensure that the register engages and that the joint faces bed down correctly all round.

3. Secure the propeller shaft, **sleeve end,** to the transfer box output flange. Tighten the nuts evenly.

4. Secure the propeller shaft to the differential input flange (with the nuts behind the input flange). Tighten the nuts evenly.

Propeller shaft (rear power take-off drive)

To refit   **Operation D/16**

1. See Section T.

DEFECT LOCATION

Symptom, Cause and Remedy

A—VIBRATING PROPELLER SHAFT

1. Balance marks out of alignment—*Check alignment of balance marks on the splined sleeve yoke and shaft.*
2. Worn splines—*Renew.*
3. Shaft out of balance—*Tighten the securing nuts; renew the shaft if still out of balance.*

B—UNIVERSAL JOINTS NOISY

1. Lack of lubrication—*Lubricate or renew bearings.*
2. Securing nuts loose—*Tighten.*
3. Worn bearings or worn spline—*Renew.*

GENERAL DATA

86 and 88 in.
Type: Hardy Spicer needle bearing
Tubular shaft—
  diameter .... 2 in. (50,8 mm.)
  wall thickness .... $\frac{3}{32}$ in. (2,4 mm.)

Overall length (face to face in neutral position)—
  Front axle drive .... 23.812 in. (654 mm.)
  Rear axle drive .... 21.812 in. (554 mm.)

107 and 109 in.
Type: Hardy Spicer needle bearing
Tubular shaft—
  diameter .... 2 in. (50,8 mm.)
  wall thickness .... $\frac{3}{32}$ in. (2,4 mm.)

Overall length (face to face in neutral position)—
  Front axle drive .... 23.812 in. (654 mm.)
  Rear axle drive .... 42.812 in. (1,087 m.)

Section E—REAR AXLE—ALL MODELS

INDEX

	Page		Page
Axle shaft assembly	E-1	Differential assembly	E-5
Axle complete	E-6	Differential pinion oil seal	E-5
Data, general	E-7	Hub, rear	E-4
Data, detail	E-7		

LIST OF ILLUSTRATIONS

Fig.		Page	Fig.		Page
E-1	Stripping and assembling half-shaft	E-1	E-4	Checking hub end-float, fully floating shafts	E-4
E-2	Layout of rear axle, semi-floating shafts	E-2	E-5	Cross-section of rear hub	E-5
E-3	Layout of rear axle, fully floating shafts	E-3			

Data, details and illustrations concerning the differential assembly will be found in Section F

Axle shaft assembly

Semi-floating type

To remove   **Operation E/2**

1. Jack up the rear of the vehicle under the chassis frame.
2. Drain off the rear axle oil.
3. Remove the road wheel and the brake drum.
4. Depress the brake pedal and wedge it in that position; detach the brake pipe at the wheel brake unit.
5. Remove the brake components. Section H.
6. Withdraw the shaft assembly complete with anchor plate.

To strip   **Operation E/4**

1. Stand the axle shaft on its splined end and press down squarely on the brake anchor plate and *bearing housing flange*, using the special annular press block, Part No. 242415 (Fig. E-1). A pressure of up to 20 tons will be required, and it may be necessary to assist the operation with sharp blows on the bearing housing, using a *brass* drift. Remove the collar.
2. Remove the oil seal and sleeve, the bearing and housing, the brake anchor plate and the distance washer, and oil retaining ring (if necessary).

3. Remove the ball bearing from the housing and the oil seal from the sleeve.
4. The road wheel studs are peened over in the axle shaft flange and the peening should be filed before withdrawing a faulty stud.

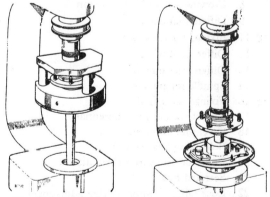

Fig. E-1—Stripping and assembling half-shaft.

To assemble   **Operation E/6**

1. Renew the road wheel studs as necessary.
2. Replace the distance washer, chamfer side down.
3. Examine the bearing for excessive side play or roughness. The bearing should be a *light press fit* in the bore of the hub and on the axle shaft.

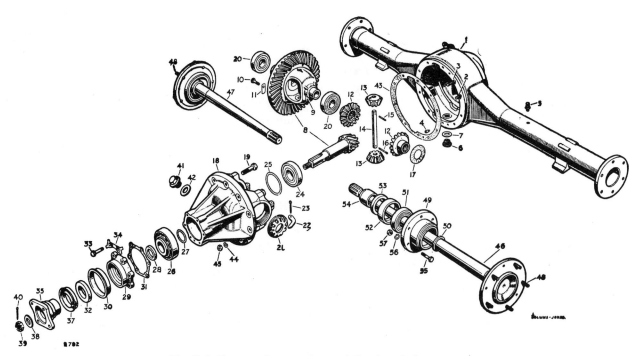

Fig. E-2—Layout of rear axle, semi-floating shafts.

1	Rear axle casing	28	Washer for bearing
2–3	Bolts fixing differential	29	Retainer for oil seal
4	Dowel locating differential	30	Mudshield for retainer
5	Breather	31	Joint washer for retainer
6–7	Oil drain plug	32	Oil seal for pinion
8	Crownwheel and bevel pinion	33–34	Fixings for retainer
9	Differential casing	35	Driving flange
10–11	Fixings for crownwheel	37	Dust shield for driving flange
12	Differential wheel	38–40	Fixings for driving flange
13	Differential pinion	41–42	Oil filler plug and washer
14	Spindle for pinions	43	Joint washer for differential
15–16	Fixings for spindle	44–45	Fixings for differential
17	Thrust washer for differential	46	Axle shaft, L.H.
18	Bevel pinion housing	47	Axle shaft, R.H.
19	Bolt fixing bearing cap	48	Stud for road wheel
20	Roller bearings for differential	49	Housing for hub bearing
21	Serrated nut	50	Distance washer
22	Lock tab }For bearing adjustment	51	Bearing for hub
23	Split pin	52	Sleeve for oil seal
24	Bearing for bevel pinion, pinion end	53	Oil seal for hub
25	Shims for bearing adjustment, pinion end	54	Retaining collar
26	Bearing for bevel pinion, flange end	55–57	Fixings for bearing housing
27	Shims for bearing adjustment, flange end		

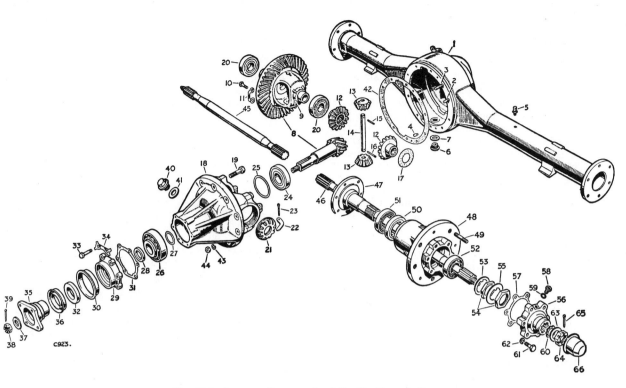

Fig. E-3—Layout of rear axle, fully floating shafts.

1	Rear axle casing	31	Joint washer for retainer
2–3	Bolts fixing differential	32	Oil seal for pinion
4	Dowel locating differential	33–34	Fixings for retainer
5	Breather	35	Driving flange
6–7	Oil drain plug	36	Dust shield for driving flange
8	Crownwheel and bevel pinion	37–39	Fixings for driving flange
9	Differential casing	40–41	Oil filler plug and washer
10–11	Fixings for crownwheel	42	Joint washer for differential
12	Differential wheel	43–44	Fixings for differential
13	Differential pinion	45	Axle shaft, R.H.
14	Spindle for pinions	46	Axle shaft, L.H.
15–16	Fixings for spindle	47	Rear hub bearing sleeve
17	Thrust washer for differential	48	Rear hub assembly
18	Bevel pinion housing	49	Stud for road wheel
19	Bolt fixing bearing cap	50	Hub bearing, inner
20	Roller bearings for differential	51	Oil seal for inner bearing
21	Serrated nut ⎫	52	Hub bearing, outer
22	Lock tab ⎬ For bearing adjustment	53–55	Fixings—for hub bearing
23	Split pin ⎭	56	Driving member for rear hub
24	Bearing for bevel pinion, pinion end	57	Joint washer for driving member
25	Shims for bearing adjustment, pinion end	58	Filler plug for hub driving member
26	Bearing for bevel pinion, flange end	59	Joint washer for filler plug
27	Shims for bearing adjustment, flange end	60	Oil seal for rear axle shaft
28	Washer for bearing	61–62	Fixings—driving member to rear hub
29	Retainer for oil seal	63–65	Fixings—axle shaft to driving member
30	Mudshield for retainer	66	Hub cap, rear

131

5. Renew the bearing or bearing housing as necessary, and fit the bearing in the housing; replace the assembly and brake anchor plate on the axle shaft.

6. Place the securing collar over the axle shaft with the chamfer towards the splined end and press it on until it abuts the bearing. A pressure of at least $2\frac{1}{2}$ tons will be required for this operation, as a suitable collar, with an interference fit of .0028 in. (0,07 mm) on the shaft, must be chosen by selective assembly. A suitable press block (Part No. 262757) is illustrated at Fig. E-1.

7. Renew the oil seal as necessary and fit it in the sleeve with the lip away from the axle shaft flange.

8. Press the oil seal and sleeve over the securing collar into the bearing housing.

To refit   Operation E/8

1. Replace the axle shaft in the axle casing, entering the splined end into the differential.

2. Replace the brake components. Section H.

3. Connect the brake pipe to the wheel cylinder.

4. Refit the brake drum and road wheel.

5. Bleed the brake system. Section H.

6. Lower the vehicle off the jack and refill the differential with oil.

Rear hub assembly, fully-floating axle

To adjust   Operation E/10

1. Adjust the end-float of the hub bearing by adjusting the hub inner nut, tightening the locknut and checking the end-float by means of a dial test indicator mounted on to one of the wheel studs (see Fig. E-4). Take the reading by pushing the hub as far as possible towards the axle centre, note the indicator reading, pull the hub outwards and again take the indicator reading, the total hub movement so measured should be .004 in. to .006 in. (0,10 mm to 0,15 mm). When the correct end-float has been obtained, bend over two tabs of the locking washer. As a safeguard, the end-float should be checked once more after locking the nuts.

To remove   Operation E/12

1. Jack up the rear of the vehicle under the chassis frame.

2. Drain off the rear axle oil.

3 Remove the road wheel and brake drum.

4. Depress the brake pedal fully, and wedge it in that position, detach the brake pipes at the wheel brake unit.

5. Remove the brake components. (Section H.)

6. Withdraw the shaft and hub assembly, complete with anchor plate, from the flange, by removing the six securing bolts, spring washers and nuts.

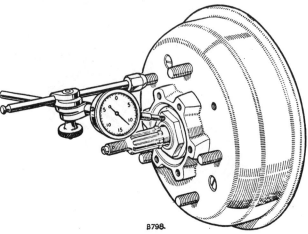

B798

Fig. E-4—Checking hub end-float, fully floating shafts.

To strip   Operation E/14

1. Remove the hub cap (*press fit*) on the driving member.

2. Remove the driving member and joint washer from the axle shaft and the hub. Remove oil seal.

3. Prise up the locking tabs and remove the locknut, lock washer and adjusting nut from the rear bearing sleeve.

4. Remove the thrust washer and hub complete with the outer roller bearing. Remove brake anchor plate. Withdraw the oil seal and bearings from the hub if necessary.

To assemble hub   Operation E/16

1. Before assembling the hub, examine the outside diameter of the inner bearing distance piece, on which the oil seal runs, for signs of damage or roughness. Renew as necessary. The distance piece should be a press fit on the rear hub bearing sleeve. Any clearance between these two parts will allow oil to leak past on to the brake linings.

2. Examine the two hub bearings and renew them as necessary. Both bearings should be an easy fit on the rear hub bearing sleeve and a *press fit* in the hub. If new bearings are slack in the hub, the hub itself should be renewed.

3. Pack the bearings with grease, using a wheel-bearing lubricator, before pressing them into the hub.

4. Examine the oil seal and renew as necessary; press the seal into the hub with the knife edge towards the inner bearing until the oil seal face

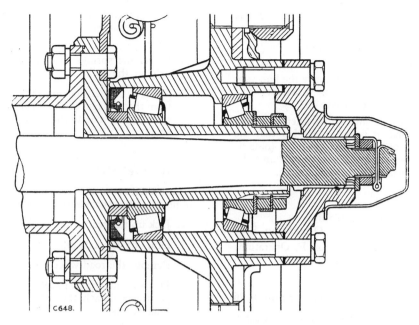

Fig. E-5—Cross-section of fully floating rear hub.

is flush with the rear face of the hub. If the seal is pressed too far in, the element will fail to register on the rear hub bearing sleeve distance piece, so allowing oil to leak past and on to the brake linings.

To assemble complete unit. Operation E/18

1. Bolt the rear hub bearing sleeve and brake anchor plate into position and then slide the complete hub on to the rear hub bearing sleeve.

2. Fit the keyed thrust washer, adjusting nut, lock washer and locknut. Adjust the hub end-float, Operation E/10.

3. Slide the axle shaft through the rear hub bearing sleeve until it locates in the splines of the differential unit. Place a joint washer on to the driving member, then slide the member on to the spline at the end of the axle shaft, securing it to the hub with the six set bolts and washers.

4. Replace oil seal and secure the axle shaft to the driving member by using the slotted nut, plain washer and split pin. Take care not to over-tighten. Tap the hub cap into place.

5. Fill the hub with one-third of a pint (0,190 litres) of oil, through the oil filler plug in the driving member. Replace the filler plug and joint washer.

6. Refill the rear axle with 3 pints (1,75 litres) of oil.

7. Replace brake components and reconnect the brake pipes, bleed and adjust the brakes (Section H).

Differential pinion oil seal

To renew   Operation E/20

Proceed as detailed under Section F, Operation F/2.

Differential assembly
Semi-floating type axle

To remove   Operation E/22

1. Jack up the rear of the vehicle.

2. Drain off the axle oil.

3. Remove the road wheels and brake drums.

4. Depress the brake pedal and wedge it in that position; detach the brake pipes at the wheel brake units.

5. Remove the wheel brake components. Section H.

6. Withdraw the shafts complete with driving member about 6 in. (150 mm) from the axle casing.

7. Disconnect the propeller shaft at the differential input flange.

8. Remove the differential assembly from the axle casing.

Fully-floating type axle

To remove the differential on the fully-floating type axle, it is only necessary to remove the hub caps and six bolts securing the driving member. The axle shafts can then be removed.

Note: If any difficulty is anticipated when adjusting the differential, it is recommended that the unit be replaced by a new assembly (obtainable from our Spares Department) and the old one returned for reconditioning.

To strip, examine and assemble
                                   Operation E/24

Proceed as detailed under Section F, Operations F/6, F/8 and F/10. *For data see Section F.*

To refit   **Operation E/26**

1. Fit the differential assembly in the axle casing.

2. Connect the propeller shaft to the input flange.

3. Push the axle shafts into the splines of the differential, and secure in position.

4. Replace the wheel brake components. Section H.

5. Replace the brake drums and road wheels.

6. Connect the brake pipes to the wheel brake units and bleed the brake system. Section H.

7. Lower the vehicle to the ground.

8. Refill the axle with oil, 3 pints (1,75 litres).

Axle complete

To remove, Method I   **Operation E/28**

1. Jack up the rear of the vehicle.

2. Remove both road wheels.

3. Depress the brake pedal and wedge it in that position. Disconnect the flexible brake pipe at the Tee-piece on the differential casing.

4. Disconnect the propeller shaft at the differential input flange. Disconnect one extremity of each check strap.

5. Disconnect one end of each shock absorber.

6. Lower the vehicle on to suitable stands placed under the chassis.

7. Jack up each of the road springs under the shock absorber plate and remove the U-bolt nuts.

8. Lower the springs so that they are relaxed but still on the jacks.

9. Remove the self-locking nuts and shackle bolts from the rear end of the springs, lower the jacks, springs, and axle to the ground, and remove the axle.

To remove, Method II   **Operation E/30**

An alternative method for removal eliminates removal of the shackle pins; proceed as follows:—

1. Jack up the rear of the vehicle.

2. Drain off the axle oil.

3. Remove the road wheels and brake drums.

4. Depress the brake pedal and wedge it in that position; detach the brake pipes at the wheel brake units.

5. Remove the wheel brake components. Section H.

6. Withdraw the shaft and hub assemblies complete from the axle casing.

7. Disconnect the flexible brake pipe at the Tee-piece on the differential casing.

8. Disconnect the propeller shaft at the differential input flange.

9. Remove the differential assembly from the axle casing.

10. Lower the vehicle on to suitable stands placed under the chassis.

11. Jack up each of the road springs under the shock absorber plate and remove the U-bolt nuts.

12. Lower the springs so that they are relaxed but still on the jacks.

13. Remove the axle casing by manoeuvring it past the road springs and check straps.

To refit   **Operation E/32**

1. Replace the axle assembly by reversing the removal procedure (Method I or II).

2. Bleed the brake system. Section H.

3. Refill the differential with oil, 3 pints (1,75 litres) and lower the vehicle off the jacking stands.

GENERAL DATA: Semi-floating type

Fitted to all 80, 86, 88 and 107 basic models. 109 models up to 121704761 and 107 Station Wagon up to 131701305.

Note: Fully floating axle shafts are fitted to 109 models from 121704770, 107 Station Wagon from 131701306; they are also available as an optional extra on the 88 models.

Oil capacity .... 3 pints (1,75 litres)

Hub bearing lubrication Pre-packed with grease

Final drive .... Spiral bevel

Ratio, axles numbered
860001 to 861319 .... 4.88 to 1

Ratio, axles numbered
861320 onwards .... 4.7 to 1

GENERAL DATA: Fully floating type

Oil capacity .... 3 pints (1,75 litres)

Hub bearing lubrication 1/3rd pint (0,190 litres)
Initial assembly only

Final drive .... Spiral bevel

Ratio .... 4.7 to 1

DETAIL DATA: Semi-floating type

Fit of retaining collar on
shaft .... .0028 in. (0,07 mm) interference (selective assembly)

DETAIL DATA: Fully floating type

Rear hub assembly:

Rear hub end-float .... 0.04 to .006 in. (0,010 to 0,16 mm)

Clearance of hub bearing in rear hub bearing sleeve .... .0002 to .0013 in. (0,005 to 0,033 mm)

Fit of hub bearing in hub .... .001 to .003 in. (0,025 to 0,075 mm) interference

Section F — FRONT AXLE — ALL MODELS

INDEX

	Page		Page
Axle casing oil seal	F-10	Stub axle	F-11
Axle complete	F-17	Stub shaft	F-12
Data	F-20	Swivel pin bearing housing	F-17
Defect location	F-19	Swivel pin housing oil seal	F-11
Differential assembly	F-5	Swivel pins	F-13
Differential pinion oil seal	F-1	Swivel pins and bearings	F-13
Front hub	F-10	Universal joint....	F-12
Half shaft	F-16	Universal joint housing assembly	F-11
Lock stop bolt	F-17		

LIST OF ILLUSTRATIONS

Fig.		Page	Fig.		Page
F-1	Layout of front axle and differential	F-2	F-20	Setting top swivel pin	F-13
F-2	Cross-section of axle (differential)	F-4	F-21	Housing for swivel pin bearing, 1948-53	F-13
F-3	Cross-section of axle (universal joint and hub)	F-4	F-22	Housing for swivel pin bearing, 1954-58	F-13
F-4	Pressing out pinion end bearing outer race	F-5	F-23	Cone bearing, 1948-53	F-13
F-5	Pinion adjustment shims	F-6	F-24	Cone bearing, 1954-58	F-13
F-6	Pinion thrust bearing pinch	F-7	F-25	Length of swivel, 1948-53	F-14
F-7	Pressing pinion end bearing outer member into pinion casing	F-7	F-26	Length of swivel, 1954-58	F-14
F-8	Bevel pinion adjustment shims	F-8	F-27	Cross-section of universal joint housing assembly	F-14
F-9	Pinion setting	F-8	F-28	Position of oil hole, 1948-53	F-15
F-10	Adjusting crownwheel backlash	F-9	F-29	Position of oil hole, 1954-58	F-15
F-11	Fitting crownwheel lockers	F-9	F-30	Checking swivel pin housing resistance to rotation	F-15
F-12	Position of lockers against differential casing webs	F-9	F-31	Removing the half-shaft roller race retaining collar	F-16
F-13	Checking crownwheel backlash	F-10	F-32	Removing the half-shaft roller race outer member	F-16
F-14	Checking hub end-float	F-10	F-33	Removing the half-shaft roller race	F-16
F-15	Cross-section of hub	F-11	F-34	Stripping half-shaft	F-17
F-16	Removing a yoke bearing (Stage 1)	F-12	F-35	Assembling half-shaft	F-17
F-17	Removing a yoke bearing (Stage 2)	F-12	F-36	Adjusting lock stop bolt	F-17
F-18	Removing the stub shaft	F-12			
F-19	Replacing a yoke bearing	F-12			

Differential pinion oil seal

To renew   Operation F/2

1. Jack up the front of the vehicle and support the chassis frame on jacking stands.

2. Drain off the oil from the differential.

3. Disconnect the propeller shaft from the differential input flange.

4. Remove the differential pinion driving flange.

5. **Axles numbered prior to 06106001 only.** Remove the oil seal and retainer and carefully preserve the shims fitted between the retainer and bearing housing. Leave the bearing housing in position, together with the shims between it and the pinion housing.

6. Remove the oil seal retainer and seal together with a joint washer. Care should be taken not to dislodge the bearings and flange end bearing washer during this operation.

7. Remove the oil seal from the retainer and fit the new seal with the lip towards the axle casing. The retainer must be warmed and the outer diameter of the new oil seal smeared with jointing compound before assembly.

8. Replace the shims or a new joint washer and the oil seal retainer.

9. Examine the input flange outer diameter for roughness or damage which may have caused failure of the original seal and rectify or replace as necessary.

Fig. F-1—Layout of front axle, late type

Key to Fig. F-1

1 Axle casing complete
2-3 Fixings—differential housing to axle casing
4 Dowel, locating housing
5 Oil seal, in casing
6 Breather
7 Oil filler plug
8-9 Drain plug and joint washer
10 Crownwheel and bevel pinion
11 Differential casing
12 Set bolt
13 Locker (double type)
14 Differential wheel
15 Differential pinion
16 Spindle for pinion
17 Plain pin } For
18 Split pin } spindle
19 Thrust washer
20 Bevel pinion housing
21 Special bolt, fixing bearing cap
22 Taper roller bearing for differential
23-24 Bearing adjustment
25 Split pin, fixing lock tab
26 Bearing for bevel pinion, pinion end
27 Shim, bearing adjustment, pinion end
28 Bearing for bevel pinion, flange end
29 Shim, bearing adjustment, flange end
30 Washer for pinion bearing
31 Retainer for oil seal
32 Mudshield for retainer
33 Joint washer for oil seal retainer
34 Oil seal for pinion
35-36 Fixings—oil seal retainer
37 Driving flange
39 Mudshield for driving flange
40-42 Fixings for flange
43-44 Oil filler plug and joint washer
45 Joint washer, differential to axle casing
46-47 Fixings—differential to axle casing
48 Half shaft
49 Stub shaft
50 Journal assembly
51 Circlip for journal

52 Housing for swivel pin bearing
53 Distance piece for bearing
54 Bearing for half shaft
55 Retaining collar for bearing
56 Joint washer for housing
57-58 Fixings—housing to front axle casing
59 Housing assembly for swivel pin
60 Special stud for steering lever and bracket
61 Stud for steering lever
62-63 Drain plug and joint washer
64 Swivel pin and steering lever
65 Cone seat for swivel pin, top
66 Cone bearing for swivel pin, top
67 Spring for cone bearing
68 Bearing for swivel pin, bottom
69 Swivel pin and bracket
70 Shim, for swivel pin bearing
71-74 Fixings—swivel pin to swivel pin housings
75 Oil seal for swivel pin bearing housing
76 Retainer for oil seal
77-81 Fixings—retainer and lock stop plate to swivel pin housing
82 Oil filler plug for swivel pin housing
83 Stub axle assembly
84 Bush for driving shaft
85 Distance piece for inner bearing
86-87 Fixings—stub axle to swivel pin housing
88 Front hub assembly
89 Stud for road wheel
90 Bearing for front hub, inner
91 Oil seal for inner bearing
92 Bearing for front hub
93 Keywasher } Fixing front hub
94 Locker } bearing
95 Special nut
96 Driving member for front hub
97 Joint washer for driving member
98-99 Fixings—driving member to front hub
100 Plain washer } Fixing driving member
101 Slotted nut } to driving shaft
102 Split pin
103 Hub cap, front

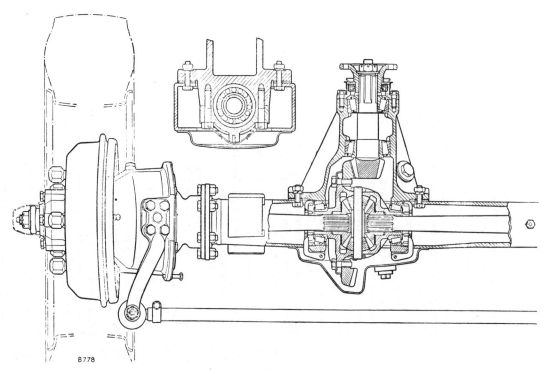

Fig. F-2—Cross-section of axle (differential), late type

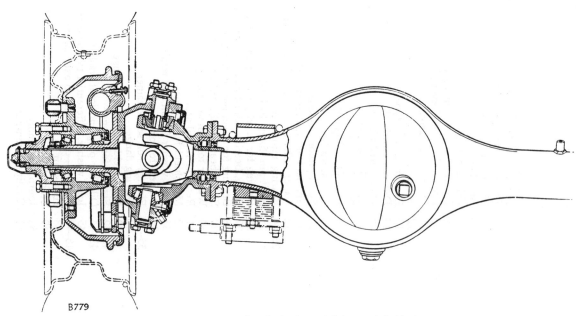

Fig. F-3—Cross-section of axle (universal joint and hub), late type

10. Refit the flange. Tighten the castle nut to 85 lb./ft. (11,75 mKg) on a torque spanner. Fit the split pin.

11. Reconnect the propeller shaft.

12. Lower the vehicle from the jacking stands and refill the differential with oil, 3 pints (1,75 litres).

Differential assembly

To remove   **Operation F/4**

1. Jack up the front of the vehicle and place jacking stands under the chassis frame.

2. Remove the road wheels.

3. Drain off the axle and universal joint housing oil; (drain and filler plugs to be removed).

4. Depress the brake pedal and wedge it in that position; detach the flexible brake pipes at the wheel brake units or at the chassis bracket.

5. Disconnect the drag link and track rod from the steering arm.

6. Withdraw each swivel pin bearing housing assembly from the axle casing, taking care not to damage the axle casing oil seals.

7. Disconnect the propeller shaft at the differential input flange.

8. Remove the differential assembly.

Note: If any difficulty is anticipated when adjusting the differential it is recommended that the unit be replaced by a new assembly (obtainable from our Spares Department) and the old one returned for reconditioning.

Differential, all types, to strip   Operation F/6

1. Remove the differential bearing caps.

2. Remove the serrated nuts.

3. Remove the differential complete with races

4. Remove the crownwheel from the differential case.

5. Remove the split pin and tap out the differential wheel spindle.

6. Remove the two differential wheels.

7. Remove the two differential pinions, together with the fibre thrust washer fitted between each wheel and the differential casing.

Pinion, early type, to strip

1. Prise up the locking tabs and remove the six set bolts securing the pinion assembly in the pinion housing.

2. Remove the pinion assembly and preserve the shims fitted between the thrust bearing housing and the pinion housing; the outer race of the pinion roller bearing is retained in the pinion housing.

3. Remove the split pin, castle nut and plain washer securing the input flange to the pinion and remove the flange.

4. Lift off the oil seal retainer and seal and preserve the shims fitted between the retainer and thrust bearing housing.

5. If the oil seal is to be renewed, press it out of the retainer.

6. Press the thrust bearing and housing from the pinion shaft and press the bearing from the housing.

7. Remove the helix distance sleeve from the pinion.

8. Remove the roller bearing inner member from the pinion.

9. Remove the two circlips retaining the pinion roller bearing outer race in the pinion housing and remove the race.

Pinion, late type, to strip

1. Draw off the two differential thrust bearings.

2. Remove the differential pinion input flange.

3. Remove the oil seal retainer and washer from the pinion housing.

4. Withdraw the pinion, remove the flange end bearing washer and the flange end bearing inner member.

5. Remove the shims for flange end bearing adjustment and press off the inner member of the pinion end bearing.

6. Press out both bearing outer members and remove the pinion bearing shims. Use the special extractor (Part No. 262757) to remove the pinion end bearing outer race.

7. Press out the oil seal from the retainer.

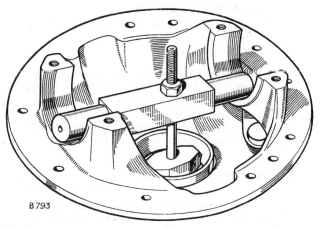

B 793

Fig. F-4—Pressing out pinion end bearing outer race, late type

To examine, all types   Operation F/8

Wash all the component parts and renew them as necessary.

The more important examination details are listed below:—

1. **Flange end pinion bearing.** This bearing should be renewed if it does not roll smoothly or if excessively worn. The pinion housing should be checked and renewed if worn in the bore. The bearing should be a *light press fit* in the housing and a *light push fit* on the pinion shaft.

2. **Pinion end pinion bearing.** This bearing should also be renewed if it does not run smoothly, or if excessively worn. It should be a *drive fit* on the bevel pinion shaft and a *light press fit* in the pinion housing.

3. **Differential thrust bearings.** These roller bearings must be renewed if any doubt exists about their condition. They should be a *light press fit* on the differential casing.

4. **Pinion oil seal.** Renew as necessary. The retainer must be warmed and the outer diameter of the seal smeared with jointing compound before assembly. The lip of the seal must be set towards the axle casing.

5. **Crownwheel and pinion.** The crownwheel and pinion are lapped and supplied in pairs with corresponding engraved markings on each component. It is absolutely essential that they are retained and fitted in pairs, otherwise it will be impossible to obtain the correct tooth bearing on assembly. Should any imperfections such as cracks or roughness be found on the teeth of either component, they must be discarded and a new factory-mated pair fitted.

   If new pinion bearings are loose on the pinion shaft (see above), both the crownwheel and pinion must be renewed.

6. **Pinion housing.** The pinion housing is supplied complete with differential caps and securing bolts; the caps are not available as separate items and must always be retained with the correct pinion housing.

   If a new pinion bearing outer member is loose in the pinion housing, the housing must be renewed complete.

7. **Differential casing.** If new differential thrust bearings are loose on the differential casing spigots, the casing must be renewed.

A larger amount of wear is permissible on the remaining differential components, but parts whose serviceability is in doubt should be renewed.

Pinion, early type, to assemble
Operation F/10

1. Fit one circlip into the pinion housing, press in the outer race of the pinion roller bearing, and fit the retaining circlip.

2. Press the inner member of the pinion roller bearing on to the pinion shaft and fit the helix distance sleeve over the shaft to abut the bearing.

3. Press the pinion thrust bearing into the bearing housing and press the assembly on to the pinion shaft, with the housing flange away from the pinion.

4. Press the oil seal into the seal retainer with its knife edge inwards and fit the retainer over the spigot on the input flange, together with the correct number of shims between the retainer and the bearing housing; these shims, to adjust the bearing nip, should be selected as described below.

5. Fit the driving flange to the pinion shaft and secure with the plain washer and castle nut.

Pinion thrust bearing pinch

6. The double-row ball thrust bearing may be either a plain Skefco or Fischer pattern, or a split Hoffmann type. Whichever type is fitted, the dimensions of the width of the bearing and the depth of the housing bore allow the bearing to stand proud by .007 in. to .012 in. (0,17 mm to 0,3 mm), so that the flange of the oil seal retainer will not meet its mating face by this amount when tightened up.

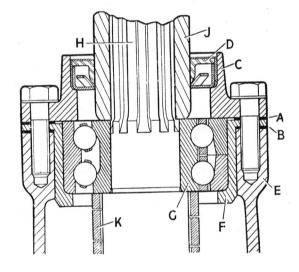

Fig. F-5—Pinion adjustment shims, early type

A—Shims adjusting bearing pinch
B—Shims adjusting pinion position
C—Oil seal retainer
D—Oil seal
E—Pinion housing
F—Thrust bearing housing
G—Thrust bearing
H—Pinion
J—Input flange
K—Helix distance sleeve

On assembly it is necessary to ascertain this clearance and select suitable shims (available .003 in. and .005 in. thick) to be fitted between the oil seal retainer and bearing housing (Fig. F-5), so that the bearing is pinched .003 in. to .004 in. (0,07 mm to 0,1 mm) when the retainer is tightened up.

7. To determine the amount by which the bearing lies above the pinion housing, press the bearing into its housing; mount the assembly on a surface plate and measure the difference in height by means of a dial test indicator (Fig. F-6).

Example:

Difference in height .011 in. (0,279 mm)

Bearing pinch required .003 in. to .004 in. (0,07 mm to 0,1 mm)

Therefore, total thickness of shims required is .007 in. to .008 in., i.e., one .003 in. and one .005 in. shims will give .003 in. (0,07 mm) bearing pinch.

8. The foregoing instructions apply to Skefco or Fischer bearings. The Hoffmann bearing has a pre-load of .001 in. to .0015 in. (0,02 mm to 0,03 mm) between the balls and tracks, thus preventing the two halves of the outer ring from meeting at the centre joint. When fitting a bearing of this type, before measuring the amount by which the bearing stands proud of the pinion housing as described above, the bearing itself must be compressed by some suitable means.

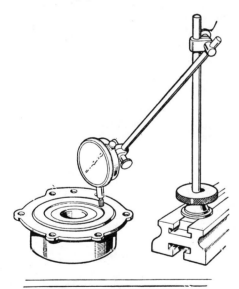

Fig. F-6—Pinion thrust bearing pinch

Pinion, to assemble, late type only

9. Press the outer member of the pinion end bearing into the pinion casing together with the shims removed on stripping (at least .020 in. (0,50 mm) should be used), using press block (Part No. 262758). Press the outer member of the flange end bearing into the pinion casing.

10. Press the inner member of the pinion end bearing on to the pinion shaft.

11. Fit the pinion shaft into the pinion case together with the shims removed on stripping (at least .020 in. (0,50 mm) should be used).

12. Fit the flange end bearing inner member into position on the pinion shaft. On early models fit helix distance sleeve to pinion.

13. Fit the flange end bearing washer and the driving flange on to the pinion shaft and retain with the nut and plain washer. The nut should be tightened to 85 lb./ft. (11,75 mkg) on a torque spanner.

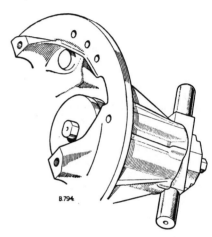

B.794

Fig. F-7—Pressing pinion end bearing outer member into pinion casing, late type

14. The loading on the bearings should be sufficient to give a reading of 6 to 10 in./lb. (0,07 to 0,11 mkg) when rotating the shaft. If the loading is incorrect, then the assembly must be dismantled sufficiently to allow shims to be either placed or removed from the front of the flange end bearing until the correct value is obtained. The required number of shims can only be found by trial and error. When the correct poundage is obtained, note the thickness of each shim used. The shims are available .003 in. (0,076 mm), .005 in. (0,127 mm), .010 in. (0,254 mm) and .020 in. (0,50 mm) thick.

Checking pinion setting, all types

15. Check the dimension from the axis of the crownwheel to the pinion face, using special gauge (Part No. 262761) (Fig. F-9). This dimension should be 3.002 in. to 3.004 in. (76,7 mm to 77,2 mm) for the 4.88 : 1 differentials or 3.00 in. to 3.002 in. (76,2 mm to 76,7 mm) for the 4.7 : 1 ratio differentials.

16. Measure the clearance between the bar and end face of the pinion with a set of feeler gauges. Adjust the position of the pinion, as necessary, by placing shims of the same value behind the pinion end bearing on the late type, and behind the bearing housing on the early type; these shims are available .003 in. (0,076 mm), .005 in. (0,127 mm) and .020 in. (0,50 mm) thick.

Late type only

17. Note the total thickness of the shims added to those already placed behind the pinion end bearing, and add a similar amount in front of the flange end bearing in addition to those already fitted to load the bearings.

18. Place the oil seal retainer and joint washer in position on the pinion shaft, but do not fit the retainer fixing bolts at this stage.

19. Recheck the torque on the pinion shaft and adjust as necessary.

20. Position the oil seal retainer and joint washer (oil hole at the bottom) and secure to the pinion housing.

Crownwheel and differential casing, all types

21. Replace the two differential wheels, together with the fibre thrust washers, which are supplied .040 in. (1,015 mm), .045 in. (1,142 mm) and .050 in. (1,270 mm) thick; they should be selected to give minimum but definite backlash between the differential wheels and pinions.

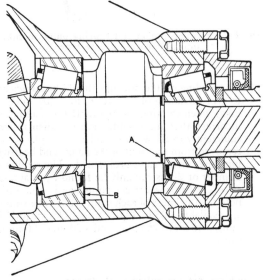

Fig. F-8—Bevel pinion adjustment shims, late type
　　A—Shims adjusting bearing preload.
　　B—Shims adjusting pinion position.

22. Replace the two differential pinions.

23. Replace the differential wheel spindle and secure with a split pin.

24. Fit the crownwheel to the differential with eight standard bolts, .375 in. (9,5 mm) dia., and two special bolts, .390 in. (10 mm) dia., and five double lockers or ten single lockers on early models.

25. The special bolts must be fitted at right angles to the differential pin in the differential casing. Tighten the bolts evenly by diagonal selection.

The locker must be held against the differential casing web opposite to the direction of bolt tightening. It must also be flattened tightly against two of the bolt head flats, not just turned up on one corner. See Fig. F-12.

When double lockers are fitted they must be fitted as shown in Fig. F-11.

26. Press on the inner members of the two differential thrust bearings.

27. Place the differential in the housing, together with the thrust bearing outer races and serrated locking nuts. Replace the bearing caps ensuring that the markings coincide and secure each with two set bolts, which must not be tightened at this stage.

28. Tighten the locking nut on the crownwheel side of the differential casing as much as possible; slacken the locking nut, then tighten once more until it just rests against the bearing. Proceed in a similar manner for the other locking nut; this ensures that all end-float has been taken up and that the bearings are not pre-loaded at this stage. The special spanner (Part No. 262759) (Fig. F-10) will facilitate this operation.

29. Slacken the locking nut on the crownwheel side of the differential casing by two serrations and tighten the opposite locking nut by the same amount. This should ensure an initial backlash of .008-.010 in. (0,20-0,25 mm) on the crownwheel.

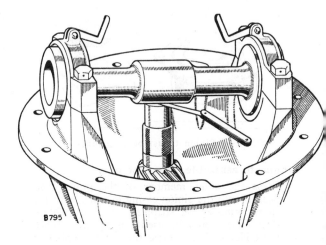

Fig. F-9—Pinion setting, all types

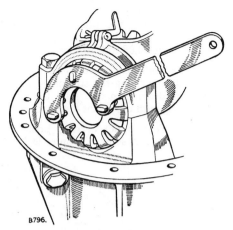

Fig. F-10—Adjusting crownwheel backlash, all types

30. Check the backlash on the crownwheel by using a dial test indicator mounted on the crownwheel teeth. See Fig. F-13. The indicator should be mounted so that the indicator plunger can be brought to bear on the securing flange of the pinion housing.

Hold the pinion shaft securely and rotate the crownwheel through its available backlash; the total movement indicated should be .008 in. to .010 in. (0,20 to 0,25 mm) or .007 in. (0,18 mm) for 1948-53 models at the tightest position.

Adjust the backlash as necessary by turning the serrated locking nuts retaining the differential thrust bearings, both in the same direction; as no tolerance is permitted and as one serration on the adjusting nut alters the backlash by approximately .005 in. (0,12 mm), it may be necessary to effect a re-location of the locking tabs to obtain the correct figure at the tightest point.

When the pinion and backlash are adjusted to these requirements the tooth bearing should also be correct.

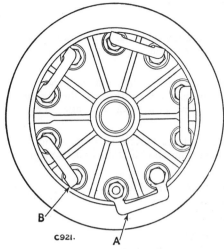

Fig. F-11—Fitting crownwheel double lockers, all types
A—Lockers before bending.   B—Locker bent in position.

31. Tighten both locking nuts by half a serration, so putting the necessary .005 in. (0,12 mm) pre-load on the bearings.

32. Lock the serrated nuts with the locking tabs; tighten the set bolts securing the thrust bearing caps, and lock the tabs and bolts with locking wire. Split pin the castle nut securing the driving flange.

To refit   **Operation F/12**

1. Secure the differential assembly, together with joint washer, to the axle casing.

2. Connect the propeller shaft to the differential input flange (nuts behind the input flange).

3. If necessary, renew the oil seals in the ends of the axle casing by prising out the oil seal from the end of the axle casing. The new oil seal must be fitted with the knife edge inwards. For further details see Operation F/14.

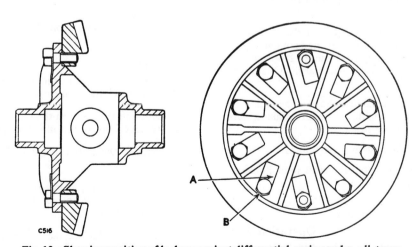

Fig. 12—Showing position of lockers against differential casing webs, all types
A—Locker to be held against the differential casing web as illustrated.   B—Flatten locker against two bolt flats

4. Place the joint washer on the axle casing joint face.

5. Replace the universal joint housing assemblies, taking care not to damage the axle casing oil seals.

6. Replace the drag link and track rod. If the ball joints have been disturbed, the lengths of the drag link and track rod must be adjusted. Section G.

7. Connect the flexible brake pipes to the wheel brake units and bleed the brake system. Section H.

8. Replace the road wheels.

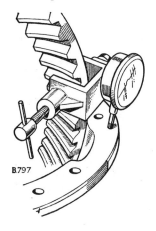

Fig. F-13—
Checking crownwheel
backlash, all types

B797

9. Lower the vehicle to the ground.

10. Replace the axle and universal joint housing drain plugs and refill with oil, 1 pint (0,5 litre).

Axle casing oil seal

To renew   **Operation F/14**

1. Remove the universal joint housing assembly from the axle casing. Operation F/4.

2. Prise out the oil seal from the end of the axle casing and fit the new seal, with the knife edge inwards.

3. Examine the retaining collar on the half shaft, on which the oil seal runs, for signs of damage or roughness which may have caused failure of the original seal; renew as necessary. Operations F/38 and F/40.

4. Replace the universal joint housing assembly by reversing the stripping procedure, taking care not to damage the seal.

5. Bleed the brake system. Section H.

6. Refill the axle and the universal joint housings with oil, 1 pint (0,5 litre).

Front hub

To adjust   **Operation F/16**

1. Remove the driving member and joint washer from the stub shaft and hub. Operation F/18.

2. Mount a dial test indicator on one of the road wheel studs using the bracket, illustrated at Fig. F-14. The total hub movement should be .003 to .004 in. (0,08 to 0,10 mm).

3. Should the end-float prove to be correct, re-assemble by reversing the stripping procedure: replace the drain plug and refill the universal joint housing with oil, 1 pint (0,5 litre).

4. If the end-float is not correct, prise up the locking tabs and unscrew the outer locknut.

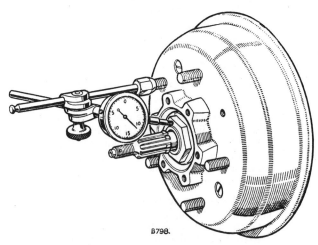

B798.

Fig. F-14—Checking hub end-float.

5. Adjust the inner hub nut, tighten the locknut and again check the end-float. When the hub movement is correct, tighten the locknut and bend over two new tabs of the locking washer. As a safeguard, the end-float should be checked once more after locking the nuts.

6. Replace the driving member and joint washer and complete the assembly by reversing the stripping procedure, taking care not to over-tighten the nut securing the driving shaft to the driving member.

7. Replace the drain plug and refill the universal joint housing with oil, 1 pint (0,5 litre).

To strip   **Operation F/18**

1. Jack up the front of the vehicle and remove the road wheel and brake drum.

2. Drain off the oil from the universal joint housing (remove both drain and filler plugs).

3. Remove the hub cap (*press fit* on the driving member).

4. Place a drip tray below the hub and remove the driving member and joint washer from the stub shaft and the hub.

5. Prise up the locking tabs and remove the locknut, lock washer and adjusting nut from the stub axle. Remove the keyed thrust washer.

6. Remove the hub complete with the inner and outer roller bearings and oil seal. Withdraw the oil seal and bearings from the hub, if necessary.

To assemble   **Operation F/20**

1. Before assembling the hub, examine the outside diameter of the inner bearing distance piece, on which the oil seal runs, for signs of damage or roughness. Renew as necessary. The distance piece should be a *press fit* on the stub axle. Any clearance between these two parts will allow oil to leak past on to the brake linings.

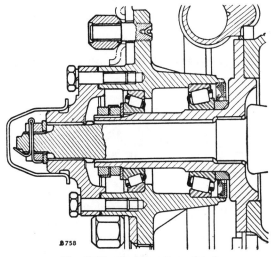

Fig. F-15—Cross-section of hub.

2. Examine the two hub bearings and renew them as necessary. Both bearings should be an *easy fit* on the stub axle and a *press fit* in the hub. If new bearings are slack in the hub, the hub itself should be renewed.

3. Pack the bearings with grease, using a wheel-bearing lubricator, before pressing them into the hub.

4. Examine the oil seal and renew as necessary; press the seal into the hub with the knife edge towards the inner bearing until the oil seal face is flush with the rear face of the hub. If the seal is pressed too far in, the element will fail to register on the stub axle distance piece, so allowing oil to leak past and on to the brake linings.

5. Replace the complete hub on the stub axle, fit the keyed thrust washer, adjusting nut, lock washer and locknut. Adjust the hub end-float and complete the assembly. Operation F/16.

   Note: It will be found that some models are fitted with driving members incorporating an oil filler plug; this is for initial filling only. During normal running the oil level is maintained from the differential and the hub requires no further attention in this respect. If the hub is replaced or has been stripped down for

any purpose, it must be filled on assembly with one-third of a pint (0,2 litre) of the same grade of oil as used in the differential.

Stub axle
To renew   **Operation F/22**

1. Remove the front hub components. Operation F/18.

2. Remove the brake anchor plate and stub axle from the swivel pin housing; swing the anchor plate back to rest on the road spring, thus obviating bleeding the brakes on reassembly.

3. Remove the stub axle and discard if unserviceable.

4. If the original stub axle is to be replaced, examine the stub shaft bush at the inner end of the axle. The clearance of the shaft in the bush should be .020 to .028 in. (0,50 to 0,70 mm). Renew the bush if necessary and ream to 1.250 in. (31,75 mm). The road wheel studs are peened over and the peening should be filed away before withdrawing a faulty stud.

5. Ensure that the joint faces of the stub axle and swivel pin housing are clean and replace the stub axle with the keyway to the top.

6. Ensure that the joint face of the brake anchor plate is clean and secure it and the stub axle to the housing. Use only the correct lock plates with the securing bolts; spring or shakeproof washers will allow the passage of oil from the housing.

7. Complete the assembly. Operation F/20.

Universal joint housing assembly
Note: The half shaft, universal joint and stub shaft assembly can be withdrawn without disturbing the universal joint housing assembly.

Swivel pin housing oil seal
To renew   **Operation F/24**

1. Jack up the front of the vehicle and remove the road wheel.

2. Depress the brake pedal and wedge it in that position; detach the flexible brake pipe at the wheel brake unit.

3. Drain off the axle and universal joint housing oil.

4. Disconnect the track rod and drag link (if applicable), from the steering arm.

5. Remove the universal joint housing assembly from the axle casing, taking care not to damage the axle casing oil seal.

6. Remove the swivel pin housing oil seal retainer, complete with seal. Discard the seal.

7. Examine the surface of the swivel pin bearing housing for signs of corrosion or damage, and renew if necessary. Operation F/44.

8. Pack the new seal with heavy grease and replace the retainer and the seal with the knife edge towards the swivel pins; ensure that the seal "wipes" the surface of the swivel pin bearing housing over its full range of travel. If not, the swivel pin shims should be equalised, i.e. the shims required should be shared between the upper and lower swivel pins. In the event of the shims not dividing equally, the greater value should be placed at the bottom of the swivel pin housings. For further details see Operation F/34.

9. Set the adjustable lock stop bolt. Operation F/46.

10. Complete the assembly by reversing the stripping procedure.

11. Bleed the brake system. Section H.

12. Refill the universal joint housing and axle with oil, 1 pint (0,5 litre).

Stub shaft

To renew   Operation F/26

1. Withdraw the stub shaft, universal joint and half shaft assembly. Operation F/36.

2. Disconnect the stub shaft from the spider journals. Operation F/28. Discard the shaft.

3. Connect the new stub shaft to the spider journals, Operation F/28, and complete the assembly, Operation F/42.

Universal joint

To renew   Operation F/28

1. Withdraw the stub shaft, universal joint and half shaft assembly. Operation F/36.

2. Dismantle the universal joint as follows:—

3. Remove the circlip.

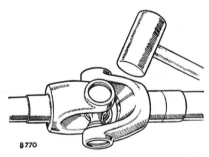

Fig. F-16—Removing a yoke bearing. Stage 1.

4. With one of the stub shaft yoke lugs uppermost tap the radius of the yoke lightly with a soft-nosed hammer.

The top bearing should then begin to emerge from the yoke.

5. Turn the joint over and withdraw the bearing.

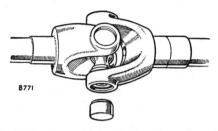

Fig. F-17—Removing a yoke bearing. Stage 2.

Always remove a bearing downwards, to avoid dropping the needle rollers.

6. Repeat these operations for the opposite bearing.

7. Part the stub shaft from the spider journals.

8. Repeat Items 4 to 7 for the half shaft bearings.

Fig. F-18—Removing the stub shaft.

9. Wash all parts and renew as necessary.

10. The parts most likely to show signs of wear after long usage are the bearing races and the spider journals. Should looseness in the fit of these parts, load markings or distortion be observed, they must be renewed complete, as oversize journals or bearing races are not supplied separately.

The bearing races should be a *light drive fit* in the yoke trunnions.

In the event of wear taking place in any of the four yoke cross holes, rendering them oval, a new stub shaft or half shaft must be fitted.

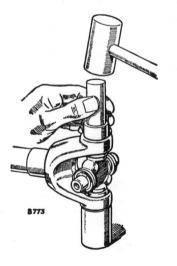

Fig. F-19—
Replacing a yoke bearing.

11. Assemble the needle rollers in the bearing races, if necessary using a smear of vaseline to retain them in place.

12. Insert the journal in the stub shaft yoke holes, and using a brass drift slightly smaller in diameter than the hole in the yoke, lightly tap the first bearing into position.

13. Repeat the operations for the other three bearings.

14. Replace the circlips and ensure that they are firmly located in their grooves. If the joint appears to bind, tap the ears slightly with a soft-nosed hammer.

15. Complete the assembly. Operation F/42.

Swivel pins
To renew **Operation F/30**

1. Remove the swivel pins. Operation F/32.

2. Thoroughly clean the boss of the steering lever or bracket with paraffin and a wire brush.

3. Drill out the grooved pin by means of a ⅛ in. (3,17 mm) drill.

4. Place the steering lever or bracket upon a solid base, i.e. between the jaws of a vice, and drive out the swivel pin from the lever or bracket boss by means of a brass drift.

5. **Top swivel pin only.** Fit the new pin, by positioning its splines in relation to the track rod lever as shown at Fig. F-20, that is with a splined groove placed in line with the longitudinal axis of the track rod lever. This is very important as it ensures that the cone is located correctly.

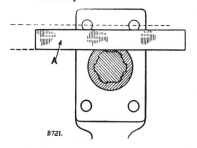

Fig. F-20—Setting the top swivel pin.
A—Straight edge.

6. Press the pin squarely into the lever or bracket.

7. Drill the lever or bracket boss and swivel pin with a 5/32 in. (3,96 mm) drill and insert a 5/32 in. grooved pin.

8. Examine the cone bearing and cone seat for wear and roughness and renew as necessary. Operation F/34.

9. Examine the bottom taper roller race for wear and renew as necessary. Operation F/34.

10. Reassemble the universal joint housing assembly. Operation F/34.

Swivel pin and bearings
To strip **Operation F/32**

1. Remove the front hub components. Operation F/18.

2. Remove the brake anchor plate and stub axle from the swivel pin housing and swing the anchor plate back to rest on the road spring, thus obviating bleeding the brakes on reassembly.

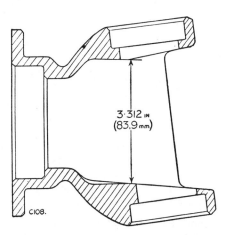

Fig. F-21—Housing for swivel pin bearing. 1948-53

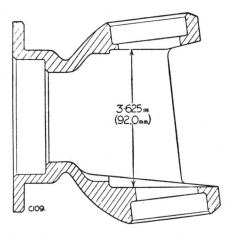

Fig. F-22—Housing for swivel pin bearing. 1954-58

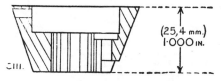

Fig. F-23—Cone bearing. 1948-53

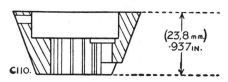

Fig. F-24—Cone bearing. 1954-58

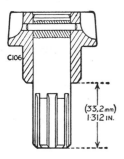

Fig. F-25—
Length of swivel pin.
1948-53

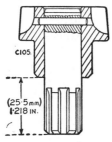

Fig. F-26—
Length of swivel pin.
1954-58

3. Disconnect the track rod and drag link (if applicable) from the steering arm.

4. Withdraw the stub shaft complete with universal joint and half shaft, taking care not to damage the oil seal in the end of the casing.

   Remove the universal joint housing assembly complete with joint washer, half shaft roller outer member and race from the axle casing.

   Remove the half shaft roller race outer member and race from the swivel pin bearing housing.

5. Remove the swivel pin housing oil seal retainer complete with seal.

6. Remove the swivel pin and steering lever assembly from the top of the swivel pin housing together with the shims, which should be preserved. Remove the cone bearing spring.

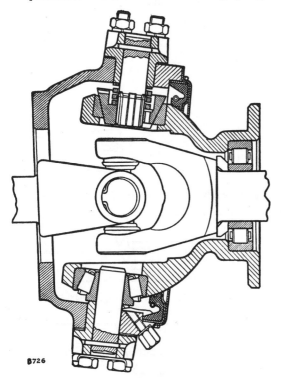

Fig. F-27—
Cross-section of universal joint housing assembly.

7. Remove the swivel pin and bracket assembly from the bottom of the swivel pin housing together with the shims, which should be preserved.

8. Part the swivel pin and swivel pin bearing housings and remove the roller race inner member and the cone bearing.

9. Drive out the race outer member and the cone seat from the swivel pin bearing housing.

To assemble   **Operation F/34**

Note: It is **most important that the correct parts are used** for the models concerned, failure to do so can result in:—

   (*a*) Fouling of half shaft joint.

   (*b*) Lack of lubrication to the swivel pin cone.

Listed below are the parts which **are not interchangeable**, together with the means of identification.

1. Front half shaft.
   1948-53 Half shaft, tracta joint and stub shaft are all separate items.
   1954-58 Half shaft, universal joint and stub shaft are connected up as one asembly.

2. Bearing for half shaft.
   1948-53 Ball   ⎱External dimensions
   1954-58 Roller   ⎰are identical.

3. Swivel pin and steering lever.
   Effective length of swivel pin as shown in Figs. F-25 and F-26.

4. Housing for swivel pin bearing.
   Internal dimension as in Figs. F-21 and F-22.

5. Cone bearing for swivel pin, top.
   External dimension as shown in Figs. F-23 and F-24.

6. Examine the bottom taper roller race and swivel pin for wear and renew as necessary. The bearing should be a *light press fit* in the housing and a *light push fit* on the swivel pin. If a new bearing race is slack in the housing, the housing must be renewed; if it is slack on the swivel pin, the swivel pin assembly must be renewed. Operation F/30.

7. Examine the upper cone seat and swivel pin for wear and roughness and rectify as necessary. The cone seat should be a *light press fit* in the housing; if a new cone seat is slack in the housing, the housing must be renewed.

8. Examine the cone bearing for wear or roughness and rectify or renew as necessary.

9. Check the cone spring: free length 1.150 in. (2,92 mm) and renew as necessary.

10. Examine the surface of the swivel pin bearing housing for signs of corrosion or damage, and renew it if necessary.

11. Press the roller race outer member and cone seat squarely into the swivel pin housing as far as possible.

12. If necessary, renew the axle casing oil seal by prising out the seal from the end of the axle casing. The new seal must be fitted with the knife edge inwards. For further details see Operation F/14.

13. Place the swivel pin housing oil seal and retainer over the axle casing flange, and fit the joint washer in position on the joint face of the flange.

14. Fit the half-shaft roller race outer member and race in the swivel pin bearing housing and fit the housing to the axle casing flange.

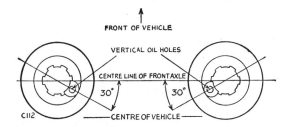

Fig. F-28—Position of oil hole. 1948-53

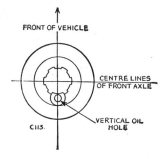

Fig. 29. Position of oil hole. 1954-58

15. Insert the cone bearing after smearing with oil, with the vertical oil hole in the bearing as shown at illustration F-28 or F-29.

16. Insert the race inner member, and holding it in position, offer the swivel pin housing to the bearing housing.

17. Replace the swivel pin and bracket assembly at the bottom of the swivel pin housing, together with the shims removed on stripping (at least .040 in.—1,0 mm—should be used). Tighten down and sharply tap the assembly to ensure positive seating. Recheck the tightness of the securing nuts.

18. Insert the cone spring in the top bearing.

19. Fit the swivel pin and steering lever assembly at the top of the swivel pin housing, with shims to the value of .040 in.—1,0 mm.

   Note: The double steering lever is fitted to the L.H. assembly on R.H.D. models and to the R.H. assembly on L.H.D. vehicles.

20. Pull down the top swivel pin securing nuts evenly in rotation until tight, then check the resistance to rotation of the steering lever measured at the track rod hole in the lever; see Fig. F-30. Add or subtract shims at the top until a figure of 14-16 lbs. (6,25-7,25 kg) is obtained.

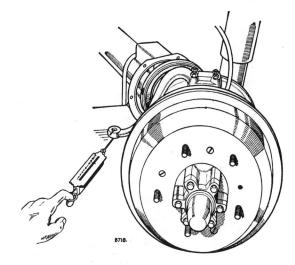

Fig. F-30—Checking swivel pin housing resistance to rotation.

21. Pack the swivel pin housing oil seal with heavy grease, and fit the seal and its retainer to the swivel pin housing.

   Check that the oil seal wipes the full surface of the bearing housing and adjust the position of the oil seal by slackening off the retainer bolts and re-setting the seal as necessary.

22. Check that there is a .050 in. (1,27 mm) clearance between the stub and half shaft yoke lugs and the swivel pin end faces. If the clearance is insufficient, increase the chamfer on the radius of the yokes.

23. Set the lock stop bolts, so that the head of the bolt protrudes ½ in. (12,7 mm) from face of oil seal retainer. See Fig. F-36.

24. Replace the half shaft, universal joint and stub shaft assembly, taking care not to damage the oil seal in the end of the casing.

25. Replace the stub axle and brake anchor plate. Operation F/22.

26. Reconnect the track rod and drag link (if applicable).

27. Replace the front hub components. Operation F/20.

28. Refill the universal joint housing with oil, 1 pint (0,5 litre).

Half shaft
To remove   **Operation F/36**

1. Remove the front hub components. Operation F/18.

2. Remove the stub axle. Operation F/22.

3. Withdraw the stub shaft, universal joint and half shaft assembly from the universal joint housing assembly.

To strip   **Operation F/38**

1. EARLY TYPE AXLES ONLY. Remove the half shaft roller bearing retaining collar by filing a flat on its outer diameter. When its thickness has been sufficiently reduced, the collar will split of its own accord (Fig. F-31). Care must be taken to prevent damage to the shaft and the roller race.

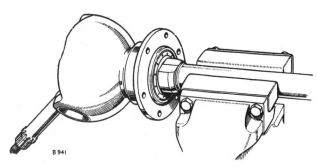

Fig. F-31—Removing the half shaft roller race retaining collar.

Withdraw the half shaft roller race outer member by tapping the joint face of the swivel pin bearing housing flange with a soft-nosed hammer (Fig. F-32).

Grip the half-shaft in a soft-jawed vice and remove the race inner member from the shaft by tapping the conical distance piece from inside the swivel pin bearing housing with a suitable drift (Fig. F-33).

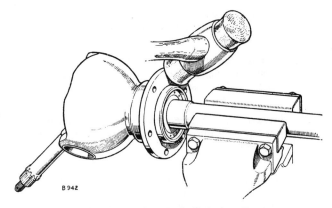

Fig. F-32—Removing the half shaft roller race outer member.

Note: On axles fitted with a plain distance piece, the race is removed by tapping the outer edge of race *inner member*; in such cases, great care must be taken to prevent damage to the race itself.

Remove the roller race inner member and race and the distance piece. Withdraw the stub shaft, universal joint and half shaft assembly from the swivel pin bearing housing.

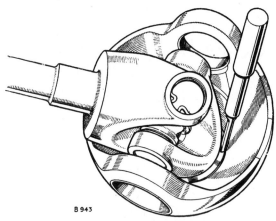

Fig. F-33—Removing the half shaft roller race.

2. Remove the two bearing races from the half shaft yoke. Operation F/28. Part the shaft from the universal joint.

3. LATE TYPE AXLES ONLY. Stand the half shaft on its splined end and press down squarely on the conical distance piece, using press blocks, A, D, J and K (Part No. 245178) (Fig. F-34).

4. Remove the collar together with the roller race inner member and the conical distance piece. Discard the retaining collar.

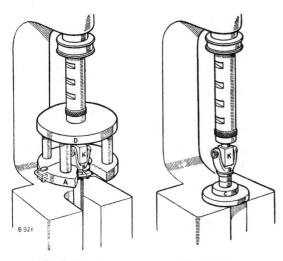

Fig. F-34—
Stripping the half-shaft.

Fig. F-35—
Assembling the half-shaft.

To assemble Operation F/40

1. Examine the bearing for excessive wear. The bearing is a *light press fit* on the shaft and a *light push fit* in the housing. Examine the external surface of the swivel pin bearing housing for signs of corrosion or damage. Renew the bearing or housing as necessary.

2. EARLY TYPE AXLES ONLY. Slide the swivel pin bearing housing over the shaft.

3. Fit the **conical** distance piece over the half shaft with the internal chamfer to the radius on the shaft.

4. Place the roller race inner member and a new retaining collar over the half shaft with the chamfer towards the splined end; stand the shaft on end and press the race inner member and collar on to the shaft until the race inner member abuts the conical distance piece. The necessary press blocks C and K, Part No. 245178, are illustrated at Fig F-35.

5. EARLY TYPE AXLES ONLY. Refit the roller race outer member into the swivel pin bearing housing.

6. Connect the half shaft to the spider journals. Operation F/28.

To refit Operation F/42

1. If necessary, renew the axle casing oil seal. Operation F/14.

2. EARLY TYPE AXLES ONLY. Reassemble the universal joint housing assembly. Operation F/34.

3. LATE TYPE AXLES ONLY. Replace the half shaft, universal joint and stub shaft assembly, taking care not to damage the axle casing oil seal.

4. Check that there is a .050 in. (1,27 mm) clearance between the stub and half shaft yoke lugs and the swivel pin end faces. If the clearance is insufficient, increase the chamfer on the radius of the yokes.

5. Replace the stub axle and brake anchor plate. Operation F/22.

6. Complete the assembly. Operation F/20.

Swivel pin bearing housing
To renew Operation F/44

1. Remove and strip the universal joint housing assembly. Operation F/32.

2. EARLY TYPE AXLES ONLY. Withdraw the half shaft, universal joint and stub shaft assembly from the swivel pin bearing housing.

3. Discard the housing.

4. Reassemble the universal joint housing and complete the assembly Operation F/34.

Lock stop
To adjust Operation F/46

1. Slacken the stop bolt locknut(s). Two locknuts are provided on 107 models.

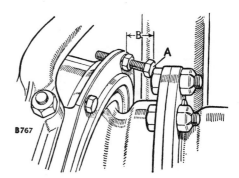

Fig. F-36—Adjusting lock stop bolt.

A—Lock stop bolt.
B—6.00 x 16 tyres: 11/16 in. (17,5 mm)
7.00 x 16 tyres: 55/64 in. (21,8 mm)
When lock stop plate is fitted:
6.00 x 16 tyres: ½ in. (12,5 mm)
7.00 x 16 tyres: 21/32 in. (16,5 mm)

2. Adjust the stop bolt so that the distance from the head of the bolt to the face of the oil seal retainer is correct.

3. Tighten the locknut(s).

Note: Early 107 models are not fitted with this adjustment, a fixed stop being provided.

Axle complete
To remove, method 1 Operation F/48

1. Jack up the front of the vehicle and place jacking stands under the chassis side member.

2. Remove both road wheels.

3. Depress the brake pedal and wedge it in that position; disconnect the flexible brake pipes at the wheel brake units.

4. Disconnect the drag link from the lower relay lever.

5. Disconnect the propeller shaft at the differential input flange.

6. Remove the self-locking nuts from the rear shackle and withdraw the shackle bolts.

7. Remove the jack with the complete axle towards the front.

To remove, method 2   Operation F/50

An alternative method for removal eliminates removal of the shackle pins; proceed as follows:—

1. Jack up the front of the vehicle and place jacking stands under the chassis side members.

2. Remove the road wheels.

3. Drain off the universal joint housing and the axle oil.

4. Depress the brake pedal and wedge it in that position; detach the flexible brake pipes at the wheel brake units.

5. Disconnect the drag link and track rod from the steering arms and lower relay lever.

6. Withdraw each half shaft complete with joint washer, universal joint housing, hub and brake gear from the axle casing, taking care not to damage the axle casing oil seal.

7. Disconnect the propeller shaft at the differential input flange.

8. Remove the differential assembly. Operation F/4.

9. Remove the U-bolts and allow the road spring bottom plates to hang on the shock absorbers.

10. Remove the axle casing by manoeuvring it past the road springs.

To refit   Operation F/52

1. Replace the axle assembly by reversing the removal procedure (Method 1 or 2).

2. Bleed the brake system. Section H.

3. Lower the vehicle off the jacking stands and refill the differential (3 pints, 1,75 litres) and universal joint housing (1 pint, 0,5 litre) with oil.

DEFECT LOCATION
Symptom, Cause and Remedy

A—VEHICLE PULLS TO ONE SIDE

1. Incorrect camber—*Check for worn bushes, settled road springs or damage to front axle unit.*
2. Incorrect or unequal castor and swivel pin inclination—*Chèck front wheel alignment. Check for damage to front axle unit and settled road springs.*
3. Uneven tyre pressures or worn tyres—*Renew tyres if necessary and check pressures. Section S.*
4. Dragging brake—*Adjust. Section H.*
5. Swivel pin tight—*Rectify or renew.*
6. Tight or dry front wheel bearings—*Inspect the wheel bearings for damage; adjust and check oil level.*
7. Incorrect toe-in on front wheels—*Adjust.*

B—VEHICLE WANDERS

1. Incorrect castor—*Check for worn bushes and damage to front suspension and axle unit; check for settled road springs.*
2. Incorrect toe-in—*Adjust.*
3. Worn swivel pins and bearings—*Renew.*
4. Worn front wheel bearings—*Renew.*
5. Tight steering assembly—*Adjust. Section G.*
6. Bent or broken frame—*Examine frame for damage. Section K.*
7. Loose axle "U" bolts—*Tighten.*
8. Unequal tyre pressures—*Section S.*
9. Unequal tyre wear—*Section S.*

C—WHEEL SHIMMY

1. Excessive castor—*Check for worn bushes and damage to the front axle or suspension; check for settled road springs.*
2. Worn ball joints—*Renew.*
3. Insufficient damping at relay unit—*Section G.*
4. Worn or loose front wheel bearings—*Adjust or renew.*
5. Steering column loose on dash—*Section G.*
6. Out-of-balance wheels—*Check, balance. Section S.*
7. Worn swivel pins and bearings—*Renew.*

8. Eccentric wheels and tyres—*Rectify or renew.*
9. Under-inflation of front tyres—*Section S.*
10. Unequal inflation—*Section S.*
11. Loose engine mountings—*Rectify or renew.*
12. Worn universal joint—*Renew. Section D.*
13. Faulty hydraulic dampers—*Renew.*
14. Insufficient damping at swivel pins—*Adjust.*
15. Broken spring leaves—*Renew.*

D—EXCESSIVE TYRE WEAR

1. Incorrect camber—*Check for worn bushes, settled road springs or damage to front axle unit.*
2. Incorrect toe-in—*Adjust.*
3. Incorrect tyre inflation—*Section S.*
4. Fast cornering—*In the hands of the operator.*
5. Wheel wobble—*Renew wheel and tyre assembly as necessary.*
6. Worn swivel pins—*Renew.*
7. Harsh or unequal brakes—*Section H.*
8. Sustained high speed driving—*In the hands of the operator.*
9. Failure to rotate tyres—*Change position of tyres, including spare—Section S.*

E—FRONT END NOISY

1. Looseness in front suspension—*Retighten and check all mountings for wear; renew as necessary. Check the front wheel alignment.*
2. Front hydraulic damper noisy—*Check damper mounting bushes for wear. If the damper itself is noisy, renew. Section J.*
3. Worn bushes—*Renew.*

F—OIL LEAKS

1. Loose drain plug—*Tighten.*
2. Worn oil seals—*Replace.*
3. Damaged joint washer—*Replace.*

Note. Modified swivel pins and bushes are available for use on models from 1954 onwards, where improved steering damping is desirable due to the vehicle having to operate under adverse conditions.

GENERAL DATA

Type:	.... Fully floating	Differential oil capacity	3 Imperial pints (1,75 litres)
Final drive	.... Spiral bevel		
Angularity of universal joint on full lock	26°	Universal joint housing oil capacity	1 Imperial pint (0,5 litre)

DETAIL DATA

Swivel pin setting: .... Resistance at steering lever eye should be:

Round section spring, no oil seal fitted .... 10-12 lb. (4,5-5,5 kg)

Round section spring, oil seal fitted .... 16-24 lb. (7-11 kg)

Rectangular section spring, no oil seal fitted .... 14-16 lb. (6,25-7.25 kg)

Rectangular section spring, oil seal fitted 18-26 lb. (8-12 kg.)

Clearance between stub and half shaft yoke lugs and swivel pin end faces .... .050 in. (1,27 mm)

Cone spring:
Number of working coils .... Three
Free length .... 1.150 in. ± .010 (29 mm ± 0,25)
Length in position .687 in. (17,4 mm)
Rate .... 660 lb/in. (7,5 mKg)
Fit of retaining collar on shaft .... .001 in. (0,025 mm) interference (selective assembly)

Differential assembly:

Pinion teeth 9
Crownwheel teeth .... 44 } Early models
Ratio .... 4.88 to 1

Pinion teeth 10
Crownwheel teeth .... 47 } Late models
Ratio .... 4.7 to 1

Backlash: crownwheel to pinion:
4.7 to 1 ratio .... .008 to .010 in. (0,20 to 0,25 mm) at the tightest point

4.88 to 1 ratio .... .007 in. at the tightest point

Backlash: differential wheels to differential pinions .... Minimum but definite backlash

Differential pinion input flange: tightening torque 85 lb./ft. (11,75 mKg)

Crownwheel fixing bolts, tightening torque .... Standard .375 in. (9,5 mm) bolts 35 lb./ft.
Special .390 in. (10 mm) bolts 45 lb/ft.

Pinion thrust bearing pinch, early type only .003-.004 in. (0,08 to 0,1 mm)

Pinion thrust bearing pre-load, late type only .... Adjust to give a torque of 6 to 10 in./lb. (0,069 to 0,115 kgm) on the pinion shaft

Crownwheel bearing pre-load .... .005 in. (0,13 mm)

Distance from crownwheel axis to pinion face:
4.7 to 1 ratio .... 3.000 to 3.002 in.
4.88 to 1 ratio .... 3.002 to 3.004 in.

Front hub and stub axle assembly

Front hub end-float .... .003 to .004 in. (0,08 to 0,10 mm)

Clearance between stub shaft and stub axle bush .... .020 to .028 in. (0,50 to 0,70 mm)

Stub axle bush bore .... 1.250 in. + .004 (31,75 mm + 0,10)

Section G
STEERING UNIT AND LINKAGE — ALL MODELS

INDEX

	Page		Page
Ball joints	G-11	Relay unit	G-8
Data	G-12	Steering column thrust bearing	G-2
Defect location	G-12	Steering control tube	G-2
Drag link	G-10	Steering unit, recirculating ball type	G-6
Drop arm	G-2	Steering unit, worm and nut type	G-1
Longitudinal steering arm	G-8	Track rod	G-11
		Wheel alignment	G-11

LIST OF ILLUSTRATIONS

Fig.		Page	Fig.		Page
G-1	Adjusting steering column thrust bearing	G-2	G-8	Relay unit	G-8
G-2	Replacing main nut in steering box	G-3	G-9	Compressing steering relay spring	G-9
G-3	Checking rocker shaft end-float	G-3	G-10	Assembling steering relay shaft assembly	G-9
G-4	Layout of steering column and linkage	G-4			
G-5	Sectional view of steering column top	G-6	G-11	Alternative method of compressing relay shaft assembly	G-10
G-6	Relative position of cam, bearings and main nut	G-7	G-12	Replacing steering relay shaft and bushes in housing	G-10
G-7	Sectioned view of rocker shaft and steering box	G-8			

WORM AND NUT TYPE STEERING UNIT

Steering control tube

To remove   **Operation G/2**

1. Disconnect the steering column wiring from the junction box on the dash panel.

2. Release the clip securing the wiring to the steering box and slide the rubber grommet (against the bottom of the steering box) off the wiring.

3. Remove the control tube clamp and joint washer from the control tube; pull the conical rubber washer in the cover plate off the wiring.

4. Pull the control tube and wiring up through the steering column and remove.

5. Remove the horn button and dipper switch unit from the control tube and disconnect the wiring from the unit as necessary. Section P.

To refit   **Operation G/4**

1. Renew the wiring, horn button and dipper switch unit and control tube bushes as found necessary.

2. Position the felt bush at the top of the tube and the two rubber bushes at equal intervals down the tube.

3. Insert the complete assembly into the steering column and pull the wiring clear at the bottom.

4. Slide the rubber washer over the bottom of the control tube; fit the clamp and joint washer on the bottom cover plate.

5. Position the control unit with the dipper switch at the bottom and secure the tube in the clamp.

6. Slide the rubber grommet over the wiring up to the clamp.

7. Reconnect the steering column wiring to the junction box on the dash panel, Section P, and secure the wiring to the steering box with a clip.

Steering wheel

To remove   **Operation G/6**

1. Remove the steering control tube. Operation G/2.

2. Remove the steering wheel from the steering inner column.

To replace   **Operation G/8**

Reverse the removal procedure.

Steering column thrust bearing

To adjust   Operation G/10

1. Remove the steering wheel. Operation G/6. The control tube and steering wheel need only be withdrawn as far as necesssary for the adjustment to be made.

2. Pull the spring and dust cover clear of the thrust adjustment.

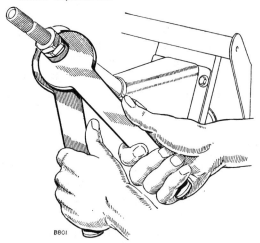

Fig. G-1—Adjusting steering column thrust bearing.

3. To remove any end-float in the inner column, unscrew the locking (upper) nut and screw down the adjusting (lower) nut until there is 7 to 9 lb./in. (0,08 to 0,10 mKg) pre-load on the thrust ball race; in practice this means that the end-float just disappears. Tighten the locking nut, using the special spanners, Part No. 263099.

4. Replace the steering wheel and control tube. Operation G/8.

Drop arm

To renew   Operation G/12

1. Remove the longitudinal steering rod ball joint from the drop arm.

   Note: If the ball joint pin is tight in the drop arm, the longitudinal steering tube and drop arm should be removed together. Operation G/22.

2. Withdraw the drop arm. Renew the drop arm if necessary.

3. Set the road wheels straight ahead and the steering unit in the midway position between full lock in each direction.

4. Fit the drop arm on the rocker shaft, selecting a suitable position on the splines, so that it lines up with the ball-joint pin.

   Note: A suitable wedge-shaped tool must be used to open the slot in the drop arm when removing and replacing it on the splined end of the rocker shaft. This avoids damage to the splines and the side cover plate.

5. Reconnect the ball joint to the drop arm.

6. Fill the steering box with clean oil.

Steering unit

To remove   Operation G/14

1. Disconnect the battery. Section P.

2. Remove the air cleaner. Section M.

3. Remove the steering control tube. Operation G/10.

4. Remove the steering wheel, dust cover and spring. Operation G/6.

5. Remove the steering column clip and rubber strip from the support bracket on the dash.

6. Remove the steering column support bracket.

7. Remove the steering column rubber grommet.

8. Withdraw the drop arm from the rocker shaft.

9. Remove the steering box from its support plate.

10. Withdraw the steering unit from under the front wing.

To strip   Operation G/16

1. Remove the bottom cover plate complete with joint washer.

2. Remove the side cover plate complete with joint washer.

3. Withdraw the rocker shaft, taking care not to damage either of its bushes.

4. Rotate the inner column to unscrew the main nut and withdraw the nut.

5. Remove the locking nut and adjusting nut from the top of the inner column, using the special spanner, Part No. 263099 (Fig. G-1); remove the eighteen 7/32in. (5,5 mm) steel balls forming the thrust race.

6. Withdraw the inner column upwards through the outer column.

   Vehicles Chassis No. 4710 series and early 5710 series.
   Remove the rocker shaft cork sealing washer and retainer from the steering box.

   Vehicles Chassis No. late 5710 series onwards.
   Remove the rocker shaft rubber sealing washer and retainer from the steering box.

8. Drive or press out the two rocker shaft bushes, if necessary.

To assemble   Operation G/18

1. Examine the inner column and main nut for wear, which will give rise to excessive play between the two parts; renew as necessary.

2. Examine the thrust race components and renew if badly worn.

3. Press in the new rocker shaft bushes if the original parts were removed. The bushes should be a *light drive fit* in the steering box and reamed in position to the dimension given in the data.

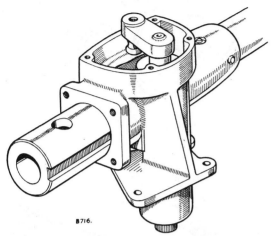

B716.

Fig. G-2—Replacing main nut in steering box.

4. Assemble the unit by reversing the stripping procedure, particular attention being paid to the following points:—

(a) Replace the nut in the steering box, *threaded portion first.*

(b) Ensure that the top face of the rocker shaft is almost flush with the top face of the side cover plate joint washer (available .010 in. and .020 in. thick) by means of a straight edge, as the rocker shaft must not have any end-float with the side cover plate in position.

(c) Replace the drop arm by using a wedge-shaped tool to slightly open the slot in the drop arm while replacing it on the rocker shaft, in order to eliminate any possibility of damage to the side cover plate.

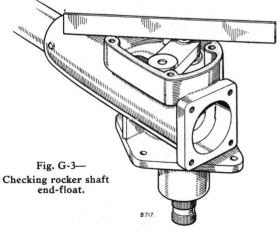

Fig. G-3—
Checking rocker shaft
end-float.

B717.

The thrust race should be packed with grease on assembly.

5. Adjust the thrust race. Operation G/10.

To refit   Operation G/20

1. Reverse the removal procedure.

2. Before connecting the drop arm to the rocker shaft, set the road wheels straight ahead and the steering inner column in the midway position between full lock in each direction.

3. Fill the steering box with oil (see Instruction Manual).

Longitudinal steering tube

To renew   Operation G/22

1. Raise the upper relay lever slightly to allow the ball joint pin to clear the lever and remove the longitudinal tube ball joint from the lever.

2. Withdraw the drop arm from the rocker shaft splines.

3. Withdraw the longitudinal tube and drop arm together towards the front of the vehicle under the radiator grille panel.

4. Disconnect the ball joint from the drop arm.

5. Unscrew the ball joints from the tube. (One left-hand and one right-hand thread.)

6. Examine the ball joints for wear in the body and pin, and renew the complete units as necessary; replace the rubber covers if damaged. Ball joints are supplied as complete units; only the rubber cover and retaining rings can be obtained separately. (Fig. G-1.) Renew the tube if necessary.

7. Fit the ball joints to the tube, leaving the clips slack at this stage.

8. Fit the drop arm to one ball joint.

9. Replace the tube and drop arm under the radiator grille panel.

10. Set the road wheels in the straight ahead position and the steering wheel in the midway position between full lock in each direction.

11. Fit the drop arm to the steering rocker shaft, Operation G/20, selecting a suitable position on the splines so that it is approximately vertical.

12. Fit the front ball joint to the upper relay lever, turning the tube to increase or decrease its effective length, so that the relay lever is not disturbed. Tighten the ball joint clips.

13. Check that the road wheels reach full lock (as determined by the limit stops on the swivel pin housings) in each direction.

14. Top up the steering unit.

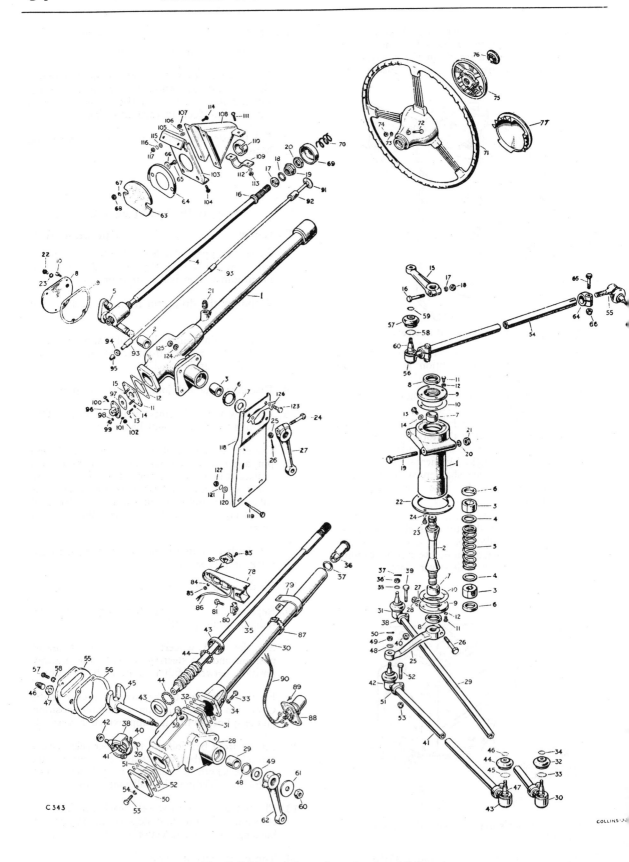

Fig. G-4—Layout of steering column and linkage.

Key to Fig. G-4

Steering Unit, Wheel and Drop Arm

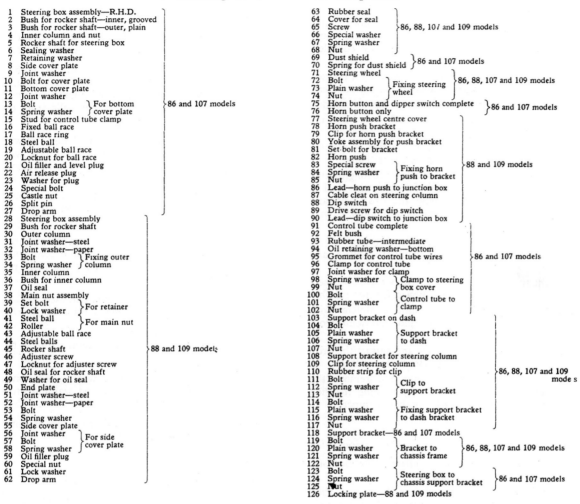

1	Steering box assembly—R.H.D.	
2	Bush for rocker shaft—inner, grooved	
3	Bush for rocker shaft—outer, plain	
4	Inner column and nut	
5	Rocker shaft for steering box	
6	Sealing washer	
7	Retaining washer	
8	Side cover plate	
9	Joint washer	
10	Bolt for cover plate	
11	Bottom cover plate	
12	Joint washer	
13	Bolt } For bottom	86 and 107 models
14	Spring washer } cover plate	
15	Stud for control tube clamp	
16	Fixed ball race	
17	Ball race ring	
18	Steel ball	
19	Adjustable ball race	
20	Locknut for ball race	
21	Oil filler and level plug	
22	Air release plug	
23	Washer for plug	
24	Special bolt	
25	Castle nut	
26	Split pin	
27	Drop arm	
28	Steering box assembly	
29	Bush for rocker shaft	
30	Outer column	
31	Joint washer—steel	
32	Joint washer—paper	
33	Bolt } Fixing outer	
34	Spring washer } column	
35	Inner column	
36	Bush for inner column	
37	Oil seal	
38	Main nut assembly	
39	Set bolt } For retainer	
40	Lock washer }	
41	Steel ball } For main nut	88 and 109 models
42	Roller }	
43	Adjustable ball race	
44	Steel balls	
45	Rocker shaft	
46	Adjuster screw	
47	Locknut for adjuster screw	
48	Oil seal for rocker shaft	
49	Washer for oil seal	
50	End plate	
51	Joint washer—steel	
52	Joint washer—paper	
53	Bolt	
54	Spring washer	
55	Side cover plate	
56	Joint washer } For side	
57	Bolt } cover plate	
58	Spring washer	
59	Oil filler plug	
60	Special nut	
61	Lock washer	
62	Drop arm	

63	Rubber seal	
64	Cover for seal	
65	Screw } 86, 88, 107 and 109 models	
66	Special washer	
67	Spring washer	
68	Nut	
69	Dust shield } 86 and 107 models	
70	Spring for dust shield	
71	Steering wheel	
72	Bolt } Fixing steering } 86, 88, 107 and 109 models	
73	Plain washer } wheel	
74	Nut	
75	Horn button and dipper switch complete } 86 and 107 models	
76	Horn button only	
77	Steering wheel centre cover	
78	Horn push bracket	
79	Clip for horn push bracket	
80	Yoke assembly for push bracket	
81	Set bolt for bracket	
82	Horn push	
83	Special screw } Fixing horn } 88 and 109 models	
84	Spring washer } push to bracket	
85	Nut	
86	Lead—horn push to junction box	
87	Cable cleat on steering column	
88	Dip switch	
89	Drive screw for dip switch	
90	Lead—dip switch to junction box	
91	Control tube complete	
92	Felt bush	
93	Rubber tube—intermediate	
94	Oil retaining washer—bottom	
95	Grommet for control tube wires } 86 and 107 models	
96	Clamp for control tube	
97	Joint washer for clamp	
98	Spring washer } Clamp to steering	
99	Nut } box cover	
100	Bolt	
101	Spring washer } Control tube to	
102	Nut } clamp	
103	Support bracket on dash	
104	Bolt	
105	Plain washer } Support bracket	
106	Spring washer } to dash	
107	Nut	
108	Support bracket for steering column	
109	Clip for steering column	
110	Rubber strip for clip } 86, 88, 107 and 109 models	
111	Bolt }	
112	Spring washer } Clip to	
113	Nut } support bracket	
114	Bolt	
115	Plain washer } Fixing support bracket	
116	Spring washer } to dash bracket	
117	Nut	
118	Support bracket—86 and 107 models	
119	Bolt	
120	Plain washer } Bracket to } 86, 88, 107 and 109 models	
121	Spring washer } chassis frame	
122	Nut	
123	Bolt } Steering box to	
124	Spring washer } chassis support bracket } 86 and 107 models	
125	Nut	
126	Locking plate—88 and 109 models	

Relay Unit and Steering Arms

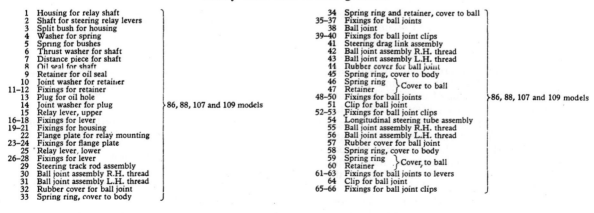

1	Housing for relay shaft	
2	Shaft for steering relay levers	
3	Split bush for housing	
4	Washer for spring	
5	Spring for bushes	
6	Thrust washer for shaft	
7	Distance piece for shaft	
8	Oil seal for shaft	
9	Retainer for oil seal	
10	Joint washer for retainer	
11–12	Fixings for retainer	
13	Plug for oil hole	86, 88, 107 and 109 models
14	Joint washer for plug	
15	Relay lever, upper	
16–18	Fixings for lever	
19–21	Fixings for housing	
22	Flange plate for relay mounting	
23–24	Fixings for flange plate	
25	Relay lever, lower	
26–28	Fixings for lever	
29	Steering track rod assembly	
30	Ball joint assembly R.H. thread	
31	Ball joint assembly L.H. thread	
32	Rubber cover for ball joint	
33	Spring ring, cover to body	

34	Spring ring and retainer, cover to ball	
35–37	Fixings for ball joints	
38	Ball joint	
39–40	Fixings for ball joint clips	
41	Steering drag link assembly	
42	Ball joint assembly R.H. thread	
43	Ball joint assembly L.H. thread	
44	Rubber cover for ball joint	
45	Spring ring, cover to body	
46	Spring ring } Cover to ball	
47	Retainer	
48–50	Fixings for ball joints	86, 88, 107 and 109 models
51	Clip for ball joint	
52–53	Fixings for ball joint clips	
54	Longitudinal steering tube assembly	
55	Ball joint assembly R.H. thread	
56	Ball joint assembly L.H. thread	
57	Rubber cover for ball joint	
58	Spring ring, cover to body	
59	Spring ring } Cover to ball	
60	Retainer	
61–63	Fixings for ball joints to levers	
64	Clip for ball joint	
65–66	Fixings for ball joint clips	

RECIRCULATING BALL TYPE STEERING UNIT

Steering unit—to remove   Operation G/24

1. Unscrew the clamp bolt and withdraw the steering wheel.

2. Disconnect the clamp securing the horn switch and support bracket to the steering outer column, then remove the assembly complete with leads.

3. Remove the spare wheel if mounted on bonnet, disconnect the support and lift the bonnet clear.

4. R.H.D. models only—Remove the air cleaner.

5. Remove the name plate and withdraw the radiator grille.

6. Loosen the bolt securing the upper relay lever to the relay unit and prise the lever clear.

7. Turn the steering wheel to allow the longitudinal steering arm to move fully forward, then slacken the clamping bolt nearest the drop arm and unscrew the longitudinal arm complete with relay lever.

8. Remove the bolts securing the steering support bracket to chassis side-member, scuttle and wing valance.

9. The support clip, rubber strip, support brackets and seal must now be removed from the dash.

10. Withdraw the steering unit complete with support plate, drop arm and ball joint from under the front wing.

11. Remove the securing screw and extract the drop arm, using special tool (Part No. 262776).

12. Unscrew the castellated nut and remove the ball joint from drop arm by tapping the side adjacent to taper smartly with a hammer.

Steering unit—to refit   Operation G/26

1. Refit the support plate to chassis side-member, scuttle and wing valance.

2. Mount the steering unit less drop arm, then secure at dash and support plate. Refit the horn switch and bracket assembly.

3. Turn the inner steering column lock to lock and select the intermediate position.

4. Replace the steering wheel with one series of spokes pointing forward and secure.

5. Screw the ball joint into the longitudinal arm and lock in the original position.

6. Fit the longitudinal arm complete with upper relay lever to the drop arm and insert the assembly along the top of chassis side-member. Connect the upper relay lever to relay unit.

7. With the front wheels positioned "straight ahead" and the steering wheel in the intermediate position, fit the drop arm to the rocker shaft. The longitudinal arm may require adjusting slightly to align the splines of drop arm and steering rocker shaft.

8. **Check the steering**, lock to lock, for correct functioning. Adjust if necessary by altering the length of the longitudinal arm.

Steering unit—to dismantle   Operation G/28

1. Remove the side cover and drain off the oil.

2. Lift off the main nut, roller, and withdraw the rocker shaft.

3. With the outer column held in a vice, unscrew the nuts holding the steering box and tap the inner column at the steering wheel end with a hide-faced hammer to partially remove the box.

4. Withdraw the box and inner column complete. The dust cover at the top of steering column will be freed by this last operation and care must be taken to ensure that this or balls from the steering box are not inadvertently lost.

5. Make provision for catching the balls, and with a hide-faced hammer, gently tap the box away from the **inner column** sufficiently to remove the outer ball race.

   Note: The main nut should be positioned approximately midway on the cam during this operation.

6. Turn the inner column to unscrew the main nut assembly and withdraw the column completely from the steering box. Remove the main nut assembly.

7. Remove the end cover, shims, ball race and any balls that may have dropped into the steering box.

8. The ball transfer tube may be removed from the main nut.

9. If oil leakage and bearing wear is excessive, remove the retaining washer, oil seal and press out the bush from steering box.

10. Remove the bush and seal from top of outer column, if excessively worn.

Steering unit—to assemble   Operation G/30

1. Press the Tufnol bush with oil seal into the top outer steering column tube.

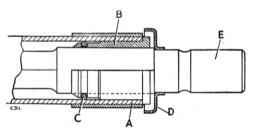

Fig. G-5—Sectioned view of steering column top.
A—Column outer tube   C—Seal
B—Tufnol bush   D—Dust cover
E—Inner shaft

2. If removed fit the rocker shaft bush to the steering box.

3. Locate the rocker shaft seal and retaining washer.

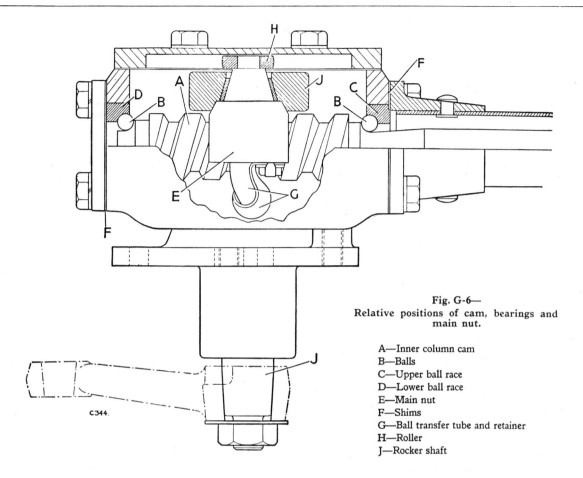

Fig. G-6—
Relative positions of cam, bearings and
main nut.

A—Inner column cam
B—Balls
C—Upper ball race
D—Lower ball race
E—Main nut
F—Shims
G—Ball transfer tube and retainer
H—Roller
J—Rocker shaft

4. Grease any thickness shim and two paper washers each side of the shim, to the flange on the outer column, then mount the outer column in a vertical position in a vice (Tufnol bush downwards).

5. Place one of the ball races, less ball bearings, over the inner column and slide the inner column into the outer column and Tufnol bush, ensuring it is free to rotate. Lift the inner column a little, grease the ball race and load with ten ball bearings, ensuring that none fall down the inside of the outer column.

6. Assemble the main nut, replacing balls as necessary and retain them in position with grease. Locate the assembly in steering box and lower on to the cam end of the inner column.

7. Carefully rotate the inner column, ensuring that the ball bearings in the main nut are not dislodged, and the steering box is up the correct way. (Filler plug towards the outer column.)

8. Grease the lower ball race and stick **ten** balls in position. Locate the outer ball race, shims, joint washer and end cover, then carefully tighten, ensuring that none of the balls are dislodged.

   Note: The inner shaft should have **no** end-float, but to ensure that the bearings are not over-stressed, sufficient shims must first be fitted to allow an end-float

reading and then shims equivalent in thickness to this reading, be removed.

The steering unit may now be elevated into a horizontal position.

9. Fit the main nut, roller, replace the rocker shaft, joint washer and cover, ensuring that the roller is correctly located in the cover slot.

10. With the main nut at mid-position on cam, tighten the adjusting screw on side cover by hand until resistance is felt as it contacts the rocker shaft; tighten a further tenth of a turn and lock the adjusting screw.

11. Refit the dust cover to top end of steering column.

Steering wheel

To remove   Operation G/32

1. Unscrew the clamping bolt at hub and withdraw the wheel.

Drop arm

To remove   Operation G/34

1. The complete steering unit must be removed before the drop arm can be extracted—see Operation G/24.

To refit

   See Operation G/26.

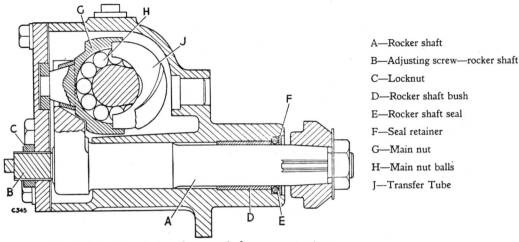

Fig. G-7—Sectioned view of rocker shaft and steering box.

A—Rocker shaft
B—Adjusting screw—rocker shaft
C—Locknut
D—Rocker shaft bush
E—Rocker shaft seal
F—Seal retainer
G—Main nut
H—Main nut balls
J—Transfer Tube

Longitudinal steering arm

To remove   Operation G/36

1. Remove the radiator grille, loosen the clamping bolt securing the upper relay lever and prise the lever off the relay unit.

2. Turn the steering wheel to allow the longitudinal steering arm to move fully forward, loosen the clamping bolt nearest to drop arm and unscrew the longitudinal arm complete with relay lever. Withdraw the assembly from the front of vehicle.

3. Unscrew the castellated nut securing the ball joint to the drop arm, then with a solid metallic object on one side of the drop arm adjacent to the taper, tap the other side with a hammer to loosen the ball joint.

4. Turn the steering wheel to move the drop arm rearwards and remove the ball joint.

To replace   Operation G/38

1. Reverse the removal procedure, ensuring that the longitudinal arm is screwed back on to exactly the former position.

2. Check the "lock to lock" movement and alter if necessary by adjusting the length of the longitudinal arm.

Steering relay unit

To remove   Operation G/40

1. Remove the air cleaner and battery. Section P.

2. Remove the bolts securing the radiator grille panel to the front wings.

3. Remove the bolts securing the grille panel to the chassis frame; remove the front apron panel; when the bolts are clear, the rubber packing pieces between the panel and frame may also be withdrawn. It will now be possible to move the radiator assembly slightly to assist in the removal of the relay unit, but care must be taken to prevent damage to the coolant hoses.

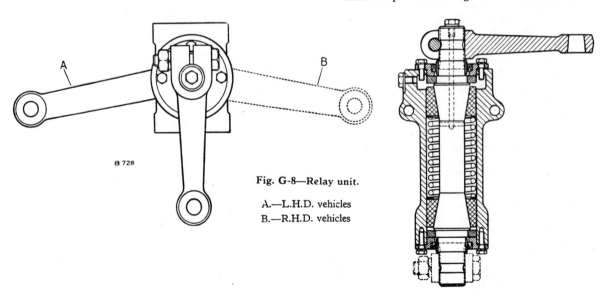

Fig. G-8—Relay unit.

A.—L.H.D. vehicles
B.—R.H.D. vehicles

4. Raise the upper relay lever slightly to allow the ball joint pin to clear the lever; disconnect the longitudinal tube ball joint from the upper relay lever.

5. Detach the lower relay lever from the relay unit shaft.

6. Remove the relay unit upwards, tapping gently with a hide-faced hammer, if necessary. The flange plate can be left in position on the under-side of the chassis cross-member.

To strip   **Operation G/42**

1. Remove the upper relay lever.

2. Drain off as much oil as possible by removing the oil filler and bleed plugs.

3. Remove the bottom plate complete with oil seal and joint washer.

   Secure a sack over the bottom half of the relay box and mount relay in a vice with the bottom pointing downwards into the sack.

   CAREFULLY tap out the shaft, Tufnol bushes and spring into the sack.

   Note: The spring is compressed to over 100 lb. (45 kg) when in position, and will cause serious damage if care is not exercised.

4. Remove the bottom end plate and brass thrust washer.

To assemble   **Operation G/44**

1. Examine the oil seals in the end caps and renew them if damaged. Examine the distance pieces on the shaft (which form tracks for the oil seals) for damage which may have caused failure of the seals; renew them as necessary.

2. Renew the split Tufnol bushes if worm or damaged.

3. Check the spring in accordance with given data. Renew the spring if necessary.

4. Fit the top end plate and joint washer to the housing.

5. Fit one split bush to the taper on the shaft and secure tightly with a suitable 2 in. hose clip (Part No. 50320).

6. Hold a suitable bar (Part No. 262768) over each end of the spring and compress it to a length of 3 in. (76 mm) in a vice, with the bars central and vertical. Place a suitable clip (Part No. 262769) over each side of the spring, as shown at Fig. G-9. Release the vice and remove the spring and clips complete.

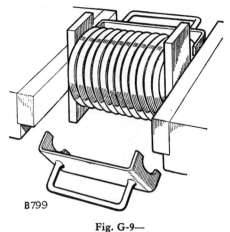

Fig. G-9—

Method of compressing steering relay spring.

7. Slide a washer over the shaft and fit the spring to the shaft so that it abuts the washer and bush.

8. Slide a second washer over the shaft and fit the second split bush to the shaft, securing it with a hose clip as for the first one (Fig. G-10).

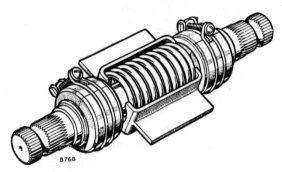

Fig. G-10—Assembling steering relay shaft assembly.

9. Remove the clips retaining the spring, slide the lower brass thrust washer over the top end of the shaft and carefully enter the assembly, top end first, into the housing; push the shaft into the housing, up towards the bleed plug end, so leaving the first hose clip free. Remove the clip and push the shaft home; release the second hose clip.

10. Fit a thrust washer to the bottom end of the shaft and fit the end cap and joint washer.

11. Fit the upper relay lever.

12. Fill the housing with oil, and fit the filler and bleed plugs and joint washers.

13. If the assembly is in order, it should need a force of at least 12 lb. (5,5 kg) to turn the relay lever and shaft, using a spring balance in the relay lever boss.

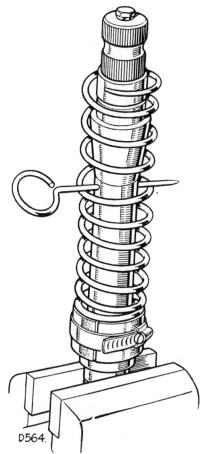

D564.

Fig. G-11—Alternative method of compressing steering relay spring

Alternative method to assemble relay unit

1. Examine all parts and renew as necessary.

2. Fit the top end plate and joint washer to the housing.

3. Fit one split bush to the taper on the bottom end of the shaft, and secure tightly with a suitable 2 in. hose clip (Part No. 50323).

4. Place a steel washer on to the shaft, next to the inner side of the Tufnol bush.

5. Place the spring over the shaft and insert the special tool (Part No. 510309) through the coils of the spring and right through the lubrication cross-drilling in the shaft.

6. The spring can now be wound down the tool until the steel washer and the split Tufnol bush can be secured to the taper on the other end of the shaft with a hose clip.

7. Remove the special tool (Part No. 510309).

8. Place a brass thrust washer on the top end of the shaft, lubricate the shaft and insert into the housing.

9. With a plastic hammer gently tap the shaft into the housing until the first hose clip slides off the Tufnol bush, remove the clip completely from the shaft.

10. Continue to tap the shaft into the housing until the second clip is freed and the shaft abuts the top end cover.

11. Fit the bleed and filler plugs, fill the unit with oil, replace the bottom end thrust washer, joint washer, end cover and tighten the retaining bolts.

12. Fit the upper relay lever.

13. If the unit is in order, it should require a force of at least 12 lb. (5,5 kg) to turn the relay shaft, using a spring balance in the relay lever boss.

To refit   **Operation G/46**

Reverse the removal procedure.

The lower relay lever must be fitted as illustrated at Fig. G-8.

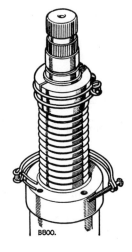

Fig. G-12—Replacing steering relay shaft and bushes in housing.

B800.

Drag link

To renew   **Operation G/48**

1. Disconnect the drag link ball joints from the lower relay lever and steering arm. Remove the drag link complete.

2. Unscrew the ball joints from the drag link tube (one left-hand and one right-hand thread).

3. Examine the ball joints for wear in the body and pin and renew the complete units as necessary; replace the rubber covers if damaged. Ball joints are supplied as complete units; only the rubber cover and retaining rings can be obtained separately. (Fig. G-1.) Renew the tube if necessary.

4. Fit the ball joints to the tube, leaving the clips slack at this stage.

5. Secure one end of the drag link to the lower relay lever.

6. Set the road wheels straight ahead and the steering wheel in the midway position between full lock in each direction.

7. Secure the other end of the drag link to the steering arm, turning the tube to increase or decrease its effective length, so that the relay lever and steering arm are not disturbed.

8. Tighten the ball joint clips.

Track rod
To renew   **Operation G/50**

1. Disconnect the track rod ball joints from the steering arms; remove the track rod complete.

2. Unscrew the ball joints from the track rod tube (one left-hand and one right-hand thread).

3. Examine the ball joints for wear in the body and pin, and renew the complete units as necessary; replace the rubber covers if damaged. Ball joints are supplied as complete units; only the rubber cover and retaining rings can be obtained separately (Fig. G-1); renew the tube if necessary.

4. Fit the ball joints to the tube, leaving the clips slack at this stage.

5. Secure the ball joints to the steering arms and adjust the toe-in. Operation G/50.

Wheel alignment
To check and adjust   **Operation G/52**

1. No adjustment is provided for castor, camber or swivel pin inclination.

2. The toe-in is adjustable; proceed as follows:

3. Set the vehicle on level ground with the road wheels in the straight-ahead position, and push it forward a short distance.

4. Measure the toe-in with the aid of a tracking stick or suitable proprietary equipment; it should be 3/64 in. to 3/32 in. (1,2 mm to 2,4 mm).

5. If correction is required to the toe-in, slacken the clips securing the ball joints to the track rod and turn the rod to decrease or increase its effective length as necessary, until the toe-in is correct.

6. Tighten the ball joint clips.

Steering ball joints
To check   **Operation G/54**

1. The steering ball joints have been designed in such a way as to retain the initial filling of grease for the normal life of the ball joint; however, this applies only if the rubber boot remains in position on the joint. The rubber boots should be checked every 3,000 miles (5.000 km) to ensure that they have not become dislodged or the joint damaged. Should any of the rubber boots be dislodged, proceed as follows:—

2. Remove the ball end from the drop arm lever by tapping smartly around the eye of the pin.

3. Remove the rubber boot.

4. Thoroughly clean all parts.

5. Place the castle nut upside down on the pin and screw on a few threads, then place the ball joint under a press or between the jaws of a vice and carefully force the pin and ball down against the spring. In this position the interior of the ball joint can be cleaned and lubricated.

6. Apply grease around the taper, and fill the rubber boot.

7. Reassemble, using new rubbers and spring rings as required.

8. When refitting track rod and ball joints to the drop arms, ensure that the ball joints are aligned with each other, in order to allow full unrestricted movement of the steering linkage.

9. When refitting longitudinal steering arm and drag link, ensure that the ball joint body is parallel with respective steering arms, in order to allow full movement.

DEFECT LOCATION

Symptom, Cause and Remedy

A—EXCESSIVE LOOSENESS OR BACKLASH IN THE STEERING

1. Steering rocker shaft incorrectly adjusted or badly worn—*Adjust or renew.*

2. Steering linkage loose or worn—*Rectify or renew.*

3. Swivel pins and bearings loose or worn—*Section F.*

4. Loose or worn front wheel bearings—*Section F.*

5. Steering box securing bolts loose—*Tighten.*

B—TIGHT STEERING

1. Low or unequal tyre pressures—*Section S.*

2. Steering box oil level low—*Replenish.*

3. Steering rocker shaft adjusted too tightly—*Adjust.*

C—RATTLE IN STEERING COLUMN

1. Steering rocker shaft incorrectly adjusted or badly worn—*Adjust or renew.*

D—VEHICLE PULLS TO ONE SIDE

1. Section F.

E—VEHICLE WANDERS

1. Section F.

F—WHEEL SHIMMY

1. Section F.

GENERAL DATA

WORM AND NUT TYPE STEERING UNIT

Type	.... Worm and nut
Ratio	.... 15 : 1
Thrust adjustment	.... 7-9 lb/in. (0,08 to 0,10 mKg) pre-load on bearing at top of column
Number of turns of steering wheel from lock to lock	2.4

RECIRCULATING BALL TYPE STEERING UNIT

Type	.... Recirculating ball
Ratio	.... Straight ahead 15.6 : 1 Full lock .... 23.8 : 1
Inner column end-float	Nil
Rocker shaft end-float	Nil
Number of turns of steering wheel from lock to lock	.... 3.3

DETAIL DATA, ALL MODELS

**Relay shaft clearances
in bushes** .... .003 to .0045 (0,08 to 0,12 mm)

Longitudinal steering tube
Ball joints
  Type .... Non-adjustable; 7/16 in. B.S.F. thread
  Tightening torque   30 lb/ft. (4 Kgm)

Steering relay unit
Bushes
  Type .... Tufnol cones

Spring:
Number of working
  coils 10
Free length .... $7\frac{1}{4}$ in. (184 mm)
Fitted length .... 3 in. (72,2 mm)
Load at fitted length.... 104 lb. (47 Kg)

Wheel alignment
Wheel camber .... $1\frac{1}{2}°$
Wheel castor .... 3°
Swivel pin inclination 7°
Toe-in .... 3/64 to 3/32 in. (1,2 mm to 2,4 mm)

Section H — BRAKE SYSTEM — ALL MODELS

INDEX

	Page			Page
Bleeding the system	H-1	Hand brake lever and linkage	H-14
Brake flexible pipe	H-5	Master cylinder	H-4
Brake pedal unit	H-4	Reservoir	H-1
Data	H-8	Transmission brake unit	H-14
Defect location	H-7	Wheel brake unit, 10 in. brakes	H-5
Foot pedal	H-4	Wheel brake unit, 11 in. brakes, front	H-10
		Wheel brake unit, 11 in. brakes, rear	H-10

LIST OF ILLUSTRATIONS

Fig.		Page	Fig.		Page
H-1	Layout of master cylinder, pedal unit and pipe lines	H-2	H-8	Plungers correctly paired	H-11
H-2	Cross-section of master cylinder	H-5	H-9	Plungers correctly located	H-11
H-3	Attachment of flexible brake hoses	H-5	H-10	Plungers incorrectly located	H-11
H-4	Layout of wheel brake unit, 10 in.	H-6	H-11	Layout of transmission brake	H-12
H-5	Wheel brake unit—front and rear, 10 in. brakes—86 and 88 models	H-7	H-12	Transmission brake unit	H-14
H-6	Layout of front wheel brake unit, 11 in. brakes—107 and 109 models	H-8	H-13	Left and right hand plungers	H-14
H-7	Layout of rear wheel brake unit, 11 in. brakes—107 and 109 models	H-9	H-14 H-15 H-16	Selection and fitting of adjuster plungers	H-15 H-15 H-16

Wheel brake system

To bleed   **Operation H/2**

If the level of the fluid in the supply tank is allowed to fall too low, or if any section of the pipeline has been disconnected, the brakes will feel "spongy", due to air having been absorbed into the system. It is necessary to remove the air-lock, bleeding the system at the wheel cylinders. Bleeding must always be carried out at all four wheels, irrespective of which portion of the pipeline is affected, starting with the wheel cylinder farthest from the master cylinder.

1. Remove the dust cover from the bleed nipple.

2. Attach a suitable length of rubber tubing, placing the lower end of the tube in a glass jar containing some brake fluid.

3. Slacken the bleed screw behind the nipple.

4. With the end of the tube held below the surface of the fluid in the jar, pump the brake pedal slowly up and down, pausing at each end of each stroke, until the fluid issuing from the tube shows no signs of air bubbles.

5. Tighten the bleed screw, with the brake pedal depressed, before removing the end of the tube from the fluid; refit the dust cover to the nipple.

6. Repeat for the three other wheels in turn.

7. It is well to continually replenish the fluid in the supply tank, to ensure that the level does not fall too low, and so cause another air-lock to be formed. Never use fluid that has just been bled from the system for topping up the supply tank, since it may be aerated.

Supply tank

To remove   **Operation H/4**

1. Drain the supply tank.

2. Disconnect the pipe to the master cylinder.

3. Remove the supply tank.

To replace   **Operation H/6**

1. Reverse the removal procedure.

2. Bleed the brakes. Operation H/2.

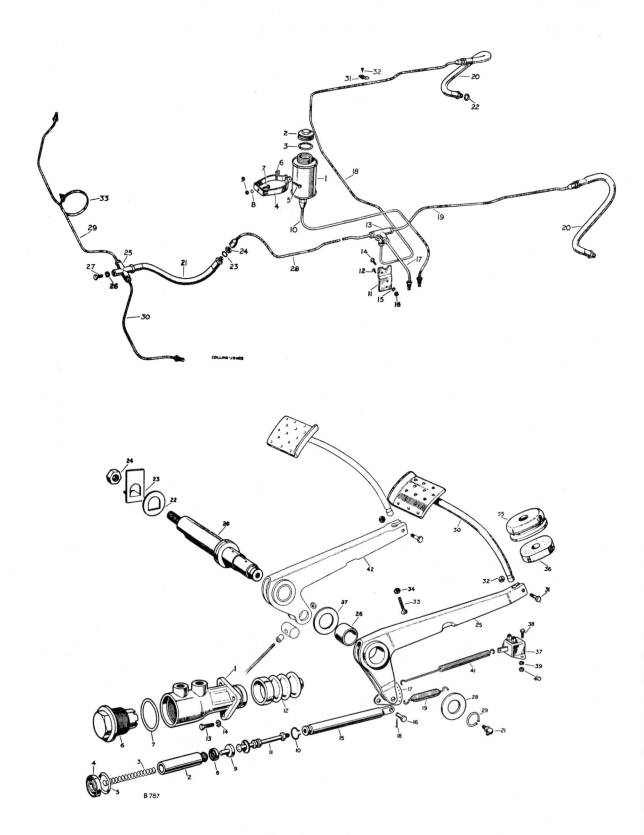

Fig. H-1—Layout of pipe lines, master cylinder and pedal

Key to Fig. H-1

1 Supply tank assembly for master cylinder
2 Filler cap for tank
3 Joint washer for cap
4 Clip for tank
5 Special bolt ⎫ Fixing clip
6 Special nut ⎭ to tank
7 Bolt ⎫
8 Spring washer ⎬ Fixing clip to dash
9 Nut ⎭
10 Brake pipe complete, for supply tank, R.H.D.
   Brake pipe complete, for supply tank, L.H.D.
11 Bracket for 4-way piece
12 Drive screw fixing bracket
13 4-way piece for brake pipes
14–16 Fixings for 4-way piece
17 Brake pipe, master cylinder to 4-way piece, R.H.D.

18 Brake pipe, 4-way to L.H. front
19 Brake pipe, 4-way to R.H. front
20 Hose complete for front wheels
21 Hose complete to rear axle
22 Joint washer for hoses
23 Shakeproof washer ⎫ Fixing hose
24 Special nut ⎭ to bracket
25 "T" piece on rear axle
26–27 Fixings for "T" piece
28 Brake pipe to rear hose
29 Brake pipe, L.H. rear to "T" piece
30 Brake pipe, R.H. rear to "T" piece
31 Clip, brake pipes to chassis frame, R.H.D.
32 Drive screw fixing clips, R.H.D.
33 Clip on rear axle for L.H. pipe

1 Master cylinder body only
2 Piston
3 Return spring for piston
4 Recuperating seal for piston, large
5 Shim washer for seal
6 End cover for body
7 Gasket for end cover
8 Rubber seal for piston, small
9 Seal retainer
10 Circlip fixing washer
11 Push rod for piston
12 Rubber boot for push rod
13 Set bolt ⎫ Fixing master cylinder
14 Spring washer ⎭ to chassis frame
15 Operating rod for brake
16 Pin for fork end ⎫
17 Spring anchor, 6 hole ⎬ Fixing operating
   type ⎪ rod to brake
18 Split pin ⎭ operating lever
19 Pull-off spring for master cylinder

20 Shaft for brake and clutch pedals
21 Grease nipple for shaft and pedal
22–24 Fixings for pedal shaft
25 Lever for brake pedal, R.H.D.
26 Bush for brake pedal lever, R.H.D.
27 Thrust washer for lever
28 Special washer ⎫ Fixing pedal lever
29 Circlip ⎭ to shaft
30 Rod and pad complete for brake pedal, R.H.D.
31–32 Fixings for brake rod
33 Special stop bolt for brakes
34 Locknut for stop bolt
35 Rubber grommet ⎫ For brake
36 Felt washer ⎭ pedal rod
37 Switch for stop lamp
38–40 Fixings for stop lamp switch
41 Spring connecting switch to brake lever
42 Clutch pedal assembly

Brake pedal

To remove   Operation H/8

1948-53 models

1. Remove the pinch bolt securing the pedal lever to the spindle and withdraw the lever from the spindle splines.

2. Disconnect the pedal return spring and the stop lamp switch operating spring.

3. Remove the split pin and joint pin securing the brake lever to the master cylinder; remove the return spring anchor.

4. Remove the pinch bolt and withdraw the brake lever from the spindle.

5. Remove the lubrication nipple from the spindle.

6. Tap out the spindle from the chassis frame.

1954-58 models

1. Remove the pad and rod from the clutch and brake pedal levers. Lift off the rubber grommets and felt pads.

2. Disconnect the clutch and brake pedal return springs and the stop light operating spring.

3. Remove the clutch operating rod from the lever on the cross-shaft.

4. Remove the brake pedal from the operating rod.

5. Remove the grease nipple.

6. Remove the circlip securing the brake and clutch pedal levers to the spindle and remove both bronze thrust washers and pedal levers.

7. If necessary, remove the bush from the brake pedal lever.

8. If necessary, withdraw the pedal spindle from the chassis side member.

To refit   Operation H/10

1948-53 models

1. The diameter of the pedal spindle should be .935 in.—.001 (23,75 mm—0,02) and the internal diameter of the bushes .938 in.—.0005 (23,8 mm —0,01), thus giving a clearance of .0025 in. to .004 in. (0,06 mm to 0,1 mm). If the spindle has excessive play in the bushes, they should be renewed and reamed as necessary.

2. Clean and replace the spindle and fit the brake lever; replace the joint pin, spring anchor and split pin securing the lever to the master cylinder.

3. Fit the brake pedal lever so that in the "off" position it does not foul the chassis or body floor and does not reduce the free play in the master cylinder piston.

4. Replace the lubrication nipple and reconnect the pull-off and stop lamp switch springs. Apply one of the recommended oils at the nipple, using a suitable gun.

5. Place the felt pad and rubber grommet on to the pedal rod and secure the rod to the pedal lever; push the grommet down to the floor.

6. Set the brake pedal stop on the chassis side member so that at the upper limit of travel of the brake pedal lever, the centre-line of the pinch bolt boss for the pedal rod is flush with the top of the chassis at the nearest point.

7. Ensure that the master cylinder piston has $\frac{1}{16}$ in. (1,6 mm) free movement in the "OFF" position.

1954-58 models

1. If necessary, renew the pedal spindle and/or its bush, reaming the bush in position to the dimension given in the data.

2. Reassemble by reversing the removal procedure.

   Note: Fit grease nipple to spindle first and position the spindle so that the nipple points downwards.

3. Lubricate with appropriate oil.

4. Ensure that the master cylinder piston has 1/16 in. (1,6 mm) free movement in the 'OFF' position. Operation H/18.

5. Set the brake pedal stop on the chassis side member so that at the upper limit of travel of the brake pedal lever it just touches the lever.

Brake master cylinder

To remove   Operation H/12

1. Disconnect the inlet pipe to the master cylinder and drain off the fluid into a suitable receptacle.

2. Disconnect the outlet pipe to the wheel cylinders.

3. Disconnect the pedal pull-off and stop lamp switch springs; remove the operating rod from the brake lever.

4. 1954-58 R.H.D. models only. Remove the operating rod from the piston push rod.

5. Remove the master cylinder from the vehicle.

To strip   Operation H/14

1. Remove the end cap and copper sealing washer from the master cylinder, and withdraw the piston return spring.

2. 1954-58 L.H.D. models only. Remove the operating rod from the piston push rod.

1948-53 models

3. Remove the fork end, locknut and rubber cover from the piston operating rod; remove the circlip and retaining washer and withdraw the operating rod.

1954-58 models

Remove the locknut and rubber cover from the piston push rod; remove the circlip and retaining washer and withdraw the push rod.

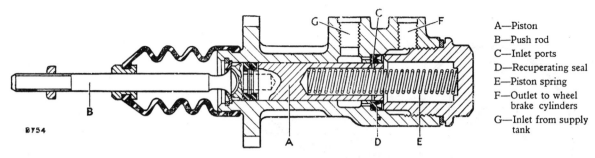

Fig. H-2—Cross-section of master cylinder.

A—Piston
B—Push rod
C—Inlet ports
D—Recuperating seal
E—Piston spring
F—Outlet to wheel brake cylinders
G—Inlet from supply tank

4. Remove the piston, piston seal carrier and seal.

5. Remove the recuperating seal and shim from the cylinder.

To assemble   **Operation H/16**

1. Clean all the component parts in Girling Cleaning Fluid or Girling Crimson Brake Fluid and assemble wet.

2. Carefully inspect the piston and recuperating seals and rubber dust cover; renew as necessary.

3. Assemble the unit by reversing the stripping procedure.

To refit   **Operation H/18**

1. Reverse the removal procedure.

2. Refill the supply tank with fluid.

3. Bleed the system at all four wheel units. Operation H/2.

4. Check for leaks and rectify as necessary.

5. Check the free play in the piston rod; if it is less than 1/16 in. (1,6 mm):—

6. Slacken off the locknut and remove the joint pin.

1948-53 models

Push back the rubber boot from the fork end, slacken off the locknut and remove the joint pin; hold the piston rod with pliers and screw the fork end further on to the rod. Tighten the locknut, replace the joint pin and check the free play again; when correct, slide the rubber boot back over the neck of the fork end. Fit the split pin.

1954-58 models

7. Hold the piston rod with pliers and screw the operating rod further on to the piston rod.

1954-58 models

8. Tighten the locknut, replace the joint pin and check the free play again; fit the split pin.

Brake flexible pipe

To remove   **Operation H/20**

1. Hold the brake pedal down to prevent loss of fluid from the supply tank.

2. Unscrew the pipe nut (A) clear of the hose adaptor.

3. Hold the adaptor nut (B) with a spanner and remove the bulkhead nut (C) and shakeproof washer (D).

4. Withdraw the hose from the chassis bracket and disconnect from the banjo on the wheel cylinder.

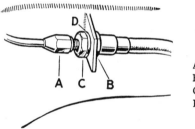

Fig. H-3—
Attachment of flexible brake hoses.

A—Pipe nut.
B—Adaptor nut.
C—Bulkhead nut.
D—Shakeproof washer.

To refit   **Operation H/22**

1. Reverse the removal procedure.

2. Bleed the brake system. Operation H/2.

Whenever any section of the pressure pipe system has been removed, a careful check should be made on replacement to ensure that all the connections and joint washers are in good condition. A faulty connection will admit air into the system, so causing poor and "spongy" braking.

Wheel brake unit, front and rear 10 in. brakes— 86 and 88 models

To adjust   **Operation H/24**

Jack up each wheel in turn. On the back face of the brake anchor plate will be found a hexagon adjustment bolt, which operates a snail cam bearing on the leading shoe. Only one of these is fitted to each wheel brake unit, thereby providing single-point adjustment. Spin the wheel and rotate the adjuster bolt until the brake shoe contacts the drum, then ease the adjuster until the wheel again rotates freely. Repeat for the other three wheels.

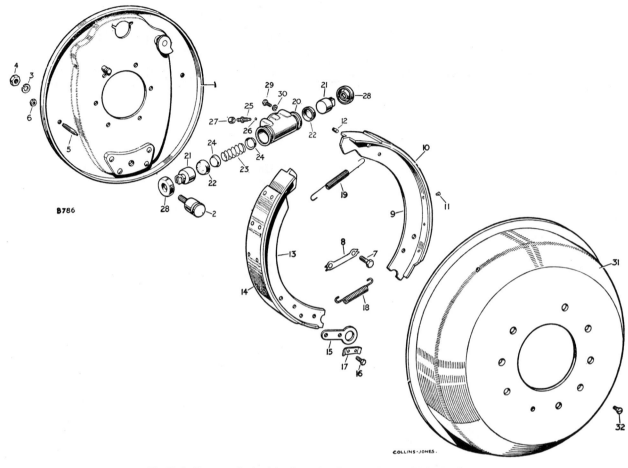

Fig. H-4—Layout of wheel brake unit—front and rear (10 in. brakes).

1 Brake anchor plate assembly, R.H.	17 Locking plate for bolt
2 Anchor pin for brake shoe	18 Pull-off spring for brake shoe
3 Spring washer ⎫ Fixing	19 Pull-off spring for leading shoe
4 Special nut ⎭ anchor pin	20 Wheel cylinder only R.H. front
5 Shoe steady post	21 Piston for cylinder, front
6 Locknut for steady post	22 Rubber cup for piston, front
7–8 Fixings for front anchor plate	23 Spring for piston, front
9 Brake shoe assembly R.H., leading	24 Washer for spring, front
10 Lining for brake shoe	25 Bleed screw
11 Rivet fixing lining	26 Steel ball for bleed screw
12 Spring post for brake shoe	27 Rubber dust cap for bleed screw
13 Brake shoe assembly, trailing	28 Rubber boot for wheel cylinder, front
14 Lining for brake shoe	29–30 Fixings for wheel cylinder
15 Anchor for brake shoe	31 Brake drum
16 Special set screw fixing anchor	32 Set screw fixing brake drum

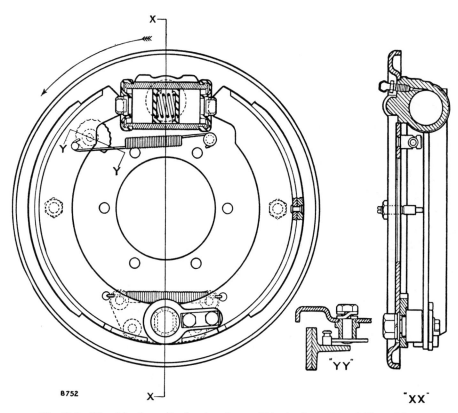

Fig. H-5—Wheel brake unit—front and rear 10 in. brakes—86 and 88 models.

To strip   **Operation H/26**

1. Jack up the vehicle.

2. Remove the road wheel and brake drum.

3. Turn back the adjuster cam to release the tension of the leading shoe pull-off spring and remove the spring.

4. Remove the trailing shoe anchor plate.

5. Remove the brake shoes together from the pivot end first; part them by disconnecting the bias reducing spring. If the wheel cylinder is not to be removed, e.g., when relining the shoes, it is well to slip the special clip Part No. 242526 over the cylinder pistons to prevent loss of fluid and admission of air to the system.

6. In cases where the unit is to be completely dismantled, the front flexible hose to wheel cylinder must be disconnected at the support bracket on frame before unscrewing from wheel cylinder, to avoid twisting and damaging of hose. The securing nut for rear wheel cylinder pipe may be unscrewed directly.

7. Depress the brake pedal to its fullest extent and wedge in that position, so preventing leakage of fluid from the supply tank; it is also advantageous to secure the loose end of the flexible hose as high as possible to reduce loss of fluid from the pipeline to a minimum

8. Remove the wheel cylinder and detach the rubber dust covers, pistons, piston cups and spring; remove the bleed nipple cover, nipple and ball.

9. Remove the brake anchor plate after first removing the hub components. Sections E and F.

To assemble   **Operation H/28**

1. Clean and replace the anchor plate.

2. Clean all the wheel cylinder components, using Girling Crimson Brake Fluid, and assemble wet.

3. Replace the bleed ball and nipple.

4. Examine the piston cups for damage or distortion and renew as necessary, replace the piston spring, cups and pistons.

5. Examine the rubber dust covers; renew if damaged.

6. Refit the wheel cylinder to the anchor plate.

7. Reconnect the bias reducing spring, renewing it if necessary; the brake shoes should be fitted together at the wheel cylinder end first (Fig. H-5).

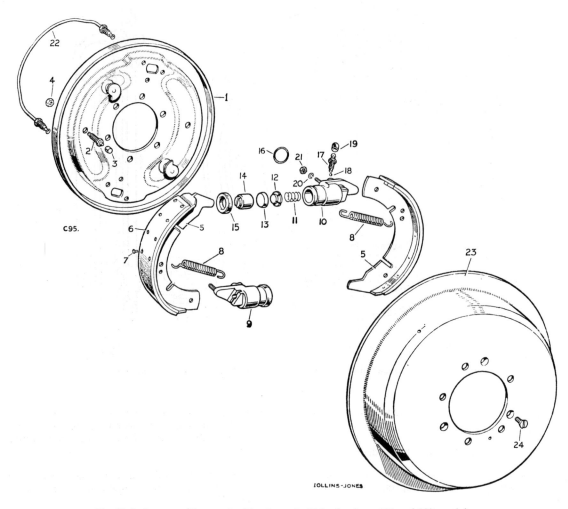

Fig. H-6—Layout of front wheel brake unit, 11 in. brakes—107 and 109 models.

1   Brake anchor plate assembly—L.H.
2   Steady post for brake shoe
3   Bush for steady post
4   Special nut—fixing steady post
5   Brake shoe assembly—L.H.
6   Lining for brake shoe
7   Rivet securing lining
8   Pull-off spring
9   Wheel cylinder assembly—L.H.
10 Wheel cylinder—L.H.
11 Spring
12 Air excluder   Part of
13 Seal   wheel cylinder
14 Piston   assembly
15 Rubber boot

16 Sealing ring for cylinder
17 Bleed screw
18 Steel ball for bleed screw
19 Rubber dust cap for bleed screw
20 Spring washer ⎫ Securing
21 Nut   ⎭ wheel cylinder
22 Connecting pipe for wheel cylinders
23 Brake drum
24 Set screw fixing brake drum

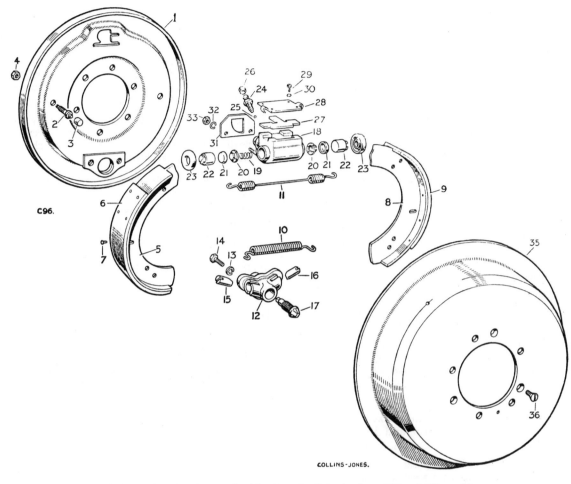

Fig. H-7—Layout of rear wheel brake unit, 11 in. brakes—107 and 109 models.

1	Brake anchor plate—L.H.	
2	Steady post for brake shoe	
3	Bush for steady post	
4	Special nut—fixing steady post	
5	Shoe assembly—leading	
6	Lining for leading shoe	
7	Rivet securing linings	
8	Shoe assembly—trailing	
9	Lining for trailing shoe	
10	Pull-off spring—adjuster end	
11	Pull-off spring—cylinder end	
12	Adjuster housing	
13	Spring washer ⎱ Securing	
14	Set bolt ⎰ adjuster housing	
15	Plunger—L.H.	
16	Plunger—R.H.	
17	Cone for adjuster	

18 Wheel cylinder—L.H. ⎱
19 Spring
20 Air excluder   ⎱ Part of wheel cylinder
21 Seal   ⎰ assembly
22 Piston
23 Seal   ⎰
24 Bleed screw
25 Ball for bleed screw
26 Rubber dust cap for bleed screw
27 Abutment plate ⎱ For
28 Dust cover plate ⎰ wheel cylinder
29 Set screw   ⎱ Securing abutment and dust
30 Spring washer   ⎰ cover plates
31 Dust cover plate for brake anchor plate
32 Spring washer ⎱ Securing
33 Nut   ⎰ wheel cylinder
35 Brake drum
36 Retaining screw

8. Reconnect the leading shoe pull-off spring, renewing it if necessary; replace it with its longest extremity hooked over the post on the shoe web.

9. Replace the trailing shoe anchor plate.

10. Examine the brake drum for scoring, ovality, and skim if required, standard diameter 10 in. (254 mm). Reclamation limit .030 in. (0,75 mm) oversize on diameter.

11. Replace the brake drum and set the leading shoe adjuster. See Instruction Manual.

12. If the brake shoe steady posts have been disturbed, they should be reset as follows:—
Screw the posts well back, clear of the shoes. Apply the brakes lightly and turn the drum by hand to centralise the shoes; continue depressing the pedal until the shoes are hard on the drum. Screw in the steady posts until they just contact the shoe webs and secure by means of the locknuts.

13. Replace the road wheel.

14. Lower the vehicle from the jack.

15. If air has entered the system during the re-lining operation, or if the unit has been completely stripped, the brake system must now be bled. Operation H/2.

Front wheel brake unit, 11 in. brakes—
107 and 109 models
To adjust   Operation H/30
Each shoe is independently set by means of an adjuster operating through a serrated snail cam.

1. With the front wheels jacked up, ensure that the wheels rotate freely; slacken off the adjusters if necessary by turning anti-clockwise.

2. Turn the adjuster for each shoe clockwise until the shoe just brushes the brake drum, then slacken off two serrations.

To strip   Operation H/32

1. Slacken wheel nuts slightly and jack up the vehicle.

2. Unscrew the wheel nuts completely and remove road wheel.

3. Turn adjuster cams at rear of brake anchor plate (anti-clockwise) to increase clearance between linings and brake drum and facilitate removal of brake drum.

4. Remove the three countersunk head screws retaining brake drum and withdraw brake drum.

5. Release brake shoes and pull-off springs by levering the trailing edge of each shoe away from the wheel cylinders.

Note: If the wheel cylinders are not to be removed, e.g., when relining brake shoes, a clip must be used to hold the pistons in position and prevent loss of fluid and admission of air to the system.

6. Release bleed nipple on bottom wheel cylinder, then depress brake pedal to fullest extent and wedge in this position, thereby preventing leakage of fluid from supply tank.

7. Disconnect union nut of brake fluid supply pipe from flexible pipe, and remove locknut securing flexible pipe to support bracket on chassis, forward of shock absorber.

8. Disconnect flexible pipe and connecting pipe from wheel cylinders.

9. Unscrew securing nuts, then remove wheel cylinders from anchor plate and detach the rubber dust covers, pistons, seals, air excluders and springs.

10. Remove the brake anchor plate and steady posts if necessary.

To assemble   Operation H/34
Clean and examine all parts and renew as necessary. If the brake linings have been renewed, the ends must be backed off. Reverse the sequence of stripping operations excepting for bleed nipple, which should be fitted to wheel cylinder before assembly to anchor plate. Finally bleed each wheel cylinder in accordance with Operation H/2.

Note: If the brake shoe steady posts have been disturbed, reset as instructed in Item 12 of Operation H/28.

Rear wheel brake unit, 11 in. brakes—
107 and 109 models
To adjust   Operation H/36
The rear brake shoes are adjusted by means of a single adjuster assembly fitted at the lower side of the brake anchor plate which allows the shoes to expand or contract equally.

1. With the rear wheels jacked up ensure that they rotate freely; slacken the adjuster if necessary, by turning anti-clockwise.

2. Apply the foot brake to ensure that the shoes are bedded in and turn the adjuster clockwise until the linings brush the brake drum, then slacken adjuster off (anti-clockwise) two clicks.

To strip   Operation H/38

1. Slacken wheel nuts slightly and jack up the vehicle.

2. Unscrew the wheel nuts completely and remove road wheel.

3. Turn adjusters at lower end of anchor plate anti-clockwise to increase clearance between linings and brake drum and thereby facilitate removal of brake drum.

4. Remove the three countersunk head securing screws and withdraw brake drum.

5. Release the brake shoes and pull-off springs by levering the shoes away from the wheel cylinder.

   Note: If the wheel cylinders are not to be removed, e.g., when relining brake shoes, a clip must be used to hold the piston in position and prevent loss of fluid and admission of air to the system.

6. Disconnect the fluid pipes from wheel cylinders and depress brake pedal to the fullest extent, then wedge in this position, thereby preventing leakage of brake fluid from supply tank.

7. Remove the securing nuts and withdraw the wheel cylinders from anchor plates, then detach the rubber dust covers, pistons, seals, air excluders and springs.

8. Remove the securing bolts and withdraw the adjuster assemblies complete with cover plates. Withdraw the plungers and unscrew the adjuster cones.

9. Unscrew the steady posts, with fibre bushes and locknuts.

10. Remove the anchor plates if necessary (see Rear Axle Section).

To assemble   **Operation H/40**

   Clean and examine all parts and renew as necessary, then reverse the sequence of stripping operations.

The following points should be observed:—

1. Lubricate the draw link, rollers, tappets and adjuster plungers with graphite grease.

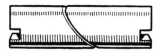

Fig. H-8—
Plungers
correctly paired.

B946.

2. Ensure that the plungers are fitted in pairs. This can be checked by placing them end to end; in this position the slots should be parallel to each other.

3. Check that the plungers are fitted to the correct bore in adjuster housing. When the plungers are fitted correctly and forced down on the flats of the adjusting cone, the slot for brake shoe web will be in line with the slots in adjuster housing and the angle of the plunger slot will coincide with the angle of brake shoe web.

4. Leave the wheel cylinder fixing nuts one turn slack so that the cylinder is free to float on the anchor plate.

5. If new linings have been fitted the ends must be backed off. The trailing shoe has the shorter lining and care must be taken to ensure it is not fitted in the leading position.

6. Finally bleed the wheel cylinders and if the brake shoe steady posts have been disturbed, reset as instructed in Item 12 of Operation H/28.

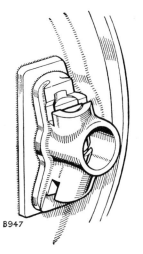 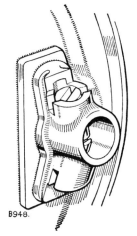

Fig. H-9—
Plungers correctly
located.

Fig. H-10—
Plungers incorrectly
located.

Where the pedal effort on the above brake systems is too high, the following modifications may be applied with advantage.

Disconnect rod from brake pedal to master cylinder at the front end.

Drill another hole of the same size $\frac{3}{4}$ in. (19 mm) above the existing hole in the short lever of the brake pedal lever assembly (241431).

Reconnect rod to lever and ensure that the correct amount of free play is present. Adjust if necessary.

On vehicles fitted with dirt excluder for master cylinder rod, which was introduced in 1955, it will, of course, be necessary to re-position the excluder to suit.

The effect of this modification is to increase the mechanical advantage of the linkage from 3.66 : 1 to 4.88 : 1. It does not, however, result in undue pedal travel, although the mileage which can be covered before brake wear renders adjustment obligatory, is slightly reduced.

It is equally applicable to the L.H.D. model, but in this case, the clutch connecting shaft will have to be removed temporarily to provide access for the drilling operation.

Wheel brake shoes

To re-line   **Operation H/42**

1. Remove the old linings from the shoes by shearing the rivets.

2. Re-line both shoes in the normal way, with the correct linings, and "back-off" both ends of each lining. Uneven braking is liable to occur if mixed sets of linings are employed.

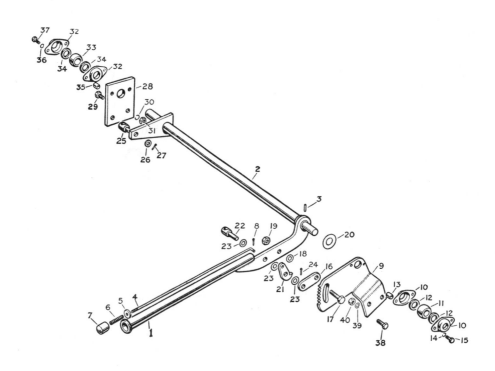

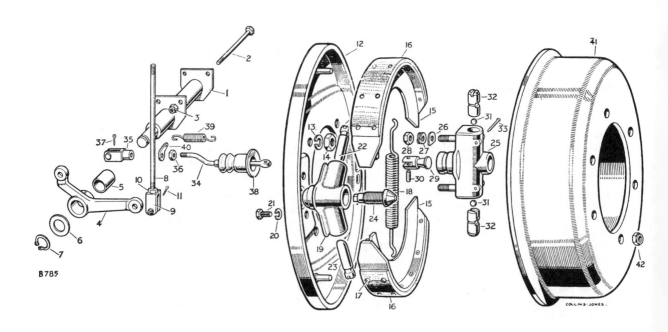

B785

Fig. H-11—Layout of transmission brake.

Key to Fig. H-11

1	Hand brake lever	17–19	Fixings for locating plate and lever
2	Cross-shaft for hand brake	20	Plain washer between lever and ratchet
3	Pin fixing lever to shaft	21	Brake catch
4	Plunger rod	22–24	Fixings for catch to lever
5	Washer for plunger spring	25	Pin for hand brake adjuster rod
6	Spring for plunger rod	26–27	Fixings for pin
7	Plunger	28	Support plate for hand brake bearing housing
8	Split pin fixing rod to catch	29–31	Fixings for support plate
9	Ratchet for hand brake	32	Housing for cross-shaft bearing
10	Housing for cross-shaft bearing	33	Spherical bearing for cross-shaft
11	Spherical bearing for cross-shaft	34	Felt ring for bearing
12	Felt ring for bearing	35–37	Fixings for housing and bearing
13–15	Fixings for bearing and housing	38–40	Fixings for hand brake lever
16	Locating plate		

1	Spindle for hand brake relay lever	23	Plunger L.H.
2–3	Fixings for spindle	24	Adjuster cone
4	Relay lever assembly for hand brake	25	Expander housing
5	Bush for relay lever	26–28	Fixings for expander housing
6–7	Fixings for lever	29	Expander cone
8	Brake rod, relay to hand brake lever	30	Pin fixing cone to brake rod
9–11	Fixings for brake rod to relay and hand brake lever	31	Roller for expander
12	Anchor plate, transmission brake	32	Plunger for expander
13–14	Fixings for anchor plate	33	Split pin fixing plunger
15	Brake shoe assembly	34	Brake rod, expander to relay lever
16	Lining for shoe	35–37	Fixings for brake rod
17	Rivet for lining	38	Dust cover for brake rod
18	Pull-off spring for brake shoe	39	Return spring for brake rod
19	Adjuster housing	40	Anchor for spring
20–21	Fixings for adjuster housing	41	Brake drum
22	Plunger R.H.	42	Self-locking nut fixing brake drum

Hand brake lever and linkage
To strip (R.H.D. models)   Operation H/44

1. Remove the centre inspection panel from the seat box.

2. Disconnect the transmission brake expander rod and vertical adjuster rod from the bell-crank lever.

3. Remove the hand brake assembly complete from the vehicle, withdrawing the lever grip carefully through the rubber draught excluder in the front of the seat box.

4. Remove the adjuster rod from the adjuster pin; remove the adjuster pin, thus releasing the brake catch and locating plate.

5. Remove the locating plate.

6. Remove the lever from the ratchet plate.

7. Remove the brake catch from the plunger rod and unscrew the plunger, plunger rod and spring from the brake lever.

1948-53 models

8. Place a jack under the transfer box, remove the right-hand rear engine support complete and the bolt from the left-hand rear support.

1948-53 models

9. Jack up and tilt the engine and gearbox unit, so that the lever may be withdrawn from the spindle.

1948-53 models

10. The spindle can only be removed from the chassis side member if the gearbox unit is first removed.

1954-58 models

11. Remove the bell-crank and spindle complete from the chassis.

1954-58 models

12. Remove the bell-crank lever from the spindle.

1954-58 models

13. If necessary, press the bush out of the lever.

To strip (L.H.D. models)   Operation H/46

1. Disconnect the transmission brake expander rod and vertical adjuster rod from the bell-crank lever.

2. Remove the hand brake and cross-shaft complete.

3. Remove the split housing from the cross-shaft support brackets, remove the felt dust seals and self-lubricating bushes supporting the hand brake cross-shaft.

4. Strip the unit. Operation H/44.

5. Remove the bell-crank lever. Operation H/44.

To assemble   Operation H/48

1. Reverse the sequence of operations detailed for stripping.

2. Renew the bell-crank lever bush and spindle if required.

3. L.H.D. models. The bushes should be greased prior to assembly and new felt seals fitted as required.

4. Set the adjuster rod by means of the locknuts at the adjuster pin, so that the hand brake lever has two ratchet clicks free movement in the "off" position.

Transmission brake unit
To strip   Operation H/50

1. Remove the centre inspection panel from the seat box.

2. Drain the transfer box.

3. Disconnect the brake expander rod from the bell crank lever.

4. Disconnect the rear propeller shaft from the transfer box output shaft.

5. Withdraw the brake drum and rear drive output flange. Remove the brake drum from the flange, if necessary.

   Note: If access is only required to the brake shoes, e.g., for re-lining, the propeller shaft may be left in position; the brake drum may then be detached from the output flange and pushed back over the propeller shaft.

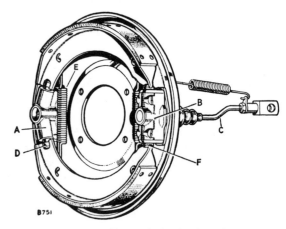

Fig. H-12—Transmission brake unit.

A—Adjuster unit   D—Adjuster plunger
B—Expander unit   E—Pull-off spring
C—Expander rod   F—Expander plunger

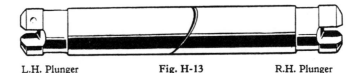

L.H. Plunger   **Fig. H-13**   R.H. Plunger

Fig. H-14—Plungers in correct bores.

6. Remove the brake shoes together with the pull-off springs, separate the shoes by detaching the springs.

7. Remove the anchor plate complete with adjuster and expander housings from the speedometer drive housing.

8. Remove the clevis also return spring, and on 1954-58 models, spring anchor and rubber dust cover from the expander rod and remove the expander housing complete. If necessary, remove the split pins from the expander housing, thus releasing the plungers, steel balls and expander cone; detach the expander rod from the cone.

9. Remove the adjuster housing, pull out the plungers and unscrew the adjuster cone from the housing.

To assemble Operation H/52

1. Clean the brake anchor plate.

2. Replace the adjuster housing, leaving the securing bolts slack at this stage; screw in the adjuster cone, leaving it in the fully "off" position.

3. Grease the adjuster plungers and replace them in the housings.
   Note: It is essential that the adjuster plungers be replaced in the correct bores of the housing. They are handed, due to the fact that in addition to the adjustment flats being at an angle of 30° when viewed vertically, they are also inclined at an angle of 15° to the plunger axes, owing to the housing bores being similarly inclined. When dismantled the plungers are not readily distinguished, and care must be taken to ensure that handed pairs are fitted.

A quick method of selecting pairs is shown at Fig. H-12. The plungers should be placed end to end with the flats mated exactly, when a correct pair will show the brake shoe slots parallel with each other. If the slots are not in line, both plungers are of the same hand, but this test gives no indication as to which hand, right or left.

Having made certain that a correct pair has been chosen, it will still be necessary to make sure that they are fitted in the proper bores, as in Fig. H-14, i.e., with the flats of the adjuster cone and plungers face to face; the slots in the ends of the plungers must be in line and vertical (parallel with the anchor plate). In this case, four distinct "clicks" will be felt for each revolution of the adjuster cone.

When assembled wrongly the brake shoes will force the plunger slots into a vertical position, throwing the plunger flat off the flat of the adjuster cone, pushing the plunger approximately 1/16 in. (1,6 mm) out of the housing and so upsetting the centralisation of the shoes.

It is possible to erect the units incorrectly in three ways:

(a) R.H. plunger in L.H. bore and L.H. plunger in R.H. bore (Fig. H-15).

In this case it is likely that no "click" will be felt when adjusting the brake.

(b) Two L.H. plungers in the housing.

(c) Two R.H. plungers in the housing (Fig. H-16).

In both these cases the correct plunger will "click" on adjustment, thus giving the erroneous impression that the assembly is in order.

Fig. H-15—Correct pair of plungers in incorrect bores.

4. Grease and replace the expander plungers, steel rollers and expander cone in the housing and locate with split pins.

5. Reconnect the expander rod to the cone and fit the complete housing to the brake anchor plate, leaving the Simmonds securing nuts one turn slack. Ensure that the housing is free to float on the anchor plate.

6. Replace the rubber dust cover (also spring anchor plate on 1954-58 models), return spring and clevis on the expander rod and mount the complete anchor plate on the speedometer drive housing.

7. Refit the brake shoes and pull-off springs together; the half-round slots in the shoe webs should be fitted to the adjuster housing.

8. Clean and replace the brake drum and rear drive output flange.

9. Reconnect the propeller shaft to the transfer box output shaft.

10. Reconnect the expander rod to the hand brake bell-crank lever.

11. To ensure correct clearance between the brake shoes and drum, turn the adjuster cone until the brake shoes are locked tightly against the drum; tighten the set bolts securing the adjuster housing (these were left slack on assembly) and slacken off the cone two clicks; give the brake a firm application to ensure that the shoes have centralised at the expander end. The brake drum should now be free to rotate.

12. Set the hand brake linkage at the vertical adjuster rod, so that the hand brake has one or two clicks free movement in the "off" position.

13. Refill the transfer box with oil, $4\frac{1}{2}$ pints (2,5 litres).

14. Replace the seat box centre inspection panel.

Transmission brake shoes

To re-line   **Operation H/54**

1. Remove the old linings from the shoes by shearing the rivets.

2. Re-line both shoes in the normal way with the correct linings, and "back-off" both ends of each lining.

Fig. H-16—Two R.H. plungers in the housing

DEFECT LOCATION

Symptom, Cause and Remedy

A—SPONGY PEDAL ACTION

1. Air in system—*Bleed the brake system.*
2. Swollen rubber components due to incorrect brake fluid—*Renew the affected parts, drain the system and refill with Girling Crimson Brake Fluid.*
3. Incorrect adjustment of brake shoes—*Adjust.*

B—CHATTERING BRAKES

1. Incorrect adjustment of brake shoes—*Adjust.*
2. Loose front wheel bearings—*Section F.*
3. Hard spots on brake drum—*Renew linings as necessary and fit a new brake drum.*
4. Distorted brake drum—*Renew linings as necessary and fit a new brake drum.*

C—LOSS OF PEDAL PRESSURE

1. Leak in master cylinder—*Renew.*
2. Leak in wheel cylinder—*Renew.*
3. Leak in brake pipes—*Renew.*

D—HARD BRAKE PEDAL

1. Incorrect lining—*Renew.*
2. Restriction in master cylinder—*Rectify.*
3. Incorrect shoe adjustment—*Adjust.*

E—BINDING BRAKE PEDAL

1. Worn or tight pedal shaft—*Rectify, renewing any excessively worn parts. Lubricate.*
2. Loose master cylinder mounting bolts—*Tighten.*

F—BRAKE PEDAL FAILS TO RETURN

1. Weak pedal return spring—*Renew.*
2. Loose master cylinder mounting bolts—*Tighten.*
3. Sticking pedal shaft—*Free the pedal shaft, renewing any excessively worn part. Lubricate.*

G—POOR BRAKES

1. Water-soaked linings—*Dry the brake linings by applying the brakes lightly whilst driving.*
2. Incorrect linings—*Renew.*
3. Glazed linings—*Renew.*
4. Incorrect shoe adjustment—*Adjust.*
5. Incorrect master cylinder adjustment—*Adjust.*

H—GRABBING BRAKES

1. Grease, oil or brake fluid soaked linings—*Replace and rectify leaks.*
2. Scored or cracked drums—*Recondition or replace.*
3. Incorrect shoe adjustment—*Adjust.*
4. Incorrect linings—*Renew.*
5. Hard spots on drums—*Renew.*

J—SIDE PULL

1. Grease, oil or fluid soaked linings—*Renew and rectify leaks.*
2. Incorrect shoe adjustment—*Adjust.*
3. Loose wheel cylinders—*Tighten.*
4. Clogged or crimped brake hose—*Clear the hose with air pressure or renew.*
5. Excessive wear in drum or scored drum—*Recondition or renew.*
6. Mixed linings—*Replace.*
7. Incorrect tyre pressures—*Section S.*
8. Water and mud in brakes—*Clean the brake assemblies, examine drums for scoring, and linings for wear. Renew as necessary.*

K—SQUEALING BRAKES

1. Incorrect linings—*Renew.*
2. Distorted brake drum—*Renew.*
3. Bent brake anchor plate—*Renew.*
4. Sprung or bent brake shoes—*Renew.*
5. Foreign bodies embedded in brake linings—*Recondition or renew.*
6. Dust or road dirt in the drums—*Clean thoroughly. If necessary, renew the linings and recondition or renew the drums.*
7. Shoes binding on the steady posts—*Adjust.*
8. Loose wheel cylinders—*Tighten. Check the brake linings and renew as necessary.*

L—BRAKES OVERHEATING

1. Brake shoes continuously in contact with drum—*Adjust.*
2. High spots on brake drums—*Recondition or renew.*
3. Defective master cylinder or swollen rubber components—*Renew.*
4. Dust or road dirt in the drums—*Clean thoroughly. If necessary, renew the linings and recondition or renew the drums.*
5. Incorrect master cylinder adjustment—*Adjust.*

M—FADING BRAKES

1. Incorrect linings—*Renew.*
2. Poor lining contact—*Adjust.*
3. Excessive heat—*Renew linings.*

N—BRAKE DRAGS

1. Incorrect brake adjustment—*Adjust.*
2. Distorted rubber boots—*Renew.*
3. Seized brake shoe—*Free the brake shoe from its anchor and smear the point of seizure lightly with grease.*
4. Weak brake shoe pull-off springs—*Renew.*
5. Loose front wheel bearings—*Section F.*
6. Restriction or obstruction in brake pipe—*Clear the pipe.*
7. Distorted brake drum—*Renew.*

P—ALL BRAKES DRAG

1. Incorrect adjustment of brakes—*Adjust.*
2. Incorrect master cylinder adjustment—*Adjust.*
3. Rubber cylinder boots swollen—*Renew.*
4. Restriction in master cylinder—*Remove, clean or recondition.*
5. Linings too thick—*Check.*
6. Weak pull-off springs—*Renew.*

Q—BRAKE LOCKS

1. Oil or brake fluid soaked linings—*Replace; rectify leaks.*
2. Torn or loose lining—*Renew and check the shoe for distortion.*
3. Loose wheel cylinders—*Tighten. Check the brake linings and renew as necessary.*
4. Swollen rubber components—*Renew.*

R—PEDAL GOES TO FLOOR BOARD

1. Linings badly worn—*Re-line.*
2. Pedal incorrectly set—*Adjust.*

DATA

1948-53 models

Brakes

Type	.... Girling
Operation	.... Hydrostatic or hydraulic

Wheel brake unit, front and rear

Lining:

Length	.... $8\frac{13}{32}$ in. (213,5 mm)
Width	.... $1\frac{1}{2}$ in. (38 mm)
Thickness	.... $\frac{3}{16}$ in. (4,75 mm)
Total braking area....	104 sq/in. (670 cm²)

Brake drum

Standard diameter	10 in. + .004 (254 mm + 0,1)
Reclamation limit	.030 in. (0,75 mm)

Transmission brake

Type	.... Girling
Operation	.... Mechanical

Lining:

Length	.... $7\frac{17}{32}$ in. (191,3 mm)
Width	.... $1\frac{1}{2}$ in. (38 mm)
Thickness	.... $\frac{3}{16}$ in. (4,75 mm)

Brake drum

Standard diameter	9 in. + .004 (228,6 mm + 0,1)

1954-58 models

Brakes

Type	.... Girling
Operation	.... Hydraulic

Foot pedal:

Fit of bush on pedal shaft, L.H.D. and R.H.D.	.... .0005 to .0025 in. (0,012 to 0,063 mm)
Bush bore: L.H.D.	1 in. + .001 (25,4 mm + 0,025)
R.H.D.	$\frac{7}{8}$ in. + .001 (22,2 mm + 0,025)

Wheel brake unit, front and rear (10 in. brakes)

Lining:

Length	.... $8\frac{1}{2}$ in. (215 mm)
Width	.... $1\frac{1}{2}$ in. (38 mm)
Thickness	.... 3/16 in. (4,75 mm)

Brake drum

Standard diameter	10 in. + .004 (254 mm + 0,1)
Reclamation limit	.030 in. (0,75 mm) oversize on diameter

Wheel brake unit, front (11 in. brakes)

Lining:

Length	.... 10.45 in. (265,4 mm)
Width	.... $2\frac{1}{4}$ in. (57,15 mm)
Thickness	.... 3/16 in. (4,75 mm)
Total braking area of front linings	.... 94 sq.in. (606 cm²)

Wheel brake unit, rear (11 in. brakes)

Finishing Axle No. 270600981

Lining:

Length—leading	10.45 in. (265,4 mm)
Length—trailing	9.6 in. (243,8 mm)
Width	.... $2\frac{1}{4}$ in. (57,15 mm)
Thickness	.... 3/16 in. ±015 (4,76 mm ± 0,38)
Total braking area of rear linings	.... 90 sq.in. (580 cm²)

Commencing Axle No. 270600982

Lining:

Length	.... 8.6 in. (218,44 mm)
Width	.... 2.25 in. (57,15 mm)
Thickness	.... 3/16 in. ±015 (4,76 mm ± 0,38)
Total braking area of rear linings	.... 77.75 sq.in. (502 cm²)

Brake drum

Standard diameter	11 in. + .004 (279,4 mm + 0,10)
Reclamation limit	.030 in. (0,75 mm) oversize on diameter

Transmission brake

Lining:

Length	.... 7.70 in. (195 mm)
Width	.... $1\frac{3}{4}$ in. (44,5 mm)
Thickness	.... 3/16 in. (4,75 mm)

Brake drum

Standard diameter	9 in. + .004 (228,6 mm + 0,1)
Reclamation limit	0.30 in. (0,75 mm) oversize on diameter

Master cylinder

Pushrod free movement	.... 1/16 in. (1,5 mm)

Section J — SUSPENSION

INDEX

	Page		Page
Bump rubber	J-7	Hydraulic damper	J-7
Data	J-1	Rear axle check strap	J-7
Front spring	J-6	Rear spring	J-6

LIST OF ILLUSTRATIONS

Fig.		Page	Fig.		Page
J-1	Front road spring, 1948-53	J-2	J-5	Rear road spring (Land-Rover 86 and 88)	J-5
J-2	Front road spring, 1954-58	J-2			
J-3	Layout of suspension	J-3	J-6	Rear road spring (Land-Rover 107 and 109)	J-5
J-4	Rear road spring (Land-Rover 80 and 88)	J-5			

SUSPENSION DATA

Front road springs

Land-Rover 80, 1948-53

Fitted to vehicles numbered	Type 1	Type 2	Type 3
	Prior to 862115	862115 to 06113529 8670001 to 06200419 8680001 to 06300030	06113530 06200420 and 06300031 onwards
Number of leaves	9	9	9
Width of leaves	$1\frac{3}{4}$ in. (44,45 mm)	$1\frac{3}{4}$ in. (44,45 mm)	$2\frac{1}{2}$ in. (63,5 mm)
Thickness of leaves	6 (upper) x .203 in. (5,16 mm) and 3 x .180 in. (4,57 mm) or 2 (upper) x .218 in. (5,56 mm) and 6 x .187 in. (4,76 mm)	6 (upper) x .203 in. (5,16 mm) and 3 x .180 in. (4,57 mm) or 3 (upper) x .218 in. (5,56 mm) and 6 x .187 in. (4,76 mm)	9 x .165 in. (4,2 mm)
Static load	617 lb. (280 kg)	755 lb. (342 kg)	524 lb. (237 kg)
Camber under static load	Flat	Flat	1.63 in. (27 mm)
Rate	200 lb./in. (2,304 kg/m)	230 lb./in. (2,649 kg/m)	190 lb./in. (2,189 kg/m)
Free camber	$3\frac{1}{2}$ in. (89 mm)	4 in. (102 mm)	4.39 in. (102,5 mm)

Land-Rover 86 and 88, 1954-58

	Driver	Passenger
Number of leaves	10	10
Width of leaves	$2\frac{1}{2}$ in. (63,5 mm)	$2\frac{1}{2}$ in. (63,5 mm)
Thickness of leaves	top plate x 11/64 in. (4,36 mm) and 9 x 9/64 in. (3,57 mm)	top plate x 11/64 in. (4,36 mm) and 9 x 9/64 in. (3,57 mm)
Static load	610 lb. (277 kg)	508 lb. (230 kg)
Camber under static load	$2\frac{1}{2}$ in. (63,5 mm)	$2\frac{1}{2}$ in. (63,5 mm)
Rate	152 lb./in. (1,74 kg/m)	152 lb./in. (1,74 kg/m)
Free camber	6.5 in. (165 mm)	5.875 in. (149 mm)

Land-Rover 107 and 109, 1954-58

	Driver	Passenger	
Number of leaves	9	9	
Width of leaves	2½ in. (63,5 mm)	2½ in. (63,5 mm)	
Thickness of leaves	9 x .165 in. (4,2 mm)	9 x .165 in. (4,2 mm)	
Static load	750 lb. (340 kg)	636 lb. (288 kg)	Up to Chassis
Camber under static load	2¾ in. (69,85 mm)	2¾ in. (69,85 mm	No. 57200469
Rate	190 lb./in. (2,19 kg/m)	190 lb./in. (2,19 kg/m)	
Free camber	6.70 in. (170,18 mm)	6.08 in. (154,43 mm)	
Number of leaves	11	11	
Width of leaves	2½ in. (63,5 mm)	2½ in. (63,5 mm)	
Thickness of leaves	11 x 11/64 in. (4,3 mm)	11 x 11/64 in. (4,3 mm)	From Chassis
Static load (vehicle unladen)	750 lb. (340 kg)	750 lb. (340 kg)	No. 57200470
Camber under static load	2¾ in. (69,85 mm)	2¼ in. (57,1 mm)	onwards
Rate	260 lb./in. (46,5 kg/cm)	260 lb./in. (46,5 kg/cm)	
Free camber	5⅝ in. (142,9 mm)	5⅛ in. (130 mm)	

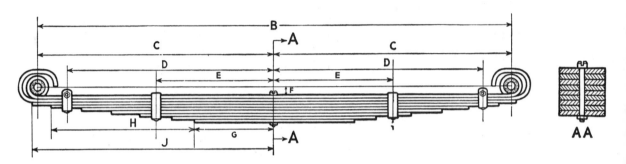

Fig. J-1—Dimensions with spring flat.

(Land-Rover 80 and 86, 1948-53)

B—36¼ in. (921 mm)   G—5 in. (127 mm)
C—18⅛ in. (460 mm)   H—5 x 2⅜ in. (5 x 60,3 mm) (Types
D—15⅞ in. (403 mm)   1 and 2) and 5 x 2¼ in. (5 x 57,2
E—8¾ in. (222 mm)   mm) (Type 3)
F—25/32 in. (19,8 mm)   J—18⅜ in. (467 mm) (Except Type 1)

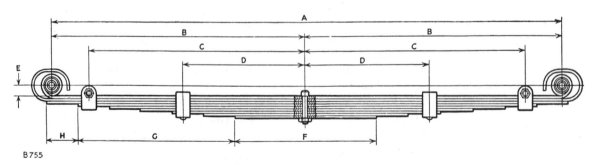

B 755

Fig. J-2—Dimensions with spring flat.

(Land-Rover 86 and 88, 1954-58—Driver and Passenger side)

A—36¼ in. (921 mm)
B—18⅛ in. (460,5 mm)
C—15½ in. (394 mm)
D—86 and 88 model 10 in. (254 mm)
     107 and 109 model 8¾ in. (222 mm)
                    10⅜ in. (263,5 mm) } Alternative
                    11 in. (279,4 mm)
E—.720 in. (18,28 mm)

F—86 and 88 model   10 in. (254 mm)
    107 and 109 model   10 in. (254 mm) } Alternative
                        9¾ in. (247,7 mm)
G—86 and 88 model   11¼ in. (286 mm)
    107 and 109 model   11¼ in. (286 mm) } Alternative
                        11⅜ in. (288,9 mm)
H—86 and 88 model   2⅛ in. (54 mm)
    107 and 109 model   2⅛ in. (54 mm) } Alternative
                        2¼ in. (57,1 mm)

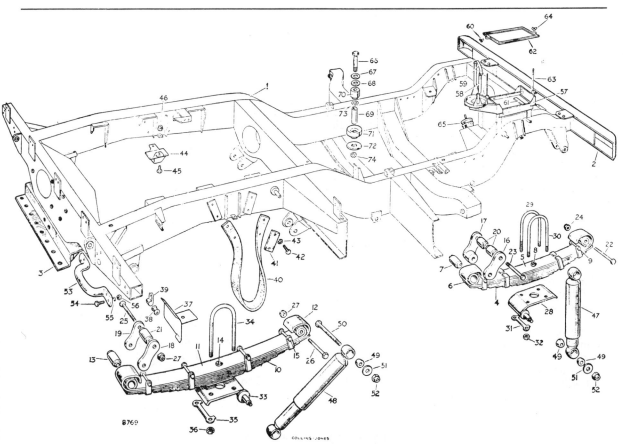

Fig. J-3—Layout of suspension.

1	Chassis frame	37	Shield for brake pipe, R.H.
2	Front bumper	38	Rubber grommet for brake pipe
3	Rear draw bar	39	Clip for grommet
4	Road spring complete, front, driver's	40	Check strap for rear axle
5	Main leaf ⎱ For front	41	Plate for check strap
6	2nd leaf ⎰ spring	42–43	Fixings for check strap
7	Bush for front spring	44	Rubber buffer for axles, front and rear
8	Dowel for front spring	45–46	Fixings for buffers
9	Bolt ⎱ For spring	47	Shock absorber, front
	Nut ⎰ clip	48	Shock absorber, rear
10	Road spring complete, rear, driver's	49	Rubber bush for shock absorbers
11	Main leaf ⎱ For rear	50–52	Fixings for shock absorbers
12	2nd leaf ⎰ spring	53	Lifting handle, rear
13	Bush for rear spring	54–56	Fixings for handles
14	Dowel for rear spring	57	Battery casing and air cleaner support complete
15	Bolt ⎱ For	58	Air cleaner clamp, side
	Nut ⎰ spring clip	59	Air cleaner clamp, top
16	Shackle plate, tapped ⎱ For	60	Wing nut for clamp
17	Shackle plate, plain ⎰ front springs	61	Rubber strip for battery
18	Shackle plate, tapped ⎱ For	62	Battery cover
19	Shackle plate, plain ⎰ rear springs	63	Battery fixing rod
20	Bush in chassis frame, front spring	64	Wing nut fixing battery
21	Bush in chassis frame, rear	65	Suspension rubber for engine. front
22	Shackle pin, front	66	Bolt, rear
23	Shackle pin, springs to frame, front	67	Plain washer, top
24	Self-locking nut, front	68	Rubber washer
25	Shackle pin, rear	69	Distance tube
26	Shackle pin, springs to frame, rear	70	Top rubber
27	Self-locking nut, rear	71	Bottom rubber
28	Bottom plate for front spring, R.H.	72	Plain washer bottom
29–32	Fixings for front springs	73	Shim
33	Bottom plate for rear spring, R.H.	74	Special nut
34–36	Fixings for rear springs		

66–74: Fixing engine unit to chassis frame at front and rear

Rear road springs

Land-Rover 80, 1948-53

	Driver	Passenger
Number of leaves	9 or 10	9 or 10
Width of leaves	1¾ in. (44,45 mm)	1¾ in. (44,45 mm)
Thickness of leaves	10 x .203 in. (5,16 mm)	10 x .203 in. (5,16 mm)
	or 7 x .218 in. (5,56 mm)	or 7 x .218 in. (5,56 mm)
	and 2 x .187 in. (4,76 mm)	and 2 x .187 in. (4,76 mm)
Static load	455 lb. (206 kg)	365 lb. (165 kg)
Camber under static load	2.38 in. (51,5 mm)	2.38 in. (51,5 mm)
Rate	180 lb/in. (2.074 kg/m)	180 lb/in. (2.074 kg/m)
Free camber	4½ in. (114 mm)	4 in. (102 mm)

Land-Rover 86 and 88, 1954-58

	Driver	Passenger
Number of leaves	11	11
Width of leaves	2½ in. (63,5 mm)	2½ in. (63,5 mm)
Thickness of leaves	top plate x ¼ in. (6,35 mm) and	top plate x ¼ in. (6,35 mm) and
	10 x 3/16 in. (4,76 mm)	10 x 3/16 in. (4,76 mm)
Static load	690 lb. (313 kg)	580 lb. (263 kg)
Camber under static load	2.5 in. (63,5 mm)	2.5 in. (63,5 mm)
Rate	166 lb./in. (1,90 kg/m)	166 lb./in. (1,90 kg/m)
Free camber	6.67 in. (154 mm)	6 in. (152 mm)
Fit of bushes in spring and chassis bores	.0025 to .0075 in. (0,065 to 0,18 mm) interference	

Land-Rover 107 and 109

	Driver	Passenger	
Number of leaves	10	10	All 107 basic models and 109 models up to vehicles numbered 121601061, and 107 Station Wagon up to 87060061
Width of leaves	2½ in. (63,5 mm)	2½ in. (63,5 mm)	
Thickness of leaves	top plate x ¼ in. (6,35 mm), 7 x 3/16 in. (4,76 mm) and 2 x 5/16 in. (7,93 mm)	top plate x ¼ in. (6,35 mm), 7 x 3/16 in. (4,76 mm) and 2 x 5/16 in. (7,93 mm)	
Static load	840 lb. (381 kg)	720 lb. (326 kg)	
Camber under static load	2.0 in. (50 mm)	2.0 in. (50 mm)	
Initial rate	145 lb./in. (1,67 kg/m)	145 lb./in. (1,67 kg/m)	
Final rate	250 lb./in.(2,88 kg/m)	250 lb./in. (2,88 kg/m)	
Free camber	7¼ in. (184 mm)	6 7/16 in. (166,6 mm)	
Fit of bushes in spring and chassis bores	.0025 to .0075 in. (0,065 to 0,18 mm) interference		

Land-Rover 109 and 107 Station Wagon

	Driver	Passenger	
Number of leaves	11	11	From vehicles numbered: 109 models 121601602 up to 121700416 107 Station Wagon 87060062 up to 131700042
Width of leaves	2½ in. (63,5 mm)	2½ in. (63,5 mm)	
Thickness of leaves	top plate x ¼ in. (6,35 mm), 6 x 3/16 in. (4,76 mm) and 4 x 5/16 in. (7,93 mm)	top plate x ¼ in. (6,35 mm), 6 x 3/16 in. (4,76 mm) and 4 x 5/16 in. (7,93 mm)	
Static load	1,158.5 lb. (525 kg)	1,015 lb. (460 kg)	
Camber under static load	2.0 in. (50 mm)	2.0 in. (50 mm)	
Initial rate	160 lb./in. (184 kg/m)	160 lb./in. (184 kg/m)	
Final rate	360 lb./in. (4,15 kg/m)	360 lb./in. (4,15 kg/m)	
Free camber	7.187 in. (182,54 mm)	6.500 in. (165 mm)	
Fit of bushes in spring and chassis bores	.0025 to .0075 in. (0,065 to 0,18 mm) interference		

Land-Rover 107, 109 and 88 Fire Tender

				Driver	Passenger	
Number of leaves	....	....	....	8	8	
Width of leaves	....	....	....	2½ in. (63,5 mm)	2½ in. (63,5 mm)	88 Fire Tender from
Thickness of leaves	....	....	....	9/32 in. (7,1 mm)	9/32 in. (7,1 mm)	111703274 onwards
Static load	....	....	....	1,158.5 lb. (525 kg)	1,015 lb. (460 kg)	109 models from
Camber under static load	....	....	....	2.0 in. (50 mm)	2.0 in. (50 mm)	121700417 onwards
Rate	....	....	....	368 lb./in. (4,2 kg/m)	368 lb./in. (4,2 kg/m)	107 models from
Free camber	....	....	....	5.187 in. (130 mm)	4.75 in. (120 mm)	131700042 onwards

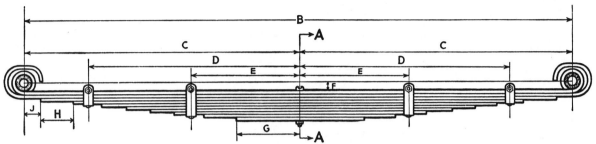

Fig. J-4—Dimensions with spring flat.

(Land-Rover 80 and 86, 1948-53)

B—42 in. (1067 mm)
C—21 in. (533 mm)
D—16⅝ in. (422 mm) (10 leaves)
    or 16⅜ in. (416 mm) (9 leaves)

E—8½ in. (216 mm) (10 leaves) or
    9⅛ in. (232 mm) (9 leaves)
F—25/32 in. (19,8 mm)

G—5½ in. (140 mm)
H—2¼ in. (57 mm)
J—1¼ in. (32 mm)

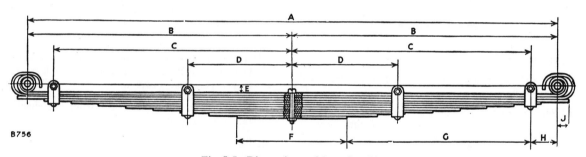

Fig. J-5—Dimensions with spring flat.

(Land-Rover 86 and 88—Driver and Passenger side, 1954-58)

A—48 in. (1,22 m)
B—24 in. (610 mm)
C—21⅜ in. (543 mm)

D—9½ in. (241 mm)
E—.780 in. (19,81 mm)
F—11 in. (280 mm)

G—17 1/16 in. (433 mm)
H—1 7/16 in. (36,5 mm)
J—1 in. (25,4 mm)

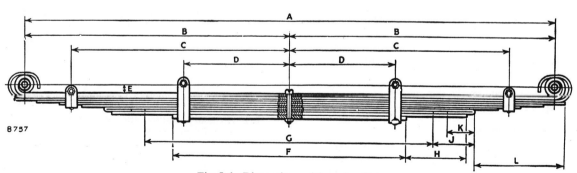

Fig. J-6—Dimensions with spring flat.

(Land-Rover 107 and 109—Driver and Passenger side, 1954-58)

A—48 in. (1,22 m)
B—24 in. (610 mm)
C—19 13/16 in. (503 mm)
D—9½ in. (241 mm)

E—.780 in. (19,81 mm)
F—26 in. (660 mm)
G—21 in. (533 mm)
H—5½ in. (140 mm)

J—3¾ in. (95 mm)
K—2½ in. (63,5 mm)
L—8¼ in. (209,5 mm)

Front springs

1948-53 vehicles

The three types of front springs are not interchangeable and must be fitted only within their respective series. On any particular vehicle, the left-hand and right-hand front springs are identical.

1954-58 vehicles

The driver side and passenger side front springs are not interchangeable, the free camber of the driver side spring being greater to compensate for the extra weight (driver, etc.) carried on that side of the vehicle.

The springs can be removed one at a time or both together as detailed.

To remove   **Operation J/10**

1. Jack up the vehicle and support it on four jacking stands.

2. Remove the front wheel.

3. Place two supports under the axle.

4. Jack up each of the road springs under the shock absorber plates and remove the U-bolt nuts. Lower the jacks so that the axle is supported by the two stands, and the springs are relaxed.

5. Remove the self-locking nut from the shackle pin in each spring eye.

6. Remove the shackle pin from the front end of the spring.

7. Remove the shackle pin from the rear end of the spring; the pin is threaded into the *inner* shackle plate.

8. Remove the road spring complete.

9. Remove the self-locking nut from the shackle pin securing the shackle plates to the chassis. Unscrew the pin from the inner shackle plate and remove it together with the two plates.

To refit   **Operation J/12**

1. If necessary, remove the shackle bushes from the chassis frame, with the aid of either a tubular drift or a suitable extractor; fit new bushes, which must be a *drive fit*.

2. If necessary, renew the rubber bushes in the spring eyes in a similar way.

Early models only

Select a suitable shim washer (available .090 in., .100 in., .110 in. and .120 in. thick) for each side of each bush, i.e., six in all, to give a definite clearance of not more than .005 in. between the shim and the shackle plate.

3. Replace the spring by reversing the removal procedure, taking care to tighten the shackle pins and locking nuts *after* the vehicle has been lowered to the ground.

Note:

IF THE SHACKLE PINS AND LOCKING NUTS ARE NOT TIGHTENED WITH THE SPRING IN THE MID-WAY POSITION, PREMATURE FAILURE OF THE BUSHES WILL OCCUR.

Rear springs

The driver side and passenger side rear springs are not interchangeable, the free camber of the driver side spring being greater to compensate for the extra weight (driver, etc.) carried on that side of the vehicle.

The springs can be removed one at a time, or both together, as detailed.

To remove   **Operation J/14**

1. Jack up the vehicle and support it on four jacking stands.

2. Remove the rear wheels.

3. Jack up each of the road springs under the shock absorber plates and remove the U-bolt nuts. Lower the jacks so that the axle is supported by its check straps and the springs are fully relaxed.

4. It is not necessary to support the rear axle on stands when removing the rear springs due to the fact that it will be supported by its check straps, as the jacks are lowered.

5. Remove the self-locking nut from the shackle pin in each spring eye.

6. Remove the shackle pin from the rear end of the spring, the pin is threaded into the *outer* shackle plate.

7. Remove the shackle pin from the front end of the spring.

8. Remove the road spring complete.

9. Remove the self-locking nut from the shackle pin securing the shackle plates to the chassis frame. Unscrew the pin from the outer shackle plate and remove it, together with the two plates.

To refit   **Operation J/16**

1. If necessary, remove the shackle bush from the chassis frame bracket with the aid of a tubular drift or suitable extractor; fit a new bush, which must be a *drive fit*.

2. If necessary, renew the bushes in the spring eyes in a similar way.

3. Replace the spring by reversing the removal procedure, taking care to tighten the shackle pins and locking nuts *after* the vehicle has been lowered to the ground.

Note:

IF THE SHACKLE PINS AND LOCKING NUTS ARE NOT TIGHTENED WITH THE SPRING IN THE MID-WAY POSITION, PREMATURE FAILURE OF THE BUSHES WILL OCCUR.

To overhaul   **Operation J/18**

1. Remove the four leaf clips; except for the inner clips on the front springs which are bent over the top leaf, all the clips are secured by bolts and nuts.

2. Remove the spring bushes. Operation J/16.

3. Remove the centre bolt and nut to release the spring leaves.

4. Clean (or preferably degrease) the leaves and carefully examine them for signs of failure or cracks. Only the main and second leaves are supplied as replacement, so that should any other leaf be faulty, the complete spring must be renewed.

5. The recambering of road springs is not advised, but if no alternative is possible, the spring should be reset, if necessary, either to a new spring or to the data set on Pages J-1 and J-3.

6. Grease each leaf with graphite grease and reassemble the spring by fitting the centre bolt and leaf clips; fit the spring bushes.

Hydraulic dampers

To renew   **Operation J/20**

If it is suspected that a shock absorber is not functioning satisfactorily, it should be removed and placed vertically in a vice, the lower eye being secured between the jaws of the vice. It should then be extended and compressed, when a uniform resistance throughout the stroke should be noted, in both directions. Should erratic or weak resistance be found, the shock absorber should be replaced.

Note: The resistance felt when extending the shock absorber is very much greater than that encountered when compressing it.

No attempt must be made to strip or adjust the hydraulic dampers; if any trouble is experienced, a new damper must always be fitted.

1. Withdraw the hydraulic damper complete with four tapered rubber bushes and retaining washers.

2. Renew the retaining washers as necessary.

3. Renew the rubber mounting bushes as necessary.

4. Fit the new damper with its outer sleeve uppermost.

The plain length of all shock absorber mounting tubes should be $1\frac{5}{16}$ in. (33,34 mm), i.e., when the securing nut is fully tightened, the compressed overall length of the two rubber bushes in the damper lug must be $1\frac{5}{16}$ in. (33,34 mm).

It is most important that this point be checked when fitting a new shock absorber or replacing the rubber bushes. If the tube is too long, suitable washers must be fitted over the tube, to reduce the compressed length of the bushes to the correct dimension.

Note:

IF THE RUBBER BUSHES ARE NOT CORRECTLY NIPPED OR IF THEY ARE NOT TIGHTENED WITH THE ROAD SPRING IN THE MID-WAY POSITION, PREMATURE FAILURE OF THE BUSHES WILL OCCUR.

On 1955-57 models the lower ends of the shock absorbers are secured to the spring bottom plates by means of plain washers and split pins.

With this type of fastening, the correct nip on the rubber bushes is predetermined by the position of the split pin hole.

A tubular piece of steel with a slot cut in it, will facilitate the compression of the rubber bushes and allow the insertion or removal of split pin.

Bump rubber

To renew   **Operation J/22**

1. Remove the bump rubber secured to the underside of the chassis member.

2. Fit the new bump rubber and secure with the two bolts and self-locking nuts.

Rear axle check strap

To renew   **Operation J/24**

1. Remove the fabric check strap, complete with two clamping plates.

2. Fit the new check strap by reversing the removal procedure; take care that the strap is fitted to the rear of the brake pipe protection plate.

Section K — CHASSIS

INDEX

	Page		Page
Battery and air cleaner support	K-1	Front bumper	K-1
Frame alignment	K-1	Rear drawbar	K-1

LIST OF ILLUSTRATIONS

Fig.		Page	Fig.		Page
K-1	Chassis frame diagonal measurements	K-1	K-4	Chassis frame dimensions (Land-Rover 107 and 109)	K-4
K-2	Chassis frame dimensions (Land-Rover 80)	K-2	K-5	Layout of chassis frame	K-5
K-3	Chassis frame dimensions (Land-Rover 86 and 88)	K-3			

Frame alignment

To check   **Operation K/10**

Figs. K-2 (Land-Rover 80, 86 and 88), K-3 and K-4 (Land-Rover 107 and 109) show the various dimensions that should be used as a guide in checking frame alignment. Fig. K-1 illustrates the diagonal measurements which may be taken to check the frame for "squareness". Extreme care must be taken when checking for malalignment.

When the body is removed, the frame may easily be checked against the measurements in Figs. K-1, K-2, K-3 and K-4. If the body is in position, measurements may be taken with the aid of a plumb-bob and chalk as follows:—

1. Place the vehicle on a level floor.

2. Hold the plumb line against one of the measuring points, with the bob slightly above the floor; mark the floor directly beneath the bob.

3. Repeat for other measuring points.

4. Move the vehicle away and measure between the chalk marks.

Care should be taken when measuring diagonals, that exactly corresponding points are used on each side of the frame.

Front bumper

The channel-section front bumper is bolted to the chassis side members, so that it may be removed to facilitate repair after accidental damage.

Rear drawbar

The rear drawbar is bolted to the chassis frame, so that it may be removed to facilitate repair after accidental damage.

Battery and air cleaner support

To remove   **Operation K/12**

1. Remove the air cleaner. Section M.

2. Disconnect the battery cables.

3. Remove the battery cover.

4. Remove the battery.

5. Remove the battery and air cleaner support from the chassis frame (this action releases the battery earth lead).

To replace   **Operation K/14**

Reverse the removal procedure.

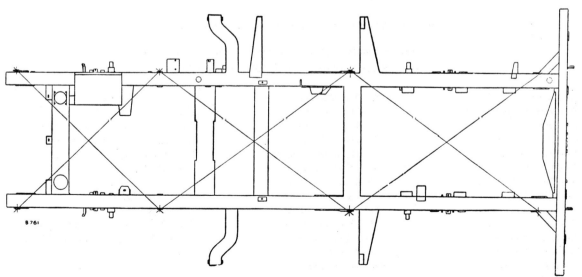

Fig. K-1—Chassis frame diagonal measurements.

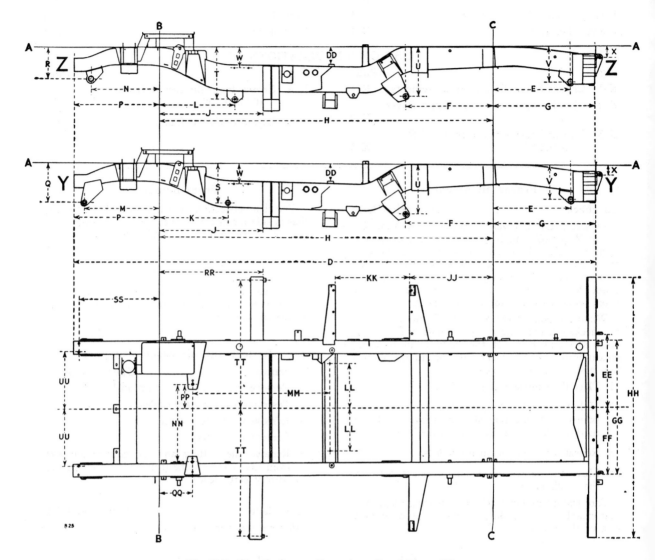

Fig. K-2—Chassis frame dimensions (Land-Rover 80)

Z—Vehicles numbered prior to 06113530, 06200410 and 06300031

Y—Vehicles numbered 06113530, 06200410 and 06300031 onwards

AA—Datum lines	Q—9 in. (228,6 mm)	JJ—20 in. (508 mm)
BB—Centre-line of front axle	R—7⅛ in. (181 mm)	KK—17¾ in. (451 mm)
CC—Centre-line of rear axle	S—9 in. (228,6 mm)	LL—10⅛ in.± 1/32 (257,2 mm±0,8 mm)
D—125 21/32 in. (3,193 m)	T—11¾ in. (298 mm)	MM—32⅞ in.± 1/32 (834,9 mm±0,8 mm)
E—19 in. (483 mm)	U—11¼ in. (286 mm)	NN—17¾ in.± 1/32 (450,7 mm±0,8 mm)
F—21 in. (533 mm)	V—7 27/32 in. (199,2 mm)	PP—5½ in. (139,7 mm)
G—25 1/16 in. (637 mm)	W—4¾ in. (120,6 mm)	QQ—8 in. (203,2 mm)
H—80 in. (2,032 m)	X—2 1/16 in. (52,4 mm)	RR—25 in. (635 mm)
J—24¾ in. (629 mm)	DD—3 29/32 in. (99,2 mm)	SS—19 11/32 in. (491 mm)
K—16⅝ in. (422 mm)	EE—16 15/16 in. (430 mm)	TT—29 7/16 in.± 1/64 (747,6 mm±0,4 mm)
L—18 in. (457 mm)	FF—15¼ in. (387 mm)	UU—13 1/16 in.± 1/32 (331,7 mm±0,8 mm)
M—18 in. (457 mm)	GG—31 in. (787 mm)	
N—16⅝ in. (422 mm)	HH—60½ in. (1,537 m)	
P—20 19/32 in. (523 mm)		

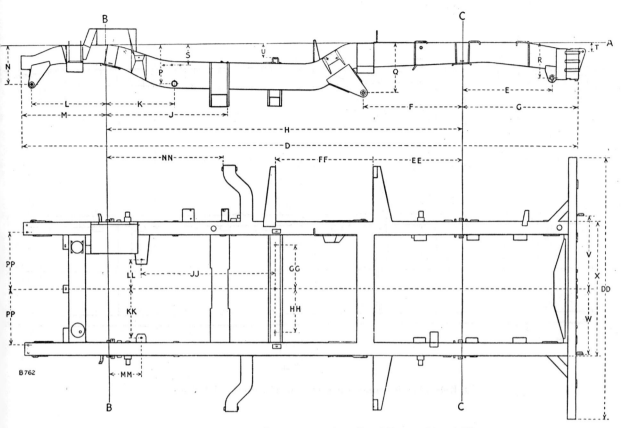

Fig. K-3—Chassis frame dimensions (Land-Rovers 86 and 88).

AA—Datum line
BB—Centre line of front axle
CC—Centre line of rear axle
D—134 $\frac{31}{32}$ in. (3,42 m)
E—21$\frac{1}{4}$ in. (540 mm)
F—24 in (610 mm)
G—28$\frac{5}{64}$ in. (713 mm)
H—86 in. (2,18 m)—86 Models
  88 in. (2,23 m)—88 Models
J—29$\frac{1}{4}$ in. (743 mm)—86 Models
  31$\frac{1}{4}$ in. (793,7 mm)—88 Models
K—16$\frac{5}{8}$ in. (422 mm)—86 Models
  18$\frac{5}{8}$ in. (473,1 mm)—88 Models
L—18 in. (457 mm)—86 Models
  17 in. (431,8 mm)—88 Models
M—20$\frac{37}{64}$ in. (523 mm)—86 Models
  18$\frac{37}{64}$ in. (472,2 mm)—88 Models
N—9 in. (229 mm)
P—9 in. (229 mm)
Q—11$\frac{7}{16}$ in. (291 mm)

R—7$\frac{13}{16}$ in. (182 mm)
S—4$\frac{3}{4}$ in. (121 mm)
T—2$\frac{1}{16}$ in. (52 mm)
U—3$\frac{11}{64}$ in. (80,56 mm)
V—16$\frac{15}{16}$ in. (430 mm)
W—15$\frac{1}{4}$ in. (387 mm)
X—31 in. (787 mm)
DD—60$\frac{1}{2}$ in. (1,53 m)
EE—21$\frac{3}{4}$ in. (552 mm)
FF—23$\frac{1}{8}$ in. (587) mm)
GG—10$\frac{1}{8}$ in. + $\frac{1}{16}$ (257 mm ± 0,8)
HH—10 in. ± $\frac{1}{32}$ (254 mm ± 0,8)
JJ—32$\frac{7}{8}$ in. ± $\frac{1}{32}$ (835 mm ± 0,8)
KK—11$\frac{9}{16}$ in. (294 mm)
LL —6$\frac{9}{16}$ in. (167 mm)
MM—8 in. (203 mm)—86 Models
  10 in. (254 mm)—88 Models
NN—28$\frac{1}{4}$ in (718 mm)—86 Models
  30$\frac{1}{4}$ in. (765,2 mm)—88 Models
PP—13$\frac{1}{16}$ in. ± $\frac{1}{64}$ (332 mm ± 0,50)

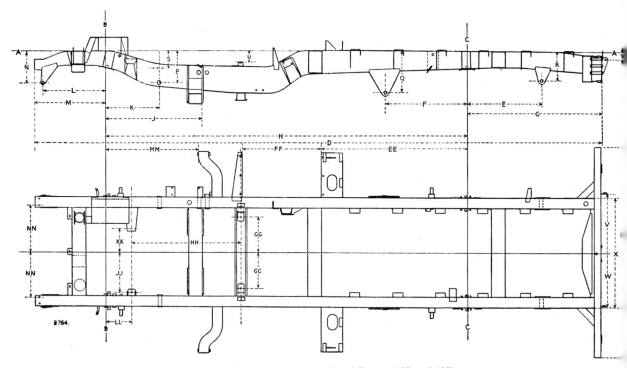

Fig. K-4—Chassis frame dimensions (Land-Rovers 107 and 109).

AA—Datum line
BB—Centre line of front axle
CC—Centre line of rear axle
D—166 $\frac{61}{64}$ in. (4,24 m)
E—21$\frac{1}{4}$ in. (540 mm)
F—24 in. (610 mm)
G—39$\frac{3}{8}$ in. (1,00 m)
H—107 in. (2,717 m)—107 Models
    109 in. (2,768 m)—109 Models
J—29$\frac{1}{4}$ in. (743 mm)—107 Models
   31$\frac{1}{4}$ in. (793,8 mm)—109 Models
K—15$\frac{5}{8}$ in. (422 mm)—107 Models
   18$\frac{5}{8}$ in. (473,1 mm)—109 Models
L—18 in. (457 mm)—107 Models
  17 in. (431,8 mm)—109 Models
M—20$\frac{37}{64}$ in. (523 mm)—107 Models
   18$\frac{37}{64}$ in. (472,2 mm)—109 Models
N—9 in. (229 mm)
P—9 in. (229 mm)
Q—11$\frac{11}{16}$ in. (297 mm)

R—8$\frac{1}{16}$ in. (205 mm)
S—4$\frac{3}{4}$ in. (121 mm)
T—2$\frac{1}{16}$ in. (52 mm)
U—3$\frac{11}{64}$ in. (80,5 mm)
V—16$\frac{15}{16}$ in. (430 mm)
W—15$\frac{1}{4}$ in. (387 mm)
X—31 in. (787 mm)
DD—60$\frac{1}{2}$ in. (1,53 m)
EE—42$\frac{3}{4}$ in. (1,086 m)
FF—23$\frac{1}{8}$ in. (587 mm)
GG—10$\frac{1}{8}$ in. $\pm$ $\frac{1}{32}$ (257 mm $\pm$ 0,8)
HH—32$\frac{7}{8}$ in. $\pm$ $\frac{1}{32}$ (835 mm $\pm$ 0,8)
JJ—11$\frac{9}{16}$ in. (294 mm)
KK—6$\frac{9}{16}$ in. (167 mm)
LL—8 in. (203 mm)—107 Models
   10 in. (228,6 mm)—109 Models
MM—28$\frac{1}{4}$ in. (718 mm)—107 Models
    30$\frac{1}{4}$ in. (768 mm)—109 Models
NN—13$\frac{1}{16}$ in. $\pm$ $\frac{1}{64}$ (332 mm $\pm$ 0,50)

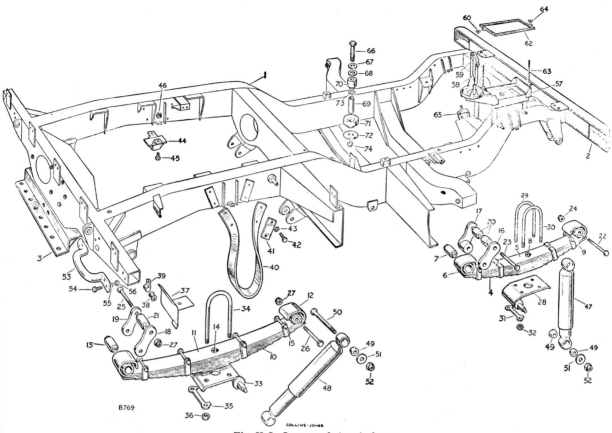

Fig. K-5—Layout of chassis frame.

1 Chassis frame	37 Shield for brake pipe, R.H.
2 Front bumper	38 Rubber grommet for brake pipe
3 Rear draw bar	39 Clip for grommet
4 Road spring complete, front, driver's	40 Check strap for rear axle
5 Main leaf ⎫ For front	41 Plate for check strap
6 2nd leaf ⎰ spring	42–43 Fixings for check strap
7 Bush for front spring	44 Rubber buffer for axles, front and rear
8 Dowel for front spring	45–46 Fixings for buffers
9 Bolt ⎫ For spring	47 Shock absorber, front
Nut ⎰ clip	48 Shock absorber, rear
10 Road spring complete, rear, driver's	49 Rubber bush for shock absorbers
11 Main leaf ⎫ For rear	50–52 Fixings for shock absorbers
12 2nd leaf ⎰ spring	53 Lifting handle, rear
13 Bush for rear spring	54–56 Fixings for handles
14 Dowel for rear spring	57 Battery casing and air cleaner support complete
15 Bolt ⎫ For	58 Air cleaner clamp, side
Nut ⎰ spring clip	59 Air cleaner clamp, top
16 Shackle plate, tapped ⎫ For	60 Wing nut for clamp
17 Shackle plate, plain ⎰ front springs	61 Rubber strip for battery
18 Shackle plate, tapped ⎫ For	62 Battery cover
19 Shackle plate, plain ⎰ rear springs	63 Battery fixing rod
20 Bush in chassis frame, front spring	64 Wing nut fixing battery
21 Bush in chassis frame, rear	65 Suspension rubber for engine, front
22 Shackle pin, front	66 Bolt, rear
23 Shackle pin, springs to frame, front	67 Plain washer, top
24 Self-locking nut, front	68 Rubber washer
25 Shackle pin, rear	69 Distance tube
26 Shackle pin, springs to frame, rear	70 Top rubber
27 Self-locking nut, rear	71 Bottom rubber
28 Bottom plate for front spring, R.H.	72 Plain washer, bottom
29–32 Fixings for front springs	73 Shim
33 Bottom plate for rear spring, R.H.	74 Special nut
34–36 Fixings for rear springs	

66 Bolt, rear ⎫
67 Plain washer, top ⎪
68 Rubber washer ⎪ Fixing engine unit
69 Distance tube ⎬ to chassis frame
70 Top rubber ⎪ at front and rear
71 Bottom rubber ⎪
72 Plain washer, bottom ⎪
73 Shim ⎭
74 Special nut

Section L — COOLING SYSTEM — ALL MODELS

INDEX

	Page		Page
Data	L-9	Thermostat, Petrol models	L-2
Defect location	L-9	Thermostat, Diesel models	L-4
Frost precautions	L-7	Visual inspection	L-7
Radiator	L-8	Water pump, Petrol models	L-1
Tests and adjustments	L-7	Water pump, Diesel models	L-2

LIST OF ILLUSTRATIONS

Fig.		Page	Fig.		Page
L-1	Cross-section of water pump, Petrol models	L-2	L-4	Layout of pump, thermostat and fan, Diesel models	L-5
L-2	Layout of pump, thermostat and coolant pipes, Petrol models	L-3	L-5	Layout of radiator and grille panel	L-6
L-3	Cross-section of water pump, Diesel models	L-4	L-6	Radiator drain taps	L-7
			L-7	Radiator filler cap	L-8

Water pump—Petrol models

To remove   **Operation L/2**

The following procedure for removing the water pump will be modified if an engine governor or heater unit is fitted. See Section T for details of these items of optional equipment.

1. Partially drain off the coolant.

2. Slacken the dynamo mounting bolts and adjusting link bolts and push the dynamo inwards.

3. Slacken the lower clip on the top hose and the clip securing the inlet manifold hose to the inlet elbow on the thermostat housing.

4. Remove the thermostat housing from the cylinder head complete with thermostat, outlet pipe, inlet elbow and joint washer.

5. Remove the copper tube and rubber joint ring from either the bottom face of the thermostat housing or the top face of the water pump casing.

6. Remove the fan blade, pulley (and distance piece if fitted).

7. Slacken the clip securing the bottom hose to the water pump inlet pipe and remove the bolt securing the pipe to the front cover.

8. Remove the water pump complete with joint washer and inlet pipe; as the pump casing is spigoted in the block, it will be necessary to oscillate it slightly as it is removed.

9. Remove the inlet pipe from the water pump.

10. The water pump may now be overhauled, Operation L/6, or exchanged for a Service Pump Assembly, obtainable from our Spares Department.

The Service Assembly comprises only the following parts:
     Water pump casing
     Spindle, fan hub and bearing complete
     Carbon ring and seal
     Impeller
     Spring washer }Locating the
     Set bolt   }spindle bearing

Pumps must be stripped to this condition before they are returned for exchange.

To strip   **Operation L/4**

1. Remove the bearing location bolt, place the pump in a vice and drift out the impeller bearing and spindle as an assembly from the pump body and from hub.

2. Cut through the seal and remove from spindle, insert the spindle into the water pump body, so that the impeller is in the position of the fan pulley. The spindle and bearing may now be drifted out of the impeller.

To assemble   **Operation L/6**

1. Examine the spindle and bearing assembly; it need not be renewed if the bearing is satisfactory and the spindle is free from excessive corrosion. Clean any corroded portion of the spindle and paint with chlorinated rubber primer to prevent further action. (Part No. 261483 for half-pint tin). As an alternative, good quality aluminium paint or other anti-corrosive paint can be used in place of a rubber primer.

2. Insert a few drops of thick oil in the location hole in the bearing.

3. Press the spindle and bearing assembly into the front of the pump body with the longer end of the spindle leading. Locate it with the set bolt and spring washer.

4. If the fan pulley hub has been removed, it must be pressed on to the spindle to a set dimension between the front face of the pulley hub and the mounting face of the water pump casing. This dimension must be: 4.140 in. (105 mm) on 1954-58 models or 4.215 in. (107 mm) on 1948-53 models.

   Care must be taken to set the hub to the correct dimension. When pressing on the hub, the spindle must be supported, to prevent pressure falling on the location set bolt.

5. On 1954-58 models, fit the carbon ring and seal into the bore of the pump body with the carbon ring to the rear, and fit the rubber water deflector washer.

   On 1948-53 models fit the carbon ring and seal into the bore of the impeller with the carbon ring to the front.

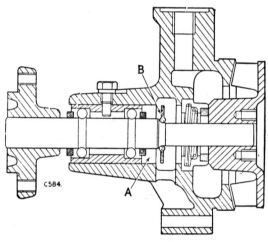

Fig. L-1. Cross-section of water pump, Petrol Models.
A—Through bore housing.
B—Water deflector washer

6. Press the impeller on to the spindle until there is .020 in. (0,5 mm) clearance between the vanes and the pump body face (check with a feeler gauge). The impeller must be a *press fit* on the spindle. If the impeller is loose on the spindle, replace either part as necessary.

7. Refit the inlet pipe to the water pump.

To refit   Operation L/8

To refit the water pump to the engine, reverse the removal procedure, noting the following points:—

1. Renew both joint washers.

2. When fitting the fan pulley, first engage the fan belt in the pulley groove.

3. On completion, run the engine and check and rectify any leaks.

Thermostat, Petrol models

If the thermostat becomes faulty in operation, overheating of the engine will usually result. To check the thermostat, remove it from its housing and run the engine; if the overheating is eliminated, the unit is faulty and must be renewed. Further tests may be made by immersing the thermostat in hot water, whereon expansion of the bellows should commence between 162°F (72°C) and 171°F (77°C) and be completed at 191°F (88°C).

To renew   Operation L/10

1. Partially drain off the coolant and remove the top hose.

2. Remove the water outlet pipe from the top of the thermostat housing.

3. Lift out the thermostat from the housing, together with a fibre joint washer, above and below its flange.

4. Fit the new thermostat, together with two new joint washers.

5. Replace the water outlet pipe and top hose.

6. Refill the coolant system to the bottom of the radiator filler neck and check for leaks.

Water pump, Diesel models
To remove   Operation L/12

1. Partially drain off coolant.

2. Slacken the dynamo mounting bolts and adjusting link bolts and push the dynamo inwards.

3. Disconnect the hoses from pump.

4. Remove the fan blade, pulley and distance piece.

5. Remove the water pump complete with joint washer.

6. The water pump may now be overhauled or exchanged for a Service Pump Assembly, obtainable from our Spares Department.

   The Service Assembly comprises only the following parts:

       Water pump casing
       Spindle, fan hub and bearing complete
       Carbon ring and seal
       Impeller
       Spring washer ⎫ Locating the
       Set bolt   ⎭ spindle bearing

   Pumps must be stripped to this condition before they are returned for exchange.

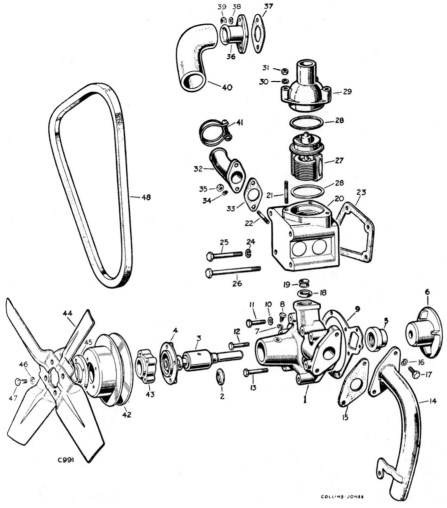

Fig. L-2—Layout of water pump, thermostat and coolant pipes, Petrol Models.

1	Water pump casing	24–26	Fixings for thermostat housing
2	Water deflector washer	27	Thermostat
3	Pump spindle and bearing	28	Fibre washer for thermostat
4	Hub for fan	29	Water outlet pipe, thermostat to radiator
5	Carbon ring and seal unit	30–31	Fixings for outlet pipe
6	Impeller for pump	32	Water inlet elbow to thermostat
7	Spring washer ⎫ Locating	33	Joint washer for inlet elbow
8	Set bolt ⎭ bearing casing	34–35	Fixings for elbow
9	Joint washer for water pump	36	Water outlet pipe from manifold
10–13	Fixings for water pump	37	Joint washer for outlet pipe
14	Inlet pipe for water pump	38–39	Fixings for water outlet pipe
15	Joint washer for inlet pipe	40	Rubber hose ⎫ Connecting water pipe
16–17	Fixings for pipe	41	Clip for hose ⎭ to inlet elbow
18	Rubber joint ring ⎫ Connecting water pump	42	Fan pulley
19	Copper tube ⎭ to thermostat housing	43	Distance piece for fan pulley
20	Thermostat housing assembly	44	Fan blade
21	Stud for outlet pipe	45	Reinforcing plate for fan blade
22	Stud for inlet pipe	46–47	Fixings for fan blade and pulley
23	Joint washer for thermostat housing	48	Fan and dynamo belt

To strip   **Operation L/14**

1. Remove the bearing location bolt, place the pump in a vice and drift out the impeller bearing and spindle as an assembly from the pump body and from hub.

2. Cut through the seal and remove from spindle, insert the spindle into the water pump body, so that the impeller is in the position of the fan pulley. The spindle and bearing may now be drifted out of the impeller.

To assemble   **Operation L/16**

1. Examine the spindle and bearing assembly; it need not be renewed if the bearing is satisfactory and the spindle is free from excessive corrosion. Clean any corroded portion of the spindle and paint with chlorinated rubber primer to prevent further action. (Part No. 261483 for half-pint tin.) As an alternative, good quality aluminium paint or other anti-corrosive paint can be used in place of a rubber primer.

2. Insert a few drops of thick oil in the location hole in the bearing.

3. Press the spindle and bearing assembly into the front of the pump body with the longer end of the spindle leading. Locate it with the set bolt and spring washer.

4. If the fan pulley hub has been removed, it must be pressed on to the spindle to a set dimension between the front face of the pulley hub and the mounting face of the water pump casing. This dimension must be: 3.453 in. (86,36 mm). Care must be taken to set the hub to the correct dimensions. When pressing on the hub, the spindle must be supported, to prevent pressure falling on the location set bolt.

5. Fit the carbon ring and seal into the bore of the pump body with the carbon ring to the rear.

6. Press the impeller on to the spindle until there is .020 in. (0,5 mm) clearance between the vanes and the pump body face (check with a feeler gauge). The impeller must be a *press fit* on the spindle. If the impeller is loose on the spindle, replace either part as necessary.

7. Refit the inlet pipe to the water pump.

To refit   **Operation L/18**

To refit the water pump to the engine, reverse the removal procedure, noting the following points:—

1. Renew joint washer.

2. When fitting the fan pulley, first engage the fan belt in the pulley groove.

3. On completion, run the engine and check and rectify any leaks.

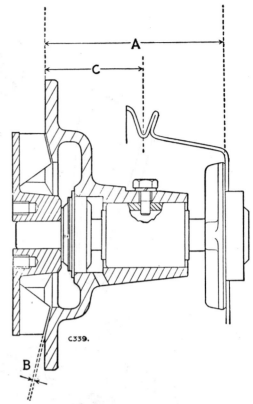

Fig. L-3—Cross-section of water pump, Diesel Models

A—3.453 in. (86 mm)   B—.020 in. (0,508 mm)
C—1.875 in. (47,625 mm)

Thermostat, Diesel models

If the thermostat becomes faulty in operation, overheating or overcooling of the engine may result. To check the thermostat, remove it from its housing and run the engine; if the coolant temperature remains unchanged, the unit is faulty and should be renewed. See important note on page L-8.

Further tests may be made by immersing the thermostat in hot water, whereon expansion of the bellows should commence between 164°F (73°C) and 173°F (78°C) and be complete at 193°F (89°C).

To renew   **Operation L/20**

1. Partially drain off the coolant, disconnect the top and by-pass hoses from the thermostat cover —also the heater hose if fitted—and remove the cover.

2. Lift out the thermostat from its housing and fit the new one.

3. Replace the top cover and re-connect the hoses.

4. Refill the coolant system to the bottom of filler neck and check for leaks.

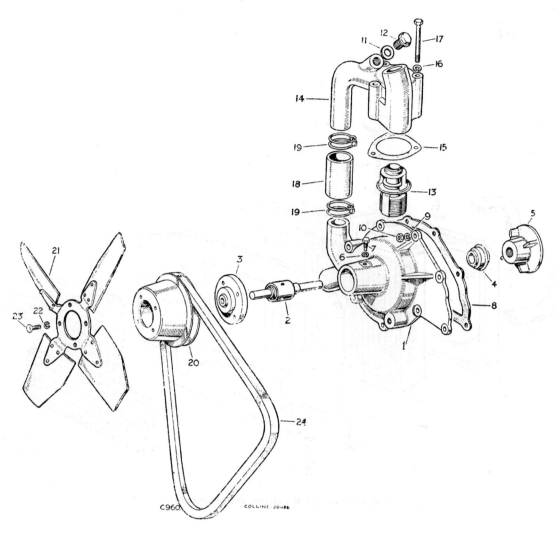

Fig. L-4—Layout of pump, thermostat and fan, Diesel Models.

1	Water pump casing	13	Thermostat
2	Spindle and bearing assembly	14	Outlet pipes and cover
3	Pulley hub	15	Joint washer for cover
4	Seal	16	Spring washer ⎫ for
5	Impeller	17	Set bolt ⎬ casing
6	Spring washer ⎫ locating spindle	18	By-pass hose
7	Set bolt ⎬ and bearing	19	Clip
8	Joint washer	20	Pulley
9	Spring washer ⎫ for	21	Fan blades
10	Nut ⎬ casing	22	Spring washer ⎫ for fan
11	Joint washer for plug ⎫ for heater return in	23	Set bolt ⎬ blades
12	Plug ⎬ water outlet pipe	24	Driving belt

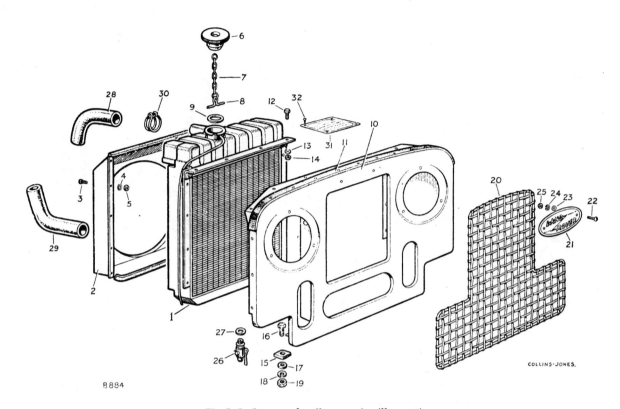

Fig. L-5—Layout of radiator and grille panel.

1	Radiator block assembly	15–19	Fixings for grille panel
2	Cowl for fan	20	Grille for radiator
3–5	Fixings for cowl	21	"Land-Rover" name plate
6	Filler cap for radiator	22–25	Fixings for grille and name plate
7	Chain for filler cap	26	Drain tap for radiator
8	Retainer for chain	27	Joint washer for drain tap
9	Joint washer for filler cap	28	Hose for radiator, top
10	Radiator grille panel assembly	29	Hose for radiator, bottom
11	Bonnet rest strip	30	Clip for radiator hoses
	Bifurcated rivet fixing strip	31	Oil recommendation plate
12–14	Fixings for radiator block	32	Drive screw fixing plate

Visual inspection

It is a good plan to inspect the cooling system at the same time as the engine oil level is checked; such care would largely prevent the possibility of a sudden and costly delay due to coolant loss and consequent engine damage. Attention should be paid to the following points:—

1. Water level in radiator—to the bottom of the filler neck.

2. Condition of all hoses—freedom from cracks and hose clips tight.

3. Any water leaks.

4. Check that the drain taps are fully closed.

As the cooling system is pressurised, the vehicle must not be run without the radiator cap in position. When removing cap follow instructions on top.

Tests and adjustments
Fan belt

The fan belt is of the "V" type, drive is on the sides of the belt and it is not therefore necessary to adjust it tightly and so put an excessive load on the water pump and dynamo bearings; the tension is correct when the belt can be depressed $\frac{5}{16}$ to $\frac{7}{16}$ in. (8 to 11 mm)—Diesel models, and $\frac{1}{2}$ to $\frac{3}{4}$ in. (12 to 19 mm)—Petrol models by thumb pressure between the fan and crankshaft pulleys. The procedure for adjustment is as follows:—

Slacken the dynamo pivot bolts and the bolt securing the dynamo to the adjusting link. Move the dynamo outwards until the tension is correct and re-tighten the bolts.

Thermostat

See pages L-2 and L-4 of this section.

Draining the cooling system

The cooling system should be drained and flushed out at least twice each year in the following manner:

1. Remove the radiator filler cap.

2. Open the water drain taps at the bottom of the radiator and on the left-hand side of the cylinder block.

3. When the water flow has ceased, insert a piece of wire in each tap to make sure that a blockage has not been caused by rust or scale.

4. Place a hose in the radiator filler neck and fill the system; adjust the flow of water to equal that draining from the taps.

5. Run the engine for a short time to ensure thorough cleaning of the whole system.

6. Stop the engine, remove the hose and close the taps. Refill the system with clean water to the bottom of the filler neck and replace the filler cap.

The total capacity of the cooling system is: Petrol and Diesel models—17 Imperial pints (9,7 litres).

Note: Use soft water wherever possible; if the local water supply is hard, clean rain or distilled water should be used.

7. Run the engine until working temperature is reached and top the water level as necessary.

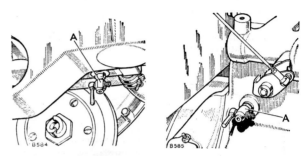

A—Drain taps—Petrol Models.

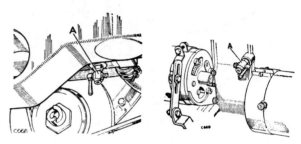

A—Drain taps—Diesel Models.

Fig. L-6—Radiator drain taps.

Cleaning radiator—externally

In the event of the cooling gills of the radiator becoming blocked with dirt, straw, etc., they should be cleaned by means of compressed air or water pressure applied from the rear, so forcing the foreign matter out through the front of the radiator. Never use a metal implement for this purpose or serious damage may result to the radiator core.

Frost precautions

In cold weather, when the temperature may drop to or below freezing point, precautions must be taken to prevent freezing of the water in the cooling system.

A thermostat is fitted in the system and it is therefore possible for the radiator block to freeze in cold weather even though the engine running temperature is quite high; for this reason the use of an anti-freeze mixture is essential.

Only high quality inhibited glycol-based solutions should be used.

When the temperature is between 32° F and 0° F (0° C and minus 17 C) use one part of anti-freeze to four parts of water.

Proceed as follows:—

1. Ensure that the cooling system is leak-proof; anti-freeze solutions are far more "searching" at joints than water.

2. Drain and flush the system. See "Draining the cooling system"

3. Mix the solution to the required strength in a separate container and refill the system.

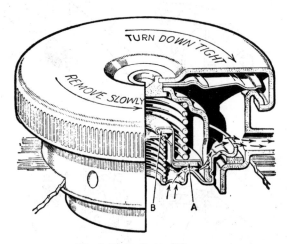

Fig. L-7—Radiator filler cap.

A—Pressure relief valve (steam escape).
B—Depression relief valve.

4. Run the engine to ensure good circulation of the mixture.

If the vehicle is to be stored in cold weather, unless it is kept in a well-heated garage or anti-freeze solution has been used, the cooling system must be completely drained.

Radiator

To remove   Operation L/22

1. Drain off the coolant.

   Note: Diesel models only—Disconnect the lead coupling the two batteries.

2. Disconnect the top and bottom hoses from the radiator.

3. On 1954-58 models disconnect the side lamp leads at snap connectors at each side of the grille panel assembly and the front lamp harness from the junction box at right-hand side of scuttle, then pull the wiring clear to front of engine.

On 1948-53 models disconnect the headlamp and horn wiring from the junction box on the dash panel and pull the wiring clear to the front of the engine.

4. Remove the radiator grille and chaff guard (if fitted) from the grille panel complete with the name plate.

5. Remove the fan blades.

6. Remove the bolts securing the front apron and remove panel. Remove the bolts securing the grille panel to the front cross-member and front wings.

7. Lift the radiator, grille panel and headlamps assembly upward, then forward to clear the vehicle.

8. Remove the rubber buffers from beneath the grille panel.

9. Remove the radiator block from the grille panel.

10. Remove the drain tap and joint washer from the bottom of the radiator block.

11. Remove the filler cap, complete with the joint washer, retainer and chain.

To refit   Operation L/24

1. Reverse the removal procedure, replacing the rubber buffers, if necessary, and connecting the wiring in accordance with the appropriate wiring diagram—Section P.

It is important to fully tighten the radiator cap. As the cooling system is pressurised, the radiator cap must be fully tightened, not left loose or just turned to the first stop, but tightened right down by turning clockwise as far as possible.

Failure to do so will result in the water rapidly boiling away with possible seizure and damage to the engine due to overheating.

It is equally important to take great care when removing the radiator filler cap, especially when the engine is hot, to avoid steam which may be blown out with considerable force.

When removing the filler cap, first turn it anti-clockwise to the stop and allow all pressure to escape before pressing it down and turning further in the same direction to lift it off.

Important

On no account must Diesel engines be run without water circulating through the cylinder block and cylinder head even for a few seconds, since lacquer formation would quickly render the injectors useless.

When water is drained a label must be attached to the steering column stating: "No water in cooling system—on no account must the engine be started until the cooling system is refilled."

DEFECT LOCATION
Symptom, Cause and Remedy

A—EXTERNAL LEAKAGE

1. Loose hose clips—*Tighten.*
2. Defective rubber hose—*Renew.*
3. Damaged radiator seams—*Rectify.*
4. Excessive wear in the water pump—*Renew.*
5. Loose core plugs—*Renew.*
6. Damaged gaskets—*Renew.*
7. Leak at the heater connections or plugs—*Rectify.*
8. Leak at the water temperature gauge plug—*Tighten.*
9. Diesel only—leak from either of the four small holes in L.H. side of cylinder block—*Fit new sealing rings to liner Section A.*

B—INTERNAL LEAKAGE

1. Defective cylinder head gasket—*Renew, check engine oil for contamination and refill as necessary.*
2. Cracked cylinder bore or liner—*Renew cylinder block (or Diesel) liner.*
3. Loose cylinder head bolts—*Tighten. Check engine oil for contamination and refill as necessary.*

C—WATER LOSS

1. Overfilling—*See Instruction Manual for filling instructions.*
2. Boiling—*Ascertain the cause of engine overheating and correct as necessary.*
3. Internal or external leakage—*See items A and B.*
4. Restricted radiator or inoperative thermostat—*Flush radiator and renew the thermostat as necessary.*

D—POOR CIRCULATION

1. Restriction in system—*Check hoses for crimps, and flush the radiator.*
2. Insufficient coolant—*Replenish.*
3. Inoperative water pump—*Renew.*
4. Loose fan belt—*Adjust.*
5. Inoperative thermostat—*Renew.*

E—CORROSION

1. Excessive impurity in the water—*Use only soft, clean water (rainwater is satisfactory).*
2. Infrequent flushing and draining of system—*The cooling system should be drained and flushed thoroughly at least twice a year.*
3. Incorrect anti-freeze mixtures—*Certain anti-freeze solutions have a corrosive effect on parts of the cooling system. Only good glycol-base solutions should be used.*

F—OVERHEATING

1. Poor circulation—*See item D.*
2. Dirty oil and sludge in engine—*Flush and refill.*
3. Radiator fins choked with chaff. mud, etc.—*Use air pressure from the engine side of the radiator and clean out passages thoroughly.*
4. Incorrect injection pump or ignition timing—*Section A.*
5. Incorrect valve timing—*Section A.*
6. Low oil level—*Replenish.*
7. Tight engine—*New engines are very tight during the "running-in" period and moderate speeds should be maintained for the first 1,000 miles (1.500 km).*
8. Choked or damaged exhaust pipe or silencer—*Rectify or renew.*
9. Dragging brakes—*Check cause—Section H.*
10. Overloading vehicle—*In the hands of the operator.*
11. Driving in heavy sand or mud—*In the hands of the operator*
12. Engine labouring on grades—*In the hands of the operator.*
13. Low gear work—*In the hands of the operator.*
14. Excessive engine idling—*In the hands of the operator.*

G—OVERCOOLING

1. Defective thermostat—*Renew.*

DATA

Capacity of cooling system—

Petrol and Diesel models
17 Imperial pints (9,75 litres)

Radiator

Filler cap pressure valve opens at:

Petrol models .... 3.25 to 4.25 lb/sq. in. (0,22 to 0,29 Kg/cm²)

Diesel models .... 10 lb/sq.in. (0,703 Kg/cm²)

Filler cap vacuum valve opens at .... 1 lb/sq.in. (0,07 Kg/cm²)

Thermostat

Type .... Bellows

Opening temperature—
Petrol models
Commences at .... 162° to 171°F (72°-77°C)
Fully open at .... 191°F (88°C)

Opening temperature—
Diesel models
Commences at .... 164° to 173°F (73°-78°C)
Fully open at .... 193°F (89°C)

Water pump
Type .... Centrifugal impeller
Dimensions between front face of pulley and mounting face of pump body:
1948-53 Petrol models 4.215 in. (107 mm)
1954-58 Petrol models 4.140 in. (105 mm)
Diesel models .... 3.453 in. (86 mm)

Clearance between impeller vanes and pump body .... .020 in. (0,5 mm)

Section M — FUEL SYSTEM — ALL MODELS

INDEX

	Page		Page
Air cleaner	M-7	Fuel pump, Diesel models	M-15
Carburetter	M-5	Fuel tank	M-9
Data	M-29	Fuel tank outlet union	M-9
Defect location	M-28	Injection pump	M-21
Filters, Diesel models	M-18	Removal, refitment and timing	M-21
Additional	M-19	Injection nozzle assemblies	M-23
Injection pump	M-21	Checking in vehicle	M-23
Main	M-19	Dismantling and cleaning	M-24
Fuel gauge tank unit	M-9	Testing	M-23
Fuel pipes, Petrol	M-10	Priming the fuel system, Diesel models	M-20
Fuel pipes, Diesel	M-10	Sediment bowl, Petrol models	M-9
Fuel pump, Petrol models	M-12	Sediment bowl, Diesel models	M-17

LIST OF ILLUSTRATIONS

Fig.		Page	Fig.		Page
M-1	Layout of carburetter, Petrol	M-2	M-21	Removing sediment bowl, Diesel models	M-17
M-2	Carburetter jets and controls, Petrol	M-4	M-22	Diagram of fuel system, Diesel models	M-18
M-3	Diagrammatic section of carburetter	M-4	M-23	Sectioned view of main fuel filter	M-19
M-4	Setting accelerator pump operating rod	M-5	M-24	Layout of twin filters	M-20
M-5	Layout of accelerator pump membrane assembly	M-5	M-25	Priming the fuel system	M-21
M-6	Layout of speed jet membrane assembly	M-6	M-26	Injection pump filter	M-21
M-7	Air cleaner, 1948-53 models	M-7	M-27	Fitting injection pump	M-22
M-8	Sectioned view of air cleaner, 1954 models	M-7	M-28	Extension shaft, revolution counter	M-22
M-9	Layout of fuel system, Petrol models	M-8	M-29	Pump control screws	M-23
M-10	Air cleaner, 1955-58 models	M-9	M-30	Pump screws adjusted and sealed	M-23
M-11	Fuel sediment bowl, Petrol models....	M-10	M-31	Testing nozzle assemblies on vehicle	M-24
M-12	Exploded view of fuel pump, Petrol models	M-11	M-32	Exploded view of injection nozzle and holder assembly	M-24
M-13	Layout of valve cage	M-12	M-33	Injection nozzle setting outfit	M-25
M-14	Contact breaker	M-12	M-34	Cleaning nozzle body oil feed passages	M-25
M-15	Feed terminal assembly	M-13	M-35	Scraping nozzle body annular recess	M-25
M-16	Armature impact washer	M-13	M-36	Removing carbon from valve seat	M-26
M-17	Armature adjustment	M-13	M-37	Cleaning Pintaux nozzle hole	M-26
M-18	Holding armature in position	M-14	M-38	Removing carbon from nozzle valve cone	M-26
M-19	Sectioned view of fuel pump, Diesel models....	M-15	M-39	Cleaning auxiliary spray hole	M-26
			M-40	Flushing nozzle body	M-26
M-20	Exploded view of fuel pump, Diesel models	M-16	M-41	Injection nozzle lapped faces	M-26
			M-42	Sectioned view of adaptor	M-27
			M-43	Nozzle spray form development	M-27

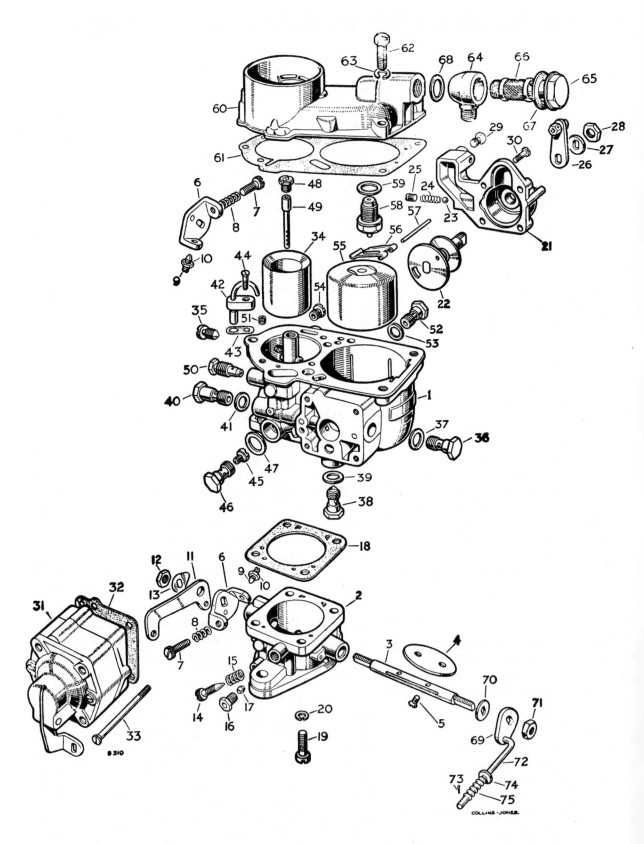

Fig M-1—Layout of carburetter, Petrol Models

Key to Fig. M-1

1	Carburetter body		39	Fibre washer for valve
2	Throttle chamber		40	Jet (75) accelerator pump
3	Spindle for throttle		41	Fibre washer for jet
4	Butterfly for throttle		42	Pump injector
5	Special screw fixing butterfly		43	Joint washer for pump injector
6	Plate, throttle abutment		44	Special screw fixing injector
7	Special screw } For slow running		45	Main jet (115)
8	Spring } adjustment		46	Bolt, main jet carrier
9	Special screw } For throttle		47	Fibre washer for bolt
10	Locknut } stop		48	Correction jet (170)
11	Throttle lever		49	Emulsion tube
12	Nut fixing throttle lever		50	Pilot jet (55)
13	Lockwasher for nut		51	Jet air bleed (1.5)
14	Special screw } For mixture		52	Starter jet, petrol (135)
15	Spring } control		53	Fibre washer for jet
16	Screwed union } For suction		54	Starter jet, air (5.5)
17	Olive } pipe		55	Float
18	Joint washer for throttle chamber		56	Toggle for float
19–20	Fixings for chamber		57	Spindle for toggle
21	Starter body		58	Needle valve complete
22	Starter valve complete		59	Fibre washer for valve
23	Ball } For starter		60	Top cover for carburetter
24	Spring } valve		61	Joint washer for top cover
25	Plug retaining starter valve spring		62	Special screw fixing top cover
26	Lever for starter		63	Spring washer for screw
27	Special washer for lever		64	Banjo union
28	Nut fixing starter lever		65	Special bolt for union
29	Special bolt fixing starter cable		66	Filter gauze for union
30	Special screw fixing starter body		67	Fibre washer, large } For
31	Accelerator pump complete		68	Fibre washer, small } union
32	Joint washer for pump		69	Lever for accelerator pump rod
33	Special screw fixing pump		70	Special washer for lever
34	Choke tube (25)		71	Nut fixing lever to spindle
35	Special screw fixing choke tube		72	Control rod for accelerator pump
36	Jet economy (50)		73	Split pin }
37	Fibre washer for jet		74	Plain washer } For control rod
38	Non-return valve		75	Spring }

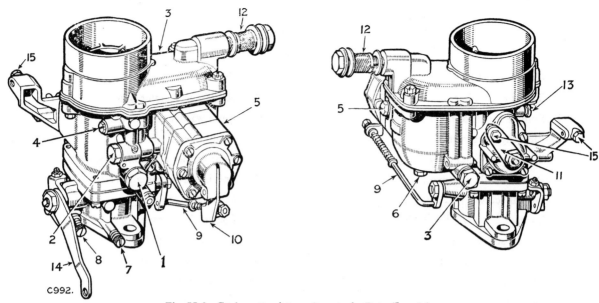

C992.

Fig. M-2—Carburetter jets and controls, Petrol models

1	Main jet	6	Non-return valve	11	Lever for starter
2	Accelerator pump jet	7	Mixture control	12	Banjo union
3	Starter jet, petrol	8	Slow running adjustment	13	Special screw fixing choke tube
4	Pilot jet	9	Pump operating rod	14	Throttle lever
5	Economy jet	10	Pump operating lever	15	Cold start cable clamping bolts

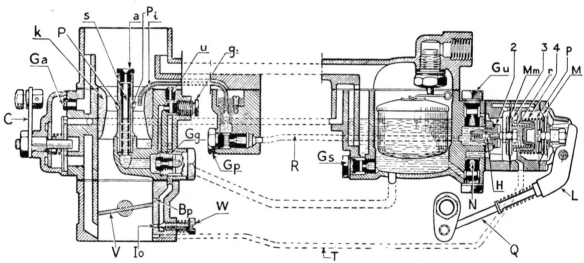

Fig. M-3—Diagrammatic section of carburetter.

a—Air correction jet
A—Slow running adjustment screw
Bp—Slow running duct
C—Bi-starter operating lever
D—Main jet carrier
g—Pilot jet
Ga—Starter air jet
Gg—Main jet
Gp—Speed jet
Gs—Starter petrol jet
Gu—Economy jet
H—Ball valve
i—Injector nozzle
Io—Slow running mixture delivery
k—Choke tube

L—Accelerator pump operating lever
M—Accelerator pump membrane
Mm—Economy action membrane
N—Non-return valve
p—Spring for membrane M.
P—Emulsion tube orifices
Q—Accelerator pump operating rod
r—Spring for membrane Mm
R—Accelerator pump delivery
s—Emulsion tube
T—Duct operating membrane Mm
u—Pilot air bleed jet
V—Throttle butterfly
W—Slow running mixture adjustment

Carburetter

To remove   **Operation M/2**

1. Disconnect the air cleaner connection from the carburetter intake orifice.

2. Remove the air cleaner.

3. Disconnect the feed pipe from the carburetter inlet banjo.

4. Disconnect the distributor suction pipe from the carburetter and pull pipe clear.

5. Disconnect the accelerator connecting rod from the carburetter throttle lever, at a ball joint.

6. Release the cold start control cable from the cold start lever on the carburetter.

7. Remove the carburetter from the inlet manifold, together with two joint washers and a packing washer.

To refit   **Operation M/4**

1. Reverse the removal procedure.

2. Renew the joint washers and packing washer.

3. Check the operation of the cold start control. (Three positions on the cold start lever.)

Carburetter jets and controls

Fault location   **Operation M/6**

1. If acceleration is bad, make sure that the speed jet is not choked (such a condition, however, will seriously affect the general performance).

2. Failure of the accelerator pump membrane will be shown by weak mixture and spitting in the carburetter on rapid acceleration.

   It can be checked by pumping the throttle with the engine running and vehicle stationary, and noting the petrol delivery from the injector tube; if the delivery is small, renew the accelerator pump membrane. Operation M/12.

3. Failure of the speed jet membrane will cause a rich mixture at all times, particularly at small throttle openings, and result in excessive fuel consumption. To rectify, renew the speed jet membrane Operation M/14.

4. At all times when accelerator pump trouble is suspected, the non-return ball valves in the pump system should be inspected for correct seating. The valves are positioned as follows: one valve in the petrol inlet to pump, the second in the injector tube, and a third in the pump assembly outlet, visible when the pump is removed from the carburetter.

To overhaul

Accelerator pump

To renew   **Operation M/8**

1. Disconnect the operating rod from the pump lever and remove the four set screws at the corners of the pump body and lift off the pump complete. Do not remove the other two set screws in the centre of the body.

2. Fit the new accelerator pump, entering the rod into the pump operating lever at the same time.

3. Adjust the pump operating rod. Operation M/10.

Accelerator pump operating rod

To adjust   **Operation M/10**

1. Remove the split pin behind the spring and allow the spring to move back along the rod.

2. Slacken the slow running screw right off.

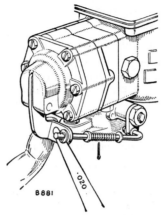

Fig. M-4—

Setting accelerator pump operating rod

B 881

3. With the throttle fully closed and the operating lever just about to operate the pump diaphragm, add washer(s) on the end of the rod up to the nearest split pin hole, ensuring that there remains .20 in. (0,5 mm) clearance between the lever and the first washer when the outer split pin is fitted.

   This clearance ensures that there is no lost movement of the lever travel.

4. Compress the spring and replace the inner split pin.

5. Check that the spring is not coilbound when the throttle is fully open.

Accelerator pump membrane

To renew   **Operation M/12**

1. Remove the outer split pin and washer(s) securing the operating rod to the pump lever (the washer(s) should be preserved).

2. Remove the four set screws at the corners of the pump body and lift off pump complete.

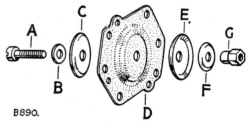

B890.

Fig. M-5—Layout of accelerator pump membrane assembly,

A—Operating rod.   D—Membrane.
B—Fibre washer.   E—Dished washer
C—Dished washer.   F—Distance washer
G—Securing nut.

3. Remove the two set screws in the centre of the body and part the pump end cover, together with the membrane assembly, from the pump body; remove the spring from the recess in the pump body.

4. Part the membrane from the outer cover and remove the operating rod from its centre. Discard the membrane.

5. Fit the operating rod to the new membrane (Fig. M-5), taking care not to twist the membrane when tightening the securing nut.
Secure the nut by staking.

6. Clean the pump body and end cover joint faces.

7. Replace the spring in the recess of the pump body. Place the end cover together with the membrane assembly in position on the pump body and insert the two set screws, which must not be tightened at this stage.

8. Depress the pump membrane by means of the operating lever and tighten the two screws fully.

9. Refit the accelerator pump unit to the carburetter, entering the rod into the pump operating lever at the same time; renew the neoprene joint washer if necessary.

10. Adjust the pump operating rod. Operation M/10.

Speed jet membrane
To renew   **Operation M/14**

1. Remove the outer split pin and washer(s) securing the operating rod to the pump lever (the washer(s) should be preserved).

2. Remove the four screws at the corners of the pump body and lift off the pump complete.

3. Remove the two set screws in the centre of the body and separate the two halves of the pump body; remove the speed membrane assembly and the spring.

4. Remove the pump shaft from the centre of the membrane and discard the membrane.

5. Fit the pump shaft to the new membrane so that the small hole for the air duct tube (E) is on the left of the securing nut (G) (Fig. M-6). Care must be taken not to twist the membrane when tightening the securing nut. Secure the nut by staking.

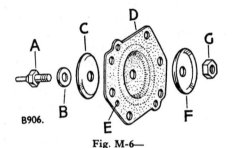

Fig. M-6—
Layout of speed jet membrane assembly.

A—Pump shaft.
B—Fibre washer
C—Dished washer
D—Membrane.
E—Air duct tube hole.
F—Dished washer.
G—Securing nut.

6. Clean the joint faces of the two halves of the pump body.

7. Place the membrane assembly in position on the inner half of the pump body, locating it by means of the small air duct tube.

8. With the spring in its recess, place the outer half of the pump body in position on the inner half and secure with two set screws.

9. Refit the accelerator pump unit to the carburetter, entering the rod into the pump operating lever at the same time; renew the joint washer if necessary.

10. If necessary, adjust the pump operating rod, Operation M/10.

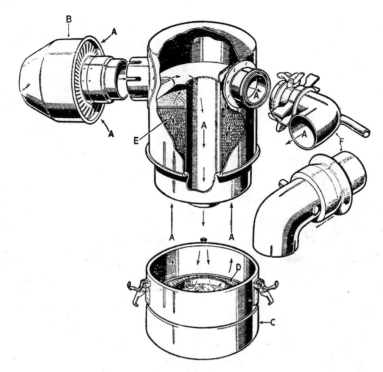

Fig. M-7—Air cleaner, 1948-53 models

A—Path of air shown ⟶ ⟶   C—Oil bath   E—Woven steel packing
B—Centrifugal pre-cleaner   D—Oil level   F—Outlet to carburetter

Air cleaner—all models

The air cleaner must be removed and cleaned at frequent intervals if an excessive rate of engine wear is to be avoided; the actual intervals will depend solely on operating conditions.

Under clean road conditions in a temperate climate, the oil bath need only be cleaned and refilled when engine oil changes are due, but when the vehicle is operated in a dust-laden atmosphere, desert, sub-tropical or tropical conditions—cleaning may be necessary twice daily.

To remove (1955-58 models) Operation M/16

1. Remove the clamping strap wing nut.

2. Disconnect the rubber connection at the carburetter.

3. Lift out the air cleaner complete with rubber connection and pre-cleaner when fitted.

To refit   Operation M/18

1. Reverse the removal procedure.

To strip   Operation M/20

1. Detach the rubber connection.

2. Remove the pre-cleaner when fitted.

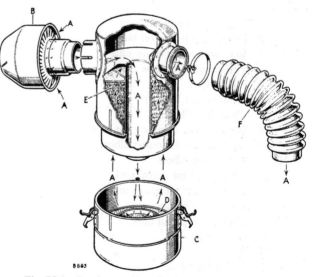

Fig. M-8—Sectioned view of air cleaner, 1954 models.

A—Path of air shown ⟶ ⟶   D—Oil level
B—Centrifugal pre-cleaner   E—Woven steel packing
C—Oil bath   F—Connection air cleaner
                                       to carburetter

3. Remove the oil bowl from the air cleaner body and empty.

4. If necessary, remove the cork washer from the air cleaner body.

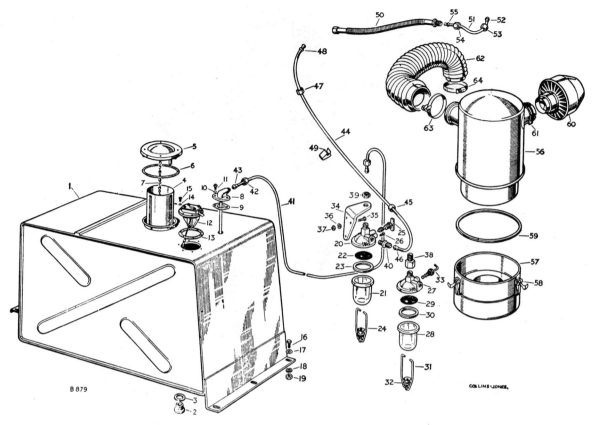

Fig. M-9—Layout of fuel system, Petrol models.

1 Petrol tank complete	31 Retainer for bowl
2 Drain plug for petrol tank	32 Screw cap for retainer
3 Joint washer for drain plug	33 Tap and gland complete
4 Telescopic filler tube	34 Bracket for sediment bowl
5 Filler cap	35–37 Fixings for bracket
6 Joint washer for cap	38 Inlet adaptor for sediment bowl
7 Chain for filler cap	39 Special nut fixing adaptor and bowl to bracket
8 Outlet elbow complete for tank	40 Outlet union for sediment bowl
9 Joint washer for outlet elbow	41 Petrol pipe complete, tank to bowl
10–11 Fixings for elbow	42–43 Fixings for pipe
12 Gauge unit for petrol tank	44 Petrol pipe complete, bowl to pump
13 Joint washer for gauge unit	45–48 Fixings for pipe
14–15 Fixings for gauge unit	49 Clip for petrol pipe
16–19 Fixings for petrol tank	50 Flexible petrol pipe complete
20 Body only	51 Petrol pipe complete, flex to carburetter
21 Bowl only	52–55 Fixings for pipe
22 Gauze for bowl	56 Filter and case
23 Joint washer for bowl	57 Oil container
24 Retainer for bowl	58 Toggle clip for oil container
25 Tap and gland complete	59 Cork washer for oil container
26 Special screw for tap	60 Centrifugal air cleaner
27 Body only	61 Clip fixing cleaners together
28 Bowl only	62 Rubber connection, air cleaner to carburetter
29 Gauze for bowl	63–64 Fixings for connection
30 Joint washer for bowl	

To assemble   **Operation M/22**

1. Clean the filter gauze and oil bowl in petrol and refill oil bowl with clean oil.

2. Reverse the stripping procedure, renewing the cork washer if necessary.

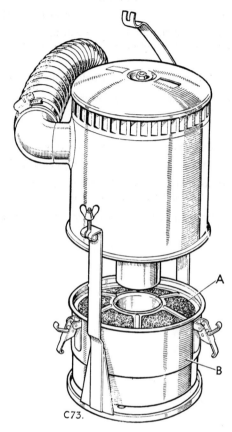

C73.

Fig. M-10—Air cleaner, 1955-58 models.

A—Removable filter gauze.
B—Oil bowl.

Note:

At all times when the diesel engine is running, it is necessary to ensure that the oil bath air cleaner is fastened securely in the vertical position.

If adjustments are made with the engine running and the oil bath air cleaner balanced on top of the engine, it is possible, should the cleaner tip to one side, for oil to be drawn into the intake manifold and hence into the engine, where it will act as a fuel and cause the engine to overspeed out of control and serious damage may result.

Should it be necessary to run the engine with the air cleaner out of the normal position, the rubber hose should be disconnected from the inlet manifold and the whole oil bath removed from the vehicle.

Fuel tank—all models

To renew   **Operation M/24**

1. Disconnect the battery.

2. Remove the right-hand seat and raise the locker lid.

3. Detach the fuel feed pipe from the outlet union on the top of the tank.

4. Disconnect the wire from the level gauge unit.

5. Drain off the fuel.

6. Remove the fuel tank and undershield, if fitted, from below.

7. Remove the outlet elbow from the tank and fit together with a new joint washer, to the replacement tank.

8. Remove the gauge unit from the tank and fit together with a new joint washer, to the replacement tank.

9. Fit the replacement tank to the vehicle by reversing the removal procedure.

Fuel gauge tank unit

To renew   **Operation M/26**

1. Disconnect the battery.

2. Drain off the fuel.

3. Remove the right-hand seat and raise the locker lid.

4. Disconnect the wire from the tank unit.

5. Remove the gauge unit from the fuel tank complete with joint washer.

6. Fit the new unit by reversing the removal procedure.

Fuel tank outlet union

To renew   **Operation M/28**

1. Remove the right-hand seat and raise the locker lid.

2. Disconnect the union nut securing the fuel feed pipe to the outlet union.

3. Remove the outlet union and suction pipe from the fuel tank complete with joint washer.

4. Fit the new union by reversing the removal procedure.

Sediment bowl, Petrol models

To remove   **Operation M/30**

1. Disconnect the inlet and outlet pipes at the sediment bowl unions.

2. Remove the sediment bowl complete from the dash bracket.

3. If necessary, remove the bracket from the dash.

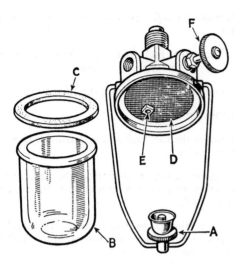

Fig. M-11—Fuel sediment bowl.

A—Thumbscrew   D—Filter gauze.
B—Glass bowl.   E—Fuel inlet.
C—Joint washer.   F—Shut-off tap.

To refit   **Operation M/32**

Reverse the removal procedure.

Fuel pipe: tank to sediment bowl, Petrol models

To renew   **Operation M/34**

1. Disconnect the union nuts securing the pipe to the fuel tank outlet elbow and sediment bowl inlet union.

2. Withdraw the pipe from below the vehicle.

3. Replace the pipe by reversing the removal procedure.

Fuel return pipe, Diesel models

To renew   **Operation M/36**

1. Remove the union nuts securing the flexible pipe to the fuel tank and leak-off pipe.

2. Remove the clips and withdraw the pipe from below the vehicle.

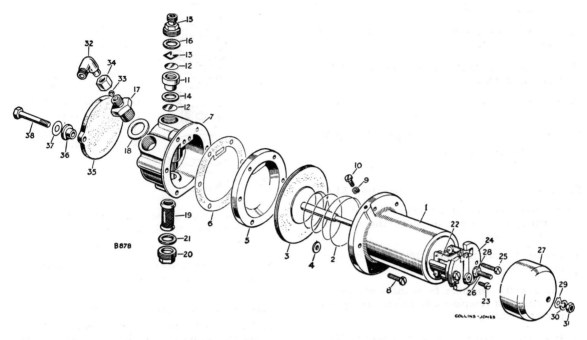

Fig. M-12—Exploded view of fuel pump, Petrol models.

1	Coil complete	18	Washer for inlet union
2	Spring for armature	19	Filter
3	Diaphragm complete	20	Plug for filter
4	Roller for diaphragm	21	Washer for filter plug
5	Plate body	22	Contact set complete
6	Joint washer for plate body	23	Special screw for contact blade
7	Body	24	Moulding for end plate
8	Screw fixing coil housing to body	25	Screw fixing moulding
9	Special spring washer } For earth	26	Terminal screw
10	Special nut	terminal screw	27	Cover for end plate
11	Valve cage	28	Terminal nut
12	Disc for valve	29	Tag for terminal
13	Spring clip retaining valve disc	30	Spring washer
14	Washer for valve cage	31	Nut
15	Outlet union	32	Elbow for pump
16	Washer for outlet union	33–34	Fixings for elbow
17	Inlet union	35–38	Fixings for electric petrol pump

Fuel pump—Petrol models

To remove   **Operation M/38**

1. Disconnect the battery.

2. Detach the inlet and outlet pipes from the elbows on the fuel pump.

3. Disconnect the feed and earth wires from the pump terminals.

4. Remove the pump.

To refit   **Operation M/40**

Reverse the removal procedure.

To strip   **Operation M/42**

Note: **Under no circumstances should any attempt be made to move the core of the magnet.**

1. Remove the cast iron body from the aluminium body.

2. Unscrew the armature from the inner rocker and remove it complete with rollers, spring and impact washer.

3. If necessary, remove the impact washer (Fig. M-16) from the recess of the armature.

4. Remove the contact blade.

5. Disconnect the earth connection (held under one of the pedestal securing screws).

6. Withdraw the outer and inner rocker hinge pin and remove the rocker assembly complete from under the pedestal.

7. Separate the two halves of the aluminium body.

8. Remove the inlet union from the rear portion of the aluminium body.

9. Remove the outlet union and withdraw the thick fibre washer, the valve cage complete with delivery valve and retaining clip, the thin fibre washer and the suction valve.

10. Remove the filter plug, fibre washer and filter.

To assemble   **Operation M/44**

1. Carefully clean all the component parts, renewing the diaphragm, contact breaker assembly and valves assembly as necessary.

Valve cage (See Fig. M-13)

2. The delivery valve (H) and suction valve (K) should both be fitted with the smooth side downwards.

3. Care should be taken that the valve retaining clip (I) in the valve cage (E) is located correctly in its groove.

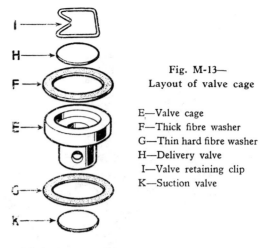

Fig. M-13—
Layout of valve cage

E—Valve cage
F—Thick fibre washer
G—Thin hard fibre washer
H—Delivery valve
I—Valve retaining clip
K—Suction valve

4. The thin fibre washer (G) should be fitted under the valve cage and the thick washer (F) above the cage.

5. Thick fibre washers are also fitted under the inlet union and the gauze filter.

Contact breaker (See Fig. M-14)

6. The contact breaker should be assembled on its pedestal in such a way that the rockers are free in their mountings, without appreciable side play.

Any excessive side play on the outer rocker would permit the points to get out of line while excessive tightness would make the contact breaker sluggish in operation.

To obtain the correct freedom, it may be necessary to square the outer rocker with a pair of thin nosed pliers. The rocker hinge pin is case-hardened and must not be replaced by ordinary wire.

The contact blade (A) should be fitted next to the bakelite pedestal, that is, underneath the tags. It should rest against the ledge (B) on the pedestal when the points are apart. The points should just make contact when the rocker is in its midway position.

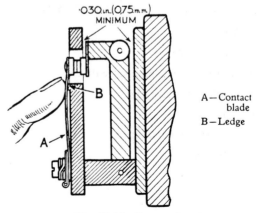

·030 in. (0.75 mm)
MINIMUM

A—Contact blade
B—Ledge

Fig. M-14—Contact breaker

7. Check the position by holding the blade in contact with the pedestal, being careful not to press on the overhanging portion (Fig. M-14); then ensure that a .30 in. (0,75 mm) feeler just slides between the white rollers and the cast iron body of the pump. If necessary the tip of the blade may be set in order to obtain the correct clearance.

8. The spring washer on the 2 B.A. screw to which the earth connection is made should be fitted between the tag and the pedestal, and the brass tag next to the head of the screw.

9. All four connections, that is, the two ends of the earthing tag and the two ends of the coil, should be soldered.

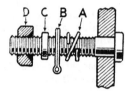

A—Spring washer
B—Tag
C—Lead washer
D—Countersunk nut

Fig. M-15—Feed terminal assembly

10. In the case of the feed·terminal screw, which holds the bakelite cover in position, the correct order for assembly is spring washer (Fig. M-15, A) next to the bakelite pedestal, then the tag (B), lead washer (C) and countersunk nut (D). Under no circumstances should this assembly be shortened by leaving out the spring washer, or in any other way, as this would probably result in distortion or breakage of the pedestal when the nut holding the cover in position is tightened.

Magnet assembly

11. Fit the armature return spring with its large diameter towards the coil. The spring must not be stretched or the action of the pump will be affected.

12. Swing the contact blade on the pedestal to one side.

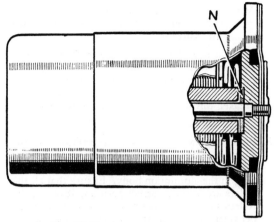

Fig. M-16—Armature impact washer
N—Impact washer.

13. Fit the impact washer (N) in the recess of the armature.

14. Screw the armature into position.

15. Fit the eleven guide rollers in position round the armature.

16. Hold the magnet assembly in the left hand in an approximately horizontal position. Push the armature in firmly but steadily, with the thumb of the right hand (Fig. M-17).

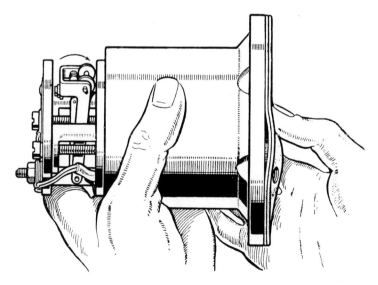

Fig. M-17—Armature adjustment

17. If the contact breaker throws over, the armature should be screwed in further until it ceases to do so. It should then be unscrewed one-sixth of a turn at a time until a position is found at which the contact breaker just throws over, care being taken to avoid jerking the armature. The armature should then be unscrewed for two-thirds of a turn, i.e. four holes; the setting is then correct.

Note: **Do not forget that this setting must be carried out with the points out of contact.**

When a new diaphragm is fitted, it is possible that considerable pressure will be required to push the armature right home. If there is any doubt about the point at which the contact breaker throws over, come back one-sixth of a turn.

18. Place the cast iron body in position on the aluminium body, with the drain hole in the cast iron member at the bottom in line with the filter plug in the aluminium body. Ensure that all the rollers are in their correct position. If one of the rollers falls out of position, it will get trapped between the two parts and cut a hole in the diaphragm.

19. Make sure that the cast iron body seats properly on the aluminium body, and insert the six screws. These screws must not be tightened up at this stage, as it is absolutely necessary to first stretch the diaphragm to its outermost position.

This is best effected by using a special forked wedge to keep the armature in its extreme position (Fig. M-18); the wedge is inserted between the white rollers of the outer rocker and pressed in under the tips of the inner rocker,

until it lifts the trunnion in the centre of the inner rocker as far as it will go. Tighten the retaining screws fully, and remove the wedge.

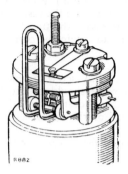

Fig. M-18—
Use of forked wedge to keep the armature in position

Note: If a wedge is not available, the diaphragm may be stretched by holding the points in contact, by inserting a matchstick under one of the white fibre rollers and passing a current through the pump; this will excite the magnet, actuate the armature, and so stretch the diaphragm.

20. Test the fuel pump. It is best to use a cut-away cover while testing the pump, as this prevents the hinge pin from falling out, and, at the same time, makes it possible to observe the action of the contact breaker. The pump should be mounted three feet above the supply tank for testing; either paraffin or petrol may be used. When switched on, the pump should prime itself promptly, and fluid should flow from the outlet union. If the pump output is restricted, the pump should slow down gradually, and if completely cut off it should stop for at least 15 seconds.

Fuel pump—Diesel

Testing fuel pump on vehicle

Ensure that there is sufficient fuel in the tank, then disconnect the fuel inlet pipe from the filter mounted on the front R.H. side of the engine. Turn the engine over by hand, with injection nozzles removed if necessary; there should be a well-defined spurt of fuel from the disconnected pipe every second revolution of the starting handle.

To remove   Operation M/46

1. Disconnect the inlet and outlet pipes, remove the securing nuts and withdraw the pump complete.

To overhaul   Operation M/48

1. Unscrew the nut at base of sediment bowl, move the retainer aside and withdraw the bowl, cork sealing gasket and gauze filter disc. Care must be taken to avoid damage to the filter disc.

2. Mark the upper and lower halves of pump casing to ensure correct alignment on re-assembly and **note the position of diaphragm**

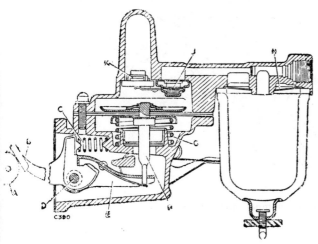

Fig. M-19—Sectioned view of fuel pump

tab. Remove the six screws securing the casings and, with the thumb pressing the diaphragm tab against the lower casing, lift the upper half clear.

3. Ease the diaphragm flexible material from the lower body joint face and holding the metal part of the diaphragm with the fingers, turn it 90° in either direction, whereon the diaphragm spring will push the diaphragm clear.

4. Remove the circlips (on late models the pivot pin is secured by two retainers), then drift the rocker arm pivot pin from the lower casing and withdraw the rocker arm, operating link, return spring and plain washers.

5. It is extremely unlikely that the hand priming mechanism will ever require replacement, but the hand lever, cork washers and hand rocker may be removed by filing the hexagon each side of the operating lever and springing the lever clear. Withdraw the cork washers and hand rocker.

   Note: If removed, the hand operating mechanism must be replaced by new parts.

6. If necessary the oil seal and retainer may be removed by filing away the spread of metal caused by the four peening marks and then drift from below.

7. Remove the retaining plate and withdraw the valves and valve gasket from the upper casing.

8. Clean all parts thoroughly in paraffin and immediately before assembly, in Shell Fusus 'A' oil.

9. Examine all parts for wear and replace as necessary. Observe the following points:

   (a) All gaskets to be renewed.

   (b) Sediment bowl filter disc must be free of damage and fit tightly round the inlet neck of the upper casing.

   (c) Renew the diaphragm assembly if any sign of hardening, cracking or porosity is present.

   (d) Only very slight wear should be tolerated at the rocker arm contact face, pivot pin, link and pull-rod slots.

   (e) Springs should be renewed, but ensure that the correct type are used.

   (f) Valves to be tested for air tightness by suction.

Early models

10. Assembly of the components is a reversal of dismantling procedure, but the location of the rocker arm, washers and operating link on a piece of .240 in. (6,1 mm) diameter rod inserted in place of the pivot pin and then driven out by the pin will facilitate this part of the operation. Replace circlips.

Late models

If rocker arm pin and related parts have been detached from pump body, re-assemble rocker arm, link and spacing washers on to pin, and refit to body, after replacing return spring. Tap the retainers into their grooves, then holding the retainers firmly against the rocker pin, peen over the ends of the grooves to ensure that they cannot work loose.

Always use replacement retainers, as these are slightly shorter than the original to allow for satisfactory fixing in the body.

11. To refit the diaphragm assembly, hold the pump lower casing with the return spring in position and the rocker arm held outwards. Position the diaphragm over the spring with the

1   Upper casing
2   Securing screws
3   Spring washer
4   Valve gasket
5   Valves
6   Retainer for valves
7   Screw securing retainers
8   Gauze filter disc
9   Cork sealing gasket
10   Sediment bowl
11   Bowl retainer
12   Diaphragm assembly
13   Diaphragm spring
14   Oil seal retainer
15   Sealing washers
16   Lower casing
17   Hand priming lever
18   Return spring for hand lever
19   Hand rocker
20   Cork washers
21   Rocker arm pivot pin
22   Operating link
23   Plain washers
24   Rocker arm
25   Return spring
26   Joint washer

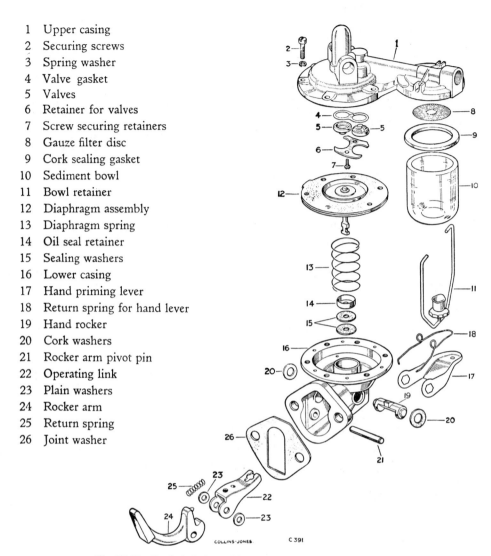

Fig. M-20—Exploded view of fuel pump, Diesel models.

flattened end of pull rod in line with the slot in operating link and the large tab on diaphragm 90° from original fitted position. Press the diaphragm assembly downward to engage the operating link slot and turn it 90° to the position noted whilst dismantling.

12. Push the rocker arm towards the pump until the diaphragm is level with the joint face, then place the upper casing assembly in position, aligning the marks made before dismantling. Fit the six securing screws and spring washers but tighten the screws just sufficiently for the heads to contact the spring washers. The rocker arm must now be pushed inward to the fullest extent before the screws are finally tightened.

Note: The diaphragm outer edges should be approximately flush with the outer edges of the pump joint faces when fitted.

Any appreciable protrusion of the diaphragm beyond the joint face edges, indicates improper fitment and necessitates the release of the six securing screws and refitment in accordance with item 12.

Fuel pump—to test without special equipment
Operation M/50

1. Immerse the pump in a bath of fuel oil or Shell Fusus 'A' oil, and operate the rocker arm several times to flush.

2. Hold the pump clear of the bath and continue to operate the rocker arm until the pump is empty, then place a finger over the inlet port ('in') and work the rocker arm several times more. A distinct suction sound should be heard when the finger is removed from the inlet port, denoting that a reasonable degree of suction has been developed.

3. Place a finger over the outlet port and again operate the rocker arm. Air pressure should be felt for two or three seconds after rocker movement has ceased. Build up the air pressure in the pump again, and with the finger held firmly over the outlet, submerge the pump completely in the paraffin or oil bath, then observe the joint face edges for signs of air leakage.

Fuel pump filter and sediment bowl

To remove and clean   Operation M/52

1. Unscrew the nut at base of sediment bowl, move the retainer aside and withdraw the bowl, cork sealing gasket and gauze filter disc. Care must be taken to prevent damage to the filter disc.

2. Clean the bowl and filter disc in petrol or (Diesel) fuel oil, directing a compressed air jet on the gauze to remove any obstinate particles.

3. Examine the cork gasket for filter bowl and renew if signs of deterioration are evident.

To replace   Operation M/54

1. Reverse the removal procedure ensuring that the gauze filter disc fits tightly round the inlet neck and is quite undamaged in any way.

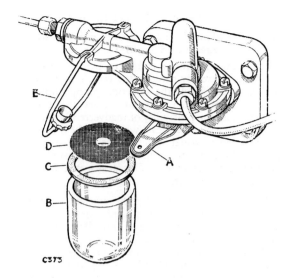

C373

Fig. M-21—Removing sediment bowl—
Diesel models

A—Hand priming lever   D—Filter gauze

B—Sediment bowl   E—Retainer for sediment
bowl

C—Cork gasket

Fuel system—Diesel models

Note: **Details of fuel lift pump will be found on Pages M-15 to M-17.**

If the injection pump is drained by disconnecting the drain pipe or by running the vehicle until all the fuel has been used, the injection pump **must** be primed before attempting to restart the engine. To minimise the possibility of inadvertently running out of fuel, a blue fuel level warning light is fitted to the instrument panel which glows when only two gallons of fuel remain in the tank and remains "on" until more fuel is added. This device is in addition to the usual fuel contents gauge.

Clean fuel is essential for the efficient operation of the fuel injection pump and injection nozzle assemblies, and for this reason four filters in all are fitted in the system. The first one is fitted in the fuel tank and requires no attention; the second—a sediment bowl and filter disc—is part of the fuel lift pump; the third is a large self-contained unit mounted on the R.H. front side of the engine, and lastly a small tubular gauze filter is fitted in the injection pump head.

An additional filter is fitted to all export Diesel Land-Rovers. This filter is dealt with in Operation M/60.

Filters

Wear of injection pump, injection nozzle parts and the subsequent loss of power and efficiency is primarily due to the presence of dirt in the fuel.

Filters are situated in the Rover system in a manner calculated to minimise the possibility of foreign matter reaching the injection pump or injection nozzles, but the element in the main filter must be renewed, the sediment bowl and filter gauze on lift pump and the filter gauze in injection pump cleaned, at appropriate intervals. These intervals vary and are dependent on operating conditions, but reference to the Owner's Instruction Manual will provide a guide.

Complete sludging up of the main filter element in an unreasonably short operating period is usually due to an excessive quantity of wax in the fuel. Attention should be paid to the method of storage (where bulk storage is used) and the advice of supplier requested. Never draw fuel from the **lowest** point of a storage tank or barrel for refuelling purposes; the lowest point should only be used for draining off sludge and other impurities which accumulate at the bottom end.

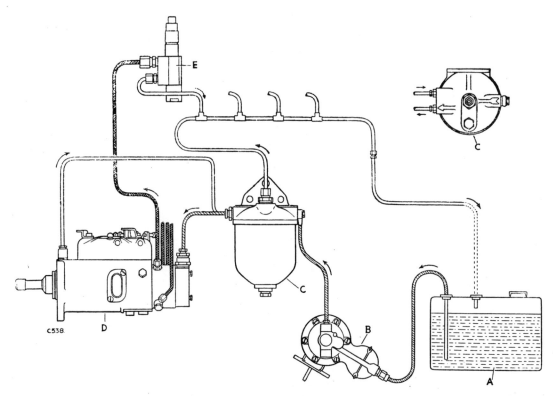

Fig. M-22—Diagram of fuel system.

A—Fuel tank
B—Fuel pump
C—Main filter
D—Injection pump

E—Injection nozzle
\\\\\\\\—Low pressure delivery
xxxxxx—High pressure delivery
========—Excess fuel spill back

Main filter

To remove   **Operation M/56**

1. Slacken the drain plug at the base of filter container and allow fuel to flow into a suitable receptacle.

2. Disconnect the fuel inlet, outlet and bleed back pipes.

3. Remove the securing bolts and lift the assembly clear.

Note: A non-return valve is incorporated in the excess fuel spill back pipe. It can be removed by disconnecting the union at the top of the filter, and withdrawing the valve complete with holder.

To refit   **Operation M/58**

1. Reverse the removal procedure and prime as in Operation M/64.

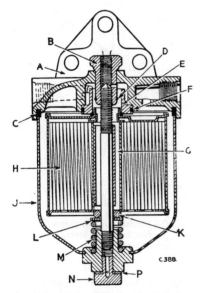

Fig. M-23—Sectioned view of main fuel filter.

A—Housing cover	H—Element
B—Cap nut	J—Container
C—Oil seal	K—Seal
D—Circlip	L—Plain washer
E—Sealing ring	M—Spring
F—Oil seal	N—Drain plug
G—Location sleeve	P—Washer

To remove element—filter in position on vehicle   **Operation M/60**

1. Slacken the plug at base of filter container and allow the fuel to flow into a suitable receptacle.

2. Disconnect the bleed back pipe from the top of filter unit.

3. Unscrew the centre cap nut at top of filter whilst supporting the container.

4. Withdraw the container complete with small sealing ring at top of element and remove the large sealing ring from the underside of filter c oer.

5. Discard the filter element, then wash the container thoroughly in fuel oil. Clean the holes in drain plug and boss with a wire. Great care should be taken to ensure that the centre spindle above lower sealing ring is absolutely clean.

6. Renew the lower sealing ring if its serviceability is in any way doubtful—a new top sealing ring is supplied with each element and should always be used.

7. Examine the large sealing gasket for container and replace if necessary.

8. Fit the new element, top sealing rings, and refit container.

9. Reconnect pipes, tighten drain plug and prime. Operation M/64.

Additional filter

All Export Diesel models are fitted with an additional C.A.V. paper element type fuel filter mounted on the engine side of the dash, in the pipe line between the fuel tank and the mechanical fuel pump. See Fig. M-24.

This means that the bowl on the additional filter becomes the water trap, therefore when two C.A.V. filters are fitted, the sediment bowl on the mechanical fuel pump and second fuel filter ('F') mounted at the front right hand side of the engine will only need cleaning and the element changed, every 24,000 (40.000 km).

The bowl of the filter mounted on the dash should be emptied and cleaned every 3,000 miles (5.000 km) and the paper element replaced every 6,000 miles (10.000 km).

If the amount of dirt and water collected when cleaning the bowl at 3,000 miles (5.000 km) appears excessive the element should also be changed; it will also indicate that more frequent checking of the filter bowl is required.

To renew additional filter element   **Operation M/62**

1. Unscrew the special bolt on the top of the filter, until the element holder can be removed.

2. Remove and discard the used element and the rubber washer.

3. Wash the container in petrol or fuel oil.

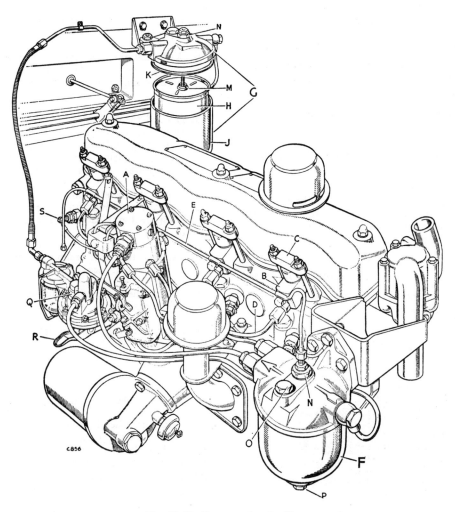

Fig. M-24—Layout of twin filters.

A—Distributor pump.	G—Fuel filter at dash.	O—Air vent plug.
B—Injector	H—Element.	P—Drain plug.
C—Clamp bar.	J—Container.	Q—Mechanical fuel pump.
D—Feed pipes.	K—Large washer	R—Hand priming lever.
E—Spill pipes.	M—Small washer.	S—Heater plug.
F—Fuel filter at engine.	N—Retainer nut.	

4. Renew the large rubber washer in the filter top, place a new element in the container, with the perforated holes to the bottom. Renew the small rubber washer on the top of the element.

5. Fit the container complete with element to the filter top and tighten the special bolt.

6. Prime the system. Operation M/64.

Priming the fuel system   Operation M/64

A—When the filter bowl has been cleaned or the paper element changed on **either** or **both** fuel filters, the system must be primed as follows:—

1. Do not attempt to start the engine hoping to draw the fuel through in this way, otherwise the full priming procedure will be necessary.

2. Slacken the air vent screw on the top of the engine filter.

3. Operate the hand priming lever in the mechanical pump until fuel free from bubbles emerges.

4. Tighten the bleed screw.

5. Operate the hand priming lever once or twice to clear the last bubbles of air into the filter bleed pipe.

6. Start the engine in the normal way and check for leaks.

B—When fuel system has been completely emptied proceed as follows:

7. Carry out operations above 1 to 5 inclusive.

8. Release air vent screw (A) on distributor pump. See Fig. M-25.

9. Operate the fuel pump hand priming lever until fuel free of air emerges. See Hand lever, Fig. M-24.

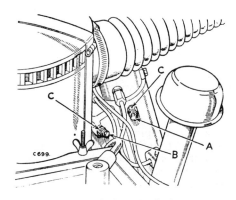

Fig. M-25—Priming the fuel system.
A—Air vent screw on distributor body.
B—Air vent screw on distributor control cover.
C—Fuel orifice.

10. Retighten the air vent screw.

11. To ensure that all air is exhausted from the pump it may also be necessary to slacken air vent screw 'B' in the distributor control cover and repeat items 9 and 10.

12. Start engine in normal way and check for leaks.

C   When distributor pump only has been drained it is only necessary to carry out operations 8 to 12 inclusive.

Note : Ensure that fuel pump lever is on the bottom of the operating cam when priming the fuel system, otherwise maximum movement of the priming lever will not be obtained.

It should not be necessary to remove additional filter, but if removed, note that it is secured to the dash by three bolts and rivnuts.

Injection pump filter

To remove and clean   Operation M/66

1. Remove the pipe filter to injection pump.

2. Unscrew the pipe connection from injection pump head and withdraw the filter.

3. Wash the filter in fuel oil.

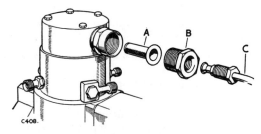

Fig. M-26—Injection pump filter.
A—Filter   B—Connection   C—Inlet pipe

To refit   Operation M/68

1. Replace the filter and pipe connection and reconnect the feed pipe at main filter end. Operate the lift pump by hand and couple the pipe to injection pump head whilst fuel flows from the pipe.

Injection pump

To remove   Operation M/70

1. Remove the air cleaner and flexible air intake pipe.

2. The fuel pipes, injection pump to injection nozzle, filter to injection pump and drain from injection pump should now be removed.

3. Disconnect the accelerator and cut-off controls.

4. Remove the securing nuts and washers then withdraw the pump.

5. Blank off all openings with special caps or adhesive tape if caps are not available.

To refit   Operation M/72

1. **Timing**

   A—Early engines
   On early engines the flywheel is marked SI.

   (i) Early, unmodified engines.

   In order to time these engines correctly, turn the crankshaft in the direction of rotation, until the timing pointer is exactly in line with the SI mark, with both valves on No. 1 cylinder closed.

   (ii) Early engines with latest type pistons and early type hot plugs.

   The injection pump timing for these engines must be altered to 17° B.T.D.C. Turn the crankshaft in the direction of rotation, until the timing pointer is 0.1 in. (2,5 mm) past the SI mark on the flywheel, with both valves on No. 1 cylinder closed.

   (iii) Early engines with latest type pistons and hot plugs.

   The correct timing for these engines is 16° B.T.D.C.

   Turn the crankshaft in the direction of rotation, until the timing pointer is 0.2 in. (5 mm) past the SI mark on the flywheel, with both valves on No. 1 cylinder closed.

   B—Late engines
   On late engines the flywheel is marked 16° and 18°.

   (i) Late engines with latest type pistons and early type hot plugs.

   The correct timing for these engines is 17° B.T.D.C.

Turn the crankshaft in the direction of rotation, until the timing pointer is exactly between the 16° and 18° mark on the flywheel, with both valves on No. 1 cylinder closed.

(ii) Late engines with latest type pistons and hot plugs.

This type of engine must be timed at 16° B.T.D.C.

Turn the crankshaft until the timing pointer is exactly in line with the 16° mark on the flywheel, with both valves on No. 1 cylinder closed.

Note: Engines fitted with late type hot plugs are identified by a splash of red paint on the cylinder head.

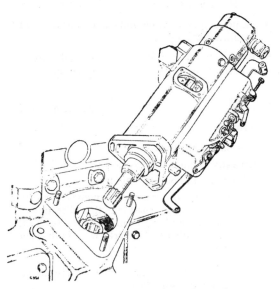

Fig. M-27—Fitting injection pump

2. Remove the inspection cover from fuel injection pump and turn the rotor until the mark (A) on drive plate is in line with the arrow on timing circlip.

3. Offer the pump to engine and fit the securing nuts and washers loosely. Observe the injection pump timing marks again and adjust if necessary by turning the pump body to align the marks.

4. Tighten securing nuts, turn the flywheel **against** direction of rotation for approximately 90° and then **in** direction of rotation until the markings (see item 1) on flywheel are again in line with the timing pointer and check finally that the timing marks in injection pump are aligned.

It is very important that the injection pump is timed as accurately as possible. Two or three degrees retardation can cause excessive white smoke when starting from cold and running at light load. Two or three degrees advance can cause excessive black smoke at low speed full load.

The timing must be checked by turning the engine until the timing marks on the pump are dead in line and then checking the timing marks on the flywheel. In this way any slight error is magnified by the 2 : 1 ratio of camshaft to crankshaft and the large diameter of the flywheel. An error of a given width on the pump markings will be 12 times that width if transferred to the flywheel.

5. Reconnect the pipes and controls; check the cut-off and throttle controls for full movement. Prime the system in accordance with Operation M/64, then refit the air cleaner and rubber connection.

6. Run the engine and adjust the slow-running control if necessary. Turn the stop screw inward to increase idling speed and outward to decrease.

The upper maximum power output stop screw setting is sealed at the works and must not be altered.

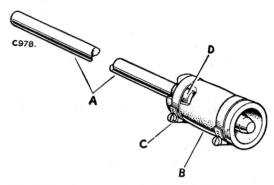

Fig. M-28—Extension shaft for revolution counter.

A—Starting handle. 26 in. (660 mm) long x .687 in. (17 mm) diameter.
B—Rubber hose. 3 in. (75 mm) long x 1¼ in. (32 mm) internal diameter.
C—Hose clips, to suit external diameter of rubber hose.
D—Rubber packing between hose and starting handle.

When a new or reconditioned distributor pump is to be fitted, it will be found that the slow running control screw is wired to the distributor pump and that the maximum output control screw is not sealed.

It is necessary, therefore, after the distributor pump has been assembled to the engine, first to fit the slow running control screw and then adjust both screws as detailed below.

Finally the maximum output control screw should be wired up and sealed as shown at Fig. M-29.

The slow running engine speed should be set at 590 r.p.m. ± 20 r.p.m.

The maximum engine speed should be set at 3,650 r.p.m. ± 20 r.p.m.

Note that the maximum engine speed corresponds to 55 m.p.h. (84 k.p.h.) in top gear, 41 m.p.h. (66 k.p.h.) in third gear and 28 m.p.h. (45 k.p.h.) in second gear.

The engine speeds should be checked with a revolution counter from the starting dog. To do this some form of extension shaft is required; a starting handle cut down with driving pin removed and modified as shown at Fig. M-28 is one method of doing this.

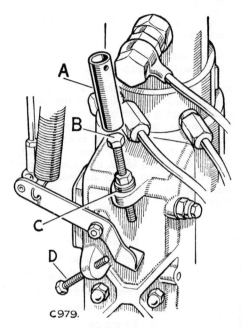

Fig. M-29—Distributor pump control screws.

A—Screw collar.
B—Maximum output control screw.
C—Screw retainer for collar
D—Slow running control screw.

To adjust the maximum output control screw, proceed as follows:—

(a) Fit extension shaft to starting dog by sliding the rubber hose over the dog, tighten by means of the hose clip.

(b) Check engine speed with revolution counter.

(c) Remove adjusting screw collar. See Fig. M-29.

(d) Slacken adjusting screw locknut; screw down to decrease engine speed and up to increase.

(e) When maximum engine speed of 3,650 r.p.m. ± 20 has been obtained, tighten locknut, replace adjusting screw collar, wire and seal screw collar as shown at Fig. M-30.

To adjust the slow running control screw, proceed as follows:—

(a) Check engine speed with revolution counter.

(b) Slacken adjusting screw locknut and screw inwards to increase speed and outwards to decrease.

(c) When a slow running speed of 590 r.p.m. ± 20 has been obtained, tighten locknut.

(d) Remove extension shaft.

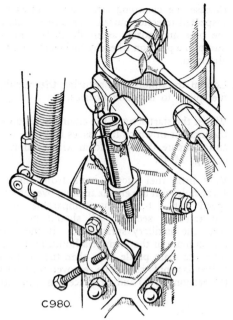

Fig. M-30—Control screws adjusted and sealed.

Fuel injection nozzles
Checking nozzle assemblies on vehicle
Operation M/74

When carrying out the first service inspection at 750 miles (1.000 km) it is important that the injectors are removed, dismantled, thoroughly cleaned, re-assembled, checked and refitted. Thereafter this procedure should be carried out every 12,000 miles (20.000 km).

This thorough checking is necessary at the first service inspection to ensure any small particles of dirt or scale which may have become detached from the pipe lines, filters, etc., are removed.

Dirt in injectors not only has an effect on performance, but also on the noise level of a diesel engine and it is therefore most important to carry out this operation.

When an injection nozzle is considered to be the cause of irregular running and loss of power, a quick check may be made by loosening the fuel feed pipe union nut on each nozzle in turn, whilst the engine is idling and again at approximately 1,000 r.p.m.

If the injection nozzle assembly being checked has been operating properly, there will be a distinct reduction in r.p.m. accompanied by obvious roughness, but a faulty injection nozzle may make little or no difference to the engine note when its fuel feed pipe is loosened.

Testing nozzle assemblies on vehicle
Operation M/76

1. Remove the fuel spill gallery pipe complete, from the injection nozzles, then disconnect the fuel feed pipe (injection pump to nozzle) from the nozzle to be tested and from the injection pump.

2. Release the clamping strap and withdraw the suspected injection nozzle assembly; reconnect the pipe and nozzle assembly to the injection pump in a position whereby fuel ejection may be observed.

3. Loosen the union nuts securing the remaining fuel pipes to injection nozzles.

4. Whilst the starter turns the engine over, observe the manner in which fuel issues from the nozzle and compare the spray form with section "A" of Fig. M-43.

Very little fuel should issue from the main spray hole with the engine turning over at starter speed but a fine spray comparable to that illustrated in section "A" should be ejected from the auxiliary spray hole. If the ejected fuel is more in the form of a liquid jet or issues from the main pintle hole, then the nozzle and holder assembly should be removed for overhaul (Operation M/78) and a replacement unit fitted.

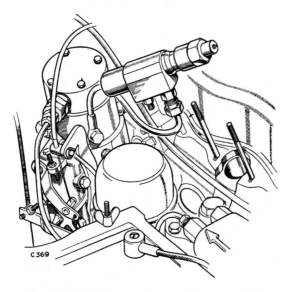

Fig. M-31—Testing nozzle assemblies on vehicle.

Bench testing of injection nozzle and holder assembly

To check a nozzle assembly and ensure that it is functioning correctly, a setting outfit as illustrated in Fig. M-33 is essential. A bench covered with linoleum or non-ferrous sheet metal is most suitable for mounting the outfit; such a surface facilitates the cleanliness essential when checking nozzle parts. Between the bench and setting outfit, a tray, also of non-ferrous metal, should be positioned to prevent spilt fuel spreading. Small containers may be attached to the bench to isolate the component parts of each assembly; these parts are carefully mated by the manufacturers and must not be interchanged. Lastly, a small bath with cover, containing Shell Fusus "A" oil for washing components, should be kept conveniently near.

The efficient operation of the injection nozzle assembly is dependent on four main conditions, as follows :—

(a) The nozzle valve must open at 135 Ats.

(b) The rate of back leakage must be within 150 to 100 Ats.

(c) Seat tightness must be sufficient to prevent leakage.

(d) Spray form must compare favourably with the illustration Fig. M-43.

Pressure setting, back leakage and seat tightness tests may be made by coupling the injection nozzle and holder assembly direct to the pressure feed pipe on setting outfit, but an adaptor must be fitted between the pipe and injection nozzle and holder assembly when testing spray form. This adaptor, described in Operation M/72, increases the pressure of fuel to the injection nozzle and holder assembly sufficiently for the main and auxiliary spray form to be determined.

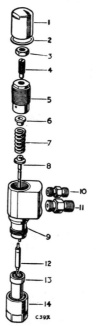

1 Protection cap
2 Copper washer
3 Locknut—adjusting screw
4 Pressure adjusting screw
5 Pressure sleeve
6 Spring cap
7 Pressure spring
8 Valve spindle and cap
9 Nozzle holder body
10 Spill-back pipe union
11 Feed pipe union
12 Nozzle valve
13 Nozzle valve body
14 Cap nut

Fig. M-32—Exploded view of injection nozzle and holder assembly.

Dismantling and cleaning   Operation M/78

A cleaning kit (Part No. 271484) is essential for removing carbon from the component parts of the injection nozzle and holder assembly. The use of special spanners (set Part No. 271482) is recommended.

1. Remove the nozzle holder protection cap and copper washer, unscrew the locknut, pressure adjusting screw and pressure sleeve, then withdraw the spring cap, spring and valve spindle. Unscrew the pipe unions and remove the copper washers.

2. Unscrew the cap nut, then remove the nozzle valve and body.

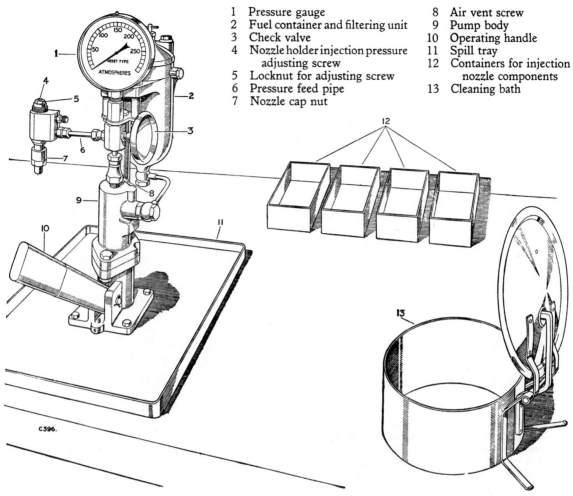

1 Pressure gauge
2 Fuel container and filtering unit
3 Check valve
4 Nozzle holder injection pressure
     adjusting screw
5 Locknut for adjusting screw
6 Pressure feed pipe
7 Nozzle cap nut
8 Air vent screw
9 Pump body
10 Operating handle
11 Spill tray
12 Containers for injection
      nozzle components
13 Cleaning bath

Fig. M-33—Injection nozzle setting outfit.

3. Soak the component parts of the assembly in Shell Fusus "A" oil to loosen carbon deposits but do **not** allow parts of any one assembly to be interchanged with those of another.

4. Brush away all external carbon deposits from component parts with a brass wire brush (Part No. ET.068) and replace them in the oil bath.

   Particular care must be exercised when cleaning the pintle and seat of nozzle valve to avoid scratching or scoring, which may result in spray distortion.

5. Clean the three oil feed passages in the nozzle body with a wire or drill of $\frac{1}{16}$ in. diameter. Remove the carbon from the annular recess with tool (Part No. ET.071) and from the valve seat, using tool (Part No. ET.070), with a rotary motion.

6. Select the appropriate size probe from the pocket of cleaning kit and secure it in the pintle hole cleaner (Part No. ET.069). Insert the probe into the bore of nozzle valve body and allow the end to extend through the main fuel outlet, then turn in a rotary manner to remove carbon.

7. Carbon may be removed from the nozzle valve cone by inserting the valve into tool (Part No. ET.072) and then rotating it alternatively in a clockwise then anti-clockwise manner whilst pressing the valve inward.

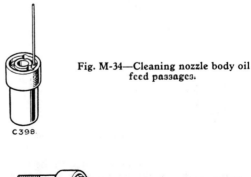

Fig. M-34—Cleaning nozzle body oil feed passages.

Fig. M-35—Scraping nozzle body annular recess.

Fig. M-36—Removing carbon from valve seat.

Fig. M-37—Cleaning Pintaux nozzle hole.

If the nozzle is blued or the seating has a dull circumferential ring indicating pitting or wear, the nozzle body and valve should be returned to a C.A.V. Service Agent and replacement parts fitted. See "Defect Location".

Do **not** attempt to lap the nozzle valve to body. This process requires special equipment and training.

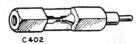

Fig. M-38—Removing carbon from nozzle valve cone.

8. Clean the auxiliary spray hole using tool (Part No. ET.120) fitted with probing wire (.008 in (0,20 mm) diameter). Allow $\frac{1}{16}$ in. (2,0 mm) only to extend from the chuck and thus minimise the possibility of the wire bending or breaking while probing. Great care must be taken to prevent breakage of the wire in the hole.

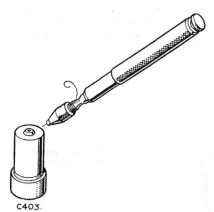

Fig. M-39—Cleaning auxiliary spray hole.

9. With flushing tool ET.427 secured to the nozzle testing outfit, fit the nozzle body (spray holes uppermost) to the flushing tool and pump test oil through vigorously. This flushing process is necessary for the removal of any tiny carbon particles which may have become lodged in the body after scraping and probing.

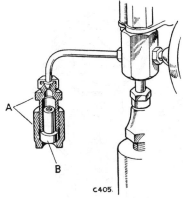

Fig. M-40—Flushing nozzle body.
A—Flushing tool.   B—Nozzle body.

10. Examine the pressure faces of nozzle body and nozzle holder to ascertain their freedom from scoring and scratches. These surfaces must be perfectly smooth. Fit the nozzle to nozzle body and check for freedom of movement.

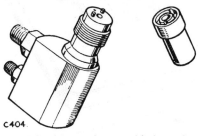

Fig. M-41—Injection nozzle assembly lapped pressure faces.

11. Immerse the nozzle body and valve in the oil bath and assemble whilst submerged. Wash the remaining components thoroughly and reverse dismantling procedure.

12. Test injection nozzle assembly in accordance with Operation M/80.

To test (Fig. M-32)   **Operation M/80**
WARNING: The injection nozzle must **not** be allowed to point towards the operator when spraying and the hands must **never** be allowed to contact the spray, which has great penetrating force.

1. Remove the cap from oil container (2) and fill with 1½ pints (0,852 litre) of Shell Fusus 'A' oil.

2. Air vent the system by removing the vent screw (8), allow oil to flow freely for a few seconds and replace the screw whilst the flow continues. Operate the pump handle until oil flows from pipe (6).

3. Connect the injector and holder assembly to the pressure feed pipe with the nozzle pointing downwards. The length and bore of this pipe is important and replacement pipes must be approximately 75 mm (2.8 in.) between the union nuts and of 3 mm (.118 in.) bore.

4. Close the check valve (6) to keep the pressure gauge out of circuit and smartly operate the hand lever (10) several times to expel all air from the system.

Back leakage

5. Open the check valve (3), move the operating handle slowly downward and note the highest pressure at which the gauge needle "flicks". This "flick" indicates the opening of the needle valve and should occur for this test at 160 to 170 atmospheres. Adjustment is made by removing the cap nut from the nozzle holder, loosening locknut (5) and turning the adjusting screw (4) clockwise to increase and anti-clockwise to decrease the opening pressure.

6. Raise the pressure in the system to just less than valve opening pressure, release the operating lever and time the pressure drop from 150-100 atmospheres. This should be not less than 5 seconds for the original nozzle and not less than 7 seconds, if a new one is to be fitted, and not more than 36 seconds for either.

7. Check externally the top and bottom of nozzle cap nut (7) and pressure pipe union nuts for signs of oil leakage. If leakage occurs at the nozzle cap nut, remove the nut and examine the pressure faces of nozzle holders and nozzle body for presence of foreign matter or surface scoring, before tightening further.

A leakproof nozzle assembly with an excessive rate of pressure drop, indicates a worn nozzle valve; the nozzle valve and nozzle body should be renewed.

Pressure setting

8. The selected **operational** opening pressure of the nozzle valve is 135 atmospheres. Readjust to this setting in the manner described in item 5.

Seat tightness

9. Wipe the bottom face of the injection nozzle dry and raise the pressure in the system to 125 atmospheres. A slight dampness on the bottom face is permissible, but blob formation or dripping indicates a badly seating valve in which case the assembly should be dismantled for further examination.

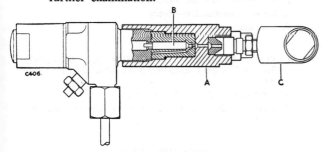

Fig. M-42—Sectioned view of adaptor (C.A.V.-E.T. 872).

A—Modified cap nut.   B—Nozzle valve (less pintle).
C—Nozzle under test.

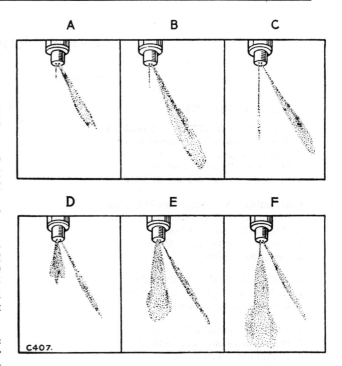

Fig. M-43—Injection nozzle spray form development
—starting to running conditions

Spray form

10. Fuel delivery to the injection nozzle assembly when testing **spray form,** must be characteristically similar to fuel delivery under normal operating conditions and to effect these conditions an adaptor (CAV Y7044872) must be fitted between the injection nozzle assembly and the pressure pipe.

The adaptor differs mainly in the cap nut and nozzle valve, from the ordinary type of injection nozzle and holder assembly as fitted to the engine; the nozzle valve has no pintle and the cap nut is extended, bored and threaded, to receive nozzles for testing.

11. Connect the adaptor assembly to the pressure pipe and adjust the opening pressure of the nozzle valve to 220 atmospheres. (See items 4 and 5.) Screw the injection nozzle and holder assembly to be tested, into the adaptor and with the check valve closed, operate the handle smartly to expel air from the system.

The auxiliary spray form may be tested at 60 strokes per minute and the main spray at 140. Spray development from starting to running speeds is illustrated in Fig. M-43; this illustration should be referred to and compared with the spray form of nozzles under test.

DEFECT LOCATION

Symptom, Cause and Remedy

PETROL ENGINES

A—NO PETROL SUPPLY TO CARBURETTER
1. Blocked pump or bowl filter—*Clean.*
2. Stoppage in pipe lines—*Clear.*
3. Sticking needle valve—*Replace.*
4. Pump inoperative—*See item* **B** *below.*

B—INOPERATIVE FUEL PUMP (ELECTRIC)
1. Broken wiring or poor connections—*Rectify.*
2. Dirty contact points—*Clean.*
3. Foreign matter in pump—*Overhaul.*
4. Faulty pump—*Renew.*

C—ELECTRIC FUEL PUMP NOISY
1. Air leak between pump and tank—*Rectify.*
2. Dirt under pump valves—*Clean.*

D—LACK OF ENGINE POWER
1. Badly adjusted carburetter—*Adjust.*
2. Blocked jets—*Clear.*
3. Needle valve sticking—*Replace.*
4. Blocked filters or pipes—*Clean.*
5. Pump inoperative—*See items* **B** *or* **F.**
6. Engine fault—*See Section A.*
7. Accelerator linkage stiff—*Lubricate*
8. Water in petrol—*Drain and clear system.*

E—HEAVY PETROL CONSUMPTION
1. Badly adjusted or worn carburetter—*Adjust or replace.*
2. Float chamber flooding—*Replace needle valve*
3. Petrol leaks—*Rectify.*
4. Wrong main jet—*Check and rectify as necessary.*

DIESEL ENGINES

Note. Various defects may be caused by replacing any of the injection equipment on this engine with equipment of the incorrect type.

LIFT PUMP

F—INOPERATIVE FUEL PUMP (MECHANICAL)
1. Fuel tank empty—*Refuel.*
2. Cork sealing gasket for sediment bowl hardened or cracked—*Renew.*
3. Sediment bowl loosely fitted—*Tighten.*
4. Filter disc clogged—*Remove and clean.*
5. Diaphragm cracked or porous—*Renew—Operation M/48.*
6. Screws securing upper and lower casings loose—*Re-set diaphragm and tighten in accordance with Operation M/48, item 12.*
7. Rocker arm excessively worn—*Renew.*
8. Springs fatigued—*Renew.*
9. Valve seating gasket or valves damaged—*Renew.*
10. Dirt on valve or valve seats—*Clean and refit.*
11. Valve retainer screws loose—*Tighten.*
12. Pipe union—tank to pump—loose—*Tighten.*

G—FUEL LEAKING FROM BASE OF PUMP
1. Diaphragm porous or cracked—*Renew.*

INJECTION NOZZLES

A—NOZZLE BLUEING
1. Nozzle holder not tightened properly—*Renew nozzle body and valve—tighten fully.*
2. Inefficient cooling—*Check cooling system—renew nozzle body and valve.*
3. Small corrugated sealing washer not fitted or damaged—*Renew nozzle and valve, fit new washer.*

B—EXCESSIVE LEAK-BACK
1. Cap nut loose—*Tighten.*
2. Pressure seats scored—*Renew nozzle and holder assembly.*
3. Nozzle valve worn—*Renew nozzle and holder assembly.*

C—VALVE LIFTING PRESSURE TOO HIGH.
1. Compression screw incorrectly adjusted—*Re-adjust.*
2. Nozzle valve sticking—*Renew nozzle valve and nozzle body.*

D—VALVE LIFTING PRESSURE TOO LOW
1. Compression screw incorrectly adjusted—*Re-adjust.*
2. Spring fatigued or broken—*Renew.*

E—SPRAY FORM DISTORTED
1. Carbon on valve seat—*Remove.*
2. Nozzle tip distorted—*Renew nozzle valve and nozzle body.*
3. Spray holes distorted—*Renew nozzle valve and nozzle body.*
4. Injection holes partially blocked with carbon—*Remove deposit.*

F—NOZZLE DRIP
1. Valve seat scored—*Renew nozzle valve and nozzle body.*
2. Spring pressure incorrectly adjusted—*Re-adjust.*
3. Carbon deposit on valve or seating—*Remove.*
4. Nozzle valve sticking—*Clean and re-check, renew nozzle valve and body if trouble is not corrected.*

MAIN FILTER

A—LEAKAGE AT CONTAINER JOINT
1. Gasket unserviceable—*Renew.*
2. Container loose—*Tighten.*

B—FUEL PUMPED TO FILTER AT NORMAL PRESSURE BUT EMERGES AT MUCH REDUCED RATE
1. Element waxed up—*Renew element.*
2. Foreign body lodged in inlet connection—*Remove and examine.*

INJECTION PUMP

A—INJECTION PUMP DEFECTIVE
1. For any reason—*Return to CAV Agent—fit a replacement unit.*

DATA — ALL MODELS

Air cleaner .... A.C. Centrifugal—oil bath

  Capacity:
    1948-53 models   .... 2 Imperial pints (1 litre)
    1954-58 models   .... 1.5 Imperial pints (0,85 litre

Carburetter

  Type   .... Solex

  Details   .... Petrol models

    Choke size:
      1948-51 models 23
      1952-58 models 25
    Main jet:
      1948-51 models 107,5
      1952-58 models 115
    Correction jet:
      1948-51 models 160
      1952-58 models 170
    Pilot jet:
      1948-51 models 45
      1952-58 models 55
    Pump jet:
      1948-51 models 50
      1952-58 models 75
    Economy jet   50
    Air bleed jet 1.5
    Starter air jet 5.5
    Starter petrol jet 135

  High speed circuit
    Petrol jet   ....
    Air bleed   ....
  Petrol level   .... $\frac{5}{8}$ in. $\pm\frac{1}{8}$ (16 mm $\pm$3) below float chamber joint face

  Exceptions to standard settings to suit various altitudes:

	1948-51 models	1952-58 models
3,000 to 6,000 feet (900 to 1800 m):		
Main jet	100	110
Air bleed jet	2.0	2.0
6,000 to 10,000 feet (1.800 to 3.000 m):		
Main jet	95	107.5
Air bleed jet	2.0	2.0
10,000 to 14,000 feet (3.000 to 4.200 m):		
Choke size	24 or 25	26
Main jet	95	107.5
Correction jet	170	180
Air bleed jet	2.0	2.0

  Exception to standard settings to suit tropical conditions:
    Main jet:
      1948-51 models 100
      1952-58 models 110

Filters

  Petrol models   .... Sediment bowl, full flow

  Diesel models, main.... C.A.V. Replaceable element, full flow

Fuel pump

  Petrol models   .... S.U. Electric

  Diesel models   .... A.C. mechanical

  Pressure, Diesel models 5 to 8 lb./sq.in. (0,351 to 0,562 Kg/cm^2)

Fuel tank

  Capacity   .... 10 Imperial gallons (45 litres). No reserve

Injection pump, Diesel models

  Type   .... C.A.V. Mechanically governed distributor

Injection nozzle assemblies   .... C.A.V. Pintaux

  Nozzle size B.D.N.O./SP6209

  Opening pressure of nozzle valve   .... 135 Ats.

  Back leakage rate, 150 to 100 Ats.:

    New nozzle   .... 7 seconds

    Original nozzle   .... 5 seconds

Section N — EXHAUST SYSTEM

INDEX

	Page		Page
Exhaust silencer, early 1954	N-1	Front exhaust pipe, late 1954 onwards	N-4
Exhaust silencer, late 1954 onwards	N-4	Intermediate exhaust pipe, late 1954 onwards	N-4
Front exhaust pipe, early 1954	N-1		

LIST OF ILLUSTRATIONS

Fig.		Page	Fig.		Page
N-1	Layout of exhaust system, early 1954	N-2	N-2	Layout of exhaust system, late 1954 onwards	N-3

Exhaust system, early 1954

Front exhaust pipe

To remove   **Operation N/10**

1. Remove the clamping flange between the front exhaust pipe and the silencer.
2. Remove four nuts and spring washers securing the exhaust pipe to the exhaust manifold.
3. Withdraw the exhaust pipe complete with joint washer.

To refit   **Operation N/12**

1. Replace the exhaust pipe by reversing the removal procedure.

Exhaust silencer (R.H.D. models only)

To remove   **Operation N/14**

1. Jack up the rear of the vehicle and place jacking stands under the rear axle casing.
2. Remove both rear wheels.
3. Disconnect front exhaust pipe from silencer.
4. Remove the clips securing the front end of silencer unit to the support plate.
5. Remove the saddle securing the tail pipe to the tail pipe support bracket.
6. Withdraw the silencer unit complete by manoeuvring it past the right-hand road spring.

To refit   **Operation N/16**

1. Replace the exhaust silencer by reversing the removal procedure.

Exhaust silencer (L.H.D. models only)

To remove   **Operation N/18**

1. Jack up the rear of the vehicle and place jacking stands under the axle casing.
2. Remove the rear left-hand wheel.
3. Disconnect the front exhaust pipe from silencer.
4. Remove the clips securing the front end of the silencer unit to the support plate.
5. Remove the two bolts and self-locking nuts securing the silencer to the rubber support strip.
6. Remove the saddle securing the tail pipe to the tail pipe support bracket.

Land-Rover 107 only—

7. Remove the saddle securing the silencer to the chassis frame.
8. Remove two bolts securing one of the extremities of the rear axle check strap to the chassis side member. Remove the shock absorber top fixing bolt and slacken the lower one. Swing the shock absorber downwards.
9. Withdraw the silencer unit complete.

To refit   **Operation N/20**

1. Replace the exhaust silencer by reversing the removal procedure, taking care to tighten the shock absorber securing bolts with the vehicle resting on the ground.

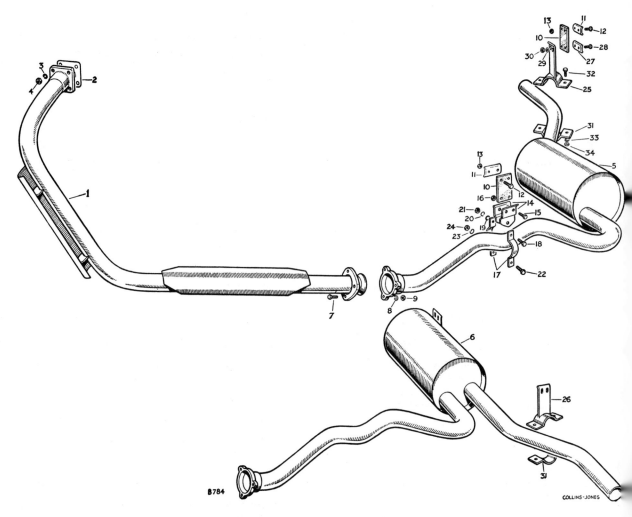

Fig. N-1—Layout of exhaust system, early 1954.

1	Front exhaust pipe complete	15–16	Fixings for plate
2	Joint washer for exhaust pipe	17	Pipe clamp
3–4	Fixings for exhaust pipe	18–21	Fixings for pipe clamp
5	Exhaust silencer complete	22–24	Fixings for pipe clamp
6	Exhaust silencer complete	25	Clamp bracket for exhaust pipe
7–9	Fixings for silencer	26	Clamp bracket for exhaust pipe
10	Flexible mounting for exhaust pipe	27–30	Fixings for clamp bracket
11–13	Fixings for flexible mounting	31	Saddle for clamp bracket
14	Plate for flexible mounting	32–34	Fixings for saddle

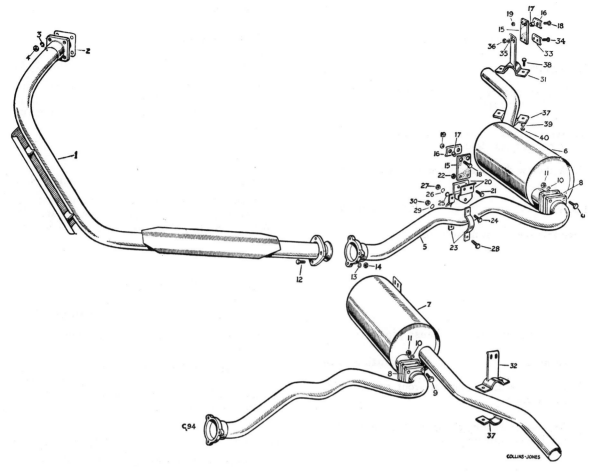

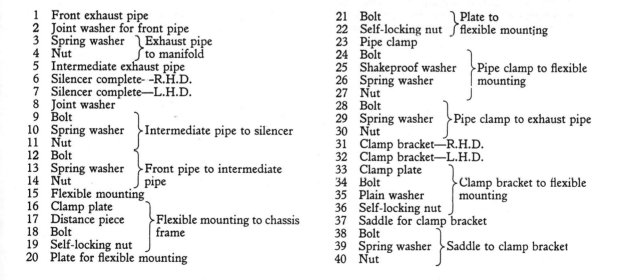

Fig. N-2—Layout of exhaust system, late 1954 onwards, Petrol and Diesel models.

1	Front exhaust pipe	
2	Joint washer for front pipe	
3	Spring washer	}Exhaust pipe
4	Nut	}to manifold
5	Intermediate exhaust pipe	
6	Silencer complete—R.H.D.	
7	Silencer complete—L.H.D.	
8	Joint washer	
9	Bolt	
10	Spring washer	}Intermediate pipe to silencer
11	Nut	
12	Bolt	
13	Spring washer	}Front pipe to intermediate pipe
14	Nut	
15	Flexible mounting	
16	Clamp plate	
17	Distance piece	}Flexible mounting to chassis frame
18	Bolt	
19	Self-locking nut	
20	Plate for flexible mounting	
21	Bolt	}Plate to
22	Self-locking nut	}flexible mounting
23	Pipe clamp	
24	Bolt	
25	Shakeproof washer	}Pipe clamp to flexible mounting
26	Spring washer	
27	Nut	
28	Bolt	
29	Spring washer	}Pipe clamp to exhaust pipe
30	Nut	
31	Clamp bracket—R.H.D.	
32	Clamp bracket—L.H.D.	
33	Clamp plate	
34	Bolt	}Clamp bracket to flexible mounting
35	Plain washer	
36	Self-locking nut	
37	Saddle for clamp bracket	
38	Bolt	
39	Spring washer	}Saddle to clamp bracket
40	Nut	

Exhaust system late 1954 onwards

Front exhaust pipe

To remove   **Operation N/22**

1. Remove securing bolts at front exhaust pipe and intermediate pipe joint.

2. Remove nuts and spring washers securing pipe at exhaust manifold.

3. Withdraw the exhaust pipe and joint washer.

To refit   **Operation N/24**

Reverse the removal procedure.

Intermediate exhaust pipe

To remove   **Operation N/26**

1. Remove securing bolts at front exhaust pipe and silencer.

2. Remove supporting clamp and withdraw intermediate exhaust pipe.

To refit   **Operation N/28**

1. Reverse the removal procedure, leaving the supporting clamps loose until the pipe has been secured firmly to front exhaust pipe and silencer.

Exhaust silencer (R.H.D. models only)

To remove   **Operation N/30**

1. Remove the bolts securing intermediate pipe to silencer and release support saddle from silencer tail pipe, keeping silencer supported by hand.

2. Withdraw silencer assembly.

To refit   **Operation N/32**

Reverse removal procedure, ensuring that the bolts securing intermediate pipe to silencer are fully tightened before finally clamping the tail pipe support.

Exhaust silencer (L.H.D. models only)

To remove   **Operation N/34**

1. Remove bolts securing intermediate pipe to silencer.

2. Keeping the silencer supported, release the supporting strap for silencer right-hand side and saddle clamp on tail pipe, then withdraw silencer assembly.

To refit   **Operation N/36**

1. Fit the silencer in position and loosely support by means of supporting strap and saddle clamp.

2. Secure the intermediate pipe to silencer.

3. Finally tighten bolts securing support strap and saddle clamp.

Section P
ELECTRICAL EQUIPMENT — ALL MODELS

INDEX

	Page			Page
Batteries	P-1	Horn button		P-24
Coil—Petrol models	P-24	Mixture control thermostat switch—Petrol		
Current voltage regulator—Diesel models	P-17	models		P-26
Data	P-28	Number plate lamp		P-23
Defect location	P-27	Side lamps		P-22
Dip switch	P-24	Starter motor		P-1
Distributor—Petrol models	P-24	Starter switch—Petrol models		P-15
Dynamo	P-15	Starter and heater switch—Diesel models		P-26
Fuel gauge tank unit	P-26	Stop lamp switch		P-25
Fuse and junction boxes	P-26	Stop and tail lamps		P-22
Headlamps	P-19	Voltage regulator—Petrol models		P-16
Heater plugs, Diesel models	P-25	Windscreen wiper		P-26
Horn	P-23			

LIST OF ILLUSTRATIONS

Fig.		Page	Fig.		Page
P-1	Exploded view of starter motor—Petrol models	P-2	P-15	Exploded view of starter drive—Diesel models	P-14
P-2	Sectioned view of starter motor—Diesel models	P-2	P-16	Undercutting commutator insulators	P-16
P-3	Wiring diagram, 1948-50 models	P-3	P-17	Checking voltage regulator	P-16
P-4	Wiring diagram, majority of 1951 models	P-4	P-18	Charging circuit	P-17
P-5	Wiring diagram, late 1951, 1952 and 1953 models	P-5	P-19	Current voltage regulator	P-17
P-6	Wiring diagram, 86 and 107 1956-58 models	P-6	P-20	Short circuiting regular contacts	P-18
P-7	Flasher wiring diagram, 1954-58 models	P-7	P-21	Voltage and current regulators	P-18
P-8	Wiring diagram, 88 and 109 1954-58 models	P-8	P-22	Cut-out relay	P-19
P-9	Wiring diagram—Diesel models	P-10	P-23	Headlamp	P-19
P-10	Checking starter brushes	P-12	P-24	Layout of lamps	P-21
P-11	Testing brush spring tension	P-12	P-25	Headlamp beam setting board	P-22
P-12	Setting pinion movement	P-13	P-26	Side lamp	P-22
P-13	Layout of the starter drive—1954 models	P-13	P-27	Stop, tail lamp, 1954 models	P-23
P-14	Layout of starter drive—1955-58 Petrol models	P-14	P-28	Stop, tail lamp, 1955-58 models	P-23
			P-29	Horn adjustment—Lucas	P-24
			P 30	Horn adjustment—Clear Hooters	P-24
			P-31	Checking heater plug circuit	P-25
			P-32	Testing heater plug circuit	P-25

Batteries

Note: Two batteries fitted to Diesel models—see Data section.

To remove   **Operation P/2**

1. Remove the air cleaner, disconnect the leads, remove the securing frame and lift battery clear (when removing one battery only—Diesel models—always remove the interconnecting battery lead completely from both batteries).

To refit   **Operation P/4**

1. Reverse removal procedure, taking care to smear the battery terminals with petroleum jelly.

    Note: The drive screws securing the battery leads are manufactured from a special non-corrosive metal and must never be replaced with ordinary drive screws, which may cause serious corrosion of the battery terminals.

Starter motor

To remove   **Operation P/6**

1. **Petrol models**—disconnect the positive lead from the battery.

    Diesel models—disconnect the negative L.H. battery lead from the battery and the leads from the starter solenoid.

2. **Diesel models**—remove the inlet and exhaust manifolds, and the dipstick and tube.

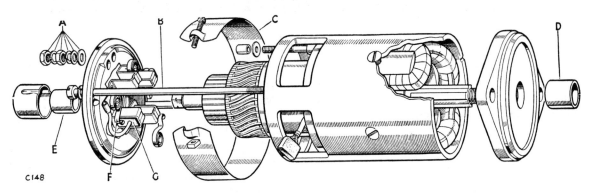

Fig. P-1—Exploded view of starter motor, Petrol models.

A—Terminal nuts and washer   C—Cover band   E—Bearing bush   G—Brush
B—Through bolt   D—Bearing bush   F—Brush spring

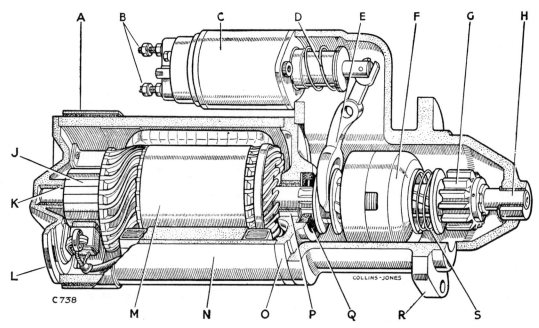

Fig. P-2—Sectioned view of starter motor, Diesel models.

A—Commutator cover band	G—Driving pinion	N—Yoke
B—Solenoid terminals	H—Porous bronze bush	O—Intermediate bracket
C—Solenoid	J—Commutator	P—Impregnated brass bush
D—Solenoid return spring	K—Porous bronze bush	Q—Brake ring
E—Engagement lever	L—Commutator-end bracket	R—Drive-end bracket
F—Clutch assembly	M—Armature	S—Cushion spring

3. 1954 models. Remove the oil filter and brackets from the cylinder block. Section A.

4. 1954 models. Detach the filter outlet pipe from the cylinder block.

5. **Petrol models**—disconnect the cable from starter.

Early models

Detach the outlet pipe from the cylinder block. Disconnect the wire to the oil pressure switch. Remove the oil pressure switch and oil pipe to the cylinder head by withdrawing two union bolts. Remove the three nuts and spring washers securing the starter housing to the flywheel housing and lift out the starter motor and housing. (If necessary, remove the large bolt locating the starter motor in the housing through the access hole in the dash panel.)

6. Remove the securing bolts and withdraw starter.

To refit   **Operation P/8**

1. Reverse the removal procedure.

2. Check the operation of the starter motor.

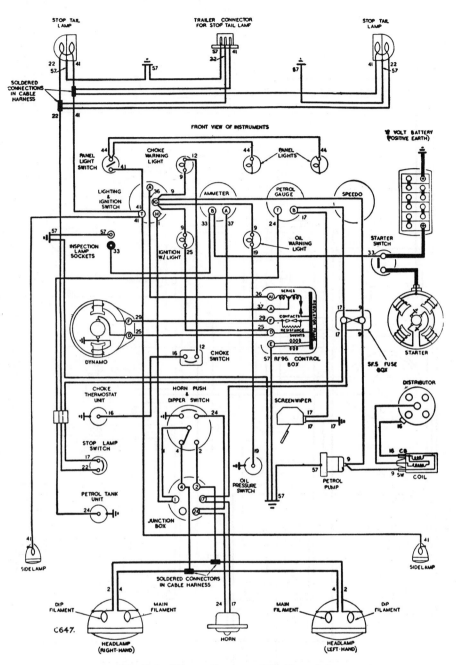

Fig. P-3—Wiring diagram, 1948-50 models

KEY TO CABLE COLOURS

1	BLUE	17	GREEN	33	BROWN	49	PURPLE
2	BLUE with RED	18	GREEN with RED	34	BROWN with RED	50	PURPLE with RED
3	BLUE with YELLOW	19	GREEN with YELLOW	35	BROWN with YELLOW	51	PURPLE with YELLOW
4	BLUE with WHITE	20	GREEN with BLUE	36	BROWN with BLUE	52	PURPLE with BLUE
5	BLUE with GREEN	21	GREEN with WHITE	37	BROWN with WHITE	53	PURPLE with WHITE
6	BLUE with PURPLE	22	GREEN with PURPLE	38	BROWN with GREEN	54	PURPLE with GREEN
7	BLUE with BROWN	23	GREEN with BROWN	39	BROWN with PURPLE	55	PURPLE with BROWN
8	BLUE with BLACK	24	GREEN with BLACK	40	BROWN with BLACK	56	PURPLE with BLACK
9	WHITE	25	YELLOW	41	RED	57	BLACK
10	WHITE with RED	26	YELLOW with RED	42	RED with YELLOW	58	BLACK with RED
11	WHITE with YELLOW	27	YELLOW with BLUE	43	RED with BLUE	59	BLACK with YELLOW
12	WHITE with BLUE	28	YELLOW with WHITE	44	RED with WHITE	60	BLACK with BLUE
13	WHITE with GREEN	29	YELLOW with GREEN	45	RED with GREEN	61	BLACK with WHITE
14	WHITE with PURPLE	30	YELLOW with PURPLE	46	RED with PURPLE	62	BLACK with GREEN
15	WHITE with BROWN	31	YELLOW with BROWN	47	RED with BROWN	63	BLACK with PURPLE
16	WHITE with BLACK	32	YELLOW with BLACK	48	RED with BLACK	64	BLACK with BROWN

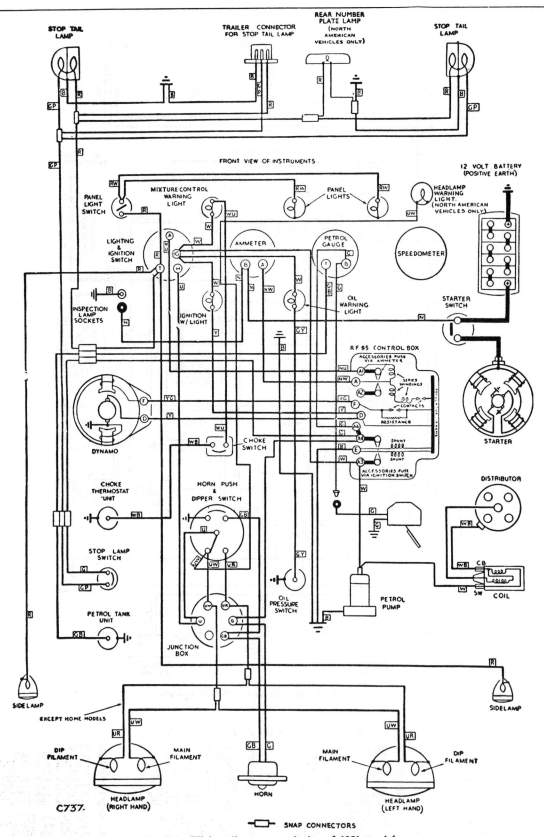

Fig. P-4—Wiring diagram, majority of 1951 models

KEY TO CABLE COLOURS

B—BLACK	N—BROWN	R—RED	W—WHITE
G—GREEN	P—PURPLE	U—BLUE	Y—YELLOW
	NU—BROWN with BLUE and so on.		

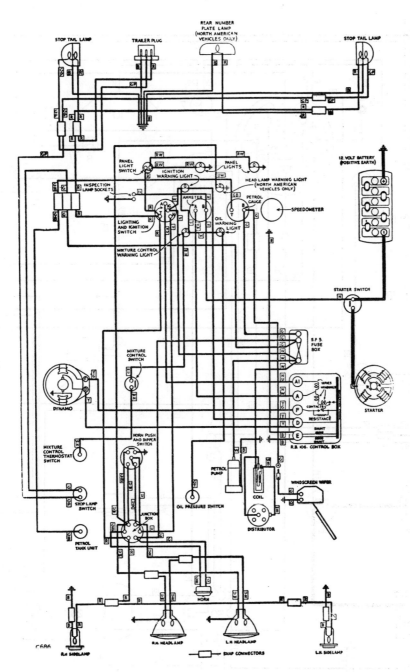

Fig. P-5—Wiring diagram, late 1951. 1952 and 1953 models

KEY TO CABLE COLOURS

B—BLACK	N—BROWN	R—RED	W—WHITE
G—GREEN	P—PURPLE	U—BLUE	Y—YELLOW
	NU—BROWN with BLUE and so on.		

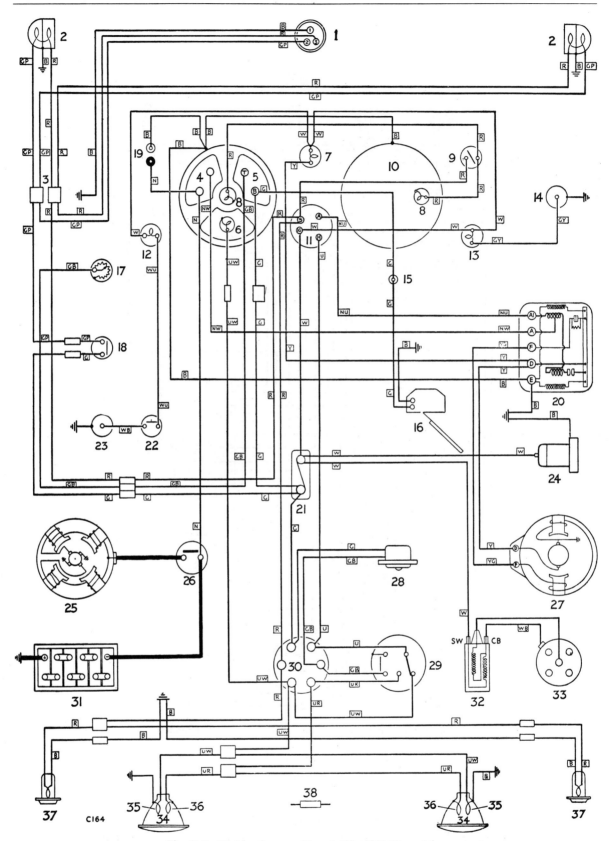

Fig. P-6—Wiring diagram 86 and 107—1956-58 models
See Page P-9 for key to wiring diagram

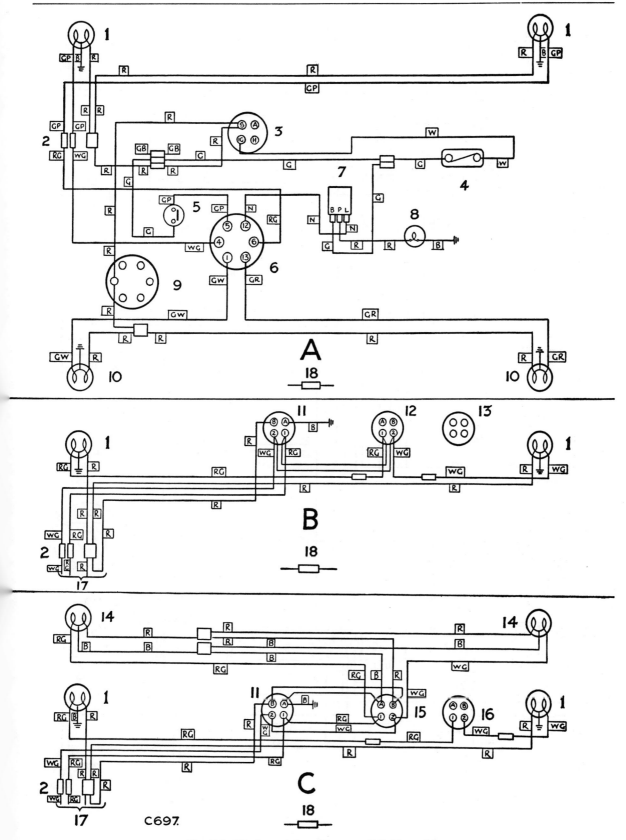

Fig. P-7—Flasher wiring diagram—1954-58 models

See Page P-9 for key to wiring diagram

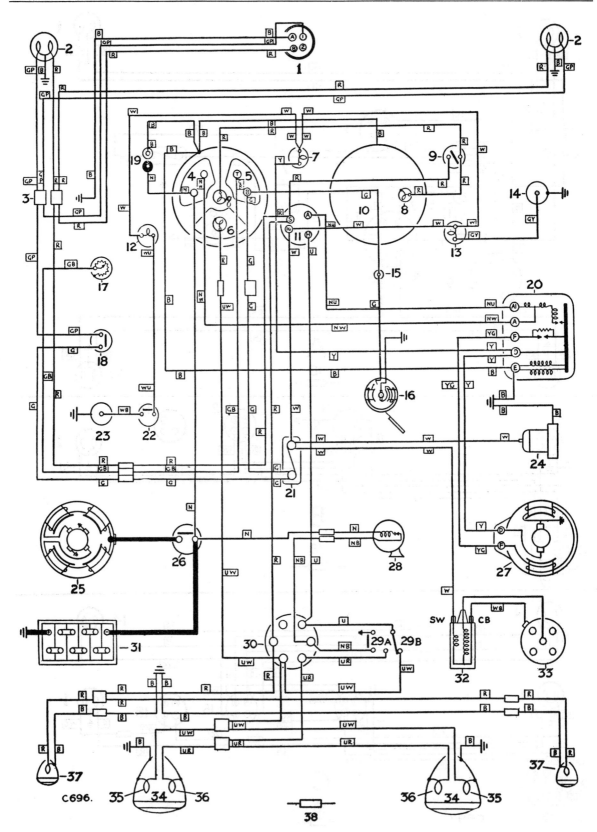

Fig. P-8—Wiring diagram 88 and 109—1954-58 models

See Page P-9 for key to wiring diagram

Key to main wiring diagrams, Figs. P-6 and P-8

1	Trailer light socket (extra equipment)	15 Windscreen wiper plug and socket	28 Horn
2	Stop, tail lamps	16 Windscreen wiper	29 Horn push and headlamp dipper switch,
3	Snap connectors for trailer light	17 Petrol tank level unit	86 and 107
4	Ammeter	18 Stop lamp switch	29A Horn push
5	Petrol level gauge	19 Inspection lamp sockets	29B Headlamp dipper switch
6	Headlamp main beam warning light	20 R.B.106 voltage control box	30 Junction box
7	Ignition warning light	21 S.F.5 fuse box (35 amp. fuse)	31 12 volt battery (positive earth)
8	Panel lights	22 Mixture control switch (at control)	32 Ignition coil
9	Panel light switch	23 Mixture control thermostat switch	33 Distributor
10	Speedometer	(at cylinder head)	34 Headlamps
11	Ignition and lighting switch	24 Petrol pump	35 Main beam
12	Mixture control warning light	25 Starter	36 Dip beam
13	Oil pressure warning light	26 Starter solenoid switch	37 Side lamps
14	Oil pressure switch	27 Dynamo	38 Snap connectors shown thus ⊣▭⊢

Note: On vehicles to the North American specification, the connections at the ignition and lighting switch are such that the sidelamps are extinguished when the headlamps are in use.

Key to flasher wiring diagram, Fig. P-7

To be used in conjunction with main wiring diagrams on Pages P-6 and P-8.

A—Wiring diagram for flashers only.

B—Wiring diagram using flashers and trailer socket. In this diagram the rear flashers are shown connected via the trailer socket and vehicle flasher plug; the plug must be in this position when trailer is not in use.

C—Wiring diagram using flashers and trailer. In this diagram vehicle flashers are disconnected and trailer plug in use, giving flashers on trailer.

1	Stop, tail lamp	7 Flasher unit	13 Dummy trailer socket
2	Snap connectors	8 Flasher warning light	14 Trailer stop, tail lamp
3	Ignition and light switch	9 Junction box	15 Trailer plug
4	Fuse box	10 Front flasher and side lamp	16 Vehicle flasher plug in dummy trailer
5	Stop lamp switch	11 Trailer socket	socket
6	Flasher switch	12 Vehicle flasher plug	17 Wiring as diagram 'A' from this point
			18 Snap connectors shown thus ⊣▭⊢

Key to cable colours

B—BLACK	N—BROWN	R—RED	W—WHITE
G—GREEN	P—PURPLE	U—BLUE	Y—YELLOW
	RN—RED WITH BROWN, AND SO ON		

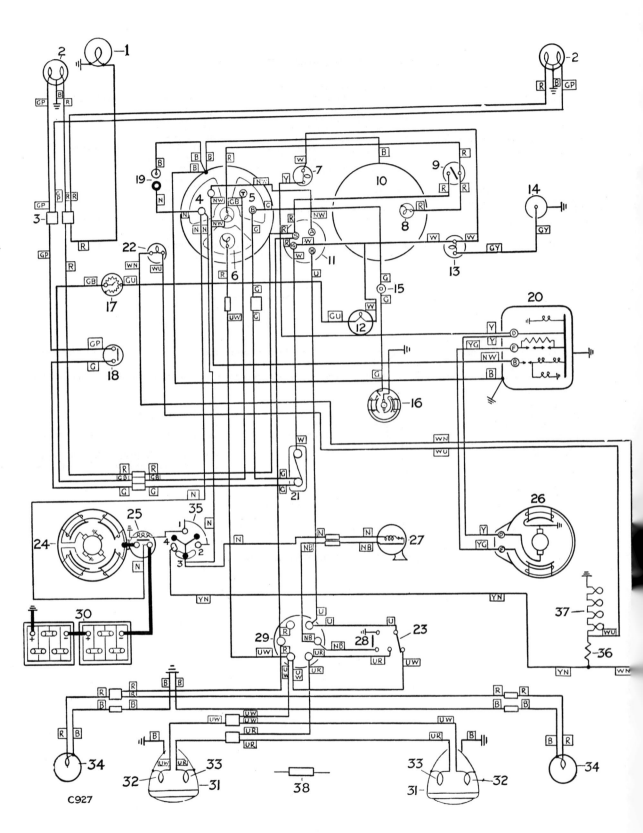

Fig. P-9—Wiring diagram, Diesel models.

C927

Wiring diagrams

Note: On vehicles to the North American specification, the connections at the lighting
switch are such that the sidelamps are
extinguished when the headlamps are in
use.

Key to cable colours

B—Black   N—Brown   R—Red   W—White
G—Green   P—Purple   U—Blue   Y—Yellow

RN—Red with brown and so on.

Key to Fig. P-9

1	Rear number plate light	20	Current control box
2	Stop, tail lamps	21	Fuse box (35 amp. fuse)
3	Snap connectors for number plate light	22	Heater plug warning light
4	Ammeter	23	Headlamp dipper switch
5	Fuel level gauge	24	Starter
6	Headlamp main beam warning light	25	Starter solenoid switch
7	Dynamo warning light	26	Dynamo
8	Panel lights	27	Horn
9	Panel light switch	28	Horn push
10	Speedometer	29	Junction box
11	Electrical services and lighting switch	30	6-volt batteries (positive earth)
12	Fuel level warning light	31	Headlamps
13	Oil pressure warning light	32	Main beam
14	Oil pressure switch	33	Dip beam
15	Windscreen wiper plug and socket	34	Side lamps
16	Windscreen wiper	35	Starter and heater plug switch
17	Fuel tank level unit	36	Resistance for heater plug
18	Stop lamp switch	37	Heater plugs
19	Inspection lamp sockets	38	Snap connectors shown thus ⊣▭⊢

To dismantle   **Operation P/10**

1. Remove the cover band, hold back the brush springs and lift the brushes from their holders.

   Petrol models

2. Remove the starter drive, by withdrawing split pin from retaining nut on end of driving shaft and unscrewing the nut.

3. Remove the driving-end bracket, by unscrewing the two through bolts.

4. Withdraw the armature from the starter yoke.

   Diesel models

5. Disconnect the copper link between the lower solenoid terminal and the starter motor casing.

6. Remove the solenoid securing bolts. Withdraw the solenoid from the drive-end bracket casting, carefully making sure that the solenoid plunger is free from the starter drive engagement lever.

7. Unscrew and withdraw the two through bolts from the commutator-end bracket, and remove bracket from the starter motor yoke.

8. Remove the rubber seal from the drive-end bracket.

9. Remove the nut securing the eccentric pin, on which the drive engagement lever pivots, and withdraw pin.

10. Split the armature and intermediate bracket assembly from the drive-end bracket.

11. Slide the drive assembly and engagement lever off the shaft, first removing the washer from the end of the armature shaft extension.

12. Slide the intermediate bracket and brake assembly off the shaft, first removing the retaining ring from the armature shaft extension.

To overhaul   **Operation P/12**

Brushes

1. Check that the brushes move freely in their holders by holding back the brush spring and pulling gently on the flexible connectors. Any tendency to stick should be corrected by cleaning with a petrol-moistened cloth, or in extreme cases by the light use of a smooth file. If a brush is damaged or worn so that it does not make good contact on the commutator, all the brushes must be renewed.

2. Check the tension of the brush springs with a spring balance. The correct tension is 30 to 40 oz. (850 to 1134 grammes) and new springs must be fitted if the tension is low.

3. The flexible connectors are soldered to terminal tags; two are connected to brush boxes, and two are connected to the free ends of the field coils. These flexible connectors must be removed by unsoldering, and the flexible connectors of the new brushes secured in their places by soldering.

The new brushes being pre-formed, "bedding" to the commutator is unnecessary.

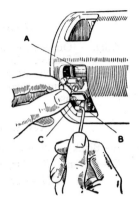

Fig. P-10—
Checking brushes.

A—Commutator.
B—Brush spring.
C—Brush.

Commutator

4. Clean the commutator with a petrol-moistened cloth. If necessary, rotate the armature and, using fine glass-cloth, remove pits and burned spots from commutator; remove abrasive dust with a dry air blast. If the commutator is badly worn, mount in a lathe, and, using a very sharp tool, take a light cut, taking care not to remove any more metal than necessary. The insulators between the commutator segments **must not be undercut.**

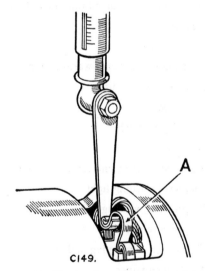

C149.

Fig. P-11—Testing brush spring tension.
A—Brush spring

Armature

5. If the armature is damaged, i.e. "lifted" conductors, or distorted shaft, it must be replaced. Never attempt to machine the armature core, or true a distorted armature shaft.

To assemble   **Operation P/14**

1. Reverse the removal procedure.

Diesel models

2. To facilitate fitting the solenoid to the drive-end bracket, ease the drive assembly forward along the armature shaft.

3. Before tightening the eccentric pivot pin securing nut, set the pinion movement as detailed below. After reassembly of the starter motor, connect the small centre terminal on the solenoid to a six-volt supply, using a switch. Connect the other side of the battery to a solenoid fixing stud. Close the switch, thus throwing the drive assembly forward into the engaged position, and measure the distance between the pinion and the washer on the armature shaft extension.

4. This movement should be made with the pinion pressed lightly towards the armature to take up any slack in the engagement linkage. This setting should be 0.20 in.-0.30 in. (0,5-0,7 mm).

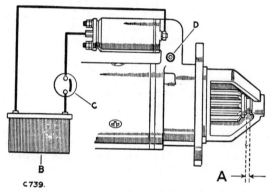

Fig. P-12—Setting pinion movement, when solenoid is energised.

A—0.20 in.-0.030 in.   C—Switch
B—6-volt battery   D—Eccentric pivot pin

To adjust the setting, slacken the eccentric pivot securing nut and turn the pin until the correct setting is obtained.

The adjustment arc is 180° and the head of the arrow, as marked on pivot pin, should be set only between the arrows on the arc described on the drive-end bracket casting.

After setting, tighten the securing nut, in order to hold the pin in position.

Starter drive, 1948-53 models
To overhaul   Operation P/16

In the event of the starter pinion becoming jammed in mesh with the flywheel, it can usually be freed by turing the starter armature by means of a spanner applied to the shaft extension at the commutator end.

If any difficulty is experienced with the starter not meshing with the flywheel, it is probable that the presence of dirt on the starter drive is preventing the free movement of the pinion on its sleeve; the sleeve and pinion should be washed in paraffin.

Should the drive have become damaged owing to misuse, it should be dismantled as detailed below, and the worn and damaged parts renewed.

1. Remove the two through bolts and withdraw the driving end bracket from the starter yoke.

2. Remove the pin from the bearing collar at the end of the starter drive.

3. Hold the squared end of the starter shaft at the commutator end by means of a spanner and unscrew the bearing collar.

4. Remove the restraining spring sleeve, restraining spring and collar.

5. Withdraw the key from the armature shaft and remove the pinion, coupling sleeve, friction washer and rubber coupling.

6. If the pinion is found to be worn or damaged, it is essential that it is renewed together with the screwed sleeve.

Starter drive—1954 models
To overhaul   **Operation P/18**

1. Remove the two through bolts and withdraw the driving-end bracket from the starter yoke.

2. Remove the shims (if fitted) from the end of the starter shaft.

3. Remove the pin from the bearing collar at the end of the starter drive.

4. Hold the squared end of the starter shaft at the commutator end by means of a spanner and unscrew the bearing collar.

5. Remove the restraining spring sleeve, restraining spring and collar.

6. Withdraw the key from the armature shaft and remove the pinion, coupling sleeve, friction washer and rubber coupling.

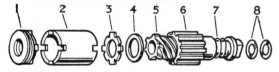

B 809

Fig. P-13—Layout of the starter drive, 1954 Petrol models.

1. Transmission plate.   5. Coupling sleeve.
2. Bendix drive sleeve.   6. Pinion.
3. Drive sleeve star washer.   7. Restraining spring.
4. Drive sleeve fibre washer.   8. Shims.

7. If the pinion is worn or damaged, renew it together with the screwed sleeve.

8. Complete the assembly by reversing the stripping procedure.

9. Check that the starter shaft has no end-float, but that it turns quite freely. Adjust the end-float by adding or removing shims in front of the bearing collar at the end of the starter drive.

Starter drive—1955-58 Petrol models

To strip   **Operation P/20**

1. Withdraw split pin from nut on end of driving shaft and unscrew nut.

2. Remove main spring, washer, pinion and sleeve assembly, collar, push-off spring and spring restraining sleeve.

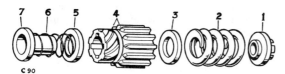

Fig. P-14—Layout of starter drive, 1955-58 Petrol models.

1. Shaft nut.
2. Main spring.
3. Washer.
4. Screwed sleeve and pinion.
5. Collar.
6. Pinion restraining spring.
7. Spring retaining sleeve.

To assemble   **Operation P/22**

1. Examine parts for excessive wear and replace as necessary. Assemble by reversing the removal procedure.

Starter drive—Diesel models

To strip   **Operation P/24**

1. Remove the drive assembly from the armature shaft.

2. Remove the lock ring from the driving sleeve.

3. Lift the two halves of the engagement bush off the driving sleeve.

4. Using a suitable circlip extractor, remove the clutch retaining circlip from the barrel unit and withdraw the driving sleeve and clutch unit.

5. The clutch assembly can now be dismantled by removing all the parts from the driving sleeve— excepting the two pressure plates which are

held in position by the ring nut. To remove the ring nut, slide the driving sleeve on to the splined armature shaft and, using soft metal jaw plates, clamp the armature in a vice, file away the peened rims and remove ring nut. This locknut should only be removed if absolutely necessary. If removed, fit a new nut and peen the rim over the notch in the driving sleeve.

6. To remove the pinion from the helically splined sleeve, knock out the pinion retaining ring securing rivet. The retaining ring, pinion, cushion spring with cup washers and sleeve can now be separated.

To assemble   **Operation P/26**

1. Reverse the stripping procedure.

   Note: The correct cushion spring tension is 11 lb. (4,9 Kg.) measured with the spring compressed to $\frac{7}{8}$ in. (22,2 mm) length and 16 lb. (7,26 Kg.) with the spring compressed to $\frac{1}{2}$ in. (12,7 mm) length.

2. Check the slipping torque of the clutch as follows; fit the drive assembly on the splined armature shaft and clamp the armature between soft metal jaw plates in a vice.

   Apply an anti-clockwise torque to the pinion with a suitable "torque wrench" fastened to the pinion teeth. The clutch should slip between 800-950 lb/in. (142,86 to 169,33 Kg/cm).

   If the clutch slips at too low a torque figure, dismantle again, and add shims one at a time until the correct figure is obtained.

   If the clutch does not slip between the torque limits given, again remove the circlip—dismantle and remove shims one at a time until the torque test gives correct figures.

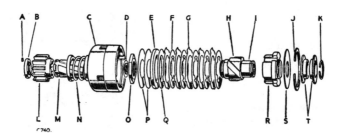

Fig. P-15—Exploded view of starter drive assembly, Diesel models.

A—Rivet	K—Lock ring
B—Pinion retaining spring	L—Pinion
C—Barrel unit	M—Helical splined sleeve
D—Thrust washer	N—Cushion spring
E—Backing ring	O—Ring nut
F—Clutch inner plate	P—Pressure plates
G—Clutch outer plate	Q—Shim
H—Helical splines	R—Moving member
I—Driving sleeve	S—Retaining washer
J—Circlip	T—Engagement bush

3. The assembled clutch unit and lever mechanism must be capable of being pushed to the full extent of the set travel. The assembly must move along the armature shaft extension smoothly and freely, but without slackness.

4. Before fitting the drive assembly to the armature shaft, lightly smear the shaft and pack the space between the indented bearings inside the pinion sleeve, with a bentonite-based grease.

Solenoid (Diesel models)—to test

The solenoid is composed of two coils, namely, a closing coil, by-passed when the plunger is fully home, and a hold-on coil to retain the plunger in the fully home position.

To test individually, remove existing connections and with the use of a 4-volt DC supply (constant voltage), proceed as below:

Closing coil

Connect the supply between the solenoid terminal marked 'S T A' and the smaller centre terminal. This should cause a current of 14.8 amps. to 17.4 amps. to pass.

Hold-on coil

Connect the supply between the solenoid body and the small centre terminal. This should cause a current of 4.5-5.6 amps. to pass.

Note: These tests should not be carried out while the solenoid is hot. Do not attempt to repair a faulty solenoid, it should always be replaced.

Starter switch—Petrol models
To remove   **Operation P/28**
1. Disconnect the battery.

2. Disconnect the three leads from the switch.

3. Screw off the switch knob and the locking nut from the switch spindle.

4. Remove the switch from the dash panel.

To refit   **Operation P/30**
Reverse the removal procedure, connecting the wires in accordance with the appropriate wiring diagram.

Starter switch—Diesel models
See Operation P/144.

Dynamo
To remove   **Operation P/32**
1. Disconnect the positive lead from the battery. Remove the air cleaner.

   Diesel only: Completely detach the lead connecting both batteries, disconnect the negative lead from the L.H. battery and remove L.H. battery.

2. Disconnect the leads from dynamo.

3. Remove the bolts securing the dynamo to adjusting and anchor brackets.

4. Remove the belt from pulley and withdraw dynamo.

To refit   **Operation P/34**
1. Reverse the removal procedure.

2. Adjust the driving belt tension: Petrol models, $\frac{1}{2}$ to $\frac{3}{4}$ in. (12-19 mm); and Diesel models, $\frac{3}{16}$ to $\frac{1}{4}$ in. (4-6 mm).

To strip   **Operation P/36**
1. Take off the driving pulley.

2. Unscrew and withdraw the two through bolts.

3. The commutator-end bracket can now be withdrawn from the dynamo yoke. Do not lose the fibre thrust washer.

4. The driving-end bracket together with the armature can now be lifted out of the yoke.

To overhaul   **Operation P/38**
Brushes
1. Lift the brushes up into the brush boxes and secure them there by positioning the brush spring at the side of the brush.

2. Fit the commutator-end bracket over the commutator and release the brushes.

3. Check that the brushes move freely in their holders by holding back the brush spring and pulling gently on the flexible connectors. Any tendency to stick should be corrected by cleaning with a petrol-moistened cloth, or in extreme cases by the **light** use of a smooth file. If a brush is damaged or worn so that it does not make good contact on the commutator, all the brushes must be renewed.

4 Check the tension of the brush springs with a spring balance. The correct tension is 22 to 25 oz. (624 to 709 grammes). In service it is permissible for this value to fall to 15 oz. (425 grammes). New springs must be fitted if the tension is low.

5. The new brushes being pre-formed, "bedding" to the commutator is unnecessary.

Commutator
6. Clean the commutator with a petrol-moistened cloth. If necessary, rotate the armature and, using fine glass-cloth, remove pits and burned spots from the commutator; remove abrasive dust with a dry air blast. If the commutator is badly worn, mount in a lathe, and, using a very sharp tool, take a light cut, taking care not to remove any more metal than necessary. Undercut the insulators between the segments to a depth of $\frac{1}{32}$ in. (0,8 mm) with a hacksaw blade ground to the thickness of the insulator.

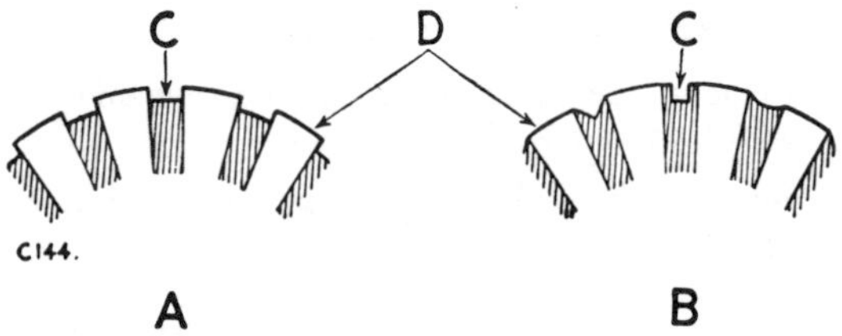

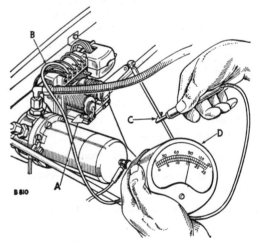
C144.

Fig. P-16—Undercutting commutator insulators.
A—Right.   B—Wrong.

To assemble   **Operation P/40**

1. Lift the brushes up into the brush boxes and secure them in that position by positioning the brush spring at the side of the brush.

2. Fit the commutator-end bracket on the armature shaft until the brush boxes are partly over the commutator. Place a thin screwdriver on top of each brush in turn and press the brush down on the commutator. The brush springs should then position themselves on top of the brushes.

3. Fit the commutator-end bracket to the yoke so that the projection on the bracket locates in the yoke.

4. Refit the two through bolts.

5. Inject a few drops of any high quality medium viscosity (SAE 30) engine oil into the hole marked "Oil" at the end of the commutator bearing housing.

To check   **Operation P/42**

1. Check the driving belt tension, ensure that it is neither too tight nor too loose; Operation P/34. Adjust if necessary by slackening the pivot and adjusting link bolts, then move the dynamo outwards from the engine to tighten belt or inwards to loosen. Re-tighten the securing bolts.

2. Disconnect the cables from terminals of dynamo and connect the two terminals with a short length of wire.

3. Start the engine and run at normal idling speed. Clip the negative lead of a moving coil voltmeter, calibrated 0-20 volts, to one dynamo terminal and the other lead to a good earthing point on the yoke.

4. Gradually increase the engine speed; the voltmeter reading should rise rapidly and without fluctuation. Do not allow the voltmeter reading to reach 20 volts nor race the engine in an attempt to increase the voltage output. An engine speed of 1,000 r.p.m. should not be exceeded.

5. If there is no reading, check the brush gear as described in Operation P/38. A low reading of approximately $\frac{1}{2}$-1 volt indicates a possible faulty field winding. Readings of 4 to 5 volts are probably attributable to faulty armature windings.

Note: If a radio suppression capacitor is fitted between the output terminal and earth, disconnect this capacitor and re-test the dynamo before dismantling. If a reading is now given on the voltmeter, the capacitor is defective and must be replaced.

6. The dynamo being found serviceable, remove the link connecting the terminals and fit them to the respective connections. Ensure that the larger terminal is connected to control box terminal marked "D" and the smaller dynamo terminal to the control box terminal marked "F".

Voltage regulator—Petrol engines

To remove   **Operation P/44**

1. Disconnect the battery.

2. Disconnect all wires from the control box.

3. Remove the control box complete from the mounting plate.

To refit   **Operation P/46**

1. Reverse the removal procedure, connecting the wiring in accordance with the appropriate wiring diagram.

B 810

Fig. P-17— Checking voltage regulator, Petrol models.
A—Piece of paper.   C—Earth.
B—D connection.   D—Voltmeter.

To check   **Operation P/48**

1. Place a piece of paper between the cut-out contacts and connect a moving-coil voltmeter to the "D" terminal on the regulator and to a good earth (not the one on the regulator box). Start the engine and increase r.p.m. until the voltage remains constant, i.e., the regulator is controlling; the voltmeter reading should be 15.8 to 16.4 volts. If the regulating voltage is not correct, the vehicle should be examined by a qualified electrician. Should the regulator be reading correctly at the commencement of this test, the earth lead of the voltmeter should be transferred to the "E" connection on the

regulator box; the reading should be the same as that obtained with the previous earth. If there is any difference, i.e., the "E" connection on the regulator gives a lower reading, it will indicate a bad earth on the regulator box.

Current voltage regulator—Diesel models
Locating faults on charging circuit

Ensure that the dynamo is functioning correctly and that the battery is in order, then proceed as follows :—

(a) Ensure that the wiring between battery and control box is in order by disconnecting the wire from control box terminal B and connecting the end of the wire removed to the negative terminal of a voltmeter. Connect the positive voltmeter terminal to an earthing point on the chassis. If a voltmeter reading is observed, the wiring is in order and the control box must be examined.

(b) If there is no reading, examine the wiring between battery and control box for defective cables or loose connections.

(c) Re-connect the wire to terminal B.

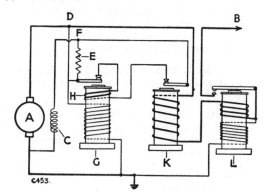

Fig. P-18—The charging circuit.

A—Armature.
B—Terminal on control box—
    to ammeter and battery.
C—Field windings.
D—Terminal on control box.
E—Resistor.
F—Terminal on control box.
G—Voltage regulator.
H—Bucking coil.
K—Current regulator.
L—Cut-out relay.

Regulator adjustments

The regulators are carefully set during manufacture to suit the normal requirements of standard equipment and, in general, further adjustments should not be necessary. However, if the battery does not keep in a charged condition, or if the dynamo output does not fall when the battery is fully charged, it may be advisable to check the settings and re-adjust if necessary.

Before disturbing any settings, it is important to check that a fault in the charging system is not due to a slipping dynamo belt or to a defective battery.

Electrical setting of voltage regulator
Operation P/50

1. Disconnect control box terminal B. Connect a first-grade moving coil 0-20 voltmeter between terminal D and earth.

2. Slowly increase the speed of the engine until the voltmeter needle flicks and steadies. This should occur at a reading between 14.2 and 14.8 volt. If it does not, stop the engine and remove the control box cover.

3. Slacken the adjustment screw locking nut (see Fig. P-20) and turn the screw in a clockwise direction to raise the voltage setting, or anti-clockwise to lower the setting. Turn the screw a fraction of a turn only at a time and re-tighten the locknut.

4. Repeat this open-circuit voltage test until the correct setting is obtained.
   Re-make the original connections.

Note: When the dynamo is run at a high speed on open circuit, it builds up a high voltage. Therefore, when adjusting the regulator, do not run the engine up to more than half throttle or a false voltmeter reading will be obtained. The adjustment should be completed within 30 seconds, otherwise heating of the regulator winding may cause an inaccurate setting to be made.

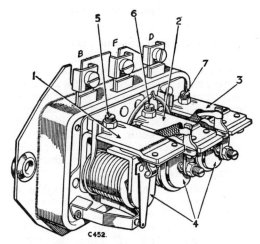

Fig. P-19—Current voltage regulator.

1 Cut-out.
2 Current regulator.
3 Voltage regulator.
4 Armature.
5 Cut-out adjusting screw.
6 Current adjusting screw.
7 Voltage adjusting screw.
B—Terminal.
F—Terminal.
D—Terminal.

Electrical setting of current regulator
on vehicle
Operation P/52

1. When setting the current regulator on the vehicle, the dynamo must be made to develop its maximum rated output, whatever the state of charge of the battery might be at the time of setting. The voltage regulator must therefore be rendered inoperative. To do this, the voltage regulator contacts should be short-circuited with a clip large enough to bridge the outer armature assembly securing screw and the insulated fixed contact bracket, as shown in Fig. P-20.

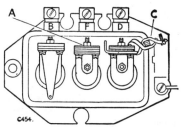

Fig. P-20—Short-circuiting voltage regulator contacts.
A—Current regulator adjusting screw.   D—Terminal.
B—Terminal.   F—Terminal.
C—Clip—short-circuiting.

2. Disconnect the cable from control box terminal B and connect a first-grade moving coil 0-40 ammeter between this cable and terminal B. Switch on all lamps and accessories. This will prevent the voltage of the system rising when the engine is started.

3. With the dynamo running at approximately 4,000 r.p.m., the ammeter needle should be steady and indicate a current of 22 amp. If it does not, the unit must be adjusted in a manner similar to that described for the voltage regulator.

Re-make the original connections.

Electrical setting of cut-out relay
                                    Operation P/54

1. Connect a first-grade moving coil 0-20 voltmeter between control box terminal D and earth. Switch on the headlamps and slowly increase the engine speed from zero. Closure of the contacts, indicated by a slight drop in the voltmeter reading, should occur between 12.7 and 13.3 volts. If it does not, the unit must be adjusted in a manner similar to that described for the voltage regulator.

   Note: When setting the cut-in voltage at a test bench, a suitable load resistor passing about 6 amperes should be connected between control box terminal B and earth. This will cause the voltmeter needle to flicker at the instant of contact closure.

2. Disconnect the cable from control box terminal B. Connect a first-grade moving coil 0-20 voltmeter between this terminal and earth. Run the engine up to speed and then slowly decelerate, noting the instant when the voltmeter reading drops to zero. This should occur between 9.5 and 10.5 volts. If it does not, adjust by carefully bowing the legs of the fixed contact post. Repeat the test and, if necessary, re-adjust until the armature releases at the voltage specified.

Cleaning contacts   Operation P/56

When cleaning the voltage or current regulator contacts, use fine carborundum stone or silicon carbide paper, followed by methylated spirits (denatured alcohol).

When cleaning the cut-out contacts, use a strip of fine glass paper—never carborundum stone or emery cloth.

Mechanical setting of air gaps—Voltage and current regulators   Operation P/58

All air-gap settings are accurately adjusted before the units leave the factory, and should require no further attention. If, however, an armature is removed for any reason, care must be taken to obtain the correct air-gap settings on re-assembly.

1. Slacken the two armature assembly securing screws so that the armature is loosely attached to the regulator frame.

2. Slacken the fixed contact locking nut and unscrew the fixed contact adjustment screw until it is well clear of the armature moving contact.

3. Slacken the voltage (or current) adjustment screw locking nut and unscrew the adjustment screw until it is well clear of the armature tension spring.

4. Using a 0.015 in. thick flat steel gauge, wide enough to cover completely the core face, insert the gauge between the underside of the armature and the copper disc. Take care not to turn up or damage the edge of this disc.

5. Press the armature squarely down against the gauge and re-tighten the two armature assembly securing screws.

6. With the gauge still in position, screw in the fixed contact adjustment screw until it just touches the armature moving contact. Re-tighten the locking nut.

7. Carry out the electrical settings, Operation P/52 or 54 as applicable.

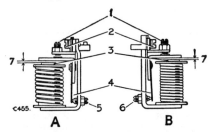

Fig. P-21—Voltage and current regulators.
A—Voltage regulator.   B—Current regulator.

1—Fixed contact adjustment   4—Armature tension springs.
   screws.   5—Voltage adjustment
2—Armature assembly securing   screws.
   screws.   6—Current adjustment
3—Cores.   screws.
       7—.015 in. (0,381 mm).

Setting cut-out relay air gap   Operation P/60

1. Slacken the two armature assembly securing screws so that the armature is loosely attached to the cut-out frame.

2. Slacken the adjustment screw locking nut and unscrew the adjustment screw until it is well clear of the armature tension spring.

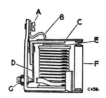

Fig. P-22—Cut-out relay.

A—Armature assembly securing screw.
B—Armature back stop.
C—Contact blade.
D—Armature tension spring.
E—Core.
F—Fixed contact post.
G—Adjustment screw.

3. Press the armature squarely down against the copper-sprayed core face and re-tighten the two armature assembly securing screws. No gauge is necessary.

4. Press the armature down against the core face and adjust the armature back stop so that a 0.018 in. (0,45 mm) gap is obtained between the tip of the back stop and the contact blade.

5. Insert a 0.010 in. (0,25 mm) thick flat steel gauge between the underside of the armature and the copper-sprayed core face. The gauge should be inserted from the side of the core nearest the fixed contact post. The leading edge of the gauge should not be inserted beyond the centre line of the core face. Press the armature down against the gauge and check the cut-out contacts. These should be just touching. If necessary adjust the height of the fixed contact by carefully bowing the legs of the fixed contact post.

6. Reset the cut-in voltage (Operation P/54) and lock the adjustment screw.

To remove   Operation P/62

1. Disconnect the positive lead of R.H. battery and the leads to regulator box.

2. Remove the securing bolts and withdraw the regulator unit.

To refit   Operation P/64

1. Reverse removal procedure, connecting wiring in accordance with the appropriate wiring diagram.

Headlamp, early models

To remove   Operation P/66

1. Remove the two bolts and clamps securing the radiator grille and lift out the grille from its sockets.

2. Slacken the fixing screw at the top of the lamp and swing it upwards. Remove the front from the top of the lamp first.

3. The reflector is secured to the lamp by means of a rubber bead and can now be withdrawn.

4. Withdraw the two screws securing the wiring and detach the wires.

5. Remove the large nut and shakeproof washer securing the headlamp to its bracket and remove the lamp.

Headlamp, late models

To remove   Operation P/68

1. Remove the securing screw from the lower side of rim and ease the rim off from the bottom.

2. Remove the dust-excluding rubber.

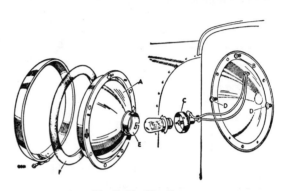

Fig. P-23—Headlamp.

A—Light unit.
B—Vertical setting adjusting screw.
C—Back shell.
D—Horizontal setting adjusting screws.
E—Bulb holder.
F—Dust-excluding rubber.

3. Press in the light unit against the tension of the screw springs and turn in an anti-clockwise direction until the heads of the screws can be disengaged through the slotted holes in the light unit rim.

4. Disconnect the wiring from the bulb socket assembly.

5. Remove the headlamp body complete with grommet from the radiator grille panel.

NOTE:

Non-split type headlamp rim

To remove   Operation P/70

Where fitted, the non-split type rim is removed by removing the set screw, located at the bottom of the rim, and then springing the rim off. The unit is then removed as in Operation P/68.

To refit   Operation P/72

Spring the rim back into position, having first replaced the dirt excluder rubber, and replace set screw and tighten.

Replacement bulbs, 1948-53

Position	Make and Type	Voltage	Wattage	
Headlamps R.H. (Home models)	Lucas No. 162	12	36 Single filament	⎫ Vertical
Headlamps L.H. (Home models)	Lucas No. 300	12	36/36 Double filament (dip to left)	⎬ fluted glass
Headlamps (R.H.D. Export models)	Lucas No. 300	12	36/36 Double filament (dip to left)	⎭ in light unit
Headlamps (L.H.D. Export models except North American vehicles)	Lucas No. 301	12	36/36 Double filament (dip to right)	
Headlamps (R.H.D. models)	Lucas No. 354	12	42/36 Double filament (dip to left)	⎫ Block glass
Headlamps (L.H.D. models except Europe)	Lucas No. 355	12	42/36 Double filament (dip to right)	⎬ in
Headlamps (Europe except France)	Lucas No. 360	12	45/35 Double filament (Duplo)	⎭ light unit
Sidelamps (dash fixing)	Lucas No. 207	12	6 Single pole	
Sidelamps (wing fixing)	Lucas No. 989	12	6 Single pole	
Stop/tail lamps (except North American vehicles)	Lucas No. 207	12	6 Single pole	
Stop/tail lamps (North American vehicles)	Lucas No. 361	12	18/6 Double filament	
Instrument panel lights	Lucas No. 207	12	6 Single pole	
Ignition and mixture control warning lights	Lucas No. 970	2.5	.5 M.E.S. ⎱ Alternatives, check	
	Lucas No. 987	12	2.2 M.E.S. ⎰ before ordering	
Oil pressure and headlamp warning lights	Lucas No. 987	12	2.2 M.E.S.	
Rear number plate lamp	Lucas No. 989	12	6 Single pole	

Replacement bulbs, 1954

Position	Make and Type	Voltage	Wattage
Headlamps (R.H.D. models)	Lucas No. 354	12	42/36 Double filament (dip to left)
Headlamps (L.H.D. models except North America and Europe)	Lucas No. 301	12	36/36 Double filament (dip to right)
Headlamps (Europe except France)	Lucas No. 360	12	45/35 Double filament (Duplo) (vertical dip)
Headlamps (France and North America)	Special	12	—
Sidelamps	Lucas No. 222	12	4
Stop/tail lamps (except North American vehicles)	Lucas No. 207	12	6
Stop/tail lamps (North American vehicles)	Lucas No. 361	12	18/6 Double filament
Rear number plate lamp	Lucas No. 222	12	4
Instrument panel lights	Lucas No. 987	12	2.2 M.E.S.
Warning lights	Lucas No. 987	12	2.2 M.E.S.

Replacement bulbs, 1955-58

Position	Make and Type	Voltage	Wattage
Headlamps (R.H.D. models)	Lucas No. 354	12	42/36 Double filament (dip to left)
Headlamps (L.H.D. models except North America and Europe)	Lucas No. 355	12	42/36 Double filament (dip to right)
Headlamps (Europe except France)	Lucas No. 370	12	45/40 Double filament (Duplo) (vertical dip)
Headlamps (France and North America)	Special	12	—
Sidelamps	Lucas No. 222	12	4
Stop/tail lamps	Lucas No. 380	12	21/6 Double filament
Rear number plate lamps (North American vehicles)	Lucas No. 222	12	4
Instrument panel lights	Lucas No. 987	12	2.2 M.E.S.
Warning lights	Lucas No. 987	12	2.2 M.E.S.

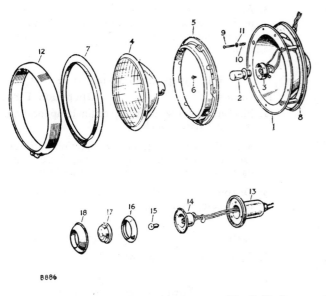

B886

Fig. P-24—Layout of lamps.

1 Body for headlamp

2 Bulb for headlamp

3 Adaptor for bulb, double contact

4 Light unit, "block-pattern" lens

5 Rim complete for light unit

6 Special screw for light unit rim

7 Rubber gasket for headlamp rim

8 Gasket for body

9 Special screw ⎫

10 Spring for screw   ⎬ Light unit adjustment

11 Cup washer for screw ⎭

12 Rim for headlamp, vehicle colour

13 Body

14 Bulb interior

15 Bulb for side lamp

16 Gasket for body

17 Glass

18 Rim complete

19 Stop tail lamp complete

20 Bulb (12v. 6w.) for stop tail lamp

21 Glass for number plate illumination, white

22 Glass for stop and tail lights, red

23 Gasket for number plate illumination glass

24 Gasket for stop tail glass

25 Spring retaining glasses

26 Screw fixing body

27 Rubber body

28 Bulb for stop tail lamp

29 Glass

30 Rim for glass

31 Number plate lamp

32 Bulb for number plate lamp

33 Glass

34 Rubber grommet for wire

35 Rubber gasket for lamp

36 Support for lamp

To refit, adjust and re-focus, early models
Operation P/74

1. Replace the headlamps by reversing the sequence of operations detailed for removal.

2. The setting of the headlamps should be checked by placing the vehicle in front of a blank wall at the greatest possible distance, taking care that the surface on which the vehicle is standing is not sloping relative to the wall. The lamps are fitted with dual filament bulbs and must be set so that the main beams of light are parallel with the road and with each other.

3. Slacken the fixing nut at the top of the lamp and move the lamp on its adjustable mounting to the required position. Tighten the locking nut. The mounting is accessible when the bonnet top panel is raised.

4. If Lucas Genuine Spare Bulbs are fitted it should be unnecessary to alter the setting of the lamp when a bulb is renewed. If, however, an ordinary bulb has to be fitted, it may be necessary to re-focus. If the lamp does not give a uniform long range beam without a dark centre, the bulb needs adjusting; when focusing it is an advantage to cover one lamp while testing the other.

To re-focus, slacken off the screw on the clip and move the bulb backwards and forwards until the best lighting is obtained.

Tighten the clamping clip after the best position for the bulb has been found.

To refit and adjust, late models
Operation P/76

1. Reverse the removal procedure.

2. Adjustment in a vertical plane is effected by turning the spring-loaded screw at the top of the lamp body.

3. Adjustment in a horizontal plane is made by means of the screw at each side of the unit.

To adjust headlamps, using beam setting board
Operation P/78

1. Mark on a board the dimensions given in Fig. P-25 and position the vehicle, unladen, on level ground.

2. Place the board 12 ft. (365 cm) in front of the headlamps, ensuring that it is at right angles to the vehicle centre line and that the centre line on board is in the same plane as vehicle centre line.

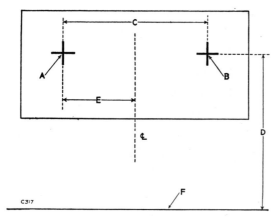

Fig. P-25—Headlamp beam setting board, 1954-58 models

A—Concentrated area of light— L.H. headlamp.
B—Concentrated area of light— R. H. headlamp.
C—20 in. (508 mm).
D—(86 and 88 models) 35½ in. (902 mm). (107 and 109 models) 37¼ in. (946 mm).
E—10 in. (254 mm).
F—Ground level.

3. Adjust the beam by turning the screws indicated in Fig. P-23 until the area of concentrated light corresponds with the marks on beam setting board.

Side lamp, dash fixing type
To remove Operation P/80

1. Slacken the screw at the top of the lamp locating it in the dash panel.

2. Turn the lamp in a clockwise direction until the tongue at the bottom is disengaged from the dash and withdraw the lamp front and reflector.

3. Disconnect the feed wire and remove the side lamp complete.

To refit Operation P/82

1. Reverse the removal procedure.

Side lamp, wing fixing type
To remove Operation P/84

1. Disconnect the leads at the snap connectors, alongside the radiator cowl.

2. Lever the rubber bead away from the lamp and remove the rim and glass from the bottom of the rim lamp.

3. If required, remove the bulb.

4. Remove the lamp and grommet from the wing.

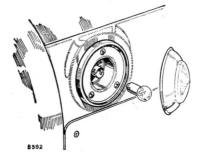

Fig. P-26— Side lamp

To refit Operation P/86
Reverse the removal procedure.

Stop and tail lamp—1954 models
(Except North American vehicles)
To remove Operation P/88

1. Slacken the securing screw and swing open the stop and tail lamp cover; disconnect the wiring from the connectors.

2. Remove the lamp complete from the rear of the body.

To refit Operation P/90

Reverse the removal procedure, reconnecting the wiring in accordance with the wiring diagram.

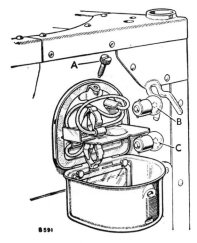

Fig. P-27—
Stop, tail lamp—
1954 models

A—Securing screw.
B—Stop bulb.
C—Tail lamp bulb.

Stop and tail lamp—1955-57 models

To remove   Operation P/92

1. Disconnect the three snap connectors securing the tail lamp harness to the main wiring harness, beneath the wheel box, adjacent to the chassis frame side member.

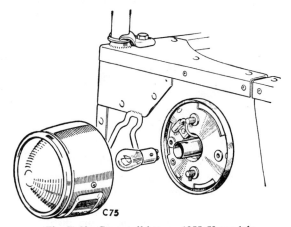

Fig. P-28—Stop, tail lamp—1955-58 models.
A—Securing bolt.
B—Double filament bulb.
C—Cover.

2. Withdraw the tail lamp harness through rubber grommet in wheel box.

3. Remove the two securing bolts and locking washers on the inside of body rear panel, then withdraw the lamp and harness complete.

To refit   Operation P/94

1. Reverse the removal procedure. Reconnect harness in accordance with wiring diagram.

Stop and tail lamp—1954 models
(North American vehicles)

To remove and refit   Operation P/96

See Operations P/88 and P/90.

Rear number plate lamp
(North American vehicles only)

To remove   Operation P/98

1. Remove the small screw in the centre of the lamp and remove the cover.

2. Disconnect the wiring.

3. Remove the lamp from the rear number plate support.

To refit   Operation P/100

1. Reverse the removal procedure.

Horn

The horn is adjusted on initial assembly and should not require attention for some considerable time.

Ascertain that horn failure or faulty note is not due to some outside source, such as a discharged battery, loose connections or loose horn mounting, before carrying out any adjustment.

Horn—80, 86 and 107 models

To remove   Operation P/102

1. R.H.D. models.   Remove the radiator grille.

2. With the ignition switched off, disconnect the wires from the horn.

3. Remove the horn complete from the front chassis cross-member.

To refit   Operation P/104

Reverse the removal procedure.

Horn—88 and 109 models

To remove   Operation P/106

1. Lift bonnet.

2. With the ignition switched off, disconnect the wires from the horn.

3. Remove horn from bonnet hinge position.

To refit   Operation P/108

Reverse the removal procedure.

Adjustment of windtone horn
Operation P/110

Lucas

1. Disconnect the leads at the snap connectors adjacent to the horn, then remove the securing bolts and withdraw the unit.

2. Remove the dome and dome securing clip, clean the points and adjust them until they are almost touching, then turn the adjusting screw **half a** turn to increase the gap.

3. If adjustment of the horn does not produce satisfactory results, the horn should be returned to the makers.

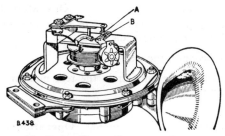

Fig. P-29—Horn adjustment. Lucas.
A—Adjustable contact.   B—Locknut.

Clear Hooters

4. Remove the horn—Operation P/106, then remove the dome and dome clip.

5. Connect the horn leads to a 12-volt battery and adjust nut (A) until maximum volume is obtained, then lock in position with nut (B). See Fig. P-30.

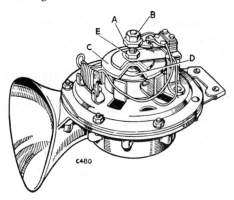

Fig. P-30—Horn adjustment. Clear Hooters.
A—Adjusting nut.   C—Armature.
B—Locknut.   D—Magnet core.
E—Locknut—armature.

6. Adjust the air gap between armature (C) and the magnet core face (D) to .045-.050 in. (1,1-1,3 mm) by slackening nut (E) and turn the armature (C) clockwise or anti-clockwise until the recommended distance is obtained, then tighten nut (E). The current consumption with horn correctly adjusted is 9 amperes.

Dip switch and horn button
To remove (86 and 107 models)
                                    Operation P/112

1. Disconnect the wires protruding from the bottom of the steering column by withdrawing the wires from the junction box on the dash.

2. Slacken the clamp bolt holding the stator tube at the bottom of the steering column.

3. Withdraw the stator tube, horn button and dipper switch complete.

4. Remove the horn button and dipper switch from the stator tube.

To refit (86 and 107 models) Operation P/114
Reverse the removal procedure, spacing the rubber and felt bushes on the stator tube before insertion in the control column, as these eliminate vibration noises.

Dip switch, to remove (88 and 109 models)
                                    Operation P/116

1. Disconnect the dip switch leads at junction box.

2. Remove the securing screws and withdraw the switch from toe board.

Dip switch, to refit (88 and 109 models)
                                    Operation P/118

1. Reverse removal procedure and reconnect the leads in accordance with wiring diagram.

Horn button, to remove (88 and 109 models)
                                    Operation P/120

1. Remove the securing screws and withdraw the horn button and leads.

2. Disconnect the leads if necessary.

Horn button, to refit (88 and 109 models)
                                    Operation P/122

1. Reverse removal procedure.

Ignition—Petrol models
Distributor
To remove   **Operation P/124**

1. Pull off the sparking plug covers and detach the plug leads; disconnect the vacuum pipe, L.T. and H.T. leads.

2. Remove the set bolt securing the distributor clamp to the distributor mounting plate.

3. Remove the distributor complete with clamp.

To refit   **Operation P/126**

1. Reverse the removal procedure; set the contact breaker gap to .014 to .016 in. (0,35 to 0,40 mm). The driving spigot on the distributor drive shaft is offset, so eliminating any possibility of mistiming the engine on replacement.

Coil
To remove   **Operation P/128**

1. With the ignition switched off, disconnect the high and low tension leads from the coil.

2. Remove the coil from the dash panel.

To refit   **Operation P/130**

1. Reverse the removal procedure.

Stop lamp switch
To remove   **Operation P/132**

1. With the ignition switched off, disconnect the two wires from the stop lamp switch.

2. Unhook the spring connecting the switch to the brake lever.

3. Remove the switch from the chassis bracket.

To refit   **Operation P/134**

Reverse the removal procedure.

Heater plugs—Diesel models

The heater plugs do not require any maintenance. However, if at any time when the heater plugs are in use, the warning light glows very brightly, a short circuit in the system is indicated. No light will indicate an open circuit.

Note: Great care must be taken not to twist the centre terminal when removing heater plug leads.

Fault location on heater plug circuit
Operation P/136

(a) Examine the fuse at terminal A3 and replace if "blown".

(b) Failure of the warning light bulb will not affect the heater plug circuit, but the bulb should be replaced when conveniently possible—Section Q.

(c) Connect one lead of the test lamp to the earth lead terminal on No. 1 heater plug and the other lead to the L.H. battery negative terminal, whereon the bulb should light. If the bulb remains unlit, a corroded, loose, or disconnected heater plug earth lead is indicated.

Move the test lamp lead from the earth terminal on No. 1 heater plug, to the terminal also on No. 1 plug, to which the inter-connecting lead is attached. If the plug is serviceable the bulb will light but a broken heater plug filament will be indicated by the lamp remaining unlit.

Check the remaining plugs in the same manner until the fault is located.

If the heater plugs are found serviceable check each terminal of the resistance unit in the same way.

Removal, cleaning and inspection of heater plugs   **Operation P/138**

The shape of the heater plug element and its position in relation to the plug body is important and care must therefore be taken when fitting, removing or cleaning the plug, to avoid distortion or damage to the element.

1. Disconnect the leads from plugs, using two spanners at each terminal to prevent the central rod or insulating tube twisting.

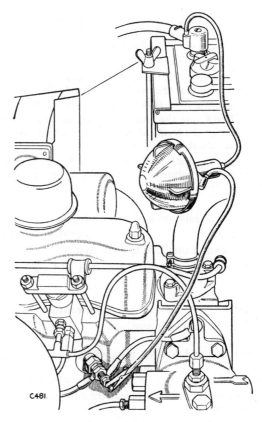

Fig. P-31—Checking heater plug circuit.

2. Remove carbon from base of heater plug to avoid possible short circuiting of the element. Do **not** sandblast.

3. Examine the element for signs of fracture or severe heat attack and the seating for scores. Plugs with fractured element must be replaced. Where scoring of the seating is sufficient to allow gas leakage or erosion of the element such that a fracture is likely to occur, then a replacement plug must be fitted.

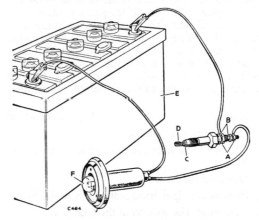

Fig. P-32—Testing heater plug circuit.

A—Terminal nuts.   D—Element.
B—Insulation.   E—12 volt battery.
C—Seating.   F—Bulb (12. v.)

4. Test the plug internal circuit for continuity, by connecting it **and** a 12 volt side-lamp bulb in circuit, to a 12 volt battery.

The inclusion of a bulb in circuit is **essential**.

5. Ensure that the terminal nuts and threads are clean and that the thread at base of plug is free of carbon, then refit the plugs and tighten.

Note: Make sure the shakeproof washers are fitted under the terminal in order to maintain good electrical contact.

Replace the leads in accordance with the wiring diagram and tighten the terminals, using two spanners to each terminal.

Resistance--heater plugs
To remove　　　　　　**Operation P/140**
1. Disconnect the leads from resistance.
2. Remove the securing screws and withdraw the unit.

To refit　　　　　　**Operation P/142**
1. Reverse removal procedure.

Starter and heater plug switch—Diesel models
To remove　　　　　　**Operation P/144**
1. Disconnect the positive lead from the right-hand battery.
2. Disconnect the leads from the back of the starter switch.
3. Remove the large securing nut from facia side of panel.
4. Withdraw switch.

To refit　　　　　　**Operation P/146**
1. Reverse removal procedure, connecting leads in accordance with the appropriate wiring diagram.

Fuel gauge tank unit
No adjustment or repair is permissible to the fuel contents gauge tank unit. If the gauge reads wrongly or—Diesel models—the fuel level warning light does not glow when two or less gallons only remain in the tank, the lead(s) at the tank unit should be checked for security. If the fault is not corrected by tightening the terminal(s), remove and test the warning light and check the tank unit by substitution.

To renew　　　　　　**Operation P/148**
1. Disconnect the battery.
   Diesel—disconnect the positive lead from R.H. battery.
2. Drain off the fuel.
3. Remove the right-hand seat and raise the locker.
4. Disconnect the wire from the tank unit.
5. Remove the gauge unit from the fuel tank complete with joint washer.
6 Fit the new unit and cork washer; complete

the assembly by reversing the removal procedure, connecting lead(s) in accordance with the appropriate wiring diagram.

Fuse and junction boxes
To remove　　　　　　**Operation P/150**
1. Disconnect the battery.
   Diesel—Disconnect the positive lead from the R.H. battery.
2. Remove the cover and disconnect the leads.
3. Remove the securing screws and withdraw the unit.

On certain early vehicles, the fuse is housed in a separate box mounted adjacent to the voltage control box. To remove, proceed as follows:—
1. Disconnect the battery.
2. Remove the fuse box cover, by springing aside the cover clip.
3. Disconnect all wires from the fuse box by loosening the grub screws.
4. Remove the two screws and nuts securing the fuse box to the mounting plate and remove the fuse box.

To refit　　　　　　**Operation P/152**
1. Reverse removal procedure and reconnect the leads in accordance with wiring diagram.

Windscreen wiper motor
To remove　　　　　　**Operation P/154**
1. Slacken the wiper arm fixing nut and tap sharply to release the clamp collet, then remove the wiper arm and blade.
2. With the key in lamp switch turned "off", disconnect the leads from wiper motor.
3. Remove the securing nuts, washers, grommets, wiper blade stop, rubber mounting block and brass brushes, then withdraw the motor.

To refit　　　　　　**Operation P/156**
1. Reverse removal procedure, but do not lock the wiper arm blade until the sweep is correctly adjusted.

Mixture control thermostat switch—Petrol engines
To renew　　　　　　**Operation P/158**
1. Disconnect the wire from the thermostat switch.
2. Remove the switch from the cylinder head rear end cover.
3. Check the switch: Contact is made at 51-54°C (124-129°F); contact is broken at 47-53°C (117-127°F).
4. Fit the new switch by reversing the removal procedure.
   Note: Renewal of the second switch in the mixture control warning light circuit (at the manual control) is dealt with in Section Q.

DEFECT LOCATION

Symptom, Cause and Remedy

A—BATTERY DISCHARGED

1. Battery unserviceable—*Renew.*
2. Battery leads corroded or loose—*Clean and tighten.*
3. Voltage or current voltage regulator faulty—*Rectify or renew.*
4. Dynamo faulty—*Rectify.*

B—DYNAMO NOT CHARGING OR CHARGING AT REDUCED RATE

1. Slipping fan belt—*Tighten.*
2. Dynamo loose on mounting—*Tighten.*
3. Continuity of circuit broken—*See Page P-16.*
4. Brushes excessively worn—*Renew.*
5. Commutator burnt or worn unevenly—*Skim the surface in lathe.*
6. Commutator glazed—*Clean with fine glass paper.*
7. Voltage or current voltage regulator faulty—*Rectify or renew.*
8. Dynamo internal circuit faulty—*Dismantle and check.*

C—LAMPS DIM WHEN ENGINE REVOLUTIONS ARE LOW.

1. Faulty earth—*Check earthing points of lamps affected.*
2. Battery in a low state of charge—*See Symptom* A.

D—BULBS FAIL FREQUENTLY

1. Battery in a low state of charge—*See Symptom* A.
2. Voltage or current voltage regulator faulty—*Rectify or renew.*
3. Loose connections—*Tighten.*
4. Wrong type of bulb used—*See bulb chart.*

E—HORN FAILURE.

1. Loose connections—*Tighten.*
2. Burnt or loose contact points—*Clean and adjust. See Page P-23.*

F—INSTRUMENT PANEL LIGHTS FAIL—*See Section Q.*

Ga—STARTER FAILS TO OPERATE—PETROL MODELS.

1. Stiff engine, indicated by inability to turn by hand—*Locate and remedy.*

   If the engine can be turned by hand, the trouble may be due to:—
2. Battery discharged—*Start by hand. Charging the battery either by a long period of daylight running, or from independent electrical supply.*
3. Broken or loose connection in starter circuit—*Check and tighten all battery, starter and starter switch connections and check the cables connecting these units for damage.*
4. Greasy, charred or glazed commutator—*Clean.*
5. Brushes worn, not fitted correctly or wrong type—*Renew.*
6. Brushes sticking in holders or incorrectly tensioned—*Rectify.*
7. Starter pinion jammed in mesh with flywheel—*Rotate the squared end of the starter shaft with a spanner to free the pinion.*

Gb—STARTER FAILS TO OPERATE—DIESEL MODELS

1. Battery discharged—*Re-charge.*
2. Starter/heater switch unserviceable—*Renew.*
3. Wiring at starter/heater switch loose—*Tighten.*
4. Solenoid unserviceable—*Renew.*
5. Wiring at solenoid loose—*Tighten.*
6. Brushes unduly worn—*Renew.*
7. Brush springs fatigued—*Renew.*
8. Commutator greasy or dirty—*Clean with petrol-moistened cloth.*
9. Commutator burnt or worn unevenly—*Remove armature, and skim.*
10. Fault in internal circuit—*Dismantle and check.*
11. Starter solenoid badly earthed—*Clean and tighten connections.*

H—STARTER OPERATES BUT ENGINE IS NOT CRANKED

1. Petrol models: Starter drive pinion not engaging with the flywheel, due to dirt on the screwed sleeve—*Clean.*

   Diesel models: Plate clutch pinion faulty—*Remove starter and dismantle to ascertain cause.*

J—STARTER PINION WILL NOT DISENGAGE FROM FLYWHEEL.

1. Petrol models: Starter pinion jammed in mesh with the flywheel—*Rotate squared end of starter shaft with a spanner until pinion flies off. On no account run the engine or serious damage to the starter will result.*

   Diesel models: Return spring in starter broken—*Dismantle starter and renew.*

K—ENGINE WILL NOT FIRE—PETROL MODELS.

1. The starter will not turn the engine due to a discharged battery—*Start the engine by hand. The battery should be recharged by running the car for a long period during daylight or from an independent electrical supply.*
2. Sparking plugs faulty, dirty or incorrect plug gaps—*Rectify or renew.*
3. Defective coil or distributor—*Remove the lead from the centre distributor terminal and hold it approximately $\frac{1}{4}$ in. from some metal part of the engine while the engine is being turned over. If the sparks jump the gap regularly, the coil and distributor are functioning correctly. Renew a defective coil or distributor.*
4. A fault in the low tension wiring is indicated by no ammeter reading when the engine is turned slowly with the ignition on. or no spark occurs between the contacts when separated quickly with the fingers with the ignition on—*Examine all the ignition cables and check that the battery terminals are secure and not corroded.*
5. Dirty or pitted contacts—*Clean.*
6. Contact breaker out of adjustment—*Adjust.*
7. Controls not set correctly or trouble other than ignition—*See Instruction Manual "STARTING PROCEDURE."*

M—ENGINE MISFIRES—PETROL MODELS.

1. See items (2), (5) and (6) under "Engine will not fire" and refer to Section A.

N—ENGINE FAILS TO START FROM COLD—DIESEL MODELS.

1. Heater plug circuit broken—*See Operation P/136.*

P—IGNITION AND MIXTURE DEFECTS—PETROL MODELS—DEFECTIVE DISTRIBUTOR.

1. Contact breaker gap incorrect or points burned and pitted—*Clean and adjust.*

2. Distributor cap cracked—*Renew.*

3. Condenser failure—*Renew.*

4. Weak or broken contact breaker spring—*Renew.*

5. Excessive wear in distributor shaft bushes, etc.—*Renew.*

6. Rotor arm pitted or burned—*Clean or renew.*

Q—MIXTURE CONTROL WARNING LIGHT FAILS TO APPEAR WHEN ENGINE REACHES RUNNING TEMPERATURE.

1. Mixture control already pushed in—*In the hands of the operator.*

2. Broken connection in warning light circuit—*Rectify.*

3. Faulty thermostat switch (at cylinder head)—*Renew.*

4. Faulty manual switch (at mixture control)—*Renew Section Q.*

5. Broken operating mechanism at manual switch—*Rectify.*

R—MIXTURE CONTROL WARNING LIGHT REMAINS ON WITH ENGINE AT RUNNING TEMPERATURE.

1. Mixture control out—*Push control right in.*

2. Faulty manual switch—*Renew. Section Q.*

3. Broken operating mechanism at manual switch—*Rectify.*

DATA

Batteries

Petrol models	.... Single 12 volt, positive earth
Capacity	.... 51 A.H.
Diesel models	.... Two 6 volt, series connected, positive earth
Capacity	.... 120 A.H.

Starter Motor

Petrol models

Nominal voltage	 12
Starting shaft end-float	.... Zero

Diesel models

Nominal voltage	 12
Starting shaft end-float	.... Zero
Lock torque	.... 32.5 lb./ft. (4,49 Kg/m)
Torque at 1,000 r.p.m.	.... 15 lb./ft. (2,14 Kg/m)

Starter motor drive

Petrol models	.... Spring-loaded pinion and sleeve
Diesel models	.... Multi-plate clutch
Slip load	.... 800 to 950 lb./in. (142,86 to 169,5 Kg/cm)

Dynamo

Petrol models

Maximum output	.... 19 amps

Diesel models

Maximum output	.... 22 amps

Control box

Petrol models	.... Compensated voltage control
Diesel models	.... Compensated current/voltage control
Voltage regulator—open circuit setting 20°C (68°F) at 2,000 r.p.m.	.... 14.2 to 14.8 volts
Current regulator—Contact opening amperage	 19
Cut-in voltage	.... 12.7 to. 13.3 volts

Distributor

Contact breaker gap	.... .014 to .016 in. (0,35 to 0,40 mm)
Distributor rotation	.... Clockwise, at drive end
Advance mechanism	.... Centrifugal/vacuum

Fuse

....	.... Protects the horn, windscreen wiper, and on early models also fuel tank level unit and stop lights.
Amperage	 35

Heater plugs

Type	.... K.L.G. B.R.Q.1 coil element—1.7 volts 36/40 amps.

Stop lamp switch

Type	.... Mechanical

Mixture control thermostat switch

Contact made at	.... 51-54°C (124-129°F)
Contact broken at	.... 47-53°C (117-127°F)

Section Q
INSTRUMENTS AND CONTROLS — ALL MODELS

INDEX

	Page			Page
Accelerator controls	Q-7 and Q-8	Instruments and switches		Q-1 and Q-2
Cut-off control	Q-9	Mixture control		.... Q-9
Hand throttle control	Q-8 and Q-9	Speedometer cable	....	.... Q-7

LIST OF ILLUSTRATIONS

Fig.		Page	Fig.		Page
Q-1	Layout of instruments and controls, 1948-53 models	Q-2	Q-6	Correct position of speedometer drive cable, 1954-58 models	Q-8
Q-2	Layout of instruments and controls, 1954-58 models	Q-3	Q-7	Layout of accelerator and linkage, 1948-53 models	Q-10
Q-3	Exploded view of instrument panel, 1948-53 models	Q-4	Q-8	Layout of accelerator and linkage (R.H.D.), 1954-57 models	Q-12
Q-4	Exploded view of instrument panel, 1954-58 models	Q-6	Q-9	Accelerator controls, Petrol models, 1958	Q-13
Q-5	Correct position of speedometer drive cable, 1948-53 models	Q-7	Q-10	Accelerator and hand speed controls, Diesel models	Q-14

Instruments and switches, 1948-53 models

To remove   **Operation Q/2**

1. Disconnect the battery.

2. Remove the four set screws and plain washers securing the panel to the dash and withdraw the panel clear of the dash.

3. Disconnect the speedometer drive cable by unscrewing the knurled union nut.

4. Remove the panel light and speedometer retaining bracket by removing two nuts and spring washers.

5. Withdraw the speedometer from the front of the panel.

6. Remove the panel light bulb from its holder.

7. Disconnect the wiring from the terminals on the petrol gauge.

8. Remove the petrol level gauge bracket, the second panel light and two earthing wires by removing the knurled nut.

9. Withdraw the petrol level gauge from the front of the instrument panel.

10. Remove the second panel light bulb from its holder.

11. Disconnect the wiring from the oil pressure warning light and pull out the bakelite bulb holder from its socket.

12. Unscrew the oil pressure warning light bulb.

13. Turn the locking ring on the oil pressure warning light case until the ring and spring can be removed.

14. Withdraw the oil pressure warning light case from the front of the panel.

15. Disconnect the wires from the rear of the ammeter.

16. Prise up the securing tabs on the case of the ammeter and remove the ammeter from the front of the panel.

17. Unscrew the ignition and mixture control warning light bezels from the instrument panel and remove the bulbs.

18. Disconnect the wires from the rear of the ignition and mixture control warning lights. (One wire on each light must be unsoldered.)

19. After compressing the retaining springs and removing the circlips, withdraw the ignition and mixture control warning lights from the front of the panel.

20. Disconnect the wires from the rear of the ignition and lamp switch.

21. Release the switch retaining clip by removing the screw and nut.

22. Withdraw the switch complete from the front of the panel.

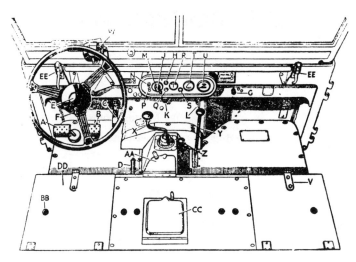

Fig. Q-1—Layout of instruments and controls—1948-53 models.

A—Clutch pedal
B—Brake pedal
C—Accelerator pedal
D—Hand brake
E—Horn button
F—Headlamp dipper switch
G—Mixture control
H—Mixture control warning light
J—Ignition switch
K—Starter switch

L—Slow-running control
M—Lamp switch
N—Instrument panel light switch
P—Lead lamp socket
Q—Charging warning light
R—Ammeter
S—Oil pressure warning light
T—Petrol level gauge
U—Speedometer
V—Access to petrol filler and brake fluid

W—Windscreen wiper
X—Main gear change lever
Y—Transfer box change lever
Z—Front wheel drive lock
AA—Access cover for gearbox filler
BB—Location hole for seat
CC—Access cover for power take-off control
DD—Tool-box
EE—Windscreen clamp

23. Disconnect the wires from the rear of the panel light switch.

24. Unscrew the knob from the panel light switch.

25. Remove the locknut securing the switch to the panel and withdraw the switch from the rear of the panel.

26. Remove the two inspection lamp sockets by removing the nuts securing the wiring at the rear of the sockets and withdrawing the sockets from the front of the panel.

27. **North American vehicles only.** Disconnect the wire from the headlamp main beam warning light; unscrew the bezel and remove the light from the rear of the panel. If necessary, remove the bulb by withdrawing from the rear of the light body.

Instruments and switches
1954-58 models

To remove　　　　　　　Operation Q/4

1. Disconnect the battery.

   Diesel—disconnect the positive lead of R.H. battery.

2. Remove the panel from the dash.

3. Disconnect the speedometer drive cable.

4. Remove the panel light bulb and holder from the speedometer. If necessary, unscrew the bulb from its holder.

5. Remove the speedometer retaining bracket (this action will also release an earth wire) and withdraw the speedometer.

6. Disconnect the wiring from the panel light switch.

7. Unscrew the knob and securing nut from the switch and remove the panel light switch from the panel.

8. Disconnect the wires from the mixture or heater plug warning light.

9. Compress the retaining spring, remove the circlip and withdraw the mixture or heater plug warning light. If necessary, unscrew the bezel from the warning light bakelite holder and withdraw the bulb.

10. Disconnect the wires from the dynamo warning light.

11. Compress the retaining spring, remove the circlip and withdraw the dynamo warning light. If necessary, unscrew the bezel from the warning light bakelite holder and withdraw the bulb.

12. **Diesel**—disconnect the wires from the fuel level warning light, unscrew the lens from the front of instrument panel and withdraw the unit. The bulb may be removed if necessary by easing the smaller diameter of the lamp body from the larger section.

   Note: Diesel—fuel level warning lamp bulb replacement can only be effected by removing the instrument panel.

13. Disconnect the wires from the ignition or auxiliary services and lamp switch.

14. Release the retaining clip and withdraw the ignition or auxiliary services and lamp switch complete.

15. Withdraw the headlamp main beam warning light bulb and holder from the multiple gauge unit. If necessary, unscrew the bulb from its holder.

16. Disconnect the wiring to the ammeter and fuel gauge and withdraw the multiple gauge illumination bulb and holder. If necessary, unscrew the bulb from its holder.

17. Remove the multiple gauge from the panel (this action will also release two earthing wires). The sections of the gauge can be removed separately.

18. Disconnect the wires from the two inspection lamp sockets and withdraw the sockets.

19. Disconnect the wires from the oil pressure warning light.

20. Compress the retaining spring, remove the circlip and withdraw the oil pressure warning light. If necessary, unscrew the bulb from its holder.

To refit, all models   Operation Q/6

Reverse the removal procedure, connecting the wiring in accordance with the appropriate wiring diagram, Section P. Replacement bulbs are listed in Section P.

Note: Care should be taken when re-connecting the lamp switch wiring on North American vehicles, as it is so arranged that the sidelamps are extinguished when the headlamps are switched on.

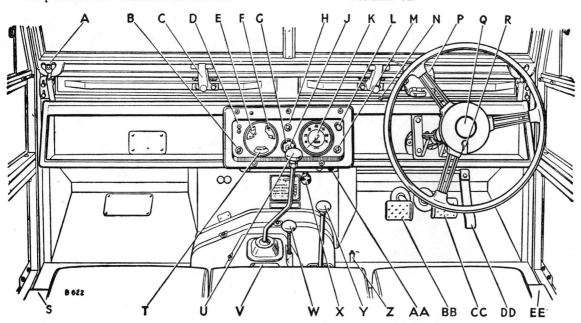

Fig. Q-2—Layout of instruments and controls—1954-58 models.

A—Wing nuts securing windscreen.
B—Oil pressure warning light.
C—Windscreen ventilators (Section R)
D—Lead lamp socket.
E—Ammeter.
F—Petrol level gauge.
G—Lamp switch.
H—Ignition warning light.
J—Ignition switch.
K—Speedometer.
L—Instrument panel light switch.
M—Mixture control warning light.
N—Wiper lead plug.
P—Windscreen wiper (Section P).
Q—Horn button (Section P).

R—Headlamp dipper switch (Section P).
S—Access to tool locker.
T—Headlamp warning light.
U—Main gear change lever (Section C).
V—Access to gearbox oil filler.
W—Front wheel drive control (Section C).
X—Starter switch (Section P).
Y—Transfer box lever (Section C).
Z—Hand brake (Section H).
AA—Mixture control.
BB—Clutch pedal (Section B).
CC—Brake pedal (Section H).
DD—Accelerator pedal (Section M).
EE—Access to petrol tank and brake fluid reservoir.

Certain items are dealt with in other sections of this manual as indicated.

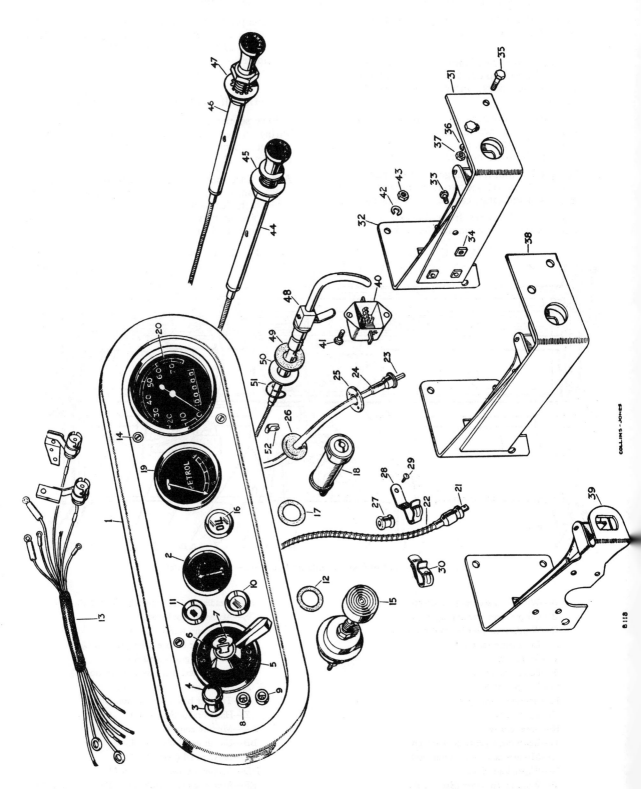

Fig. Q-3—Exploded view of instrument panel—1948-53 models

Key to Fig Q-3

1 Instrument panel
2 Ammeter
3 Panel light switch
4 Knob for switch
5 Lamp and ignition switch
6 Barrel lock for ignition switch
7 Key for lock
8-9 Inspection lamp sockets
10 Ignition warning light
11 Mixture control warning light
12 Washer for warning lights
13 Panel harness
14 Screw fixing panel
15 Starter switch
16 Oil pressure warning light
17 Washer for warning light
18 Headlamp warning light
19 Petrol level gauge
20 Speedometer
21 Inner cable } Speedometer
22 Outer cable } drive*

23 Inner cable } Speedometer
24 Outer cable } drive†
25 Retainer plate for cable†
26-27 Rubber grommets for cable
28-30 Clips for cable grommets
31 Bracket for mixture control } **
32 Support for bracket
33-34 Fixings: support to bracket
35-37 Fixings for brackets
38 Bracket for mixture control††
39 Bracket for mixture control‡
40 Switch for warning light
41-43 Fixings for switch
44 Mixture control } ‡‡
45 Washer for mixture control
46 Mixture control } †
47 Shakeproof washer for control
48 Hand throttle control
49 Cork washer for control
50-51 Fixings for hand throttle
52 Clip for throttle cable

*—Vehicles numbered prior to 06105831, 06200141 and 06300031
†—Vehicles numbered 06105831, 06200141 and 06300031 onwards
**—Vehicles numbered prior to 06104683, 06200107 and 06300022
††—Vehicles numbered 06104683 to 06111527, 06200107 to 06200311 and 06300022 to 06300030
‡—Vehicles numbered 06111528, 06200312 and 06300031 onwards
‡‡—Vehicles numbered prior to 06111528, 06200312 and 06300031

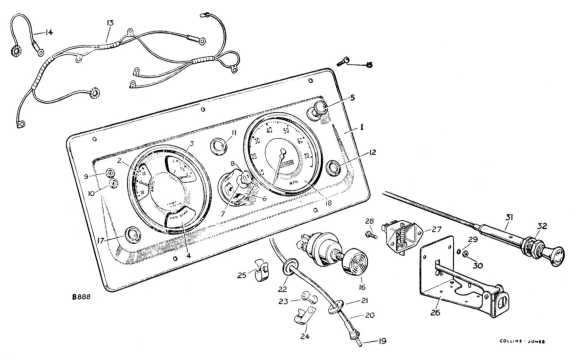

Fig. Q-4—Exploded view of instrument panel—1954-58 models

1	Instrument panel	16	Starter switch—Petrol models
2	Ammeter	17	Warning light, oil
3	Fuel gauge	18	Speedometer
4	Warning light for headlamp beam	19	Cable, inner
5	Switch for panel lights	20	Cable, outer
6	Switch for lamps	21	Retaining plate for cable
7	Barrel lock for ignition or electrical services	22	Rubber grommet, in dash
8	Key for lock	23	Rubber grommet, on cable
9	Socket for inspection lamp, black	24	Clip
10	Socket for inspection lamp, red	25	Clip
11	Warning light, dynamo	26	Bracket for mixture control
12	Warning light, mixture or heater plugs	27	Switch for mixture warning light
13	Panel harness	28–30	Fixings for switch
14	Lead, ammeter to inspection socket	31	Mixture control complete
15	Fixings for instrument panel	32	Shakeproof washer for control

22/23 } For speedometer cable

24/25 } For speedometer cable

26–32 } Petrol models

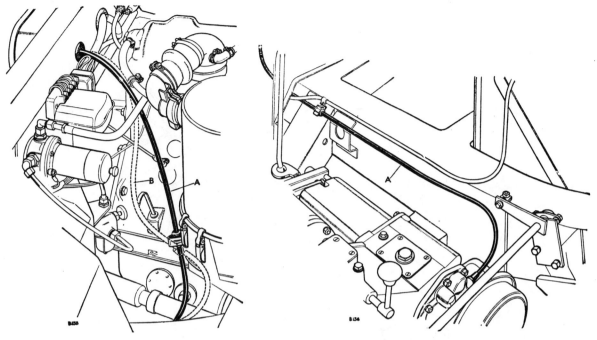

Fig. Q-5—Correct position of speedometer drive cable—1948-53 models.

A—Correct position of cable. B—INCORRECT position of cable.

Speedometer drive cable

To remove **Operation Q/8**

1. Disconnect the battery.

   Diesel—disconnect the positive lead of R.H. battery.

2. Withdraw the instrument panel clear of the dash.

3. Disconnect the speedometer drive from the speedometer head.

4. Free the cable by withdrawing the end from the dash and pushing the rubber grommets from the securing clips on the air cleaner and the cross-member (1948-53 models) and on the flywheel housing, chassis side member and transfer casing (1954-58 models).

5. Disconnect the speedometer cable at the gearbox end. (If necessary, remove the centre seat panel.)

6. Withdraw the inner cable from the outer casing.

To replace **Operation Q/10**

1. Thoroughly clean the inner cable and smear suitable grease over its entire length.

2. Insert the cable in the outer casing.

3. Replace the speedometer drive by reversing the removal procedure, care being taken to avoid acute curves. The inner shaft end must be located in the square or slot of the speedometer pinion before the drive is secured to the housing.

4. If the clips holding the securing grommet have been moved, the drive should be correctly positioned before these clips are tightened.

Accelerator controls, 1948-53 models, to remove **Operation Q/11**

1. Remove the two throttle return springs (one off only when engine governor is fitted).

2. Detach the control rod from the accelerator shaft to the cross-shaft at the ball socket connections.

3. Slacken the top bolt securing the pedal housing, slide the pedal stop to one side and withdraw the pinch bolt and nut securing the pedal to the shaft; remove the pedal.

4. Withdraw the accelerator shaft and lever assembly; if necessary, remove the lever.

5. Remove the two bolts, spring washers and nuts securing the pedal housing, pedal stop and return spring anchor (L.H.D. models only).

6. **R.H.D. models only:** Remove the two bolts, spring washers and nuts securing the pedal shaft bracket, harness clip and return spring anchor.

7. Detach the control rod from the cross-shaft to the carburetter bell-crank at the ball socket connections.

8. Remove the four bolts, spring washers and nuts securing the cross-shaft and brackets.

9. If necessary, remove the two levers from the cross-shaft.

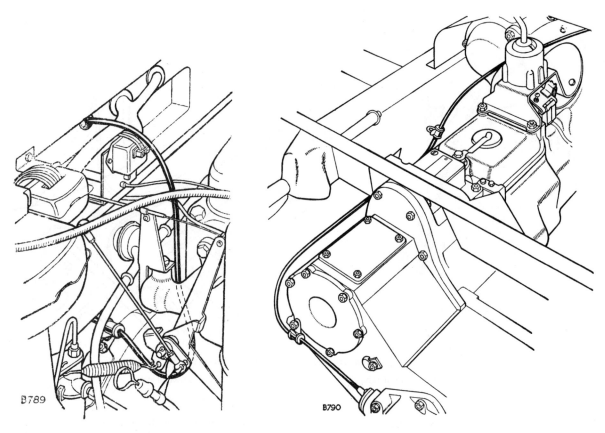

Fig. Q-6—Correct position of speedometer drive cable—1954-58 models.

Accelerator controls

To remove (see Figs. Q-7 and Q-8) **1954-58 Petrol and 1958 Diesel models**   Operation Q/12

1. Remove the throttle return springs.

2. Detach the control rods from the shaft levers.

3. Loosen the clamping bolt, securing lever on accelerator pedal shaft. then withdraw the lever.

4. Remove the accelerator shaft and pedal stop housing.

5. Detach the pedal shaft support bracket from the the toe-box and remove the shaft and pedal complete.

   Note: On L.H.D. models, the accelerator pedal, pedal shaft and distance piece may be withdrawn without removing the support bracket.

6. Remove the cross-shaft, bracket(s) and distance washers.

7. If necessary, remove the two levers from the cross-shaft.

To refit, all models   Operation Q/14

1. Reverse the removal procedure. If disturbed, adjust the lengths of the control rods as necessary.

Hand throttle control, 1948-53 petrol models
To remove   Operation Q/16

1. Disconnect the operating wire from the hand throttle lever at the carburetter.

2. Withdraw the handle and wire from the driver's side of the dash.

3. Release the outer case from the abutment bracket by removing the securing clip, screw, nut and spring washer.

4. Remove the circlip, plain washer and cork washer securing the outer case to the dash, and withdraw the case from the driver's side of the dash.

To replace   Operation Q/18

Reverse the sequence of operations detailed for removal, taking care that a small amount of clearance is left between the throttle lever and the bell crank on the carburetter linkage.

Hand throttle control—Diesel models

To remove—see Fig. Q-10   **Operation Q/20**

1. Disconnect the control rod, quadrant to cross-shaft, at the quadrant ball joint, inside vehicle.

2. Remove the securing bolts, quadrant to scuttle.

3. Remove instrument panel and remove securing bolts, quadrant upper bracket to dash bottom centre panel.

4. Withdraw complete unit.

To refit   **Operation Q/22**

1. Reverse removal procedure.

2. Check for correct functioning and set the hand speed lever as necessary by adjusting the operational lengths of the control rod, quadrant to cross-shaft.

Mixture control—Petrol models

To remove   **Operation Q/24**

A plunger switch is incorporated in the mixture control; it is wired in series with a bi-metal thermostat switch at the rear of the cylinder head and the amber warning light on the instrument panel.

1. Disconnect the battery.

2. Disconnect the wiring from the mixture control warning light switch.

3. Disconnect the operating wire from the lever at the carburetter.

4. Withdraw the inner wire and knob from the driver's side of the dash. See Figs. Q-3 and Q-4.

5. Loosen the screw holding the outer cable at the carburetter.

6. Remove the cold start control outer cable, bracket and switch from the dash by removing the securing nut on the driver's side of the dash.

7. If necessary, remove the warning light switch from the bracket.

8. If necessary, remove the control outer cable from the bracket by unscrewing the cable through the securing locknut.

To refit   **Operation Q/26**

Reverse the removal procedure, taking care that the carburetter cold start lever is fully closed when the control knob is pushed right in, and that the three positions of the control knob are definite.

Note: For further details of the mixture control warning light system, see Section P.

Cut-off control—Diesel models

To remove   **Operation Q/28**

1. Disconnect the control cable from the injection pump cut-off lever and outer cable support.

2. Unscrew the securing nut from the engine side of scuttle and withdraw the cut-off control cable complete.

To refit   **Operation Q/30**

1. Secure the control to the scuttle and the outer cable to the clamping clip on injection pump; locate the inner cable in the cut-off lever clamping screw, then, pressing the lever firmly downward, tighten the clamping screw.

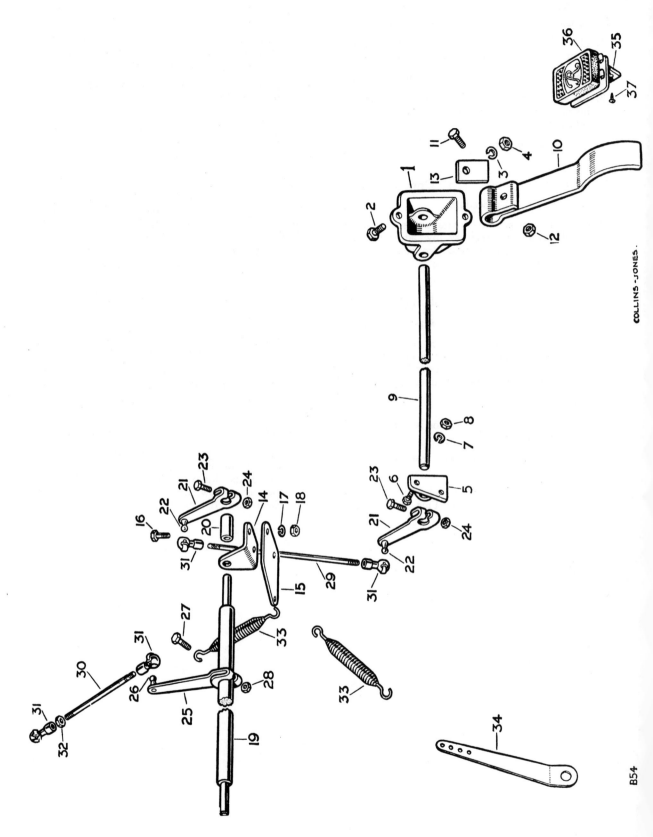

Fig. Q-7—Layout of accelerator and linkage, 1948-53 models.

Key to Fig. Q-7

1	Housing for accelerator pedal shaft
2–4	Fixings for housing
5	Bracket for accelerator pedal shaft
6–8	Fixings for bracket
9	Shaft for accelerator pedal
10	Accelerator pedal
11–12	Fixings: pedal to shaft
13	Stop for pedal
14	Bracket for accelerator cross-shaft
15	Anchor for throttle return spring
16–18	Fixings for bracket and anchor
19	Cross-shaft for accelerator
20	Distance piece for cross-shaft
21	Accelerator levers
22	Ball ends for levers
23–24	Fixings for levers
25	Cross-shaft lever
26	Ball end for lever
27–28	Fixings for lever
29	Control rod, pedal to cross-shaft
30	Control rod, cross-shaft to engine
31	Ball joint sockets for rods
32	Locknuts for sockets
33	Throttle return springs
34	Spring anchor on flywheel housing
35	Foot support for accelerator pedal
36	Rubber pad for support
37	Drive screw fixing support

35, 36, 37 } Optional equipment

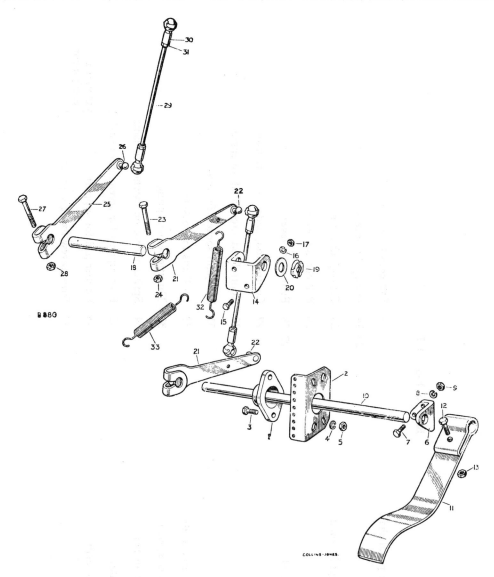

Fig. Q-8—Layout of accelerator and linkage (R.H.D.)—1954-57 models.

1	Housing for accelerator pedal shaft	20	Distance washer for lever
2	Anchor for throttle return spring	21	Lever assembly for accelerator
3–5	Fixings for housing and anchor to dash	22	Ball end for lever
6	Bracket for accelerator pedal shaft	23–24	Fixings for levers
7–9	Fixings for bracket	25	Lever assembly for cross-shaft
10	Shaft for accelerator pedal	26	Ball end for lever
	Distance piece for pedal shafts	27–28	Fixings for lever
11	Accelerator pedal	29	Control rod for accelerator levers
12–13	Fixings for pedal	30	Ball joint socket for rods
14	Bracket for accelerator cross-shaft	31	Locknut for socket
15–17	Fixings for brackets and anchor	32	Return spring for throttle
18	Cross-shaft for accelerator	33	Return spring for pedal
19	Special clip locating shaft		

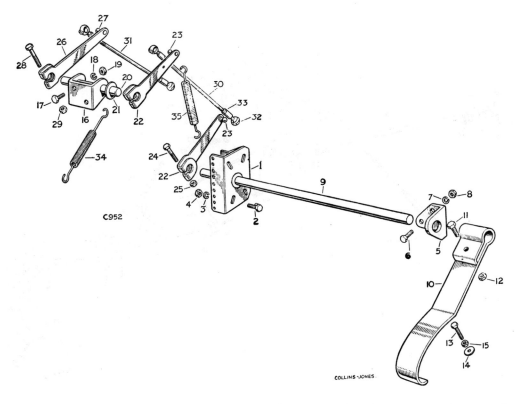

Fig. Q-9—Accelerator controls—1958 Petrol models

1	Accelerator shaft and pedal stop housing	23	Lever ball end
2-4	Fixings—housing and pedal stop to dash	24-25	Fixings—levers and stop clip to shaft—2 litre; levers to shaft—2¼ litre
5	Accelerator pedal shaft bracket		
6-8	Fixings—bracket to dash	26	Cross-shaft lever assembly
9	Accelerator pedal shaft	27	Lever ball end
10	Accelerator pedal	28-29	Fixings—lever to cross-shaft
11-12	Fixings—pedal to shaft	30	Control rod, pedal shaft to cross-shaft
13-15	Pedal stop, in floor	31	Control rod, cross-shaft to engine
16	Accelerator cross-shaft bracket	32	Ball joint socket for rods
17-19	Fixings—bracket to dash	33	Locknut for socket
20	Accelerator cross-shaft	34	Return spring for throttle—2 litre Return spring for pedal—2¼ litre
21	Lever distance washer		
22	Accelerator lever assembly	35	Return spring for pedal—2 litre

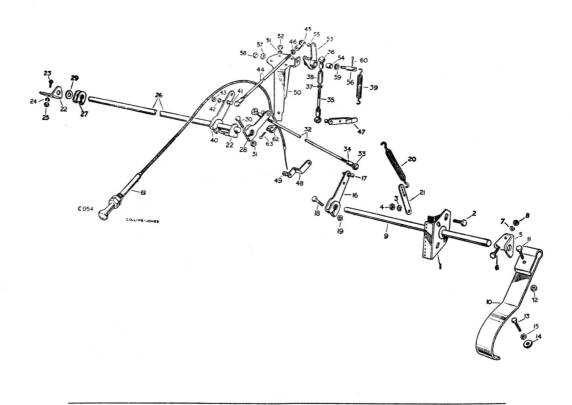

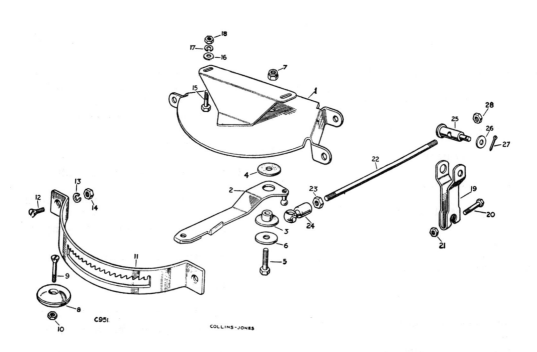

Fig. Q-10—Accelerator and hand speed controls—Diesel models

Key to Fig. Q-10

1 Accelerator shaft and pedal stop housing	35 Control rod, bell crank to accelerator lever
2–4 Fixings—housing and pedal stop to dash	36–38 Ball socket, nut and adjusting nut—bell crank control rod
5 Accelerator pedal shaft bracket	39 Distributor levers return spring
6–8 Fixings—bracket to dash	40 Lever, cross-shaft to engine
9 Accelerator pedal shaft	41–43 Fixings—ball end to accelerator lever
10 Accelerator pedal	44 Control rod, cross-shaft to bell crank
11–12 Fixings—pedal to shaft	45–46 Ball joint and locknut for control rod
13-15 Pedal stop, in floor	47 Distributor pump accelerator control lever
16 Accelerator lever assembly, pedal shaft	48 Distributor stop lever
17 Lever ball end	49 Stop lever swivel clamp
18–19 Fixings—lever to shaft	50 Distributor pump bell crank bracket
20 Pedal return spring	51–52 Fixings—bracket to distributor pump
21 Return spring anchor	53 Distributor pump bell crank
22 Accelerator cross-shaft bracket	54 Bell crank bush
23–25 Fixings—bracket to dash	55 Bell crank ball end
26 Accelerator cross-shaft	56 Bell crank pin
27 Cross-shaft stop clip	57–58 Fixings—pin to bell crank bracket
28 Accelerator lever assembly, cross-shaft	59–60 Fixings—bell crank lever to pin
29 Cross-shaft distance washer	61 "Engine stop" control
30-31 Fixings—levers and stop clip to cross-shaft	62–63 Fixings—control outer cable to pump abutment bracket
32 Control rod, pedal shaft to cross-shaft	
33–34 Ball joint socket and locknut—for rod	

1 Housing for governor control quadrant	15–18 Fixings—control to dash
2 Control lever and ball end	19 Hand engine speed control operating lever
3 Lever bush	20–21 Fixings—operating lever to accelerator cross-shaft
4 Lever washer	22 Control rod for engine speed control
5–7 Fixings—control lever to housing	23 Nut ⎫ For
8 Lever knob	24 Ball socket ⎭ control rod
9–10 Fixings—knob to lever	25–27 Fixings—engine speed control rod
11–14 Fixings—quadrant plate to housing	28 Nut—fixing control rod to joint pin

Key to Fig. O-?

Section R
BODY — ALL MODELS

INDEX

	Page		Page
Back rest for rear seat	R-20	Radiator grille panel	R-5
Body repairs	R-1	Rear body	R-22
Bonnet	R-5	Rear door, Station Wagon	R-20
Cab	R-16	Rear seat	R-20
Cab (De Luxe), interior trim	R-19	Riveting body panels	R-1
Cab body back rest panel	R-16	Roof and sides	R-20
Cab sliding backlights	R-16	Seat base	R-11
Dash panel	R-14	Sidescreen window	R-9
Door	R-9	Tailboard	R-22
Door lock	R-13	Tropical roof, cab	R-19
Front floor	R-13	Tropical roof, hard top	R-21
Front wing	R-5	Ventilator	R-14
Hard top	R-20	Windscreen	R-14
Hard top window glass	R-21	Windscreen glass	R-14
Paint process for body panels	R-5	Windscreen ventilator	R-14

LIST OF ILLUSTRATIONS

Fig.		Page	Fig.		Page
R-1	Layout of seat base, seats, front floor, wings and bonnet, 1948-53 models	R-2	R-9	Layout of hard top and tropical roof	R-18
R-2	Layout of seat base, seats, front floor, wings and bonnet, 1954-58 models	R-4	R-10	Canopy side brackets	R-19
R-3	Layout of tailboard, doors and sidescreens, 1948-53 models	R-6	R-11	Fitting filler strip in window weather strip	R-21
R-4	Layout of tailboard, doors and sidescreens, 1954-58 models	R-8	R-12	Layout of rear body unit—86 and 88 models	R-23
R-5	Layout of dash panel, windscreen and ventilators, 1948-53 models	R-10	R-13	Layout of rear body unit—107 and 109 models	R-24
R-6	Layout of dash panel, windscreen and ventilators, 1954-58 models	R-12	R-14	Rear door, seals and rear step	R-25
R-7	Door gusset plate	R-13	R-15	Layout of Station Wagon roof and sides	R-26
R-8	Layout of cab and tropical roof	R-17	R-16	Layout of Station Wagon De Luxe trim	R-27

General body repairs

With the exception of the dash panel, which is steel, the body panels are constructed througho ut from Birmabright, with steel cappings and corn er brackets; all steel parts are galvanised.

Riveting

Three types of rivet are used on the body:

1. Aluminium pop or "blind" rivets are used only on box sections or where it is difficult or impossible to use any other type because of limited working space; these rivets are "snapped-up" from one side only. The setting is controlled by the breaking of a headed steel mandrel which passes through the tubular rivet; the mandrel break occurs only when the thicknesses being riveted have been pulled together tightly and the rivet head on the blind side fully formed. The mandrels are either of the break stem or break head type, the latter being used in positions where the mandrel head is free to fall away after the rivet head is set. Where it is required to retain the broken-off portion of the mandrel within the headed-up part of the rivet, as for example in box sections (where a loose mandrel head would rattle) or for sealing the rivet with filler or stopper, the break stem type is used. Either a mechanical or pneumatic hand tool can be used for fixing pop rivets.

2. Bifurcated or "split" rivets are used for securing rubber and canvas together or to metal. The rivet is passed through the materials to be joined, a boss cap is placed over the tongues of the rivet, and these tongues then spread with a suitable drift.

3. Various sizes and lengths of round head rivets are used, and for these a suitably indented dolly is needed for the rivet head, while the tail of the rivet is peened over with a hammer, operated manually, electrically, or by compressed air.

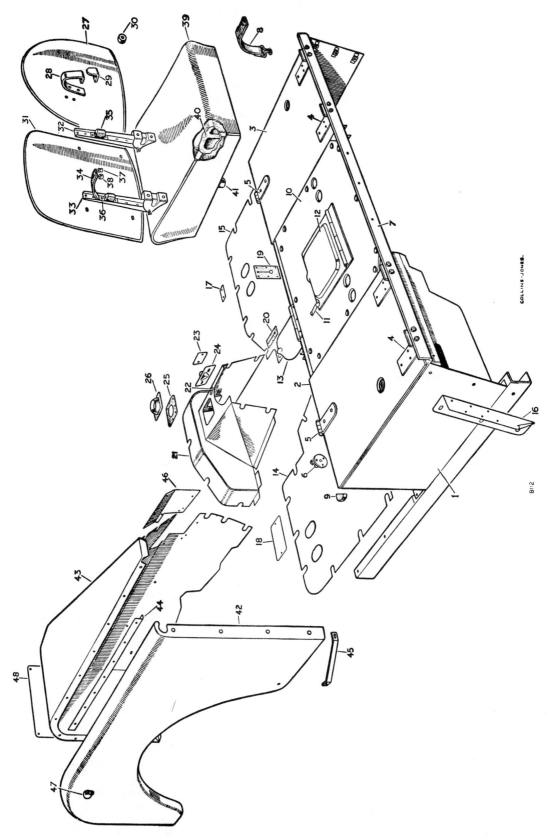

Fig. R-1—Layout of seat base, toe plates and front wings, 1948-53

Key to Fig. R-1

1 Seat base assembly
2 Lid for tool locker
3 Lid for petrol tank access
4 Hinges for lids
5 Hasps for lids
6 Turnbuckle for lid hasp
7 Angle plate, seat base to rear body
8 Retaining strap for locker lid
9 Rubber corner piece for lid (extra equipment)
10 Centre cover panel
11 Spring clip for power take-off access cover
12 Access cover for power take-off
13 Inspection cover for gearbox
14 Toe plate, left hand
15 Toe plate, right hand
16 Corner fixing angle
17 Cover plate for pedal adjuster (early vehicles)
18 Cover plate for pedal holes
19 Rubber cover for handbrake slot
20 Rubber cover for transfer lever slot
21 Gearbox cover
22 Spring clip for gearbox cover

23–24 Cover plate for gearbox cover (alternatives)
25–26 Rubber seal for gear lever (alternatives)
27 Seat back rest
28 Bracket for back rest
29 Reinforcing bracket for bracket
30 Rubber buffer for back rest
31 Seat back rest
32–33 Hinges for back rest
34 Retaining strap for back rest
35 Rubber buffer
36 Securing plate for buffer
37–38 Fixings for strap
39 Seat cushion
40 Rubber interior for cushion
41 Rubber dowel locating seat
42 Front wing side
43 Front wing top and valance
44 Seal for wing joint
45 Stay for wing
46 Cover plate for wing valance
47 Rubber buffer (door stop)
48 Registration plate

* Vehicles numbered prior to 06110305 and 06300031.

† Vehicles numbered 06110305 and 06300031 onwards.

291

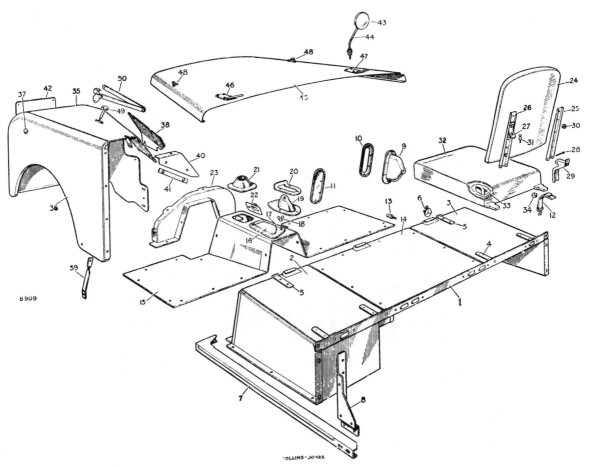

Fig. R-2—Layout of seat base, seats, front floor, wings and bonnet, 1954-58

1	Seat base and floor assembly	27	Retaining strap for seat back rest
2	Lid for tool locker	28	Split pin
3	Lid for petrol tank	29	Support bracket for front seat back rest
4	Hinge for lids	30	Buffer for seat back rest
5	Hasp for locker lids	31	Stud for retaining strap
6	Turnbuckle for locker lids	32	Seat cushion complete
7	Sill panel, L.H.	33	Rubber interior for seat
8	Corner bracket, L.H.	34	Rubber dowel locating seat
9	Rubber cover for hand brake	35	Front wing, top, L.H.
10	Retainer for rubber cover		Front wing, side, R.H.
11	Cover plate for hand brake slot	36	Front wing, side, L.H.
12	Access cover for P.T.O.	37	Rubber buffer in wing for door
13	Stud for cushion retaining strap	38	Cover plate for wing valance, L.H.
14	Centre cover panel complete	39	Stay for front wing
15	Front floor complete	40	Bracket, L.H.
16	Inspection cover for front floor	41	Bolt plate
17	Stud plate for inspection cover wing nut	42	Number plate, L.H.
18	Wing nut	43	Mirror only
19	Seal for transfer gear lever	44	Arm for mirror
20	Retainer for transfer lever seal	45	Bonnet top panel
21	Rubber seal for gear lever	46	Hinge for bonnet, L.H.
22	Cover plate for operating rod	47	Hinge for bonnet, R.H.
23	Gearbox cover complete	48	Staple for bonnet and windscreen fastener
24	Seat back rest, trimmed	49	Bonnet fastener
25	Hinge complete for seat back rest, R.H.	50	Prop rod for bonnet
26	Hinge complete for seat back rest, L.H.		

Paint touching-up process for body panels

Body panels are finished in stoving synthetic enamel and a special technique, detailed below, must be followed when touching up the paint finish after repair work.

Preparatory work

Thoroughly clean the damaged portion; all traces of wax polish, etc., should be removed with a suitable solvent such as White Spirit.

The surrounding edges of the paint film must be correctly feather edges, using a wooden block and suitable paper.

Colour

(a) Small damaged areas:

Prepare the correct colour finish by thinning to 40 parts finish to 60 parts thinner by volume.

Apply a built-up coat by spray and allow to air dry for four to six hours.

(b) Large damaged areas (complete wings or panels):
Prepare the correct colour finish by thinning 50/50 with thinner.

Apply one or two full spray coats; allow 15 to 30 minutes between coats and four to six hours (or preferably overnight) after the final application.

Half-hour air drying colour finish and thinners are obtainable from our Spares Department.

Polishing

After the recommended drying period, lightly polish with any good smooth polishing compound and finally clear, if necessary, with any good quality wax polish.

Notes

1. When spraying in small areas and in order to minimise dry spray, it is recommended that the air pressure for spraying be reduced to 30-40 lb/sq.in. (2,1-2,8 kg/cm²).

2. When touching up stoved synthetic finishes, no advantage is to be gained by mist-coating the patch. Instead, the edges of the patch should be faded out during application and any resultant dry spray removed during polishing with any good polishing compound.

3. It is not always easy to blend a patch or touch-up; to do so successfully and lose the edges requires practice by a skilled operator. In cases where the damage is on a conspicuous part of the vehicle, it is recommended that the operator sprays out the entire damaged part, e.g., door panel, wing, etc.

4. In certain instances, the materials listed are available locally. We can furnish additional information in this respect on demand, providing the serial numbers of vehicles concerned are quoted.

Bonnet

To remove   **Operation R/2**

1. If fitted, remove the spare wheel from the bonnet.

2. Unhook the bonnet fasteners, disconnect the bonnet prop rod, if fitted, lift the bonnet to its highest position and slide it out to the left, from its hinges.

3. Remove the hinges from the bonnet panel.

4. Remove the bonnet fasteners and the staples.

5. Place the new bonnet panel in position on the vehicle and the hinges in position in the brackets on the dash.

6. Using the hinges as templates, drill the eight holes in the panel, and secure the panel to the hinges.

7. Complete the assembly by reversing the removal procedure.

Radiator grille panel

To renew   **Operation R/4**

1. Lift off the grille and nameplate and, if fitted, the chaff guard. Remove the cover from the junction box on the dash panel and disconnect the horn and headlamp harness; unclip the harness from the wing.

2. Remove the bolts, spring washers, nuts, rubber packing pieces and plain washers securing the grille panel to the second chassis cross-member.

3. Remove the bolts, spring washers and nuts securing the radiator block to the grille panel and to the wings; disconnect the wiring from the horn and lift off the grille panel complete with headlamps and wiring.

4. Remove the headlamps.

5. Remove the bonnet rest strip from the grille panel.

6. Remove the headlamp and horn harness from the panel, together with the rubber grommets and cable clips.

7. Assemble and replace the new grille panel by reversing the sequence of Items 1-6.

Front wings

To remove   **Operation R/6**

1. Remove the bonnet.

2. Disconnect the side lamp harness at the snap connectors in the engine compartment.

3. On R.H.D. vehicles, remove the valance cover plate near the exhaust pipe.

4. Remove the wing stay from the dash.

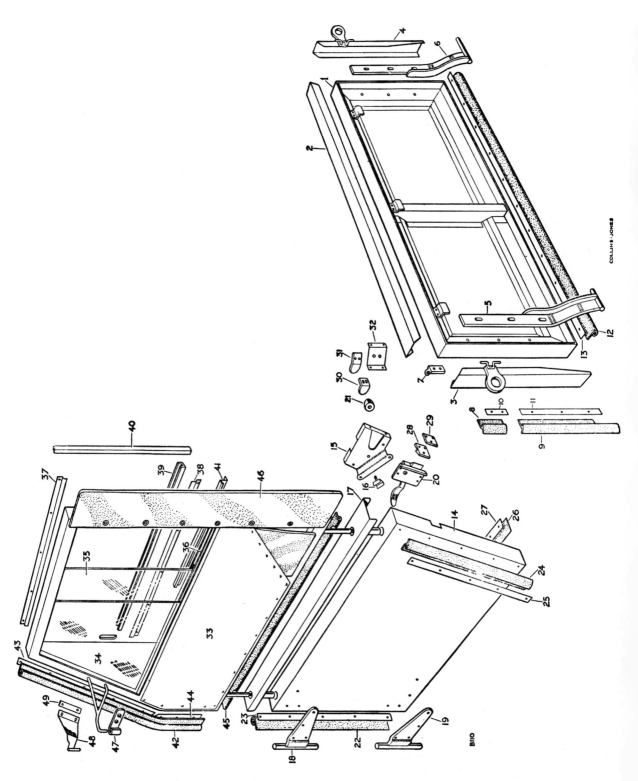

COLLINS · JONES

B110

Fig. R-3—Layout of tailboard, doors and sidescreens, 1948-53

Key to Fig. R-3

1 Tailboard
2 Top capping for tailboard
3–4 Side cappings for tailboard
5–6 Hinges for tailboard
7 Hook for tailboard chain
8–9 Weather strips for tailboard, sides
10–11 Retainers for weather strips
12 Weather strip for tailboard, bottom
13 Retainer for weather strip
14 Front door
15 Gusset plate for door
16 Bolt and plate for gusset plate
17 Top capping for door
18–19 Hinges for door
20 Door lock
21 Rubber buffer for door
22 Weather strip for door, front
23 Retainer for weather strip
24 Weather strip for door, rear
25 Retainer for weather strip
26 Weather strip for door, bottom

27 Retainer for weather strip
28 Striking plate for door
29 Tapped plate fixing plate
30–31 Stops for door buffer (alternatives)
32 Reinforcement for stop
33 Side screen
34 Fixed window
35 Sliding window
36 Channel for windows
37–38 Retainers for channel } *
39 Channel for windows, bottom
40 Channel for windows, rear
41 Filler for fixed window } †
42 Rubber draught strip at front edge
43–44 Retainers for draught strip
45 Rubber draught strip at lower edge
46 Rear flap
47 Hinge for sidescreen
48 Hinge plate } Service modification
49 Back plate } for sidescreen hinge

*—Vehicles numbered prior to 8666250.

†—Vehicles numbered 8666250 onwards

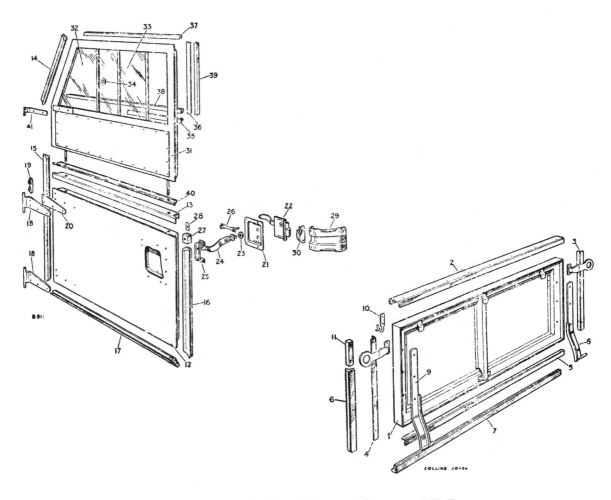

Fig. R-4—Layout of tailboard, doors and sidescreens, 1954-58

1 Tailboard assembly	22 Door lock, L.H.
2 Top capping for tailboard	23 Washer, handle to cover
3 Angle for rubber seal, R.H. side	24 Handle, L.H.
4 Angle for rubber seal, L.H. side	25 Bracket for door handle
5 Angle for rubber seal, bottom	26 Captive plate
6 Sealing rubber, side	27 Rubber buffer for doors
7 Sealing rubber, bottom	28 Fixing plate
8 Hinge for tailboard, R.H.	29 Support bracket for door striking plate
9 Hinge for tailboard, L.H.	30 Striking plate for door lock
10 Hook for tailboard chain, L.H.	31 Sidescreen assembly, L.H.
11 Rubber buffer for tailboard	32 Fixed window, front
12 Front door assembly, L.H.	33 Sliding window, rear
13 Top capping for door	34 Knob for sliding window
14 Seal for door, front upper, L.H.	35 Filler, top and bottom ⎫ For
15 Seal for door, rear lower, body	36 Filler, rear ⎭ windows
16 Seal for door, front lower, dash	37 Channel, top
17 Seal for door, bottom, sill	38 Channel, bottom
18 Hinge complete, L.H.	39 Channel, rear
19 Nut plate for hinge	40 Sealing strip for sidescreen
20 Packing plate for hinge	41 Hinge plate, L.H.
21 Mounting plate for door lock	

5. Withdraw the bolt, spring and plain washers and nuts securing the wing to the dash pillar, to the dash and radiator grille frame; lift off the wing complete.

6. If necessary:—

   (a) Remove the driving mirror.

   (b) Remove the sidelamp, harness and grommet from the wing.

   (c) Remove the bonnet fastener.

   (d) L.H. wing only. Remove the bonnet prop rod.

   (e) Remove the R.H. wing valance plate.

   (f) Remove the wing stay.

   (g) Remove the registration plate.

   (h) Separate the wing top and valance from the wing side.

To refit   Operation R/8

1. Reverse the removal procedure.

Sidescreen windows

Sliding window

To renew   Operation R/10

1. Move the sliding window to allow access to the screws securing glass run channel—top and bottom—then remove the screws from inside channel.

2. Withdraw the top run channel and sliding window.

3. Renew the bottom run channel if necessary.

4. Fit new parts as necessary and assemble by reversing the removal procedure.

Fixed window

To renew   Operation R/12

1. See Operation R/10, items 1-3 inclusive.

2. Ease the fixed glass clear of frame, after removing the screws securing front retainer on 1954-58 models.

3. Apply new Prestik sealing strip to window frame, renewing parts as necessary and assemble by reversing the removal procedure.

Note: Two-piece door only—if necessary, the complete assembly can be removed by removing the nuts, plain washers and spring washers securing the assembly to the door.

Sidescreen hinge, to modify, 1948-53

1. A special hinge plate has been designed as a Service replacement in cases where the fabricated wire hinge on the sidescreen has fractured.

2. The hinge plates and fittings are available from our Parts Department under the following part numbers:—

Description		Qty.	Part Number
Hinge plate, right hand	....	1	301916
Hinge plate, left hand	....	1	301917
Backing plate for hinge	....	2	301918
Bolt ($\frac{1}{4}$ in. x $1\frac{3}{4}$ in.) ⎱ Fixing		4	250518
Spring washer ⎱ hinge plate		4	3074
Nut ($\frac{1}{4}$ in.) ⎱ to sidescreen		4	2823

3. Remove the door complete with sidescreen from the vehicle.

4. Mark off and drill the two $\frac{1}{4}$ in. (6,5 mm) clearance fixing holes for the new hinge plate in the sidescreen frame. The plate, which has slotted fixing holes, must be so positioned that its hinge pin is accurately in line with the two door hinge pins; the use of a straight edge is essential for this operation.

5. Secure the hinge plate on the outer side of the sidescreen, with a backing plate on the inside, by means of the two bolts, spring washers and nuts.

6. Replace the door and sidescreen and adjust the hinge bracket on the windscreen so that there is no strain on the new hinge.

Front door

To remove and refit   Operation R/14

1. Remove the sidescreen.

2. Swing the door panel forward until parallel with the front wing and lift from its hinges.

3. If necessary, remove the door hinges.

4. Replace the door by reversing the removal procedure, renewing the sealing rubbers as necessary.

Door gusset plate, to fit, 1948-53

1. On early vehicles it may be found that the upper rear corner of the door panel is fractured, owing to vibration of the rear edge of the sidescreen placing an excessive strain on the door capping. A gusset plate is now fitted to strengthen the door.

2. If required, these plates can be obtained from our Parts Department under Part Numbers 302335—left hand and 302334—right hand.

3. Remove the sidescreen.

4. Remove the door from the vehicle.

5. Remove the upper buffer from the door.

6. Shear the two rearmost rivets securing the top capping.

7. Secure the free end of the clip to the gusset plate by means of the bolt and plate, spring and plain washers and nut provided.

8. Fit the gusset plate in position as shown at **Fig. R-7**.

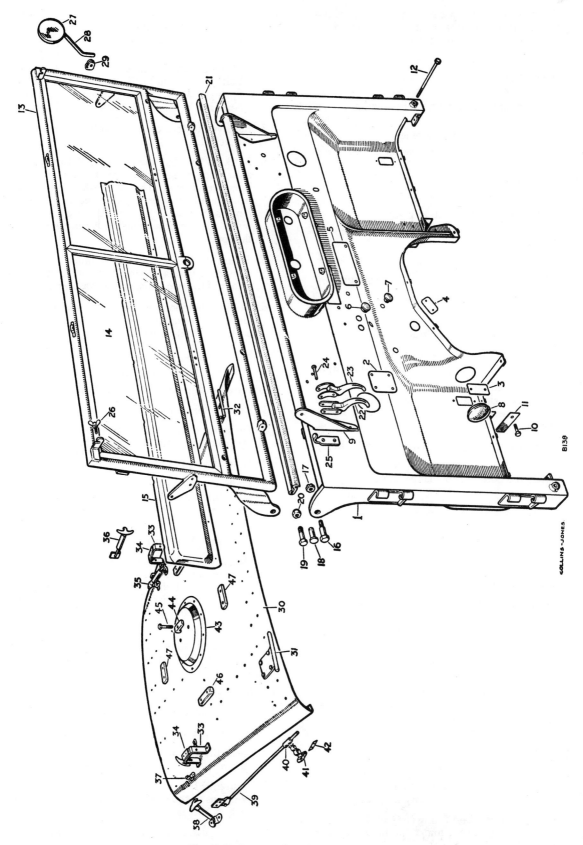

Fig. R-5—Layout of dash panel, 1948-53

Key to Fig R-5

1 Dash panel
2 Cover panel for steering cut-out
3 Cover plate for accelerator pedal hole
4 Access plate for exhaust rocker shaft
5 Cover plate for governor quadrant hole
6–7 Rubber blanking plugs for heater holes
8 Rubber blancking plug for starter access hole
9 Hand rail
10–12 Fixings, dash to chassis
13 Windscreen
14 Glass for windscreen
15 Bottom panel for windscreen
16–20 Pivot bolts for windscreen (alternatives)
21 Rubber sealing strip for windscreen
22–23 Fasteners for windscreen (alternatives)
24 Joint pin fixing fastener
25 Catch for fastener
26 Wing bolt in windscreen for hood

27 Driving mirror
28 Arm for mirror
29 Clip for arm
30 Bonnet panel
31–32 Hinges for bonnet
33 Support for windscreen
34 Tape for support
35–36 Clamps for windscreen (alternatives)
37 Staple for bonnet and windscreen clamp
38 Bonnet fastener
39 Prop rod for bonnet
40 Rubber tube for rod
41 Spring clip for rod
42 Tapped plate fixing clip
43 Support for spare wheel
44 Clamp for spare wheel
45 Bolt for clamp
46–47 Rubber support blocks for wheel

Extra equipment

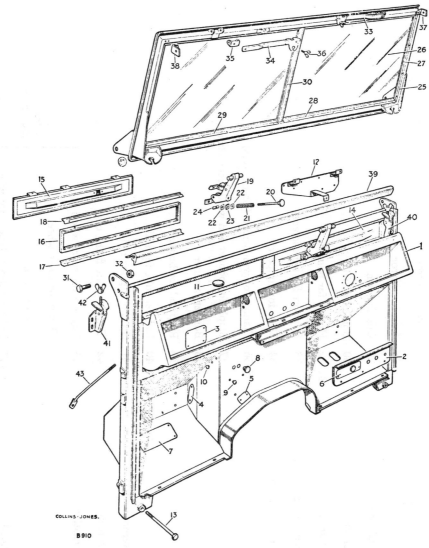

Fig. R-6—Layout of dash panel, windscreen and ventilators, 1954-58

1 Dash complete
2 Panel for controls
3 Cover panel for steering column
4 Cover plate for accelerator pedal hole
5 Access plate for bottom rocker shaft
6 Cover panel for governor cutout in dash
7 Cover plate for pedal holes
8 Rubber plugs, large, heater pipe holes
   Rubber plug, medium, heater wiring holes
9 Rubber plug, small, heater bolt holes
10 Rubber plug, redundant accelerator holes
11 Rubber grommet for demister holes
12 Mounting plate for sump
13 Tie bolt
14 Ventilator lid for dash, R.H.
15 Ventilator lid for dash, L.H.
16 Seating rubber for ventilator lids
17 Retainer, bottom ⎫ For sealing
18 Retainer, top   ⎭ rubber
19 Operating lever assembly for ventilator
20 Adjusting screw for ventilator

21 Spring
22 Square washer ⎫ For adjusting
23 Rubber washer ⎬ screw
24 Trunnion pin   ⎭
25 Windscreen complete assembly
26 Glass for windscreen
27 Retainer for windscreen glass, vertical
28 Retainer for windscreen glass, R.H. ⎫ Upper and
29 Retainer for windscreen glass, L.H. ⎭ lower
30 Cover for centre strip
31–32 Fixings for windscreen
33 Pivot arm, R.H.
34 Pivot arm, L.H.
35 Pivot bracket, pivot arm to windscreen
36 Winged screw
37 Bracket, R.H. ⎫ For hood, cab and
38 Bracket, L.H. ⎭ hard top attachment
39 Rubber sealing strip for windscreen
40 Fastener for windscreen, R.H.
41 Fastener for windscreen, L.H.
42 Wing nut for fastener
43 Tie bar for dash support

9. Drill two ¼ in. (6,5 mm) clearance holes in the door panel and secure the plate by means of the two ¼ in. bolts, spring washers and nuts provided.

10. Drill the plate through the rivet holes in the top capping and secure the capping and plate, using two new rivets.

11. Drill two holes in the door shut flange, using the gusset plate as a guide and secure with the two 2 B.A. screws, spring washers and nuts provided; the screw heads should be on the outside of the door.

12. Secure the plate to the door reinforcement by means of the two pop rivets provided.

13. Tighten the clip against the sidescreen fixing tube by means of the nut fitted at Item 7.

14. Replace the rubber buffer.

15. Replace the door and sidescreen.

16. Repeat Items 3—15 for the other door.

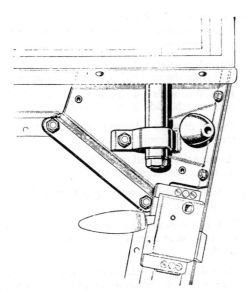

Fig. R-7--Door gusset plate

Door lock
(Two-piece and full length)
To renew   Operation R/16

1. Remove the door lock from the door.

2. If required, remove the striking plate from its support bracket.

3. Renew the lock and plate as necessary and refit by reversing Items 1 and 2.

4. Adjust the position of the striking plate as necessary, so that the door draught excluders and buffers are slightly compressed.

Front floor, 1954-58
To remove   Operation R/18

1. Remove the transfer lever knob and dust excluder.

2. Remove the four wheel drive lever knob, spring and ferrule.

3. Remove the floor board securing bolts and lift off the front floor complete.

4. If necessary, remove the gearbox cover from the dash panel.

To refit   Operation R/20

1. Reverse the removal procedure.

2. Adjust the four wheel drive lever.

Toe plates, 1948-53
To remove

1. Withdraw the pinch bolts securing the brake and clutch pedals to the levers and remove the pedals, felt pads and rubber grommets.

2. Remove the transfer lever knob and locknut. On early models, remove the front wheel drive lock ring from the operating wire.

3. After lifting out the seat cushions, remove the seat centre cover panel, by withdrawing the set bolts and plain washers.

4. Remove the bolts, spring washers and nuts securing the hand brake to the chassis, and swing the hand brake out of the way to the rear.

5. Remove the securing set bolts, spring and plain washers, and lift off the toe plates.

To refit

1. Reverse the removal procedure.

2. Before fitting new toe plates, secure the transfer lever rubber cover to the underside of the right-hand plate by means of six bifurcated rivets and boss caps, and the pedal hole cover plate by means of four drive screws.

Gearbox cover, 1948-53
To remove

1. Remove the toe plates, as detailed above.

2. On vehicles with the four-wheel drive control protruding from the gearbox cover, remove the knob, locknut, spring and bush from the control rod.

3. Unclip the gearbox filler plug cover and swing the cover to one side.

4. Remove the set bolts, spring and plain washers and lift off the gearbox cover.

To replace

1. Reverse the sequence of operations detailed for removal.

2. Before fitting a new cover on early vehicles, secure the gear lever seal to the cover by means of eight bifurcated rivets and boss caps.

Windscreen

To remove   **Operation R/22**

1. Remove the doors and sidescreens complete.

2. Remove the hard top or cab; if a soft hood is fitted, release the front straps from the support stays at the top of the windscreen and disconnect the top drain channels or tie tubes from the windscreens.

3. Remove the windscreen wiper positive lead plug from its socket or disconnect the lead from the wiper motor on early 1948-53 models.

4. Slacken the wing nuts at the bottom corners of the windscreen, or release the windscreen clamps.

5. Remove the windscreen pivot bolts and remove the windscreen complete.

To refit   **Operation R/24**

1. Reverse the removal procedure, renewing the windscreen sealing strip if necessary.

Windscreen glass

To renew   **Operation R/26**

1. Remove windscreen.

2. If necessary, remove the windscreen wiper blade; disconnect the wiper motor earth wire and remove the wiper motor from the windscreen.

1948-53

3. Remove the twenty-one round-headed screws securing the windscreen in the tubular frame and remove the windscreen complete.

1948-53

4. Withdraw the twenty-one countersunk screws securing the cappings round the glass and prise away the cappings; remove the glazing strip from the screen, together with the support angles and remove the glass or glasses as necessary.

1954-58

5. Withdraw the drive screws securing the retainers round the glass and prise away the retainers; remove the glass or glasses as necessary. Apply "Prestik" strip $\frac{1}{2}$ in. (12,7 mm) wide, round the outside on both faces of the new glass.

To refit

1. Reverse the stripping procedure.

Ventilator, 1954-58

To remove   **Operation R/28**

1. Remove the bolts securing the ventilator lid operating lever to the dash.

2. Remove the bolts and nuts securing the ventilator lid hinges to the dash and remove the lid complete with operating lever.

3. Remove the operating lever from the lid.

4. If necessary, remove the ventilator lid sealing rubber from the dash.

5. If necessary, unscrew the adjusting screw from the operating lever and remove the spring, square washer, rubber washer and trunnion pin from the lever.

To refit   **Operation R/30**

1. Reverse the removal procedure, renewing sealing rubbers as necessary.

Dash panel

To remove   **Operation R/32**

1. Remove the front floor, or toe plates, gearbox cover, doors, windscreen, bonnet and wings.

2. Remove the pedals, felt pads and rubber grommets.

3. Disconnect the battery.
   Diesel models—disconnect the lead coupling both batteries.

4. **Petrol models**—disconnect the starter motor lead from the terminal on the switch or motor.
   Diesel models—disconnect the starter/heater plug switch leads from the switch.

5. **Petrol models**—disconnect the distributor low tension wire from the coil.

6. Remove the knurled nut and disconnect the high tension cable from the coil.

7. Disconnect the oil warning light wire from the oil pressure switch.

8. **Petrol models**—disconnect the mixture warning light wire from the switch on the cylinder head.

9. **Petrol models**—disconnect the petrol pipe (pump to carburetter) at the pump. Disconnect the petrol pipe (tank to sediment bowl) at the bowl.

10. Disconnect the accelerator linkage by disconnecting the control rod, at the carburetter or injection pump. Disconnect the throttle return spring on 1948-53 models.

11. **Petrol models**—if fitted, disconnect the engine governor operating rod at the quadrant.

12. **Diesel models**—disconnect the engine hand speed control rod at the cross-shaft by removing the retaining nut and locknut.

13. If fitted, disconnect the heater water pipe hoses, disconnect the leads and remove the heater unit complete.

14. **Disconnect the dynamo leads.**

15. **Petrol models**—if fitted, disconnect the engine governor operating rod at the quadrant.

16. Disconnect the mixture control wire from the carburetter.

17. If fitted, disconnect the hand throttle wire from the bracket on the cylinder head and the hand throttle lever.

18. Disconnect the speedometer drive from the transfer box; release the cable from its securing clips.

19. Extract the split pin, remove the nut and bolt securing the drop arm to the steering rocker shaft and lower the drop arm.

1954-58

Remove the drop arm from the steering rocker shaft, using extractor, Part No. 262776.

20. Disconnect the headlamp and horn wires at the junction box on the dash.

21. Part the frame and dash section of the main harness at the snap connectors.

22. **Diesel L.H.D.**—disconnect the additional filter pipes at the filter.

23. Remove the bolt securing the steering box support bracket to the chassis in 1954-58 models; remove the two tie bolts, plain washer and nuts fixing the dash to the chassis; remove the nuts and bolts securing the dash to the extremities of the sill panels or the reinforcing brackets. Lift off the dash panel complete.

To renew   Operation R/34

1. Remove the dash panel.

    1948-53

2. Withdraw four set bolts and spring washers and remove the hand rail.

3. Lift off the junction box and disconnect the wiring; remove the junction box from the dash.

4. Withdraw the horn button and dipper switch, stator tube and horn and dip switch wires from the steering column.

5. Draw off the steering wheel, spring and dust shield.

6. Remove the steering column clip and rubber strip; remove the steering column support bracket; remove the steering column rubber seal.

7. Remove the bolts and nuts securing the steering column and withdraw it from the dash.

    1954-58

8. Remove the steering column support brackets and tie rod from the dash.

9. Disconnect and remove the petrol pipe (pump to sediment bowl).

10. Disconnect the wiring from the petrol pump, voltage control box and the fuse box; remove the mounting plate complete with pump, voltage control box and the fuse box.

11. **Diesel models**—disconnect the wiring from the control box and the fuse box; remove the mounting plate complete with control box and fuse box.

12. **Petrol models**—disconnect the wiring from the mixture control warning light switch and remove the bracket, switch and mixture control.

13. **Diesel models**—disconnect the wires and remove the heater plug resistance.

14. **Petrol models**—if fitted, remove the hand throttle control; if fitted, remove the engine governor control quadrant assembly.

15. **Diesel models**—remove the engine hand speed control.

16. **Petrol models**—disconnect the wiring from the coil and remove the coil from the dash; after disconnecting the cables from the starter switch, screw off the starter knob and locknut. Withdraw the switch from the dash.

17. Remove the petrol sediment bowl and bracket.

18. Unhook the throttle return springs, and remove the two control rods (accelerator pedal to cross-shaft and cross-shaft to carburetter).

19. **Diesel models**—disconnect the leads and remove the starter/heater plug switch by removing the large securing nut from facia side of panel.

20. Remove accelerator linkage with pedal and brackets.

    R.H.D. models—detach the pedal shaft bracket from the dash panel complete with shaft and pedal.

    L.H.D. models—withdraw the pedal shaft complete with pedal and distance piece.

    Diesel L.H.D.—remove the additional filter from the dash panel.

21. Remove the accelerator cross-shaft, levers and bracket(s).

22. If fitted, remove the engine governor control quadrant assembly.

23. Disconnect the speedometer drive from the speedometer head and withdraw it from the dash; disconnect all the wiring from the instruments and controls on the instrument panel, Section Q, and remove the main harness.

24. Remove the windscreen sealing strip. Remove the windscreen fastener catches from the dash panel.

25. Remove the transfer lever instruction plates; remove the rocker shaft access plate.

26. Remove the governor cut-out panel and the pedal hole covers.

27. Remove the ventilators and operating controls. Operation R/28.

28. Remove the harness clip.

29. Remove all remaining rubber grommets and plugs; remove the steering column blanking plate and refit it on the new dash panel.

30. Transfer all the dash fittings to the new panel by reversing the removal procedure, referring to appropriate sections and connecting the wiring in accordance with the appropriate wiring diagram. Section P.

To refit   **Operation R/36**

1. Reverse the removal procedure.

2. Connect the wiring in accordance with the appropriate wiring diagram.

3. Adjust the accelerator, mixture or cut-off control and throttle linkage by reference to appropriate sections.

4. Set the road wheels straight ahead and the steering wheel in the midway position between full lock in each direction before securing the drop arm to the steering box rocker shaft.

Seat base

To remove   **Operation R/38**

1948-53

1. Remove the toe plates and gearbox cover.

2. Remove the bolts, spring washers and nuts securing the seat box and locker lid hinges to the rear body; remove the locker lids.

3. Remove the set bolts, spring and plain washers securing the body corner brackets to the seat base, and the set bolts, spring and plain washers securing the heel boards to the chassis.

4. Disconnect the hand brake linkage and pull the hand brake lever upwards in its slot as far as possible.

5. Lift off the seat base.

1954-58

1. Lift out the seat cushions.

2. Remove front floor. Operation R/18.

3. Remove the bolts securing the seat base and locker lid hinges to the back rest and sill panels; remove the locker lids.

4. Lift off the seat base, manoeuvring the hand lever grip carefully through the rubber draught excluder in the front of the seat base.

To refit   **Operation R/40**

1. Reverse the removal procedure.

1948-53

2. Adjust the hand-brake linkage.

Cab 1954-58

To overhaul   **Operation R/42**

1. Remove the bolts and nuts securing the cab at the windscreen, and the nuts securing it at the hood sockets and at the best rest panel capping.

2. Lift off the cab complete, then remove the roof panel and sealing rubber from the rear panel.

3. Remove the draught excluders and retaining strips from the top of the front door apertures.

4. Remove the rear upper front door seals and cappings and the capping draught pads from the front edge of the side panels.

5. If necessary, remove the rear bottom sealing strip and draught filler pieces from the back rest panel capping.

6. If necessary, remove the sealing rubber and retaining strip from the front edge of the roof.

7. If necessary, remove all mounting brackets.

8. Renew the sliding backlights as necessary. Operation R/44

9. Assemble the unit by reversing Operations 1 to 7, renewing the rubber draught strips and fittings as necessary.

Note: All 1957 models fitted with cabs, hard tops and hoods, including Station Wagons 88 and 107:

Slight alterations have taken place concerning the fixing brackets used to secure cabs, hard tops and hoods to the windscreen, but stripping and assembly operations are similar to those listed above.

Cab sliding backlight, 1954-58

To renew   **Operation R/44**

1. Withdraw the drive screws securing the bottom channel to the cab rear panel (the drive screws are inside the channel).

2. Remove the bottom run channel and sliding backlight.

3. If necessary, remove the top run channel, the rubber sealing strips and the backlight stops.

4. If necessary, remove the catches from the backlights.

5. Renew the rubber sealing strips, fittings and sliding lights as necessary. Refit by reversing the removal procedure.

Cab body back rest panel, 1954-58 (Land-Rover 107 and 109 only)

To remove   **Operation R/46**

1. Remove the cab. Instruction Manual.

2. Remove the seat cushions.

3. Remove the bolts securing the seat base to the back rest panel. Operation R/38.

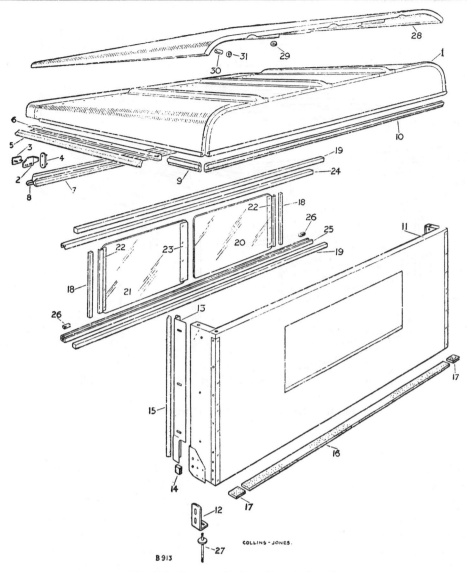

B 913   COLLINS-JONES.

Fig. R-8—Layout of cab and tropical roof.

1	Cab roof assembly	20	Sliding backlight, R.H. half
2	Adjustable bracket, L.H.	21	Sliding backlight, L.H. half
3	Stud plate	22	Finger pull for backlight
4	Adjustable link	23	Draught strip for L.H. half
5	Rubber seal for door	24	Channel, upper ⎱ For
6	Retaining strip, L.H.	25	Channel, lower ⎰ backlight
7	Rubber seal for canopy	26	Stop for backlight
8	Stiffening strip for canopy seal	27	Mounting stud
9	Rubber seal, roof to side	28	Tropical roof panel
10	Rubber seal, roof to back		Screw (2 B.A. x ½" long)
11	Cab rear panel assembly		Plain washer
12	Mounting bracket	29	Rubber washer
13	Capping for front door rear seal, L.H.		Shakeproof washer
14	Draught strip for capping		Nut (2 B.A.)
15	Front door seal, rear upper		Screw (¼" x 2" long)
16	Sealing strip at rear, bottom		Plain washer
17	Rubber draught filler piece for corner	30	Distance piece
18	Rubber sealing strip, side	31	Rubber washer
19	Rubber sealing strip, upper and lower		

18 Rubber sealing strip, side ⎱
19 Rubber sealing strip, upper and lower ⎰ For backlight

29 Rubber washer / Shakeproof washer / Nut (2 B.A.) ⎱ Fixing roof at end of stiffeners

Screw (¼" x 2" long) / Plain washer ⎱ Fixing roof

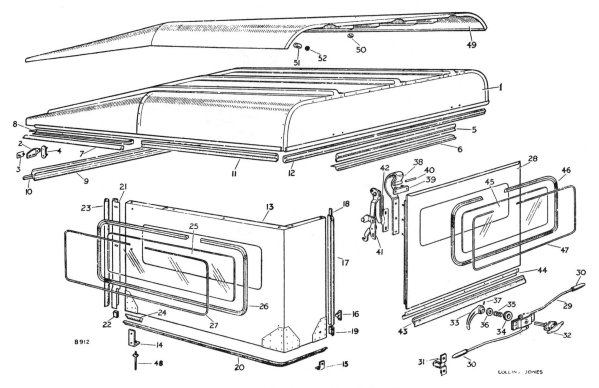

Fig. R-9—Layout of hard top and tropical roof.

1	Roof assembly	25	Weather strip for glass
2	Adjustment bracket, L.H.	26	Filler strip for weather strip
3	Stud plate	27	Rear lid assembly
4	Adjustable link	28	Lock complete for rear lid
5	Rubber seal for rear lid, top	29	Bolt end for lock
6	Retaining strip for rear seal	30	Guide for rear lid lock
7	Rubber seal for door	31	Handle for rear lid, outer
8	Retaining strip, L.H., for door seal	32	Handle for rear lid, inner
9	Rubber seal for canopy	33–36	Boss, fixings for handles
10	Stiffening strip for canopy seal	37	Hinge leaf for rear lid
11	Rubber seal, roof to side	38	Hinge bracket for rear lid
12	Rubber seal, roof to back	39	Pin for rear lid hinge
13	Side panel assembly, L.H.	40	Quadrant complete, L.H.
14	Mounting bracket, front	41	Spring for quadrant
15	Mounting bracket, rear	42	Rubber sealing strip for rear lid, bottom
16	Socket for rear lid lock bolt	43	Retaining strip for bottom seal
17	Rubber sealing strip for rear lid, side	44	Glass for rear lid
18	Reinforcing strip for rear lid seal	45	Weather strip for backlight
19	Rubber buffer for rear lid, side	46	Filler strip for weather strip
20	Rubber sealing strip, lower edge to body	47	Fixings for hard top
21	Capping for front door rear seal, L.H.	48	Tropical roof panel
22	Draught strip for capping	49	Fixings for panel to roof at end of stiffener
23	Seal for front door—upper	50–51	Fixings for roof to panel
24	Glass for side window		

4. Remove the two bolts securing the rear extremities of the sill panels to back rest panel corner brackets.

5. Remove the cab body back rest panel complete.

6. If necessary :—

   (a) Remove the seat back rest support brackets and buffers.

   (b) Remove the door lock striking plates and support brackets.

   (c) Remove the clips for the starting handle and jack handle.

   (d) Remove the sealing strip at the bottom rear of the cab.

   (e) Shear the rivets securing the rear lower door seals and remove the seals.

   (f) Withdraw the drive screws and remove the door rubber buffers.

   (g) Remove the corner brackets.

To refit   **Operation R/48**

Reverse the removal procedure.

Cab tropical roof, 1954-58

To remove   **Operation R/50**

1. Remove the screws, spring and plain washers, nuts, distance pieces and rubber washers securing each side of the panel to the roof.

2. Remove the screws, spring, plain and rubber washers and nuts securing the tropical panel stiffeners to the cab roof both at the front and at the back, then lift off the tropical roof panel.

3. Withdraw the drive screws or shear the pop rivets securing the tropical panel stiffeners to the cab roof, and lift off the tropical roof panel.

To refit   **Operation R/52**

1. Reverse the removal procedure.

Cab (De Luxe Model) interior trim panels, 1954-58

To remove   **Operation R/54**

1. Remove the rear squab complete (four drive screws at the bottom and two at the top), and the seat cushion.

2. Remove the yellow knob from the front wheel drive control, and the wing nut and washer from the gearbox access cover, and remove the floor covering. Remove the four carpet clips and refit the dome-headed bolts.

3. Remove the canopy central support bracket by withdrawing two drive screws.

4. Remove the two canopy mouldings by withdrawing the four drive screws securing them to the side brackets and windscreen retainers.

5. Remove the canopy moulding side brackets from the lower stud on the brackets securing the roof to the windscreen. Replace the plain washers, spring washers and nuts on the studs.

6. Remove the drive screw securing each quarter side panel angle flap to the body cappings.

7. Withdraw the two drive screws securing each of the lower quarter panels to the body cappings, and remove the panels.

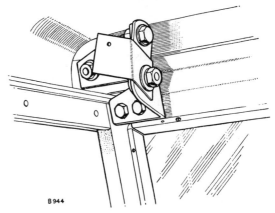

B944

Fig. R-10—Canopy side brackets.

8. Swing the quarter side panels forward and withdraw the bifurcated rivets securing each of them to the front door rear seal cappings.

9. Withdraw the drive screw securing each of the quarter back panels at its top inner edge, and remove the panels.

10. Disconnect the roof light earth wire.

11. Withdraw the four drive screws securing the top rear upper panel to the support channels and remove the panel complete with roof lamp.

12. If necessary, remove the roof lamp from the panel.

13. Withdraw the two bolts securing the support channels to the cab rear panel, and remove the channels; refit the bolts.

14. Remove the two covered spire clips securing the inside ends of the glove boxes to the instrument box; fold the sides, bottom and top of the glove boxes inwards and remove the glove boxes complete.

15. Remove the felt pads secured to the outside ends of the glove boxes with a suitable adhesive.

16. Remove the steering column cover by withdrawing three drive screws.

17. Disconnect the windscreen wiper plug from its socket and remove the three glove box shelf panels, secured each with one drive screw; replace the windscreen wiper plug.

18. Disconnect the wire at the top of the R.H. windscreen pillar from the wire inside the roof trim; disconnect the wire from the instrument box from the wire emerging from the right-hand windscreen pillar, and remove. Withdraw the wire in the R.H. pillar.

19. Remove the drive screws and plain washers securing the two roof lining retainers and the roof lining itself to the roof panel, and remove the roof lining. The front and rear edges of the lining are secured to the roof panel with a suitable adhesive.

20. Open the doors to the front wings, withdraw the five drive screws securing each door trim panel, and remove the panels from the rear.

21. Remove the sidescreens from the door panels, withdraw the nuts and shakeproof washers securing each armrest to the sidescreen frame.

22. Remove the sidescreen trim panels from the sidescreens by withdrawing four drive screws.

23. Remove the top and side dash floor covering retainers from the dash by withdrawing ten drive screws; remove the transfer lever instruction plates and the starter switch knob; detach the floor covering from the dash. Replace the instruction plate and the starter switch knob.

24. Clean off the adhesive compound from the dash, roof panel and glove box outside ends with petrol.

To refit   Operation R/56

1. Reverse the removal procedure.

Station Wagon—all models, 1954-58
Rear door
To remove and dismantle   Operation R/58

1. Remove check strap anchor bolt from rear body floor.

2. Open door to fullest extent and lift clear of hinges.

3. Unscrew the nuts securing the door upper half to lower half and withdraw top section, then remove the sealing strip.

4. Remove the bolts securing hinges, packing plates and check strap.

5. Remove retainer—inner, for door lock handle—inner, then unscrew partially the ring nut securing the private lock and catch, using a special "C" spanner. Slackening of the ring nut will allow the door lock, mounting plate and handles to be removed complete.

6. Unscrew the drive screws securing vertical and horizontal retainers for door glass. Pull off glazing strip from edges of door glass and ease glass away from frame.

To assemble and replace   Operation R/60

1. Reverse "remove and dismantle" procedure.

2. Adjust lock striking plate.

   Note: Door seals should be examined and replaced as necessary before refitting door.

Rear seat
To remove   Operation R/62

Remove the bolts securing the seat pivot brackets to wheelarch box and withdraw the seat complete.

To refit   Operation R/64

Reverse removal procedure.

Back-rest for rear seat
To remove   Operation R/66

Remove bolts securing back-rest brackets to upper body and lower body capping, then withdraw back-rest.

To refit   Operation R/68

Reverse removal procedure.

Roof and sides
To remove   Operation R/70

1. Remove the bolts securing the roof at windscreen corners and bolts securing sides to lower body at front doors, rear corners and adjacent to rear door.

2. Disconnect the roof lamp wire at the snap connector on top of windscreen.

3. Lift roof and sides complete from vehicle.

4. Remove the bolts securing roof to sides and lift roof clear.

To refit   Operation R/72

Reverse removal procedure ensuring that the seals are in good condition before replacing. Before finally tightening roof to sides, spread rubber seal over side panel top edges.

Hard top
To overhaul   Operation R/74

1. Remove the nuts securing the hard top to the windscreen and hood sockets, and the bolts at the rear body cappings.

   Lift off the hard top complete.

2. Detach the spring-loaded rear door quadrants from the side panels. Remove the rear door hinges from the roof panel and remove the door complete with hinges and quadrants.

3. Remove the roof panel and sealing rubbers from the side panels.

4. Remove the draught excluders and retaining strips from the top of the front door apertures.

5. Remove the draught excluders and cappings from the front edges of the side panels.

6. Remove the draught excluder and retaining strip from above the rear door.

7. If necessary, remove the rear door quadrants and hinges from the door frame.

   Note: On assembly, care should be taken to fit the quadrants to the lower captive bolts, with the springs to the inside.

8. If necessary, remove all mounting brackets.

9. If necessary, slide out the rubber mounting strip from the lower edge of the side panels. When refitting, the strip should have its free edge on the inside.

10. If required, remove the sealing rubber and retaining strip from the front edge of the roof.

11. Remove the rear door seal strips from the side panels.

12. If necessary, detach the sockets for the rear door lock bolts. On assembly, fit the sockets with the chamfered face to the inside, to facilitate entry of the bolt.

13. To remove the door lock, remove the inner handle by depressing the spring-loaded boss and push out the locking pin; remove the handle, boss, cap and spring. Withdraw the screws, spring and plain washers and nuts securing the lock to the door panel; remove the bolts and plain washers securing the bolt guides to the door panel, remove the outer handle and lift off the lock complete. On assembly, it will be necessary to adjust the position of the bolts by slackening the locking nuts, to obtain adequate entry into the sockets.

14. If necessary, remove the rubber sealing strip and retainer from the lower edge of the rear door.

15. Renew the window glasses as necessary. Operation R/76.

16. Assemble the unit by reversing Operations 1 to 14, renewing the rubber draught strips and fittings as necessary.

Hard top window glass
To renew   **Operation R/76**

Note: As some difficulty may be experienced in carrying out this operation, it will be found advantageous, where possible, to remove the panel in which the glass is to be fitted, and lay it flat on a suitable bench or stand.

1. Prise out the rubber filler strip from the glass weather strip; push the glass and weather strip from the panel aperture.

2. Square off one end of the rubber weather strip, and, starting at the bottom centre, fit the narrow groove of the strip to the panel aperture with the locking groove to the weather side.

3. Force the strip well into the aperture corners, and, allowing about one inch overlap, square off the other end of the moulding. Compress the moulding around its length until the ends can be joined. (This overlap is important, as otherwise a gap will appear between the moulding ends when the glass is fitted.)

4. Fit the glass into the moulding, using a flat piece of metal to pull the lip over the glass.

5. Square off one end of the filler strip, and, starting opposite the joint in the moulding, insert the filler strip in the groove in the weather strip by means of the special tool, Part No. 262771. Allowing about $\frac{1}{4}$ in. overlap, square off the end of the filler strip, and force the overlap into the weather strip groove.

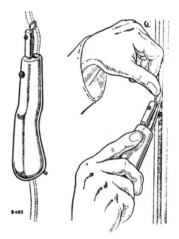

Fig. R-11—

Fitting filler strip in window weather strip.

Hard top tropical roof, 1954-58
To remove   **Operation R/78**

1. Remove the screws, spring and plain washers, nuts, distance pieces and rubber washers securing each side of the panel to the roof.

2. Remove the screws, spring, plain and rubber washers and nuts securing the tropical panel stiffeners to the hard top roof, both at the front and at the back.

3. Remove the drive screws or shear the pop rivets securing the panel to the hard top stiffeners, and lift off the tropical roof panel.

To refit   **Operation R/80**

1. Reverse the removal procedure.

Tailboard

To remove and refit   **Operation R/82**

1. Release the tailboard keys and drop the tailboard.

2. North American vehicles only. Disconnect the rear number plate lamp wiring before removing the tailboard.

3. Unhook the tailboard chains; remove the plain washer, spring washer and split pin from the R.H. hinge pin and slide out the tailboard to the left.

4. If necessary, remove the tailboard hinges and the chain hooks.

5. Refit by reversing items 1 to 3.

Rear body

To remove   **Operation R/84**

1. Remove the hood and hood sticks or the hard top.

2. Remove the spare wheel if fitted in the rear body.

3. **80, 86 and 88 models**: remove the seat cushions.

4. Remove the tailboard. Operation R/82.

1948-53 models

5. After disconnecting the battery, slacken the stop-tail lamp cover screw, swing open the cover and disconnect the wiring; remove the two nuts and detach the clip and earth wire from the body bracket. Repeat for the other lamp.

1954-58 models

6. Disconnect the stop/tail lamp harnesses at the snap connectors below the rear corners of the body floor and the earth wires from the chassis.

1948-53 models

7. Remove the twelve nuts, bolts and spring washers securing the body to the chassis; remove the thirteen nuts, bolts and spring washers fixing the body to the seat box, eight of which also secure the locker lids; remove the six bolts and plain washers securing the body to the side of the seat box and remove the rear body complete.

1954-58 models

8. Remove the bolts, plain washers, spring washers and nuts securing the body to the chassis; remove the rear body complete.

9. If necessary :—

(a) Remove the stop-tail lamps, leads and grommets.

(b) Remove the spare wheel clamp, brackets and tyre rests.

(c) Remove the hood strap staples.

(d) Remove the tailboard chain brackets, the chains and keys, the Land-Rover nameplate and the number plate.

(e) Remove the protecting strip from the rear of the body.

(f) Remove the tailboard rubber buffers, if fitted.

(g) Remove the rubber buffers from the underside of the body floor, if fitted.

1954-58 models

(h) Remove the seat base corner brackets.

(j) Land-Rover 80 and 86 only. Remove the seat back rest support brackets, buffers and retaining strap studs.

Remove the door lock striking plates and support brackets.

Remove the clips for the starting handle and jack handle.

1954-58 models

Shear the rivets securing the rear lower door seals and remove the seals.

1954-58 models

Withdraw the drive screws and remove the door rubber buffers.

(k) Land-Rover 107 and 109 only. Remove the floor tread plates.

1954-58 models

Remove the locker lids and turnbuckles.

1954-58 models

Remove the wheel arch box support stays.

To refit   **Operation R/86**

Reverse the removal procedure.

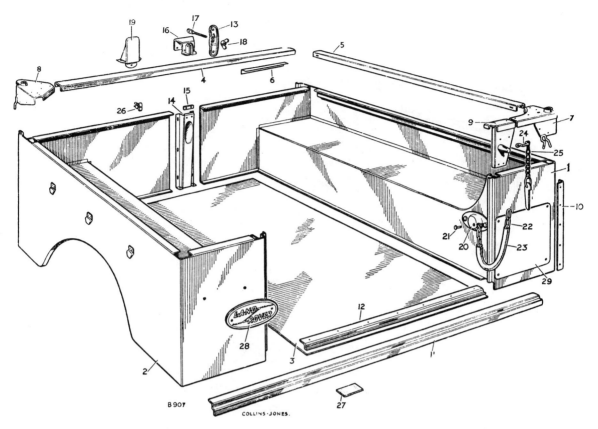

Fig. R-12—Layout of rear body unit (Land-Rover 86 and 88).

1 Side and wheel arch complete, R.H.	16 Pivot bracket for spare wheel clamp
2 Side and wheel arch complete, L.H.	17 Tie bar for spare wheel clamp
3 Rear floor complete	18 Wing nut
4 Capping for body back rest panel	19 Bracket, spare wheel tyre rest
5 Capping for body top, sides	20 Bracket for tailboard chain
6 Corner strengthening angle	21 Pin, fixing tailboard chain to bracket
7 Hood socket complete, rear corner, R.H.	22 Chain for tailboard
8 Hood socket complete, front corner, L.H.	23 Sleeve for chain
9 Corner bracket and tailboard dowel, L.H.	24 Staple for hood strap
10 Rear protection angle	25 Key and chain for tailboard
11 Rear mounting angle	26 Clip for starting handle and jack handle
12 Protecting strip at rear of floor	27 Rubber buffer, floor to chassis
13 Clamp for spare wheel	28 "Land-Rover" nameplate
14 Reinforcement bracket for clamp	29 Registration plate
15 Tapped plate for pivot bracket	

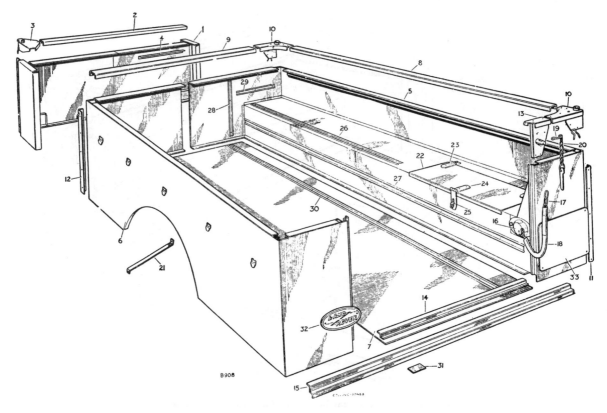

Fig. R-13—Layout of rear body unit (Land-Rover 107 and 109).

1 Cab body assembly, lower, front
2 Capping for cab body, top
3 Socket, L.H.
4 Corner strengthening angle
5 Side and wheel arch complete, R.H.
6 Side and wheel arch complete, L.H.
7 Rear floor
8 Capping for body top, sides
9 Capping for body top, front
10 Hood socket, R.H.
11 Corner protector angle, rear
12 Corner protecting angle, front, L.H.
13 Corner bracket and tailboard dowel, R.H.
14 Protecting strip at rear of floor
15 Rear mounting angle
16 Tailboard chain bracket
17 Chain for tailboard

18 Sleeve for chain
19 Staple for hood strap
20 Tailboard key and chain
21 Support stay
22 Locker lid for wheel arch box
23 Hinge for locker lid
24 Hasp for locker lid
25 Turnbuckle for locker lid
26 Tread plate, wheel arch box, top
27 Tread plate, wheel arch box, sides
28 Tread plate, inner, front panel
29 Tread plate, outer, front panel
30 Tread plate for rear floor
31 Rubber buffer, floor to chassis
32 "Land-Rover" nameplate
33 Registration plate

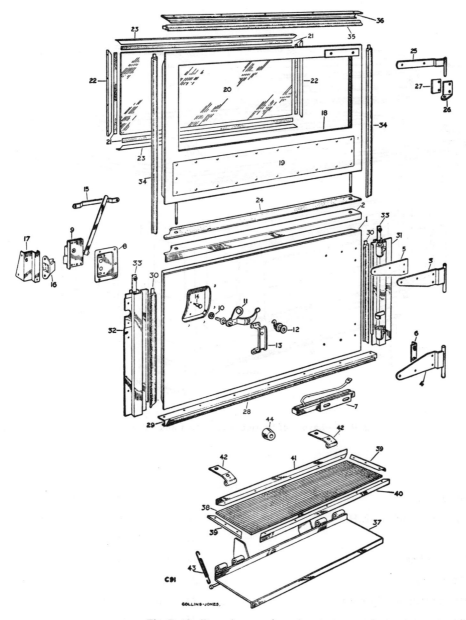

Fig. R-14—Rear door, seals and rear step.

1 Rear door assembly—lower	17 Support bracket for striking plate	30 Seal for rear door side—lower
2 Top capping for door—lower	18 Rear door assembly—upper	31 Seal retainer-R.H. ⎫ For lower
3 Hinge, top	19 Filler panel for rear door—upper	32 Seal retainer-L.H. ⎭ rear door
4 Hinge, bottom	20 Glass window	33 Nut retainer
5 Packing plate for hinge	21 Glazing strip	34 Rubber sealing strip—door side upper
6 Nut plate for hinge	22 Retainer for glass—vertical	35 Seal for door top
7 Check strap complete	23 Retainer for glass—horizontal	36 Retainer for seal
8 Mounting plate for door lock	24 Rubber sealing strip	37 Rear step
9 Door lock	25 Hinge plate ⎫ For rear door	38 Rubber mat ⎫
10 Rubber washer, handle to cover	26 Top pivot ⎬ —upper	39 Retainer—side ⎪
11 Handle and catch bracket	bracket ⎭	40 Retainer—front ⎪
12 Private lock and catch	27 Packing for top pivot bracket	41 Retainer—rear ⎬ For rear
13 Bracket for door handle	28 Seal for rear door bottom	42 Hinge centre ⎪ step
14 Locking pillar for catch	29 Retainer for seal	43 Spring ⎪
15 Retainer for door handle		44 Buffer ⎭
16 Striking plate for rear door		

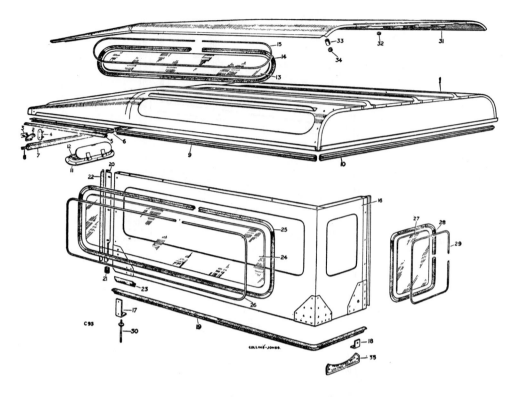

Fig. R-15—Layout of Station Wagon roof and sides.

1	Roof complete	19	Rubber sealing strip
2	Adjustment bracket—L.H.	20	Capping for front door seal— L.H.
3	Stud plate	21	Draught strip for capping
4	Adjustable link	22	Seal for front door
5	Seal for door	23	Draught strip for corner plate
6	Retaining strip for door seal	24	Window glass—side
7	Rubber seal for canopy	25	Weather strip
8	Stiffening strip for seal	26	Filler for weather strip
9	Rubber seal—roof to side	27	Window glass—rear
10	Rubber seal—roof to back	28	Weather strip
11	Roof ventilator	29	Filler for weather strip
12	Sealing rubber for ventilator	30	Mounting stud
13	Side light for roof	31	Tropical roof panel
14	Weather strip	32	Rubber washer
15	Filler for weather strip	33	Distance piece
16	Side panel assembly—L.H.	34	Rubber washer
17	Mounting bracket—front	35	"Station Wagon" name plate
18	Mounting bracket—rear		

33 Distance piece ⎫ Panel to roof
34 Rubber washer ⎬ at sides

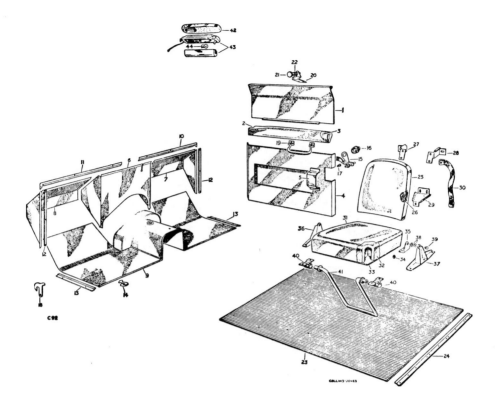

Fig. R-16—Layout of Station Wagon De Luxe Trim.

1	Trim casing for sidescreen—R.H.	23	Rubber mat
2	Side armrest complete—R.H.	24	Retainer for mat
3	Rubber topping	25	Rear seat back-rest complete
4	Trim casing for door—R.H.	26	Pad for seat back-rest
5	Trim casing for door lock	27	Bracket (R.H.)—upper
6	Dash covering—centre	28	Bracket (L.H.)—upper > For seat back-rest
7	Dash covering—R.H.	29	Bracket—lower
8	Dash covering—L.H.	30	Retaining strap
9	Floor covering	31	Rear seat complete
10	Retainer for dash covering—R.H. top	32	Rubber interior
11	Retainer for dash covering—L.H. top	33	Seat base
12	Retainer for dash covering—side	34	Rubber buffer
13	Retainer for floor covering—side	35	Cushion pivot bracket—seat
14	Clip for floor covering	36	Cushion pivot bracket (L.H.) on wheel arch box
15	Door handle and catch bracket	37	Cushion pivot bracket (R.H.) on wheel arch box
16	Private lock and catch	38	Plain washer
17	Locking pillar for catch	39	Special rivet
18	Safety catch for L.H. door lock	40	Support tube bearing
19	Pull handle for front door	41	Support tube
20	Bracket for door light locking screw	42	Packing block for roof lamp
21	Locking screw	43	Roof lamp complete
22	Spring	44	Bulb

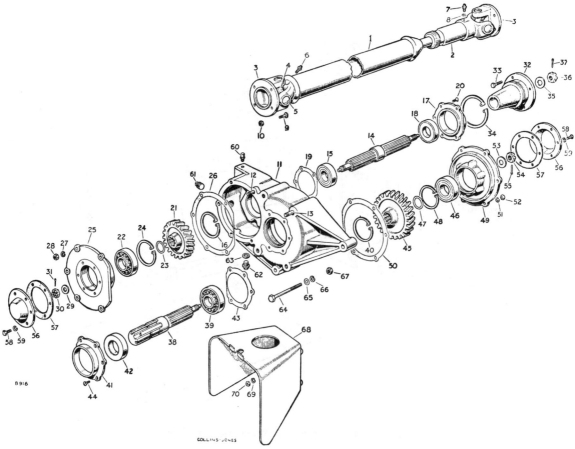

Fig. T-6—Layout of rear power take-off unit.

1	Propeller shaft, P.T.O. drive	33	Special bolts for propeller shaft
2	Splined end ⎱ For propeller	34	Circlip retaining bolts to flange
3	Flange ⎰ shaft	35–37	Fixings for flange
4	Journal complete for propeller shaft	38	Output shaft for P.T.O. 6-spline
5	Circlip for journal	39	Bearing for output shaft, rear
6	Grease nipple for journal	40	Circlip for bearing
7	Grease nipple for propeller shaft, .250 in.	41	Retainer for oil seal ⎱ For output
	(6,35 mm) dia.	42	Oil seal ⎰ shaft
8	Washer for nipple	43	Joint washer for retainer
9–10	Fixings for propeller shaft	44	Screw fixing retainer
11	Housing assembly for P.T.O.	45	Gear wheel, 24 teeth
12	Stud for bearing housing	46	Bearing for output shaft, front
13	Stud for pulley housing or guard	47	Shim, for front output shaft bearing
14	Input shaft for P.T.O.	48	Circlip, bearing to housing
15	Bearing for input shaft, front	49	Housing for output shaft front bearing
16	Circlip, bearing to housing	50	Joint washer for bearing housing
17	Retainer for oil seal ⎱ For input	51–52	Fixings for bearing housing
18	Oil seal ⎰ shaft	53–55	Fixings for front bearing
19	Joint washer for retainer	56	Cover plate for bearings
20	Screw fixing retainer	57	Joint washer for cover plate
21	Gear wheel, 20 teeth	58–59	Fixings for cover
22	Bearing for input shaft, rear	60	Breather for casing
23	Shim for rear input shaft bearing	61	Filler plug
24	Circlip, bearing to housing	62	Drain plug for casing
25	Housing for rear input shaft bearing	63	Fibre washer for plug
26	Joint washer for rear bearing housing	64–67	Fixings for P.T.O. assembly
27–28	Fixings for bearing housing	68	Guard for P.T.O. spline
29–31	Fixings for rear bearing	69–70	Fixings for guard
32	Flange for P.T.O. input shaft		

Section S—WHEELS AND TYRES—ALL MODELS

INDEX

	Page			Page
Changing tyre positions	S-2	Tyre removal and fitting		S-2
Defect location	S-4	Tyre and tube repairs	....	S-2
Factors affecting tyre life	S-2	Tyre treads	....	S-2
Tyre pressures....	S-1	Wheel balance	....	S-3

LIST OF ILLUSTRATIONS

Fig.			Page
S-1	Changing wheel positions	....	S-2
S-2	Divided wheel	....	S-3
S-3	Tightening sequence	....	S-3

Tyre pressures

Careful attention must be given to the question of correct tyre pressures if maximum tyre life and performance are to be obtained.

TYRE PRESSURES—1948-53

For **normal road and cross-country** work, tyre pressures must be maintained at:—

Front	Rear
20 lb. per sq.in.	26 lb. per sq.in.
(1,4 kg/cm²)	(1,8 kg/cm²)

When **loads in excess of 550 lb.** (250 kg) are carried in the rear of the vehicle, pressures in the **rear tyres only** must be raised to 30 lb. per sq.in. (2,1 kg/cm²).

Should it be desired to traverse **exceptionally soft ground,** the tyre pressures may be **reduced** to

Front

6.00 x 16: 15 lb. per sq.in. (1,05 kg/cm²)
7.00 x 16: 13 lb. per sq.in. (0,9 kg/cm²)

Rear

6.00 x 16: 20 lb. per sq.in. (1,4 kg/cm²)
7.00 x 16: 18 lb. per sq.in. (1,25 kg/cm²)

These reduced pressures must only be employed when absolutely essential and the pressures **must be returned to normal** immediately after the soft ground has been negotiated.

1. For **normal road and cross-country** work, tyre pressures must be maintained at:—

Front and Rear

25 lb. per sq.in. (1,75 kg/cm²)

When **loads in excess of 550 lb.** (250 kg) are carried in the rear of the vehicle, pressures in the **rear tyres only** must be raised to 30 lb. per sq.in. (2,1 kg./cm²).

2. Should it be desired to traverse **exceptionally soft ground,** the tyre pressures may be **reduced** to

Front and rear

6.00 x 16 tyres: 15 lb. per sq.in. (1,05 kg/cm²)
7.00 x 16 tyres: 13 lb. per sq.in. (0,9 kg/cm²)

When loads in excess of 550 lb. (250 kg) are carried in the rear of the vehicle, pressures in the **rear tyres only** must be raised to :—

6.00 x 16 tyres: 20 lb. per sq.in. (1,4 kg/cm²)
7.00 x 16 tyres: 18 lb. per sq.in. (1,25 kg/cm²)

TYRE PRESSURES—1954-58

Careful attention must be given to the question of correct tyre pressures if maximum tyre life and performance are to be obtained.

1. For **normal road and cross-country** work, tyre pressures must be maintained at:—

Land-Rover, all models
Front and Rear

25 lb. per sq.in. (1,75 kg/cm²)

When **loads in excess of 550 lb.** (250 kg) are carried in the rear of the vehicle, pressures in the rear tyres only must be raised to:

Land-Rover 86 and 88:
30 lb. per sq.in. (2,1 kg/cm²)

Land-Rover 107 and 109:
32 lb. per sq.in. (2,25 kg./cm²)

2. Should it be desired to traverse **exceptionally soft ground,** the tyre pressures may be reduced to:—

Land-Rover 86 and 88
Front and Rear:

6.00 x 16 tyres: 15 lb. per sq.in. (1,05 kg/cm²)
6.50 x 16 tyres: 15 lb. per sq.in. (1,05 kg/cm²)
7.00 x 16 tyres: 13 lb. per sq.in. (0,9 kg /cm²)

When **loads in excess of 550 lb.** (250 kg.) are carried in the rear of the vehicle, pressures in the **rear tyres only** must be raised to:—

6.00 x 16 tyres: 20 lb. per sq.in. (1,4 kg/cm²)
6.50 x 16 tyres: 20 lb. per sq.in. (1,4 kg/cm²)
7.00 x 16 tyres: 18 lb. per sq.in. (1,25 kg/cm²)

Land-Rover 107 and 109

Unladen   **Front and Rear**
16 lb. per sq. in. (1,15 kg/cm²)

Laden   Front: 18 lb. per sq. in. (1,25 kg/cm²)
Rear: 24 lb. per sq. in. (1,7 kg/cm²)

Reduced pressures must only be employed when absolutely essential and the pressures must be returned to normal immediately after the soft ground has been negotiated.

Pressures should be checked and adjusted weekly, paying attention to the following points:

1. Whenever possible, check the tyres cold, as the pressure is about 2 lb. (0,1 kg) higher at running temperature.

2. Always replace the valve caps, as they form a positive seal on the valves.

3. Any unusual pressure loss (in excess of 1 to 3 lb. (0,05 to 0,20 kg) per month) should be investigated and corrected.

4. Always check the spare wheel, so that it is ready for use at any time.

5. At the same time, remove embedded flints, etc., from the tyre treads with the aid of a penknife or similar tool. Clean off any oil or grease on the tyres, using petrol sparingly.

Tyre treads

The tread form of the Standard 86 and 88 and Special tyres makes them uni-directional. They must be fitted with the V in the tread pattern pointing forwards at the top of the wheel, to ensure maximum grip and efficient tread cleaning when operating on soft ground. For this reason it may be found necessary to reverse the spare tyre on its wheel (dependent on which side it is to be fitted) when putting it into service.

Changing tyre positions

In the interests of tyre mileage and even wear, it is recommended that the wheels are changed round every 3,000 miles (5.000 km) as follows:

Spare to left-hand front; left-hand front to left-hand rear; left-hand rear to right-hand front; right-hand front to right-hand rear and right-hand rear to spare.

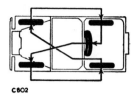

C802

Fig. S-1—Changing wheel positions.

Factors affecting tyre life

1. Incorrect tyre pressures.

2. High average speeds.

3. Harsh acceleration.

4. Frequent hard braking.

5. Warm, dry climatic conditions.

6. Poor road surfaces.

7. Impact fractures caused by striking a kerb or loose brick, etc.

8. Incorrect front wheel alignment. Alignment should be checked periodically.

Tyre and inner tube repairs

Minor tyre injuries, such as from nails, require no attention other than removal of the object, but more severe tread or wall cuts require vulcanised repairs.

Avoid the use of gaiters or liners except as a temporary expedient. As "Butyl" synthetic tubes are used, all repairs must be vulcanised.

Tyres

Well base rims (*Standard on all models*)

To remove   **Operation S/2**

1. Remove the valve cap and core (extractor provided in tool kit) and deflate the tyre.

2. Press each bead in turn off its seating. Insert a lever at the valve position and, while pulling on this lever, press the bead into the well, diametrically opposite the valve.

3. Insert a second lever close to the first and prise the bead over the wheel rim. Continue round the bead in small steps until it is completely off the rim.

4. Remove the inner tube and pull the second bead over the rim.

To refit   **Operation S/4**

1. Place the cover over the wheel and press the lower bead over the rim edge into the well.

2. Inflate the inner tube until it is just rounded out, dust with French chalk, and insert it in the cover, with the white spots near the cover bead coinciding with the black spots on the tube.

3. Press the upper bead into the well diametrically opposite the valve and lever the bead over the rim edge.

4. Push the valve inwards to ensure that the tube is not trapped under the bead, pull it back and inflate the tyre.

5. Check the concentricity of the fitting line on the cover and the top of the wheel flange. Deflate the tube completely and re-inflate to the correct pressure, to relieve any strains in the tube.

Divided wheels (*fitted as optional equipment on 88 models*)

To remove   **Operation S/6**

Note: Do not touch the nuts securing the two halves of the wheel together before the tyre is deflated or serious personal injury may result.

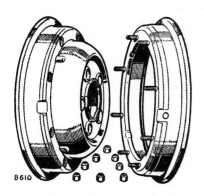

Fig. S-2— Divided wheel

1. Remove the valve cap and core to deflate the tyre.

2. Press each bead in turn away from the flange, using levers and working round the tyre in small steps. Two or three circuits of the tyre may be necessary to free the beads completely.

3. Slacken and remove the clamping nuts. Remove the upper half of the wheel. Push the valve through the lower half of the wheel and remove the cover and tube.

To refit   **Operation S/8**

1. Thoroughly examine the cover for nails, flints, etc., and ensure that no loose objects have been left inside. Clean the wheel rim flanges and seatings.

2. Inflate the inner tube until it is just rounded out, dust with French chalk and insert it in the cover with the white spots near the cover bead coinciding with the black spots on the tube.

3. Fit the protection flap, starting at the valve position. Make sure that the edges of the flap are not turned over inside the cover and that it lies centrally between the beads. See that the flap fits closely against the tube round the valve.

4. Lay the studded half of the wheel on the floor or bench with the studs pointing upwards. Fit the cover over the wheel and thread the valve through the hole, making sure that it points downwards.

5. Fit the other half of the wheel and tighten the clamping nuts lightly. Finally tighten the nuts in the sequence illustrated. Check that the valve is free and inflate the tyre to the recommended pressure.

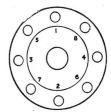

Fig. S-3— Tightening sequence.

Wheel and tyre

To balance   **Operation S/10**

Wheel and tyre units are accurately balanced on initial assembly with the aid of small weights secured to the inner side of the wheel slot flanges by means of set bolts. In the interests of smooth riding and even tyre wear, it is advantageous to check the balance whenever a tyre is refitted, on suitable proprietary equipment.

DEFECT LOCATION
(Symptom, Cause and Remedy)

A—EXCESSIVE WEAR ON FRONT TYRES

1. Tyres under-inflated—*Refer to "Recommended Tyre Pressures".*
2. Tyre positions not changed regularly—*Change every 3,000 miles (5.000 Km).*
3. Incorrect toe-in—*Section G.*
4. Harsh or unnecessary use of brakes—*In the hands of the operator.*
5. Incorrectly adjusted brakes—*Section H.*
6. Eccentric brake drum—*Section H.*
7. Front wheels or tyres out of balance—*Rebalance the wheel assembly.*

B—RATTLES FROM FRONT WHEELS

1. Loose wheel bearings—*Adjust and examine for damage, Section F.*
2. Broken wheel bearings—*Renew. Section F.*
3. Brake shoes or anchor plate loose—*Check and retighten. Section H.*

C—SQUEAKS FROM FRONT WHEELS

1. Wheel stud nuts loose—*Examine studs for damage and tighten.*
2. Lack of lubrication to front wheel bearings—*See Section F.*
3. Front wheel bearings adjusted too tightly—*Adjust and examine for damage.*
4. Damaged front wheel bearings—*Renew. Section F.*

D—OTHER NOISES FROM THE FRONT WHEELS

1. Variation in tread surface due to patch or damage—*Renew outer cover.*
2. Type or condition of tyre tread giving a noise similar to gear growl—*Renew with tyres of the recommended type.*
3. Under-inflated tyres also giving a noise similar to gear growl—*Inflate to the pressures recommended.*
4. Foreign body embedded in tyre—*Extract the embedded matter and repair the tyre as necessary.*
5. Wear in differential—*Section F.*

E—OVERHEATING OF FRONT WHEEL BEARINGS

1. Insufficient lubricant.—*See Section F*
2. Use of a poor quality or incorrect grade of lubricant—*Replenish.*
3. Front wheel bearings adjusted too tightly—*The end-float in the front hub bearings must be correct. Adjust and examine for damage. Section F.*
4. Damaged front wheel bearings—*Renew. Section F.*
5. Heat transfer from brake drums due to dragging brakes—*Adjust. Section H.*
6. Excessive use of the brakes—*In the hands of the operator.*
7. Foreign matter in the bearings—*Clean and renew bearings.*

F—EXCESSIVE WEAR ON REAR TYRES

1. Under-inflated tyres—*Refer to "Recommended Tyre Pressures".*
2. Rear wheels out of alignment—*Check that the rear spring centre dowel is not sheared. Check for a broken rear spring main leaf. Check for a damaged chassis frame. Rectify.*
3. Rear wheel run-out or wobble—*Check for loose wheel nuts. Check for a damaged wheel or incorrectly fitted tyres. Rectify.*
4. Harsh and unnecessary use of brakes or high speed driving—*In the hands of the operator.*
5. Wheels or tyres out of balance—*Rectify.*

G—REAR WHEEL NOISE

1. Wheel hub nuts or drum studs loose—*Rectify.*
2. Interference of brake drum with brake shoes—*Check the shoes for damage or warping and rectify. Check the brake drum for scoring. Rectify or renew.*
3. Brake back plate loose—*Rectify. Check shoes and drum for damage.*
4. Type or condition of tyre tread—*Renew with suitable tyres.*
5. Wear in the differential—*Section E.*

Section T—EXTRA EQUIPMENT—ALL MODELS

INDEX

	Page		Page
Capstan winch, front	T-18	Oil cooler	T-25
Capstan winch, rear	T-22	Power take-off, centre	T-2
Cover plates for propeller shafts	T-35	Power take-off, rear	T-4
Data	T-58	Propeller shaft joint cover plates	T-35
Defect location	T-58	Rear seats	T-44
Door handles, locking	T-44	Spare wheel carrier	T-45
Engine governor, Petrol models .... T-11 and	T-18	Three-quarter length hood	T-47
Fire fighting equipment	T-48	Towing attachments	T-45
Flashing indicators	T-37	Trafficators	T-39
Full length hood	T-45	Trailer plug and socket	T-42
Hand engine speed control, Petrol models	T-24	Ventilator flyscreens	T-47
Heater unit, Petrol models	T-33	Water temperature and oil pressure gauge	T-31
Heater unit, Diesel models	T-35	Windscreen wiper—extra	T-44
Locking door handles	T-44	Window catches	T-44

LIST OF ILLUSTRATIONS

Fig.		Page	Fig.		Page
T-1	Installation of centre power take-off	T-2	T-24	Additional drillings in grille panels	T-27
T-2	Layout of gearbox drive unit and centre pulley	T-3	T-25	Layout of oil cooler—Diesel models	T-28
T-3	Cutting and drilling inspection panel	T-4	T-26	Installation of oil cooler—Petrol models	T-29
T-4	Cross-section of gearbox drive unit and centre pulley	T-5	T-27	Installation of oil cooler—Diesel models	T-30
T-5	Rear power take-off and drive pulley	T-5	T-28	Water temperature and oil pressure gauge—Petrol models	T-31
T-6	Layout of rear power take-off unit	T-6	T-29	Water temperature and oil pressure gauge—Diesel models	T-32
T-7	Rear power take-off propeller shaft centre bearing assembly	T-7	T-30	Layout of heater unit—Petrol models	T-34
T-8	Cross-section of rear power take-off	T-7	T-31	Layout of heater unit—Diesel models	T-36
T-9	Cross-section of rear pulley unit	T-9	T-32	Propeller shaft joint cover plates	T-37
T-10	Layout of rear pulley unit....	T-10	T-33	Cover plates in position	T-37
T-11	Layout of engine governor	T-12	T-34	Position of flasher mounting bracket	T-38
T-12	Installation of engine governor	T-13	T-35	Layout of trafficators	T-39
T-13	Layout of speed limit governor	T-15	T-36	Flasher and trailer plug wiring diagrams	T-40
T-14	Layout of front capstan winch	T-16			
T-15	Rivnut ready for fitting	T-19	T-37	Additional drillings in front wings	T-42
T-16	Rivnut fitting	T-19	T-38	Layout of rear seats	T-43
T-17	Installation of front winch	T-19	T-39	Bonnet panel carrier dimensions	T-45
T-18	Rear winch	T-22	T-40	Towing attachments	T-46
T-19	Cross-section of rear capstan winch....	T-22	T-41	Flow chart, fire tender	T-48
T-20	Layout of rear capstan winch	T-23	T-42	Pump and controls	T-50
T-21	Layout of hand throttle	T-24	T-43	Arrangement of governor control	T-52
T-22	Layout of oil cooler, 2 litre Petrol	T-26	T-44	Exploded view of pump	T-54
T-23	Location and drilling of tapping plates	T-27	T-45	Sectioned view of pump	T-56

Hood, early type

To convert   **Operation T/2**

Should it be required to fit the later (rope-fixing) type of hood to vehicles numbered 860001 to 8666000, a complete kit of parts can be obtained from our Spares Department under Part No. T1968.

To fit the new hood in place of the original (strap-fixing) hood, proceed as follows:—

1. Remove the original hood complete with all straps, leaving the hood sticks in position.

2. Drill two $\frac{3}{16}$ in. (4,8 mm) fixing holes in the tapered end of each retaining plate supplied.

3. Fit the new hood over the hood sticks and secure the front hood eyes to the windscreen. Secure the front straps to the windscreen and the long rear straps to the staples on the rear of the body. Secure the hood side curtains to the front hood stick by means of the short straps on the curtains. Position the hood neatly.

4. Drill a $\frac{3}{16}$ in. (4,8 mm) hole in the outside of each front hood socket on the centre-line of the door buffer stop and $\frac{3}{4}$ in. (19 mm) from the front (sloping) face of the socket. Fit the hood side rope hooks in these holes.

5. Pull the hood side ropes taut from the rear; fit two retaining plates on each bodyside panel, to correspond with the visible rope loops, with the top edge of each plate on the centre-line of the rope. Secure each plate with two screws, spring washers and nuts. Loop the ropes under the plates.

6. Pull the rear curtain bottom rope taut. Fit a retaining plate in each upper corner of the tailboard panel, to correspond with the rope loops. Secure each plate with two screws, spring washers and nuts. Loop the rope under the plates.

7. Fit a rope cleat on each body rear panel, against the diagonal edge of the rear hood socket and secure with two screws, spring washers and nuts.

8. Insert the triangular side flaps on the rear curtain in the pockets on the side curtains and secure with the straps provided.

9. Place the loop on one end of the rear curtain bottom rope over the adjacent rope cleat, wind the rope round the hook at the lower rear corner of the side curtain, pull the rope taut under the plates on the tailboard, round the hook on the other side curtain and secure on the adjacent rope cleat.

10. Secure the side curtain bottom ropes and the rear curtain side ropes round the rope cleats. Adjust the whole hood as neatly as possible.

Centre power take-off—86 and 88 models

To fit   **Operation T/4**

1. Remove the centre inspection panel from the seat box.

2. Remove the top cover plate complete with joint washer from the transfer casing.

3. Remove the mainshaft rear bearing housing assembly and joint washer from the rear of the transfer casing.

4. Fit the power take-off drive unit assembly and joint washer to the rear of the transfer casing with the oil drain hole in the housing at the bottom.

5. Fit the power take-off selector assembly and joint washer to the top face of the transfer casing; ensure that the selector fork engages with the dog clutch on the drive shaft.

6. Land-Rover 86 only. Fit the three-groove driving pulley over the flanged drive shaft.

7. Mark out and cut one hole 7 in. (177,8 mm) diameter and two slots $\frac{1}{8}$ in. (3,17 mm) wide and $2\frac{1}{16}$ in. (52,38 mm) long, and drill one hole .204 in. (5,18 mm) diameter in the panel as illustrated in Fig. T-3.

8. Rivet the cover retaining clip to the panel by means of the rivet and the plain washer, which should be placed between the clip and the panel. Engage the tongues of the cover in the slots cut in the panel.

9. Replace the seat box inspection panel.

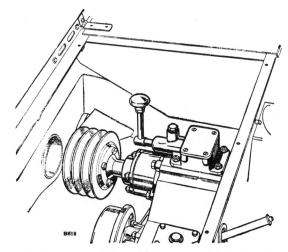

Fig. T-1—Installation of centre power take-off unit.

Note: The centre power take-off must only be used in conjunction with an engine governor. Operation T/26. A special type of centre power take-off is supplied for use with certain items of special equipment. It may be recognised by the fact that the drive housing is extended to the rear, to enable the drive pulley to be fitted the opposite way round to the standard unit. In this manner the load from the drive belts is brought directly over the rear bearing in the drive housing. Overhaul instructions are similar to those for the standard type.

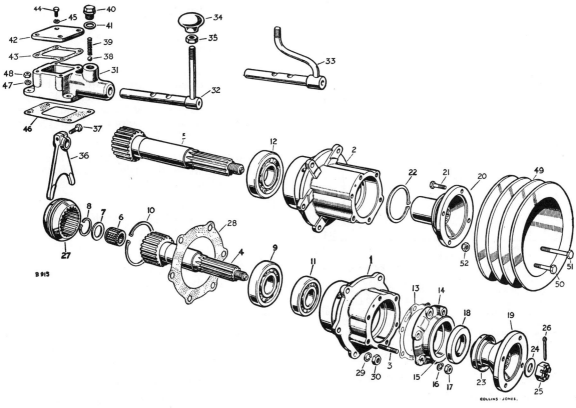

Fig. T-2—Layout of gearbox drive unit and centre pulley.

1 Housing assembly for drive bearing
2 Housing assembly for drive bearing (with welder, compressor etc.)
3 Stud for oil seal housing
4 Shaft for P.T.O. drive
5 Shaft for P.T.O. drive (with welder, compressor etc.
6 Bearing for gearbox mainshaft
7 Retaining plate for bearing
8 Circlip fixing retaining plate
9 Bearing for drive shaft, front
10 Circlip, bearing to housing
11 Bearing for drive shaft, rear
12 Bearing for drive shaft, rear (with welder, compressor etc.)
13 Shim for bearing
14 Housing for oil seal
15 Mudshield for housing
16-17 Fixings for oil seal housing
18 Oil seal for drive shaft
19 Flange for P.T.O. drive shaft
20 Flange for P.T.O. drive shaft ⎫ With welder,
21 Bolt for flange ⎬ compressor,
22 Circlip retaining bolts ⎭ etc.
23 Mudshield for flange

24–26 Fixings for flange
27 Dog clutch for P.T.O. shaft
28 Joint washer for housing
29–30 Fixings for housing
31 Housing for P.T.O. selector
32 Selector shaft and rod for P.T.O.
33 Selector shaft for rod and P.T.O. (with welder, compressor etc.)
34 Knob for rod
35 Locknut for knob
36 Fork for selector shaft
37 Set bolt fixing fork to shaft
38 Steel ball ⎫ For selector
39 Spring ⎭ shaft
40 Plug for spring
41 Joint washer for plug
42 Cover plate for housing
43 Joint washer for plate
44–45 Fixings for plate
46 Joint washer for housing
47–48 Fixings for housing
49 Pulley for centre power take-off
50–52 Fixings for pulley

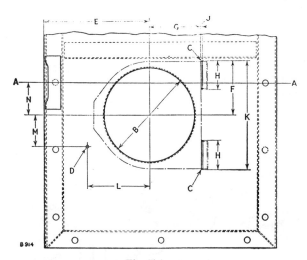

Fig. T-3—
Cutting and drilling seat box centre inspection panel.

AA—Centre line of body.	G—4 in. (101,56 mm).
B—7 in. (177,8 mm).	H—2 $\frac{1}{16}$ in. (52,38 mm).
C—Two slots as shown.	J—$\frac{1}{8}$ in. (3,17 mm).
D—One hole .204 in. (5,18 mm).	K—8 $\frac{1}{16}$ in. (204,77 mm).
	L—4 $\frac{3}{4}$ in. (120,60 mm).
E—7 $\frac{15}{16}$ in. (201,6 mm).	M—2 $\frac{1}{4}$ in. (57,12 mm).
F—4 $\frac{1}{32}$ in. (103,94 mm).	N—2 $\frac{1}{2}$ in. (63,46 mm).

To overhaul   **Operation T/6**

1. Remove the centre inspection panel from the seat box.

2. Slacken the adjustment and remove the driving belts; identify the belts so that they may be replaced in their original grooves.

3. Withdraw the driving pulley from the drive shaft flange.

4. Remove the selector assembly complete with a joint washer from the top of the transfer casing.

5. Remove the drive unit complete with a joint washer and dog clutch from the rear face of the transfer casing.

Strip the units as follows:—

Selector unit

6. Remove the brass plug and joint washer from the top of the selector housing and lift out the selector spring and ball.

7. Remove the housing cover plate and joint washer.

8. Withdraw the shaft and selector fork from the housing.

9. If necessary, remove the knob and locknut from the selector shaft.

Drive unit

10. Slide the dog clutch off the power take-off shaft.

11. Grip the gearbox end of the shaft in a soft-jawed vice: remove the driving flange.

12. Remove the oil seal housing from the drive housing together with shims (if fitted) which should be preserved. Drift out the oil seal from the housing.

13. Remove the unit from the vice. Remove the circlip retaining the drive shaft front bearing; place the protection cap (Part No. 243241) on the threaded portion of the shaft and drive out the shaft from the housing. Drift the rear bearing from the housing.

14. Remove the internal circlip from the bore of the shaft and lift out the plain retaining washer and the gearbox mainshaft bearing.

15. Renew any worn parts and reassemble by reversing the stripping procedure, paying particular attention to the following points:—

Selector unit

16. Assemble by reversing the stripping procedure.

Drive unit

17. The front (large) ball bearing must be a *light drive fit* on the shaft and in the housing.

18. The rear ball bearing must be a *light drive fit* on the shaft and in the housing.

19. The oil seal must be replaced with its knife edge inwards and with the plain face flush with the lower edge of the chamfer in the seal retainer. When fitting the retainer to the drive housing, the oil drain slot in the retainer must be in line with the drain hole in the housing.

20. The end-float of the shaft must be adjusted to nil on assembly by means of shims between the oil seal retainer and drive housing; these shims are available .003 in. and .005 in. (0,076 mm and 0,12 mm) thick.

21. The dog clutch must be fitted with its recessed end towards the gearbox.

22. Refit the drive unit. Operation T/4.

Rear power take-off
To fit   **Operation T/8**

1 If not already fitted, install the power take-off drive and selector units on the transfer casing. Operation T/4.

2. **86 and 88 models:** Secure the propeller shaft to the input flange of the rear take-off unit with the sliding joint at the front.

Pass the sliding joint end of the propeller shaft forwards through the holes provided in the rear and centre chassis cross-members. Secure the power take-off unit to the rear cross-member, with the fixings provided

Secure the front end of the propeller shaft to the flanged drive shaft on the gearbox.

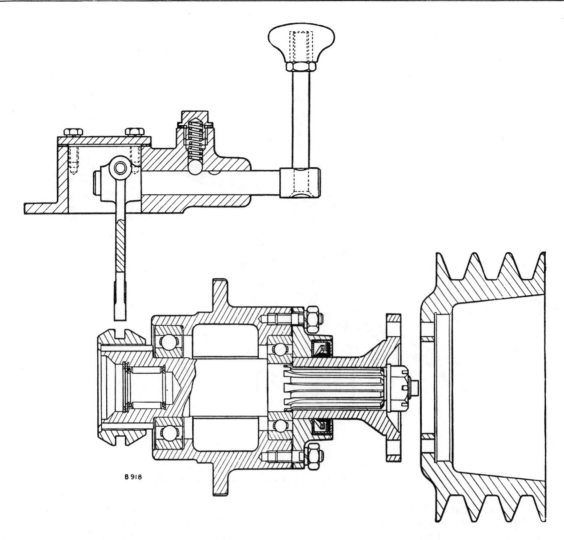

Fig. T-4—Cross-section of gearbox drive unit and centre pulley.

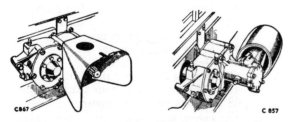

Fig. T-5—Rear power take-off and rear drive pulley.

Note: **86 and 88 models:** If a centre power take-off pulley is also fitted, four bolts 1$\frac{23}{32}$ in. (43,7 mm) long must be used to secure the propeller shaft.

3. **107 and 109 models only.** Secure the cross-member intermediate bearing support to the brackets welded to the chassis side members, using the bolts, spring washers and nuts provided. (Fig. T-7.)

Pass the universal joint end of the front propeller shaft forward through the hole provided in the centre chassis cross-member, and secure the front end of the shaft to the flanged drive shaft on the gearbox.

Secure the centre bearing housing to the cross-member intermediate bearing support by means of the rubber bushes, bolts, nuts, plain and spring washers provided.

When tightened, the rubber bushes on the centre bearing housing are compressed to a length of 1$\frac{1}{2}$ in. (38 mm); the bearing housing flange must be adjusted by means of shims which are supplied .048 in. thick, so that it lies centrally in the rubber bushes.

Secure the rear end of the rear propeller shaft to the input flange of the rear take-off unit, with the sliding joint at the front.

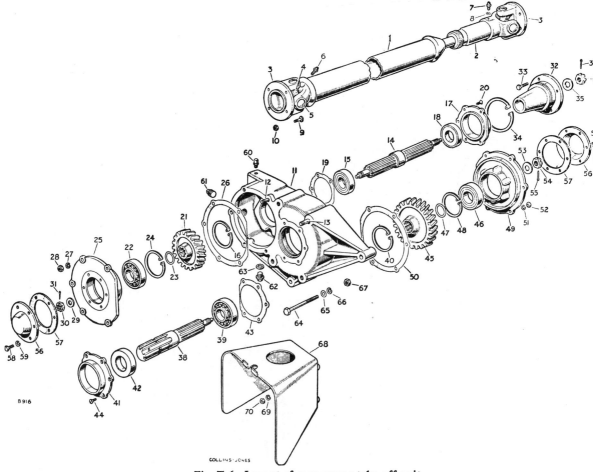

Fig. T-6—Layout of rear power take-off unit.

1 Propeller shaft, P.T.O. drive	33 Special bolts for propeller shaft
2 Splined end ⎱ For propeller	34 Circlip retaining bolts to flange
3 Flange ⎰ shaft	35–37 Fixings for flange
4 Journal complete for propeller shaft	38 Output shaft for P.T.O. 6-spline
5 Circlip for journal	39 Bearing for output shaft, rear
6 Grease nipple for journal	40 Circlip for bearing
7 Grease nipple for propeller shaft, .250 in. (6,35 mm) dia.	41 Retainer for oil seal ⎱ For output
	42 Oil seal ⎰ shaft
8 Washer for nipple	43 Joint washer for retainer
9–10 Fixings for propeller shaft	44 Screw fixing retainer
11 Housing assembly for P.T.O.	45 Gear wheel, 24 teeth
12 Stud for bearing housing	46 Bearing for output shaft, front
13 Stud for pulley housing or guard	47 Shim, for front output shaft bearing
14 Input shaft for P.T.O.	48 Circlip, bearing to housing
15 Bearing for input shaft, front	49 Housing for output shaft front bearing
16 Circlip, bearing to housing	50 Joint washer for bearing housing
17 Retainer for oil seal ⎱ For input	51–52 Fixings for bearing housing
18 Oil seal ⎰ shaft	53–55 Fixings for front bearing
19 Joint washer for retainer	56 Cover plate for bearings
20 Screw fixing retainer	57 Joint washer for cover plate
21 Gear wheel, 20 teeth	58–59 Fixings for cover
22 Bearing for input shaft, rear	60 Breather for casing
23 Shim for rear input shaft bearing	61 Filler plug
24 Circlip, bearing to housing	62 Drain plug for casing
25 Housing for rear input shaft bearing	63 Fibre washer for plug
26 Joint washer for rear bearing housing	64–67 Fixings for P.T.O. assembly
27–28 Fixings for bearing housing	68 Guard for P.T.O. spline
29–31 Fixings for rear bearing	69–70 Fixings for guard
32 Flange for P.T.O. input shaft	

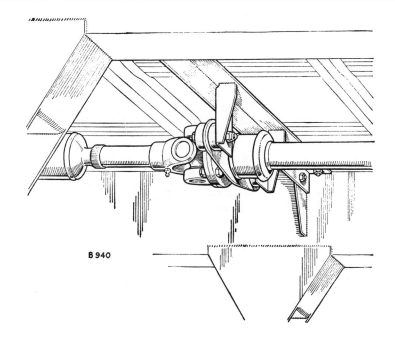

Fig. T-7—
Rear power take-off pro-
peller shaft centre bearing
assembly, 109 models only.

Pass the sliding joint end of the propeller shaft forward through the holes provided in the rear and No. 5 (front bumper is No. 1 cross-member) cross-members and secure the power take-off unit to the rear cross-member with the fixings provided.

Secure the front end of the rear propeller shaft to the front shaft flange.

4. Fill the unit with oil, 1 pint (0,5 litre).

To overhaul   Operation T/10

1. **86 and 88 models** only. Disconnect the front end of the propeller shaft from the flanged drive shaft on the gearbox.

2. **107 and 109 models** only. Disconnect the rear propeller shaft from the front shaft.

3 Remove the unit complete with propeller shaft from the rear chassis cross-member.

4. **107 and 109 models** only. Remove the front propeller shaft complete with centre bearing assembly.

5. Disconnect the propeller shaft from the input flange. To overhaul the propeller shafts see Section D.

6. Remove the output shaft guard.

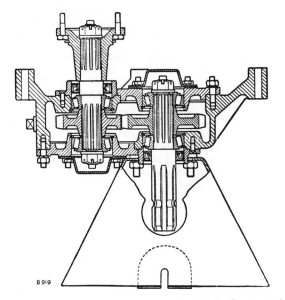

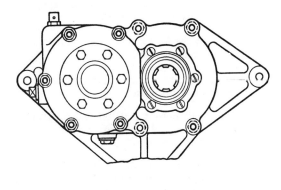

Fig. T-8—Cross-section of rear power take-off unit.

7. Drain off the oil from the power take-off and secure the unit in a vice by means of the input flange.

8. Remove the input shaft rear bearing cover plate and joint washer.

9. Remove the breather.

10. Remove the split pin, castle nut and plain washer securing the input shaft rear bearing; remove the bearing inner race and shims, which should be preserved.

11. Remove the input shaft rear bearing housing complete with circlip and outer race and a joint washer. If necessary, remove the circlip and drift the race from the housing.

12. Withdraw the 20-tooth gear and front inner race from the input shaft.

13. Lift off the complete unit from the input shaft and set aside.

14. Remove the external circlip retaining the propeller shaft bolts in the input flange and remove the bolts. Remove the split pin, castle nut and plain washer securing the flange to the shaft and drift the flange from the shaft.

15. Secure the complete unit in a soft-jawed vice by means of the output shaft.

16. Remove the input shaft oil seal retainer complete with oil seal and joint washer. Drift the seal from the retainer.

17. Remove the output shaft front bearing cover plate and joint washer.

18. Remove the split pin, castle nut and plain washer securing the output shaft front bearing; remove the bearing inner race and shims, which should be preserved.

19. Remove the output shaft front bearing housing complete with circlip and outer race and a joint washer. If necessary, remove the circlip and drift the race from the housing.

20. Withdraw the 24-tooth gear and rear inner race from the output shaft.

21. Lift off the power take-off housing, leaving the output shaft in the vice.

22. Remove the output shaft oil seal retainer complete with oil seal and joint washer. Drift the seal from the retainer.

23. To remove the bearing outer races remaining in the housing, remove the two internal circlips, heat the housing in water and tap out the races.

24. Wash all the component parts thoroughly and lay them out for inspection. Renew all joint washers and split pins.

25. Check all the bearings for wear and damage and renew them as necessary.

26. Check the gears for damage marks and rectify or renew as necessary; the gears must only be replaced as a pair.

27. Examine the housings for signs of damage or cracks and renew them as necessary. A housing may also be scrap as a result of excessive wear in a bearing bore; such wear will be obvious during the course of assembly.

28. Assemble the unit by reversing the stripping procedure, paying particular attention to the following points:—

29. The two bearing outer races must be a *warm tap fit* in the take-off housing.

30. The other bearing outer races must be a *light drive fit* in the bearing housings.

31. The bearing inner races must all be an *easy tap fit* on the input and output shafts.

32. The backlash between the gears must be .008 in. to .012 in. (0,20 to 0,30 mm).

33. The recess in the splined bore in each gear must be fitted adjacent to the centre flange on each shaft. The input shaft gear must be fitted on the longer end of the shaft.

34. Each oil seal must be pressed into its retainer until the plain face is approximately 5/16 in. (8 mm) below the outer face of the retainer.

35. When replacing the shafts, a piece of shim steel or stiff paper should be wrapped round the shaft splines, to prevent damage to the oil seals.

36. Adjust the bearings in the following manner:—

   (a) When both shafts are in position with the castle retaining nuts pulled up tightly, tap both ends of each shaft to settle the bearings.

   (b) Rotate each shaft in turn; it should turn quite freely, but no end-float must be present. Adjustment to achieve this condition is provided by the shims adjacent to the bearing inner race which are available .005 in., .010 in. and .020 in. (0,12 mm., 0,25 mm and 0,50 mm) thick. To reduce the end-float, shims must be removed; if the bearings have too much interference, suitable shims must be added to bring the setting correct.

Power take-off gears

To transpose   Operation T/12

1. Remove the rear pulley unit (if fitted).

2. Drain off the oil from the take-off unit.

3. Remove the take-off unit from the chassis frame.

4. Remove the input shaft cover plate.

5. Remove the split pin, castle nut and plain washer from the end of the input shaft.

6. Remove the input shaft bearing housing complete with bearing.

7. Remove and preserve the shims from the input shaft and withdraw the 20-tooth gear.

8. Withdraw the 24-tooth gear from the output shaft in a similar manner.

9. Transpose the gears and reassemble the unit by reversing the stripping procedure.

10. It is most important that the two sets of shims removed be replaced on their original shafts.

11. Refill the unit with oil, 1 pint (0,5 litre).

Rear drive pulley

To fit   **Operation T/14**

1. Remove the output shaft guard from the rear power take-off casing.

2. Offer the pulley unit to the power take-off by entering the splined output shaft into the pulley sleeve and secure it by means of the nuts and spring washers.

3. Fill the unit with oil, $\frac{3}{4}$ pint (0,5 litre).

4. It is most important to ensure alignment of the driving belt in the centre of the pulley and also

to obtain the correct tension of the belt; the belt tension is correct when the hand brake will hold the vehicle and the two sides of the belt cannot be compressed completely together by hand at a point midway between the vehicle and the driven machine.

To overhaul   **Operation T/16**

1. Remove the pulley unit from the rear drive unit.

2. Drain off the oil from the pulley unit.

3. Remove the pulley from the bevel pinion shaft.

4. Remove the pinion shaft housing from the drive housing complete with shims, which should be preserved.

5. Tap the pinion shaft from the housing, complete with one inner race, distance tube and shims, which should be preserved; the second inner race can only be withdrawn after the oil seal is removed. Slide the shims, distance tube and inner race off the pinion shaft.

6. Warm the housing in hot water, drift out the oil seal, remove the second inner race and drift out the outer races.

7. Remove the bevel wheel bearing end plate from the drive housing, complete with the bearing outer race and shims, which should be preserved.

If desired, the outer race can be removed from the end plate by heating the plate in hot water.

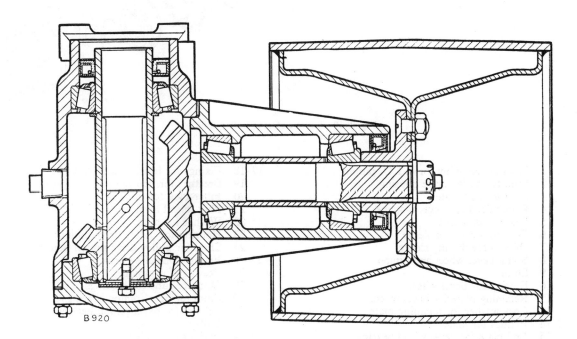

B 920

Fig. T-9—Cross-section of rear pulley unit.

8. Remove the drive shaft and bevel wheel complete with the bearing inner races from the housing.

9. Remove the set bolt and spring washer securing the bevel wheel retaining plate, lift off the plate and cork washer and slide off the bevel wheel complete with an inner race and shims which should be preserved. Drift the inner race from the bevel wheel.

10. Drift the second inner race from the drive shaft and remove the retaining circlip.

11. Warm the drive housing in hot water and drift out the oil seal and outer race.

12. Wash all the component parts thoroughly and lay them out for inspection.

13. Check all the bearings for wear and damage and renew them as necessary.

14. Check the gears for damage marks and rectify or renew them as necessary; the gears must only be renewed as a pair.

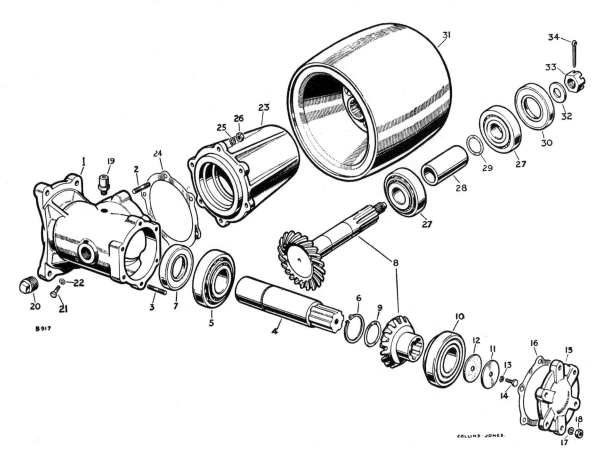

Fig. T-10—Layout of rear pulley unit.

1	Housing assembly for P.T.O. pinion	17–18	Fixings for bearing end plate
2	Stud for pulley drive housing	19	Breather for housing
3	Stud for end plate	20	Filler plug for housing
4	Pinion driving sleeve, 6-spline	21	Plug for oil level
5	Bearing for sleeve	22	Washer for plug
6	Circlip, bearing to sleeve	23	Housing for pulley drive pinion
7	Oil seal for driving sleeve	24	Shim for pulley drive pinion housing
8	Spiral bevel wheel and pinion	25–26	Fixings for pulley drive
9	Shim	27	Bearings for pinion
10	Bearing for bevel wheel	28	Distance tube for bearings
11	Retaining plate for bevel wheel	29	Shim for bevel pinion bearings
12	Cork washer for retaining plate	30	Oil seal for bevel pinion bearings
13–14	Fixings for plate	31	Pulley
15	End plate for bevel wheel bearing	32–34	Fixings for pulley
16	Shim for bevel wheel end plate		

15. Examine the housings for signs of damage or cracks and renew them as necessary. A housing may also be scrap as a result of excessive wear in a bearing bore; such wear will be obvious during the course of assembly.

16. Assemble the unit by reversing the stripping procedure, paying particular attention to the following points:—

17. The two drive shaft bearing outer races must be a *warm tap fit* in the drive housing and end plate.

   The two inner races must be a *light drive fit* on the drive shaft and bevel wheel.

18. The pinion shaft bearing outer races must be a *warm tap fit* in the pinion housing. The inner races must be an *easy tap fit* on the pinion shaft.

19. The drive housing, end cover and pinion housing should be warmed to facilitate fitting the bearing outer races.

20. The small shims (available .005 in., .010 in. and .020 in. (0,12 mm, 0,25 mm and 0,50 mm) thick) behind the bevel wheel, provide adjustment for alignment of the bevel wheel and pinion teeth; the original shims should be correct if the original gears, etc., are replaced.

21. The drive housing oil seal must be fitted with its sealing lip inwards.

22. The drive shaft must be able to turn quite freely, no end-float must be present. Adjustment to achieve this condition is provided by the shims under the end cover, which are available .005 in., .010 in. and .020 in. (0,12 mm, 0,25 mm and 0,50 mm) thick. To reduce the end-float, shims must be removed.

23. The pinion housing oil seal must be fitted just below the housing end face with its sealing lip inwards.

24. Adjust the pinion shaft bearings as follows:—

   (a) With the pulley fitted and the pinion shaft retaining nut pulled up tightly, tap both ends of the shaft to settle the bearings.

   (b) Rotate the shaft; it should turn quite freely, but no end-float must be present. Adjustment to achieve this condition is provided by the shims on the shaft between the distance tube and outer bearing, which are available .005 in., .010 in. and .020 in. (0,12 0,25 mm and 0,50 mm) thick. To reduce the end-float, shims must be removed.

25. The shims between the pinion and drive housings, available .005 in., .010 in. and .020 in. (0,12 mm, 0,25 mm and 0,50 mm) thick, are provided for adjustment of the backlash between the bevel wheel and pinion. There must be definite backlash at all positions of a complete revolution, but this must not exceed .004 in. (0,10 mm) at any point. Excessive backlash can be corrected by removing suitable shims.

Engine governor—Petrol models

To fit **Operation T/18**

1. Disconnect the bonnet prop rod from the bonnet.

2. Remove the bonnet.

3. Fit the governor bracket support on top of the dynamo support bracket, using the bolt already securing the dynamo bracket. Turn the support to the rear and leave the bolt slack.

4. Fit the governor to the bracket (three bolts and spring washers).

5. Slacken the dynamo adjusting bolt to relieve the tension on the fan belt.

6. Remove the original fan pulley and distance piece from the hub of the water pump spindle, and fit the new double groove pulley and distance piece.

7. Remove the three set bolts securing the thermostat housing and in their places fit the three studs using the existing spring washers.

8. Readjust the fan belt tension.

9. Place the governor driving belt over the fan pulley and round the governor pulley. Fit the mounting bracket and governor to the extension studs on the front of the thermostat housing, securing the bracket with the three special nuts and shakeproof washers, leaving the nuts slack.

10. Secure the mounting bracket to the support with one bolt, spring washer and nut, leaving the nut slack.

11. Carefully bend the distributor vacuum pipe to clear the governor and bracket.

12. Hold the governor out to tension the belt, (it should be possible to depress the belt ½ in. (12,5 mm) by thumb pressure midway between the pulleys) and tighten the nuts and bolts holding the governor mounting bracket and support.

13. Check the oil level in the governor, by removing the filler plug at the top front and the level plug at the R.H. side. Replenish as necessary with engine oil through the filler hole until the level is to the bottom of the level plug hole. Replace both plugs.

14 Remove and discard the throttle return spring between the bell crank lever and the anchor on the petrol filter bracket.

15. Remove the cover plate on the dash panel immediately below the instrument panel.

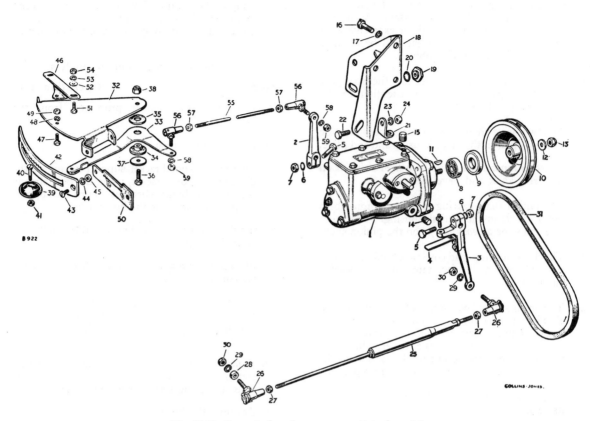

B 922

Fig. T-11—Layout of engine governor, Petrol models.

1	Engine governor complete	28	Distance piece, bell crank lever end
2	Lever, governor to quadrant	29–30	Fixings for rod
3	Lever, grommet to bell crank	31	Belt for governor drive
4	Spring blade for bell crank	32	Housing for governor control quadrant
5–7	Fixings for levers	33	Lever for control
8	Bearing, large ⎫ For engine Bearing, small ⎭ governor	34	Bush for lever
		35	Washer for lever
9	Oil seal for pulley end	36–38	Fixings for control lever to housing
10	Pulley for governor	39	Knob for lever
11	Woodruff key for pulley	40–41	Fixings for knob
12–13	Fixings for pulley	42	Quadrant plate
14	Level plug for governor	43–45	Fixings for quadrant plate
15	Filler plug for governor	46	Support for governor control
16–17	Fixings for governor	47–49	Fixings for support
18	Bracket for governor	50	Rubber draught excluder
19–20	Fixings for bracket	51–54	Fixings for control
21	Support for bracket	55	Operating rod, quadrant to governor
22–24	Fixings for support	56	Ball joint for rod
25	Control rod, governor to bell crank	57	Locknut for ball joint on rod
26	Ball joint complete for rod	58–59	Fixings for operating rod
27	Locknut for ball joint		

16. Insert the governor control quadrant in the rectangular hole uncovered, and bolt it to the dash, using the fixings originally securing the cover plate and with the rubber draught excluder between the quadrant housing and the dash.

Leave the nuts slack at this stage.

17. Remove the instrument panel complete, without disconnecting the instruments.

18. Secure the quadrant bracket to the underside of the instrument box. Tighten the nuts securing the quadrant to the dash and then the nuts fixing the bracket to the instrument box.

19. Replace the instrument panel.

20. Fit a ball joint to each end of the governor operating rod and attach the rod to the control quadrant lever, using a spring washer and nut. Loosen the governor throttle control (R.H.) lever on its shaft and place the quadrant lever in the inoperative (extreme R.H.) notch. Push the governor loading (L.H.) lever forward until a marked resistance is felt, indicating that the internal mechanism is against the stop in the rear end cover. With the loading lever in this position, adjust the length of rod and connect it to the loading lever, using a spring washer and nut. Tighten the ball joint locknuts.

21. Fit the collapsible control rod between the bell crank lever and the governor throttle control (R.H.) lever; secure it at the governor end, and

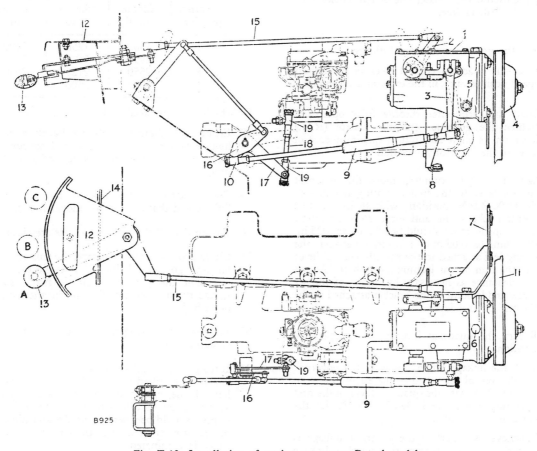

Fig. T-12—Installation of engine governor—Petrol models

A—Inoperative position.   B—1,500 R.P.M.   C—3,000 R.P.M.

1	Engine governor	11	Drive belt
2	Loading lever	12	Control quadrant
3	Throttle control lever	13	Operating lever
4	Governor pulley	14	Draught excluder
5	Oil level plug	15	Governor operating rod
6	Oil filler plug	16	Relay lever
7	Bracket for governor	17	Carburetter bell crank
8	Support for bracket	18	Rod, bell crank to carburetter
9	Collapsible control rod	19	Adjustable ball joint for rod
10	Adjustable ball joint for rod		

at the bell crank end with two spring washers, nuts and one distance piece to be fitted between rod and bell crank.

Note.—Before fitting, ensure that there is no free play in the collapsible control rod.

22. Check that the carburetter throttle is fully open when the accelerator pedal is fully depressed. If this is not so, the throttle lever on the dash cross-shaft should be adjusted as necessary.

    Note.—The Amal adjustable ball joints on the linkage should be adjusted as follows:—

    (a) Tighten the ratchet screw at the head of the joint until the ball is held solidly in its cup.

    (b) Unscrew the ratchet one or two clicks until the ball is free.

Setting the governor control linkage

23. Place the quadrant control lever in its highest speed position, i.e., in the extreme L.H. notch.

24. Hold the carburetter throttle fully open and tighten the governor throttle control (R.H.) lever on its shaft and return quadrant control lever to the inoperative position

25. With the engine running, move the quadrant control lever to the first operating notch, i.e., the 1,500 R.P.M. position; with the lever in this position, check the anti-surge stop clearance. The stop clearance should be .020 in. to .025 in. (0,50 mm to 0,65 mm) measured between the spring leaf attached to the throttle control lever and the cam on the loading lever shaft. Adjust the clearance as necessary by means of the set screw and locknut in the bracket attached to the throttle control lever.

26. Return the quadrant lever to the inoperative position.

    With the linkage set in this way, the governor should control the speed of the engine between 1,500 R.P.M. with the quadrant lever in the first operating notch, and 3,000 R.P.M. in the extreme L.H. notch.

    Whenever any part of the governor linkage is disturbed for any reason, the complete linkage must be reset.

Checking the engine speed with the governor in position.

27. It is possible to check the governed speed of the engine with the governor in operation, by measuring the rear power take-off speed with a revolution counter.

    The relationship between the engine speed and the rear power take-off speed is shown in the following tables:—

(a) Rear power take-off pulley:—

		Pulley Speed	
Governor position	Engine speed	5:6 Power take-off ratio	6:5 Power take-off ratio
1	1500	1070	1540
4	1950	1390	2000
8	2550	1820	2630
11	3000	2145	3100

(b) Rear power take-off drive shaft:—

		Drive shaft speed	
Governor position	Engine speed	5:6 Power take-off ratio	6:5 Power take-off ratio
1	1500	1250	1800
4	1950	1625	2350
8	2550	2125	3050
11	3000	2500	3600

Points to be checked if the governor surges.

28. Ensure that there is negligible backlash in the linkage between the governor and carburetter. Such backlash must not exceed .010 in. (0,25 mm).

29. Ensure that there is no drag at any point in the linkage and that the throttle moves freely.

30. Ensure that all the carburetter jets are clean.

31. Check and correct as necessary, the tension in the fan and governor belts. If it is necessary to retension the governor belt, it may also be necessary to reset the linkage in the manner described.

32. Fit the new spring to the accelerator pump actuating rod.

33. If the governor still surges after attentions 28-32, it can be rectified by inserting 2 B.A. washers behind the spring on the accelerator pump actuating rod. Washers to the thickness of ⅛ in. (3 mm) should be inserted initially and additions of one washer at a time then made until the surge is eliminated:—

    (a) Remove the nut securing the pump lever to the carburetter throttle spindle.

    (b) Slide the lever off the spindle and unscrew it from the pump actuating rod, counting the number of turns of the lever to unscrew.

    (c) Remove the split pin holding the spring abutment washer.

    (d) Thread the new washers up the pump rod, screw the lever on the pump actuating rod, giving the same number of turns as when removed, and reassemble on the carburetter.

Note: On no account must the split pin be removed from the end of the pump rod, as this is set to give the correct pump action.

Only just enough washers to rectify the surge should be incorporated, as their addition pre-loads the governor linkage.

In any case, no further washers should be inserted after the point when the spring is compressed to $\frac{1}{2}$ in. (12,5 mm) length with the throttle fully open.

34. Replace the bonnet and reconnect the prop rod.

To remove **Operation T/20**

1. Disconnect the operating rod at the governor end by removing the nut and spring washer.

2. Disconnect the control rod at the governor end by detaching the adjustable ball joint.

3. Remove the governor unit complete with mounting bracket and support,

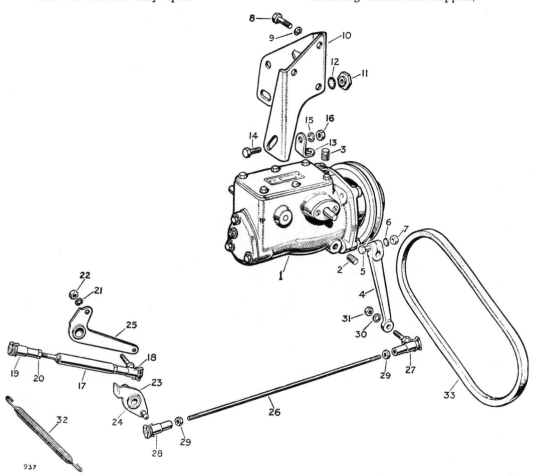

Fig. T-13—Layout of speed limit governor, Petrol models.

1	Engine governor complete
2	Level plug
3	Filler plug
4	Lever, governor to relay
5–7	Fixings for lever
8–9	Fixings for governor
10	Bracket for governor
11–12	Fixings for bracket
13	Support for bracket
14–16	Fixings for support
17	Control rod complete, accelerator cross-shaft to engine
18	Ball joint complete
19	Ball joint body
20	Locknut for ball joints

21–22	Fixings for control rod
23	Relay lever for governor
24	Bush for lever
25	Bell crank lever for carburetter
26	Control rod, relay lever to governor
27	Ball joint complete
28	Ball joint body
29	Locknut for ball joint
30–31	Fixings for control rod
32	Return spring for throttle
33	Belt for governor drive
	Fan pulley and governor drive
	Special stud for governor
	Distance washer for fan pulley

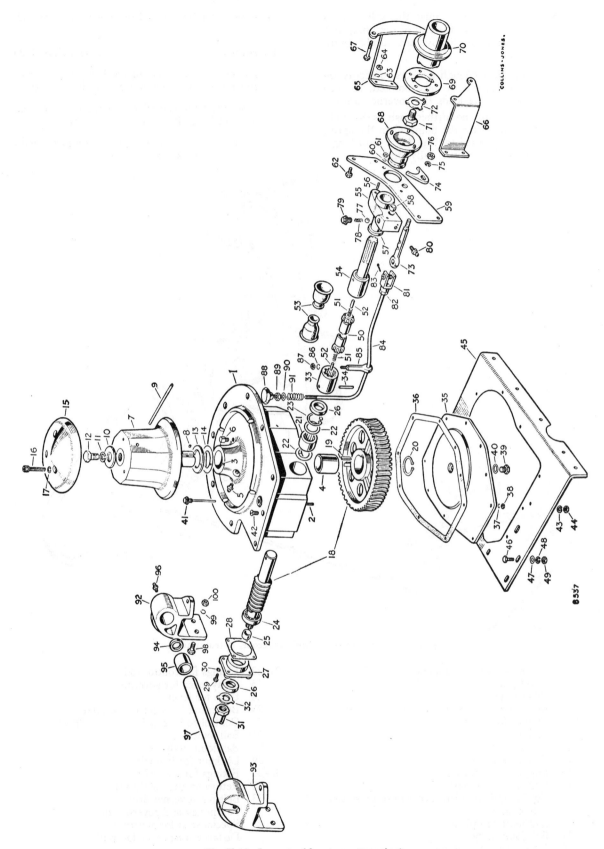

Fig. T-14—Layout of front capstan winch.

Key to Fig. T-14

1 Casing assembly for front winch
2 Stud for bottom cover
3 Dowel for thrust washer
4 Bush for bollard shaft
5 Grease nipple for shaft
6 Breather cup for housing
7 Bollard and shaft assembly
8 Dowel for shaft
9 Pin for bollard
10-12 Fixings for bollard
13 Thrust washer } For
14 Shim } bollard
15 Cap for bollard
16-17 Fixings for cap
18 Worm wheel and worm complete
19 Special key for worm wheel
20 Circlip fixing worm wheel
21 Roller bearing for worm
22 Washer for bearing
23 Circlip fixing bearing to casing
24 Ball bearing for worm shaft
25 Distance piece for worm shaft
26 Oil seal for worm shaft
27 Retainer for oil seal
28 Joint washer for oil seal retainer
29-30 Fixings for oil seal retainer
31 Starting dog
32 Lock washer for starting dog
33 Universal joint sleeve
34 Special pin fixing sleeve to worm
35 Bottom cover for winch casing
36 Joint washer for bottom cover
37-38 Fixings for bottom cover
39 Drain plug for front winch
40 Joint washer for drain plug
41 Filler plug and dipstick
42-44 Fixings for front winch
45 Support plate for front winch
46-49 Fixings for support plate
50 Propeller shaft for front winch

51 Plunger spring } For propeller shaft
52 Plunger }
53 Dust cover
54 Driving shaft for front winch
55 Winch shaft housing assembly
56 Stud for support plate
57 Bush for winch driving shaft
58 Bush for control shaft
59 Support plate for winch shaft
60-61 Fixings for housing
62-64 Fixings for support
65 Bracket for winch shaft support plate, R.H.
66 Bracket for winch shaft support plate, L.H.
67 Set bolt fixing brackets to front cover
68 Driving flange for front winch
69 Winch driving plate
70 Driving flange for fan pulley
71-72 Fixings for driving flange and plate
73 Control shaft for driving flange
74 Selector fork for control shaft
75-76 Fixings for fork
77 Steel ball
78 Spring } For control shaft
79 Plug for spring }
80 Grease nipple for control shaft
81-83 Fixings for control rod
84 Control rod for winch
85 Eyebolt for winch control rod
86-87 Fixings for eyebolt
88 Knob for control rod
89 Locknut for knob
90 Plain washer for spring
91 Spring for control rod
92 Rope guide bracket assembly, R.H.
93 Rope guide bracket assembly, L.H.
94 Thrust washer
95 Bush for guide bar
96 Grease nipple for bush
97 Guide bar for winch rope
98-100 Fixings for rope guide

35 m.p.h. speed limit governor

To fit   **Operation T/22**

1. Disconnect the bonnet prop rod from the bonnet.

2. Remove the bonnet.

3. Fit the governor bracket support on top of the dynamo support bracket, using the bolt already securing the dynamo bracket. Turn the support to the rear and leave the bolt slack.

4. Fit the governor to the bracket (three bolts and spring washers).

5. Slacken the dynamo adjusting bolt to relieve the tension on the fan belt.

6. Remove the original fan pulley and distance piece from the hub of the water pump spindle and fit the new "double groove" pulley and distance piece.

7. Remove the three set bolts securing the thermostat housing and in their place fit the three studs, using the existing spring washers.

8. Readjust the fan belt tension.

9. Place the governor driving belt over the fan pulley and round the governor pulley. Fit the mounting bracket and governor to the extension studs on the front of the thermostat housing, securing the bracket with the three special nuts and shakeproof washers, leaving the nuts slack.

10. Secure the mounting bracket to the support with one bolt, spring washer and nut, leaving the nut slack.

11. Carefully bend the distributor vacuum pipe to clear the governor and bracket.

12. Hold the governor out to tension the belt (it should be possible to depress the belt ½ in. (12,5 mm) by thumb pressure midway between the pulleys) and tighten the nuts and bolts holding the governor mounting bracket and support.

13. Check the oil level in the governor. See Instruction Manual.

14. Remove and discard the two original throttle return springs.

15. Fit the spring between the accelerator lever and the spring anchor on the toe box side.

16. Remove and discard the control rod between the accelerator relay lever and the carburetter relay lever.

17. Detach the control rod, between the bell crank and the carburetter, at the bell crank.

18. Remove the split pin and plain washer from the spindle in the inlet manifold. Withdraw and discard the relay lever and bell crank lever, first removing and retaining the ball pin, spring washer and nut from the bell crank lever.

19. Fit the new bell crank lever (long arm forward, short arm upwards) and the new relay lever (ball end downwards and towards the outside) on the spindle and secure, using the existing plain washer and split pin.

20. Fit the ball pin (previously removed from the old bell crank lever) on the inside of the long arm of the new bell crank lever and secure with the spring washer and nut.

21. Connect the control rod to the carburetter, to the bell crank ball pin.
    Note: The Amal adjustable ball joints on the linkage should be adjusted as follows:—
    (*a*) Tighten the ratchet screw at the head of the joint until the ball is held solidly in its cup.
    (*b*) Unscrew the ratchet one or two clicks until the ball is free.

22. Fit the control rod between the accelerator relay lever and the shorter arm of the bell crank lever, securing it at the bell crank end with the distance piece, spring washer and nut.

23. Fit the control rod between the relay lever and the governor lever, securing at the governor lever with a spring washer and nut.

24. Adjust the two new control rods as necessary to ensure correct opening and closing of the throttle.

25. Slacken the governor lever on its spindle and retighten so as to ensure full throttle opening. The throttle should only just open fully (i.e., the rods must be set to the correct length) otherwise the governor will not operate correctly.

26. Replace the bonnet and secure the bonnet prop rod.

27. Road test the vehicle, when the governor should operate at approximately 35 m.p.h. (55 k.p.h.) in top gear on level ground.

To remove   **Operation T/24**

1. Disconnect the control rod at the governor end by detaching the adjustable ball joint.

2. Remove the governor unit complete with mounting bracket and support.

Front capstan winch—all models

Note 1: A hand throttle must be fitted and used in conjunction with the front capstan winch, on Petrol models.

Note 2: New heavy duty front springs should be fitted to 2 litre Petrol models. See Section J for removal and refitting procedure.

To fit   **Operation T/26**

1. Remove the grille panel and radiator complete (Section L).

2. Remove the four set bolts and spring washers and withdraw the fan.

3. Mark off a point on the front face of chassis second cross-member $3\frac{9}{32}$ in. (83,3 mm) from the top face and mid-way between the side-members.

Use a pilot drill first, then drill the front face only of the cross-member to $\frac{27}{64}$ in. (10,318 mm).

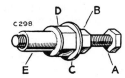

Fig. T-15—Rivnut ready for fitting.

A—Set bolt.   C—Plain washer.
B—$\frac{5}{16}$ in. U.N.F. nut.   D—Distance piece.
            E—Rivnut.

4. Fit a nut and plain washer to a $\frac{5}{16}$ in. U.N.F. set bolt having a threaded length not less than $1\frac{1}{2}$ in. (38,1 mm). Drill or file the thread clear, of a $\frac{3}{8}$ in. U.N.F. nut, and slide it on to the set bolt, then screw on a Rivnut. Adjust so that $\frac{1}{8}$ in. (3,2 mm) of the set bolt extends beyond the Rivnut and then lock the assembly. Insert the Rivnut into the hole in second cross-member and then, keeping the set bolt and distance nut stationary, turn the $\frac{5}{16}$ in. U.N.F. nut clockwise $2\frac{1}{4}$ turns. Remove set bolt, nut, plain washer and distance nut.

5. Assemble the winch support plate temporarily to the cross-member, securing it with a set bolt and spring washer.

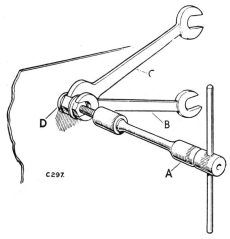

Fig. T-16—Rivnut fitting.

A—$\frac{5}{16}$ in. U.N.F. spanner.   C—$\frac{3}{8}$ in. U.N.F. spanner
B—$\frac{5}{16}$ in. U.N.F. spanner.   D—Rivnut.

Note: 86 and 107 models only, should have a packing washer fitted between the support plate and Rivnut.

Using the support plate as a template, mark off and drill the other four holes as in item 3, and five $\frac{5}{16}$ in. (8 mm) clearance holes in the front bumper.

6. Remove the winch support plate and front bumper. Fit the other four Rivnuts to second cross-member.

7. Relieve the fan belt tension.

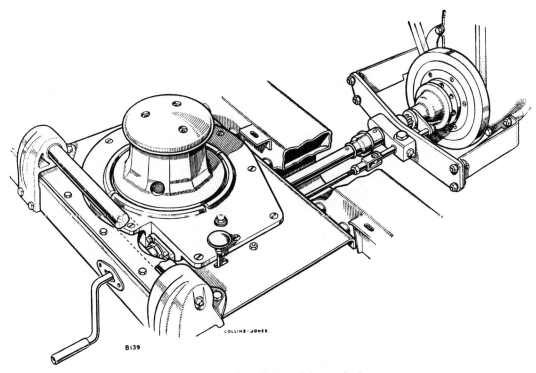

Fig. T-17—Installation of front winch

8. Prise up the tabs on the starting dog lock washer and remove the dog and washer.

9. **Petrol models:** Using a suitable extractor, withdraw the vibration damper from the crankshaft. Withdraw the six screws from the damper and remove retaining plate, shims, rubber disc and remove the existing driving flange. Reassemble the damper, using the new driving flange; it will be necessary to true the damper between centres by adjusting the six fixing screws. (Section A.)

   Diesel models: Fit new driving plate, complete with special plug and shakeproof washer.

10. Secure the two shaft plate brackets to the engine front cover, replacing the original four bolts or studs with the four new bolts or studs.

11. **Petrol models:** Replace the vibration damper, securing it to the crankshaft by means of the winch driving plate, locking washer and special set bolt. Readjust the fan belt tension.

12. Secure the shaft housing to the shaft support plate. Grease the driving shaft and insert it in the housing, sliding the driving flange on to its spline. Insert the control shaft in the housing and secure the selector fork to the control shaft and in the groove of the flange by means of a spring washer and nut. Push the steel ball into the hole, holding it in position by the spring and the plug. Fit the grease nipple in the shaft housing.

13. Bolt the housing and support plate to the brackets.

14. Slide two rubber dust covers on to the propeller shaft and fit a spring and plunger into each end of the shaft; insert one end of the shaft into the driving shaft held in the shaft housing; slide the dust cover over the joint.

15. Bolt the winch support plate to the front bumper.

16. Fit the winch to the support plate. Offer the winch, plate and bumper into position; engage the propeller shaft with the universal joint sleeve on the winch; secure the winch and plate to the cross-member. Secure the bumper to the chassis. Slide the second dust cover over the propeller shaft joint.

   Note: Plain washers $\frac{1}{8}$ in. (3,2 mm) thick, must be fitted between the support plate and the Rivnuts on **86** and **107 models.**

17. Slide the eyebolt on to the control rod and fit the locknut and clevis to the end of the rod.

18. Pass the rod through the hole in the cross-member and secure it to the support plate with a spring washer and nut on the eyebolt; fit the spring, plain washer, locknut and knob on the rod.

19. Fit the clevis to the control shaft in the shaft housing and adjust it so that the driving flange in engaged and disengaged fully, when the rod is moved in its slot to the "drive" and "free" positions, located by the selector ball.

20. Mount the rope guide brackets and guide bar on the support plate. Making sure that the bar turns freely, drill four holes through the brackets into the front face of the bumper; secure the brackets to the bumper.

21. Fill the unit with oil, to the mark on the dipstick, using an S.A.E. 40 oil.

22. Turn the unit (by means of the short starting handle supplied) until the hole in the side of the bollard exposes a grease nipple provided for lubrication of the bollard shaft and apply grease, using a suitable gun.

23. Grease all moving parts and apply grease, by means of a gun, to the nipples provided on the rope guide brackets and the drive shaft housing.

24. Replace the fan blade.

25. Replace the grille panel and radiator. Section L.

   Note: It may be necessary to tighten the starting dog on the front of the winch shaft and secure it by means of the lock washer.

To overhaul   Operation T/28

1. Remove the control knob and locknut, plain washer and spring from the control rod; remove the nut and spring washer securing the control rod eyebolt to the support plate and drop the control rod, slide back the dust cover from the front universal joint on the winch propeller shaft.

2. Remove the nuts, spring and plain washers securing the support plate to the chassis cross-member, and the bolts, plain washers and self-locking nuts securing the front bumper to the chassis; remove the bumper, support plate, rope guide and winch complete, at the same time disengaging the propeller shaft from the universal joint sleeve on the winch. The spring and plunger in the propeller shaft will be freed at this stage and care should be taken that these are not lost.

3. Remove the winch from the support plate.

4. Slide the rear dust cover along the propeller shaft and withdraw the propeller shaft from the sleeve of the driving shaft, care being taken that the second spring and plunger are not lost.

5. Extract the driving shaft from the shaft housing and remove the driving flange from engagement with the selector fork.

6. Disconnect the control rod clevis from the control shaft and remove the drive shaft support plate, housing and control shaft complete from the brackets.

7. Remove the selector fork from the control shaft; remove the plug, spring and ball from the drive shaft housing and withdraw the control shaft; remove the shaft housing from the plate.

8. Remove the radiator and grille panel assembly—Section L.

9. **Petrol models:** Remove the driving plate from the crankshaft vibration damper; remove the vibration damper (Section A).

10. Remove the two support plate brackets.

11. **Diesel models:** Remove the driving plate from the fan driving pulley or vibration damper.

12. If necessary, remove the two rope guide brackets and rope guide from the front bumper and support plate.

   If necessary, remove the bushes from the brackets.

13. Remove the drain plug and filler plug and drain off the oil.

14. Drive out the Mills pin securing the universal joint sleeve to the rear of the worm shaft and remove the sleeve.

15. Unscrew the dog from the front of the worm shaft; slide off the lock washer.

16. Remove the oil seal retainer, oil seal and joint washer from the casing. If necessary, remove the oil seal from the retainer.

17. Turning the shaft to disengage the worm from the worm wheel, drive the worm shaft, ball bearing and distance piece from the casing. Drift the bearing and distance piece from the shaft.

18. Remove the bottom cover and joint washer from the casing.

19. Withdraw the three Allen screws and spring washers and lift off the bollard cap.

20. Remove the set bolt, spring washer and plain washer from the end of the bollard shaft; drift out the safety pin securing the bollard to the shaft and remove the bollard.

21. Remove the thrust washers and shims, which should be preserved and withdraw the worm wheel and shaft from the casing.

22. Remove the circlip securing the worm wheel and press the shaft from the wheel; if necessary, remove the peg and key from the shaft.

23. If necessary, press the two bollard shaft bushes from the casing; remove the worm shaft oil seal from the casing; remove the roller retaining circlip, a distance washer, the roller bearing, and a further washer; remove the grease nipple, the breather cup and the thrust washer peg, leaving the bare casing.

24. Wash all the component parts thoroughly and lay them out for inspection.

25. Check all the bearings for wear and damage and renew them as necessary.

26. Check the gears for damage marks and rectify or renew them as necessary; the gears must only be renewed as a pair.

27. Examine the casing for signs of damage or cracks and renew as necessary. The casing may also be scrap as a result of excessive wear in a bearing bore; such wear will be obvious during the course of assembly.

28. The bollard and shaft are only supplied as an assembly.

29. Assemble the unit by reversing the stripping procedure, paying particular attention to the following points:—

30. The roller bearing must be a *push fit* in the casing and on the worm shaft. The ball bearing must be a *light press fit* in the casing and on the worm shaft.

   Renew the bearings, casing or shaft as necessary.

31. If necessary, renew the bollard shaft bushes, which must be a *press fit* in the casing and a *sliding fit* on the bollard shaft. They must be reamed to 1.312 in. (33,4 mm).

   The upper bearing must stand $\frac{1}{8}$ in. (3,17 mm) proud of the top face of the casing.

32. The bollard shaft must be well greased on assembly.

33. The worm shaft oil seals must be replaced with their knife edges inwards.

34. The worm shaft must be able to turn quite freely, but no end-float must be present.

35. The shims between the bollard thrust washer and the casing, available .005 in. thick, are provided for adjustment of the bollard shaft end-float, which must be set on assembly to .003 in. to .005 in. (0,075 to 0,125 mm).

36. If necessary, renew the bushes in the rope guide brackets.

   The old bushes may be removed by screwing a suitable size tap into the bearing and then extract; a thrust washer is fitted behind each bush.

   The new bushes must be a *light press fit* in the brackets. The guide bar must be able to rotate freely in the bushes, which must be reamed in position to 1.390 in. (35,3 mm).

37. If necessary, renew the drive shaft bush in the shaft housing. The bush must be a *press fit* in the housing. After fitting, ream the bush to .750 in. (19,05 mm) and drill the lubrication hole through the nipple side of the bush. The drive shaft must be a *sliding fit* in the bush.

38. If necessary, renew the two control shaft bushes in the housing, the bush on the studded side of the housing should stand 3/32 in. (2,38 mm) proud of the housing face.

39. Complete the assembly and installation. Fill the winch with oil—3½ pints (2,0 litres). Apply grease at the nipples on the rope guide, bollard shaft and drive shaft housing. Smear all moving parts liberally with grease.

Rear capstan winch

To fit   **Operation T/30**

1. Assuming that a rear power take-off unit is already installed, to fit the capstan winch, proceed as follows:—

2. Remove the rear pulley unit or output shaft guard from the power take-off casing.

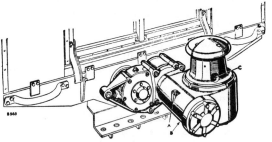

Fig. T-18—Rear winch.
A—Filler plug and dipstick.
B—Oil drain plug (under casing).
C—Access hole for bollard shaft nipple.

3. Offer the capstan winch to the power take-off, with the bollard upwards, by entering the splined output shaft into the drive sleeve and secure it by means of the nuts and spring washers provided.

4. Fill the unit with oil. See Instruction Manual.

5. Turn the unit until the hole in the side of the bollard exposes a grease nipple provided for lubrication of the bollard shaft and apply grease, using a suitable gun.

To overhaul   **Operation T/32**

1. Remove the winch unit complete.

2. Drain off the oil.

3. Remove the end cover from the winch casing, together with shims, which should be preserved. If it is desired to remove the bearing outer race, the end cover must be warmed in hot water.

4. Withdraw the worm complete with the two bearing inner races. Drift the races from the worm shaft.

5. Remove the bollard cap.

6. Remove the set bolt, spring and plain washers retaining the bollard to the shaft; drift out the safety pin and remove the bollard. Lift off the bollard thrust washer and shims, which should be preserved.

7. Remove the bottom cover and cork joint washer from the casing.

8. Remove the bollard shaft from the casing, complete with the worm wheel.

9. Remove the set bolt, spring and plain washers, securing the worm wheel to the bollard shaft; drift the shaft from the wheel, complete with the locating key and remove the peg from the shaft.

10. Remove the breather and bollard shaft grease nipple from the casing.

11. Warm the casing in hot water and remove the oil seal and remaining bearing outer race. If necessary, drift the two bollard shaft bushes from the casing.

12. Wash all the component parts thoroughly and lay them out for inspection.

13. Check all the bearings for wear and damage and renew them as necessary.

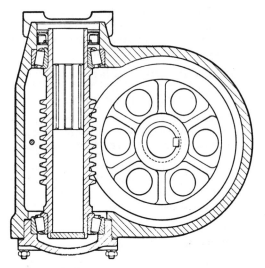

Fig. T-19—Cross-section of rear capstan winch.

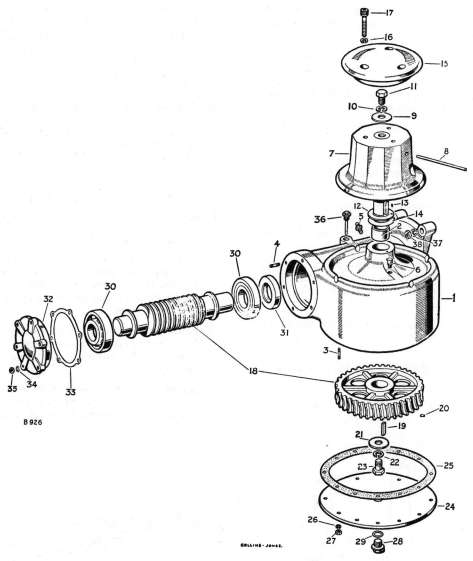

B 926

COLLINS · JONES.

Fig. T-20—Layout of rear capstan winch.

1	Winch casing	19	Key for worm wheel
2	Bush for bollard shaft	20	Peg for worm wheel key
3	Stud for bottom cover	21–23	Fixings for worm wheel
4	Stud for end cover	24	Bottom cover for casing
5	Grease nipple for bollard shaft	25	Joint washer for cover
6	Breather for casing	26–27	Fixings for bottom cover
7	Bollard and shaft assembly	28	Drain plug
8	Safety pin for bollard	29	Joint washer for plug
9–11	Fixings for bollard	30	Taper roller bearings for worm
12	Thrust washer for bollard	31	Oil seal for worm shaft
13	Peg for thrust washer	32	End cover for casing
14	Shim adjusting bollard shaft	33	Shim adjusting worm shaft bearings
15	Cap for bollard	34–35	Fixings for end cover
16–17	Fixings for cap	36	Filler plug and dipstick
18	Worm wheel and worm	37–38	Fixings for winch unit

14. Check all the gears for damage marks and rectify or renew them as necessary; the gears must only be renewed as a pair.

15. Examine the casing for signs of damage or cracks and renew as necessary. The casing may also be scrap as a result of excessive wear in a bearing bore; such wear will be obvious during the course of assembly.

16. The bollard and shaft are only supplied as an assembly.

17. Assemble the unit by reversing the stripping procedure, paying particular attention to the following points:—

18. The two worm shaft bearing outer races must be a *warm tap fit* in the casing and end plate. The two inner races must be a *light drive fit* on the worm shaft.

19. The two bollard shaft bushes must be a *press fit* in the casing and a *sliding fit* on the bollard shaft. They must be reamed to the dimension given in the data.

20. The drive housing and end cover should be warmed to facilitate fitting the bearing outer races.

21. The worm shaft oil seal should be fitted with its knife edge inwards.

22. The bollard shaft must be well greased on assembly.

23. The worm shaft must be able to turn quite freely, but no end-float must be present. Adjustment to achieve this condition is provided by the shims under the end cover, which are available .005 in., .010 in. and .020 in. thick. To reduce the end-float, shims must be removed.

24. The shims between the bollard thrust washer and the capstan casing, available .005 in. thick, are provided for adjustment of the bollard shaft end-float, which must be set on assembly to .003 in. to .005 in. (0,075 to 0,125 mm).

Hand throttle—Petrol models

To fit   **Operation T/34**

1. Remove the air cleaner and connecting tube.

2. Disconnect the control rod between the accelerator relay lever and the carburetter relay lever, the rod between the carburetter lever and the bell crank lever, and the return spring from the bell crank lever.

3. Remove the bell crank lever and the relay lever from the bell crank spindle, unscrew the spindle from the inlet manifold, and replace with the new spindle.

4. Secure the abutment bracket to the tapped hole in the top rear face of the inlet manifold, using a set bolt, spring washer and plain washer.

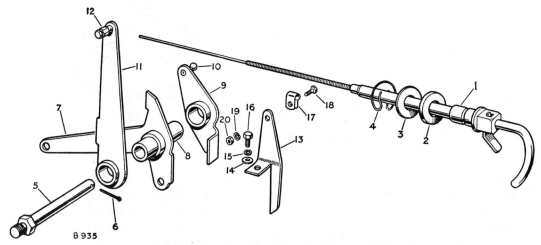

Fig. T-21—Layout of hand throttle, Petrol models.

1–4	Hand throttle control
5–6	Spindle for bell crank
7–8	Bell crank lever
9–10	Relay lever
11–12	Hand throttle lever
13	Abutment bracket for hand throttle

14	Plain washer	} Fixing abutment bracket
15	Spring washer	
16	Set bolt	
17	Cable clip	} Fixing hand throttle cable to abutment bracket
18	Screw	
19	Spring washer	
20	Nut	

5. Remove the ball pin from the original bell crank lever and fit it in the same position on the new bell crank lever.

6. Fit the hand throttle lever, the new bell crank lever, and the new relay lever to the spindle, using the original plain washer and split pin.

7. Replace the control rod between the carburetter lever and the bell crank lever, and connect the return spring to the bell crank lever.

8. Drill a $\frac{19}{32}$ in. (15 mm) dia. hole in the control panel $1\frac{3}{16}$ in. (30,16 mm) from the right-hand edge of the panel and $1\frac{3}{8}$ in. (9,52 mm) from the bottom.

9. Place the hand throttle control in the hole drilled in the panel and secure with the fixings provided.

10. Secure the control outer casing to the abutment bracket with a clip, screw, spring washer and nut.

11. Connect the control inner cable to the hand throttle lever, using the fixings provided. Position the abutment bracket so that the control cable lies in smooth curves.

12. Connect the control rod between the accelerator relay lever and the carburetter relay lever. Adjust the control rods until there is $\frac{1}{16}$ in. (1,58 mm) clearance between the hand throttle lever and the bell crank lever, and between the bell crank lever and the relay lever.

13. Test the operation of the control and replace the air cleaner.

Oil cooler—Petrol and Diesel models

To fit **Operation T/36**

1. Disconnect the bonnet prop rod from the bonnet by removing the split pin, plain and spring washers, then remove the bonnet.

2. Drain the oil from the sump into a suitable receptacle.

3. Remove the dipstick, then remove the sump.

4. **Diesel models:** Remove the oil relief plug from the pump, then fit new plug complete with joint washer; fit the new crankcase sump complete with drain plug and replace the dipstick.

5. **Petrol models:**

   (a) Slacken the locknut securing the oil pressure relief valve, then screw out the valve, complete with spring, plunger and ball. Discard

the screw and spring. Remove the locating screw and withdraw pump, leaving the pump driving shaft in position in the distributor shaft housing.

   (b) Dismantle the pump and fit the new gears (Section A). Fit the new pump cover with the new bolts and split pins. Fit a new split pin fixing the oil strainer.

   (c) Fit the reassembled pump to the engine, using the original locating screw. Replace the oil pressure relief valve, using the new adjusting screw and spring.

   (d) Fit the new crankcase sump complete with drain plug and replace the dipstick.

6. Secure the flexible oil pipe to the sump by means of the banjo centre and two joint washers. Do not fully tighten.

7. Remove the air cleaner body, oil reservoir and flexible pipe.

8. Remove the battery or batteries and carrier top(s).

9. Drain the coolant from the radiator.

10. Remove the radiator, and grille panel complete with headlamps. (Section L.)

11. Ease the tension on the fan belt. Remove and discard the fan, and (Petrol models) distance piece.

12. Drive screw the two tapping plates to the chassis front cross-member, as illustrated in Fig. T-23.

13. Drill and tap the four holes in the tapping plates to $\frac{1}{4}$ in. U.N.F.

14. Fit the oil relief valve to the top union of the oil cooler.

15. Remove and discard the inner left-hand nut and bolt, securing the grille panel assembly to the top of the radiator, then detach earth clip from the bolt in the top panel, and re-tighten the bolt.

16. Mark out and drill the L.H. side panel as illustrated in Fig. T-24.

17. Remove the lower securing nut and bolt, then mark out and cut away the section of the R.H. side panel indicated in Fig. T-24. Drill a hole above the cut-out, through the panel and radiator bracket, and refit securing nut and bolt.

18. **Petrol models:** Remove and discard the fan cowl and replace with the new one.

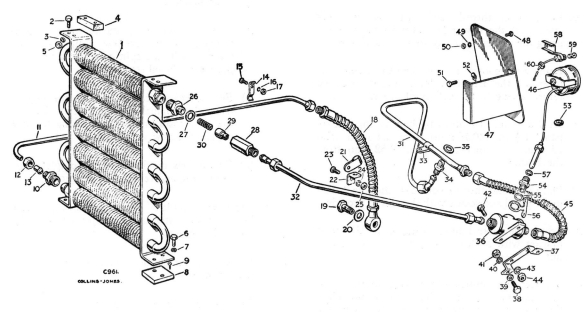

Fig. T-22—Layout of oil cooler, Petrol models.

1	Oil cooler	26	Oil union
2–5	Fixings—oil cooler to radiator	27	Joint washer for union
6–7	Fixings—oil cooler to frame	28	Body
8	Tapping plate for oil cooler	29	Plunger
9	Drive screw fixing plate to frame	30	Spring for plunger
10	Oil return pipe union	31	Oil pipe, union to flexible pipe
11	Oil return pipe	32	Oil pipe to relief valve
12–13	Union fixings—for return pipe	33	Clip for pipe—union to flexible pipe
14	Oil return pipe clip	34	Union for oil pipe
15–17	Fixings—for clip	35	Joint washer for union
18	Flexible oil pipe, return to sump	36	Thermometer pocket complete
19–20	Fixings—flexible pipe to sump	37–41	Not required
21	Flexible pipe clip	42–44	Fixings—pocket to wing valance
22	Clip bracket	45	Flexible pipe—pump to pocket
23–25	Fixings—for clip	46	Oil temperature gauge
		47	Mounting bracket for gauge
		48–52	Fixings—mounting bracket to dash.
		53	Grommet for pipe in dash

Oil release valve (items 26–30)

On oil filter adaptor (items 34–35)

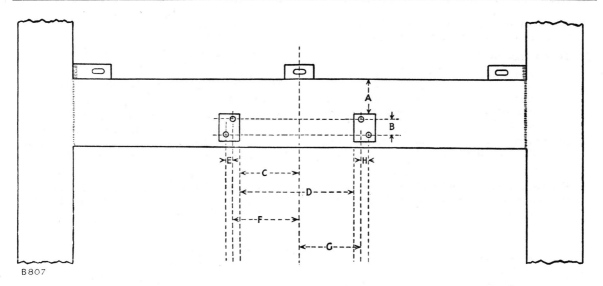

Fig. T-23—Location and drilling of tapping plates.

A—1 $\frac{15}{16}$ in. (49,2 mm)   C—4 $\frac{7}{8}$ in. (123,8 mm)   E—$\frac{1}{2}$ in. (12,7 mm)   G—4 $\frac{3}{8}$ in. (111mm)

B—1 $\frac{1}{4}$ in. (31,7 mm)   D—8 $\frac{1}{4}$ in. (209,5 mm)   F—5 $\frac{7}{8}$ in. (149,2 mm)   H—$\frac{1}{2}$ in. (12,7 mm)

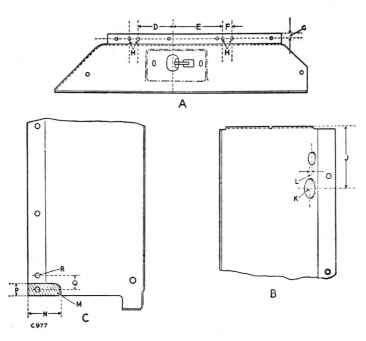

Fig. T-24—Details of additional drillings in grille panels.

A—Top panel
B—L.H. side panel
C—R.H. side panel
D—3 $\frac{15}{16}$ in. (100 mm)
E—5 $\frac{7}{16}$ in. (138 mm)
F—1 $\frac{15}{16}$ in. (23,8 mm)
G—$\frac{9}{16}$ in. (14,3 mm)
H—Four new holes $\frac{9}{32}$ in. (7,1 mm) dia.
J—3 $\frac{1}{4}$ in. (82,5 mm)

K—One new hole 1 $\frac{1}{8}$ in. (28,6 mm) dia.
L—$\frac{1}{8}$ in. (3,2 mm)
M—Shaded area represents section to be cut away
N—1 $\frac{3}{4}$ in. (44,4 mm)
P—$\frac{5}{8}$ in. (15,8 mm)
Q—$\frac{1}{2}$ in. (12,7 mm)
R—One new hole $\frac{9}{32}$ in. (7,1 mm) dia.

19. **Petrol models:** Remove and discard the radiator cap, and replace with the new one.

20. **Diesel models:**

 (a) Remove the starter dog and withdraw the damper assembly. Replace with the new double pulley assembly and secure to the crankshaft with the starter dog and a new lock washer.

 (b) Remove the dynamo, and withdraw the pulley; fit the new double pulley and refit the dynamo

21. Replace the radiator and grille panel assembly, securing with the original nuts and bolts. Do not fully tighten.

22. **Petrol models:** Fit the new fan to the pulley and refit the belt.

 Diesel models: Fit the new fan to the new double pulley and fit two new belts.

23. Mark out and drill the radiator grille panel top, as shown in Fig. T-24.

24. Secure the oil cooler to the radiator and grille panel assembly, using the four holes drilled in the top panel and secure with the nuts, bolts, washers and distance pieces supplied.

25. Drill a further $\frac{9}{32}$ in. (7,1 mm) dia. hole in a suitable position in the grille top panel, and using the sherardised nut and bolt supplied, fit the earth clip.

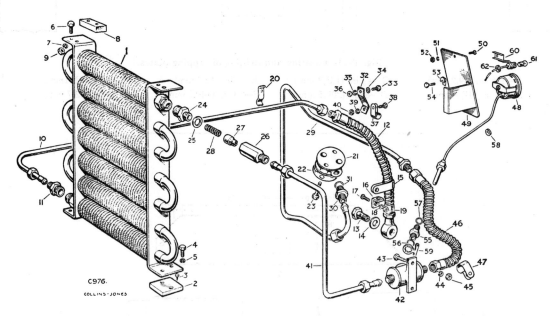

Fig. T-25—Layout of oil cooler, Diesel models.

1	Oil cooler	26	Body
2	Tapping plate	27	Plunger
3	Drive screw, plate to frame	28	Spring for plunger
4–5	Fixings—cooler to chassis frame	29	Oil pipe, union to flexible pipe
6–9	Fixings—cooler to radiator and grille panel	30	Union for oil pipe
10	Oil return pipe	31	Joint washer for union
11	Union for return pipe	32	Bracket for clip
12	Flexible oil pipe, return to sump	33–36	Fixings—bracket to front engine lifting bracket
13–14	Fixings—flexible pipe to sump	37	Clip for union to flexible oil pipe
15	Clip, for flexible oil pipe	38–40	Fixings—clip to bracket
16	Bracket for clip	41	Oil pipe to relief valve
17–19	Fixings—return pipe clip to bracket	42	Thermometer pocket complete
20	Clip for oil return pipe	43–45	Fixings—thermometer pocket to valance
21	Adaptor for engine oil filter	46	Flexible oil pipe, pump to pocket
22	Joint washer for adaptor	47	Clip fixing flexible pipe to L.H. battery support
23	Bolt, fixing adaptor		
24–25	Oil union and joint washer		

26. Tighten all nuts and bolts.

27. Fit the union to the oil cooler lower R.H. side and fit the right-angled end of the oil return pipe to the union and secure the other end of the flexible pipe already fitted to the sump. Figs. T-26 and T-27. Secure the non-flexible pipe to the battery carrier (R.H. on Diesel), using a clip, screw, nut and spring washer.

28. Tighten the banjo bolt securing the flexible pipe to sump and secure the pipe to a convenient sump securing stud, using a bracket, clip, screw, nut and spring washer—Figs. T-22 and T-25.

29. Fit the oil pipe relief valve to the thermometer pocket, but do not fully tighten the union; connect the pipe to the foremost end of the thermometer bulb pocket—see Figs. T-22 and T-25. Secure the flexible oil pipe to the pocket.

30. Fit the oil pipe, flexible pipe to oil filter adaptor and—Petrol models: secure it with a clip to the thermostat housing stud, or—Diesel models:

fit a bracket to the engine lifting bracket, then secure the pipe to the bracket with a clip—see Figs. T-22 and T-25.

31 Using the thermometer pocket as a guide, drill two holes ¾ in. (5 mm) dia. in the L.H. wing valance, or—Diesel models: L.H. battery valance, and secure the pocket, using two bolts, nuts and spring washers.

32. **Petrol models:** Remove plug from oil filter adaptor and fit a union and joint washer. Fit the pipe, connecting flexible pipe to adaptor, to the union, and connect the other end to the flexible pipe.

33. **Diesel models:** Remove the engine oil filter and fit the adaptor and joint washer between it and cylinder block, and secure with the new bolts and original spring washers; fit the union and joint washer. Fit the pipe, connecting flexible pipe to adaptor, to the union and connect the other end to the flexible pipe.

34. Mark and cut out a 1 in. (25,4 mm) hole in the L.H. glove box, approximately 3 in. (75 mm) from the base and 2 in. (50,8 mm) from R.H. side of glove box.

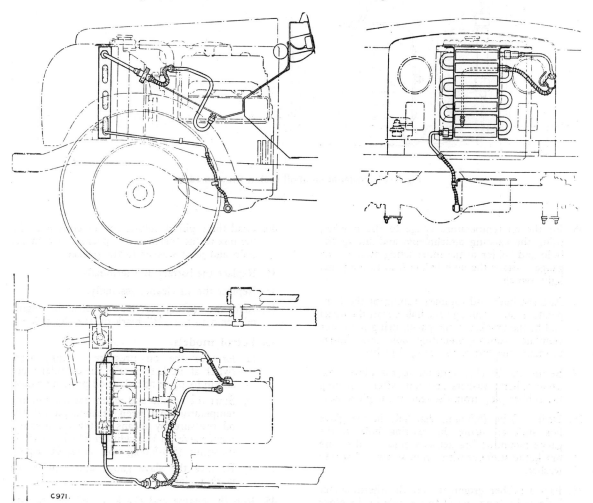

C971.

Fig. T-26—Installation of oil cooler, Petrol models.

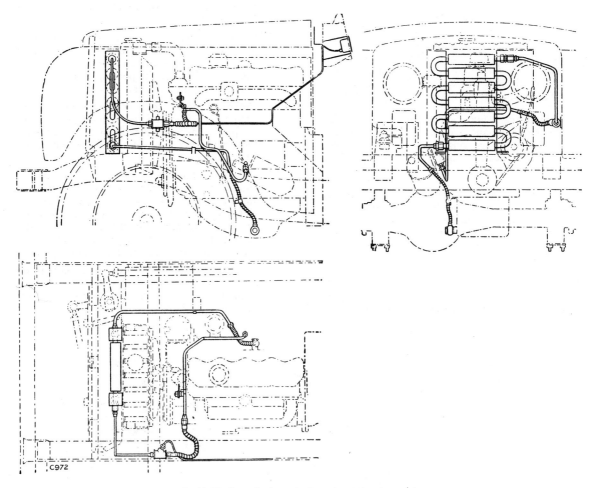

Fig. T-27—Installation of oil cooler, Diesel models.

35. Fit the oil temperature gauge to the bracket, using the existing attachments and fitting the bulb and holder to the inner fixing stud on the gauge. Attach the bulb holder lead to the panel light switch.

36. Pass the bulb and capillary tubing of the temperature gauge through the hole cut in the panel and fit the bracket to the panel, using the lower ventilator control mounting hole and fixings to secure the top of the gauge bracket.

37. Secure the bracket stiffener to the glove box, using a bolt, washers and nut, after removing the rubber plug from the rear of the glove box.

38. Drill a $\frac{7}{32}$ in. (5,5 mm) dia. hole in the glove box stiffener, using the existing hole in the gauge mounting bracket as a guide, and secure bracket to stiffener with a nut, screw and spring washer.

39. Pass a rubber grommet over the thermometer bulb and tubing and fit to the hole in the glove box.

40. Lead the capillary tubing conveniently over the toe box to the thermometer pocket, then fit the bulb and joint washer to the pocket.

41. Replace the battery and terminals.

42. Replace the air cleaner assembly.

43. Refill the cooling system, and then the engine oil sump to the "H" mark on the dipstick.

44. **Petrol models:**

    (a) Remove the oil pressure warning light switch at the L.H. rear of the cylinder block and in its place fit a slave oil pressure gauge.

    (b) Start the engine and when normal running temperature has been reached, adjust the oil pressure by means of the oil pressure relief valve on the cylinder block, to 75-80 lb./sq.in. (5,3-5,6 kg/cm^2) at 2,500 r.p.m.

    (c) Remove the slave gauge and replace the warning light switch.

45. Run the engine and check for oil and coolant leaks, then refit bonnet.

Water temperature and oil pressure gauge— all models

To fit   Operation T/38

1. Disconnect the bonnet prop rod from the bonnet by removing the split pin, plain and spring washers, then remove the bonnet.

2. Drain the coolant from the radiator into a suitable receptacle.

3. Mark and cut out a 1 in. (25 mm) dia. hole in the L.H. glove box, approximately 3 in. (75 mm) from the base and 2 in. (50 mm) from R.H. side of glove box.

4. Fit the combined water temperature and oil pressure gauge to the gauge-mounting bracket using the existing attachments, and fitting the bulb and holder to the inner fixing stud on the gauge. Attach the bulb holder lead to the panel light switch.

5. Fit the oil pipe to the union on the gauge.

6. Pass the oil pipe and the bulb pipe of the temperature gauge through the 1 in. (25,4 mm) dia. hole cut in the panel and secure the bracket to the coil mounting and glove box, using the same bolt.

7. Drill a $\frac{7}{32}$ in. (5,5 mm) dia. hole in the glove box stiffener, using the existing hole in the gauge-mounting bracket as a guide, and secure bracket to stiffener with a nut, screw and spring washer.

8. Pass a rubber grommet over the thermometer bulb and tubing and fit to the hole in the glove box.

9. **Petrol models:**

   (a) If fitted, remove the governor (Operation T/20) and remove the thermostat housing. Strip the old housing, discard and fit parts to new housing.

   (b) Fit the plug and washer to the larger tapped hole in the new thermostat housing and fit the union and washer to the other hole. Fit the locker over the union, and tighten the union until the holes in the locker are in line with the holes in the right-hand side of the housing.

   (c) Fit the new thermostat housing complete to the engine and secure with the existing bolts and spring washers, ensuring that the rubber seal is in position between the water pump and the housing.

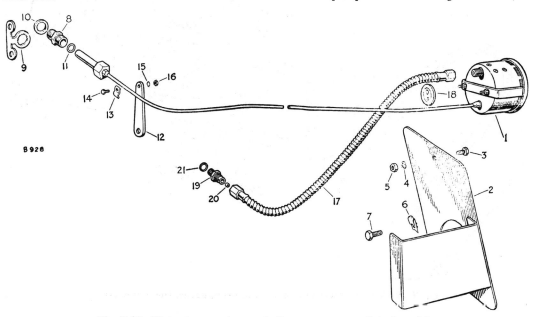

Fig. T-28—Water temperature and oil pressure gauge, Petrol models.

1 Water temperature and oil pressure gauge	13 Thermometer pipe clip
2 Mounting bracket for gauge	14–16 Fixings for clips
3–7 Fixings—mounting bracket to dash	17 Oil pipe for gauge
8 Union for thermometer bulb	18 Grommet for pipe, in dash
9 Locker for union	19 Union for oil pipe
10 Washer for union	20 Meter valve
11 Washer for thermometer bulb	21 Washer for union
12 Thermometer pipe support bracket	

(d) Refit the governor (if fitted).

(e) Form the thermometer pipe to pass to the left of the coil, down over the toe box and along the wing valance to the thermostat housing. Coil the excess thermometer pipe neatly, adjacent to the bulb and to the L.H. wing valance, tape both coils at the top, then fit the bulb to the union, using the joint washer provided.

(f) Fit the bracket under a convenient bolt on the engine front cover, fit a clip over the pipe and secure it to the bracket.

(g) Secure the pipe to the L.H. wing valance and toe box at two suitable points, using the remaining clips, bolts, spring washers and nuts. On a L.H.D. vehicle secure the pipe to the steering column using two clips, and on a R.H.D. vehicle secure the pipe to the tie bar for the dash support, using the rubber cleat.

11. **Diesel models:**

(a) Remove the plug from the L.H. rear of the cylinder head, discard, then replace with a union and joint washer.

(b) Drill two $\frac{7}{32}$ in. (5,5 mm) holes in dash for mounting thermometer pipe clip bracket. The holes to be 6 in. and $7\frac{7}{8}$ in. (152 and 200 mm) from R.H. side of L.H. toe box, and in a position to be approximately level with the top of the cylinder head.

(c) Secure the bracket to the engine side of the dash, using two nuts, screws and spring washers. Coil the thermometer pipe neatly into approximately a 3 in. (76,2 mm) coil, tape at the top and clip to the bracket.

(d) Lead the thermometer pipe along the L.H. side of the vehicle, and fit the bulb to the union, using the joint washer provided.

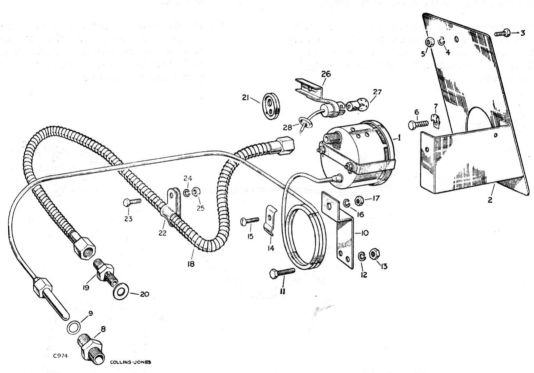

Fig. T-29—Water temperature and oil pressure gauge, Diesel models.

1	Water temperature and oil pressure gauge	18	Oil pipe for gauge
2	Mounting bracket for gauge	19	Union for oil pipe
3–7	Fixings—mounting bracket to dash	20	Joint washer for union
8	Union for thermometer bulb	21	Grommet for oil pipe in dash
9	Joint washer for gauge bulb	22	Clip for pipe
10	Support bracket for pipe clip	23–25	Fixings—clip to dash
11–13	Fixings—bracket to dash	26	Panel light adaptor
14	Clip for thermometer pipe	27	Bulb
15–17	Fixings—pipe clip to support bracket	28	Grommet for lead

12. **Petrol models:**

   (a) Disconnect the feed wire from the oil pressure switch at the L.H. rear of the cylinder block and carefully cover the wire with insulating tape. Remove and discard the switch, then replace with a union and joint washer.

   (b) Clip the flexible oil pipe to the dash panel at a convenient point and connect the oil pipe to the union.

13. **Diesel models:**

   (a) Remove the banjo bolt fixing the valve gear feed pipe at the R.H. rear of the cylinder block, discard and replace with a union and joint washer.

   (b) Clip the flexible oil pipe to an existing hole in the dash panel, located approximately $7\frac{1}{2}$ in. (190 mm) down and 4 in. (101 mm) to left of the thermometer pipe clip bracket previously secured to the dash.

   (c) Lead the oil pipe along the dash panel and clip again to the panel about $2\frac{1}{2}$ in. (63,5 mm) to the right of the vehicle centre line. Secure the pipe to the R.H. toe box side panel, using the remaining clip and fixings, and connect the oil pipe to the union.

14. Refill the cooling system.

15. Start the engine and check for leaks (both coolant and oil).

16. Refit the bonnet.

Heater unit and demister tubes
Unit fitment   Operation T/40
Petrol models:

1. Disconnect the bonnet prop rod from the bonnet.

2. Remove the bonnet.

3. Drain off the coolant.

4. Disconnect the bottom water hose at the inlet pipe to the pump end. Remove the inlet pipe from the pump and discard the pipe.

5. Fit the new inlet pipe to the pump with the joint washer and secure it, using the existing bolts, spring washers and clip.

6. Fit the reducing union and joint washer to the pipe.

7. Disconnect the top water hose from the thermostat housing and disconnect the water hose to the inlet elbow.

8. Remove the thermostat housing from the cylinder head. Completely strip and discard the housing.

9. Fit the parts removed from the old housing to the new thermostat housing.

10. Fit the plug and joint washer to the smaller tapped hole in the housing, and to the large tapped hole fit the water supply valve and joint washer.

11. Fit the thermostat housing complete to the cylinder head, ensuring that the rubber seal is in place on the top of the water pump, and secure, using the existing set bolts and spring washers.

12. Remove the rubber plugs, one from the front face of the control panel and the other from the L.H. side of the control panel box.

13. Fit to the heater switch the feed wire and also a suitable length of wire to connect the heater switch to the terminal with the single green wire in the fuse box.

14. Remove the knob from the switch and fit the switch to the face of the control panel, using the existing hole. Refit the knob.

15. Remove the two large, and three small rubber plugs from the dash centre panel.

16. Fit the rubber seal to the heater over the water pipes.

17. Fit the rubber hoses to the water pipes and secure.

18. Remove the nuts, spring washers and plain washers from the three studs on the heater and fit to the studs the three brackets. Fit the heater to the dash and secure, using the existing nuts, spring washers and plain washers.

   Note: Before fully tightening the nuts ensure that the mounting brackets are lying radially outwards from the studs.

19. Connect the feed wire to the snap connectors on the heater lead.

20. Fit the two union nuts, one to the water inlet pipe and one to the water outlet pipe.

21. Fit the remaining two clips, one to each hose on the heater and fit the inlet and outlet pipes to the hoses. Secure the pipes to the water supply valve and the reducing union. Secure the pipes to the hoses, using the two clips.

22. Fit the two spire nuts to the blanking cap and fit the blanking cap to the heater, securing by means of the two acme screws.

   Note: This operation is eliminated if demisters are to be fitted.

23. Refill the cooling system.

24. Open the water supply valve and check the functioning of the heater.

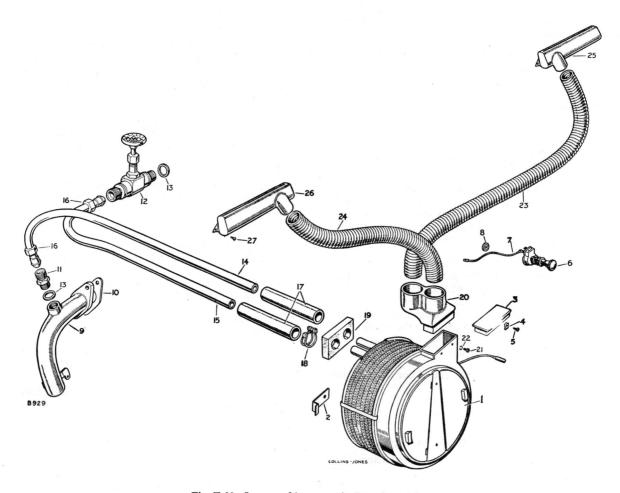

Fig. T-30—Layout of heater unit, Petrol models.

1	Heater	
2	Bracket for heater	
3	Blanking cap	} Not required
4	Spire nut } Fixing	} with
5	Acme bolt } blanking cap	} demisters
6	Switch for heater	
7	Feed wire for heater	
8	Grommet for heater leads	
9	Inlet pipe for water pump	
10	Joint washer for pipe	
11	Reducing union for pipe	
12	Valve for water supply	
13	Joint washer for valve and union	

14	Water outlet pipe
15	Water inlet pipe
16	Union nut for heater pipe to valve and union
17	Hose for water pipes
18	Clip for hose
19	Rubber seal for pipes
20	Junction box for demister tubes
21–22	Fixings: junction box to heater
23	Tube for demister, R.H.
24	Tube for demister, L.H.
25	Nozzle for demister, R.H.
26	Nozzle for demister, L.H.
27	Drive screw fixing nozzle

Diesel models

1. Disconnect the bonnet prop and remove the bonnet complete.

2. Drain off the coolant.

3. Unscrew the plug from L.H. side of water outlet pipe and fit the union for hose with a copper sealing washer interposed.

4. Remove the plug from rear L.H. corner of cylinder head top and fit the flow control valve and copper joint washer.

5. Remove the rubber plug from R.H. side of control box panel face and another from L.H. side of control box.

6. Part the lead connected to the heater at the snap connector and connect the eyeletted end to one terminal of the rheostat switch. Connect the eyeletted end of the lead with bared opposite end, to the switch second terminal. Remove the control knob from switch and fit to hole in R.H. side of control panel, then lock in position. Replace knob.

7. Fit a rubber grommet to the hole in L.H. side of control box and pass both leads from the rheostat switch through the grommet.

8. Remove the two large and three small rubber plugs from the L.H. side of the scuttle centre panel.

9. Fit the sponge rubber seal over the heater pipes, then remove the nuts, plain and spring washers from the securing studs—leave the earth lead terminal on the lower stud.

10. Position a steady bracket to each mounting stud and offer the unit to the scuttle. Fit the nuts, spring and plain washers, but before tightening ensure that the steady brackets are extending radially outward.

11. Fit to the heater switch the feed wire and also a suitable length of wire to connect the heater switch with the terminal with the green wires in the fuse box.

12. Fit the "Z"-shaped hose to the control valve and heater inner pipe, then secure. The "L"-shaped hoses should now be fitted to the water outlet pipe, then the hose and pipe assembly connected to the heater and water pump adaptor.

13. Fit the support clip for water outlet pipe and secure it loosely to the manifold securing stud. Adjust the hoses and pipe as necessary and secure.

14. Refill the coolant system, open the water valve and check the functioning of heater.

To fit demisters Operation T/42

1. Remove the blanking cap (if fitted) from the heater and fit the junction box for demister tubes.

2. Remove the rubber plugs from the top of both glove boxes.

3. Petrol models: Disconnect the battery.

   Diesel models: Disconnect the positive lead of R.H. battery.

4. Remove the securing screws and withdraw the instrument panel complete with controls and wiring.

5. Pass the R.H. demister tube through the hole in R.H. glove box top, through the hole in R.H. side of instrument box, over the wiring, on through the hole in instrument box, L.H. side, and fit the tube to one pipe of the demister junction box.

6. Insert the L.H. demister tube into the hole in L.H. glove box top, pass it through the L.H. side of instrument panel and through the hole in L.H. bottom of instrument box. Fit the tube to the other pipe on the demister junction box.

7. Fit the demister nozzles to their respective tubes and using the holes in the nozzles as pilots, drill $\frac{7}{64}$ in. (2,77 mm) dia. holes in windscreen frame, then secure the nozzle with drive screws.

8. Refit the instrument panel and battery lead, then test heater and demister for correct functioning.

9. Refit the bonnet and prop rod.

Propeller shaft joint cover plates

To fit Operation T/44

1. Protect the rear shaft rear joint by placing a cover plate under the rear axle differential housing, with the slots in the retaining strap located in the stiffening webs of the housing; retain it with a strap over the housing and secure by means of two bolts and nuts.

2. Protect the front shaft front joint in a similar manner.

   Protect the front shaft rear joint by means of a plate which should be secured under the transfer box, between No. 3 and No. 4 chassis cross-members (front bumper is No. 1 member) as follows:—

3. Position the plate centrally beneath the front shaft rear joint, with the two right angle brackets abutting the rear of No. 3 cross-member.

4. Bend the plate to the contour of the cross-members and drill three $\frac{9}{64}$ in. (3,57 mm) dia. holes in the front member, and three in the rear member, using the plate as a template ; the holes should be the three outermost at each end of the plate.

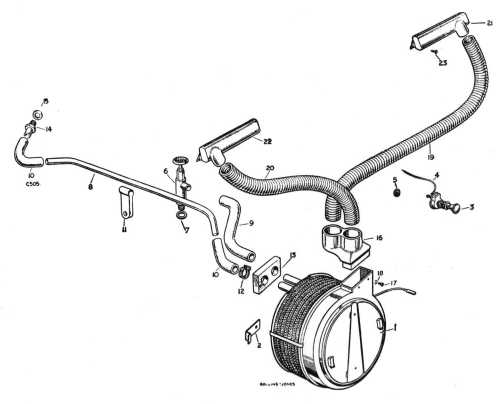

Fig. T-31—Layout of heater unit, Diesel models.

1	Heater	12	Clip for hose
2	Bracket for heater	13	Rubber seal for pipes
3	Switch for heater	14	Union outlet pipe to pump
4	Feed wire for heater	15	Washer
5	Grommet for heater leads	16	Junction box for demister tubes
6	Valve for water supply	17–18	Fixings: junction box to heater
7	Joint washer for valve and union	19	Tube for demister, R.H.
8	Water outlet pipe	20	Tube for demister, L.H.
9	Water inlet pipe	21	Nozzle for demister, R.H.
10	Hose for water outlet pipe	22	Nozzle for demister, L.H
11	Clip for hose pipe	23	Drive screw fixing nozzle

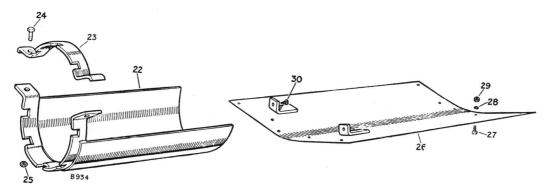

Fig. T-32—Layout of propeller shaft joint cover plates.

22   Cover plate for joint at differential housings
23   Top strap for cover plate
24–25 Fixings for cover plates
26   Shield for joint at transfer box
27   Bolt   ⎫
28   Spring washer ⎬ Fixing
29   Nut   shield
30   Drive screws ⎭

5. Secure the plate in position with six drive screws; disregard the two right angle brackets which are not used when fitting the plate with the gearbox and transfer box unit in position.

6. The rear shaft front bearing is effectively screened by the transmission brake unit.

Flashing indicators—All models

To fit   **Operation T/46**

1. Remove the five screws and lower the instrument panel, drill one hole .189 in. (4,8 mm) dia. (No. 12 drill) in accordance with the dimensions in Fig. T-34 for mounting the flasher unit.

2. Drill one hole $\frac{3}{4}$ in. (18,05 mm) dia. in the dash, as shown in Fig. T-34.

3. Make the connections from the end of the flasher harness to the flasher switch and warning light, as indicated in the wiring diagram. The green lead connected to the X terminal on the flasher unit should be plugged into the spare hole in the petrol gauge snap connector.

4. Mount the flasher unit to the dash, behind the instrument panel, using a drive screw and refit the instrument panel.

5. Fit the switch and warning light to the mounting bracket.

6. Secure the bracket to the upper glove box stiffener channel, by using the lower ventilator control fixings. Using the existing hole in the bracket as a guide, drill a $\frac{9}{32}$ in. (7,1 mm) dia. hole in the lower stiffener channel and secure bracket with a screw, washers and nut.

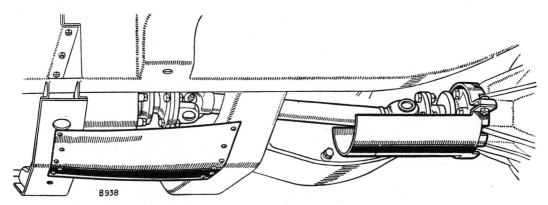

Fig. T-33—Propeller shaft joint cover plates in position.

Note: The flasher switch and warning light mounting bracket is fitted to the R.H. side of the instrument panel on R.H.D. models and on the L.H. side on L.H.D. models.

L.H.D. models fitted with oil pressure and/or water temperature gauge have the mounting bracket fitted between the steering column and the gauge panel, which means that the ventilator control fixing cannot be used and a further $\frac{9}{32}$ in. (7,1 mm) hole must be drilled as shown in Fig. T-34.

7. Fit a rubber grommet to the $\frac{3}{4}$ in. (19,05 mm) dia. hole in the dash and feed the harness through. Clip the harness to the dash panel.

8. Feed the flasher harness for the rear lamps through the side member, the harness emerging at the rear of the member with the rear light harness.

Note: It will be found that the best method of feeding the lead through the chassis member is to disconnect the wires of the frame harness at the rear of the vehicle, then attach a length of soft iron wire to the leads and withdraw leads and wire back through the side member. Attach the flasher harness to the iron wire and pull wire and harness back through the chassis.

9. Cut out two holes $1\frac{7}{16}$ in. (36,5 mm) dia. in the rear body panel to take rear flasher lamps. The cappings are pre-drilled to the correct size.

10. Connect the harness to the lamps and fit the lamp to the body. Connect the earth terminal to the rear cross-member.

11. Drill the wings as shown in Fig. T-37.

12. Move the side lamps to the inner hole.

13. Pass the harness through the wing valances and connect to flasher lamps.

14. Fit the lamps to the wings in the position vacated by the side lamps.

15. Check flasher system for correct operation.

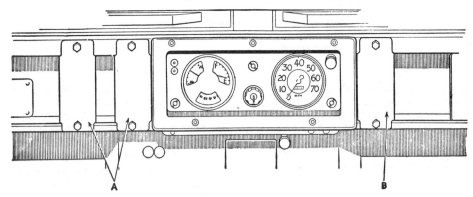

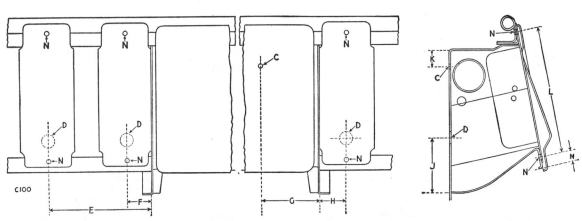

Fig. T-34—Position of flasher mounting bracket.

A—Alternative position of bracket on L.H.D. models.
B—Position of bracket on R.H.D. models.
C—Hole in dash for flasher unit mounting .189 in. dia. (4,80 mm)
D—Hole in dash for flasher harness $\frac{3}{4}$ in. dia. (19,1 mm)
E—5$\frac{5}{16}$ in. (134,9 mm)
F—1$\frac{5}{16}$ in. (33,3 mm)

G—3 in. (76,2 mm)
H—1$\frac{5}{16}$ in. (33,3 mm)
J—2$\frac{1}{2}$ in. (63,5 mm)
K—$\frac{3}{4}$ in. (19,8 mm)
L—6$\frac{1}{4}$ in. (158,8 mm)
M—$\frac{7}{16}$ in. (11,1 mm)
N—Hole in glove box stiffener $\frac{9}{32}$ in. dia. (13,5 mm)

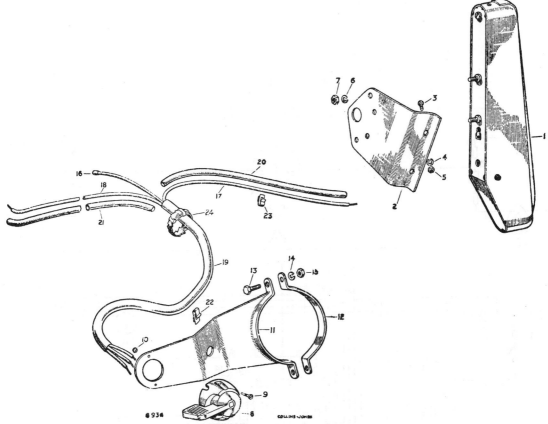

Fig. T-35—Layout of trafficators.

1	Trafficator
2	Bracket for trafficator
3–5	Fixings for bracket
6–7	Fixings for trafficator
8	Switch for trafficator
9–10	Fixings for switches
11	Bracket for trafficator switch
12	Clamp for bracket
13–15	Fixings for bracket and clamp
16	Feed lead to switch
17	Short lead ⎱ Switch to trafficator
18	Long lead ⎰
19	Sheath, trafficator lead to switch
20	Sheath, trafficator leads in hand rail
21	Sheath, trafficator leads in windscreen
22	Cable clip on switch bracket
23	Cable clip at glove box
24	Cable cleat at steering column

Trafficators

To fit   **Operation T/48**

1. Fit a bracket to the top of both windscreen side members, and secure at the countersunk holes with two screws, spring washers and nuts to each bracket.

2. Dismantle the trafficators and connect to each of them a lead covered by a sheath (short lead to the one for the driver's side).

3. Secure the trafficators to the brackets using spring washers and nuts.

4. Feed the leads from the trafficators through the holes just below the brackets, down the windscreen side members behind the rubber seals, cover the longer with a sheath inside the hand rail, enter the holes at the back of the hand rail to emerge at the hole in line with the steering column, and down through the hole in the glove box top. Sufficient slack must be left in the cables between the windscreen and the hand rail, to allow for folding of the windscreen.

5. Lower the instrument panel.

6. Connect the switch feed lead to the two-way connector in the green cable to the petrol gauge terminal "B", feed this lead through the windscreen wiper grommet and secure in the clip.

7. Secure the switch bracket horizontally to the steering column, using a clamp, bolts, spring washers and nuts.

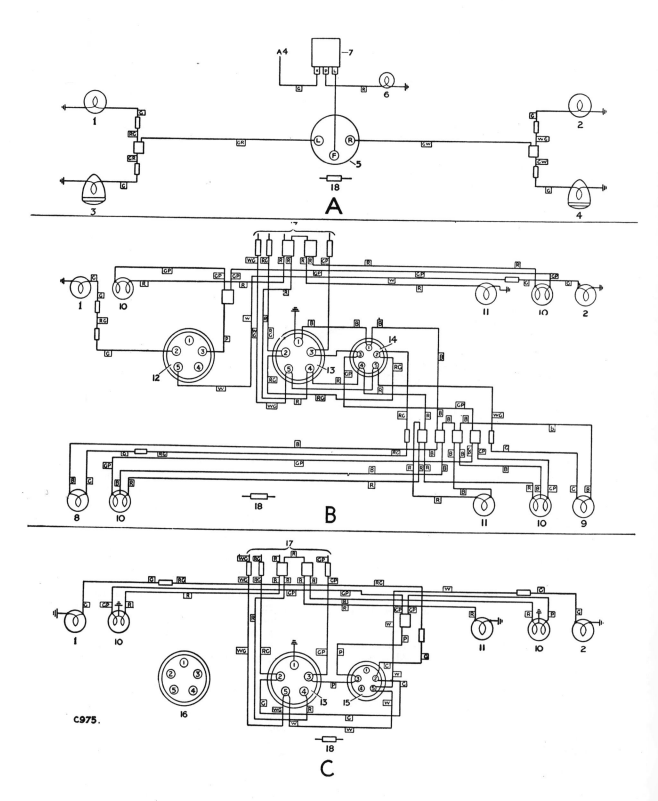

Fig. T-36—Flasher and trailer plug wiring diagrams.

Key to Fig. T-36

A—Wiring diagram for flashers only.

B—Wiring diagram, using trailer and flashers. On this diagram, flashers are disconnected and trailer plug is in use, giving flashers on trailer.

C—Wiring diagram, using flashers and trailer socket. On this diagram, the rear flashers are shown connected via the trailer socket, and vehicle flasher plug; the plug must be in this position when the trailer is not in use.

1	Rear flasher lamp L.H.	10	Stop and tail lamp
2	Rear flasher lamp R.H.	11	Number plate illumination lamp
3	Front flasher lamp L.H.	12	Vehicle flasher plug, in dummy trailer socket
4	Front flasher lamp R.H.	13	Trailer socket
5	Self-cancelling switch	14	Trailer plug
6	Warning light	15	Vehicle flasher plug
7	Flasher unit	16	Dummy trailer socket
8	Trailer flasher lamp L.H.	17	Wiring as diagram "A" from this point
9	Trailer flasher lamp R.H.	18	Snap connectors shown thus: ⊣▭⊢

KEY TO CABLE COLOURS

B—Black	N—Brown	R—Red	W—White
G—Green	P—Purple	U—Blue	Y—Yellow
	RN—Red with Brown and so on.		

8. Pass the three leads, covered with a suitable sheath, through the large hole in the switch bracket and connect to the switch. The feed wire from the instrument panel is connected to the central terminal. The other two wires are connected so that the driver's side trafficator operates when the switch is down.

9. Secure the switch to the bracket, using the fixings provided.

10. Secure the leads to the switch bracket with a clip and to the steering column support bracket with a cleat.

11. Secure the slack cable between the windscreen and hand rail with a clip at the end face of each glove box.

Trailer plug and socket

To fit   **Operation T/50**

Note: Appropriate cable colours in parenthesis. See wiring diagram.

1. Using the dummy socket bracket as a template, mark off two mounting holes on rear cross-member, $1\frac{5}{8}$ in. (41,5 mm) from inner face of step mounting bracket to centre of socket aperture and 1 in. (25,4 mm) down from the bottom of the cross-member.

2. Drill two holes, $\frac{11}{64}$ in. (5 mm) and secure bracket to cross-member, using self-tapping screws.

3. Mark a point, $1\frac{3}{4}$ in. (44,5 mm) from the centre of the rear plug socket, towards the outer edge of cross-member, $1\frac{1}{4}$ in. (32 mm) from bottom edge, and drill a $\frac{15}{32}$ in. (12 mm) hole.

4. Fit a rubber grommet to the hole, then fit dummy socket to bracket, and thread flasher plug lead through grommet.

5. Fit the trailer socket and leads to rear cross-member.

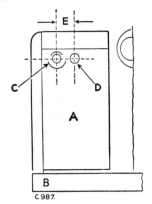

C 987

Fig. T-37—
Additional drillings in front wings.
A—Wing.
B—Bumper.
C—Existing side light position.
D—One new hole, $1\frac{7}{16}$ in. (36,5 mm) dia.
E—$3\frac{1}{4}$ in. (82,6 mm)

Fitting vehicle flasher plug (items 6-12 inclusive)

6. Remove R.H. rear wheel and disconnect flasher and rear light wires from snap connectors under wheelarch.

7. Fit double snap connectors to main tail lamp lead from harness (red) and reconnect rear lamp wire.

8. Connect the stop and tail light wires from the lamps (green and purple) to the flasher plug wire (yellow) with a snap connector.

9. Connect the R.H. flasher wire (white and green) to the flasher plug wire (buff) with a snap connector.

10. Connect the L.H. flasher wire (red and green) to the flasher plug wire (purple) with a snap connector.

11. Connect the flasher plug earth wire (blue) to the existing earth wire on the rear cross-member, using an earth bridge lead.

12. The flasher plug wire (white) is for the rear lamps. Leave disconnected as the lamps are coupled direct from the main harness.

Trailer socket wiring (items 13-19 inclusive)

13. Connect trailer socket wire (red) to main loom wire (red) with a two-way snap connector.

14. Connect L.H. and R.H. tail lamp wires (red) to connectors (13).

15. Using tail lamp bridge lead, connect snap connectors (14) together.

16. Connect the trailer socket wire (green and purple) to the main loom wire (green and purple) with a snap connector.

17. Connect the R.H. flasher trailer socket wire (white and green) to main loom wire (white and green) with a snap connector.

18. Connect the L.H. flasher trailer socket wire (red and green) to the main loom wire (red and green) with a snap connector.

19. The trailer socket wire (black) goes to earth on rear cross-member with the main loom earth connection, using the earth bridge lead.

Fitting trailer plug and lead (items 20 and 21)

20. Pass the trailer plug wires through the retaining clip along the draw bar.

21. Connect the rear lamps, stop lamp and flashers to the terminals. See wiring diagram.

To use trailer plugs

22. Trailer not in use: remove trailer plug and fit flasher plug into trailer socket at rear cross-member.

23. Trailer in use: fit trailer plug from draw bar to trailer socket on rear cross-member and fit flasher plug into dummy socket.

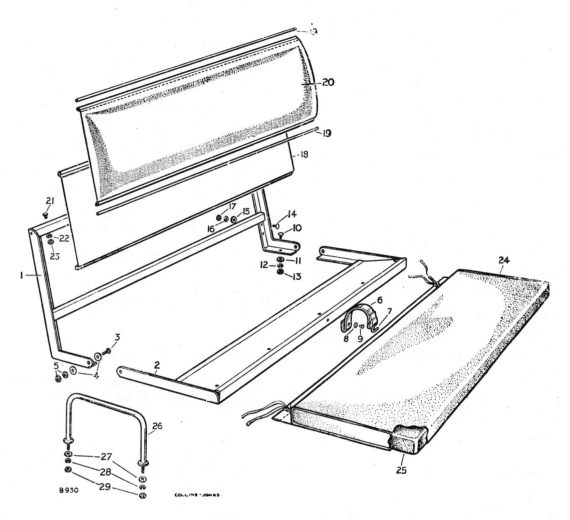

Fig. T-38—Layout of rear seats.

1	Rear seat back frame	18	Back rest panel
2	Hinged seat base	19	Retaining rod for back rest pad
3–5	Fixings—seat base to back frame	20	Back rest pad
6	Retaining strap for seat base ·	21–23	Fixings for back rest
7	Hook for strap	24	Rear seat cushion
8–9	Fixings for strap	25	Pad for cushion
10–13	Fixings—seat frame to wheel arch box	26	Guard rail ⎫ Land-Rover
14–17	Fixings—seat back frame to body cappings	27–29	Fixings for guard rail ⎬ 86 and 88 ⎭ only

Rear seats—all models

To fit   **Operation T/52**

1. Place each rear seat frame in position on the wheelarch box, and on early models secure to the holes already drilled in the top capping; on late models secure by the spring clips.

2. Drill two ¼ in. (6,5 mm) dia. holes in the wheelarch box, using the frames as a guide, and secure each seat frame to the wheelarch box by means of bolts, plain and spring washers and nuts.

3. **Land-Rover 107 and 109 only.** When fitting rear seat units at the rear end of the wheelarches, plain washers equal to the height of the wheelarch box tread plates should be inserted between the rear seat frame vertical members and wheelarch boxes.

4. Secure backrest panels to the seat back frames with bolts, spring washers and nuts.

5. Place each seat cushion in position and attach to the seat frame with the tapes provided.

6. **Land-Rover 86 and 88 only.** Drill two 9/16 in. (15,1 mm) holes in the top of the rear body panels through the holes in the rear capping corner brackets, on each side of the vehicle, to receive the rear guard rails.

7. Fit the rear guard rails in position on the rear body cappings and secure by means of plain washers, spring washers and nuts.

Locking door handles—all models

To fit   **Operation T/54**

1. Remove both door handles complete with locks and mounting plates.

R.H. door lock (locking)

2. Withdraw the key from the door lock and remove the locking plate, loosely secured by a pin; remove the lock securing nut.

3. Fit the lock to the new door handle with the key slot serrations facing downwards (unlocked) and the plain washer between the lock and bracket.

4. Replace the lock securing nut, but do not fully tighten.

5. Refit the locking plate so that the hooked part is uppermost.

6. Fit the pin to the locking plate, check the operation of the lock, and peen over the end of the pin.

7. Screw the slotted nut back to the locking plate.

8. Remove the exterior handle support bracket from the original door lock, transfer the rubber washer from the old handle to the new, and discard the old handle.

9. With the catch in the unlocked position, fit the handle to the door lock, securing with the support bracket and original fittings. The screw heads must be to the door interior.

10. Fit the handle and lock complete to the R.H. door, using the original fixings, then tighten the slotted nut securing the catch lock, using a special 'C' spanner, Part No. 248877.

11. Open out the centre inner hole at the rear of the mounting plate to $\frac{3}{16}$ in. (4,76 mm).

12. Secure the pillar in the drilled hole, using a plain washer, spring washer and nut.

13. Check the operation of the lock.

L.H. door lock (with catch)

14. Remove the top front screw, securing the lock to the mounting plate.

15. Secure the catch to the vacant hole, using a screw, plain washer and nut.

16. Ensure that the catch moves freely, and prevents the door handle from being lifted when in the lowered position.

Window locks

17. With the side screws shut, position the brackets of the catch assembly on the bottom rail, so that the screws are just clear of the rear of the sliding windows.

18. Drill two ⅜ in. (5 mm) holes through each bracket into the bottom rail and secure each bracket with the two pop rivets provided.

Extra windscreen wipers—all models

To fit   **Operation T/56**

1. Remove the blanking piece and washer from the passenger's side windscreen after withdrawing the two screws, spring washers and nuts.

2. Fit the new windscreen wiper motor to the windscreen, with the escutcheon and seal on the outside, using the fixings provided.

3. Remove the rubber plug and fit the plug socket in the hole in the glove box top.

4. Withdraw the five screws and lower the instrument panel.

5. Connect the feed lead to the two-way connector in the green lead to the fuel gauge terminal 'B'.

6. Replace the rubber plug in the instrument box side with a grommet; pass the feed lead through the grommet and, with a cap placed on the lead, connect it to the plug socket.

7. Clip the feed lead to the rear of the glove box, using a clip.

8. Cut the feed lead with plug at a point 4 in. from the terminal end and bare the wire at the ends.

9. Connect the section of the lead with the plug between the wiper motor and the plug socket and the other portion with the terminal to a drive screw on the windscreen rail to act as an earth.

10. Fit the wiper arm to the motor, and the blade to the arm.

11. Adjust the blade position and test the wiper operation.

12. Replace the instrument panel.

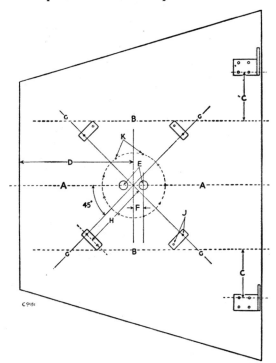

Fig. T-39—
Bonnet panel spare wheel carrier dimensions.

    A—Centre line.
    B—Guide lines.
    C—$7\frac{1}{2}$ in. (190,5 mm).
    D—$18\frac{1}{8}$ in. (460,4 mm).
    E—2 new holes, $1\frac{1}{2}$ in. (38 mm) dia.
    F—$1\frac{11}{16}$ in. (42,8 mm).
    G—Diagonals.
    H—$11\frac{1}{8}$ in. (282,6 mm).
    J—Eight new holes $\frac{7}{32}$ in. (5,5 mm) dia.
    K—Nine new holes—No. 6 drill .204 in.
        (5,1 mm) dia.

Spare wheel carrier on bonnet—all models

Note: The following items are for fitting a spare wheel carrier to the existing bonnet on all models. The clamps are reversible to accommodate 6 in. or 7 in. tyres.

To fit   **Operation T/58**

1. Mark a centre line, with a pencil, along the bonnet from front to rear.

2. **86 and 88 models:** Mark a guide line on each side of this line, $7\frac{1}{2}$ in. (190,5 mm) from each inner hinge fixing. See Fig. T-39.

3. Mark and centre pop the centre line at $18\frac{1}{8}$ in. (460,4 mm) from the front edge of the bonnet, and using this as a centre, mark off a point either side at $1\frac{11}{16}$ in. (42,8 mm) and cut two $1\frac{1}{2}$ in. (38,1 mm) dia. holes.

4. **86 and 88 models:** Mark out from the centre pop, four diagonal lines, 45° to the centre line, as shown in Fig. T-39, then mark each line at $11\frac{1}{8}$ in. (282,6 mm) and drill a $\frac{7}{32}$ in. (5,5 mm) dia. hole.

5. Fit two bolts and clamps to the support plate, then secure a split pin to each bolt.

6. Locate the spare wheel support, complete with clamp to bonnet, ensuring that the two bolts are over the centres of the two $1\frac{1}{2}$ in. (38,1 mm) dia. holes.

7. Using the support plate as a template, drill nine .204 in. (5 mm) dia. holes (No. 6 drill) and rivet assembly to bonnet.

8. **86 and 88 models:**

    (*a*) Position the four rubber support blocks on the diagonal lines, and secure with a screw, large plain washer, small plain washer, spring washer and nut to the hole previously drilled. Do not fully tighten.

    (*b*) With the outer lower edge against the guide line, and using the hole in the block as a guide, drill four more $\frac{7}{32}$ in. (5,5 mm) holes. Secure to bonnet, and tighten.

Towing attachments—all models

To fit   **Operation T/60**

1. All towing attachments can easily be fitted, using the nuts, bolts, spring and plain washers provided.

Full length hood—all models

The soft hood completely encloses the vehicle and can be opened at the rear to facilitate loading. It is available with plain sides or, for Export territories only, with side windows.

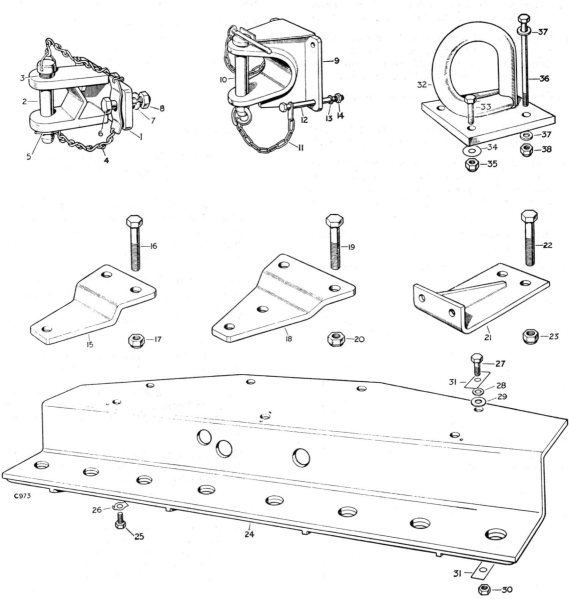

Fig. T-40—Towing attachments.

1	Towing jaw assembly	18	Rear tow plate
2	Pintle pin for jaw	19–20	Fixings—tow plate to rear draw bar
3	Spring for pin		For use with combine harvester only
4	Retaining chain for pin	21	Anchor plate for towing jaw
5	Spring clip for chain	22–23	Fixings—tow plate to rear draw plate
6–8	Fixings—jaw to chassis frame		Only required when power take-off is fitted
9	Towing jaw	24	Rear tow plate
10	Towing jaw pin	25–31	Fixings—towing plate to rear cross-member
11	Chain for towing jaw pin	32	Lifting and towing ring
12–14	Fixings—jaw to chassis	33–35	Fixings—towing ring to front bumper
15	Rear tow plate	36–38	Fixings—towing ring and bumper to frame
16–17	Fixings—tow plate to rear draw bar		

Standard equipment

To fit   **Operation T/62**

1. Fit the two hood sticks in the sockets at the corners of the rear body and secure with clamp arms, bolts, washers and nuts.

2. Secure the tie tube between the sticks by means of self-locking nuts.

3. Fit the intermediate hood stick between the tie tube, securing it with locknuts.

   On 109 models the intermediate hood stick is full length and should be secured to the body side cappings, using four bolts and two nut plates.

4. Secure the top drain channels to the front hood stick, using bolts, plain washers and self-locking nuts. Fit the adjustment plate between the top drain channel and the windscreen top rail.

6. If not already fitted, secure the door rear drain channels to the front hood stick with bolts, plain washers and self-locking nuts.

7. Secure the two rope hooks (one L.H., one R.H. —the hook towards the door jamb) to the body sides, $\frac{1}{4}$ in. (6,3 mm) from the door jamb, with the top of the rope hook touching the capping, using the 2 B.A. nuts, screws and washers provided.

8. Secure the two staples to the tailboard cotter brackets by removing the second pair of rivets down on each bracket. Fix the staples to the brackets with the $\frac{3}{4}$ in. (19 mm) long 2 B.A. screws, nuts and washers provided.

9. Place the hood over the sticks and secure it to the windscreen top rail.

10. Secure the front support straps to the staples on the windscreen top rail.

11. Secure the rear hood straps to the staples on the body, and the side curtain straps to the front hood stick.

12. Pass the side ropes round the hooks at the front corner of the body, secure under the side hooks, and together with the rear ropes, to the hooks at the rear of the body.

13. Push the rear curtain side flaps through the side pockets and secure.

Three-quarter length hood—all models

The soft hood encloses the vehicle rear body, behind the cab, and can be opened at the rear to facilitate loading. It is available with plain sides or, for Export territories only, with side windows.

To fit   **Operation T/64**

1. Position the drain channels against the cab rear panel so that with the lower edge resting on the rear body front capping, each drain channel protrudes approximately $\frac{1}{8}$ in. (32 mm) out from the body side capping. The drain channels are shaped to go round the hood stick.

2. Using the drain channels as templates, drill six holes $\frac{17}{64}$ in. (6,7 mm) dia. and secure the channels to the cab rear panel, using the fixings provided.

3. Position the hood mounting frame centrally against the cab rear panel and resting on the drain channels.

4. Using the mounting frame as a template, drill twelve holes $\frac{17}{64}$ in. (6,7 mm) dia. and secure the frame to the cab rear panel, using the fixings provided.

5. Fit the rear hood sticks in the sockets at the rear corner of the body and secure with clamp arms, bolts, washers and nuts.

6. Fit the front hood sticks in the sockets in the front corners of the body and secure with bolt plates, spring washers and nuts.

7. Secure the tie tubes between the sticks, using self-locking nuts.

8. Fit the intermediate hood stick between the tie tubes, securing it with self-locking nuts and, 109 models, securing the hood stick flanges to the pre-drilled holes in the body side cappings, using the fixings provided.

9. Mark a centre 9 in. (229 mm) from the door jamb and 2 in. (50,8 mm) down from the top of the rear body capping, and using the front rope hooks as templates, drill four holes and fix the rope hooks to the body sides, using the 2 B.A. nuts, screws and washers provided.

   Note: Two rope hooks, one L.H., one R.H.— the hook should be towards the door jamb.

10. Secure the two staples to the tailboard cotter brackets by removing the second pair of rivets down on each bracket. Fix the staples to the bracket with the $\frac{3}{4}$ in. (19 mm) long 2 B.A. screws, nuts and washers provided.

11. Place the hood over the sticks and secure to the mounting frame. The hood retaining strips should be inserted in the top and side channels of the mounting frame. Peg the upper retaining strip into the side strip.

12. Fit the lower ends of the two side retaining strips to the staples on the mounting frame and secure with the short straps.

13. Fasten the two straps over the intermediate hood stick, secure the ropes to the rope brackets on the body sides and, together with the rear ropes, to the hooks at the rear of the body.

14. Secure the rear curtain straps to the two staples fitted to the rear of the body.

15. Push the rear curtain side flaps through the side pockets and secure.

Ventilator flyscreens

To fit   **Operation T/66**

1. The flyscreens may be fitted, an inner and an outer to each ventilator orifice, by using the screens as templates and drilling twenty $\frac{7}{64}$ in. (2,8 mm) dia. holes and then fixing in position over each orifice, using the drive screws provided.

FIRE FIGHTING EQUIPMENT
(Petrol models only)

Land-Rover Fire Tenders are basically the same as standard models and maintenance procedure, generally, is unchanged.

The pump, mounted at the rear of vehicle, is a two-stage, self-priming, high-pressure impeller type. A single shaft, supported on a plain bearing at the rearmost end and a ball bearing at the driving end, carries three impellers. The first impeller, furthest from the driving end of pump, withdraws air from the suction pipe, causing the necessary depression to induce a flow of water to the pump. The two main impellers maintain and pressurise the water flow.

An engine speed governor and oil cooler, details of which are included in the Workshop Manual, are used in conjunction with the pump; drive is taken from the rear of gearbox transfer casing by propeller shaft.

All details peculiar to the Fire Tender, are dealt with in the following pages.

To prime the pump (Fig. T-42) Operation T/68

1. Select the "Priming" position with lever (1) and remove wing cap (2); pour water into the filler neck until it flows from the exhaust pipe (3), then replace the wing cap. See Fig. T-42.

To engage the pump drive (Fig. T-42)
Operation T/70

1. Start the engine with the transfer gear lever in neutral position; depress the clutch, select top gear with main gear lever and move the "power take-off" selector (early models, beneath centre seat box; late models, knob on heelboard) forward, then release the clutch pedal. Control engine r.p.m. by means of the governor control lever (8).

To pump from first-aid tank (Fig. T-42)
Operation T/72

1. Fit a blanking cap (4) to suction port and ensure that main delivery valves (5) are closed.

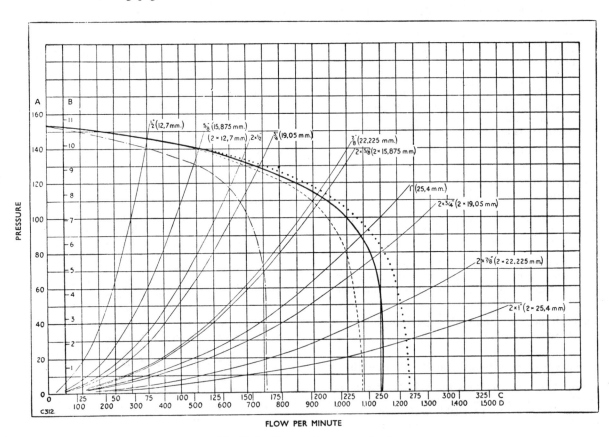

Fig. T-41—Flow and pressure chart.

(Pump speed 2,850 r.p.m.   Water temp. 42°F.   Air temp. 46°F.)

A—Pounds per square inch	— — — 15 ft. (4,6 metres) lift, 3 in. (76 mm) suction
B—Kilogrammes per square centimetre	·········· 10 ft. (3 metres) lift, 3 in. (76 mm) suction
C—Gallons per minute	▬▬▬ 6 ft. (1,8 metres) lift, 3 in. (76 mm) suction
D—Litres per minute	············ Zero lift, 3 in. (76 mm) suction
	——— Nozzle sizes

2. Open first-aid suction control valve (6) and pressure control valve (7) and select "Working" position with lever (1).

3. Start the engine and engage the drive.

4. Increase engine r.p.m. to suit output requirements.

5. To decrease the flow from delivery hoses reduce the engine r.p.m.

To fill first-aid tank from a hydrant (Fig. T-42)
Operation T/74

1. Connect the suction hose to the hydrant.

2. Open first-aid suction control valve (6) and ensure that delivery valves are closed.

3. Open hydrant valve.

4. When first-aid tank is full, shut off the hydrant.
   Note: The pump is not under power during this operation.

To pump from a static water supply (Fig. T-42)
Operation T/76

1. Prime pump.

2. Connect the suction and main delivery hoses; ensure that a strainer is fitted to the suction hose to prevent impurities entering the pump.

3. Close the delivery valves.

4. With lever (1) at "Priming" start the engine and engage the drive.

5. Move the governor control quadrant to the fully open position. The vacuum gauge (9) should indicate an increasing depression, and when water flows from exhaust pipe (3), the delivery valves must be slowly opened. When the pressure gauge (10) indicates rising pressure, move the lever (1) into "Working" position.

6. To decrease the flow from delivery hoses, reduce the engine r.p.m.

To pump from a hydrant or gravity feed supply (Fig. T-42)   Operation T/78

1. Connect the suction and delivery hoses and open the delivery valves.

2. Select "Working" position with lever (1).

3. Open the valve of tank or hydrant.

4. Start the engine and engage the pump drive.

5. Increase the engine r.p.m. to suit delivery requirements.

6. To decrease flow from delivery hoses, reduce the engine r.p.m.

   Note: When the pump is working for a prolonged period it is desirable from time to time to close the delivery valve, reduce the engine r.p.m. and select the "Priming" position with lever (1), so changing the water in the priming pump and avoiding overheating.

To temporarily stop output (Fig. T-42)
Operation T/80

1. Move governor control lever to extreme right-hand-side to allowe engine to idle and close delivery valves.

   Periodically select "Priming" position with lever (1) in order to allow the water in pump to be changed and thereby avoid overheating.

To stop pumping   Operation T/82

1. Close the valve of supply tank or hydrant, reduce engine speed and close delivery valves.

2. Disengage the drive to pump and disconnect the delivery and suction hoses.

Precautions to be taken when pumping
(Fig. T-42)   Operation T/84
A strainer in a wicker basket should be used on the end of the suction hose when the supply is being taken from open water. Care should be taken to ensure that as the water level falls the suction hose is kept far enough below the surface to ensure no air is drawn in. Suction hose joints must be screwed up tightly to avoid reduced delivery, and if necessary the hose must be secured to prevent kinking.

Rate of flow and pressure of the pump must be regulated by varying engine speed and **not** by partially closing the valves.

Should the suction hose be leaking and air is drawn in, the lever (1) should be left in the "Priming" position so that any air is passed through the exhaust pipe together with water from the priming pump. In this case a hose may be connected to the exhaust pipe to carry excess water away.

Frost precautions   Operation T/86

1. Under cold weather conditions, where freezing may occur, the drain cocks must be opened when pumping is concluded. Complete drainage will be ensured if the pump is kept running for a few minutes after the suction hose is disconnected and whilst the cocks are open.

2. To ensure that the pump will be ready for instant use, prime with "anti-freeze mixture" instead of water alone.

Periodic checks

After every operation .... Remove and clean filter in prim-**ing funnel**.

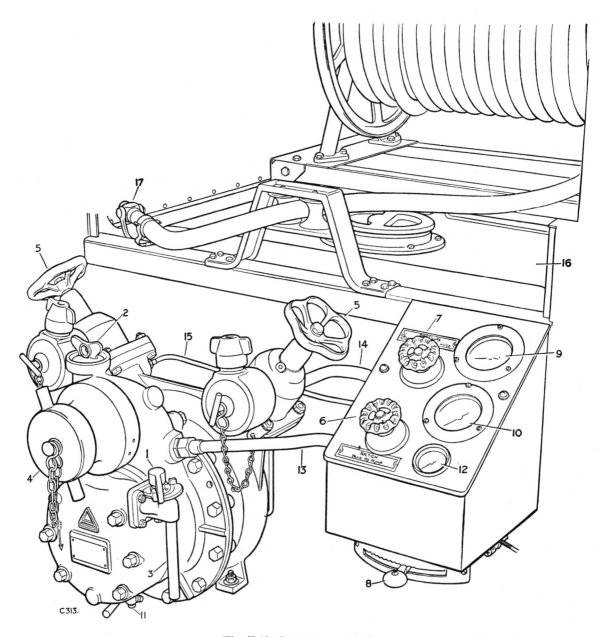

Fig. T-42—Pump and controls

1	Priming lever	7	First-aid pressure control valve	13	First-aid suction pipe
2	Filler cap	8	Governor control lever	14	First-aid delivery pipe
3	Exhaust pipe	9	Vacuum and pressure gauge	15	Pressure gauge pipe
4	Blanking cap	10	Pressure gauge	16	First-aid tank
5	Main delivery valves	11	Drain cock	17	First-aid hose nozzle
6	First-aid suction control valve	12	Oil temperature gauge		

After every operation and every seven days inoperative .... Ensure that the priming pump casing is full.

Note: See Frost precautions.

After pumping water containing impurities (lake, canal, sea water, etc.) .... Thoroughly scavenge the pump with clean fresh water.

Every ten hours running and every fourteen days inoperative Top up the filler pipes, protruding from the pump mounting ring, with engine oil. At the same time check the effectiveness of the mechanical seal by removing the oil drain plug from underneath the driving flange end of the pump. An undue proportion of water flowing out with the oil indicates a damaged seal, which should be replaced.

Every 1,000 hours running .... (a) Remove the pump, driving flange and end cover. Syringe the ball bearing with petrol and re-pack one-third full with good quality non-acid grease.

(b) Apply a suitable oil to the pump driving propeller shatf nipples, one on each universal joint and one on the sliding sleeve.

At convenient intervals (dry suction test) .... Ensure that the priming casing is full of water; close all valves and blank off the suction port. With lever (1) at "Priming" run the engine for **not** more than two minutes with the control quadrant lever fully open and note the depression registered by the vacuum gauge. The gauge should soon show 24-28½ inches of mercury if the system is air tight. Move the exhaust lever to "Working" position and stop the engine.

The vacuum gauge should record a drop of not more than three inches of mercury per minute if the pump is air tight.

Governor control cable—inner, to remove
(see Fig. 43)   **Operation T/88**

1. Disconnect the ball joint at control quadrant and remove it from the rod.

2. Unscrew the adjusting rod and body from tube and plug assembly.

3. Remove the locking spring from inner cable.

4. Withdraw the tube and plug assembly.

5. Take out the split pin securing the inner cable and slider assembly to the governor arm (left-hand) and withdraw the assembly from the swivel.

6. Grease the new cable assembly and feed it into the swivel assembly attached to support bracket on governor. Turn the cable occasionally to overcome any slight resistance which may be felt.

7. When fully inserted, the trunnion of the inner cable assembly should be attached to the governor arm again with a plain washer and split pin.

8. Press the governor arm fully forward. Pass the tube and plug assembly over the inner cable extending from the outer tube, until it is ½ in. (12,5 mm), 2 litre; ¾ in. (19 mm), 2¼ litre, from the shoulder of swivel coupling on chassis side member.

9. Screw the locking spring over the inner cable until it is $\frac{1}{16}$ in. (1,5 mm) from the end of tube and plug assembly, and cut the surplus inner cable off with a small hacksaw.

   Note: Ensure that the governor arm is extended fully forward before finally cutting the cable.

10. Screw the body tightly on to tube and plug assembly, position control quadrant in the fully closed position, screw the adjusting rod with ball joints and locknuts into body and adjust to fit quadrant. Open and close the quadrant lever fully and check for correct adjustment.

First-aid hose reel, to remove   Operation T/90

1. Unscrew the nozzle from end of hose and withdraw the hose from fairleads.

2. Remove the union securing the delivery pipe to reel centre shaft.

3. Unscrew the breather pipe from first-aid tank.

4. Remove the bolts securing the supporting feet and lift the hose and reel assembly clear.

First-aid hose reel, to fit   Operation T/92

1. Reverse removal procedure.

Reel support and first-aid tank, to remove
    Operation T/94

1. Remove the first-aid hose reel.

2. Disconnect the pressure pipe "reel to control cock" at the cock, and withdraw.

3. Disconnect the suction pipe "tank to control cock" at the tank and cock, then withdraw.

4. Unscrew the two bolts from the first-aid tank steady straps and move the tank centrally in the rear body.

5. Remove the bolts securing the reel support to the wheel arch box sides, then lift the support clear and remove the tank.

Reel support and first-aid tank, to refit
Operation T/96

1. Reverse removal procedure.

Vacuum or pressure gauge, to remove
Operation T/98

1. Disconnect the pipe from rear of gauge.

2. Remove the screws securing bezel to the instrument panel and withdraw the gauge.

   Note: In some cases it may be necessary to raise the instrument panel slightly, to gain access to the rear of instruments

with a spanner. To raise the panel, remove the control wheels and rubber grommets, withdraw the screw securing panel and instruction plates.

Oil temperature gauge, to remove
Operation T/100

1. Disconnect the ball joint at the control quadrant and remove the bolts securing quadrant to support bracket; lower quadrant.

2. Unscrew the knurled nut securing the oil temperature gauge to instrument panel.

3. Disconnect the capillary tubing from the oil pipe union on left-hand front wing valance and release the supporting clips from chassis side and cross-member.

4. Withdraw the gauge and capillary tubing, ensuring that the tubing is not bent unnecessarily, nor twisted.

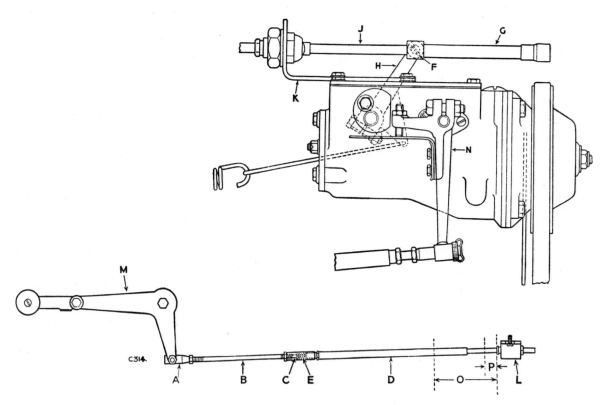

Fig. T-43—Arrangement of governor control

A—Ball joint
B—Adjusting rod
C—Body
D—Tube and plug assembly
E—Locking spring
F—Split pin
G—Inner cable and slider assembly
H—Governor arm
J—Swivel assembly
K—Support bracket for swivel assembly
L—Swivel coupling
M—Control quadrant lever
N—Governor arm (R.H.)
O—Control fully open:
  2 litre, $3\frac{1}{16}$ in. (78 mm)
  $2\frac{1}{4}$ litre, $2\frac{1}{2}$ in. (63,5 mm)
P—Control inoperative:
  2 litre, $\frac{1}{2}$ in. (12,5 mm)
  $2\frac{1}{4}$ litre, $\frac{3}{4}$ in. (19 mm)

Oil temperature gauge, to refit
Operation T/102

1. Reverse removal procedure, again taking great care to bend the tubing only where necessary; do not twist it.

Pump, to remove   Operation T/104

1. Drain the pump and then remove the rearmost water drain plug or tap.

2. Disconnect from pump the first-aid delivery and suction pipes and also the pressure gauge pipe.

3. Remove the bolts securing the driving propeller shaft to the power take-off driving flange at rear of gearbox.

4. Ensure that the pump is suitably supported (with a sling, etc.), then remove the three bolts securing pump to rear cross-member and the two bolts to support plate.

5. Withdraw the pump and propeller shaft complete and lower. Unscrew the foremost drain tap as soon as possible to avoid damage, then disconnect the propeller shaft.

Pump, to dismantle (see Fig. T-44)
Operation T/106

1. Unscrew the lubricating pipes (1) and oil drain plug and extension (53, 55). Drain off oil. Remove the nuts and washers securing mounting ring (2) and withdraw the ring.

2. Remove the delivery valve securing bolts and withdraw the valve assemblies (3). Take out the spindle and seal assembly (6) and (7) and spring (8). A peg spanner will be required to unscrew the lower plate of the spindle and seal assembly if a new disc type rubber seal (7) is required.

3. The discharge valves may be dismantled completely by unscrewing the nuts securing control wheel (5), withdrawing the wheels, pressing the spindle body (11) downwards and extracting the body. Circlip (9) and spindle seal (10) may now be removed from the discharge valve casting.

4. Unscrew the cap nuts and gently tap the priming pump cover (12) off with a hide-faced hammer. Carefully remove the gasket (17). If necessary remove the grub screw (15) and extract the bush (16).

5. Slide the priming pump impeller (19) from the shaft (18) and take out the impeller key.

6. Remove the cap nuts and withdraw the suction casing (20) with sealing "O" ring. If necessary withdraw the shaft seal (22).

7. Tap the locking washer (32) down and unscrew the impeller nut. Withdraw the suction impeller (33) and remove the key from the shaft.

   Note: A metal strip, bent hook shape, will facilitate the removal of impeller.

8. Using the hooks if necessary, draw the diffuser (34) from housing and shaft. Remove distance piece (36), pressure impeller (37) and pressure impeller key.

9. Remove the split pin, washer and nut (**left-hand thread**) securing the driving flange (72), then withdraw the flange and key.

   Note: The shaft should be positioned vertically between two pieces of wood and clamped in a vice when unscrewing the flange nut. *Do not* grip the shaft between metal jaw protectors or allow it to be held in the horizontal position. The weight of the main casing (38) plus the torque exerted by the operator on the flange nut, whilst the shaft is held horizontally, might cause distortion.

10. Using an "Allen" key, unscrew the socket-headed bolts (71) securing bearing cover (69).

11. Tap the shaft on the impeller side of main casing (38) with a hide-faced hammer to remove it complete with bearing cover and ball bearing (65). The fibre washer (62), "O" ring (63) and mechanical seal (61) may be withdrawn as the shaft is taken from the casing.

12. Remove the bearing cover, securing circlips, spacer and ball bearing from the shaft.

13. The seal (70) in bearing cover, seals (46) and stationary sealing ring (40 or 41), joint washer or sealing ring (42 or 43) and seal cover (47), if fitted, may now be removed if necessary, from the main casing.

14. Remove the priming cock and exhaust pipe assembly (76) from the priming pump cover.

Checking pump component parts for wear
(Fig. T-45)   Operation T/108

1. Check the bush in priming pump cover for excessive wear, see data section. If necessary remove the bush as instructed in Item 4 of the dismantling procedure, and fit a new one. Wear at this point must not be allowed to become excessive, since a corresponding amount of wear will take place in other components mounted on the shaft.

2. Note the end-float of priming pump impeller. Any increase on 0,2 mm (.008 in.) will result in reduced suction capacity. To check the end-float, place the impeller in position in priming casing with an already compressed gasket in place. Lay a straight-edge over the gasket and impeller and check the clearance with a feeler gauge.

3. Examine shaft seal in suction casing and renew if necessary.

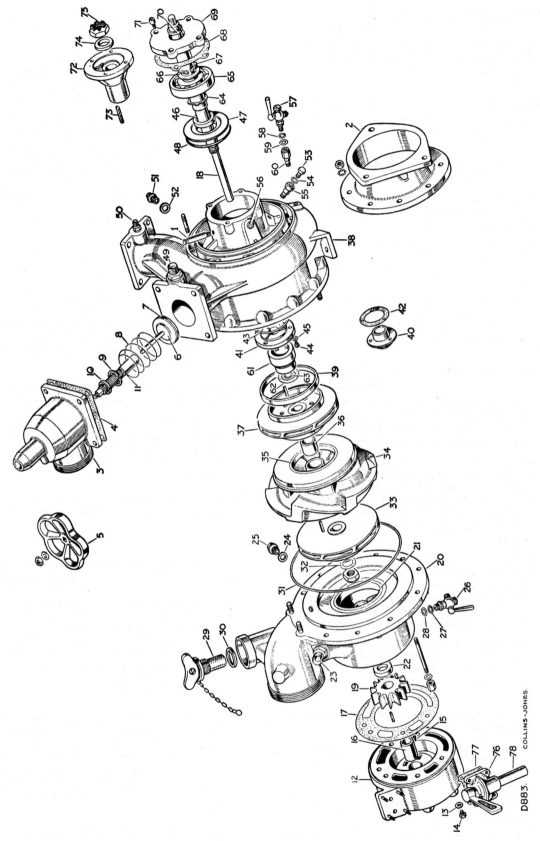

Fig. T-44—Exploded view of pump

Key to Fig. T-44

1 Oil filler tube
2 Mounting ring
3 Delivery valve
4 Joint washer for valve
5 Control wheel
6 Spindle and seal assembly
7 Rubber seal
8 Spring
9 Circlip
10 Seal
11 Spindle body
12 Priming casing
13 Washer } For priming
14 Plug } casing
15 Grub screw, securing bush
16 Bush for shaft
17 Gasket for priming casing
18 Shaft with washers and keys
19 Priming impeller
20 Suction casing
21 Wearing ring
22 Seal (in suction casing) for shaft
23 Suction pipe union, first aid
24 Washer } For suction
25 Plug } casing
26 Drain cock
27 Fibre washer
28 Copper washer
29 Cap and filter assembly
30 Washer for cap
31 Rubber "O" ring
32 Locking washer
33 Suction impeller
34 Diffuser ring
35 Wearing ring
36 Distance piece
37 Suction and pressure impeller
38 Main casing
38 Main casing
39 Wearing ring

40 Stationary sealing ring
41 Stationary sealing ring
42 Joint washer
43 Sealing ring
44 Screw } For sealing
45 Washer } ring
46 Seal
47 Cover for rear seal
48 Sealing ring
49 Union for delivery pipe, first aid
50 Union for pressure gauge pipe
51 Plug
52 Washer for plug
53 Plug, oil drain
54 Joint washer
55 Extension tube
56 Grease nipple
57 Drain cock
58 Fibre washer } For drain
59 Copper washer } cock
60 Extension for drain cock
61 Mechanical seal
62 Fibre washer
63 Rubber "O" ring
64 Circlip
65 Ball bearing
66 Distance piece
67 Circlip
68 Joint washer
69 Bearing cover
70 Seal
71 Screw for cover
72 Driving flange
73 Key for flange
74 Washer } For
75 Nut } flange
76 Priming cock
77 Joint washer for cock
78 Exhaust pipe

375

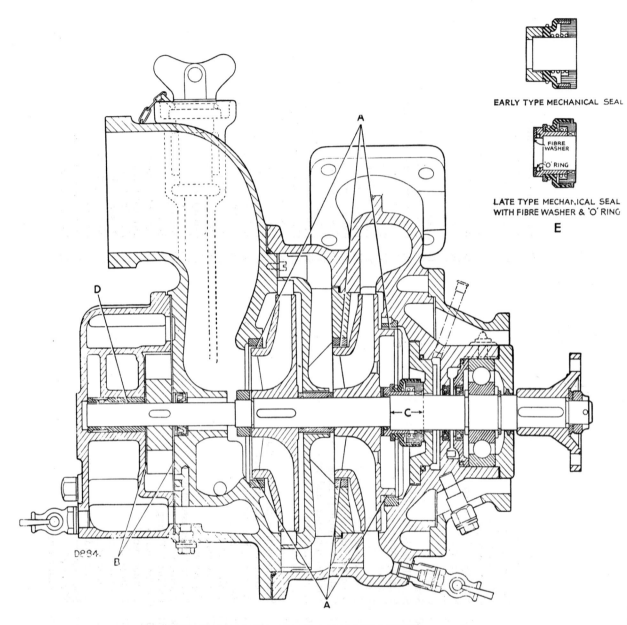

EARLY TYPE MECHANICAL SEAL

LATE TYPE MECHANICAL SEAL
WITH FIBRE WASHER & 'O' RING

E

Fig. T-45—Sectioned view of pump, Serial No. A745060 onwards

A—Wearing ring clearance 0,25 mm (.010 in.)   B—Impeller total end-float 0,2 mm (.008 in.
C—28 mm—0,3 (1.102 in.—.012)

4. Check the internal diameter of wearing rings, and the external diameter of shoulders on suction and pressure impellers. A *radial* clearance of 0,25 mm (.010 in.) is normal. A clearance in excess of 0,5 mm (.020 in.) will necessitate the regrinding of impeller shoulders and the fitment of suitably oversize wearing rings.

5. The fibre washer and "O" ring seal (see Fig. T-44) must be replaced if any sign of deterioration exists.

6. If the mechanical seal has worn unduly and is to be renewed, the stationary sealing ring must also be replaced.

Ensure that the dimension from friction face of the stationary seal and the shoulder of shaft when in position is 28 mm±0,3 (1.102 in.±.012).

Note: On pumps prior to Serial No. A745060 if the early type mechanical seal having a large distance piece and no fibre washer or "O" ring is fitted, it may be replaced by the latest type complete with fibre washer and "O" ring. When fitting the latest type mechanical seal the original seal distance piece as well as the seal should be discarded (see 'E', Fig. T-45).

7. When a new stationary sealing ring is fitted it must be secured in the main casing by the three fixing screws and then accurately turned and lapped in position.

8. Check the seals in pressure casing and bearing cover and replace if necessary. If a felt ring type of seal is fitted in the bearing cover, the new or old one must be soaked in engine oil before replacement.

9. The ball bearing should be renewed if its serviceability is in any way doubtful.

10. Thoroughly clean the exhaust cock and check for correct functioning.

Pump, to assemble   Operation T/110

1. Reverse the dismantling procedure and note that the mechanical seal should be tapped on to the shaft (after ensuring that the seal splines are correlated), using a piece of tubing and a hide-faced hammer.

   When the mechanical seal is against the shaft shoulder, the end of the shaft key-way for pressure impeller will be 4 mm (.196 in) from the face of the mechanical seal.

2. Use grease throughout assembly and top up with oil, using the filler tube at driving end, when assembly is complete.

3. After fitting pump to the vehicle, a dry suction check should be made. See "Periodic checks"

DEFECT LOCATION (*Fire fighting equipment*)

Symptom, Cause and Remedy

A—PUMP NOT DELIVERING. HIGH VACUUM READING WITH VALVES CLOSED BUT NO PRESSURE BUILD UP.

1. Strainer or suction pipe completely blocked—*Remove and clear.*

B—PUMP NOT DELIVERING. VACUUM READING LOWER THAN CORRESPONDING STATIC SUCTION LIFT. AIR CONTINUALLY ESCAPING FROM EXHAUST PIPE

1. Badly leaking hose—*Rectify.*
2. Leaking delivery valve—*Rectify.*
3. Leaking mechanical seal—*Rectify.*

C—PRESSURE INDICATED BY GAUGE BUT LITTLE OR NO DELIVERY FROM HOSE.

1. Obstruction in suction hose—*Clear.*
2. Foreign matter in pump or at intake due to damaged strainer—*Dismantle, clean and rectify.*
3. Pressure gauge unserviceable—*Renew.*
4. Higher suction lift due to water level at supply failing—*Set pump at lower level if possible.*

D—VACUUM FALLS AFTER PROLONGED RUNNING WITH CLOSED VALVES.

1. Water in priming pump overheated—*Drain off hot water by opening drain cock in priming casing. Refill and re-prime pump.*

E—NO VACUUM INDICATED. AIR CONTINUALLY ESCAPING FROM EXHAUST PIPE

1. Delivery valve open—*Close.*
2. Drain cock in main casing open—*Close and prime*

F—NO VACUUM INDICATED. NO AIR ESCAPING FROM EXHAUST PIPE

1. Priming pump contains too little or no water—*Refill and re-prime pump.*
2. Filler strainer choked—*Clean.*
3. "Priming" lever in "Working" position—*Re-set to "Priming" position.*

G—WATER EMERGES FROM OIL FILLER TUBE OR AT DRIVING FLANGE.

1. Worn mechanical seal or scored stationary seal. *Dismantle pump and replace.*

DATA

Centre power take-off

Drive shaft end-float.... .003 to .005 in. (0,07 to 0,12 mm)

Rear power take-off

Backlash between gears .008 to .012 in. (0,20 to 0,30 mm)

Input and output shaft end-float   .... Zero

Rear drive pulley

Drive shaft end-float   Zero

Pinion shaft end-float   Zero

Backlash: bevel wheel to pinion   .... .004 in. (0,10 mm)

Front capstan winch

Bollard shaft bushes

Bush bore   .... 1.311 in. + .002 (33,31 mm + 0,050)

Bollard shaft end-float   .... .003 to .005 in. (0,075 to 0.125 mm)

Reamed bore   .... 1.390 in. + .004 (35,306 mm + 0,10)

Drive shaft housing bush

Reamed bore   .... .750 in. + .002 (19,05 mm + 0,050)

Fire fighting equipment

General

Capacity of first aid tank   40 gal. (182 litres) approx.

Length of first aid hose   120 ft. (40 metres)

Maximum permissible nozzle size when both delivery ports are in use   One $\frac{7}{8}$ in. (22 mm) and a 1 in. (25 mm)

Delivery port   .... $2\frac{1}{2}$ in. B.S.P. thread

Suction port   .... $4\frac{1}{2}$ in. B.S.P. thread

Delivery port adaptor   .... Suitable for standard British instantaneous $2\frac{1}{2}$ in. hose coupling

Suction port adaptor   .... Screwed to B.S.S. 336/1954 for 3 in. (76 mm) hose

Maximum self-priming suction lift   .... 26 ft. (8 metres)

Pump

Type   .... Two-stage impeller, self-priming high-pressure

Drive   .... Propeller shaft from gear-box at engine speed

Maximum R.P.M. (governed)   3,000

Threads   .... Metric

Priming pump impeller end-float   .... 0,2 mm (.008 in.)

Face of stationary seal to shoulder on shaft   .... 28 mm±0,3 (1.102 in ± .012)

Radial clearance between wearing rings and impeller shoulders   .... 0,25 mm (.010 in.)

Section V —
RECLAMATION SCHEMES—ALL MODELS

Flywheel

A. Wear or scoring on the flywheel pressure face

1. Remove the clutch bolts and dowels from the flywheel.

2. Machine the *whole* pressure face, not merely inside the bolts and dowels, until the score marks are removed.

   The maximum amount of metal which may be removed from the flywheel face is .030 in. (0,75 mm). If the face is not satisfactory after machining to these limits, the flywheel must be scrapped.

   Minimum thickness after refacing is as follows:

   Petrol models:
   88 models, 1956-58 .... 1.204 in. (30,5 mm)
   Other models, 1948-56 1.047 in. (26.5 mm)

   Diesel models: 1.330 in. (33,8 mm)

Petrol models

B. Starter ring excessively worn or damaged

1. Remove the scrap starter ring by securing the flywheel in a vice fitted with jaw protectors, then drill a $\frac{3}{16}$ in. (4,76 mm) dia. hole axially between the root of any one tooth and the inner diameter of the starter ring $\frac{13}{32}$ in. (10,3 mm) deep. Care must be taken to prevent the drill entering the flywheel.

2. The operator should then stand in the position indicated by Fig. V-1, place a chisel immediately above the drilled hole, and strike it sharply.

   Important Note: The starter ring will normally split harmlessly but on remote occasions rings have been known to fly asunder when split; it is therefore important that the operator should be in the position indicated and as an additional precaution, a cloth may be laid over the upper part of the starter ring.

3. Heat the starter ring uniformly to between 220°C and 225°C but do not exceed the higher temperature.

4. With the flywheel placed on a suitably flat surface, position the ring on to the flywheel with the square edge of the teeth against the flange.

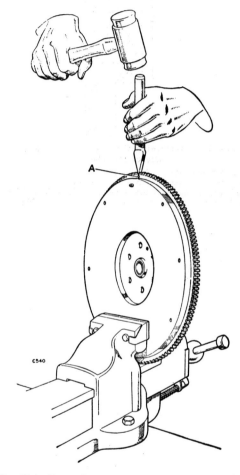

Fig. V-1—Removing an unserviceable starter ring, Petrol models.

A—Drilled hole.

There should be a clearance of $\frac{1}{16}$ to $\frac{1}{8}$ in. (1,5 to 3 mm) between the inner diameter of ring and flywheel if the temperature is correct. Press the starter ring firmly against the flange until the ring contracts sufficiently to grip the flywheel.

5. Allow the flywheel assembly to cool gradually; do not hasten cooling in any way and thereby avoid the setting up of internal stresses in the ring which may cause fracture or failure in some respect.

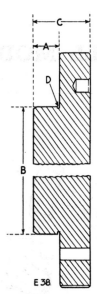

Fig. V-2—Machining flywheel for ring gear (Diesel models)

A—Depth of spigot .... .625 in. (15,87 mm).
B—Spigot diameter .... 9.624 in. (244,44 mm).
C—Minimum thickness after refacing .... 1.330 in. (33,8 mm).
D—Undercut .... .062 in. wide × .031 in. (1,58 × 0,79 mm)

Diesel models

1. Remove the clutch bolts, dowels and primary pinion bush.

2. Machine the flywheel teeth off flush and turn the gear ring spigot to the dimensions shown in the illustration (Fig. V-2).

3. Fit the ring gear to the flywheel, using the original clutch cover fixing bolts. (These must be renewed if in poor condition.)

4. Replace the dowel and renew the primary pinion bush if necessary.

Clutch pressure plate

When worn or scored, a maximum of .010 in. (0,25 mm) may be machined off the face of the clutch pressure plate.

Brake drums

If scored or worn, .030 in. (0,75 mm) may be machined off the brake drums.

Printed and distributed by Brooklands Books Ltd., PO Box 146, Cobham, Surrey KT11 1LG, England Phone: 01932 865051 Fax: 01932 868803

ISBN 0 90 073 980   Ref: B LR10WH